SCHAUM'S OUTLINE OF

THEORY AND PROBLEMS

of

BUSINESS LAW

•

DONALD A. WIESNER, J.D., LL.M.
Chairman and Professor of Business Law
University of Miami

NICHOLAS A. GLASKOWSKY, Jr., M.B.A., Ph.D.
Professor of Management and Logistics
University of Miami

•

SCHAUM'S OUTLINE SERIES
McGRAW-HILL, INC.

New York   St. Louis   San Francisco   Auckland   Bogotá
Caracas   Lisbon   London   Madrid   Mexico   Milan
Montreal   New Delhi   Paris   San Juan   Singapore
Sydney   Tokyo   Toronto

To Bev and Liz

DONALD A. WIESNER is currently Chairman and Professor of Business Law, School of Business Administration, University of Miami (Florida). His many articles appear in law reviews and business journals. Educated at the Universities of Arizona and Miami, he holds a J.D. (1953) and LL.M. (1961) from the latter institution. He is a specialist on purchasing law and negotiations and delivers seminars on such topics to national corporations.

NICHOLAS A. GLASKOWSKY, JR. has degrees in International Law and Relations (A.B., Harvard, 1948) and Business Administration (M.B.A., 1954, and Ph.D., 1960, both from Stanford University). He is the author of several college textbooks including *Business Logistics* and *Highway Transportation Management*. He is currently Professor of Management and Logistics at the University of Miami (Florida). He frequently testifies as an expert witness in court cases and at transportation regulatory hearings.

Material from *Uniform CPA Examination Questions and Unofficial Answers*, Copyright © 1981, 1980, 1979, 1978, 1977, 1976, 1975, 1974, 1973 by the American Institute of Certified Public Accountants, Inc., is reprinted (or adapted) with permission.

Schaum's Outline of Theory and Problems of
BUSINESS LAW

5 6 7 8 9 10 11 12 13 14 15 SH SH 9 8 7 6 5 4 3 2

ISBN 0-07-069062-6

Sponsoring Editor, Elizabeth Zayatz
Editing Supervisor, Marthe Grice
Production Manager, Nick Monti

Cover design by Amy E. Becker.

Library of Congress Cataloging in Publication Data

Wiesner, Donald A.
   Schaum's outline of theory and problems of
business law.

   (Schaum's outline series)
   Includes index.
   1. Business law -- United States.   I. Glaskowsky,
Nicholas A.   II. Title.
KF889.6.W54   1985   346.73'07   84-14335
ISBN 0-07-069062-6   347.3067

Preface

The purpose of this outline is to offer in a clear and systematic manner the information needed for an understanding and appreciation of business law as it is taught in colleges and universities. This volume presents material that is usually found in a first course in business law. It is intended as an aid to understanding current business law texts by offering statements and examples which clarify and reinforce an understanding of the subject. It is also a review for accounting students who must take the commercial law examination administered by the American Institute of Certified Public Accountants (AICPA).

Each chapter begins with a presentation of main principles and illustrative examples. This is followed by a section called Black Letter Law, which is a set of summary statements of the major principles just studied.

The problems which follow each chapter are of two types: multiple choice and essay questions. These are similar, and in some cases identical, to the problems in the commercial law examination given to certified public accounting candidates. The solutions to the multiple choice statements provide more than the correct answer, however, as they elaborate on what might be a wrong interpretation suggested by the other possible answers. All the solutions to the multiple choice problems and essay questions are the authors'. They are not the product of the American Institute of Certified Public Accountants.

Except for Part I: Introduction, each part of the outline (Contracts, Sales, etc.) ends with a topic test containing essay questions. These sets of questions test the student's ability to identify a specific legal issue without the assistance of a chapter heading. The ability to identify and characterize issues is of critical importance in the development of the decision-making skills required of the business student.

The reader is strongly reminded that decisions of courts are made by applying the law to a set of facts. The court (judge) will state the law in a case being tried. The jury (or the judge in a nonjury trial) will be the trier of fact and thus determine the outcome of the case in favor of the plaintiff or defendant under the law. As to business transactions, the law is ordinarily relatively clear. Through precedent and codification, such as the Uniform Commercial Code, it is usually possible to say generally what the law is. The more difficult problem is determining the facts.

Basically, a lawsuit can produce three different outcomes and two of the three are bad for the plaintiff. This is true because under our legal system *the burden of proof is on the plaintiff*. Briefly stated, the three possible outcomes are:

1. The *plaintiff* proves his or her case and *wins*.
2. The *plaintiff* fails to prove his or her case and *loses*.
3. The *defendant* proves his or her case and the *plaintiff loses*.

Proving the plaintiff's case is occasionally easy, often difficult, and sometimes practically impossible despite the plaintiff's perhaps justified belief in the righteousness of his or her cause. Very frequently the trier of fact must sort out sharply conflicting testimony and often it comes down simply to which party's testimony is believed or given greater weight. The plaintiff will win *only* if the court determines from all the evidence put before it that the plaintiff's allegations, statements, and/or contentions *are* the facts. The burden of proof is on the plaintiff, *not* on the defendant.

Throughout this book we state the facts of a situation in case examples and review questions. The reader should understand that these facts are what the trier of fact has found or will find to *be* the facts of the case. Here we must necessarily present the facts of each example or case as *given* so that we can proceed with the purpose of this book: reviewing with you, the reader, the manner in which the law is applied to the facts of business situations.

Finally, it is customary at this point for authors to thank those who have assisted them in typing and editing their manuscript. But since we used our personal computers and word processing software to create, edit, and print out the entire manuscript we have only ourselves to thank. Naturally, however, that means we are truly wholly accountable for any errors or omissions, and for these we must take full responsibility.

DONALD A. WIESNER
NICHOLAS A. GLASKOWSKY, JR.

Coral Gables, Florida

Contents

CONTENTS

CONTENTS

CONTENTS

CONTENTS

nics' Liens. 25.11 Purchase Money Security Interests. 25.12 Priorities. 25.13 Proceeds. 25.14 Rights of Secured Parties: Generally. 25.15 Right of Repossession. 25.16 Right of Disposal and Sale. 25.17 Termination-Continuation Statements.

26.1 Introduction. 26.2 Principal-Agent. 26.3 Master-Servant. 26.4 Employer-Employee. 26.5 Independent Contractors. 26.6 Independent Contractor: Dangerous Work. 26.7 Independent Contractor: Careless Selection and Excessive Control. 26.8 Agents: Other Meanings. 26.9 Capacity to be an Agent. 26.10 Principals. 26.11 Formation of the Agency Relationship. 26.12 Agents' Authority Generally. 26.13 Actual, or Real, Authority. 26.14 Express Authority. 26.15 Implied Authority and Incidental Authority. 26.16 Ratification. 26.17 Apparent, or Ostensible, Authority. 26.18 Contract Between Principal and Agent. 26.19 Agency Contract: Compensation. 26.20 Contract: Reimbursement to Principal. 26.21 Agency Duties: Generally. 26.22 Agent's Duty: Loyalty. 26.23 Agent's Duty: Obedience. 26.24 Agent's Duty: Accounting. 26.25 Principal's Duties of Reimbursement and Indemnification.

27.1 Introduction. 27.2 Agent's Conduct. 27.3 Agent Buying and Selling. 27.4 Agents: Possession and Notice. 27.5 Undisclosed Principals. 27.6 Unnamed or Partially Disclosed Principals. 27.7 Undisclosed Principal: Third Party's Election. 27.8 Injuries to Third Parties: Tort Liability. 27.9 Agents and Third Parties. 27.10 Third Parties and Nonexistent Principals. 27.11 Torts and Agent Liability. 27.12 Criminal Responsibility. 27.13 Termination: Principal and Agent. 27.14 Agency Coupled with an Interest: Termination. 27.15 Third Parties: Notice of Termination.

28.1 Partnerships: Definition. 28.2 An Association. 28.3 Two or More Persons. 28.4 Carrying on a Business. 28.5 As Co-Owners. 28.6 Intention to Share Profits. 28.7 Articles of Partnership. 28.8 Partnership Name. 28.9 Oral Partnership Agreements. 28.10 Partnership by Estoppel. 28.11 Kinds of Partners and Partnerships. 28.12 General and Limited Partnerships. 28.13 Universal Partnership. 28.14 Silent, or Dormant, Partnership. 28.15 Retiring Partners and Incoming Partners. 28.16 Surviving Partner. 28.17 Nominal Partners. 28.18 Partnership Goodwill. 28.19 Partnership Capital. 28.20 Partnership Property: Dedication. 28.21 Rights in Partnership Property. 28.22 Partner Relations. 28.23 Partnership Not an Entity.

CONTENTS

CONTENTS

Chapter 1

Law and Business

1.1 OVERVIEW

A course in business law is taught in nearly all colleges and universities in the United States. Such courses are offered for the purpose of informing the professional business student and the layperson of the legal environment within which each must live and operate.

This book includes material which is traditionally taught in a first college course. Naturally, institutions vary as to the topics which they choose to include in a first course, and some topics included in a particular school's first course in business law may not be found in this volume.

1.2 SOURCES OF LAW

Law is both a system of conduct and the method by which this conduct is enforced. In the United States law comes from a number of sources which include constitutions, treaties, statutes, administrative regulations, executive orders, ordinances, and common law.

EXAMPLE 1. Warren was arrested for depositing garbage on the street. A police officer cited him for violating Section 1090 of the City Ordinance. This ordinance is *legislation* (a *statute*) enacted by the city government. State constitutions and state statutes confer on cities the power to enact certain laws.

EXAMPLE 2. Margo promised that when she terminated employment with Sarget, Inc., she would not compete with them for 1 year. After leaving, she immediately began competing with Sarget. Sarget sued her for breach of contract. The rules under which Margo will be judged are generally found in *case law*, that is, previously reported court decisions addressed to the same or similar question. Case law is also called *common law*, *precedent*, or *judge-made* law.

1.3 JURISDICTIONS

There are, in effect, 51 "nations" or jurisdictions in the United States which exercise lawmaking power. These include the 50 sovereign states and the federal government. While the federal government is important and supreme in critical areas of society, day-to-day legal implications are frequently regulated by the states.

EXAMPLE 3. Toby is charged with slandering Spring's Burger Shop by telling others that it is rat-infested. The shop successfully sued Toby for slander (a civil wrong, or tort) in the state civil court. The state appeals court refused to disturb the result. Toby threatens that she "will take this case all the way to the U.S. Supreme Court." Usually the Supreme Court has no interest in, or jurisdiction over, this type of case. The state supreme court would be the final court, as no federal question appears to be involved.

EXAMPLE 4. Lanson brought an action against ILM for damages to his property when ILM was digging up the street. At the trial the court refused to permit Lanson's attorney to cross-examine a hostile witness. Lanson lost in the state trial court and state appeals court. If Lanson preserved his claim that his federally protected constitutional right to due process was violated, the issue is one that the U.S. Supreme Court could consider if it wished. When it wishes to do so, the Supreme Court grants *certiorari* (to be informed of).

1.4 BUSINESS-LAW PRINCIPLES

The principles of business law come from multiple sources. When the subject of contracts is studied, for example, the common law and case law will be seen as the most usual sources of the relevant legal principles. These principles are found in the reported decisions of the judges of the state and federal systems. In the field of business law, many common-law principles have been restated and modified by legislation. The most comprehensive legislation in this area is found in the Uniform Commercial Code (UCC). The UCC has in the main been enacted into legislation in all the states with the exception of Louisiana which, while it has enacted several UCC articles, has its own commercial code based on the early French law, commonly known as the Napoleonic Code.

The UCC modified many principles of commercial law, and this book will note such changes and repeat such principles in the appropriate sections.

EXAMPLE 5. Grant agreed to construct a swimming pool for Lash for $12,000. When Grant was half finished, he needed money and demanded that Lash pay him an additional $2,000. Fearful that Grant would abandon the job, Lash agreed to pay the extra amount. Under the common law this new promise to pay extra is unsupported with consideration and therefore it would not be enforceable. If, on the other hand, the original contract was for the sale of personal property (goods), the result could be different. Modification of a sales contract under Section 2-209 of the UCC generally does not require new consideration. The UCC changed existing common-law principles in regard to certain contracts such as the sale of personal property, or goods.

In this book statutory modifications and codification of the common law will be seen more extensively in some subjects than in others. The law of sales, as mentioned above, has been changed and is contained in a statute: Article 2 of the UCC. Principles governing commercial paper are found in Article 3, bank deposits and collections in Article 4, and secured transactions in Article 9. In all, eight areas of substantive law are treated in the UCC.

EXAMPLE 6. Gena issues a check to a department store, stops payment on it, and is successfully sued by the store. She settles the dispute by promising to make payments and giving a lien on her household furniture as security. The legal principles governing the check are found in Article 3 (commercial paper), the principles which apply to the stop-payment order are found in Article 4 (bank deposits and collections), and the security agreement by which she created the lien is treated in Article 9 (secured transactions).

This does not necessarily mean that statutory provisions are the last word. These provisions must be applied by the courts. Such interpretations and applications become the new case law, the definitive law on the point.

EXAMPLE 7. A 2-year-old boy died of burns suffered when boiling water erupted from a defective vaporizer loaned to the family by an aunt who had just purchased the unit from a drugstore. Generally, only those who contract can sue for breach of contract, a breach of warranty here. However, since this is a sale of goods, Article 2 of the UCC is applicable. It provides (Section 2-318) in most states that a member of the purchaser's family may also sue. A state supreme court ruled that under these circumstances, a nephew was a member of the family within the meaning of the statutory language. This court decision, interpreting Section 2-318 of the UCC, is now precedent, or case law, in that state.

Not all statutory modifications of the common law are as extensive and comprehensive as the UCC. Statutes are frequently enacted to address specific problems.

EXAMPLE 8. After a particularly hard sell, a builder obtained Larson's signature on a home improvement contract. Once they have signed, both parties are bound under contract law. Because of abuses reported, state legislatures in some states enacted a law calling for a cooling-off period. This statute allows the homeowner, but not the builder, to call off the agreement within 3 days of making it. This statutory rule does not disturb other principles of contracts for home improvements. It only expresses a special rule to carry out a particular public policy.

1.5 THE TOPICS

This text presents material on contracts, sales, commercial paper, secured transactions, agency, partnerships, and corporation law. Contracts and agency principles are generally founded on common law. The other subjects, while governed generally by the common law, have been modified by attempts to cause the states to adopt so-called uniform codes or acts. It should be noted, however, that even where all or many of the states have adopted these uniform codes or acts, the provisions adopted often differ in detail among the adopting states. These differences in detail may be important in particular legal situations.

As mentioned previously, the common-law principles of sales, commercial paper, and secured transactions have been restated and modified by the UCC. Partnership rules have been restated in most states by the enactment of the provisions of the Uniform Partnership Act and the Uniform Limited Partnership Act. Corporation law also has been the subject of numerous attempts to make it uniform; the most prominent of these attempts is the Model Business Corporation Act. Reference to statutory modification (the code type as well as other attempts at uniformity) will be made in appropriate sections of this volume so as to provide the reader with the current sources of many of the basic principles of business law.

EXAMPLE 9.   Certain basic principles govern the concept of agreement (offer and acceptance) in contracts. Although the sale of goods is treated under Article 3 of the UCC, certain parts of sales law will be noted under the general topic of contracts in respect to agreements involving the sale of goods. Those principles will, however, be repeated and elaborated upon later in the section on sales.

1.6 TORTS AND CRIMES

This outline does not concentrate on the topics of torts and crimes. However, such legal effects do occur from time to time in business settings. A *tort* is a civil wrong for which the injured party can sue for damages. Such a suit is a private civil action. A *crime* is an offense against society for which the state seeks from the accused a fine, his freedom, or even his life. It is a public action in which the state is the prosecutor. An incident may contain facts indicating both a tort and a crime.

EXAMPLE 10.   Randle took a camera from a store display window without the retailer's permission. If such taking was done under circumstances the state defines as a crime, Randle may be prosecuted for larceny. However, whether or not Randle's action has criminal consequences, the retailer has a right under tort law to sue in a civil case for damages or the return of the camera. Randle's action was a civil wrong, a tort called *conversion*.

1.7 TORTS

Torts may be classified as *personal* torts or *property* torts. The former refers to those acts causing injury to one's person, one's reputation, and, in some cases, even to one's feelings. A property tort, on the other hand, describes an economic injury to property caused by the civil wrong. The person committing the tort is called a *tortfeasor*. Personal torts include acts constituting negligence, assault, battery, slander, libel, false arrest, and even emotional distress. Torts against property are trespass, conversion, and wrongful interference with a contractual relationship.

EXAMPLE 11.   Barret had a busy day. Lying, he told his barber that his banker was a thief (slander). On his way to flag a taxi he beat out another person by raising his fist until the other surrendered his claim to the cab (assault) and then pushed an elderly woman out of the way for the cab (battery). He borrowed his secretary's gold pen and now refuses to return it (conversion) and agreed to pay his supplier an extra $1,000 if the supplier would quit doing business with another company despite the supplier's contract (wrongful interference with a contractual relationship). Further, without permisssion Barret parked his car in his neighbor's driveway (trespass).

The most frequent tort actions involve negligence. Negligence is proved when the plaintiff shows that the defendant owed a duty to the plaintiff, that the defendant fell below the standard of care of a reasonable person, and that such act proximately caused the injury complained of.

EXAMPLE 12.   A supermarket owner has a produce section with green beans piled high on the display counter. A customer picks out the beans, and some beans fall to the floor. A different customer walks by, fails to see a bean on the floor, slips on it, falls, and injures herself. The retailer had a duty to maintain safe premises. A failure to correct the dangerous situation in timely fashion may mean falling below the standard of care. If such omission was the proximate cause of the injury (a broken bone, for example), the retailer would be liable for negligence.

In the above example the defendant might raise the question of the plaintiff's negligence in not watching where she was walking. This would be a charge of *contributory negligence*. If found to be true, it could be a complete defense. Many states have abolished contributory negligence as a complete bar to a plaintiff's recovery, substituting instead the *doctrine of comparative negligence*. Under this principle, each party bears some of the consequences.

EXAMPLE 13.   Tuttle was driving unsafely, and Berenson was walking carelessly. Except for both acts Berenson would not have been struck by Tuttle's automobile. Both were negligent. Under contributory negligence Berenson would collect nothing from Tuttle. Berenson, who suffered $10,000 in injuries, would receive $6,000 under comparative negligence if, for example, the jury found him 40 percent negligent and Tuttle 60 percent.

The plaintiff's negligence does not always operate to diminish recovery. This is seen where the "last clear chance" doctrine applies.

EXAMPLE 14.   A minor was skipping down the center of a school driveway (negligence) when she saw a car approaching. She tried to stop but slipped and fell, leaving her left foot extended onto the driveway. The car ran over her foot. The driver cannot use this negligence against the minor if the last clear chance doctrine applies. Such applies when a plaintiff puts herself in peril by her own negligence, the driver becomes aware (or should have been aware) of the peril from which the plaintiff cannot or is not extricating herself, and the defendant has a reasonable opportunity to save the other from harm but fails to do so.

Negligence actions are numerous and expensive. Therefore some jurisdictions have enacted a so-called no-fault doctrine in dealing with automobile cases. Economic losses are collected from one's own insurance company irrespective of fault. Main goals of the plan include the establishment of a system which provides prompt and certain payment for reasonable loss.

EXAMPLE 15.   An injured motorist claimed that the no-fault statute deprived him of his right to full recovery in tort. The new statute exempted a negligent driver from liability for up to $2,000 to the extent that the injured's own insurance covered the loss. The injured motorist contended that he would have recovered $800 for "pain and suffering" under tort law but for the new statute. The court held the no-fault statute constitutional. It noted that the plan created bore a reasonable relation to legislative objectives (e.g., relieving court congestion), that the plan pared the high cost of automobile insurance, and that the prompt recovery features provided a reasonable substitute for rights abrogated or modified.

1.8   CRIMES

Criminal law is written in statutes and describes antisocial behavior and the sanctions which follow conviction. More serious offenses are called *felonies*; less serious ones are termed *misdemeanors*. Felonies provide grave consequences to the convicted, usually requiring incarceration in a state penal facility for a period of more than a year. Further, some civil rights are suspended, such as the right to vote or hold public office. Felonies include the crimes of treason, murder, rape, arson, robbery, embezzlement, burglary, and other offenses proscribed by federal and state governments. Criminal trials are quite technical and require the state to prove every element of the crime.

EXAMPLE 16. Assume that the state statute defines larceny as (1) taking and (2) carrying away (3) the personal property (4) of another (5) with specific intent to deprive the true owner of it permanently. Starr, aged 17 years, lived next door to Farro, who has just purchased a new car. It was parked in Farro's driveway. Starr looks it over, admires it, and spots the keys in the car. He cannot resist. Starr jumps in the car for a ride. The car never returns in one piece, as it is wrecked on the next block. The state could prove that Starr was guilty of taking and carrying away the personal property of another, but the circumstances do not suggest that Starr meant to take it permanently. Technically, there is no showing of larceny, as one element is missing. Starr may be guilty of a lesser crime, i.e., "using an automobile without the owner's permission," which is a lesser felony or misdemeanor in some states.

Misdemeanors are less serious offenses. State or federal statutes describe whether the crime is a felony or a misdemeanor. Generally the punishment prescribed suggests the characterization. As a rule of thumb, an offense calling for imprisonment in other than a state prison, or for less than a year, is probably a misdemeanor rather than a felony.

Chapter 2

Legal Systems

2.1 FUNCTION OF THE LEGAL SYSTEM

The rules about to be studied arose out of conflict. However, if every contract would be effective only after a lawsuit, the legal system could not operate effectively. It is the expectation that the legal system will generally be obeyed that brings both private and public order. The operation of the legal system, and the results it produces, provides guidelines accepted by society. Therefore, one studies the legal system because it plays a prominent role in announcing and enforcing principles by which one lives and does business.

2.2 APPELLATE AND TRIAL COURTS

An *appellate court* is one in which judges decide whether a lower court committed a legal error in rendering a judgment, decree, or other order. It is a court of error. The party appealing is called the *appellant*; the one resisting is the *appellee*. A *trial court*, on the other hand, functions to hear evidence, determine the facts, apply the law to the facts, and render a judgment or decree.

EXAMPLE 1. Bramer sued Sutter for breach of an oral contract to deliver wheat. Sutter admits to such a contract but contends that he promised to deliver Grade B wheat. Bramer disagrees, maintaining that it was Grade A. The court refuses to allow Bramer to introduce into evidence a typed note he claims to have received from Sutter. The note does mention Grade A. There is no signature or other identifying mark on the note. Bramer wants to bring in a typewriting expert to testify. The court refuses to allow this. The jury returns a verdict for Sutter, and the court enters judgment in his favor, i.e., not guilty of breach of contract. Bramer files an appeal to an appellate court. He is the appellant. He contends that it was legal error for the court not to allow the expert witness to testify and for the jury to decide his credibility. The appellate court, consisting of from three to nine judges (as in the U.S. Supreme Court), will decide whether the court below, here the trial court, committed a legal error. If it rules that an error was made, the appellate court would probably reverse the judgment and order a new trial. If it finds no error, it will affirm the judgment of the lower court.

There are many ways to claim error (called *assignments of error*). These include ruling on the introduction of certain evidence, application of the wrong law, or error in instructing the jury on what law to apply, or what presumptions to entertain. Generally, a court is exclusively a trial or an appellate court, but there are a number of exceptions.

2.3 THE ADVERSARY SYSTEM

Litigation is a struggle. Adversaries oppose each other and are usually represented by professional counsel. The court, which represents society, is assigned a somewhat passive role. The burden of presenting and defending a case rests primarily on the competing parties in both criminal and civil trials.

EXAMPLE 2. A defendant was convicted of transporting stolen vehicles across state lines. A coconspirator pleaded guilty and testified against the defendant. During the trial the judge conducted an extensive examination of the witnesses. The defendant was convicted. He appealed, charging that there was undue participation of the court in the trial. The appellate court agreed and reversed the conviction. The court noted that a trial judge may, in the furtherance of justice, question a witness, or even call and question a witness not used by either party. A trial judge should, however, be careful to preserve an attitude of impartiality and guard against giving the jury any impression that the court held an opinion about the defendant's guilt. A judge may believe that he or she can assist in developing the evidence by participating in the interrogation of the witnesses, but ordinarily the judge would do well to forgo such intrusions upon the functions of counsel. In reversing the conviction, the appellate court noted that all courts, whether trial or appellate, should at all times adhere to an atmosphere of cold neutrality.

2.4 ISSUES OF FACT

The "trier of the facts"—the jury, or the judge where a jury trial has been waived or where no jury is permitted—decides what happened, occurs, or will occur. Such trier need have no training in legal rules. He or she must consider and examine only the evidence presented and then draw conclusions about the actuality of such facts as are claimed.

EXAMPLE 3. Talbot claimed she paid Salas $50 down on a stereo which Salas agreed to sell for $100. Salas's attorney contends that Talbot paid no money, that no agreement was reached, and that the only time the parties spoke to one another occurred at a bar when Salas was too intoxicated to understand anything. Talbot will testify under oath where, when, and how the agreement was reached and will offer to introduce a witness who will testify that he saw Talbot talking to Salas at the decisive time. Salas will testify that he has no money now; that his wife doesn't know of any money he received; and that he had talked to a number of persons at the bar the night of the alleged agreement before he passed out, but he does not remember Talbot being present. Further, several patrons at the bar will testify to the condition of Salas at the decisive time. The trier of the facts will hear some of the proffered witnesses but not others, it being within the power of the court to decide whether the proffered evidence is relevant and material.

In the above example the trier of the facts will determine from the evidence the decisive facts. Did the parties state language of agreement? If so, what were its terms? Was money paid down? What was the state of Salas's mind from the evidence?

2.5 ISSUES OF LAW

Triers of facts render verdicts, but only judges issue judgments. If certain facts are found, the court can then rule as a matter of law that the party is entitled to judgment. Issues of law will be the main subject of this outline. If the trier of the facts has some evidence on which to base a decision, the appellate court will not disturb the finding.

2.6 JURISDICTION OF COURTS

The term "jurisdiction" has a number of legal meanings. *Jurisdiction* may mean the power of a court to affect the defendant, the plaintiff, or certain property. It also identifies the territorial limits of a particular court, the monetary limits of disputes, or the type of case the court may hear and rule upon.

Courts have jurisdiction over the plaintiff when he or she files suit in the case and over the defendant by process. If the defendant is personally served by an official in the state, the court gains *in personam* jurisdiction over him or her.

EXAMPLE 4. Adam owed Tower $5,000 which he refused to pay, and Tower filed an action in Los Angeles civil court where Tower lives. Adam is from Arizona but travels to Los Angeles frequently. If a sheriff or other officer serves court papers including a copy of the complaint (and thereby obtaining personal service of process) on Adam while he is in California, such court has *in personam* jurisdiction over Adam.

EXAMPLE 5.   Fallon died and left a number of heirs, few of whom were on friendly terms. Fallon owned a mine in Colorado which is quite valuable. It is not clear who has title to the mine. This issue can only be decided by a Colorado court, as the subject matter, the land, is within the sole jurisdiction of the place where it is located.

Some parties are within a court's jurisdiction despite lack of personal service at the time and place of the lawsuit. A resident, for example, can be personally bound by service at his residence although he himself is not present. Further, a foreign business person doing business in the state, or a nonresident motorist causing an accident, can be subject to jurisdiction though not personally served in the state.

EXAMPLE 6.   Tarr resides in Arkansas but travels extensively. As a jobber she sells insulation material in Illinois, where, on her last trip, she was involved in an automobile collision. A Chicago customer is upset over Tarr's failure to deliver quality goods. And back in Little Rock, Tarr's dentist is about to sue her for an overdue bill. Even if the Arkansas sheriff or other officer cannot find Tarr at her residence, a summons and copy of the complaint can be left there in care of an adult member of the household. Further, both the Chicago buyer and the injured Illinois motorist can obtain *in personam* jurisdiction over Tarr by following statutory guidelines.

Where personal jurisdiction is not possible, an *in rem* jurisdiction may exist if the defendant has property in the state. Each state has jurisdiction over the property within its boundaries, and the *in rem* power exists to the extent of the defendant's ownership. Simply illustrated, one's summer cottage in a neighboring state can be subject to such jurisdiction. The owner could suffer a judgment to the extent of the value of his or her (the defendant's) interest in the cottage.

2.7   THE FEDERAL COURT SYSTEM

Three main federal courts are the district courts, the circuit courts of appeals, and the Supreme Court of the United States. District courts function primarily as trial courts and the others as appellate courts. Every state has at least one district court. These courts handle both civil and criminal cases involving a federal statute, and where parties are residents from different states, a civil suit can be brought in the federal system. This jurisdiction is based on diversity of citizenship but requires that the amount in dispute exceed $10,000.

Courts of appeal (12 circuits) hear from the district courts and also review decisions of the federal administrative agencies. The Supreme Court is mainly an appellate court, but it does have trial or *original jurisdiction* in a few instances. These include a dispute between two states or where a foreign representative (e.g., ambassador) is involved. Attempts by most litigants to go all the way to the Supreme Court are mostly made by a petition for *certiorari*. The Court has discretion as to whether it will hear the case. Very few such petitions are granted.

EXAMPLE 7.   A black person filed suit in federal district court, had a trial, and lost. He had believed all along that the jury was against him because he was black. He charged that, because there was no black on the jury, his civil rights were denied. He appealed to the circuit court of appeal, which affirmed the lower court. He then filed a petition for *certiorari* to the Supreme Court. The Supreme Court refused to hear the case and thereby denied *certiorari*. Typically, less than 3 percent of such petitions are granted by the Supreme Court.

Other federal courts include the Tax Court, Court of Customs, Court of Customs Appeal, and Court of Claims. These specialized courts handle cases of the types suggested by their names.

2.8   STATE COURT SYSTEMS

Both tradition and the amount of business combine to determine the makeup of state court systems. They too have trial and appellate courts with different names, and their functions are similar to the federal system described above. However, most states provide a special court for criminal cases. Also, they have numerous special courts. Probate courts, juvenile courts, and small claims courts are the names of some of these special state courts.

EXAMPLE 8.   Farnsworth's aunt died, leaving no children but a number of nephews and nieces. To settle her estate there would usually be no litigation, but a court proceeding may be needed to determine her proper heirs, collect her property, pay her creditors, and distribute the remainder of her estate according to her will if she left one, otherwise as provided by law. Farnsworth may have to file a petition in probate court seeking settlement of these affairs.

2.9   COURT PROCEDURE

Most civil cases begin with the plaintiff filing a *complaint*, a writing setting forth basic facts entitling the plaintiff to legal relief. The court system will then serve *process*, i.e., notice, on the defendant by which he or she is notified to defend by filing an answer, a motion to dismiss, or other appropriate response.

EXAMPLE 9.   A plaintiff filed a complaint suing the defendant, charging that on December 1, 19X3, the sum of $5,000 was delivered to and received by the defendant from the plaintiff. The plaintiff demands its return. The defendant files a *motion to dismiss*. In effect, this admits the facts alleged but says, "so what?" and thus challenges the plaintiff to state upon what legal ground should the money be returned. The defendant would win his or her motion and the case would be dismissed if the plaintiff could not state a reason why the money should be returned, such as a loan or an advance against expenses not incurred.

If the complaint did state a legal complaint, the defendant would answer it and perhaps deny some of the facts alleged. This would put the case *at issue* for which the trier of the facts would decide the facts. Additionally, the defendant might have his or her own complaint and express it in a counterclaim. Before the trial the parties may engage in *discovery*. This includes depositions (taking testimony outside of court), requests for admissions, interrogatories, production of documents, and, in personal injury actions, even physical and mental examinations of persons.

Where preliminary procedures do not settle the dispute, the case goes to trial, and in jury cases, a panel is selected from the community. Such *petit jurors* are called to determine the facts. Each side can challenge prospective jurors in the *voir dire* (i.e., to speak the truth). A juror can be challenged for *cause* or through the exercise of the *right of peremptory challenge*. If counsel can successfully challenge for cause, counsel need not use up one of his or her limited number of peremptory challenges. These exist in both civil and criminal trials.

EXAMPLE 10.   A defendant was convicted of armed robbery, and he appealed. The prosecutor for the state used six of seven peremptory challenges to remove prospective jurors who belonged to the same race as the defendant. The defendant objected to such use. The court ruled that this was no error. The essential nature of a peremptory challenge is that it may be exercised without a reason stated and without being subject to the court's control. Challenges for cause permit rejection of jurors on a narrowly specified provable and legally cognizable basis (e.g., bias, interest) of partiality.

At trial each party puts forth a case. Testimony and documents which are relevant and material to the issue are evidence. *Relevant* means that the evidence offered tends to prove what it is intended to prove, while *material* refers to a fact which would have some bearing on the outcome.

EXAMPLE 11.   A defendant offers to introduce a birth certificate reflecting a birth date of 1920 in a trial which questions the age of the plaintiff in a will contest. This would be relevant evidence. However, if such certificate was introduced only to show the age of the plaintiff, and that point was not in issue in the litigation, it would not be material.

The jurors' verdict is not a judgment; the court may enter judgment only after being satisfied the verdict complies with the law. Judgments can order a number of things, and in civil cases the more usual is a command to pay money. Extraordinary relief, e.g., injunctions, specific performance, is granted in equity courts. This will be studied in the chapter on contract remedies.

2.10 ARBITRATION

Parties are permitted to settle civil disputes outside of legal institutions. When they formally attempt such, they enter into arbitration. An arbitration clause is found in some business contracts. An agreement to submit to arbitration is generally valid, as is the submission of an existing dispute to arbitration. Arbitration hearings are, in most instances, informal. Many arbitrators are not lawyers, and the parties may not even be represented by counsel. The rules of procedure regarding evidence, admission of testimony, and documents are somewhat relaxed. Records are usually maintained, but official written arguments to a point (briefs, for example) are rarely submitted.

There is a trend toward an increasing use of arbitration in business disputes. This is not only because it may save the parties the time and expense of litigation, but also because the dealings in question may involve special or particular trade customs or technical questions which the parties consider would be more expertly understood and ruled upon by an arbitrator who is experienced in the matters involved.

2.11 ADMINISTRATIVE AGENCIES

As society became more complex, not all disputes could be settled by lawsuits. The regulation of business and other aspects of society has, in large measure, passed to administrative agencies by legislative action. The widow's claim under social security and the veteran's benefit are both handled through administrative procedures. Business practices are monitored by such agencies as the Federal Trade Commission and working conditions by the Wage and Hour Division of the Department of Labor. Regulatory agencies include those of the federal, state, and local governments.

EXAMPLE 12. Tuff Trucking rents and buys new cars for different purposes and pays no sales tax on cars it buys for its executives. The State Sales Tax Commission challenges this omission and has notified Tuff of a tax deficiency in its monthly sales tax return. Tuff contends that such purchases are exempt under the sales tax law. Usually neither the state nor Tuff would file a lawsuit in this matter. Such a dispute would normally be settled through administrative proceedings. These would include a review by the local agent, a review by his or her supervisor, and maybe a hearing before an administrative judge. The dispute would likely be settled at one of these levels. A lawsuit, while ultimately possible, is rarely invoked in such circumstances.

Solved Problems

2.1   Filbert of Tucson, Arizona, and Task are cousins and have been engaged in business dealings over the years but have become estranged since Task moved to Idaho. Task still owes Filbert $5,000 on the Fury Project, which is not doing well. Filbert is demanding repayment. Task gets nasty and refuses to return Filbert's phone calls. Filbert has made up his mind to sue Task in Arizona. Under these circumstances

(a) an Arizona court will have *in personam* jurisdiction over Task if Task's wife is served by legal process while visiting Arizona.

(b) an Arizona court can obtain *in personam* jurisdiction over Task if Task has a savings account in a Phoenix, Arizona, bank.

(c) Filbert cannot sue a nonresident such as Task in an Arizona court.

(d) Task's financial interest in the Arizona Fury Project can be the subject of *in rem* jurisdiction over Task.

Usually personal jurisdiction over the defendant occurs when the defendant is served in the state with judicial process or, in exceptional cases, in respect to doing business or in regard to vehicular accidents. Serving process on Task's wife in Arizona will not achieve *in personam* jurisdiction over Task. However, if Task has property in Arizona, his interest there can be the subject of an *in rem* jurisdiction. The answer is (*d*).

2.2   It became important at a trial to determine whether the defendant dropped a letter in the corner mailbox on June 3, 19X3, at approximately 11:30 p.m. This "fact" will be decided by

(*a*)   a jury in a jury trial.

(*b*)   a judge in a jury trial.

(*c*)   the date stamped on the envelope by the post office.

(*d*)   evidence about whether the letter was received by the addressee.

Statement (*a*) is correct. A jury is the trier of fact in a jury trial and decides whether such an alleged event as above actually took place. Since the issue is whether the letter was deposited, and at the time stated, the latter two statements are not helpful.

2.3   Adam was sued by Eve for divorce. Adam defended on the grounds that there was no marriage in the first place. Eve countered with the claim that there was a common-law marriage by which each agreed to live with the other, forever. Adam wants to put Eve's cousin on the stand. She will testify that Eve's real name is Sara. The cousin has known Eve for over 30 years. Adam is offering evidence that is

(*a*)   immaterial.

(*b*)   material.

(*c*)   relevant.

(*d*)   irrelevant.

The answer is (*a*). The issue for the court is apparently whether an agreement was made between the parties constituting a common-law marriage. It is not helpful to the solution if Adam proves that Eve is an assumed name. If the agreement was made between the parties, that defense is not good. Accordingly, even if Adam proves the alias, it will not aid the court; it is therefore immaterial. Adam's evidence would be material if he wished to prove he was defrauded by Eve's impersonation, and further, offering the testimony of a cousin who knew her would be relevant since it would tend to prove what is intended to be proved, i.e., impersonation.

2.4   Kramer is a prospective witness. At the *voir dire* (the examination of the jurors) the defendant's attorney learns that Kramer is a business associate of the plaintiff. The defendant's attorney should

(*a*)   exercise one of his peremptory challenges to remove Kramer.

(*b*)   challenge Kramer for cause.

(*c*)   ask for a mistrial.

(*d*)   permit Kramer to be selected, and if the defendant loses, then challenge her qualifications.

A prospective juror can be removed by the court either as a result of a successful challenge for cause or arbitrarily by one side using one of its limited number of peremptory challenges. Here the attorney should first try to urge her removal for cause, i.e., bias, as she is on friendly terms with the plaintiff. The *voir dire* is the proper time to exercise these rights, not after the trial. Choice (*b*) is the answer.

2.5 A civil suit involving no federal statute or question can be brought in a federal court provided

(*a*) the amount in controversy exceeds $10,000.

(*b*) the plaintiff and defendant are citizens of different states.

(*c*) both (*a*) and (*b*).

(*d*) a labor union is involved.

The diversity of citizenship rule allows civil suits to be tried in a federal court provided the plaintiff and the defendant are citizens of different states and the amount in controversy exceeds $10,000. Choice (*c*) is the answer.

Chapter 3

Introduction

3.1 GENERAL

Contracts have for their objective the accomplishment of some business purpose as distinguished from a purely social one. The legal rule governing contracts is primarily concerned with the creation and transfer of property rights through the exchanged promises of at least two parties. These promises are not always expressly made, but they do involve a commitment that something shall or shall not happen in the future.

3.2 DEFINITION

There is no one definition of a contract. A contract is, of course, "a legally enforceable agreement," but has been described more formally as a "promise or a set of promises for the breach of which the law gives a remedy, or the performance of which the law in some way recognizes as a duty" (Restatement of Contracts, 2d ed., Section 1). Not all promises are legally enforceable. Some types of agreements do not qualify as contracts, while others legally fail because the parties did not observe some rule of contract law.

EXAMPLE 1. Larson and Taylor agree to meet for lunch at the Regency at 12 noon, Wednesday. Larson changes his mind and doesn't show up. Larson suffers no legal liability for his failure to appear. Social agreements are not binding at law.

EXAMPLE 2. An owner shows his home to a prospective buyer. They find themselves in complete agreement about the terms of the deal and shake hands on the contract. This is an agreement that could be binding. This contract, although for a business purpose and otherwise complete, is not enforceable since contracts for the sale of real estate must be in writing.

3.3 ELEMENTS OF A CONTRACT

In addition to the requirement of a signed writing for certain agreements, there are other reasons why an apparent agreement may not be a contract. The requirements of a contract are

(1) offer and acceptance

(2) reality of consent

(3) consideration

(4) legality

(5) contractual capacity

(6) possible requirement of a writing

These elements must be considered when determining whether a contract is enforceable. Most litigated cases address only one of these areas, but all must be observed. Each of these elements will be discussed in detail later in this book.

EXAMPLE 3.   Alan is out of work. Alan and Burt agree that Burt will pay Alan $500 a month and Alan will accept it until he finds work. This agreement is unenforceable since Alan neither gave up a legal right nor suffered a legal detriment, i.e., did not give consideration, for Burt's promise. Further, if instead of merely promising to accept the money, Alan also promises to supply Burt with lobster that he would illegally catch out of season, the agreement would now fail on another ground, that of illegality.

3.4 CONTRACT LAW IS BASIC

The law of contracts is considered to be the basic law for understanding many other legal transactions. There are, of course, special rules in some commercial areas, but a knowledge of contract law is necessary in order to understand fully the legal principles governing sales, commercial paper, secured transactions, real property, agency, and other fields of business law discussed in later parts of this volume.

EXAMPLE 4.   Linda signed an application for life insurance, submitted to the medical examination, and now awaits the decision of the insurance company. When or whether the policy comes into force is basically a contract-law question. However, an understanding of insurance law, for instance whether or not the written policy must be delivered, may provide a more complete response to the question.

Chapter 4

Classification of Contracts

4.1 INTRODUCTION

Contracts are classified in a number of ways which assist in understanding how contracts are created, operate, or otherwise function. The usual classifications are (1) executed and executory contracts, (2) bilateral and unilateral contracts, (3) express and implied (in fact or in law) contracts, (4) valid, voidable, void, and unenforceable contracts, and (5) formal and informal contracts.

4.2 EXECUTED AND EXECUTORY CONTRACTS

When all the terms of the contract have been fully performed by both parties, the contract is said to be an *executed contract*. If the terms have not been fully performed, or one or both of the parties remain obligated to do or not to do something in the future, the contract is referred to as an *executory contract*.

EXAMPLE 1. A seller delivered goods to a buyer on credit. The seller has performed her duty; her part is executed. The buyer's performance, to pay, is in the executory stage. If the seller and buyer only exchanged promises to perform in the future, there is a contract; it is wholly in the executory stage, but it is a binding obligation nonetheless.

4.3 BILATERAL AND UNILATERAL CONTRACTS

A *bilateral contract* is one in which both parties exchanged promises to perform in the future. A *unilateral contract* is one in which only one party made a promise for an act or performed an act for a promise.

EXAMPLE 2. Many daily contracts are unilateral in nature. When a homeowner offers to pay $25 to have his lawn mowed, the act of the worker in mowing the lawn results in a unilateral contract. The customer made a promise to pay, and the worker accepted by an act, here mowing the lawn.

4.4 EXPRESS AND IMPLIED CONTRACTS

Commitments may be expressed in clear, understandable terms, either in writing or in speech. These are *express contracts*. Situations arise, however, in which the terms of the agreement are not expressed and must be inferred from the conduct of the parties. An *implied contract* is one in which the terms have not been expressed or declared by the parties in speech or in writing but are to be implied or inferred from their conduct or acts. Moreover, implied contracts can be implied *in fact* or implied *in law*. Only the implied-in-fact contract is a "true" contract.

EXAMPLE 3. The customer who places himself in the barber chair implies his intention to purchase a haircut. The barber's response of cutting the hair is the acceptance he implies. Neither party expressed his intention through speech or writing. Had both engaged in a dialogue regarding their intentions before their actions, the contract would be express and bilateral and would be in the executory stage.

15

An implied-in-law contract is commonly called a *quasi contract*. It differs from the implied-in-fact contract in that there is no requirement that the court be satisfied that the parties intended to contract. The rule is generally used in cases in which the court is attempting to prevent unfairness, fraud, unjust enrichment, or other wrongdoing. Parties, for example, who sue to recover money, goods, or compensation for valuable services delivered to another by mistake would invoke the theory of quasi contract or implied-in-law contract.

EXAMPLE 4. A senior citizen, with no intention of contracting, gains admittance and free room and board in a home for the elderly by misrepresenting himself as a poor citizen. He would be liable for the reasonable value of the supplied room and board under the theory of quasi contract. The basis for the recovery is that a benefit was conferred upon the citizen and it would be inequitable for him not to pay for the benefit.

The principle of implied-in-law contract cannot be invoked by a party who is negligent on his or her own part. For example, this is seen where a party sent to repair a roof works at the wrong address. The owner of the repaired roof who did not see or approve this act would not be liable in quasi contract.

4.5   VALID, VOIDABLE, VOID, AND UNENFORCEABLE CONTRACTS

Contracts may also be classified in accordance with their binding effect on the parties. A *valid contract* is one which all the parties are bound to honor. A *voidable contract*, however, is an agreement which is valid and binding until it is avoided or disaffirmed by the party entitled to avoid or disaffirm it. This power to avoid contracts applies, for example, to agreements made by parties of youthful age (i.e., minors), those defrauded, or those in other circumstances where the law permits disaffirmance. It must be remembered, however, that the voidable contract is a binding agreement at all times until it is avoided by the party having such power to disaffirm the contract.

A *void contract* is no contract at all. It is an agreement which is unenforceable. While the term seems to be a contradiction, the classification is used to distinguish those agreements which appear to be contracts but, because of some grave defect, are void. Illegal bargains, many times masquerading as true contracts, are the most common examples of void contracts.

EXAMPLE 5. Benson agreed to buy a used car for $3,000. Benson had no business talent. The car could have been purchased for $2,200 with a little negotiating. This may be a bad bargain, but it is a valid contract.

EXAMPLE 6. Benson agreed to buy the car for $3,000 even though he knew the price to be a bit high, but the seller said that the car "had been owned by an old schoolteacher from Pasadena." This was a lie. Benson believed it, and it was his reason for paying so much. Fraud may have been committed here. If so, Benson may avoid or disaffirm the contract since it is a voidable one.

EXAMPLE 7. Benson hired Taylor to find a purchaser for Benson's house, agreeing to pay Taylor a 7 percent commission. Taylor is successful and demands the 7 percent. Benson refuses to pay. Taylor is not a licensed broker as required by state regulatory law and is therefore acting illegally. This seemingly good agreement is an illegal or void contract. Taylor will recover nothing.

Courts label certain contracts *unenforceable* when by reason of certain technical rules the law will not allow a remedy if the other party raised the rule in defense. Common types of contracts which are unenforceable include those in which the statute of limitations has run out, in which the debt was discharged in bankruptcy, or where the Statute of Frauds requiring certain proof (generally written evidence) was not observed. The defense of statute of limitations maintains that the claim is too old, that the plaintiff waited too long to bring an action, while the defense of bankruptcy maintains that the defendant has been discharged of his or her obligation in a federal bankruptcy proceeding. The *Statute of Frauds* is the name given to the state statutes which prescribe certain forms of proof in order for a contract to be binding.

EXAMPLE 8.   Handl ran a grocery store and sold goods on credit to X and Y in 1979 and orally agreed to sell his building to Z. The statute of limitations on open accounts in the state is 1 year. Y went bankrupt and was discharged of all his debts in 1981. Z changed her mind and backed out of the deal a month after she told Handl she would buy the store. If Handl sued all of them, X could defend on the grounds of the statute of limitations, Y on the same grounds or on bankruptcy discharge, and Z on the grounds of the Statute of Frauds, that is, the contract was not in writing. At that stage all the contracts could be classified as unenforceable.

4.6 FORMAL AND INFORMAL CONTRACTS

Some contracts are enforceable by reason of the formality under which they are signed or made. Three types are recognized: a contract under seal, a contract of record, and simple contracts. Simple contracts are informal contracts, while sealed contracts and contracts of record are known as formal contracts. A contract under seal is one evidenced by a writing and having a special impression, seal, paper wafer, or the like attached to the instrument. Today, it is frequently seen as a printing of a wafer after the contracting party's signature with the word "Seal" or the letters "L.S." (for the Latin phrase *locus sigilli*, meaning "place of the seal") placed after the signature. The fact that a party "sealed" a document had great legal significance under the common law. It made the requirement for consideration unnecessary, and by statute in many states it permitted, and still does in some, the period during which one may sue on a sealed document to be considerably longer than on most other contracts.

The UCC repeals the effect of seals in regard to the sale of goods, and in many states the effects of seals have been abolished by statute for other types of obligations as well.

A *contract of record* refers to those acknowledgments made by a party before a court. A promise made by a defendant in a criminal case declaring that he or she will appear for trial is one such contract, commonly called a *recognizance bond*.

Most contracts today are *simple contracts*. They are neither contracts of record nor sealed contracts. Any agreement, whether in writing or oral, which is not a contract of record or a sealed contract is a simple contract.

Black Letter Law
A Summary

1.   Executed and executory contracts describe the state of the performance of the parties to a contract.

2.   An agreement in which each party exchanged promises to perform is called a bilateral contract, while a promise for an act or an act for a promise is labeled a unilateral contract.

3.   Express contracts are created by the language of the parties; an implied-in-fact contract is created by their other conduct.

4.   When a court uses a contract approach to prevent unfairness or unjust enrichment, it applies the principle of a contract implied in law, or quasi contract.

5.   A voidable contract refers to an agreement in which one may rescind the contract for causes such as infancy, mistake, fraud, or wrongdoing.

6.   An agreement which has no legal effect at all is called void.

7. If a previously valid contract is no longer capable of being proved, it is called unenforceable.

8. Special contracts, such as negotiable instruments or written agreements under seal, are called formal contracts; all others, whether oral or written, are simple contracts.

Solved Problems

4.1 Marie telephoned M. Pierre, hairstylist, for a 10:00 a.m. appointment and obtained such time for her hairstyling.

(*a*) This is a purely social agreement, not a legal one.

(*b*) Marie has entered into a formal contract.

(*c*) Unless M. Pierre recorded the telephone call, he could not prove this agreement.

(*d*) The parties entered into a simple contract.

   The answer is (*d*). This oral agreement was created by language and is therefore an express and simple contract. It is not a sealed writing or other special type of written contract and therefore does not qualify as a formal contract. This was not a social agreement, but a legal one. As to proof, a tape recording is not necessary as the parties may testify about their oral agreement. The testimony of the parties would determine the establishment of the agreement.

4.2 Hone agreed to sell his house to Taswell for $120,000. This oral agreement was reached after 3 hours of intense negotiation in which all the terms were considered carefully.

(*a*) Contract law alone will govern this transaction.

(*b*) This is an unenforceable contract since the sale of land must be in writing under the Statute of Frauds.

(*c*) This is an executed contract.

(*d*) The parties entered into an implied-in-law or quasi contract.

   Statement (*b*) is the correct answer. A contract for the sale of land requires a writing, the lack of which would make this an unenforceable contract if contested. While the rules of contract might dominate certain questions in this transaction, real property law would also have to be consulted. The parties intended to contract and used language; therefore the contract is not implied but express.

4.3 The board of directors of the Mico Corporation voted to award a construction contract to the Mills Construction Company. The board authorized the company president to carry out the resolution by entering into a written contract. The facts in this case

(*a*) indicate that an implied-in-fact contract is contemplated.

(*b*) suggest that only corporation law will be involved.

(*c*) reflect a void contract.

(*d*) would be examined in the light of corporation law, contract law, and agency law.

   Statement (*d*) reflects the concern of a lawyer. Corporation law, for example, would govern the acts of the board, agency law would govern the acts of the president in carrying out the board's instructions, and the terms of the construction contract agreement would be examined under contract principles.

4.4 The seller delivered a Model XL compressor to the buyer, who paid the full purchase price of $500. Under these circumstances, (*a*)   the contract is voidable on grounds of fraud.

(*b*)   this contract is fully executed.

(*c*)   the performance is fully executory.

(*d*)   this agreement is void.

The answer is (*b*). Both parties appear to have fully performed. The contract has been executed on both sides and is at rest. If the buyer had merely agreed to pay in the future and the seller delivered the compressor, the contract would be said to be partly executory and partly executed.

4.5   Dr. Fell happened upon an accident scene and rendered valuable medical assistance to one of the unconscious victims. Under these circumstances Dr. Fell could try to prove

(*a*)   an executory contract.

(*b*)   an implied-in-fact contract.

(*c*)   an implied-in-law or quasi contract.

(*d*)   a formal contract.

The answer is an implied-in-law or quasi contract, statement (*c*). A court may believe that, in order for justice to be done and to avoid unjust enrichment, the doctor should be entitled to some compensation. However, since the victim had no opportunity to refuse the help, the court may be reluctant to imply a duty to the accident victim under law. An implied-in-fact contract cannot occur since both parties did not intend to contract; the victim could not do so under the circumstances. The doctor executed his or her performance but is yet to be paid.

4.6   Powers, aged 17 years, orally agreed to take dancing lessons for a period of 2 years from Ace Studio. Ace obtained this agreement by falsely misrepresenting that its teachers had taught Fred Astaire how to dance. Which of the following elements of contract law would not be an issue under these facts?

(*a*)   Offer and acceptance.

(*b*)   Capacity of the parties.

(*c*)   Formality, the Statute of Frauds.

(*d*)   Reality of consent, fraud.

There would be no question of whether there was an offer and acceptance, statement (*a*). The parties clearly appear to have agreed. The consent of Powers, however, may not be real, as fraud was involved. The contract dealing with a long-term arrangement, over 1 year, should have been in writing under the Statute of Frauds. Powers might also raise the question of his infancy, the capacity of one of the parties, as he is a minor.

Chapter 5

Offer and Acceptance

5.1 GENERAL

Every contract must have the mutual agreement of the parties. Commonly, one party, the offeror, makes an offer to the offeree, who receives the offer and accepts it. This mutual agreement is manifested by their conduct such as oral statements, writings, or "other acts." Other acts are those actions which the law infers reflect mutual agreement, as in implied-in-fact contracts.

EXAMPLE 1. "I'll pay you $300 for the stereo," says the offeror. When the offeree hears of, or learns of, this, the offer is made. The offeree nods his head in agreement. The court can reasonably find a manifestation of the agreement by this conduct, the acceptance as reflected by the head movement of the offeree. Only an offeree can accept an offer.

5.2 PRELIMINARY NEGOTIATIONS

An offer is the communicated intention of the offeror to contract with the offeree. The parties must seriously intend to make a binding agreement. Preliminary negotiations, general in nature, are not legal offers. Accordingly, invitations to bid, advertisements, catalog information, price tickets in stores, circulars, and incomplete proposals are actions suggesting that a contract is to be entered into later. These are not legal offers that a party can accept. Parties who respond to such statements in a serious and definite manner are not offerees who accept, but are at most offerors.

EXAMPLE 2. Able has before him three writings: the morning newspaper advertising the model refrigerator he wants "on sale for $650," a mail-order catalog showing a Bonica camera for $350, and a letter from his friend stating that she "is ready to sell her boat if she can get at least $3,500 for it." Able's actions in attempting to hand over to the sales clerk $650 for the refrigerator, in mailing out an order blank with check enclosed for the Bonica camera, and in telephoning his friend that he "accepts the offer regarding the boat" are not acceptances, but are at most merely offers to contract.

The law does not absolutely prohibit advertisements and the like from being offers, but unless there is clearer evidence of a serious intent to contract, come one or all, the law takes the wise position that these actions are merely invitations to negotiate. If, however, an advertisement, for example, is specific enough so that a court can assume that the advertiser did mean to contract with anyone who appeared in response to the advertisement, an offer can be said to have been made.

EXAMPLE 3. The *Daily Tribune* prints a Baker Department Store advertisement which reads, "Five Model No. 723 TVs, $175 each, first come, first served." Courts have held this to be a legal offer allowing the first five customers tendering their money to be acceptors of the offer.

5.3 DEFINITENESS

Offers must be definite, because vague or incomplete terms generally result in no contract when the offeree "accepts." This is not to say that some terms may be unspoken or untreated by the parties. Major terms of contracts, such as the performance expected, should be expressed or be obvious enough to permit a court to know what to enforce. At times, terms such as price, time of performance, and other major terms may be supplied by the courts when finding that the parties agreed by implication to "reasonable" terms, especially when the agreement was executed by one of the parties.

EXAMPLE 4. Harriet has a dangerous broken front porch step which she "orders" repaired by the local carpenter "as soon as possible." The exact time of performance and rate of pay are not mentioned by the parties. In a dispute the court could rule that a contract was made and that a "reasonable" price must be paid such as is paid to carpenters in the community for like services. A reasonable time limit would be a matter of several days due to the facts of the case, i.e., dangerous condition and the words "as soon as possible."

In dealing with the sale of personal property the UCC has greatly liberalized the "definiteness" requirement. As will be seen in Part III (Sales), even if "one or more terms are left open a contract for sale does not fail for indefiniteness if the parties have intended to make a contract and there is a reasonably certain basis for giving an appropriate remedy," UCC, Section 2-204(3).

5.4 SECRET INTENTION

A contract is the result of a meeting of the minds of the parties. This meeting of the minds is measured, however, by an objective rather than a subjective standard. Secret intentions of one of the parties which the other party could not reasonably discern from the other's conduct will not prevent a court from ruling that a meeting of the minds existed. For example, an offer or acceptance made as a joke may reasonably, or objectively, be taken seriously by the other party. In such a case a contract has been formed.

EXAMPLE 5. Adam informs his two friends that by pretending to offer his 19X1 Honda for sale at $1,000 he can "get Baker excited." Baker listens to the offer, is excited over the bargain, and accepts, as a reasonable person might do. Adam can easily prove his secret intention of a "joking offer," but a court could allow the agreement to stand under the objective theory of contracts.

5.5 COMMUNICATION OF THE OFFER

Offers become legal offers only upon communication to the offeree and may be revoked or withdrawn by the offeror at any time before the communication of acceptance by the offeree. One cannot accept an offer not addressed to him or her, and further, one cannot accept an offer without knowing about it. For example, two letters that pass in the mail, each containing the language of an agreement between the parties, are only considered to be two offers, each to the other. That is, the acceptance must be induced by the offer.

Generally, the power of the offeror to revoke the offer persists even if the offeror agreed to keep the offer open for a definite future period. There are some exceptions to this rule: options, firm offers, and some public bidding cases. In an option the offeror cannot withdraw within the time granted because an option is itself a contract to keep an offer open. A contract requires legal consideration, an element discussed in a later section. Options, given for legal consideration, are therefore enforceable. Firm offers are those made by merchants for the sale of goods, that is, personal property. Under the UCC, Section 2-205, a firm offer is one made in writing by a merchant promising to keep an offer open for a period not in excess of 3 months. This offer cannot be revoked despite the absence of consideration. Further, a unilateral offer made to another who is acting on such an offer may not be revoked. Here the doctrine of *promissory estoppel*, i.e., relying on the offer to one's detriment, provides the basis for such a result. Finally, offers in the form of bids made to public agencies in response to an advertisement for bids are not revocable in some states by statute or case law.

EXAMPLE 6. Laslow needed time to find financing for the purchase of Olson's house. Olson promised in writing to keep the offer open for 30 days. Ten days later Olson found another buyer and notified Laslow. The offer was revoked when Laslow was notified, or otherwise learned, of the sale. However, if Laslow had made a deposit of, say, $100 (called *consideration*) for Olson's promise to keep the offer open, an option would have been created. Options cannot be revoked.

EXAMPLE 7.   The U.S. Navy advertised for bids for the construction of 30 supply huts. Standard Construction submitted a sealed bid. Before the bid opening, Standard decided to revoke its bid. It cannot revoke despite the fact that this is not an option. Generally, bids to the federal government cannot be revoked. Some states also enforce this rule.

Once the offer has been accepted, the contract is formed and neither party may unilaterally sever the agreement. It is important, however, that the parties be properly identified as offeror or offeree in some particular negotiating situations. An auctioneer, for example, is the offeree and the bidder is the offeror. Unless the auction is announced as "without reserve," the auctioneer may withdraw the article from the auction even after bids have been made. Since the bidder is the offeror, he or she too can revoke a bid any time before the acceptance of the bid by the auctioneer.

5.6   TERMINATION OF OFFER

An offer does not remain open indefinitely. It ends if there is communication of rejection, if a counteroffer is made, or if the offer is revoked, as well as if one of the parties dies or becomes insane or if a reasonable amount of time has passed since the offer was made. An offeree's negative response is a rejection, as is his or her proposal to change the terms through a counteroffer. The death of either party terminates the offer whether the other is aware of the death or not.

Termination by reason of the passage of a reasonable length of time poses most of the problems in determining whether an effective acceptance was made. The law assumes that the offer remains open for the period specified by the offeror or, in the absence of such, for a reasonable length of time according to the circumstances. In this regard there are some guidelines: An offer to buy or sell an item whose price fluctuates widely and quickly has a short life, sometimes only hours. Where the subject matter is not changing in value or demand, a longer time is assumed, certainly for the day the offer was received and, in some circumstances, much longer. However, an offer made in conversation with another is short-lived because it terminates at the end of the conversation.

EXAMPLE 8.   A corporate president called in her two out-of-town engineers for a Friday afternoon conference and criticized their operations. Both engineers had long-term employment contracts. Disturbed by the criticism, the engineers offered to resign. The president did not respond but continued to deal with other matters. Later, the meeting broke up. Back home on Monday morning the engineers found telegrams from the president "accepting your gracious offers to resign." The engineers were forced to leave, and they sued, claiming there was no contract of resignation. The court ruled that the "offers to resign" had terminated at the end of the conversation on Friday afternoon and could not be accepted thereafter.

A legal revocation occurs, except in public offer cases, only when, and if, before the offer has been accepted the offeree learns it is no longer valid. The offeree may learn either directly or indirectly that an offer is no longer valid. For example, an offeree may learn of an offer's revocation by implication, as in the case of seeing notice of the sale of goods previously offered to the offeree. An offeree who communicates his or her acceptance in a timely manner before receiving a previously dispatched revocation has made a valid contract.

EXAMPLE 9.   Taylor received an offer by mail and is seriously considering accepting. Unknown to Taylor the offeror had second thoughts and has already dispatched a letter (or telegram) of revocation. The offer is not revoked until Taylor receives the notice of revocation or otherwise learns of the withdrawal of the offer.

EXAMPLE 10.   Taylor reads in his local newspaper of a patent attorney's offer to pay a fee to anyone who witnessed a demonstration of a new cattle feeder at a recent trade show. Taylor had attended the show and decides to accept. The next day's newspaper contains a notice by the attorney revoking the offer; Taylor did not see this. Taylor cannot now accept the offer since a public offer can be revoked in the same manner as the offer was made despite the offeree's ignorance of the revocation.

The rejection of an offer communicated to the offeror terminates the offer. Some communicated thoughts to the offeror may not be negative enough to be called rejections. A clear counterproposal by the offeree is a rejection, but language or conduct indicating a request for further information, or an inquiry about other concessions, may prevent the offeree's response from being a rejection. The UCC, Section 2-207, in dealing with additional or different terms made by an offeree, does not regard them as rejections in the sale of goods.

EXAMPLE 11. A developer offers a housepainter $600 per house for the four houses he will paint, $500 in advance, the balance on completion, and work to commence this week. The housepainter may reply in a number of ways: "No" (rejection); "Yes, but $1,000 down" (a counteroffer and also a rejection); "Sounds okay, but can you raise it a bit?" (neither an acceptance nor a rejection); "Yes. Is it okay if I begin next week?" (acceptance, accompanied by inquiry).

EXAMPLE 12. A purchasing agent orders 500 Model X electric motors for AMX Supply, "$75 each, delivery 30 days, 90 days credit." AMX Supply acknowledges the order at the $75 price, but states "60 days delivery and 60 days credit." This is a sale of goods between merchants under Section 2-217 of the UCC; it is not a rejection but an acceptance. (See Section 5.9 for information on acceptance and sale of goods.)

Offers are also terminated by intervening illegality of the subject matter. Therefore, an offer to provide polygraph (lie detector) services to a firm would terminate if the state should prohibit such services.

5.7 ACCEPTANCES

A contract has been formed when the offer has been accepted. This is a legal reality even if neither party has yet performed and, occasionally, even when one of the parties is not yet aware of the acceptance. The facts which constitute acceptance of the contract depend on the particular behavior of the parties. If, for example, the offeror expressly orders that he hear the words of acceptance from the offeree's own mouth or from a communicated writing, the law will honor such direction and find no contract exists until this communication occurs. It is therefore dependent on the express intentions of the offeror, or, in their absence, what courts interpret to be the reasonable implications of the offeror's intentions, which control the question of whether a legal acceptance has been made.

The general rule has always been that the acceptance must be identical to the offeror's terms. This is sometimes called the *mirror image* or *mirror principle* and is still the rule in all but contracts for the sale of goods governed by Article 2 of the UCC.

At times it becomes important to determine the exact moment a contract is made, that is, when the offeree's intention to accept becomes the legal act of acceptance. This occurs more suddenly when a unilateral contract, rather than a bilateral contract, is contemplated by the parties.

EXAMPLE 13. Harold, by sitting in the barber chair, offers to pay the barber $6 for a haircut. The barber cuts Harold's hair. That is the act of acceptance of a unilateral contract.

Harold offers to sell his stamp collection to Favia for $1,200. Favia says, "OK," which is the verbal act of acceptance of a bilateral contract.

EXAMPLE 14. Harold completes a catalog mail-order form for a $700 camera depicted on page 354. He signs the form, encloses a money order, and sends it to the company. Upon receipt by the company, Harold's order becomes an offer. If the company promptly ships the camera, its conduct in shipping is the act of acceptance, forming a unilateral contract. Since Harold did not specify the method of acceptance, the offeree, a seller of goods, may do what is reasonable under law. The UCC, Section 2-206(1)(b), provides that such an offer invites acceptance "either by a prompt promise to ship or by the prompt . . . shipment."

5.8   SILENCE AS ACCEPTANCE

Generally an acceptance cannot be made by the silence of the offeree even if the offeree meant his silence as an assent. However, silence can be acceptance if the parties have previously agreed that silence constitutes acceptance or if, by their previous conduct, the parties have impliedly agreed to silence as acceptance. Previous conduct of the parties is the most common grounds upon which silence is alleged to constitute acceptance.

EXAMPLE 15.   Con, a sharp operator, mails out 100 letters to various monied parties. Con offers to sell them a widget for $50 and warns that "If I don't hear from you within 30 days, I assume you have accepted my offer; a stamped, self-addressed envelope is enclosed for your answer." Ninety persons ignore the letter and peel off the stamp, seven mail in a loud "no," and three persons who want to buy the widget remain silent. There is no contract for any of the 100 addressees. One can't be forced to contract. Those that remained silent cannot use that as an acceptance since there was no previous understanding that silence would constitute an acceptance.

EXAMPLE 16.   For the past 4 years a tobacco farmer has been buying two or three tobacco flues each year from Miller Supply. Several flues arrive unsolicited in early October, and the farmer has been paying for the flues he keeps and returning the unwanted flues by Thanksgiving Day. This year the farmer waited until Christmas to return the flues he didn't want. His unusual silence constitutes an acceptance since he had a duty to speak earlier, based on the history of dealings between himself and Miller Supply.

For unsolicited goods received by mail, the Federal Postal Reorganization Act (1970) protects the recipient of unsolicited merchandise. This law provides that if one mails unordered goods to a person, that person does not have to make payment and does not have to return the goods. This law does not apply to charities.

5.9   ACCEPTANCE AND SALE OF GOODS

The rule that an acceptance to be effective must conform exactly to (i.e., "mirror") the terms of the offer has been modified by the UCC for the sale of goods. The mirror-image principle is not always applicable to this particular type of contract. The UCC assumes that parties to the sale of goods intend to contract despite apparently different language employed in their acceptances. Under Section 2-207(1) of the UCC, "a definite and seasonable expression of acceptance or a written confirmation . . . operates as an acceptance even if it states terms additional to or different from those offered or agreed upon" unless the acceptor had clearly made his or her acceptance conditional on those other terms. If it does not appear the offeree means to make a counteroffer or reject the offer, a contract exists.

The question is then whether these different or additional terms of the offeree become the contract terms. The different terms won't be, but the additional terms that do not "materially alter" the offer can become part of the contract if both parties are merchants (generally, parties that regularly deal in the goods in question) and the offeror did not previously object or reject within a reasonable time after receipt of the acceptance. This conflict and search for the complete terms of the contract has been called the "battle of the forms." This is in deference to the habit of commercial firms swapping printed forms while contracting. Such forms usually have a number of clauses considered to be beneficial to buyer or seller. The buyer's form is commonly known as the *purchase order* and the seller's form is an *acknowledgment*.

EXAMPLE 17.   A purchasing agent orders 500 Shafer ball valves from Roma Iron Foundry. The purchase order list price is $10 each, FOB Detroit, Central Trucking, and 90 days credit. The iron foundry receives the order, decides to accept, and mails out its acknowledgment which provides for 60 days credit and demands an audited financial statement within 15 days. There is a contract since neither party made its terms conditional to contracting. The 90-day credit period will probably remain the term since this is different from the 60 days offered by the seller. The financial statement requirement is a new or "additional" term and could become part of the contract within a short time. If the court were to hold that the term doesn't materially alter the offer, and if the purchasing agent does not communicate his objection to the additional term of the iron foundry, it becomes a part of the contract.

5.10 DISTANCE AND COMMUNICATION

If parties intend to sign an agreement or, in the presence of each other, exchange promises of agreement, problems of communication of acceptance, rejection, or revocation do not occur. However, much contracting occurs at a distance by mail or telegram, which is considerably less than instantaneous communication. When this delay in communication is present, the intentions of the offeror or offeree are not immediately known by the other, leaving the possibility of contract formation unknown to one of the parties. Generally, the intention to offer, reject, or revoke must be communicated to the other before such intention becomes legally effective. Acceptances, however, form an important exception: acceptances may be constructively communicated if the offeror expressly or impliedly allows this to occur. In effect, acceptance can be formed at the time the offeree dispatches the acceptance rather than when it is received by the offeror.

EXAMPLE 18.   An offeror mails an offer to an offeree who receives it. The offeror changes her mind and quickly telegraphs her withdrawal or revocation of the offer. Until this telegram reaches the offeree, the offer is still open for acceptance.

EXAMPLE 19.   The offeror mails an offer to an offeree who receives it. The offeree mails back a letter of rejection, but before the offeror receives the letter of rejection the offeree telephones his acceptance to the offeror. A contract is formed. Rejection becomes legal only when communicated to the offeror.

The *deposited acceptance rule*, sometimes called the *mailbox rule*, the *implied agency rule*, or the *doctrine of constructive communication of acceptance*, is generally approved in the United States. Further, in sale-of-goods contracts the implication is believed to have been extended further. The UCC, Section 2-206(1)(a), expressly authorizes the offeree, in communicating acceptance, to do so "in any manner and by any medium reasonable in the circumstances." It appears that modern courts apply this rule to more than just the sale of goods.

EXAMPLE 20.   An offeror mails an offer of employment to an offeree. The offeree promptly telegraphs her reply of acceptance. The telegram is misdelivered and doesn't reach the offeror. There was no contract under the implied agency rule, as the risk of the agency not delivering was on the party who employed the agency, here the offeree. Had she used the mail, by implication the contract would be formed whether or not the letter goes astray because she used the same method of communication that was used by the offeror. Recent law suggests that if the telegram was a *reasonable medium* under the circumstances, the contract was formed upon dispatch of the telegram.

EXAMPLE 21.   An offeror mails an offer to sell *goods* to an offeree. The offeree telegraphs her acceptance, and under the business practice, this was reasonable. The telegram of acceptance never arrives. The UCC Section 2-206(1)(a), implies that this is a valid acceptance.

If an offeree attempts to reject before an acceptance, the dispatch of the acceptance will not complete the contract. Contract formation is now dependent upon whether the acceptance reached the offeror before the rejection.

Black Letter Law
A Summary

1. A contract is formed when there is a manifestation of assent to enter into a binding agreement having definite terms.

2. A legal offer is a communicated serious intention to contract with the offeree.

3. Only the party receiving the offer, the offeree, can accept an offer.

4. An acceptance of an offer can be manifested by express language, by other conduct, and, where there was a duty to speak, by the silence of the offeree.

5. Under the reasonable medium, implied agency, or mailbox rule, it is possible for an acceptance to take place without the offeror being aware of the contractual moment.

6. Offers can be revoked anytime before acceptance and through any means by which they are received by the offeree.

7. Except for public offers, a revocation must be communicated to the offeree before it is effective.

8. A rejection of an offer by the offeree becomes effective upon notice to the offeror.

9. Offers lapse at the end of a stated period, by the passage of a reasonable time, and by the death or insanity of the offeror or offeree.

10. A promise to keep an offer open for a specified period of time for a consideration is a contract called an option; it is not merely an offer that can be revoked.

11. Silence by the offeree can constitute an acceptance provided it was previously agreed to be an acceptance or if past dealings would clearly imply such.

12. Under the Uniform Commercial Code an acceptance of a contract for the sale of goods can contain additional or different terms and yet constitute a lawful acceptance.

Solved Problems

5.1 Normally, the offer initiates the process by which a contract is created. Therefore, the offer is critical in satisfying basic contract-law requirements. Which of the following statements is incorrect?

(*a*) The offer may only be expressed in words.

(*b*) The offer must be communicated to the other party.

(*c*) The offer must be certain enough to determine the liability of the parties.

(*d*) The offer must be accepted by the other party.

(*Adapted from AICPA Examination, May 1978*)

Offers may be expressed by conduct other than just merely words; therefore, statement (*a*) is the answer. The other statements reflect basic principles of contract law.

5.2   Almovar Electronics was closing out several lines of electronic parts which were becoming outdated. It sent a letter on March 8 to Conduit Sales & Service Company, one of its largest retail customers, offering the entire lot at a substantial reduction in price. The offer indicated that it was for "immediate acceptance." The terms were "cash, pick up by your carrier at our loading dock, and not later than March 15." It also indicated that the terms of the offer were not subject to variance. The letter did not arrive until March 10, and Conduit's letter accepting the offer was not mailed until March 12. The letter of acceptance indicated that Conduit would take the entire lot, would pay in accordance with the usual terms (2/10, net/30), and would pick up the goods on March 16. Which of the following *best* describes the legal relationship of the parties?

(*a*)   The acceptance was not timely; hence no contract.

(*b*)   The different terms of the acceptance are to be construed as proposals for changes in the contract.

(*c*)   The different terms of the acceptance constituted a rejection of the offer.

(*d*)   Since both parties were merchants and the changes in the acceptance were not material, there is a valid contract.

(*AICPA Examination, May 1979*)

   The answer is statement (*c*). An offeror may demand that only certain terms be made part of the contract which cannot be changed by the offeree. The language here is quite explicit on this point. Otherwise, the acceptance might have been timely, as the mailbox or deposited acceptance rule could have been applied. This was a sale of goods, and the argument that Section 2-207(1) of the UCC, allowing certain acceptances between merchants to be valid despite additional or different terms in the acceptance, is being made by statements (*b*) and (*d*). In this case, however, the clear language of the offer excluded the operation of Section 2-207(1).

5.3   On March 1, Wilkins wrote Connor a letter and offered to sell him her factory for $150,000. The offer stated that the acceptance must be received by her by April 1. Under the circumstances, Wilkins's offer

(*a*)   will be validly accepted if Connor posts an acceptance on April 1.

(*b*)   may be withdrawn at any time before acceptance.

(*c*)   may not be withdrawn before April 1.

(*d*)   could not be validly accepted since Wilkins could assert the Statute of Frauds.

(*Adapted from AICPA Examination, May 1981*)

   Generally, offers may be revoked any time before acceptance, statement (*b*). The mailbox rule is not applicable since the offeror specifically demanded that the acceptance would be effective only upon receipt by the offeror. The Statute of Frauds requirement of a writing was met since Wilkins wrote a letter.

5.4   An outstanding offer to sell a tract of real property is terminated at the time

(*a*)   the buyer learns of the seller's death.

(*b*)   the seller posts his revocation if the original offer was made by mail.

(*c*)   the buyer posts a rejection of the offer if the original offer was received by mail.

(*d*)   the buyer learns of the sale of the property to a third party.

(*AICPA Examination, November 1974*)

Offers can be revoked in a number of ways. Knowledge that the item for sale has been sold is notice of revocation, statement (*d*). A notice of revocation is effective whichever way accomplished. Offers also terminate upon rejection, but an intent to reject becomes a rejection only when it is received by the offeror.

5.5   Donaldson Retailers engaged in lengthy negotiations for the purchase of an office building from Universal Real Estate, Inc. The parties reached an impasse on the price. Universal's written offer to sell was $150,000. Donaldson replied by telegram, offering $140,000—"take it or leave it." Universal filed the telegram away for future reference but did not respond. Donaldson then sent a letter stating that Universal was to disregard its prior communication and that it accepted the offer at $150,000. Universal wrote back stating, "The price is now $160,000—take it or leave it." Donaldson promptly telegraphed Universal that it held Universal to its original offer of $150,000. Under these circumstances,

(*a*)   the purported contract is unenforceable in any event under the Statute of Frauds.

(*b*)   no contract was formed.

(*c*)   there can be no contract, since the same means of communication was not used throughout the transaction.

(*d*)   Donaldson's reply offering $140,000 constituted a mere counterproposal which did not terminate the original offer.

No contract was formed on these facts, statement (*b*). Universal's first offer was rejected by a counteroffer. Donaldson's second thought to accept was merely a new offer which was never accepted. The manner of communication played no role in this case, nor did the Statute of Frauds. On the latter point, writing was used by both parties, and had there been agreement, the Statute of Frauds would have been satisfied.

5.6   Unless the offer specifies otherwise, an acceptance is generally effective when it is

(*a*)   signed by the offeree.

(*b*)   received by the offeror.

(*c*)   delivered by the communicating agency.

(*d*)   dispatched by the offeree.

(*AICPA Examination, May 1976*)

Statement (*d*) reflects the general rule. This rule is called by various names. They include the mailbox rule, the implied agency rule, the doctrine of constructive communication of acceptance, reasonable medium, and the deposited acceptance rule.

5.7   An offer is generally effective when it is

(*a*)   dispatched.

(*b*)   signed.

(*c*)   mailed.

(*d*)   received.

(*AICPA Examination, May 1976*)

The offeror's intention to offer is not an offer. Only when this intention is communicated to the offeree does it become a legal offer, statement (*d*). Offers must be actually, not constructively, communicated to the offeree, as an offeree cannot accept an offer of which he or she has no knowledge.

5.8   Maurice sent Schmit Company a telegram offering to sell Schmit a 1-acre tract of commercial property located adjacent to Schmit's warehouse for $8,000. Maurice stated that Schmit had 3 days to consider the offer, and in the meantime the offer would be irrevocable. The next day Maurice received a better offer from another party, and he telephoned Schmit informing him that the offer was revoked. The offer was

   (*a*)   irrevocable for 3 days upon receipt by Schmit.

   (*b*)   effectively revoked by telephone.

   (*c*)   never valid, since the Statute of Frauds applies.

   (*d*)   not effectively revoked because Maurice did not use the same means of communication.

   (*Adapted from AICPA Examination, May 1981*)

   This offer was effectively revoked before acceptance, statement (*b*). The fact that the offeror promises to hold the offer open for a stated period of time does not change the rule. Any means by which the offeree learns of the revocation is an effective notice.

5.9   Harper is opening a small retailing business in Hometown, U.S.A. To announce her grand opening, Harper places an advertisement in the newspaper quoting sales prices on certain items in stock. Many local residents come in and make purchases. Harper's grand opening is such a huge success that she is unable to totally satisfy the demand of the customers. Which of the following correctly applies to the situation?

   (*a*)   Harper has made an offer to the people who read the advertisement.

   (*b*)   Harper has made a contract with the people who read the advertisement.

   (*c*)   Harper has made an invitation seeking offers.

   (*d*)   Any customer who demands the goods advertised and tenders the money is entitled to them.

   (*Adapted from AICPA Examination, May 1981*)

   Generally advertisements are invitations seeking offers, statement (*c*). An advertisement can be drawn specifically enough to qualify as an offer but usually is not so phrased or intended. Regulatory statutes which prohibit false advertising do not invalidate the rule, but an advertiser who violates the rule might suffer criminal penalties only.

5.10   Dustin received a telephone call on Monday from his oil supplier. The supplier offered him 1,000 barrels of heating oil at $48 a barrel, the current price in a rapidly changing market. Dustin said he would take the offer under advisement. The next day, the market price rose to $50 a barrel, and Dustin sent the supplier a letter late that afternoon accepting the offer at $48 a barrel. The letter arrived in the usual course on Thursday morning, by which time the market price had moved to $56 a barrel. The supplier called Dustin and said she would not accept his order. Dustin insisted that he had a contract. Which of the following is correct?

   (*a*)   Acceptance took place on dispatch of Dustin's letter.

   (*b*)   Acceptance did not take place upon dispatch as the offer had already expired.

   (*c*)   Acceptance did not take place because the only means of acceptance Dustin could use was the phone.

   (*d*)   Acceptance could only be made by a signed writing.

   (*AICPA Examination, November 1981*)

   Statement (*b*) is correct, as the offer had lapsed by passage of a reasonable time. Reasonable time is judged by the actions of the parties and other circumstances. A telephone offer regarding a subject with a rapidly fluctuating price is short-lived. This is so in this case. The acceptance could have been communicated in any manner provided it was timely. A signed writing would have been necessary if the other party raised the issue of the Statute of Frauds.

5.11 The waterworks had a long-standing policy of offering employees $100 for suggestions actually used. Due to inflation and a decline in the level and quality of suggestions received, the waterworks decided to increase the award to $500. Several suggestions were under consideration at that time. Two days before the public announcement of the increase to $500, a suggestion by Farber was accepted and put into use. Farber is seeking to collect $500. Farber is entitled to

(a) $500 because the waterworks had decided to pay that amount.

(b) $500 because the suggestion submitted will be used during the period that the waterworks indicated it would pay $500.

(c) $100 in accordance with the original offer.

(d) nothing if the waterworks chooses not to pay since the offer was gratuitous.

(*Adapted from AICPA Examination, November 1981*)

An acceptance must have been induced by the offer, statement (*c*). Farber intended to accept the $100 offer, not the later offer of which he had no notice. This was not a gift situation. The employer was willing to pay for the employee's suggestion. The fact that the suggestion would now be worth more than it had been originally is not relevant to contract law.

5.12 Nichols wrote Dilk and offered to sell Dilk a building for $50,000. The offer stated it would expire 30 days from July 1, 19X1. Nichols changed his mind and does not wish to be bound by his offer. If a legal dispute arises between the parties regarding whether there has been a valid acceptance of the offer, which of the following is correct?

(a) The offer will not expire before the 30 days even if Nichols sells the property to a third person and notifies Dilk.

(b) If Dilk categorically rejects the offer on July 10, Dilk cannot validly accept within the remaining stated period of time.

(c) If Dilk phoned Nichols on August 1 and unequivocally accepted the offer, it would create a contract, provided he had no notice of withdrawal of the offer.

(d) The offer cannot be legally withdrawn for the stated period of time.

(*Adapted from AICPA Examination, May 1981*)

Offers terminate upon rejection even in cases where a stated time for acceptance is given, statement (*b*). Offers also terminate by a timely revocation or by the expiration of the stated time. This is not an option which binds the offeror to hold it open for the option period.

5.13 Markom invented a new potholder and agreed to allow Tewer Corporation to manufacture and sell the item for a "reasonable royalty" per unit. Under which of the following grounds will this agreement be most challenged?

(a) Failure to state a time for the license.

(b) Failure to state when the invention's details are to be delivered to Tewer Corporation.

(c) Failure to state a royalty price.

(d) Failure to set forth who will apply for the patent.

While the absence of a price in many agreements can be supplied by the court applying "reasonable price," the parties have here used a term that might be incapable of determination, statement (*c*). If this particular class of invention earned a fairly uniform royalty rate, the term could be found. The other suggested answers would cause little difficulty to a court. A reasonable time could be found for delivery. The other points could also be clarified by a court. This agreement would probably fail for want of "definiteness."

5.14   Fennimore owned a ranch which was encumbered by a 7 percent mortgage held by the Orange County Bank. As of July 31, 19X0, the outstanding mortgage amount was $83,694. Fennimore decided to sell the ranch and engage in the grain storage business. During the time that he was negotiating the sale of the ranch, the bank sent out an offer to several mortgagors indicating a 5 percent discount on the mortgage if the mortgagors would pay the entire mortgage in cash or by certified check by July 31, 19X0. The bank was doing this in order to liquidate older unprofitable mortgages which it had on the books. Anyone seeking to take advantage of the offer was required to present payment at the Second Street branch on July 31, 19X0. Fennimore, having obtained a buyer for his property, decided to take advantage of the offer since his buyer was arranging his own financing and was not interested in assuming the mortgage. Therefore, on July 15 he wrote the bank a letter which stated: "I accept your offer on my mortgage; see you on July 31, 19X0. I'll have a certified check." Fennimore did not indicate that he was selling the ranch and would have to pay off the full amount in any event. On July 28, the bank sent Fennimore a letter by certified mail which was received by Fennimore on July 30 which stated: "We withdraw our offer. We are oversubscribed. Furthermore, we have learned that you are selling your property and the mortgage is not being assumed." Nevertheless, on July 31 at 9:05 in the morning Fennimore walked in the door of the bank, holding his certified check. Vogelspiel, a bank mortgage officer, approached him and stated firmly and clearly that the bank's offer had been revoked and that the bank would refuse to accept tender of payment. Dumbfounded by all this, Fennimore nevertheless tendered the check, which was refused.

Answer the following, setting forth reasons for any conclusions stated: In the eventual lawsuit that ensued, who will prevail? (*Adapted from AICPA Examination, May 1980*)

If the bank and its mortgagor should be involved in a lawsuit, the issue would be whether the bank's legal offer to Fennimore to satisfy an existing mortgage at a 5 percent discount was effectively revoked by the bank before the requested act of acceptance by Fennimore, the offeree. The court will look to the terms of the offer in order to determine whether the offeree made an effective acceptance. In this case the bank appeared to request an act of acceptance, not a promise. In other words, the offeror intended to enter into a unilateral rather than a bilateral contract. If the offer demanded an act as the acceptance, an attempted acceptance by a promise would not qualify. The bank in its offer demanded the tender of the certified check on July 31, 19X0. The fact that Fennimore attempted to accept by a promise before that date does not change the offeror's terms under which it will contract. The offer can only be accepted by the tendering of the requested act on July 31, 19X0. Unfortunately for Fennimore, the offer was revoked before that date. Offers can be revoked anytime before acceptance. Fennimore will lose the lawsuit, and the bank will win.

5.15   Austin wrote a letter and mailed it to Hernandez offering to sell Hernandez his tuna canning business for $125,000. Hernandez promptly mailed a reply acknowledging receipt of Austin's letter and expressing an interest in purchasing the cannery. However, Hernandez offered Austin only $110,000. Later Hernandez decided that the business was in fact worth at least the $125,000 that Austin was asking. He therefore decided to accept the original offer tendered to him at $125,000. The telegram reached Austin before Hernandez's prior letter, although the letter arrived later that day. Austin upon receipt of the telegram telegraphed Hernandez that as a result of further analysis of the worth of the business, he was not willing to sell at less than $150,000. Hernandez claims a contract at $125,000 resulted from his telegram. Austin asserts either that there is no contract or that the purchase price is $150,000.

Answer the following, setting forth reasons for any conclusions stated: If the dispute goes to court, who will prevail? (*AICPA Examination, November 1980*)

Hernandez claims a contract by virtue of his telegram of acceptance which the offeror, Austin, received before the previously mailed rejection and counteroffer. Offers can be accepted before their revocation, rejection, or lapse. A letter of rejection does not become a legal rejection until it is received. Since the action of the offeree, Hernandez, was prompt, the communication of an acceptance before the legal rejection completes the contract which is formed by this act of acceptance. The fact that the offeree used a different means of communication of acceptance does not affect the validity of the acceptance. If the means and timeliness were reasonable, the acceptance stands provided the offeror did not prohibit such means. In a dispute between Hernandez and Austin, Hernandez (the offeree) will succeed in proving that a contract was formed.

5.16   Florida residents found a piece of property in Florida and, after learning that the owner lived in Texas, prepared a contract for sale. They listed the terms, signed the contract, and mailed it to the Texas owner with instructions that if the owner approved, to send the contract to the attorney for the Florida residents. The owner was pleased with the written offer, signed it, and, as instructed, deposited it in the mail. Before the receipt of the contract by the Florida residents, the Texas owner had a change of mind. He immediately telephoned the Florida attorney informing him that the offer was rejected. Upon receipt of the contract the Florida residents recorded the document and treated the contract as made and accepted. The Texas owner sued to clear title to his land which he claims he did not sell to the Florida residents.

Who will prevail in this lawsuit? Give reasons for any conclusions stated.

Every offer must be accepted before a contract is formed. Where parties deal at a distance, and mail or telegraph is used to communicate, the doctrine of constructive communication of acceptance, sometimes called the mailbox rule, provides the answer. The contract can be formed at the place where the offeree acted to accept. If the offeror does not expressly prohibit it or otherwise indicate that the mailbox rule cannot apply, the offeree's timely act in responding to the offer by the same means as used in the offer constitutes the act of acceptance. In this case the Florida residents made an offer by mail. They did not state how the acceptance was to be communicated. The Texas owner, as offeree, had the power to cause an acceptance by his agreement to its terms which he attempted to communicate by the same means as the offeror. His act of depositing the letter of acceptance in the mail is considered to be the act of acceptance. A subsequent attempted rejection by him is no longer possible. The Texas owner entered into a contract by reason of a rule that is known by various names: the constructive communication of acceptance rule, the mailbox rule, or the implied agency rule. This principle arose from the famous English case in which it was first announced, *Adams v. Lindzell* (1818). The buyers, the Florida residents, will prevail over the Texas owner. A binding contract was formed.

Chapter 6

Reality of Consent

6.1 INTRODUCTION

Every contract must have mutual consent. This consent must be voluntary, as the presence of the offer and acceptance does not necessarily prevent a deeper inquiry into the degree of voluntariness of consent. Conduct by one of the parties may have been such that the other party may rescind or disaffirm the contract and, in some instances, seek damages. Voluntariness of consent is examined under the subject called *reality of consent*. Reality of consent is questioned on the following grounds: fraud, misrepresentation, mistake, duress, undue influence, and, under the UCC, unconscionability.

EXAMPLE 1. A seller agreed in writing, before witnesses, to sell his land to the buyer. In fact the document expressly provided that "This contract is signed freely without fraud, disabililty, or under duress, or any other ground." The seller now contends that he was threatened with exposure of his criminal past by the buyer unless he signed. The buyer maintains that the seller "agreed." The seller can offer oral testimony that he signed without real consent, under duress, that his agreement was not voluntary. He would be allowed to disaffirm the contract on grounds of duress, i.e., lack of reality of consent.

6.2 FRAUD

A contract can be avoided, or damages received, if it was induced by misrepresentation of a material fact by one party which was relied upon by the other to his or her injury or loss. The requirements for a fraud action are not precisely defined by the courts. This is based on the principle that definiteness might allow some specific techniques of wrongdoing to escape the legal consequences of bad conduct.

Most courts, however, require a number of facts to be shown if the contract is to be construed as fraudulently induced. (1) In the first place there must be a false statement, active concealment, or silence when there is a duty to speak. (2) A material fact must be involved in the false statement, active concealment, or silence. (3) There must be an intention to deceive the other party by means of a false statement, active concealment, or silence, and there must be knowledge of the falsity or concealment. (4) The person deceived must have reasonably relied upon the other party to make an accurate statement or to make a complete disclosure. (5) This reasonable reliance must have resulted in an injury. All elements of the cause of action must be proved, as the absence of any one element prevents avoidance on the ground of fraud.

EXAMPLE 2. Cord was a shady boat dealer. In selling boats to X, Y, and Z, he told X that the 16-foot *Columbia* was a 1982 model, he puttied over the knothole in the 12-foot dinghy he sold to Y, and he remained silent when Z wanted a boat that didn't "tip easily." Cord lied to X; the boat was a 1979 model. Y or anyone else couldn't have spotted the knothole filled and painted over. Cord knew that while the vessel sold to Z was fast, it capsized easily except in the hands of an expert. In all three sales the parties were defrauded if they relied on Cord's conduct and if the features of each boat were important, that is, material to the sale.

6.3 FRAUD: FALSE STATEMENT

The party alleging fraud must show that the other party made a false statement, actively concealed some fact, or remained silent when the law required one to speak. Representing a product as "all wool" or as "100 percent silk" when it is not is an obvious example of a false statement.

Proof that a statement is false is necessary. The law, however, does not limit fraudulent conduct to false statements but includes any behavior which misleads another in an important, i.e., material, way. Active concealment is conduct by which one purposely conceals an important fact about the proposed contract; it frequently occurs in the sale of property.

EXAMPLE 3. A beam in a house is infested with termites. Caulking and painting over the beam disguises the potentially dangerous structural problem. This would be active concealment, as would be setting back the mileage (odometer) in a used car.

The duty to speak, or improperly keeping silent, is not easily shown as fraudulent conduct. Generally one has no duty to tell prospective contracting parties the bad features of the proposed contract. The old adage "let the buyer beware," while not the general broad principle it once was, is a reminder that contracting is not a friendly endeavor. Both parties are expected to look after their own interests. Accordingly, the seller's knowledge that his home is in the middle of a high-crime neighborhood does not by itself place upon him the duty to tell this to a prospective buyer. However, it does not take many additional facts to require a duty to speak. For example, where the silent party stands in a fiduciary or confidential position to the other, or even in those instances where one party knows that the other is under a mistaken view of certain facts, the duty to speak may be present.

EXAMPLE 4. Adam is Eve's stockbroker. Adam's knowledge that a particular company is in bad financial condition requires Adam to speak should Eve express an interest in investing in that company. This would be a fiduciary or confidential relationship between Adam and Eve, requiring utmost good faith.

EXAMPLE 5. During negotiations for the sale of a motel the prospective buyer stated that he was a "born-again-Christian" and would not want a motel which had the "hourly trade," that is, was a rendezvous for sex. The seller says nothing and changes the subject. The seller has a duty to speak since he definitely knows that the buyer would not be interested in this motel if he knew the facts.

A fiduciary relationship is one which the law views as based on trust and confidence. Contracts between lawyer and client, or between partners, are particularly susceptible to the "duty-to-speak" requirement.

6.4 FRAUD: MATERIAL FACT

The most difficult question in fraud cases is determining what is a material fact. The fraudulent conduct must involve something factual and important to the party who is misled. Generally, opinions and promises to do something in the future are not material facts.

EXAMPLE 6. Atterlee makes the following statements: "The motor in this car has been completely rebuilt" (statement of fact); "Don't worry, if you buy this car we will completely overhaul the motor" (promise); "I think that the motor was completely overhauled" (opinion).

This is not to say that an opinion (e.g., the "value" of something) or a promise can never be grounds for fraud. An opinion by an expert to a nonexpert, or by one in a superior position, has been held to be fraudulent conduct, especially if the speaker did not really hold such an opinion. Further, a promise can be an affirmation of fact and therefore be a warranty. A person making such a promise could be liable for a breach of contract under appropriate circumstances. In this same connection, a promise which the promisor never intended to keep could be a false statement of a fact, provided the injured party proves such a false intention.

EXAMPLE 7. The seller of a motel states that "It is my opinion that, with the owner present full time, the occupancy rate could be doubled." The buyer had no motel experience, and the seller held no such opinion, as the motel is a white elephant that he wishes to dispose of. This is fraud.

EXAMPLE 8. The motel buyer is induced to buy on the seller's promise to get the zoning changed to permit a nightclub operation within 3 months of the sale. If, at the time of the contract, the seller had no intention of carrying out the promise, the promise is "factual." Note that the state of one's mind is as much a fact as the state of one's digestion.

At common law a misstatement about the law was not considered to be a misstatement of fact, as the law is a matter of common knowledge. Therefore, it is generally held that a misstatement of local or state law will not allow for a rescission, but a misstatement of foreign (another state or nation) law has been held to be a misstatement of a fact. The law is changing, and some recent cases tend to treat statements about the law, whether of the state of residence or another state or nation, as factual.

6.5 FRAUD: JUSTIFIABLE RELIANCE

The party alleging fraud must have relied on the fraudulent conduct of the other party. A party who undertakes an independent investigation of the subject is not contracting in reliance on the fraudulent conduct. It is sometimes stated that no reasonable person should have believed the party who is charged with fraud. While the reliance by the defrauded party must be reasonable, courts generally rule that if *in fact* the party believed the fraudulent conduct to his or her injury, reliance is shown. The distinguishing aspect of these doctrines is whether the information was available to the person without going to some effort or expense to discover the truth.

EXAMPLE 9. A farmer showed a city dweller a parcel of land, stating that it was "5 acres of good muck land." It was closer to 3 acres and quite rocky. If the city dweller really believed the farmer, a jury could find that justifiable reliance was present. However, some investigation, a second opinion for example, would have quickly revealed the true quantity and quality of the land.

6.6 FRAUD: INTENTION TO DECEIVE

Intention to deceive is present where the party acted in such a manner as to create a substantially false impression. Half-truths qualify as such behavior, as well as statements made with reckless disregard of the truth. While neither the court nor the jury can read another's mind, the facts and circumstances can lead reasonable persons to infer bad intent or knowledge, or *scienter* (that is, guilty knowledge). Wanton statements, i.e., the speaker doesn't know whether they are true or false, are instances of fraudulent conduct.

EXAMPLE 10. A stockbroker felt he was the last word in knowing it all. There wasn't a stock he hadn't heard of. His customer asked about Marling Corporation, and rather than admit his ignorance, the broker replied that it was a "fine company" and took an order for 200 shares. Unknown to the broker, the company had been reported in financial trouble. Simple inquiry would have revealed this. The broker's statement was a wanton or reckless act qualifying as a statement made with the intention to deceive.

6.7 FRAUD: INJURY

The false statement of a material fact made with the intention to deceive and justifiedly relied upon does not establish fraud without a showing than an injury or damage resulted. There must be a causal connection between the conduct and the injury, which in most cases is not difficult to establish. If, however, the conduct did not cause a loss, there is no remedy for fraud.

EXAMPLE 11. Jones sells a "gold" watch for $300. If it were gold, it would have been worth at least $450. The watch is actually worth $150. Smith, the buyer, is injured by this conduct to the extent of $300, the difference in value between what he contracted for and what he received. The fraudulent conduct is the proximate cause of the loss or injury.

EXAMPLE 12. A seller represents that her motel is rated AAA by the motel association, which is a lie. Shortly after the sale the business shrinks due to the opening of two new motels in the neighborhood. The motel is now less valuable. The cause of the loss in value is not the lack of rating but new competition. The fraudulent conduct did not cause the injury. There is no fraud recovery.

Fraud is also a tort as well as a grounds for contract rescission. This permits the defrauded party an additional remedy besides rescission. Generally, money damages occur in a fraud action. This measure is determined by attempting to give such defrauded party the benefit of his or her bargain. In Example 11, above, the watch was represented as gold. If it really had been gold, the watch was worth $450. The injured party is entitled to the benefit of his bargain, that is, a gold watch for $300. Since the watch he received is worth only $150, his damages would be the difference between the value of what he contracted to buy ($450) and the value of what he received ($150). The recovery would be the difference, that is, $300. He also keeps the watch he received. Further, since a wanton statement is tortious behavior, punitive damages (as a punishment) might also be awarded.

6.8 INNOCENT MISREPRESENTATION

Not all conduct involving an untruth is fraudulent, but the law nevertheless provides a remedy in the action for innocent misrepresentation. Innocent misrepresentation of a material fact relied upon by the other party to his or her injury permits an action for rescission of the contract. This lawsuit involves the innocent, but false, statements one believes to be true. There is no requirement that an intention to deceive be shown.

EXAMPLE 13. Linda wants a fast sports car. She understands that the seller has a car that has broken several speed records. The seller acknowledges that this is true and to push the sale states that "this little baby has moved 132 miles per hour on six occasions." Linda is impressed with that statement and buys the car. Unknown to the seller, the speedometers on those models are defective and overstate the speed by 10 miles per hour. The car cannot go 132 miles per hour and never did. This is an innocent misrepresentation. The seller misstated the facts. Had he only reported what he *saw*, i.e., the speedometer showing a speed of 132 miles per hour, he would have been making a true statement.

Unlike fraud, an action for innocent misrepresentation only allows the other party to rescind the contract. It does not provide for money damages.

6.9 MISTAKE

A contracting party can disaffirm a contract on grounds of mutual mistake of a material fact and, in some exceptional circumstances, for reasons of a unilateral mistake. Like the actions of fraud and misrepresentation, the mistake must be material and factual. Mistakes occur when the mind of one or both of the parties is not in agreement with the facts. They come in a variety of ways, from a simple arithmetical miscalculation to grievous error over the subject matter itself.

Mutual mistakes occur most commonly in situations where both parties make a mistake about the existence of the subject matter or in situations where contract language is capable of several different meanings and each party takes a different meaning.

EXAMPLE 14. A cemetery company agrees to purchase granite in the amount of 50,000 perch from the local quarry. Unknown to both parties, there is only 40,000 perch in the quarry. This is a mutual mistake about the existence of the subject matter, i.e., a quarry having at least 50,000 perch of granite.

EXAMPLE 15. An owner of a house on Laurel Street contracts by mail to sell it to a Chicago buyer. The owner has two houses on Laurel Street, one within the Albuquerque city limits and the other outside. Each party has a different house in mind. The term "house on Laurel Street" in this negotiation is capable of two meanings. Each party takes a different meaning. A mutual mistake occurs.

An action for mutual or bilateral mistake is not common, and the law does not rescue on such grounds someone who has simply made a bad bargain. The sale of one's stock two days before a new oil field is discovered by the corporation is a business mistake and bad luck. Further, one's expectations about the value of a contract can be unrealized, but unless they come within the rather stringent rules on mistake, the contract is not avoidable.

At common law a mistake of domestic law made by both parties does not allow for rescission. A mistake of law occurs when a person knows the facts but is ignorant of the legal consequences of those facts. A mistake of foreign law, however, is considered to be a mistake of fact. Also, some jurisdictions still honor the distinction by denying relief where the mistake is only of local or state law. Many other states have by case law or statute abolished the distinction.

Unilateral mistakes are one-sided mistakes. The other contracting party fully understood the contract and wants to retain it. The law does not allow broad avoidance on the grounds of unilateral mistake. However, there are circumstances under which avoidance is possible. First, where one party enters into a contract by mistake and the other party was aware of this misimpression, the law can allow rescission. This is by reason of mistake, or possibly by reason of fraud, that is, failure of the duty to speak. Secondly, there are situations where the court will allow disaffirmance for reasons of *equity*. Here the court must be satisfied on a number of grounds: that the mistake is substantial, the mistaken party is not guilty of gross negligence, no third parties are involved, and the parties can be restored to the *status quo ante*.

EXAMPLE 16. Ace construction contracts to place pilings at the Waterfront Hotel, believing that the land has subsoil similar to that in the surrounding area. The hotel knows of this wrong impression held by Ace and is pleased to get the contractor at this price. This might be a case of snapping up an offer too good to pass up. The court may allow rescission.

EXAMPLE 17. Marlowe Supply, in response to a public invitation for bids, submitted a price of $40,000. Others filed bids of $52,000 and $71,000. The state agency awarded the contract to Marlowe which now learns how far off its bid was. An error of $15,000 was caused by a misplaced decimal point in the calculations of some of the items. This is a substantial error, representing nearly 40 percent of the bid price. The court could apply the equity considerations theory and allow rescission if there was no gross negligence, if no third parties are involved, and if the parties can be restored to their positions before contracting. The last requirement may not be met on these facts in some states.

6.10 DURESS

Improper conduct by one party which forces another to contract is duress and allows the other to avoid the agreement. The will of the other party must, of course, have been overcome by this improper conduct. Usually there is little difficulty in proving whether the will was actually overcome, but a problem of proof and law exists on the issue of what is improper conduct.

Certain conduct is always improper. A threat to kill, to harm physically, or to imprison another, or his loved ones, is always condemned behavior. Further, threats to criminally prosecute another or to reveal scandalous secrets qualify. This is generally so even if the other party deserves to be criminally prosecuted. The law normally prohibits the use of the criminal process for civil ends. Additionally, conduct less than that just described above can be improper in unconscionable circumstances. A threat of civil process is normally not duress. However, it has been held improper in a case where the party had no chance to preserve his legal rights because he was recalled into the army during an emergency.

EXAMPLE 18. Gary is an extortionist and a bully. He threatens to expose his boss as a homosexual, to expose his stockbroker as a thief, and to beat up his creditor. If he forced all of them to contract with him, each would have a possible action for rescission.

EXAMPLE 19. A dentist's 17-year-old receptionist was an embezzler. Upon discovery, the dentist threatened the girl's parents with prison for the girl unless the money was replaced. They had to mortgage their home to pay the money. The parents later attempted to breach their agreement. A threat to use criminal process for civil ends is duress, especially where the party using a threat gained some advantage. This contract can be rescinded.

6.11   UNDUE INFLUENCE

Contracting is generally between legal strangers, and parties are presumed to have contracted at arms' length. Accordingly, the fact that the bargain is a bad one is not grounds for avoidance, as bad bargains are enforceable. Sometimes, however, parties do not contract at arms' length, but rather they contract with persons much weaker than themselves or where parties stand in some fiduciary or confidential relationship to each other. One's relationship with a partner, for example, is a fiduciary relationship as to certain dealings. An elderly mother whose daily life and business are taken over by her bossy, but competent, daughter might suggest a confidential relationship. In either fiduciary or confidential relationships the law can examine whether there is indeed dominance on one side and dependence on the other. Basically, the courts attempt to determine whether there was a real difference in bargaining ability resulting in the weaker party being unable to protect himself or herself against an aggressive party who gained the weaker party's trust or confidence. Contracting between such parties is the common type of undue influence case.

It is generally stated that if the fiduciary or confidential relationship exists, and if a contract is entered into that is unfair for the dependent party, there is a presumption of undue influence. This finding means that the dominant party, or the one in a fiduciary relationship, must prove that he or she *did not* unduly influence the other.

EXAMPLE 20. An elderly mother has money, but all business and personal affairs are handled by her competent daughter. The daughter's advice and counsel are not only sought, but followed. The daughter advises her mother to sell her car to the daughter at a price well below market. This otherwise valid contract is unfair and may be set aside on grounds of undue influence.

EXAMPLE 21. A tax lawyer advises his client to lease a building to him on a lease-back arrangement. The lawyer has a fiduciary duty to his client, and if the contract is unfair, undue influence could allow a rescission.

6.12   UNCONSCIONABLE BARGAINS

Courts sometimes refuse to enforce an agreement because its terms are too harsh or severe. Generally there is reality of consent, but by reason of equity it would be unjust to allow the court process to be used in this manner. In the sale of goods, Section 2-302 of the UCC authorizes the court to consider the question of unconscionability. If the court finds the contract or any clause in it to have been unconscionable at the time it was made, it may "refuse to enforce the contract, or it may enforce the remainder of the contract without the unconscionable clause" so as to avoid any unconscionable result.

There is no agreement on what contracts, or contract clauses, are unconscionable. Cases involving excessive time payments for merchandise are frequent subjects of the rule.

EXAMPLE 22. Lane lived in a poor neighborhood. Credit was hard to obtain, but the Sun Furniture Company gave it under exceptionally hard credit terms. Sun had no cash price. The company demanded that other furniture not purchased there must also be included in the mortgage. Upon default, Lane might show not only that the price was unconscionable, but also that the security provisions were onerous. The courts have modified some of these contracts on the grounds of unconscionability and denied foreclosure on such other furniture.

6.13 EFFECT OF UNREALITY OF CONSENT

A contract entered into by reason of fraud, misrepresentation, duress, mistake, or undue influence may be rescinded or set aside provided the injured party acts within a reasonable time. Failure to act in timely fashion, or behavior suggesting approval of the contract, causes an otherwise voidable contract to be ratified. Further, only fraud allows money damages in lieu of an action for rescission.

Ratification of a voidable contract by reason of passage of time cannot occur if the facts which caused the contract to be created still exist. However, delay when the disability is removed, or performance of acts inconsistent with avoidance, is a waiver and ratifies the contract.

EXAMPLE 23.   Adler's wife was wealthy and considerably older than Adler. Insecure, she threatened to leave Adler unless he "proved his love" by waiving all right of inheritance should she predecease him. He signed away his rights. She died 10 years later. Adler attempted to assert his rights to her estate, but his "contract" was used against him. Adler contended he signed under duress. The executor of the estate admitted that but charged that Adler's inaction and silence for 10 years constituted ratification of the voidable contract. The court ruled that because he was continuously under the threat, Adler couldn't be held to have ratified by silence or inaction. Adler's waiver of his rights was made under duress, and hence the contract could be rescinded.

It is important to note that there is no time limit on when such a contract can be avoided because the duress is continuous. An action for rescission of such a voidable contract is therefore not bound by the states' statutes of limitations.

Black Letter Law
A Summary

1. Despite a manifestation of consent, a contract may be avoided on the ground of unreality of consent.

2. Consent is said not to be real where fraud, misrepresentation, mistake, undue influence, or duress occurred in the formation of the contract.

3. In order to use fraud in avoidance, the injured party must show each and every element of fraud.

4. While fraud is never conclusively defined, the following elements must be present: (*a*) a false statement, active concealment, or silence when there was a duty to speak; (*b*) the involvement of a material fact; (*c*) the intention to deceive, including wanton statements; (*d*) reasonable reliance that the statement is accurate or that there is full disclosure; (*e*) injury resulting from the reasonable reliance.

5. Statements of value or opinion are generally not considered to be statements of fact.

6. A party who makes an independent investigation of a statement made by the other party cannot be said to have relied on the false statement.

7. A successful fraud action permits the injured party either to avoid the contract or to sue for the value that was misrepresented.

8. Misrepresentation allows the injured party to rescind the contract and requires a showing of the elements of fraud except the intention to deceive.

9. There are two kinds of mistakes alleged in lawsuits: unilateral, or one-sided, mistakes and mutual mistakes.

10. Generally unilateral mistakes of a material fact do not permit avoidance unless the other party knew or should have known that a mistake was being made.

11. A mutual mistake permits rescission of the contract and occurs when the parties use language capable of several meanings and each has taken a different meaning, or in instances when the parties are in error about the existence of the subject matter of the contract.

12. Mistakes of law, while still generally not treated as mistakes of fact, are now being treated differently in a growing number of states.

13. Improper conduct by one party which forces another to contract is duress and allows for rescission.

14. Improper conduct includes actions or threats that leave the victim believing that he or she has no reasonable alternative but to contract.

15. A threat to criminally prosecute another is duress, but a threat to bring a proper civil action usually is not.

16. Where a contract is entered into under undue influence, it may be disaffirmed.

17. There is a presumption of undue influence when it is shown that one of the parties is in a dominant or fiduciary position with the other who is subservient and that the contract they enter into is unfair to the subservient party.

18. In the case of a contract greatly favorable to one of the parties, where it can be shown that the parties are equals, no presumption of undue influence is created, as bad bargains are enforceable.

19. Certain agreements which are shockingly unfair may be modified or set aside on grounds of unconscionability.

20. The Uniform Commercial Code recognizes the doctrine of unconscionability for cases that do not meet the requirements of relief on grounds of reality of consent.

Solved Problems

6.1 Parties must show conduct of mutual assent in order to contract. This consent must be real, however. Which of the following does *not* permit avoidance of the contract?

(a) Bad bargain

(b) Fraud

(c) Undue influence

(d) Mutual mistake

Generally one is free to make a foolish or bad bargain, statement (a). What the court will not enforce, however, is an agreement made as a result of overreaching or other wrongdoing. The other three grounds are recognized by courts as being sufficient cause to permit relief to the injured party.

6.2 The law does not generally permit mistake as a defense to a contract. Under what circumstances will a court allow such a defense?

(a) Mutual mistake of fact

(b) Mutual mistake of value

(c) Unilateral mistake of a material fact

(d) Unilateral mistake of law

Statement (a) is the correct answer. An error as to the value of a bargain is rarely grounds for relief, nor is a mistake about an agreement's legal consequences. A unilateral mistake of a material fact does provide an excuse in certain types of cases which usually occur where the other party knew, or should have known, that the other was making a mistake. Generally, however, a unilateral mistake is not an adequate cause to disturb the obligations of a contract.

6.3 X and Y were partners in the lumber business where X was the manager and in charge of the books. Y came to realize that X was stealing money and sharing it with Barbara, his girlfriend. If X and Barbara agree in writing to pay the partnership $10,000, which of the following threats inducing such a promise would *not* be duress?

(a) Y threatened X and Barbara with civil lawsuit for the recovery of the missing money unless they signed the promise.

(b) X and Barbara signed the promise under Y's threat to send both to jail.

(c) X and Barbara signed the promise under Y's threat to beat up Barbara.

(d) X and Barbara signed the promise under Y's threat to tell X's wife that X was an embezzler who had a girlfriend.

Improper conduct includes threatened criminal action or physical acts against the person or property of the other. Choice (a) is the answer; threatening to bring a civil action is generally proper. A threat to bring a civil suit is not wrongful conduct unless it would be on an unfounded claim where the lawsuit could cause great damage. A threat of criminal prosecution, even where there are grounds for such, is usually considered to be an improper means to use to enforce one's rights in a civil action. Wrongful conduct always includes criminal or tortious acts and sometimes just unconscionable conduct. The facts indicated in statement (d) would probably qualify as wrongful conduct.

6.4 Martha married Toby after having been through a bitter divorce with her husband. Toby had been married before and wanted to leave all his estate to his children. He demanded that Martha waive her rights in his estate; otherwise he would divorce her. Toby had no grounds for divorce, but Martha feared an additional scandal. Martha signed the release and waiver. Several years later the tables were turned, and Toby was begging Martha not to divorce him. She gained a number of concessions from him during this period, but she did nothing about her release and waiver. Toby died, and his estate contends that Martha signed away her rights. Which is the *incorrect* statement?

(a) Toby's threat was improper conduct which overcame the will of Martha and thus constituted duress.

(b) Martha may have ratified the voidable release by failing to disaffirm the release when the threat was removed.

(c) Martha waived the duress by failure to file suit within the period of the statute of limitations.

(d) Martha could not ratify a contract entered into under duress until the threat was removed.

All but (c) are correct statements. The statute of limitations does not govern the time within which actions must be brought on duress actions. The passage of time can be interpreted as ratification, provided the threat which induced the contract is removed. Normally the injured party is allowed a reasonable time to disaffirm a voidable contract. In this case, it is likely that Martha ratified the release by her silence much earlier than the period a general statute of limitations would allow.

6.5 The buyer of a motel was induced to purchase it when the seller stated that the motel business "for the past 2 years increased 10 percent." One month after the motel was purchased, it was destroyed by fire and there was insufficient insurance coverage. Which is the *correct* statement?

(a) If the seller honestly believed the false statement he made was true, he could *not* be guilty of misrepresentation.

(b) Since the loss was not caused by fraud or misrepresentation, there was no injury and therefore no action against the seller.

(c) The seller's statement was only an opinion, not one of fact.

(d) Under no circumstances could the seller's statement be considered a statement of a material fact.

A successful fraud action requires that the loss be suffered as a result of the fraud, statement (b). Here an independent event, the fire, caused the injury. If the seller had not intended to lie and yet the statement was untrue, he could be sued for misrepresentation. The statement regarding past business was factual, not an opinion, and it was important to the buyer, thus material to the buyer.

6.6 The difference between an action for fraud and an action for misrepresentation is the presence of

(a) material fact.

(b) injury.

(c) scienter.

(d) reliance.

All actions for fraud must be proved by a showing of the intention to deceive, or scienter (c). Its absence in misrepresentation litigation distinguishes the two forms of unreality of consent which both require, in addition to the other elements mentioned, a false statement or similar conduct.

6.7 Mrs. Tower, aged 81, regarded her neighbor Franco as the last word in business sagacity. Having funds to invest and being uninformed about safe investments, she consulted Franco. He told her that first mortgages on real property were one of the safest forms of investment and offered her a first mortgage on business property owned by him. The mortgage was signed by him for $60,000 (the price he had just paid for the property) at 7 percent interest. The prevailing rate was 13 percent. If Mrs. Tower wishes to rescind the contract, which of the following is the *correct* statement?

(a) She should charge undue influence, showing her age, confidential relationship with Franco, and the unfairness of the contract.

(b) Mrs. Tower should allege that the statement about mortgages is false.

(c) Franco should try to show that while first-mortgage loans are not usually given for the amount of the value of the security, in this case it was fair because he would look out for her.

(d) Mrs. Tower has a clear case of mutual mistake of fact.

Statement (a) is the answer; there was a clear difference in the bargaining ability between the parties which the law attempts to protect by the doctrine of undue influence. The representation about the value of first mortgages is probably true, but the fact that Franco might look out for Mrs. Tower is irrelevant. The bargain was unfair when the terms of the interest rate are examined. There was no mistake on the part of either contractor.

6.8   In fraud actions a statement by the seller about the value of the property being sold is

(a) considered a statement of a material fact.

(b) generally not evidence of a fraudulent statement.

(c) a material fact if over the sum of $500.

(d) a material fact if placed in a signed writing.

A mere statement of opinion, here the value of an item, does not generally qualify as a fraudulent statement of fact; the answer is (b). However, where such representations are made by an expert or professional, the line between opinion and fact is not so clear. Usually, however, value is considered to fall in that category called sales talk, or puffing.

6.9   The parties contracted for a cargo of cotton to arrive in Liverpool by the steamship *Peerless* from Bombay. Two ships by that name sail from Bombay at different times, and each party had in mind a different ship. Either party could rescind the contract on the grounds of

(a) unilateral mistake of a material fact.

(b) a mutual mistake about the identity of the subject matter.

(c) a mutual mistake of foreign law.

(d) a unilateral mistake known to the other party.

Both parties made a mistake about the identity of the subject matter, statement (b). As both erred, it was not a unilateral mistake. If each party had a different ship in mind, a mutual mistake occurred. Either party can disaffirm such a contract. There was no question of mistake of law in this case.

6.10 Some courts allow rescission of unilateral mistakes providing certain elements are shown. Which of the following is *not* necessary?

(a) The mistake must be substantial, and no gross negligence has occurred.

(b) The mistake must involve goods only, not services.

(c) Rights of third parties have not intervened.

(d) It is possible to put the other party in the *status quo ante*.

All the factors except that mentioned in statement (b) contribute to relief on the grounds of unilateral mistake. Mistakes in public bidder cases, for example, are commonly one-sided, unilateral. When the mistaken bidder can show that the error was substantial, that he or she was not guilty of gross negligence, that third-party rights are not involved, and that the *status quo ante* can be restored, some courts will grant a rescission of the contract on grounds of unilateral mistake.

6.11 Townsend was interested in selling certain properties and visited Barney, a broker. While there, he signed, without reading, certain papers Barney handed to him. Later, he learned that he had granted Barney an exclusive listing for several years. Townsend's best chance of rescinding this agreement would be

(a) charging Barney with fraud in his silence as to the meaning of the papers.

(b) charging undue influence in that Barney was a professional.

(c) charging unilateral mistake, alleging that he was not grossly negligent, that no third parties are involved, and that the broker has done nothing yet.

(d) claiming that this is an unfair contract.

Townsend may be liable on this contract since he did not read what he signed, and neither fraud nor undue influence are grounds in this case. Unfairness is never a ground by itself, but unconscionability might be. Accordingly, the mistake doctrine, statement (c), may be Townsend's only possibility for relief from the onerous tems.

6.12 The seller sold the buyer goods after falsely stating that "similar goods sold last week for $30 each." In an action to set aside the contract, which of the following would be the seller's *best* defense?

(a) The goods are truly worth that much, but there is an absence of buyers who need the goods.

(b) The seller would go broke unless she gets that price.

(c) The buyer is the only witness to the false statement.

(d) The buyer didn't rely on the false statement in entering into the contract.

It is not enough that the statement be false, involve a material fact, and be intentionally made (scienter). It must be relied upon by the other party; statement (d) is the answer. Worth or value is generally not relevant, and the seller's need plays no role in determining fraud. Fraud is not usually committed in front of witnesses save the injured party. The absence of other witnesses, therefore, is no bar to recovery.

6.13 Madison advertised for the submission of bids on the construction of a parking lot. Kilroy submitted a bid of $112,000. There were nine other bids. Kilroy's bid was $45,000 less than the next lowest bid. The discrepancy was due to the omission of a $46,000 item on the part of Kilroy's staff. Madison accepted the bid and demands either performance or damages from Kilroy. Kilroy is

(a) bound by the acceptance at $112,000.

(b) not bound by the acceptance but only if Madison knew of the mistake.

(c) not bound by the acceptance if the mistake should have been known by Madison.

(d) not bound by the bid submitted because there was *no* subjective meeting of the minds.

(*AICPA Examination, November 1981*)

Generally, unilateral mistakes are not grounds for rescission. A notable exception to the rule exists where the other party knew or should have recognized the mistake. Here, Madison, seeing such a substantial difference between Kilroy's bid and the others, should have recognized the mistake, bringing this case within the exception, statement (c). A subjective meeting of the minds is not necessary, an objective meeting being sufficient.

6.14 Mistake of law, generally, is no ground for avoidance of a contract. Modern law has seen some modification of this rule. Which of the following statements is *incorrect*?

(a) Some states by statute have allowed statements of law to be treated as statements of fact.

(b) A mistake of foreign law is frequently treated as a statement of fact.

(c) A mistake about the meaning of a particular legal rule is always grounds for avoidance.

(d) A mistake of domestic law is generally no grounds for avoidance.

A mistake about the meaning of a particular legal rule is a mistake of law and does not qualify as grounds for relief, statement (*c*). Foreign law, however, is treated as factual, and in some states by statutes, the law makes no distinction between law and fact.

6.15 Mabel's husband deserted her and their three children. Her job paid only enough for necessaries. She needed a new stove. Only Sander's Stoves offered to sell her one on credit. The cash price was $500. Sanders charged $700, plus interest; required a credit life insurance policy at $200; and demanded that Mabel mortgage her living-room furniture and refrigerator as further security for the credit purchase. Under what legal grounds could this contract be questioned?

(*a*) Fraud

(*b*) Undue influence

(*c*) Unconscionability

(*d*) Duress

Under Section 2-302 of the UCC, the law might examine this contract on the grounds that it is unconscionable, statement (*c*). The higher price for credit, plus interest; the credit life insurance requirement; and the additional security from a struggling homemaker in an unequal bargaining position suggest unconscionability. A court could refuse to enforce this contract, either wholly or in part.

6.16 A father had five sons, and as the children grew, he had many business dealings with them. The father could not read or write the English language, and his eldest son advised him on business matters and handled many of his father's affairs as he grew older. When the father was 80 years of age and his health had deteriorated, he sold his farm to his eldest son for the price that he had paid for it 20 years previously. This was $100,000 less than the present market value.

If the father sought to set aside this sale of the farm, what would be his best legal grounds? State your decision and any conclusions you reach.

The best grounds would be one alleging undue influence. The father, or his representative, must show evidence of a confidential or fiduciary relationship. This occurs when one has gained the confidence of the other and appears to act or advise with the other's best interest in mind. This confidence on one side and the resulting superiority and opportunity for influence created on the other require the court to examine critically the transaction between the two parties. It is not an arms' length transaction. If the bargain entered into is not fair to the party who reposed this trust, the court will require the superior or dominant party to prove that he did not unduly influence the other party. Under the circumstances in this situation, the sale would probably be set aside.

6.17 Lacy was not educated, but she was careful. She truly believed that "diamonds are a girl's best friend." Accordingly, she worked hard and invested her savings in diamonds. She purchased her first diamond from a well-known jeweler for $1,050 and demanded a statement in writing setting forth its cut, weight, and wholesale value. The jeweler complied and, under "value," stated that the diamond had "a present wholesale value of $900 to $1,100." Lacy was happy with that and purchased other diamonds from the same store while continuing to be ignorant of diamonds, their value, and character. One day an expert examined her collection and called it "unimpressive." He appraised the first diamond she had bought as being "worth no more than $400, now or ever." Furious, Lacy wants to sue the diamond store.

What success will Lacy have against the store? State the decision and your reasons for your conclusion.

The alleged false representations of the store relate to the value of the diamond purchased. Ordinarily, representations of value are regarded as expressions of opinion not constituting the basis of fraud. There are exceptions, however. If, for example, a party states a matter which might otherwise be only an opinion but affirms it as an existing fact, the court may treat it as factual. Here the jewelry store was an expert and, in effect, gave an expert opinion to a layperson in no position to appraise the stone and make her own determination of its true value. If the store's agent made the statement knowingly, an action of fraud might lie. If the other elements of fraud are also proved, Lacy could disaffirm the contract on grounds of fraud.

6.18 Middle School District invited bids for the supply of milk for the school year. The bid invitation clearly announced that "no bidder may withdraw a bid after the date announced for opening." Sellon Milk filled out a bid form offering the specified quantity at 7.5 cents per pint. This was a clerical error as that number was really an undelivered price for another buyer. When the bids were opened, Sellon realized its error and immediately requested that the bid be rejected. Middle instead accepted the bid, although it was more than one-half cent below the other bids. Sellon quickly found another seller willing to sell at the bid price, but after several months this new seller refused to deliver any more milk. Sellon obtained another substitute, but again it was only temporary. Now the Middle School District demands that Sellon finish out the year's contract. Sellon believes that it has a legal excuse.

What success will Sellon have in being relieved of its contract? State the decision and reasons for your conclusion.

There is no doubt that unilateral mistakes are hard to undo, as the law does not favor their unraveling. But where the mistake is substantial, there was no gross negligence, no rights of third parties have intervened, and the parties can be restored to the *status quo ante*, the courts will listen. However, they expect the party seeking rescission to act promptly. If a party fails to take steps to rescind within a reasonable time and instead follows a course inconsistent with rescission, the court could conclude that the party has waived its right of rescission. If the court characterizes Sellon's actions in getting others to do its job as consistent with living up to the contract, the right of rescission has been waived and the contract will stand as ratified. Sellon would probably lose this decision.

Chapter 7

Consideration

7.1 GENERAL

Consideration is a legal benefit or advantage to the promisor or a legal detriment or disadvantage to the promisee as a result of the promise. It is a requirement of every contract, and it must be legal and of some value. The law will not ordinarily weigh the value because adequacy of consideration is immaterial, except in particular situations. In bilateral contracts the mutual promises of each party form the consideration for the other's promise.

EXAMPLE 1. A builder promises to build a house for an owner according to certain specifications. The owner agrees to pay $70,000. If the builder should refuse to build, he could be successfully sued. If the builder were to contend that he received no consideration for his promise to build, his argument would fail because the law considers the owner's promise to pay $70,000 as being a legal benefit to the promisor. It is also a legal detriment to the promisee. Most bilateral contracts comply with the benefit and detriment rule, but both are not necessary.

In unilateral contracts, an act for a promise, or a promise for an act, is both a manifestation of assent and the consideration.

EXAMPLE 2. A doctor treats a patient for the patient's promise to pay her fee. Doctors rarely formally promise to treat, but perform instead. The doctor's act in treating is technically the act of offer (or an acceptance) and the consideration she provides to make the contract binding.

Most business agreements are for the pecuniary advantage of both parties and possess valid consideration. There are instances, however, in which the presence of consideration is questioned. A closer examination of consideration and its exceptions requires inquiry into gratuitous promises, charitable subscriptions, past consideration, promissory estoppel, preexisting duty, forbearance, debt satisfaction, voucher checks, and composition agreements.

7.2 GRATUITOUS PROMISES

A promise to bestow a gift, called a *gratuitous promise*, is unenforceable. This is true whether in writing or not.

EXAMPLE 3. An uncle promises in writing to give his nephew $5,000 on his eighteenth birthday. The nephew has made great plans for this money, including a contract for an expensive camera he has always wanted. During the eighteenth birthday celebration the uncle is offended by the nephew's drinking. The uncle tears up the $5,000 check he was about to deliver to his nephew. This was a gratuitous promise and is not enforceable.

In Example 3 the uncle made a promise of something of value, but he received no legal benefit from the nephew and the law does not recognize mere reliance the nephew suffered as a result of the promise. The nephew suffered a detriment in incurring a contract liability because of his expectations, but this is not considered a legal detriment unless the promisor (here the uncle) expressly, or by reasonable implication, induced the promisee (the nephew) to incur such liability.

The promisor must promise something of value, as illusory promises do not provide consideration for the contract. An illusory promise is one so worded that performance is left to the election of the promisor.

EXAMPLE 4.   A retailer signed a form contract with a radio station by which the retailer agreed to buy 30 commercial spots at $60 per spot. On the reverse side of the form, the station "reserved the right to cancel this contract at any time." Since the radio station is not bound to run the spots, their promise is illusory. An illusory promise does not supply consideration for the other's promise to perform. Accordingly, the retailer is *likewise not bound*.

7.3   CHARITABLE SUBSCRIPTIONS

Promises or pledges to charitable drives for religious, education, health, or scientific purposes are tested in most states by the principle of consideration. There is, however, strong public policy honoring such pledges, and some jurisdictions will enforce a bare promise to pledge without any consideration. Fortunately for charities, the "reliance" principle works well for pledges.

The premise assumed by the courts in cases of charitable subscriptions is that parties who pledge expect or should expect that the charity will rely on the pledge to its legal detriment. This reliance on the pledge, the detriment to the charity, is the necessary consideration.

EXAMPLE 5.   Cotton pledged $10,000 to the hospital drive for a new wing. The hospital then hired an architect to design the building. This hiring, incurring a legal liability to the architect, is an act the pledgor should have expected to occur in this situation. Accordingly, the hospital's change of legal position—liabilty to the architect— is the "legal detriment suffered by the promisee as a result of the promise," and the law views that it was impliedly bargained for.

Not all charitable pledges are enforced using the detriment principle. Some pledges are more simply enforced by exchange of valuable promises. A pledge made to a charity on condition of another's promise also to pledge is enforceable.

EXAMPLE 6.   Austin's son was killed while in college. Austin pledged $100,000 to the college if it would name the library after the son. The college agreed. There are mutual promises of something of value, and these are enforceable promises.

EXAMPLE 7.   A company promises to match gifts made by its employees to the local community chest. Employee Mace promises to donate $50. Mace's promise to donate is the consideration for the company's promise to donate and vice versa.

7.4   PAST CONSIDERATION

Past consideration is not legal consideration. For example, occasionally a promise is made to one "in consideration of years of faithful service." If no new consideration is present, this is a gratuitous promise. The promise to pay another for a favor rendered without request, and without expecting any payment, is without consideration.

EXAMPLE 8.   While working on his car, Aaron found his neighbor at his side. The neighbor, attempting to help, solved the problem. Aaron, in a burst of enthusiasm, states that "next payday I am giving you $50." There is no present consideration for this promise; it is past consideration only and is unenforceable.

Some apparent past consideration can form the basis of valuable consideration. If an act was previously requested by the promisor under circumstances in which no gift was intended, or where there was a valid obligation which is now discharged or unenforceable, the promise may be enforceable without new consideration. A promise to pay an old debt which had been made unenforceable by long delay (the statute of limitations), if in form required by law, does not fall under the past consideration doctrine.

EXAMPLE 9. A debtor owed a creditor $500 for over 5 years. The state statute of limitations for this debt is 4 years, and the debtor could defend on that statute. If the debtor now promises to pay the old debt, no new consideration is needed.

EXAMPLE 10. Todd needs help with his tax return. His buddy is a tax expert and, upon Todd's request, helps him. Later Todd promises to pay the expert $400. Since Todd previously requested the act, the later promise has valuable consideration, provided the parties did not understand that the services originally were to be a gift.

7.5 PROMISSORY ESTOPPEL

This is a principle used to enforce agreements in which no legal consideration is present, but the reliance of the other party is such that it would be inequitable to deny a remedy. If the promisor would reasonably expect the promisee to take some action or forbearance relying on the promise, the promise is enforceable despite the absence of consideration. Many charitable subscription cases fit this model, but the doctrine is not limited to them.

EXAMPLE 11. Lori Builders is bidding on a public housing project for a state agency. It will need several subcontractors to complete the job. In assembling its bid, Lori received a contract price from Toledo Plumbing of $30,000. Relying on that figure, Lori bids and gets the contract. Toledo now says that $50,000 is the price. Lori may invoke the doctrine of promissory estoppel when Toledo contends that it received no consideration for its promise to keep the offer of $30,000 open and firm.

7.6 PREEXISTING DUTY

A promise to do something one has a legal right to do is valuable consideration. However, a promise to perform what one is already under obligation to do, or not to do, is never legal consideration for the new promise. Preexisting duties either arise by operation of law or are voluntarily undertaken. Whatever the source, the promise to do what one already must do cannot be the basis of consideration for a new promise.

A father's duty to support his minor child is placed upon him by the law. His duty to work 8 hours a day for his employer is self-imposed by his contract. Accordingly a father's promise to feed his child if his uncle promises the father $300 a week would not be enforceable against the uncle. Likewise, if the father tells his uncle that he isn't going to go to work each day and the uncle promises him $300 if he would do his duty, another unenforceable promise is made.

EXAMPLE 12. A builder wants a promise of an additional $3,000 or else he will walk off the job. The owner promises to pay the $3,000. The builder finishes the job and demands the additional $3,000. The owner's promise is unenforceable since there is no consideration. The builder had a preexisting duty to build according to specification and for the original contract price.

Sometimes unforeseen difficulties cause one to promise additional consideration without receiving anything in return. If the difficulties are truly extraordinary and not reasonably foreseeable, a promise to pay additional money may be enforceable.

EXAMPLE 13. Unknown to builders and others in the area, pockets of quicksand exist on a job site. After contracting, a builder refuses to continue when he learns of the quicksand and calculates the added cost of building on the site. The owner agrees to pay the extra cost. This new promise may be enforceable without new consideration. The unforeseen difficulties rule may apply.

The preexisting duty rule does not deprive the parties of the right to rescind the original agreement for a different consideration. This results in some courts holding the amendment as an implied cancellation or implied rescission of the original agreement, thereby holding the agreement as amended valid even though no additional consideration was given. Indeed, in sales contracts under the Uniform Commercial Code, Section 2-209(1), no new consideration is needed for an agreement modifying a sales contract.

7.7 FORBEARANCE

A promise to *forbear*, not to do something one has a legal right to do, is consideration. Promises not to sue, not to compete, not to drink, for examples, are promises to forbear. A promise not to sue is consideration, provided the promisor reasonably believes he has a legal claim. Anyone has the power to sue by filing a law action, but pressing a frivolous law action is not a legal *right* to sue.

EXAMPLE 14. Harlow honestly believed that Thomas had slandered him at a lodge meeting. From what was actually said at the lodge meeting, it is doubtful that slander was committed. Nevertheless, if Thomas promised $500 for Harlow's promise not to sue, Thomas would be bound to pay the money. Harlow's promise to forbear suing is valuable consideration for Thomas's promise to pay the $500.

7.8 DEBT SATISFACTION

In satisfying a liquidated debt already due, any payment less than the amount of debt will not discharge the debt. A *liquidated debt* is one in which there is neither a dispute about liability nor a dispute about the exact amount owed. On the other hand, an agreement for any consideration paid in attempting to satisfy an *unliquidated*, or disputed, debt is full payment and satisfaction. A promise to pay $350 for a freezer, a promise to pay the plumber his daily rate, or an agreement in respect to most commercial undertakings usually results in the creation of a liquidated debt. On the other hand, a bona fide dispute about the terms of a contract, or some claim made in regard to purchased goods or services, can change an otherwise liquidated debt into an unliquidated debt or even a disputed claim.

EXAMPLE 15. A debtor owes X $600, and she owes Dr. Y $500 for a medical bill she honestly disputes should be no greater than $300. The doctor insists on $500. If the debtor gets X to agree to accept $350 in full payment and Dr. Y to take $400 in full payment, only the doctor's bill is completely satisfied. X can sue for the balance of the $600 debt because it is a liquidated debt. A sum of $400 is not valuable consideration for $600. The doctor's bill, however, is not liquidated, and any consideration agreed upon within the disputed area, $300 to $500, satisfies the obligation.

Generally the adequacy of consideration is immaterial. Accordingly, if one agrees to sell a $5,000 car for the sum of $5, the law would enforce the promise in the absence of fraud or other wrongdoing. But an agreement by which the parties exchange the same type of consideration, but in differing amounts, can be inadequate as a matter of law and unenforceable.

EXAMPLE 16. Mary wished to make an enforceable future gift to her niece. Accordingly, she promised in writing "to pay $5,000 in consideration of the payment of $5, receipt whereof is hereby acknowledged from my niece." The sum of $5 promised, or received, is inadequate to support the promise to pay $5,000. Mary's promise is unenforceable by reason of the absence of consideration.

7.9 VOUCHER CHECKS

A *voucher check* contains a notation identifying the debt and providing that the cashing of the check "is an acceptance and full payment." The rules of consideration are not suspended because of the use of a voucher check. The acceptance and cashing of a voucher check drawn for a sum less than the amount due, in the absence of any consideration for a release, does not prevent the collection of the balance due. Some states have validated written debt settlement agreements for a lesser amount, but the use of a voucher check for that purpose is generally prohibited. Section 3-408 of the UCC is sometimes advanced for the proposition that a voucher check could provide a final settlement for less than the full amount of the debt.

EXAMPLE 17.   Fay has two creditors, X and Y. They claim that Fay owes each $4,000. Fay honestly disputes Y's claim. Fay delivers two personal checks in the amount of $3,000 to each. Each check contains the legend that "the cashing of this check is acceptance of payment in full." X and Y cash their respective voucher checks. The cashing of the check by Y satisfies the claim since this was a disputed, or unliquidated, debt. X's claim, however, was liquidated and not in dispute. Partial payment of a liquidated debt does not discharge the debt regardless of the proof of agreement. X may sue for the $1,000 balance remaining.

7.10   COMPOSITION AGREEMENT

At common law a *composition agreement* is one between a debtor and two or more of his or her creditors who agree to take, for the sake of immediate payment, a sum less than the whole amount of their claims to be distributed, pro rata to joining creditors, in full satisfaction of the debts. Simply stated, what a debtor could not accomplish with a creditor "one on one," he can achieve when two or more creditors settle with him in one agreement.

EXAMPLE 18.   Danny is hard-pressed and has but $6,000 available to pay his creditors, X Y, and Z. Danny agrees to give the entire amount to them in settlement of all their claims totaling $20,000. X wants no part of the deal. Y who is owed $6,000 agrees, as does Z who is owed $12,000. Proportionally, Danny pays Y $2,000 and Z $4,000. Later, Danny's uncle dies and leaves Danny money. X, who was owed $2,000 and didn't join in the composition agreement, can sue. The claims of Y and Z were discharged by the composition agreement.

7.11   ACCORD AND SATISFACTION

An *accord* is an agreement in which one party promises to give a substituted performance in satisfaction of an existing legal duty when the other party has already executed his or her performance. When this promise is fully performed, the obligation is then satisfied, hence the term "accord and satisfaction."

EXAMPLE 19.   Malinas, a retailer, owed her supplier $550 for goods but had difficulty in paying the debt. The supplier, anxious to have Malinas stock a new line of goods, offered to forgive the debt if Malinas promised to stock the new line. This agreement is the accord. When Malinas actually stocks the goods, a *satisfaction* occurs and the original debt is discharged.

Some courts have used the term "accord and satisfaction" to describe situations where an agreement was reached to settle a disputed or unliquidated debt, as in the voucher check situations.

Black Letter Law
A Summary

1.   Every simple promise requires valuable consideration.

2.   Consideration is a legal benefit to the promisor or a legal detriment suffered by the promisee; it must be bargained for.

3.   Mutual promises to do something of value are consideration.

4. A promise to bestow a gift, whether in writing or not, is generally unenforceable.

5. A promise to donate to a charity can be enforceable under the consideration doctrine, the detriment principle, or promissory estoppel.

6. Past consideration is generally no consideration.

7. Exceptions to the past consideration doctrine include promises made after an act was previously requested and in old obligations which by law may be revived by a new promise.

8. Promissory estoppel occurs when the promisor expects, or should have expected, the other party to rely on the promise to his detriment.

9. A promise to do what one is already legally bound to do by contract or law is not valid consideration.

10. A promise to forbear from doing what one has a legal right to do is valuable consideration.

11. Partial payment of a liquidated debt already due for money alone will not discharge the full debt.

12. Voucher checks with the "payment-in-full notation" do not alter the liquidated debt rule, but are effective for unliquidated, or disputed, debts.

13. A liquidated debt is one in which there is neither a dispute about liability nor a dispute about the amount owed.

14. A common-law composition agreement is an exception to the consideration doctrine and allows discharge of the full debts by partial payments to creditors in their pro rata amounts.

Solved Problems

7.1   X and Y enter into an agreement by which X is to sell a product to Y at a price of $100 per unit of product for a period of 1 year. In exchange, Y promises "to purchase as many as he might want during that period." Which statement is correct?

   (a) Such an agreement is a requirements contract.
   (b) This agreement is an output contract.
   (c) Y's promise is illusory and binds no one.
   (d) Y has given valuable consideration.

        A promise to purchase as many as you might *want* promises nothing of value and therefore (c) is the answer. This type of promise is illusory and therefore is no consideration. Requirements contracts are different, as the buyer promises to buy what he or she "needs" or "requires" during the period. This is a valuable promise. If the buyer needs or requires the goods, the buyer *"must* buy them from the seller." This is a valuable promise and constitutes consideration.

7.2   Matson is a better negotiator than Torque. She manages to get Torque to agree to buy 1,000 fasteners at $80 per unit. The market price for such units is generally between $61 and $73. Which is the correct statement?

(a) Bad bargains are enforceable.

(b) This agreement fails by reason of inadequacy of consideration.

(c) Matson is supplying past consideration.

(d) Gross inadequacy of consideration alone allows rescission of the contract.

Each party is free to bargain as he or she pleases, and since the law does not protect one from making a foolish bargain, (a) is correct. The adequacy of consideration is important only in cases of fraud or where parties use the same exchange medium for consideration, such as money for money, wheat for wheat, etc. Past consideration is seen where one promises to pay for something that was done for free in the past.

7.3 Three old classmates each promised to donate $14,000 to their university's fund-raising drive for an addition to the library. Under which conditions would the pledges be *unenforceable*?

(a) If each pledged in consideration of the others' pledging

(b) If the pledges are in writing and notarized

(c) If the university hired an architect to design the building after the university received the pledges

(d) If, upon request of the classmates, the university agreed to name the addition after them

Most courts still require some form of consideration or promissory estoppel to be shown for charitable pledges. Statement (b) is the answer, although some courts would enforce it on public policy alone. A promise to bestow a gift does not become enforceable just because one can prove the promise was made, which is all the writing would show. In all three other situations, either consideration was given or the university changed its legal position in reliance on the promised gifts in a way that the donors should have expected.

7.4 Which of the following is *not* a liquidated debt?

(a) Debt evidenced by a promissory note

(b) A customer claim on a department store for a refrigerator which failed while under warranty

(c) An account stated

(d) A dentist bill unpaid for 6 months

A customer claim on a department store for a refrigerator which failed while under warranty is the most likely claim that is unliquidated, statement (b). A promissory note is certain in amount, as is an "account stated," which results when a statement is not objected to by the debtor. A dentist bill that is unpaid for 6 months and which is not objected to is also likely to be a liquidated debt.

7.5 An air cadet promised to name his mother beneficiary of his life insurance policy if she promised to pay the proceeds to his girlfriend if he should die. The mother promised, and the air cadet named her the beneficiary. When the air cadet died and the mother received the insurance proceeds, she refused to turn the money over to the girlfriend. Can the mother's promise be enforced?

(a) Yes, because the cadet suffered a legal detriment by naming his mother the beneficiary.

(b) No, because the girlfriend gave no valuable consideration.

(c) No, because his mother received no valuable consideration for her promise.

(d) Yes, because his mother promised in writing.

The answer is statement (a). The contracting parties were the cadet and his mother. The cadet did not have to name his mother as the beneficiary but did so relying on her promise to deliver up the proceeds. Consideration can be a legal detriment suffered by the promisee. The cadet was the promisee.

He suffered a legal detriment, promising to name his mother as beneficiary. This supplies the consideration for the enforcement of the mother's promise to deliver up the proceeds to the girlfriend. The promisor, the mother, does not necessarily receive benefit to herself. It is sufficient that the promisee, the cadet, suffered a detriment as a result of the promise.

7.6   Consideration to support a contract generally requires

(*a*)   an adequate exchange.

(*b*)   a bargained exchange.

(*c*)   a reasonable price.

(*d*)   an adequate price.

(*AICPA Examination, May 1976*)

The answer is a bargained exchange, statement (*b*). It is essential that the parties bargained for what each received and that this something, or promise of something, was of some value no matter how small. A "reasonable" price is not necessary. This term is used where the parties agreed to pay but no amount was mentioned. That is a problem of offer and acceptance, or terms, but not of consideration.

7.7   Which of the following will *not* be sufficient to satisfy the consideration requirement for a contract?

(*a*)   The offeree expends both time and money in studying and analyzing the offer.

(*b*)   The offeree makes a promise which is a legal detriment to him.

(*c*)   The offeree performs the act requested by the offeror.

(*d*)   The offeree makes a promise which benefits the offeror.

(*AICPA Examination, November 1979*)

Consideration is a benefit to the promisor or a legal detriment suffered by the promisee. Statement (*a*) is the answer. While the offeree is suffering some disadvantage or detriment by studying the offer, the offeror did not request or expect such to be done as a condition to contracting. Accordingly, the law does not recognize such efforts as a legal detriment sufficient to supply consideration. The other statements describe the traditional acts which constitute consideration.

7.8   The common-law contract doctrine of consideration

(*a*)   requires that consideration have a monetary value if it is to be valid.

(*b*)   recognizes that the forbearance from a legal right constitutes consideration.

(*c*)   has been abolished in most jurisdictions if the contract is made under seal.

(*d*)   requires a roughly equal exchange of value by the parties to the contract.

(*AICPA Examination, November 1976*)

The correct statement is (*b*). It is not necessary that one gives up something to the other contractor. It is enough if one gives up something one has a legal right to do. To promise to forbear suing, for example, is an act which qualifies as consideration. Statement (*c*) reminds the reader that at one time a seal created an evidentiary presumption that consideration was given, or that such was not necessary. This rule is no longer generally true.

7.9   In order to be valid, consideration must

(*a*)   be stated in the contract.

(*b*)   be based upon a legal obligation as contrasted with a moral obligation.

(c)   be performed simultaneously by the parties.

(d)   have a monetary value.

(*AICPA Examination, November 1976*)

   Consideration must be legal in character as stated in (b). A nephew's present promise to pay his aunt who is now penniless "upon consideration of the many acts of kindness toward me during my youth" may be based on sound moral grounds but does not supply consideration. The nephew's promise would not be enforceable.

7.10   A written option to buy land generally *cannot* be revoked before acceptance if the offer

(a)   is supported by consideration from the offeree.

(b)   allows a specific time for acceptance.

(c)   is made exclusively to one person.

(d)   by its terms is *not* revocable before acceptance.

(*AICPA Examination, May 1976*)

   Options are contracts and accordingly require consideration, statement (a). Consideration makes the agreement binding as a contract. Offers can be revoked but not a promise to hold an offer open for consideration, which is what an option is.

7.11   Montbanks's son, Charles, was seeking an account executive position with Dobbs, Smith, and Fogarty, Inc., the largest brokerage firm in the United States. Charles was very independent and wished *no* interference by his father. The firm, after several weeks deliberation, decided to hire Charles. It made him an offer on April 12, 19X9, and Charles readily accepted. Montbanks feared that his son would *not* be hired. Being unaware of the fact that his son had been hired, Montbanks mailed a letter to Dobbs on April 13 in which he promised to give the brokerage firm $50,000 in commission business if the firm would hire his son. The letter was duly received by Dobbs, and the firm wishes to enforce it against Montbanks. Which of the following statements is correct?

(a)   Past consideration is *no* consideration; hence there is *no* contract.

(b)   The preexisting legal duty rule applies and makes the promise unenforceable.

(c)   Dobbs will prevail since the promise is contained in a signed writing.

(d)   Dobbs will prevail based upon promissory estoppel.

(*AICPA Examination, May 1979*)

   Montbanks received no consideration for his promise to Dobbs, statement (a). Dobbs never gave a legal benefit to Montbanks or suffered a legal detriment as a result of Montbanks's promise. The son had already been hired. This is a typical case where the only consideration Dobbs could offer is past consideration. Past consideration will not bind the other's promise. A signed writing does not validate an otherwise ineffective agreement. Promissory estoppel is not applicable because Dobbs did not change its position as a result of the father's promise; the firm had already employed the son.

7.12   Which of the following offers for the sale of the Lazy L Ranch is enforceable?

(a)   The owner tells the buyer she will sell the ranch for $35,000 and that the offer will be irrevocable for 10 days.

(b)   The owner writes the buyer offering to sell the ranch for $35,000 and stating that the offer will remain open for 10 days.

(c) The owner telegraphs the buyer offering to sell the ranch for $35,000 and promises to hold the offer open for 10 days.

(d) The owner writes the buyer offering to sell the ranch for $35,000 and stating that the offer will be irrevocable for 10 days if the buyer will pay $1. The buyer pays.

(Adapted from AICPA Examination, November 1981)

Offers made without consideration are sometimes called "naked" offers, which may be revoked at any time before acceptance. Where the offeror asks for and receives consideration to keep his or her offer open, an option occurs. Options are contracts and remain binding for the agreed term. Statement (d) is correct. The payment of $1 as requested by the offeror is the consideration supplied by the offeree to make the option binding. All other statements only describe offers which may be revoked before acceptance.

7.13 Smith contracted to perform for $500 certain services for Jones. Jones claimed that the services had been performed poorly. Because of this, Jones sent Smith a check for only $425. Marked clearly on the check was "payment in full." Smith crossed out the words "payment in full" and cashed the check. Assuming that there was a bona fide dispute about whether Smith had in fact performed the services poorly, the majority of courts would hold that

(a) The debt is liquidated and Smith can collect the remaining $75.

(b) The debt is liquidated, but Jones by adding the words "payment in full" canceled the balance of the debt owed.

(c) The debt is unliquidated, and the cashing of the check by Smith completely discharged the debt.

(d) The debt is unliquidated, but the crossing out of the words "payment in full" by Smith revives the balance of $75 owed.

(AICPA Examination, May 1981)

This is a voucher check situation, and the effectiveness of the settlement depends on whether the debt was liquidated or unliquidated. The facts suggest a bona fide dispute, and therefore the debt is unliquidated. Any agreement the parties reach will settle the debt in such cases. "Paid in full," the voucher situation, is the debtor's offer to settle the dispute at that amount. The cashing of the check under such a condition is the acceptance. The debt is settled. Statement (c) is correct. Smith had no right to cross out the condition on the check. If Smith did not want to contract, he should have returned the check. Statements (a) and (b) are not applicable if one assumes that this is an unliquidated, or disputed, debt.

7.14 Williams purchased a heating system from Radiant Heating, Inc., for her factory. Williams insisted that a clause be included in the contract calling for service on the heating system to begin *not* later than the next business day after Williams informed Radiant of the problem. The service was to be rendered free of charge during the first year of the contract and for a flat fee of $200 per year for the next 2 years thereafter. During the winter of the second year, the heating system broke down and Williams promptly notified Radiant of the situation. Due to other commitments, Radiant did *not* send anyone over the next day. Williams phoned Radiant and was told that the $200-per-year service contract was uneconomical and the company could not get a person over there for several days. Williams in desperation promised to pay an additional $100 if Radiant would send someone to repair the heating system that day. Radiant did so and sent a bill of $100 to Williams. Is Williams legally required to pay this bill and why?

(a) No, because the preexisting legal duty rule applies to this situation.

(b) No, because the statute of frauds will defeat Radiant's claim.

(c)   Yes, because Williams made the offer to pay the additional amount.

(d)   Yes, because the fact that it was uneconomical for Radiant to perform constitutes economic duress which freed Radiant from its obligation to provide the agreed-upon service.

(Adapted from AICPA Examination, May 1979)

Under the terms of the original contract, Williams has a right to have the services she demanded. The other party's promise to do what it is already obligated to do does not provide consideration for Williams's second promise. Statement (a) is correct. The other statements refer to the existence of Williams's promise, which is not in question. Even if she admits making the promise, the issue is its enforceability by reason of lack of consideration.

7.15   Keats Publishing Company shipped textbooks and other books for sale at retail to Campus Bookstore. An honest dispute arose of Campus's right to return certain books. Keats maintained that the books in question *could not* be returned and demanded payment of the full amount. Campus relied upon trade custom, which indicated that many publishers accepted the return of such books. Campus returned the books in question and paid for the balance with a check marked "account paid in full to date." Keats cashed the check. Which of the following is a correct statement?

(a)   Keats is entitled to recover damages.

(b)   Keats's cashing of the check constituted an accord and satisfaction.

(c)   The preexisting legal duty rule applies, and Keats is entitled to full payment for all the books.

(d)   The custom-of-the-industry argument would have *no* merit in a court of law.

(AICPA Examination, May 1979)

Where the debt is in dispute, or unliquidated, the doctrine of accord and satisfaction easily applies. An agreement and execution of the agreement, here by payment under a voucher check, satisfy the obligation. Statement (b) is the answer. The custom of the industry, called trade custom under the Uniform Commercial Code, is a relevant source for settling legal disputes. Therefore, it is incorrect to state that it would have no merit in a court of law.

7.16   Novack, an industrial designer, accepted an offer from Superior Design Corporation to become one of its designers. The contract was for 3 years and expressly provided that it was irrevocable by either party except for cause during that period of time. The contract was in writing and signed by both parties. After a year, Novack became dissatisfied with the agreed compensation which he was receiving. He had done a brilliant job, and several larger corporations were attempting to lure him away.

Novack, therefore, demanded a substantial raise, and Superior agreed in writing to pay him an additional amount as a bonus at the end of the third year. Novack remained with Superior and performed the same duties he had agreed to perform at the time he initially accepted the position. At the end of the 3 years, Novack sought to collect the additional amount of money promised. Superior denied liability beyond the amount agreed to in the original contract.

Answer the following, setting forth reasons for any conclusions stated: Can Novack recover the additional compensation from Superior? *(AICPA Examination, November 1978)*

The facts indicate that the original employment contract was binding and not breached at the time Novack wanted to change its terms. Of course, both parties could have modified the contract by mutual agreement supported by consideration. However, the second agreement lacked consideration in that Novack supplied no new consideration for Superior's promise to pay a bonus for work Novack was already legally bound to do. The rule governing preexisting duty applies in this case. Novack's promise to live up to his contract was a promise to do no more than he was legally obligated to do. This is the general rule and is only modified in the case of the sale of goods. Section 2-209 of the UCC does permit good-faith modifications of sales contracts without the need for additional consideration. This case involves an employment contract, however, not one for the sale of goods.

7.17 Terry Barr executed a pledge of $50,000 to the Mount Hope Hospital Fund Drive in 19X5. The pledge was delivered to Mount Hope Hospital and provided: "In consideration of and to induce the subscriptions of others, I (we) promise to pay to Mount Hope Hospital or order the sum of Fifty Thousand and No/100 dollars ($50,000), $5,000 of which is paid herewith, the balance to be paid in nine equal monthly installments commencing on January 1, 19X6." Terry had made payments totaling $20,000, which were applied to the pledge, before she died in late March 19X6. Terry's estate refused to pay the balance of $30,000, and Mount Hope Hospital is using legal language such as "detriment" and "promissory estoppel" in their claim.

Can Mount Hope Hospital succeed on the above facts? Answer, setting forth reasons for any conclusions stated.

The hospital will not succeed on the above facts. Charitable subscriptions generally require a showing of consideration or promissory estoppel. In the absence of evidence that others subscribed because Terry subscribed, and that is why she pledged, the statement in the notes will be ineffective to show consideration. Further, there is no showing that the hospital acted to its legal detriment as a result of the promise. Simply spending money received is no legal detriment. Terry's promise apparently did not induce the hospital to change its position to its legal detriment. Accordingly, the doctrine of promissory estoppel would not apply.

7.18 The rock group Curtains entered into an agreement with Dex Record Company, the terms of which provided that the rock group was to record exclusively for Dex for a period of 3 years. The only consideration given to Curtains was a check in the amount of $2,500, which had noted on it that it was "an advance against royalties." Following some early successes, the group decided to contract with a competing recording studio. Dex resisted, claiming that Curtains was required to fulfill the 3-year contract. Curtains contended that it received no consideration for its promise to Dex in that the $2,500 was later paid back to Dex out of royalties.

Was the first contract binding? Answer, setting forth reasons for any conclusions stated.

The adequacy of consideration is generally immaterial in the absence of fraud, other wrongdoing, or gross inadequacy such as would shock the conscience of the court. The $2,500 advance was sufficient consideration for the agreement. The law will not consider whether or not it was a good bargain. The fact is that even if the $2,500 was an advance against royalties, there was no assurance at the time of the contract that royalties would occur. By making the advance, Dex Record Company suffered a legal detriment and the rock group received a legal advantage. It is not the function of the court to review the amount of consideration except as noted above.

Chapter 8

Illegal Agreements

8.1 NATURE OF AGREEMENTS

An agreement whose object is contrary to common law, constitutional law, statute, or public policy is illegal and unenforceable. Constitutional and statutory enactments seldom prohibit particular types of contracts. Rather, they identify antisocial behavior and provide criminal sanctions. Agreements arising out of these expressly prohibited activities are, by implication, void and, while not subject to criminal sanction, are illegal bargains. Further, agreements created within the broad range of behavior prohibited by "public policy" as defined by the courts are also treated by the courts as illegal bargains.

EXAMPLE 1. Luster gave the poker winner a $500 check for poker losses. State statute prohibits poker and fines those who so engage. The check is therefore for an illegal purpose. The winner cannot enforce payment of the $500 check.

EXAMPLE 2. Lott wants to marry Craig's wife. He promises Craig $5,000 if Craig will divorce his wife. Craig agrees. Lott now refuses to pay the $5,000. There is no statute covering this, but most courts would say that it is against public policy for a court to enforce an agreement whose purpose is to break up a marriage.

Illegal bargains are frequently tested in the courts. They occur in business and interpersonal situations including Sunday contracts, gambling and wagering, usury, licensing, antitrust, and covenants not to compete.

8.2 SUNDAY CONTRACTS

A bargain made on Sunday or other legal holidays can be illegal and unenforceable if the state or local law so provides. There is no uniformity except for the general trend which sees these "blue laws," as they are called, becoming less of a factor in present-day practice. Further, even an agreement made on Sunday in a state which enforces such laws can be adopted, ratified, or accepted on the following secular days. It is only when a Sunday contract is in its executory stage that it may be unenforceable. Works of necessity, public welfare activities, and sales of goods have contributed to the decline of the Sunday bargain rules. Many state and local statutes provide numerous exceptions including entertainment and sports presentations.

EXAMPLE 3. State statute prohibits used-car sales on Sunday and legal holidays. An agreement signed on Sunday performed Monday by either party is an "adoption" of the Sunday bargain, making it enforceable.

8.3 GAMBLING AND WAGERING

Like Sunday bargains, public policy on gambling and wagering is generally found in state statutes. Some states allow gambling by license, such as horse racing, while prohibiting private gambling. Gambling is an agreement where the parties involved will gain or lose depending upon the outcome of some uncertain event in which they have no material interest except their gain or loss.

EXAMPLE 4. A football fan bets $50 on the outcome of a game on Sunday television. The only interest he has is *on* what he may win. This is an illegal bargain, a wager which is not enforceable.

EXAMPLE 5. Brown "bets" Ace Insurance Company that her house will burn down during the year. Brown pays a premium of $400, and Ace agrees to pay up to $90,000 if the house burns down. It would cost that much to replace the house. This is not a wager. Brown owns the house and has therefore a material interest in the subject of the "bet". This interest is in seeing that the house is preserved. Brown has an "insurable interest" in the property, a necessary element in insurance contracts. Without an insurable interest, this would have been a bet and would be illegal. Taking out insurance on one's neighbor's house is a bet, a gamble. One would recover nothing should the neighbor's house burn down.

An agreement to purchase stock or a commodity in which one never intended to take title or where the other never intended to deliver is illegal. Accordingly, an agreement to buy a futures contract, for example the delivery of 5,000 bushels of wheat, could be unenforceable if the agreement did not provide for delivery or the buyer could take cash in lieu of delivery.

EXAMPLE 6. X and Y read the stockmarket page in the newspaper every day. They hate to pay brokers' commissions. They agree that X will honor all Y's buy and sell orders. Each month they will strike a balance as to how much one owes the other. X records the orders but has no stock to sell or deliver. This is an illegal bargain and is unenforceable.

8.4 USURY

Usury is the taking of, or the agreement to take, a greater interest for use of money than is permitted by law. Usury is highly regulated, and few states have the same rate limits or penalties for violation. Most states have a general usury statute that states the maximum allowable rate of interest and then lists numerous exceptions. Common types of lenders or transactions having exceptional or special maximum rates are:

(1) Retail stores: revolving accounts for the sale and purchase of consumer items, sometimes called the *time-price differential*

(2) Credit unions

(3) Small loan companies

(4) Commercial bank discount rates

(5) Savings and loan associations

(6) Automobile loans

For some of these exceptions a special license must be obtained. This is so, for example, in the case of small loan companies. They are authorized to charge a high rate because their customers are traditionally poor credit risks and the lenders have high administrative costs in relation to the size of the average loan. In other cases the usury exception applies to a particular type of transaction, such as used-car sales. Usury laws are for the protection of the borrowers, and accordingly, each state has its sanctions against an offending lender. In many cases the penalty is forfeiture of interest, or double interest, and sometimes the principal itself cannot be collected by the lender. There are also criminal penalties provided for particularly outrageous behavior such as shylocking (extortionate interest, usually accompanied by physical threats to enforce collection), which is punishable by fine and imprisonment.

The party charging another with usury must show that the lender intended to charge a usurious rate, not that he or she intended to violate the law. A common trap for a lender is to charge as "expense" what the court later characterizes as interest. Expenses related to making a loan are allowed provided they are necessary and are reasonable in amount. Sometimes, even if reasonable in amount, an expense charged may be considered to be *disguised interest*. If so, this may bring the total interest charge over the usury limit.

EXAMPLE 7.   A bank loans a developer $100,000 for 3 years at 18 percent interest in a state where 18 percent per annum is the maximum lawful rate for such loans. The expenses charged by the bank include attorney's fee $770, credit check $300, document preparation $500, survey by the bank's clerk $350, and site inspection by the bank vice president $900. This transaction is usurious. Only expenses necessary to the loan and reasonable in amount are not considered interest. Typing up documents is a lender's normal job. Site inspection by a bank officer is a normal duty and would be interpreted as interest. However, if the bank had paid an outside inspector, and the inspection was necessary for the protection of the loan, and the amount was reasonable, this could be a legitimate expense.

8.5   LICENSING

A state or local license or permit is commonly required of parties before they may engage in particular types of business. Performing services without the required license is generally punishable by fine or imprisonment. Regulatory licenses are generally required of and issued to such persons as doctors, dentists, lawyers, real estate brokers, craftspeople, and others where the state determines it is in the public interest that certain qualifications be met by practitioners. Contracts made by unlicensed persons are unenforceable if the statute is regulatory, that is, enacted for the protection of the public.

If the required license is intended for revenue purposes only, the offender may be subject to a fine but could nevertheless recover for services performed under the contract.

EXAMPLE 8.   Mark needed a welder for repairs on his garage door. The city required welders to have a license costing $75 and obtainable only *after* showing that one could weld competently. The city also required anyone engaging in a retail business to have a business license, which cost $25 and could be obtained simply by applying for it. The welder's license is regulatory; the retail business license is for revenue. If a welder contracted with Mark, performed the work, and had to sue for the fee, the welder could not recover unless he or she had a welder's license.

If a retail salesperson sold a vacuum cleaner on credit to Mark without the business license, the salesperson could be fined but could legally collect the purchase price. The retail business license in this case is for revenue purposes since the license statute requires that no competence be shown to protect the public interest.

8.6   ANTITRUST

Both the federal government and the states enact legislation regulating business activity and its effect upon the open market. The federal antitrust laws, because of their broad reach, are the more important. However, there are also actions at common law providing relief from illegal business practices.

EXAMPLE 9.   Adam is an overly aggressive retailer. He falsely states that Brown's product is defective (disparagement), induces Taylor to break his employment contract with Neary (interference with contractual relations), falsely represents that his goods are Benson's product (mislabeling), and employs customer lists and procedures he appropriated from his former employer (trade secrets). The common law provides these injured parties with a remedy for such violations.

If a sale of goods or delivery of service occurs in interstate or foreign commerce, federal antitrust law attempts to preserve competition and prevent control of economic power. The Sherman Act of 1890 declares illegal every contract in restraint of trade (Section 1) and punishes every person who monopolizes or attempts to monopolize any part of trade or of commerce (Section 2). The Clayton Act of 1914, building on the Sherman Antitrust Act, prohibits price discrimination, restraints or tie-in sales, stock acquisitions of competitors, and interlocking directorships of corporations, if these acts lessen or tend to lessen competition.

EXAMPLE 10.   Zed Printing manufactures and sells comic books. It deals in interstate commerce. The New England area is the lifeblood of the comic book market. In a successful attempt to stifle competition in this area,

Zed sells comic books to only its favorite retailers at 10 percent less than other retailers are charged. In other areas Zed demands that jobbers and retailers not use or buy any other brand of comic book as a condition of Zed's selling to them. The stock of Mace, Inc., Zed's competitor in California, is being quietly purchased by Zed. Two of Zed's directors are also board members of a corporation that competes with Zed. If Zed's conduct tends to lessen competition, or create a monopoly, Zed Printing has violated Section 2 of the Clayton Act by price discrimination, Section 3 by tie-in restrictions, Section 7 by purchase of a competitor's stock, and Section 8 by interlocking directorates.

Good-faith dealing or ignorance does not insulate firms from the criminal and civil sanctions of federal antitrust laws. Fine and imprisonment of company officers can result, as well as treble damages to the business injured. The Federal Trade Commission Act of 1914 specifically empowers the commission to enforce sections of the Clayton Act and the Sherman Antitrust Act. Amendments followed in the Robinson-Patman Act (1936), which strengthened price discrimination rules and yet also allowed some price discrimination, where warranted by reasonable quantity discounts and other mitigating factors.

8.7 COVENANTS NOT TO COMPETE

In addition to federal and state legislation dealing with monopolistic practices and unfair competition, a common commercial agreement, called a *covenant not to compete*, is greatly used and subject to much litigation. Generally, a covenant not to compete is a restraint of trade and is illegal unless it is *ancillary* to an otherwise proper agreement and reasonable as to both time and geographic restrictions. However, an outright restraint of trade, whether reasonable or not, is illegal per se.

EXAMPLE 11. A theater owner, fearing competition from a property holder who was about to build, obtained the holder's promise, for a valuable consideration, that the holder "would not open a theater within 5 miles of the city for a period of 5 years." The theater owner cannot enforce this promise. It is an outright restraint of trade. It is tied to no other proper agreement, nor is it ancillary to another agreement.

A restraint of trade is considered unreasonable unless it is authorized by statute or is necessary to protect the interest of the party in whose favor it is imposed. It cannot create a monopoly, control prices artificially, limit production, or impose hardship on the promisor. The common legitimate use or purpose of this covenant is to protect purchased goodwill, or at least an opportunity to capture it. This frequently occurs in employment contracts and the purchase of businesses.

EXAMPLE 12. May Kay drives a small truck which carries prepared sandwiches and snacks for the city industrial area. She is a mobile caterer. When Lunch Box Company hired her, she signed a promise that "upon leaving the company I will not compete in the industrial area for 1 year." Bob is purchasing Ted's Golf Shop, which includes the inventory and the "goodwill." Ted says he is retiring. Bob wants a chance to retain Ted's old customers. Ted promises not to compete within 5 miles of the shop for 3 years. Both of these restraints of trade are ancillary to another agreement: May, her employment; Ted, the sale of the business. They appear reasonable as to time and area. Both are valid and enforceable.

Where, however, an employer or the buyer of a business drives too hard a bargain and gains what the court considers excessive restraint, the entire covenant falls and the other party is generally left with no promise to enforce. Some states will amend or modify the excessive restriction to "reasonable restriction."

8.8 EXCULPATORY CLAUSES

Some contracts contain a clause exempting one party from his or her own negligence (a tort). These are called *exculpatory clauses*. They are not favored by the law. It is only when the parties are seen to be bargaining from equal positions, and there is full disclosure, that such a clause could be enforceable. Accordingly, exculpatory statements on the reverse side of parking lot tickets, or placed on residential lease contracts, for example, are generally not binding.

EXAMPLE 13. A widower with two children, who lived on a rent subsidy, signed a lease which contained a paragraph exempting the landlord from "any damage or injury to tenant occurring on the premises." The widower tripped over a rock which was lying on a common stairway of the apartment building and injured himself. The landlord contended he could not be sued for such a defective condition since the lease clearly exempted the landlord. The court disagreed, citing a number of tests for the acceptance of such clauses. These included situations where one was performing a duty of a matter of practical necessity (i.e., housing, a basic human requirement), superior bargaining position (the landlord), and the use of a standardized adhesion ("take it or leave it") contract containing such an exculpatory clause with no provision whereby a purchaser could pay additional fees and obtain protection against negligence. The lease failed *all* of these tests. The widower won.

8.9 EFFECT OF ILLEGALITY

Where the bargain is illegal, the court generally leaves the parties where it finds them, but there are exceptions to this rule. If the agreement is illegal by a statute which attempts to protect a particular class, a member of that class will not be denied its remedy because it was a partner in the bargain. This is illustrated in the usury cases where the borrower may be relieved of interest payments, recover double interest, or even, in the exceptional case, obtain a pardon from the principal debt. Likewise, a party who entered into an agreement under a mistake of fact will *not* be considered in *equal fault* (*in pari delicto*) and can enforce his or her rights. This may be observed in a lawsuit by a stage actor who performs in a play where the producer failed to obtain a necessary license. If the actor performed in ignorance of this violation, the producer may not use illegality as a defense to the payment of the actor's fee.

EXAMPLE 14. A traveler in a hurry to the airport can only make his flight if the taxi driver runs at least three red lights. The traveler promises the driver $50 and the costs of any fines if the driver gets him to the airport in time to catch the flight. The driver agrees, speeds, runs several red lights, and succeeds. The traveler refuses to pay anything but the fare. The court will not assist either party in carrying out an illegal bargain. It leaves the parties where it finds them: here, the driver without the promised $50. If the driver had demanded prepayment and then honored every red light, the court would not assist the traveler in retrieving the money the driver did not "earn" by having the traveler miss the flight.

Public policy honors the repentant by providing court access to a party who has an illegal bargain but changes his or her mind before the performance of the illegal part. Also, if the parties had separated legal parts from illegal parts when contracting, the court will allow enforcement of the severable or divisible legal portions. However, if the parts are viewed as one bargain by the parties at the time of the contract, the court will not attempt to sever the legal from the illegal. It will totally deny recovery.

EXAMPLE 15. Denton Furnace Supply sells and installs iron furnaces. The company has competent workers but no regulatory license to install these heating devices. It has, however, a business license to sell furnaces. Denton contracted with a homeowner for the *sale* and *installation* of a Model XL iron furnace for the "total installed price of $1,700." The list price for the unit was $1,200, but this was not stated in the agreement or invoice. The furnace was installed. A dispute arose between the parties, and Denton sued for the balance. The homeowner defended on the grounds that Denton did not have the required regulatory license. Denton admits it cannot recover for the installation, which it estimates is worth $500, but wants the $1,200 for the furnace. The parties did not separate the legal from the illegal. Hence, the court will not. It is not a divisible contract. On these facts, Denton loses.

Black Letter Law
A Summary

1. An illegal bargain is unenforceable.

2. A bargain can be illegal by common law, by statute, or by public policy.

3. Bargains that are illegal include Sunday agreements, gambling, usury, and anticompetitive acts.

4. Sunday bargains are made illegal in various states and localities by statutes and ordinances, but an adoption of the contract on a secular day makes the bargain binding.

5. Gambling is an agreement whereby the parties involved gain or lose on the happening of some uncertain event that they have no material interest in except that which may occur from the possibility of such gain or loss.

6. Gambling can take many forms; the statutes of each state define prohibited gambling activity.

7. Usury is the taking of, or the agreement to take, a greater interest for the use of money than is permitted by law.

8. Usury is determined by each state statute as to transactions, exceptions, maximum rates, and penalties.

9. Not everyone who performs services without an appropriate license is prevented from enforcing the bargain.

10. Where a license is required for revenue purposes only rather than regulatory purposes, compensation earned without the license can be recovered at law.

11. A bargain made for the sole purpose of preventing competition is not enforceable.

12. The Sherman Antitrust Act, the Clayton Act, and the Robinson-Patman Act are federal statutes monitoring agreements and practices that might restrain or impair competition in interstate or foreign commerce.

13. A covenant not to compete is an agreement that may be enforceable if it does not unreasonably restrain competition and is ancillary to the sale of a business or to an employment contract.

14. A covenant not to compete as ancillary to the sale of a business or to an employment contract will be enforced if the court finds it reasonable as to the time and area restrictions.

15. Not all illegal bargains are void, because the doctrines of repentance, not *in pari delicto*, and severability allow exceptions.

16. In an executory bargain if the party who is to perform the illegal act repents and attempts to rescind the agreement, the law will entertain the action.

17. Parties not in equal fault (not *in pari delicto*), such as a performer who unknowingly performs in an unlicensed play, may have recourse to the courts.

18. If, at the time of the bargain, the parties separated the legal parts from the illegal parts, the court will enforce the severable lawful terms of the agreement.

Solved Problems

8.1   An illegal bargain always results in

   (a)   a voidable contract.

   (b)   fine or imprisonment against one of the parties.

   (c)   a void contract.

   (d)   a valid contract.

   Statement (c) is correct. An illegal bargain is no contract from the beginning; hence it is void. Not all illegal bargains that have the elements of a crime as a bargain may merely be against public policy.

8.2   Usury statutes

   (a)   establish the amount of interest the lender must charge.

   (b)   set a maximum rate of permissible interest which may be agreed upon between the parties.

   (c)   are enacted to protect the lender.

   (d)   are not applicable if the lender and borrower have equal bargaining power.

   A usury statute sets the maximum rates at which money can be loaned, statement (b). It is for the protection of the borrower and is not concerned with the relative bargaining power of the parties.

8.3   James borrowed money in a state in which the maximum interest for this particular type of loan was 20 percent per annum. As a condition to the loan, however, James was required to take out a life insurance policy as security for the loan. James was charged 19 percent interest for the loan. The yearly insurance premium, if considered to be additional interest, made the loan interest rate 22 percent per annum. Which is the correct statement?

   (a)   The lender has clearly entered into a usurious contract.

   (b)   If the lender and the insurance company are the same party, the loan is usurious.

   (c)   If James pays the interest for over a year without complaint, he has waived the charge of usury.

   (d)   James and the lender are *in pari delicto*.

   Requiring additional security such as an insurance policy is not improper or illegal. However, if it is made a condition of the loan, the additional cost—here the insurance premiums—could be labeled interest; and so the correct statement is (b). If another insurance company were involved, the loan could be proper. By statute the lender and borrower, as regards the charging of interest, are not considered in equal fault (*in pari delicto*). The borrower is the protected party.

8.4   A steelworker was out of work and started painting houses in his neighborhood. The city required housepainters to possess a painting license. The city charged a modest fee and required the applicant to take a written test on different paints and wood surfaces. The steelworker, without a license, painted three local houses on credit. If he had to sue for payment of his services, what would be the likely result?

   (a)   These are valid and enforceable contracts.

   (b)   These contracts are voidable at the election of the homeowners.

   (c)   The steelworker would be unsuccessful, as this license was a regulatory license.

   (d)   The steelworker would succeed, as the required license was for city revenue purposes only.

If the license is required by the city to protect its residents from unqualified persons, a contract made by an unlicensed person is void, statement (c). Such a license is called regulatory rather than revenue. The fact that some knowledge of painting skills was required by the city suggests that protection of the citizens rather than mere collection of taxes or revenue is the object of the law. If a painter had only to pay a fee in order to be issued the license, it would clearly be revenue only.

8.5   There are numerous antitrust statutes. The more prominent ones are the federal laws. Which of the following is *not* an antitrust law?

(a)   Robinson-Patman Act

(b)   Sherman Antitrust Act

(c)   Wagner Act

(d)   Clayton Act

Statement (c) is the answer. The Wagner Act is also known as the National Labor Relations Act. It regulates collective bargaining for workers engaged in interstate commerce. The Sherman Antitrust Act was the first major federal legislation proscribing anticompetitive behavior. The Clayton Act added to the Sherman Act. The Robinson-Patman Act, dealing mainly with price discrimination, amended the Clayton Act.

8.6   Kramer is a partner in an engineering and designing firm. Her partnership contract contains a clause which states that should Kramer leave the firm, she agrees not to compete with the firm for 1 year, either as an individual or as a member of another designing firm, anywhere within the city limits of Los Angeles. The firm does most of its business with clients in the states of California, Oregon, and Washington. The clause would be held

(a)   legally enforceable by most courts.

(b)   an illegal restraint of trade under the Sherman Antitrust Act.

(c)   illegal, thereby invalidating the entire contract.

(d)   unconscionable under the Uniform Commercial Code.

Reasonable restraints of trade are permitted if ancillary to an otherwise valid contract and reasonable in both time and geographical restrictions, and so statement (a) is correct. In this case the covenant is tied to a proper agreement, the partnership articles, and its restriction is appropriate to the protection of partnership interest. A restriction of 1 year within the city in which the employee works for a firm having clients in a three-state area is not unreasonable. The Uniform Commercial Code is not applicable to this type of contract.

8.7   Tiny was a petty businessman. He envied and feared his competitors. However, he was usually a shrewd judge of goods and would call the goods as he saw them. Sometimes he went too far, making untruthful remarks about his competitors' products. When he does so, what common-law action could be brought against Tiny?

(a)   Mislabeling

(b)   Disparagement

(c)   Wrongful interference with contractual relations

(d)   Violation of trade secrets

Tiny could be charged with disparagement, statement (b). Disparagement is to the goods of others what slander is to another's reputation. It allows an action for damages. Wrongful interference relates to activities which disturb relationships others have. Inducing a party to breach his or her distributorship contract with another so that the party would deal only with you would be the offense charged under that name.

8.8 Hobble Drugs ran an all-night drugstore which sold controlled as well as uncontrolled drugs. Tunney made a credit purchase for controlled drugs and at the same time one for uncontrolled drugs. Tunney was not allowed to purchase the controlled drugs, taking them under circumstances which were illegal. The price of the purchases on his charge account read "drugs, $110" and no other figure or words. Under these circumstances,

   (*a*) Hobble can collect the legal part of the contract, $30, the market value of the legal drugs.

   (*b*) since there were legal purchases with the illegal, the entire contract is legal.

   (*c*) the entire purchase is void if the parties did not sever the legal from the illegal consideration.

   (*d*) if the controlled drugs could have been obtained by Tunney taking the trouble to get a valid prescription for them, this absence does not make the entire contract void.

   If a part of the agreement is legal and part is illegal, the courts will enforce the legal part if it can be separated from the illegal part. Here the parties did not separate the items and the court will not do it for them; statement (*c*) is the answer. The fact that one could have made a legal transaction, but didn't, does not rescue a bargain already made.

8.9 For a covenant not to compete to be enforceable it must be ancillary to an otherwise proper agreement. Which of the following would not be ancillary?

   (*a*) An employee's promise not to compete upon termination.

   (*b*) A business seller's promise not to compete against his buyer.

   (*c*) A new barber's promise to a local barber that he would not start up a barbershop in the town.

   (*d*) A retiring partner's promise not to compete with the old partnership.

   All promises are tied to another proper contract except (*c*). The new barber's promise in such circumstances is an outright promise to stifle competition and is illegal. It would serve no purpose but to prevent competition. The other promises attempt to protect a proper interest the other has in the subject matter.

8.10 Not all parties stand equally guilty before the law when the question of an illegal bargain is raised. These parties are said not to be in equal fault (not *in pari delicto*). Which of the following would more likely qualify as a party not *in pari delicto*?

   (*a*) A minor against an adult in a bargain

   (*b*) A party induced to contract by greed

   (*c*) A party induced to contract by fraud of the other

   (*d*) A lender under a usury statute

   Whether parties are equally at fault is a fact question. However, parties who have been defrauded by the other sometimes qualify provided the victim's own behavior does not involve moral turpitude; the answer is (*c*). The usury statute is for the protection of the borrower as a matter of law, not the lender. Greed offers no excuse to a participant in an illegal scheme, and the fact that one is a minor does not by itself immunize the participant.

8.11 Cary and Mary Chang decided to refinance their apartment building. The Journal Mortgage Company agreed to loan them $200,000 at 15 percent interest. The state maximum rate was 20 percent per annum. The penalty for violation was forfeiture of all interest. As a further condition to the loan, Journal required that Cary and Mary form a limited partnership and deed the apartment to the firm. Journal was to be the only limited partner and would receive

25 percent of the profits for a capital contribution of $500. During the first 5 years of the loan $12,000 a year was paid to Journal by reason of its partnership ownership. The Changs finally realized that their dealings with Journal cost them over 23 percent per year if the "profits" given to Journal were considered interest on the loan. They determined that they would have been better off borrowing money from their bank at 18½ percent per year. The Changs have now decided to sue, charging usury.

What success will the Changs have? Answer the question and state reasons for any conclusions reached.

In order to prove usury one must prove a loan of money that is payable absolutely in return for which a greater amount is charged than the interest allowed by statute with intent to violate the law. The issue in this case is whether the partnership agreement was a sham by which the lender required more on its loan. Courts do not hesitate to look beneath the form of the transaction to see the real transaction. Journal's argument that its profits under the partnership were not absolute would be measured by the reality of apartment rentals, the only source of profit for the partnership. Usury is proved if it was a successful holding and the intent of Journal was to receive more than the loan agreement provided, regardless of the maximum rate allowed. It is likely that Journal is guilty of usury, as it required an additional sweetener in the form of a partnership with a nominal capital contribution. The lender, Journal, could lose all its interest (i.e., limited partnership "profits"), past and present.

8.12 Cable TV Troubleshooters was a new and aggressive company. It directed its attention to a common need of new cable TV companies by providing professional assistance in solving difficult technical problems encountered in installing cable TV lines in residential communities. Troubleshooters hired highly qualified engineers at top money. The company looked to have a nationwide company in 5 years. Accordingly, the employed engineers were required to sign a covenant not to compete upon termination of employment for a period of 5 years within 1,000 miles of the home office in Chicago. At the time of John Center's termination with Troubleshooters, the company had already expanded to all of Illinois and half of the state of Indiana. Center intends to compete in a part of Iowa which is within the 1,000-mile radius of Chicago. Troubleshooters threatens Center with a lawsuit seeking an injunction against Center.

Can Troubleshooters prevent Center from opening up an office in Iowa? State your answer and give reasons to support any conclusions you reach.

Covenants not to compete are generally enforceable if they are ancillary to an otherwise proper contract and the restraint is reasonable to both time and area restrictions. These last points are the questionable issues in most litigation. First, to deprive an individual of 5 years of employment in his or her field is generally too long a period. Second, area restraint is intended to protect existing rights, not future plans. The fact that Troubleshooters intends to go nationwide is not relevant. It does not have such capability now and is not doing business in Iowa. The area restriction is therefore unreasonable. Troubleshooters would not have good success with its lawsuit.

8.13 Farrel, a highly competent technician, worked in a research laboratory having a government contract. He was suspected of industrial espionage in regard to some of the government work. Farrel was both popular and articulate, and the laboratory did not wish to press the matter with insufficient evidence. Nevertheless, it intended to get rid of Farrel. After some negotiation, Farrel agreed to a layoff provided the laboratory closed the case and agreed not to resist any claim Farrel might put in for unemployment compensation. The laboratory agreed. Farrel later applied for unemployment compensation, and the laboratory resisted the claim by stating that Farrel was fired for misconduct. Farrel, unable to receive unemployment compensation, sues the laboratory for breach of its agreement.

What principle of law could the laboratory invoke to resist this contract action? What success would the laboratory have? State reasons for any conclusions reached.

Illegal bargains are unenforceable, and the courts leave the parties where they find them. In this case it would mean that Farrel receives neither unemployment compensation nor damages for breach of contract. The reason why a person is laid off is important government information and relevant to whether or not a claim for unemployment compensation is allowed. When the parties agreed to withhold this information from the government, they attempted to contract in violation of a public policy which is set by statute. Accordingly, when the laboratory supplied the truthful information to the state agency, it was only doing its legal duty. The bargain the laboratory made with Farrel was illegal.

Chapter 9

Capacity

9.1 GENERAL

Few persons are completely denied the right to contract. Except for imprisoned felons and adjudicated incompetents, all persons have the power or capacity to contract. However, some classes of persons are especially protected by law from making improvident contracts. These persons include infants (minors) and those incapable of understanding the nature of the contract because of mental disease, drugs, alcohol, etc. These persons possess the power to avoid or disaffirm their contracts.

9.2 MINORS OR INFANTS

At common law, minors could disaffirm all contracts except for necessaries anytime during their minority or a reasonable time after attaining majority. Each state decides what is a legal minor (or infant) for contract purposes. This is set by state statute. The age of 18 years is the majority age in most states, although some states have established 19 years as adulthood.

9.3 DISAFFIRMANCE

An otherwise valid contract with an infant can be set aside by conduct expressing disaffirmance or avoidance. This can occur during the period of minority or a reasonable time after majority by informing the other party of such intention, refusing to honor the contract on that ground, or exhibiting any other behavior consistent with disaffirmance.

EXAMPLE 1. Gato, age 17, signed up for 6 months of dance lessons at $50 a month. After the second month of dancing and paying, Gato was tired of dancing. He refused to pay any more money and refused the lessons. Gato is disaffirming the contract, which he can do as a minor.

EXAMPLE 2. Wendy, age 17, agreed to sell her stamp collection 9 months hence to Olson, an adult and collector, for $1,500. Five months later Wendy turned 18 years in a state in which that is the age of majority. She then decided to sell her stamp collection to Alfred without notice to Olson. The sale to Alfred is a disaffirmance of the first contract with Olson, and if a reasonable time did not elapse after majority, it is an effective avoidance. Four months after majority is generally well within a reasonable time.

Minors can disaffirm contracts provided they offer to return to the other party any property or consideration they received and still possess. The entire contract must be disaffirmed; a partial avoidance is not permitted. All contracts of infants in their purely executory state can be disaffirmed, even those for necessaries, as there is no consideration received to be returned. In a few jurisdictions an older minor, by statute, cannot disaffirm unless he or she can restore the adult to the *status quo ante* where tangibles have been received from the adult.

EXAMPLE 3. Rolf, a minor, purchased a motor bike for $900 from an adult. Rolf lost it in the lake in a bridge accident. In most states Rolf, as a minor, can demand the $900 back despite the fact that he has not retrieved the bike for return to the store. He may not have this right in some states as he cannot place the adult back into the position the adult was in at the time the contract was made. If Rolf retrieved the bike from the lake and offered to return it, the minority rule requires Rolf to give the adult the difference in value between what the damaged bike is now worth and the $900 (restoration of the *status quo ante*).

9.4 RESTRICTIONS ON DISAFFIRMANCE

There are a growing number of restrictions on the minor's right to disaffirm. Some are placed by statute and others by case law. A minor who induces an adult to enter into a contract by falsely misrepresenting his or her age does not, in the majority of jurisdictions, lose the right to disaffirm. However, recent decisions show a trend the other way. Further, even where the contract can be disaffirmed, the minor may be held liable for any damage to the consideration returned. Some other contracts have public policy overtones that outweigh the infant rule. These include contracts of enlistment into the armed services, marriage contracts, and statutorily protected interests such as life insurance contracts, educational loans, and other contracts in which the public's interest is interpreted to be superior to the minor's right to disaffirm. The major restriction on infant disaffirmance involves contracts for necessaries. Minors are liable for the reasonable value of necessaries actually supplied and used. Technically they are not liable for the contract price, but must pay a reasonable price.

Necessaries of life for minors include those goods or services falling within a certain group and befitting one's station in life. Food, shelter, clothing, and needed medical care are the major classes. Today, other items may be included, but courts have been reluctant to extend these classifications.

EXAMPLE 4.   Elise, age 17, is from a well-to-do family. She purchases an automobile on credit. She needs it to "keep up with her crowd." Despite her family's wealth, this would not be a necessary, certainly not in this instance. Cars have been held to be necessaries in some recent cases where they were needed for work for the minor to support himself or herself.

EXAMPLE 5.   Launcelot Lavelle, 17-year-old member of a wealthy family, purchased a $500 cashmere sport coat from Classy Retailers. Launcelot had no other sport coats; his dress habits had involved either jeans and tee shirts or suits for formal occasions. He wanted the sport coat to attend a garden party where such attire was "correct." At the party, his girlfriend told him the coat looked tacky. Upset, Launcelot attempted to return the coat to Classy Retailers and disaffirm his contract. The store refused to take the coat back. On the facts of this case, the store is likely to prevail: clothing is a necessary, cashmere is appropriate to Launcelot's station in life, he needed a sport coat, and he used it. He would be liable for the reasonable value of the coat.

The minor must need the goods or services and must use or consume them, as purely executory contracts for necessaries can always be disaffirmed.

9.5 RATIFICATION

A contract made by a minor cannot be ratified until he or she attains majority, as an attempted ratification may be disaffirmed like any other contract. Minors' contracts are voidable, not void. As such, they remain enforceable until the party having the right to disaffirm so acts. Ratification can be either expressed or implied by the use of the consideration for a reasonable period of time after majority. Mere passage of time, or silence, can be ratification only in rare situations where there is other conduct indicating approval.

EXAMPLE 6.   A 17-year-old buyer bought a watch on a conditional sales contract by which he was to make monthly payments. He did not make any payments. Three years later the buyer was sued for the balance. It was revealed that the watch was lost or stolen while the buyer was still a minor. The court ruled that ratification is not implied by the party's mere silence and inaction, no matter how prolonged after reaching majority.

Since ratification can occur only after majority, the conduct of the ex-minor after majority must be examined to find ratification. It is not necessary, however, to prove that the ex-minor knew that he had the right to disaffirm or ratify.

EXAMPLE 7.   A buyer purchased a car while a minor. Two months after attaining majority she attempted, unsuccessfully, to sell the car to another buyer. Ratification occurred when she attempted to sell the car after attaining her majority.

9.6 MINOR'S TORTS

A minor is responsible for torts he or she commits against another, except in the case of mental disability. A minor cannot disaffirm a tort liability. Occasionally, adults attempt to use this rule to enforce a contract indirectly, but one cannot enforce a minor's contract by a suit in tort.

EXAMPLE 8. Attle, age 17, falsely misrepresented his age in buying goods from a seller. The goods were consumed or destroyed without payment. The seller sued Attle in tort for fraud in the inducement and seeks damages. In this case, the damages would be the worth of the goods. The seller would lose, as this is an attempt to enforce a contract indirectly which he could not enforce directly in the face of the minor's disaffirmance.

Minors commit torts not connected with contracting. When this occurs, an action for damages occurs and the minor's conduct will be measured according to his age and understanding.

EXAMPLE 9. A neighbor's picture window is smashed by a baseball negligently thrown by Tommy, age 10 years. At this age, most minors appreciate duty to others and their property. Neighbor could sue Tommy for negligence (tort) and recover from Tommy's assets, if he has any, or later when Tommy possesses assets.

The parents of a minor are generally not liable for the torts committed by the minor. The exceptions include instances in which the act was done under the direction of the parent, or where there was a failure to properly supervise a minor with a propensity for causing damage, or where a legislature has placed a special liability on the parent. Examples involve a parent's automobile and cases where the minor vandalized property.

9.7 EMANCIPATION

Emancipation is the severing of all, or parts, of the reciprocal duties and rights between parent and minor child. Generally, parents have a duty to support their minors and are entitled to obedience and services. The parent who abandons the minor child loses this right but is not necessarily released from the duties.

EXAMPLE 10. A minor, age 17, leaves home and supports himself by working at a factory. The parent does nothing. The minor is emancipated to the extent that the parent could not demand that the paycheck from the factory be paid directly to the parent. At common law the money earned by a minor belongs to the parent, but the parent may waive such right by action or inaction.

By statute and case law in many states, marriage emancipates the minor. Further, in most states, marriage removes the disability of age and the minor's right to disaffirm contracts. Even where they do not marry, emancipated minors might be held to contracts for items that otherwise would not qualify as necessaries.

There is no direct relationship between the law of majority for contractual disaffirmance and the rights of minors to perform other acts. A person can be a major for contractual purposes but be incapacitated to perform other acts. Much of this behavior is regulated by age. An 18-year-old may be an adult for the purpose of losing his right to disaffirm a contract, but may be denied the right to attend horse races, drink intoxicating beverages, vote, hold public office, or have immunity from criminal liability.

EXAMPLE 11. Bart turned 18 years old and the next evening was arrested for consuming whiskey in a bar in a state in which such sales were prohibited to those under 20 years. Bart is a major for contract purposes, but he is under-age for certain regulatory purposes, such as consuming whiskey in a bar.

9.8 THIRD PARTIES

At common law an innocent third party could be injured by the minor's act of disaffirmance. If a minor sold goods to another who resold them, the innocent transferee who did not contract with the minor could be required to turn the goods over to the disaffirming minor. Under Section 2-403 of the UCC, however, the infant seller could lose the property if the buyer resold it to a "good-faith purchaser for value." Further, money or property a minor invested in a partnership (called the *capital* of a partnership) could be lost to the claims of creditors in the event of insolvency.

9.9 INCOMPETENCY

The law requires that a person have sufficient mental capacity to understand the nature and character of a transaction. This capacity may be impaired by mental weakness, mental disease, injury, drugs, alcohol, or any other cause which prevents the necessary understanding. If a court has declared one incompetent in a special competency hearing, all attempts by that person to contract are void, not voidable.

The more common situation occurs where no competency judgment was made, but the party's mental capacity is definitely impaired, i.e., a factual incompetent. In such cases the incompetent's contract can be disaffirmed provided he or she returns any consideration received. This duty of restoration of consideration which the person no longer possesses is not required where the other party knew of the incompetency, or took unfair advantage of the party.

It is quite possible for affected parties to have lucid intervals during which they are, or become, aware of a contract they made. Conduct during a lucid period recognizing or approving the contract can act as a ratification of the contract.

EXAMPLE 12. Samantha had troubles that required several visits to a mental sanitarium. Her relatives were unsuccessful in having her declared incompetent though she admittedly had a "mental weakness." Samantha deeded some land to a buyer. A bank was asked later to give a mortgage but refused, claiming the deed to the buyer was void. If anything, the deed was voidable as there was no decree of incompetency. Mere mental weakness is not, by itself, incompetence. It would have to be shown that Samantha did not understand the nature of the transaction, the contract, and the sale of land.

EXAMPLE 13. Smedley was visibly intoxicated. He left the bar where he had been drinking and wandered down the street, eventually finding a watch repair shop where he sold his gold watch. Sober the next day, he found the sales ticket in his pocket and attempted to retrieve the watch. The watch repair shop was not an innocent party, and Smedley can retrieve the watch after returning what, if any, consideration he still had.

Black Letter Law
A Summary

1. Only a few people lack the legal capacity to contract, such as adjudicated incompetents and imprisoned felons.

2. Minors, incompetents, and others like situated are not incapacitated but have the power to avoid or disaffirm contracts for nonnecessaries.

3. Minors are parties under the legal age as prescribed by state law, which ranges from 18 years to 21 years.

4. Minors may avoid most contracts except for necessaries anytime during their minority or a reasonable time after majority.

5. A minor's contract can only be ratified when he or she is an adult, or major.

6. Disaffirmance and ratification are proved by conduct including express statements of the party possessing the right.

7. Generally, a minor may still avoid a contract even if the minor no longer has the consideration he or she received from the adult.

8. In some jurisdictions the older minor's right of disaffirmance is conditioned on placing the adult in the *status quo ante* or making some adjustment for the depreciated or damaged consideration to be returned.

9. Generally the misrepresentation of age by the minor does not deprive him or her of the right to disaffirm.

10. A minor is liable for his or her torts, but tort law cannot be used indirectly to enforce a minor's contract.

11. Emancipation refers to the rights and duties of the parent or guardian and the child, generally the duty of the child to obey and supply service and the parent's duty to support the child.

12. Emancipation by itself does not terminate the infant's right to disaffirm contracts.

13. In contract cases there are two types of incompetence: adjudicated incompetence and factual incompetence.

14. A party who is adjudicated an incompetent in an incompetency hearing can no longer contract and an attempted contract is void, but previous contracts are not automatically disaffirmed.

15. A party who successfully defends a contract action on the grounds of incompetency succeeds only in that action; the outcome has no legal effect on any other contract.

16. A person is incompetent if, at the time of the contract, he or she does not appreciate the nature and character of the transaction.

17. Generally, a factual incompetent is not as benefited by the law as a minor, as the incompetent must restore the other party to the *status quo ante*.

18. The sane party in contract actions in which incompetency is alleged may offer to show that the other side had lucid intervals during which the contract was ratified by conduct, including silence.

Solved Problems

9.1 A minor or infant is a party

  (*a*) under the age of 21 years.

  (*b*) under 19 years of age.

  (*c*) who by state statute is declared a minor.

  (*d*) under 18 years of age.

   The term "minor," or "infant," is a legal term, statement (*c*). Each state is free to decide the age at which one becomes an adult for contract purposes. Until the 1970s, the usual age of majority was 21 years. Today, most states, by statute, set the age at 18 years.

9.2 The right of disaffirmance of a minor's contract

    (*a*) is unrestricted.

    (*b*) must be exercised during the period of minority.

    (*c*) is available to the minor's parent for the parent's own interest.

    (*d*) is not conditioned on whether the minor is being fair to the adult.

      The right to disaffirm is not a reward for good behavior. It is based on a public policy directed toward preventing a minor from making an improvident bargain; the answer is (*d*). Not all infant contracts are voidable, however, and even if a contract belongs to that class, some restrictions may be present. Restoration of the *status quo ante* and rights of innocent third parties are typical restrictions in certain situations.

9.3 Vidal, a stockbroker, sold 100 shares of corporate stock to Rabin, age 17 years, who paid $10,000 for it. Vidal then became concerned because Rabin was a minor, and Vidal offered to return the money for the stock. Rabin would have none of it and, in fact, agreed in writing that he ratified the contract for a consideration of $100 paid by Vidal. Which is the correct status of this transaction?

    (*a*) Vidal was clever, as this was an effective ratification.

    (*b*) Rabin was not bound on the first contract but is bound on the ratification agreement because fraud is now involved.

    (*c*) Rabin could still disaffirm both contracts, as minors' contracts can only be affirmed, or ratified, after majority.

    (*d*) Stock transactions are an exception to the rule that minors may disaffirm contracts.

      If the contract of a minor is one that can be disaffirmed, the only effective ratification occurs after majority; (*c*) is the answer. These facts show no fraud, and even if they did, one cannot enforce a contract indirectly by prosecuting a tort action. Like the stock purchase contract itself, the ratification agreement may be disaffirmed. While stock exchange regulations may prohibit sales to minors, such ownership is neither illegal nor against public policy.

9.4 After having purchased 100 shares of stock from Vidal for $10,000, Rabin, age 17 years, now wants to disaffirm the purchase because the stock has dropped $3,000 in market value. Rabin offers to return the stock to Vidal. Under these circumstances,

    (*a*) Rabin cannot disaffirm the purchase since he cannot put the other party in the *status quo ante*.

    (*b*) Rabin can disaffirm the contract and obtain his purchase price of $10,000 back.

    (*c*) Rabin can disaffirm under the majority rule but recover only the sum of $7,000.

    (*d*) the courts will not aid either party in such transactions since it is illegal for a minor to purchase stock.

      Answer (*b*) is correct. Under the rules followed in most states, the infant can recover all his consideration provided he returns what he possesses. In some states the minor must restore the other party to the *status quo ante*. In such a state Rabin could recover only $7,000. It is not illegal for a minor to buy stock.

9.5 Rabin fraudulently misrepresented his age in purchasing $10,000 worth of stock from Vidal, a stockbroker. Rabin was only 17 years old but appeared to be 20 years old. Rabin showed Vidal a driver's license reflecting his age as an adult. Under these circumstances

    (*a*) in most states Rabin could disaffirm the purchase contract.

    (*b*) Rabin is estopped, i.e., prevented, from proving his real age.

(c) Rabin could not be prosecuted for obtaining property under false pretenses or fraud.

(d) estoppel would not apply against Rabin if he truly felt that he was fully capable of handling his own affairs.

Most courts permit the minor to disaffirm the contract despite his fraudulent misrepresentation of age, statement (a). In recent years some courts have denied the minor such a right, or have allowed it but require that the infant restore the other party to the *status quo ante*. Minors are responsible for their torts and crimes. The adult, for example, could sue to disaffirm the contract on the grounds of fraud but generally cannot use the fraud to defend the infant's suit for disaffirmance.

9.6   Emancipation of a minor

(a) prevents a minor from disaffirming future contracts.

(b) limits the goods and services that are considered necessaries.

(c) increases the number of goods and services that are considered necessaries.

(d) always releases the parent from the duty of supporting the minor.

Generally, emancipation does not disturb the minor's right to disaffirm contracts, but it may increase the number of items which might be called a necessary, statement (c). Some state statutes prescribe marriage as an act of emancipation and loss of a minor's right to disaffirm contracts. Parents of emancipated minors may, nevertheless, still be liable for their support.

9.7   Necessaries are those goods and services required to maintain one's station in life and to provide for the minor's continued health and safety. A contract for necessaries can fix liability on the minor for their reasonable value. What element need *not* be shown to prove an item or service is a necessary?

(a) Need

(b) Use

(c) Class, i.e., food, shelter, clothing, medical care, etc.

(d) Fairness of the price

Statement (d) is the answer. A minor is liable only for the reasonable value of furnished necessaries; the actual price charged is not relevant. The other elements must be shown, but class (c) has been enlarged under modern circumstances. However, the classification doctrine still prevents jewelry and the like from being considered a necessary, irrespective of the minor's station in life.

9.8   Granat had personality trouble for years. He was, however, a crackerjack salesman when he wasn't in "one of his moods." His sister finally had him declared incompetent in a competency hearing on August 13, 19X3. Which is the correct statement?

(a) All contracts he entered into before August 13, 19X3, are void.

(b) All contracts he entered into before August 13, 19X3, are voidable.

(c) All contracts he enters into after August 13, 19X3, are void.

(d) Contracts he entered into before August 13, 19X3, cannot be avoided in individual actions.

The answer is (c). For contract purposes, an incompetency hearing determines the capacity of the person for the future. Accordingly, attempted contracts subsequent to the decree of incompetency are not voidable, but void. Earlier contracts are not automatically affected, but the guardian may bring individual actions to avoid them if the guardian can prove that the declared incompetent was such at the time of the contract.

9.9   A minor contracted with a life insurance company for a $15,000 policy naming his girlfriend as beneficiary. Upon his death his mother was appointed personal representative of his estate. As such she had the legal right to exercise the minor's right of disaffirmance on behalf of his estate. The state law did not make insurance contracts binding on infants. Which is the correct statement under these circumstances?

(a)   The mother can disaffirm the policy on grounds of the minor's incapacity and recover all the paid premiums.

(b)   The mother can affirm the contract but disaffirm the beneficiary designation.

(c)   The mother can sue the insurance company for contracting with a minor.

(d)   The girlfriend can collect the insurance proceeds even if the mother decided to disaffirm the contract.

   Answer (a) is correct; one can only disaffirm the entire contract, not just part of it. As personal representative for her deceased son, the mother can exercise the right of avoiding the contract on grounds of infancy. But the right cannot be used in an attempt to revoke the beneficiary designation only. Such would be an attempt to partly disaffirm while ratifying the entire contract of insurance.

9.10 Barrow was a subtle drunk. He was aptly described as the party in the old joke, "I didn't know my roommate drank until one night he came home sober." Barrow, while intoxicated to such a degree that he did not know the nature and character of the transaction, purchased an expensive piece of business property. The next day he was sober and accepted congratulations on his "shrewd business move." He acknowledged the feat after being informed of what he had done and even began to brag about it. Several weeks later he had a change of mind. What is the seller's best defense to Barrow's attempt to disaffirm the contract?

(a)   A reasonable person would not have recognized that Barrow was drunk and therefore the contract should stand.

(b)   Barrow ratified the contract during a sober period after learning what he had done.

(c)   The contract was fair and was in fact a bargain for Barrow.

(d)   The contract was in writing, and Barrow's signature was steady.

   Since Barrow was aware of the contract after becoming sober and acted as if he approved what he had done, this voidable contract has been ratified, statement (b). Intoxicated persons can avoid their contracts provided they place the other party in the *status quo ante*. This rule assumes that the sober party did not know that the other was so disabled. On the other hand, improper conduct by the sober party could allow the intoxicated party to disaffirm the contract even without restoring the other party to the *status quo ante*.

9.11 Roberts, age 19, lost his job shortly after getting married; his wife was employed. Unable to find a new position, he signed a contract with Allene Employment Agency under which he agreed to pay a sum equal to 2 months of his starting salary should Allene find him work. Allene was good on its promise and found Roberts a job paying $1,200 monthly. Roberts was pleased with the job but not with the payments to Allene. After making $200 in payments to Allene, he stopped paying. Allene sues Roberts for the $2,200 balance. Roberts defends on the grounds that the age of majority in his state is 20 years.

   (a) What contentions can Allene bring in this case to show that Roberts should pay? (b) What argument can Roberts use in his defense?

   (a) Allene is aware that Roberts is technically a minor and is permitted to disaffirm most contracts. In some states, however, marriage, by statute, not only emancipates the minor but also removes his disability as a minor. If such is the case here, Allene can collect the remainder of its fee. Even if this rule is not available, Allene should contend that the contract was for a necessary. Business contracts are generally not necessaries, but a married minor is considered as having an expanded scope of needs. Getting a job to support one's family might be a necessary for Roberts.

(*b*) Roberts is not without argument on this position. Even if the court rules the job to be a necessary, Roberts can charge that he is liable only for the reasonable value of the supplied necessary. Accordingly, the fee of $2,400 for a job paying $1,200 a month may be more than reasonable or fair value. It is likely that a more modest fee can be collected under this theory.

9.12 Bart was 17 years old when he and his buddies were involved in a fracas in a neighboring town and arrested. Getting released in a strange town was not easy, and Bart remembered that he had to sign a lot of papers. Unknown to Bart, one of the papers was a promissory note. He signed such a note in favor of a bailbondsman in the sum of $3,000. The promissory note contained a confession of judgment clause, a provision that allowed the bondsman to obtain a judgment with little notice and quite quickly. Bart straightened out and by age 22 was on his way to success. He was married and in the process of buying a townhouse. During this transaction, he learned that there was a $3,000 judgment of record against him in favor of the bondsman. The judgment had been entered 4 years ago, but this was Bart's first knowledge of the fact. The age of majority is 18 in Bart's state. Bart wants to disaffirm the promissory note on grounds of infancy.

What are the respective legal contentions of Bart and the bailbondsman? State your conclusions and your reasons which support them.

Minors may disaffirm contracts during their minority or a reasonable time after attaining majority. The bailbondsman's contention will be that a period of 4 years since majority is beyond a reasonable time. Bart will argue that mere passive behavior alone, silence here, is insufficient evidence of ratification of the contract. While the fact that Bart may not have known that he had a right to disaffirm is no defense, there is an excuse if the infant did not know that he had made a contract under circumstances in which the adult's behavior was less than open. Bart will probably be permitted to disaffirm this promissory note.

9.13 Mary, age 79 years, owned a large greenhouse left to her by her husband, who had died 20 years earlier. During those years Mary ran the business. She made some big mistakes, but the business survived despite her erratic behavior. On two occasions during the past 10 years her two daughters unsuccessfully attempted to have her declared incompetent. Her most serious setback occurred when a medical examination revealed that she suffered from a heart blockage that caused seizures, blackouts, and involutional psychosis resulting in depression. During this period Mary entered into a transaction with Payne Florists, a national concern, by which Mary's business would be merged with Payne over a 2-year period. The critical agreements were signed after a particularly bad day for Mary in which it appeared that she had lost consciousness 2 hours before the signing. Six days later she collapsed on the street and died of a heart attack. Her estate sues to rescind the merger agreement with Payne.

What evidence must the estate show in order to succeed in having the contract disaffirmed?

The test of contractual capacity is whether or not a person is able to understand the nature of her action and comprehend its consequences. This capacity is measured at the time of the execution of the contract. The estate must disprove that fact. There is a presumption of capacity, and the previous unsuccessful attempts to prove her incompetent suggest competency rather than incompetency. Further, even if the doctors could prove that she was incapable at certain times, this does not deny the possibility of lucid intervals during which she possessed the requisite capacity. Neither old age, nor illness, nor extreme emotional distress is sufficient, of itself, to negate such capacity. The estate will have a heavy burden to prove incapacity to set aside this contract.

Chapter 10

Writing

10.1 BACKGROUND

There is no basic requirement that contracts be in writing signed by all the parties. There is, however, a long history of statutory requirement that *certain contracts* be proved by a signed writing or some other special form of evidence. The history is reflected in the term "Statute of Frauds" in deference to the 1677 English statute which singled out certain contracts as requiring writing or special forms of proof.

However, even if a particular contract requires a writing, this does not mean that both parties must sign it or that the signing occur at the time of contracting. The Statute of Frauds is only concerned with the proof of the contract.

10.2 STATUTE OF FRAUDS

The English Statute of Frauds addressed five types of contracts which were commonly subject to perjured testimony. These were (1) promises to answer for the debt of another (*guaranty contracts*); (2) agreements involving real property; (3) agreements that could not be performed within a year; (4) marriage settlement contracts; and (5) special promises to be personally responsible for the debts of an estate (decedent). A sixth type of contract requiring a writing, also identified under an English statute, deals with the sale of goods, that is, personal property.

These statutes were enacted, in substance, in the United States. Further, certain states have added to these statutes other types of contracts, such as those involving life insurance, magazine subscriptions, realtors' listings, and representations regarding corporate stock.

EXAMPLE 1. Tyndal orally employed Rauls, a real estate broker, to find a purchaser for Tyndal's home. Rauls found Bennet, who went over all the terms in the contract of sale in Rauls's office with Tyndal. They shook hands on the "firm deal" but signed no paper. Three real estate salespeople in the office witnessed this event. Either Tyndal or Bennet could refuse to carry out the sale of realty if they defended on the Statute of Frauds. However, in many states Rauls has earned her commission and must be paid. In other states, however, listing contracts must be in writing and Tyndal could escape the liability arising from this oral employment contract.

10.3 GUARANTY CONTRACTS

A promise to answer for the debt of another is within the Statute of Frauds and requires a writing signed by the promisor. This guaranty contract is also called a *secondary promise* or *collateral promise*. On the other hand, a promise to make a debt one's own is an *original* or *primary promise*, and does not require a writing under this section.

EXAMPLE 2. A customer telephones a store and orders a $300 silver dish to be delivered to a prospective bride. The store charges the customer. This oral contract is enforceable. This was intended as an obligation of the customer, not as another's debt. It was an original promise.

EXAMPLE 3. A woman brought a prospective buyer to a retailer and orally asked the retailer to sell goods *to* the buyer for which she (the woman) "would stand good." In reliance on such statement, the retailer sold goods to the buyer and charged them to the buyer. After making some payments, the buyer defaulted. The retailer cannot hold the woman on her oral promise to answer for the debt of another. Such collateral promises require a writing signed by the promisor.

There are some exceptions to the rule that collateral promises require a writing. If the promisor agrees to become liable for the debt of another because of some pecuniary advantage he or she may gain from the arrangement, no writing is required. This exception, enforced under the *main purpose doctrine*, is treated as an original promise and is enforceable despite the absence of a writing.

EXAMPLE 4. Brown's car was damaged by fire to the extent of $650. The bank had a mortgage on the car. Brown was employed by a garage, but the garage refused to repair the car on credit unless the bank guaranteed the payment. The bank gave its oral okay, and the repairs were made. It was to the pecuniary benefit of the bank that the car be repaired. The oral promise is enforceable.

Further, an oral agreement is enforceable in cases where the promisor takes over an existing debt and makes it his or her own. This is a *substitution agreement*, a form of novation—that is, a new agreement—in which the creditor releases the old debt in consideration of the promise of the new third party who takes over this obligation. No writing is required in that situation.

10.4   AGREEMENTS INVOLVING REAL PROPERTY

An agreement concerning land, or any real interest in land, must generally be in writing to be enforceable under the Statute of Frauds. Land is real property, real estate, and immovable. It is space on earth and those things the legal system considers "permanently attached" to that space. Very little could be said to be permanently attached in the scientific sense, but the law attempts to distinguish between those things which do or do not ordinarily form a part of the "permanent nature" of the land.

EXAMPLE 5. Able owns 100 acres of land. It has growing timber, crops, and minerals on or in it. A house is situated thereon and includes a kitchen with a built-in oven and refrigerator. The barn's equipment includes a large pasteurization machine which is quite heavy, is bolted to the floor, and could be removed only by taking out part of the wall. Able rents out 10 acres of the south section to a neighbor for pasturage. Able permits his north neighbor use of the two north acres for pasturage for his cows. With the exception of the crops (goods), timber, and minerals (which can be goods under certain contracts), the above reflects interests in land requiring a writing when contracting for their transfer or use.

Today, by statute, most lease agreements are governed by special proof requirements of the states, including writing. On the other hand, crops are treated as goods and require no writing under this section, but may require special proof under Article 2 of the UCC.

Growing crops and timber, if sold apart from the land, are goods within Section 2-107 of the UCC, which also provides rules for determining whether other properties on the land are goods or realty. Minerals or the like, or a structure or its materials to be removed from realty, are treated as goods if, under the contract, the seller is to sever them. Where the buyer is to sever them, the item is realty. All other things attached to realty are considered goods, provided they are capable of severance "without material harm" to the realty.

EXAMPLE 6. Barney was ordered by a divorce judge to sell his farm and split the proceeds with his ex-wife. Bitter, Barney quickly and orally sold as much of the real property as possible. Barney sold all phosphate on the land to X for $5,000, X to dig it up (realty severance test). The peanut crop he sold to Y (goods—crops). Ten acres of standing pine he sold to Z, Barney to deliver (goods). The Japanese rock garden with waterfall, an integral part of the farm residence entrance, Barney sold to his neighbor (realty removal causes material harm). Only the oral contracts to sell the crops and pine are enforceable if they meet special proof requirements under the UCC.

Part performance of an oral land contract is one of the more litigated aspects of this section of the Statute of Frauds. The statute is inapplicable to fully performed, executed contracts, as there is nothing for the court to enforce. Oral sales of realty in a partly executed state, however, are governed by less certain rules. Generally, if the buyer of land under an oral contract made partial payment, was given possession, and made valuable and substantial improvements on the property, the contract is enforceable without a writing. Some states will even enforce oral contracts if part payment was made and possession given to the buyer. Part payment alone on an oral contract to purchase realty is insufficient part performance and does not qualify as an exception to the rule.

EXAMPLE 7.   Barry was pursued by his creditors. He sought and obtained an immediate transfer. He hurriedly sold his townhouse to Loeffler for $7,000, $2,000 cash down, $5,000 balance by the end of the year and assumption of the mortgage. Loeffler took possession eagerly. He transformed the interior into a bachelor's pad by removing a wall, put in a loft, and added a picture window two stories tall. This all cost $10,000. Several months later Barry returned to the city and demanded his townhouse back. Barry offered to return the money and pay Loeffler a reasonable sum for the improvements. Barry claims this is an unenforceable oral contract. However, part payment, possession, and substantial improvements qualify for the exception. Loeffler can enforce the oral contract.

10.5   ONE-YEAR CLAUSE

An agreement requiring performance beyond 1 year from the date of the contract is within the Statute of Frauds and requires a writing. The period of a year expires on the anniversary date of the contract. If the parties did not expressly contemplate performance for more than a year, many courts will enforce the oral contract.

EXAMPLE 8.   A lender orally agreed to finance a promoter's plan to develop and manage a transportation business on the Columbia River. The plan could not be put in operation until the completion of a certain dam, the completion of which turned out to be delayed 3 years beyond its previously anticipated completion date 10 months hence. The lender contends that it is not bound by its oral promise. The court ruled otherwise, stating that under the express terms one "cannot say that the terms of this contract made performance impossible within a year." The oral promise was enforceable.

The fact that full and complete performance is unlikely or improbable within the year does not necessarily place the promises within the Statute of Frauds. It is a "possibility test." If it was possible, the agreement need not be in writing. An express statement regarding time (more than a year) does place the agreement within the Statute of Frauds.

EXAMPLE 9.   Harris Company orally hires X and Y. It promises X a lifetime job as a printer and Y a 2-year position as advertising manager. Harris has to lay off both after 6 months. X can prove her oral contract since her death *could* "complete her performance." Y cannot prove his contract since by its express terms it requires 2 years for complete performance.

Full performance by one party is generally considered to take the contract out from under the Statute of Frauds.

10.6   MARRIAGE SETTLEMENTS AND ESTATE DEBTS

A promise made upon consideration of marriage is within the Statute of Frauds. The father's promise to pay the groom upon marriage to the daughter is a historical example of this promise, requiring a writing. Today, it is more likely seen in cases where one intending to marry another demands that, as a condition to marriage, the other promise to adopt a child by a previous marriage. Also, a man's promise to pay his ex-wife money if she would marry another and thereby terminate alimony payments is a promise made in consideration of marriage. Certain promises of personal representatives are unenforceable unless reduced to writing. An example of such a promise requiring a writing is where the personal representative of a decedent's estate orally promises that debts of the decedent will be paid, even if the representative must personally pay them.

10.7 NATURE OF THE WRITING

A written agreement, containing the major terms of the contract, signed by both parties satisfies the Statute of Frauds, but such complete evidence is not necessary. It is enough if the party being charged with the promise has signed it and sufficient information is present allowing a court to infer that a contract was entered into. This signed writing can be a note, memorandum, letter, or any other tangible evidence of agreement. Further, the signing need not be formal if the mark was intended as authentication. Therefore, an initialing, or even a letterhead on printed stationery or invoices, can be considered to be the signature required under the statute. Even a letter denying the contract can provide the evidence.

EXAMPLE 10.   Danner orally sold his hunting lodge to Yorick, an old hunting buddy, for $5,000. The pair had a falling out, and Danner mailed a bitter letter to Yorick which ended "I agreed to sell the lodge to you for $5,000, but everybody knows that since it is not in writing there is no deal." This letter can bind Danner, but since Yorick did not sign it he cannot be bound, as it must be signed by the party charged.

There is no specific rule about the quality of the writing. The writing need only indicate that a contract was made between the parties and the subject matter was identified with reasonable certainty, as well as the essential terms of the unperformed promises. In the above example, the paucity of details expressed in the letter did not prevent the writing from qualifying. And while real property is frequently set forth by a "legal description," the term "lodge" is sufficient if the seller owned only one lodge.

10.8 THE UCC AND THE SALE OF GOODS

Section 2-201 of the UCC provides that a contract for the sale of goods for the price of $500 or more requires a writing or other special proof of the agreement. The writing must be sufficient to indicate that a sale between the parties took place and is signed by the party sought to be charged. The specific "other forms of proof" are treated in Part III (Sales) of this book. However, it may be helpful to note here that it is easier to comply with the UCC requirements than with the Statute of Frauds. For example, under the UCC, the necessary writing need contain only one contract term, "quantity."

Black Letter Law
A Summary

1. When writing or some special form of evidence is required to prove a contract, the issue is said to be within the Statute of Frauds.

2. Not all contracts are within the Statute of Frauds, as each state has its own requirements, though most states have enacted laws requiring special proof in six types of contracts.

3. Under the Statute of Frauds, guaranty contracts, marriage settlements, promises of executors, multiyear contracts, land contracts, and the sale of goods over a particular dollar amount require writing or certain special type of proof.

4. A fully executed contract which did not comply with the Statute of Frauds remains settled, but executory promises to perform in any of the six types require a special proof; part performance rarely qualifies.

5. A promise to answer for the debt of another is a collateral promise and requires a writing, whereas a promise to make a debt one's own is original and needs no writing.

6. A contract which by its terms is not contemplated to be performed within a year of the making of the contract requires a writing.

7. While land contracts, or any interest therein, require a writing, a buyer who is given possession and makes valuable improvements under an oral contract may generally enforce the agreement.

8. An executory contract for the sale of goods at the price of $500 or more generally requires a writing.

9. An oral contract to sell goods at the price of $500 or more can be proved without writing in certain situations.

10. An oral contract to sell goods at the price of $500 or more is enforceable if the goods have been received and accepted, or paid for, or if they are specially manufactured goods.

11. If a signed writing is required under the Statute of Frauds, any writing indicating that a contract was formed, whether initialed or not, will suffice if the signature or mark is that of the party attempting to breach the contract.

Solved Problems

10.1 The purpose of the Statute of Frauds is to render agreements unenforceable unless they are

    (*a*) legal.

    (*b*) not fraudulent.

    (*c*) written.

    (*d*) supported by consideration.

(*AICPA Examination, May 1976*)

    The Statute of Frauds refers to the manner of proof of a contract. In most instances a writing signed by the party being charged is required; statement (*c*) is the answer.

10.2 The Statute of Frauds

    (*a*) does not require that all the terms and provisions of the agreement of the parties be contained in a single document.

    (*b*) requires that both parties sign the written contract.

    (*c*) defines what constitutes fraudulent conduct by a party in inducing another to make a contract.

    (*d*) applies to all contracts that by their terms require the payment of $500 or more.

(*AICPA Examination, November 1974*)

Since proof of the contract is the main purpose of the Statute of Frauds, a court is interested in all writings that pertain to the formation of the transaction. A single document is not necessary; the answer is (a). The name "Statute of Frauds" comes from the original English statute, which labeled it such for the prevention of fraud and perjured testimony. The $500 requisite has reference to sales of goods contracts, not all other contracts.

10.3   On May 1, 19X6, James Arthur orally agreed to a contract as a sales representative of Wonder Insurance Company. The contract terminates April 30, 19X7, and provides for $10,000 salary plus 1 percent of the insurance premiums charged by the company on the policies which he writes. Under these circumstances,

(a)   Dean wins since he was astute enough to prepare a writing.

(b)   the contract in question is not subject to the Statute of Frauds.

(c)   Arthur would be permitted to delegate his performance to another equally competent person.

(d)   Arthur's contract is too indefinite and uncertain to be enforceable.

(*AICPA Examination, May 1976*)

The facts suggest an employment contract, a type that does not come within the Statute of Frauds unless its full performance is to exceed a year; the answer is (b). Since the performance is finished within a year, an oral agreement may be proved. There is no suggestion in the case of an undisclosed principal, nor of any indefiniteness. Since this appears to be a personal appointment, it is unlikely that Arthur could delegate his duties to another without the permission of the company.

10.4   Albert and Dean were men of action. They struck a deal on the sale of Dean's farm for $200,000 over the dinner table. They shook hands but used no pen and paper for the transaction. The following day Dean wrote and delivered a note to Albert reminding him of the transaction and stating that he will be ready to close the transfer of the farm at an early date. Albert, upon reading the letter, has cooled on the deal and now refuses to live up to his oral promise to purchase the farm. What is the result?

(a)   Dean wins since he was astute enough to prepare a writing.

(b)   Albert wins since the signed writing must be executed at the time of the contract.

(c)   Albert wins as the Statute of Frauds requires that the signed writing must be that of the party charged, that is, the party now refusing to honor the oral agreement.

(d)   Albert wins because neither party was bound by this oral agreement as both parties were required to sign the memorandum.

With Albert refusing to honor his oral promise to purchase the farm (land), Dean must have a memo signed by Albert. Only Dean signed the memo. This means that only Dean could be liable on this oral contract; statement (c) is the answer.

10.5   Wilson was a valued customer of the Lodge of Three Seasons, a luxury resort. Wilson took his mother to the lodge for a stay. The manager informed Wilson that a large deposit for new guests was required. Wilson pointed out that such would be unnecessary and stated that he would "be good for the bill if Mother doesn't pay." Relying on those words, the manager relented, and the mother was registered without having to put down a deposit. Unfortunately, the mother skipped out without paying her bill. Under these circumstances,

(a)   Wilson is liable for the bill since he made a primary, or original, promise to pay the bill.

(b)   Wilson is not liable without a writing since this oral promise is a typical collateral promise to answer for the debt of another.

(c)   Wilson would be liable on his promise because the guest was his mother.

(d)   Wilson would be liable because the manager relied on Wilson's oral promise to the manager's detriment.

The promise to answer for the debt of another, a guaranty contract, requires a writing signed by the guarantor; statement (b) is correct. It is important to identify the exact commitment of the speaker. Here, Wilson said he would pay *if* his mother didn't. Such is a secondary, or collateral, promise and is within the Statute of Frauds. Had Wilson ordered the manager to charge the account to Wilson (i.e., made the debt his own), the result would be different, as such would be an original promise and require no writing.

10.6   Sometimes an oral contract for the sale of land may be enforced under the performance doctrine. In order to qualify for such an exception, which of the following would *not* be necessary?

(a)   Full payment of the purchase price

(b)   Possession by the purchaser

(c)   Valuable and substantial improvements made by the buyer

(d)   Some payment of the purchase price

Oral contracts for the sale of real estate can be enforced if there is some payment by the buyer, possession is transferred to the buyer, and the buyer has made valuable and substantial improvements on the land. Full payment is not required, statement (a).

10.7   Rabett has 200 acres of standing timber on her timber farm. If she wanted to sell some or all of the timber for over $500, which rule regarding evidence of the contract is applicable?

(a)   The Statute of Frauds regarding land.

(b)   The Statute of Frauds, Article 2 of the UCC, regarding the sale of goods.

(c)   The parol evidence rule.

(d)   The specially manufactured goods rule under Article 2 of the UCC.

Answer (b) is right. Timber is goods and is governed by Article 2 of the UCC. The parol evidence rule refers to the inadmissibility of other evidence which contradicts the terms of a complete written contract.

10.8   Preston hired Ganley as a private detective on March 1, 19X2, when he visited Ganley's city. Preston orally promised Ganley 8 months of employment at $2,000 a month, beginning September 1, 19X2, when Ganley would be available. Under these circumstances,

(a)   no writing is required since this is an 8-month contract.

(b)   the entire oral contract is enforceable under the performance doctrine if Ganley started work in September and continued for 2 months.

(c)   an oral contract is unenforceable if by its own terms it is incapable of full performance within a year of its making.

(d)   Ganley can sue for fraud if Preston attempts to breach this oral contract.

The year clause of the Statute of Frauds requires full performance within a year of making of the contract. In this case, full performance would end on May 1, 19X3, or 14 months after the execution of the contract; statement (c) is the answer. This agreement is unenforceable by reason of the Statute of Frauds.

10.9   The writing and signature requirements of the Statute of Frauds are not burdensome. Which of the following would *not* qualify as a signature?

(a)   A rubber stamp with the party's name.

(b)   An "X" mark made by the party.

(c)   Letterhead on the party's stationery or invoice.

(d)   A forged signature.

   The Statute of Frauds merely requires an act of authentication by the party being charged; the answer is (d). All except the forgery qualify as an act of authentication if that was the party's intent.

10.10   Which of the following statements suggests a collateral promise within the meaning of the Statute of Frauds?

(a)   Ship the wedding gift to Mary, and bill me.

(b)   Sell her the dress, but bill us both.

(c)   We will stand behind Able, as he is supplying us on our contract.

(d)   Of course Taylor is a good credit risk; we will back him.

   It is not always easy to identify a collateral credit risk as contrasted with an original promise. But a statement that one will back up another is generally a statement of guaranty; the answer is (d). Making a debt one's own is an original promise, as is making it a joint debt. And a promise to stand behind another for your own benefit, sometimes called the main purpose doctrine, is also considered to be an original promise and not within the Statute of Frauds.

10.11   Adam was admitted to the hospital, suffering from a severe gastric hemorrhage. As his condition worsened, his sons had numerous discussions with hospital personnel. No writing was signed, however. The sons pointed out to the hospital that their father had no funds to pay for treatment, but as the situation grew more serious, they did state "Spare no expense. Go ahead; we will pay." Further, they assured the hospital that "Father has some property back in Kentucky, and when we sell the property we will pay the entire balance in full." The sons did make some payments on the bill, which totaled over $5,000. After making $300 in payments, the sons refused to honor the debt. The sons pointed out that their father was admitted to the hospital on his own as they did not sign him in. The hospital demands the balance from the sons on the basis of the oral promises they made.

   What success will the hospital have against the sons? State your reasons for your conclusion.

   The language and other conduct of the promisor are examined to determine whether this was a collateral promise or an original promise. In the beginning, of course, the sons had no duty to pay for their father's debts. However, it was at the sons' request that the hospital proceeded to furnish services for the benefit of the sons, who used language indicating that they were assuming the financial obligation. The transactions with the sons reveal that they contracted for the additional services, and as such, the promise to pay was an original undertaking and outside the Statute of Frauds.

10.12   West, a former professor of computer science, established a trade school under the corporate name of Computering, Inc. West had all the common stock and one-half of the preferred stock issued to herself. The remaining preferred stock was purchased by her friends. In the beginning the school prospered, but a slowdown in students forced West to engage Media Press, a public relations firm, to undertake a media blitz for the new school year. Media agreed, provided West assured it that the contract price of $6,000 would be paid. West orally stated, "Don't worry, if the bill to the school is not paid within 30 days, I will personally pay for it." The campaign ran, but the school nevertheless failed. Media is suing West personally for the $6,000 bill.

   What success will Media have? State your answer and give reasons for your conclusions.

This seems clearly to be an oral promise to answer for the debt of another which, under the Statute of Frauds, requires a signed writing by West. There is, however, an exception to the rule, which is known as the main purpose doctrine. Whenever the main purpose and object of the promisor are not to answer for the debt of another, but to subserve some pecuniary or business purpose of one's own, a promise is not within the Statute of Frauds. This is so even if the promise is otherwise in the form of a promise to pay the debt of another. Here, Media can offer that the benefit is personal and direct to West. West was not merely an officer and stockholder of the corporation. In effect she *was* the corporation, and a jury could reasonably find a direct and personal benefit to West. West would be liable under the main purpose doctrine for her oral promise to pay the bill.

10.13 Thompson, a contractor, was bidding on a huge townhouse project and had been in the practice of using Telec Industries, an electrical contractor. Thompson asked Telec to submit an offer on the electrical part of the project. On August 5, 19X2, Telec replied on letterhead stationery that "We are happy to offer to perform the necessary wiring on the project for $250,000, beginning when the facilities are ready for wiring but no earlier than February 5, 19X3, with completion 15 months from commencement." Thompson received this bid on August 7, 19X2, was delighted at the low figure, and immediately telephoned Telec accepting the offer. Thompson then bid on the project and won the award. However, Telec had miscalculated its project workload and was unable to find time to start the electrical work for Thompson. Thompson sued Telec for breach of contract.

What success will Thompson have in this suit? State your reasons for any conclusion you reach.

Agreements, by the terms of which performance cannot be executed within 1 year from the date of the making of the contract, require a writing signed by the party to be charged. Since there was no way that performance was contemplated to be finished within a year, the Statute of Frauds applies. Thompson's contention that the August 7, 19X2, letter qualifies as a writing signed by Telec fails. It is true that the letterhead could constitute a signature; however, the writing must indicate that a contract was made. Here the letter indicates only that an offer containing all the terms was made. An offer is not a contract. Thompson will not succeed if Telec relies on the Statute of Frauds as a defense.

Chapter 11

Terms and Interpretation

11.1 OTHER CONTRACT ISSUES

Contract disputes involve more than the question of validity of the contract and rights of third parties. Issues arise over the contract terms involving such topics as conditions, the parol evidence rule, interpretation and construction, time of performance, and satisfactory performance.

11.2 CONDITIONS

A *condition* in a contract is a clause which has for its object the suspension, rescission, or modification of the principal duty or obligation. Three types of conditions are conditions precedent, conditions concurrent, and conditions subsequent. A *condition precedent* is one which must be performed before the agreement goes into effect or a right accrues. *Concurrent conditions* are those which are mutually dependent; they are to be performed at the same time. A *condition subsequent* refers to a future event or act, the occurrence of which discharges the obligation.

Conditions are valuable provisions in contracts and are considered material, so that a breach affects the entire contract. A condition precedent is frequently created by the words "on the condition that," "provided however," "if," or similar language. A condition may also be implied.

EXAMPLE 1. An engineering company agreed to develop and manufacture wrapping machines for a sales company which would sell them. The contract provided that the "development costs are to be paid from the proceeds of the sale of the machines." The engineering company spent over $60,000 in development costs and billed the sales company. The sales company authorized its agents to pay all the proceeds from the sale of the first six machines to the engineering company. The engineering company, unpaid, sued the sales company, which defended on the grounds that no machines had yet been sold. The court held that the payment of the development costs was "conditioned" on the sale of the machines. The sale was a condition precedent to recovery of the costs.

Conditions subsequent are the opposite of conditions precedent. The agreement provides that the contract is in existence but is capable of termination by the occurrence of the condition subsequent.

EXAMPLE 2. Hanson, in writing, agreed to purchase Albert's house for $110,000. One of the terms of the contract stated that "In the event that Hanson is unable to obtain financing of a sum no less than $90,000 at an interest rate of no more than 14 percent per annum, within 60 days from date, this contract is terminated and void, and all sums advanced as deposits by Hanson will be returned." Such a clause expresses a condition subsequent.

Many contracts contain implied concurrent conditions; the agreed performances are to take place at the same time.

EXAMPLE 3. A seller agrees to supply and deliver 100 electric fans for $3,000. In the absence of an agreement to the contrary, these are implied conditions concurrent. The seller must tender the electric fans at the same time as the buyer must tender the purchase price.

11.3 PAROL EVIDENCE RULE

When parties have intended the written agreement to be the complete understanding of the parties, the parol evidence rule prohibits any other written or oral evidence to vary, alter, or modify any term.

EXAMPLE 4.   At the time of the signing, paragraph 9, which provided "delivery by the seller," was objected to by the seller. The buyer orally agrees he will pay the cost of delivery. The writing is not changed, however. The written terms stand. An attempt to change this term of the contract by other evidence is prohibited by operation of the parol evidence rule. The seller's only grounds would be to charge fraud, which is doubtful under these few facts.

The parol evidence rule operates to bar other evidence of agreement occurring before the execution of the document as well as evidence occurring during the execution. It does not, however, prohibit other evidence in a number of common situations. Either oral or written evidence can be introduced to prove that the contract was not to take effect until the happening of a condition precedent.

EXAMPLE 5.   An owner signed a listing contract with her realtor. The owner claimed that she signed on the condition that this would not take effect until the owner's husband also signed. He never signed. The realtor found a purchaser and sued the owner for a commission. Oral evidence about when the written listing agreement became binding is admissible under an exception to the parol evidence rule.

There are, in addition, three other exceptions to the parol evidence rule. (1) The parol evidence rule does not apply to evidence of misbehavior of one of the parties whch qualifies as a legal excuse for the other party. Accordingly, charges of fraud, mistake, undue influence, duress, and other claims of injustice can be proved by evidence, oral or written, contrary to the written document. (2) Parol evidence is admissible if the terms of the contract are ambiguous or the terms are incomplete. (3) Modification of a contract—that is, an amendment after the execution of the writing—is not subject to the parol evidence rule. Of course, if oral evidence is offered to prove modification of a written agreement, the rules of formality must also be honored, if they apply. This means that if the amended contract is of a type within the Statute of Frauds, the oral evidence would be inadmissible on *that* ground, not by reason of the parol evidence rule.

11.4 INTERPRETATION AND CONSTRUCTION

A contract may contain language whose meaning is not clear to the court. A court *interprets* when it explores the text for meaning or attempts to *construe* the agreement by looking beyond the text. In either attempt, the court is asked to determine the agreement of the parties. There are several rules which courts use to assist in making such determinations. These rules have as their objective the determination of the common intention of the parties to the contract:

The rules of construction include the following:

(1) When possible, the court will attempt to uphold the contract rather than render it void.

(2) When there is more than one writing, the court will attempt to construe them together.

(3) Doubtful or ambiguous language is to be construed against the party who drew the contract or chose the language.

(4) Words and phrases are to be given their normal meaning.

(5) Where a contract is partly written and partly printed, the writing controls.

(6) Typewriting will prevail over printing, and handwriting over typewriting.

EXAMPLE 6.   A credit card contract provided that "the customer is liable for charges made on a lost or stolen card until Store receives notice of loss by certified mail." The customer lost her card and saw unauthorized purchases on her monthly statement at which time she notified the store. The store claims she is liable for unauthorized purchases incurred before notification. The customer contends plain language says she is liable "until she notifies." She notified; therefore she is no longer liable. The court agreed, stating that "the language was chosen by the store" and *literally* it has that meaning.

11.5 TIME OF PERFORMANCE

If the time specified in the contract is of the essence, failure to perform in timely fashion is a material breach of the contract. If it is not and a breach occurs, there can be an action for damages but no complete excuse from the contract. Time is of the essence when the parties expressly say so in the contract or where, under the circumstances, the parties should have understood it to be. Further, in certain types of contracts time is traditionally of the essence by implication, such as notes payable, whether installment or otherwise.

EXAMPLE 7. A home buyer was selling his house and buying a more expensive one. An additional down payment for the new house was $20,000, due in 60 days. The proceeds from the sale of his present house were to be the source of the $20,000, but the contract did not state so. His sale was delayed, and he failed to tender the $20,000 on the due date. The seller claims the contract was discharged by the material breach. The court ruled that no material breach occurred. In the absence of express terms, sales of real property are not contracts where time is of the essence by implication.

The fact that a specific time is stated in the contract does not make that contract one in which time is of the essence. The phrase itself, "time is of the essence," is generally used to activate the rule, though its general use in printed contracts does not conclusively assure enforcement. Sometimes the facts are so obvious that the courts imply time as a condition. A printer's promise to deliver wedding invitations by May 1, 19X3, for a wedding scheduled for June 1, 19X3, needs no express terms to make time of the essence.

11.6 SATISFACTORY PERFORMANCE

A party expressly promises to perform "to the satisfaction of the other." The contract now contains a condition precedent. When this occurs the court must decide whether or not to apply the test literally. The issue is whether the subjective good-faith judgment of the promisee is the standard or, alternatively, a peformance that would satisfy a "reasonable person" is acceptable. The general rule is that where a contract calls for "satisfactory performance," all that is required is that which would satisfy a reasonable person unless personal taste, judgment, or fancy is involved.

EXAMPLE 8. Magic Cola granted a license to a bottler upon the condition that the bottler develop an increase in sales "satisfactory to Magic." Magic notified the bottler that it was dissatisfied with the small increase in sales. The bottler claims unfair termination. If Magic's dissatisfaction was genuine and made in good faith, Magic's judgment was conclusive under the terms of the agreement.

Some contracts by their nature involve personal taste or judgment, requiring only good-faith dissatisfaction. Contracts with artists and interior decorators are obvious examples if personal satisfaction was guaranteed. However, many times the performance is mechanical or is governed by such definite specifications that an objective standard will be applied, unless the contract makes it clear that subjective judgment was intended as controlling.

A builder who agrees to perform to the satisfaction of the owner generally will be measured by an objective standard.

EXAMPLE 9. A subcontracting firm in a government contract promised that it would lay sewer pipe, mains, and sewer lines and that the contract could be terminated if such work proved "unsatisfactory to the general contractor." The performance would be measured as performance satisfactory to a reasonable person.

Black Letter Law
A Summary

1. A condition is a contract clause which has for its object the suspension, rescission, or modification of the principal duty or obligation.

2. Three types of conditions are found in contracts: conditions precedent, conditions subsequent, and concurrent conditions.

3. Where something must be done or occur before the contract becomes effective, a condition precedent is identified, whereas the condition subsequent refers to those matters which occur to release the obligation.

4. Where parties have intended the written contract to be the complete understanding, the parol evidence rule prohibits any other written or oral evidence to vary, alter, or modify any terms.

5. The principal exceptions to the parol evidence rule include misbehavior in the formation of the contract in the nature of fraud, duress, etc.; ambiguity in the document; agreements subsequent to the contract; and oral proof of the existence of a condition precedent as to the effectiveness of the entire contract.

6. Rules of interpretation and construction of contracts are aids to the court in applying the contract language to the dispute where such language is not explicit.

7. Time of performance of a contract can be a material contract term allowing rescission for failure to perform where time is of the essence either by express terms or by reasonable interpretation.

8. In contracts calling for satisfactory performance, a performance which satisfies a reasonable person is all that is required unless personal taste or fancy is involved.

Solved Problems

11.1 Barnes agreed to purchase from Damion 1,000 shares of Excelsior Photo, Inc., stock at $100 per share. Barnes was interested in obtaining control of Excelsior, whose stock was very closely held. The stock purchase agreement contained the following clause: "This contract is subject to my [Barnes's] obtaining more than 50 percent of the shares outstanding of Excelsior Photo stock." In this situation

(a) the contract is *not* binding on Damion because it lacks consideration on Barnes's part, i.e., unless she obtained more than 50 percent, she is *not* liable.

(b) the contract is subject to an express condition precedent.

(c) specific performance would *not* be available to Barnes if Damion refuses to perform.

(d) while the contract is executory, Damion *cannot* transfer good title to a third party who takes in good faith.

(*AICPA Examination, May 1975*)

A condition precedent requires that until the condition is fulfilled, the contract has no binding force; the answer is (b). Here the parties used typical words in creating an express condition precedent, i.e., "this contract is subject to . . . ." Despite the clause the contract reflects consideration, and if the stock was important for control, a breach of the agreement could subject the other to an action for specific performance. The fact that the contract is in its executory stage does not necessarily mean that the owner of the subject matter to be transferred does not retain power over its disposal.

11.2 Ames and Bates have agreed that Bates will sell a parcel of land to Ames for $10,000 if the land is rezoned from residential to industrial use within 6 months of the agreement. Bates agreed to use his best efforts to obtain the rezoning, and Ames agreed to make a $2,000 good-faith deposit with Bates 2 weeks after the date of the agreement. What is the status of this agreement?

(*a*) No contract results because the event is contingent.

(*b*) The agreement is probably unenforceable because Bates would be required to attempt to influence governmental action.

(*c*) The parties have entered into a bilateral contract subject to a condition.

(*d*) Ames is *not* obligated to make the deposit at the agreed time even though Bates has by then made an effort to procure a rezoning.

(*AICPA Examination, May 1978*)

There are no set words in a contract which establish a condition precedent. The simple word "if" in the context of this agreement creates the condition; the answer is (*c*). Many contracts are drawn with contingencies without losing their validity as contracts. Just as long as each party must do something absolutely, the promise is binding and is not illusory. No illegal bargain is suggested by the promise to get a different zoning as this could be done legally. The law will not infer criminal intent merely because that would be one of the possible ways to have the zoning changed.

11.3 On July 25, 19X8, Archer, the president of Post Corporation, with the approval of the board of directors, engaged Biggs, a CPA, to examine Post's July 19X8, financial statements and to issue a report in time for the annual stockholders' meeting to be held on September 5, 19X8. Notwithstanding Biggs's reasonable efforts, the report was not ready until September 7 because of delays by Post's staff. Archer, acting on behalf of Post, refuses to accept or to pay for the report since it no longer served its intended purpose. In the event Biggs brings a legal action against Post, what is the probable outcome?

(*a*) The case would be dismissed because it is unethical for a CPA to sue for his or her fee.

(*b*) Biggs will be entitled to recover only in quasi contract for the value of the service to the client.

(*c*) Biggs will *not* recover since the completion by September 5 was a condition precedent to his recovery.

(*d*) Biggs will recover because the delay by Post's staff prevented Biggs from performing on time and thereby eliminated the timely performance condition.

(*AICPA Examination, November 1978*)

Not all conditions in contracts are expressly set forth by the parties. Frequently, the courts must read them into the agreement. In this case an implied condition existed; the answer is (*d*). It is understood that if one party must rely on the other party in performing, a failure of that party to perform cannot be used against the party failing to deliver on time or at all. While it is true that the September deadline does suggest a "time of the essence" duty, if the failure of one party prevents the performance of the other, an excuse is shown.

11.4 A buyer and seller agree to the purchase and sale of 1,000 bushels of wheat for $4,500. Which of the following is correct as to the status of performance?

(a) The buyer must tender the money before the seller must tender the wheat.

(b) The performances of each are concurrent.

(c) The seller must tender the wheat before the buyer must tender the money.

(d) This is a credit sale.

   This is a usual type of bilateral contract in which the parties fail to specify who shall perform first. In such an event, if no other implication is present, the contract is interpreted as calling for concurrent performance, answer (b). Credit is never implied unless there is some evidence or trade custom suggesting otherwise.

11.5 Walker and White entered into a written contract involving the purchase of certain used equipment by White. White claims that there were oral understandings between the parties which are included as a part of the contract. Walker pleads the parol evidence rule. This rule applies to

(a) subsequent oral modifications of the written contract by the parties.

(b) additional consistent terms, even if the contract was *not* intended as a complete and exclusive listing of all terms of the agreement.

(c) a contemporaneous oral understanding of the parties which contradicts the terms of a written contract intended as the final expression of the agreement between the parties.

(d) evidence, based upon the performance by Walker, in support of the oral modification.

(AICPA Examination, November 1976)

   Where parties have entered into a written contract and indicate that such is the final and complete understanding of the parties, oral agreements at that time inconsistent with the written contract, even if proved to have occurred, cannot be introduced into evidence, answer (c). The other statements reflect exceptions to the parol evidence rule.

11.6 The parol evidence rule does *not* apply to

(a) prior oral agreements which would normally have been included in the written contract.

(b) oral agreements relating to and made contemporaneously with the written contract.

(c) written agreements intended by the parties as the final expression of their agreement of the terms included in the written contract.

(d) written agreements which were obtained by fraud.

(AICPA Examination, November 1973)

   While the law discourages introduction of evidence to contradict a complete written contract, it cannot permit a party to benefit from his or her misconduct. Accordingly, evidence of fraud is always admissible to contradict the validity of the written contract, answer (d). All the other statements refer to the type of evidence properly excluded by the application of the parol evidence rule.

11.7 Austin is attempting to introduce oral evidence in court to explain or modify a written contract he made with Wade. Wade has pleaded the parol evidence rule. In which of the following circumstances will Austin *not* be able to introduce the oral evidence?

(a) The contract contains an obvious ambiguity on the point at issue.

(b) There was a mutual mistake of fact by the parties regarding the subject matter of the contract.

(c) The modification asserted was made several days after the written contract had been executed.

(d) The contract indicates that it was intended as the "entire contract" between the parties and the point is covered in detail.

(*AICPA Examination, May 1979*)

The answer is (d). Nowhere is the court more insistent in looking only to the definite terms of the written contract than where the parties expressly indicated that the document reflected the "entire contract." This clause in written contracts is known as the *entireties clause*.

11.8   Mary employed a draper to recommend and install drapes for her new home. She was quite discriminating and demanded that the draper perform to "her entire personal satisfaction." Which is the correct statement?

(a) If Mary is truly dissatisfied with the performance, she need not pay for the work.

(b) If the draper's performance would satisfy a reasonable person, Mary must accept the job and pay for it.

(c) If Mary was personally satisfied but could find that a reasonable person would not be satisfied, she could be relieved of the contract.

(d) Such agreements are against public policy.

This is a personal satisfaction contract. Personal satisfaction, however, is generally interpreted by the courts as that degree of satisfaction a reasonable person would demand unless personal taste or fancy is involved. The nature of the work, in this case, and the position or attitude of Mary regarding personal taste suggest that a subjective test is to be applied. Accordingly, as stated in answer (a) if Mary is truly dissatisfied, she may be excused from paying.

11.9   Lanson and Severs entered into an agreement after hours of negotiations. The original draft was typewritten but was well marked up by the time the parties signed the document. Later, the parties noticed that paragraph 7, as typewritten, called for "all vacations to be taken in June and July only." By ink, in cursive writing, the paragraph called for the month of July only. A dispute arose about when vacations could be taken. Which is the correct statement?

(a) Vacations are in June and July since that was the first term in the typewritten contract.

(b) July is the vacation month since writing controls typewriting.

(c) Vacations are in June since that term was unchanged.

(d) Since the typewritten contract is all marked up, the contract is void.

The rules of interpretation and construction are merely tools to assist the court in finding the intention of the parties. In this case, the rule that favors writing over typewriting would assist the court in determining that July is the month intended for vacations, statement (b). Statement (a) is of assistance in contracts where there are conflicting terms set forth in the same document, which is not the case here.

11.10 Nichola purchased a Model 120 Peach computer from Hudson's Computer Island Store for $4,250. The written contract contained an 18-month warranty, provided the unit was returned to the manufacturer or one of its dealers. The contract also contained an effective disclaimer of any other warranties and concluded with the language that the contract "represented the entire agreement and understanding of the parties." Nichola can prove that during the sale negotiation, the clerk orally assured Nichola that a 1-year extension of the warranty could be purchased for $100 if paid for within 60 days of the sale. On the fifty-ninth day after the sale Nichola offered Hudson's Computer Island Store $100 for the warranty extension. Hudson's refused. Which of the following is the best legal defense for Hudson's should Nichola press for the additional warranty?

(a) The "entireties" clause permits no evidence whatsoever to contradict or add to the written contract.

(b) The parol evidence rule.

(c) The inadequacy of consideration.

(d) The fact that the clerk had no express authority to make such an offer.

The answer is (b). This type of agreement made at the time of the contract is the proper subject of the parol evidence rule. The entireties clause normally cuts off argument that additional terms were intended by the parties, but not incorporated in the written contract. However, such a clause is not effective to bar other types of evidence, such as fraud, mistake, etc. Accordingly, statement (a) goes too far. The fact that the clerk had no express authority (d) to offer the additional warranty does not bar the presence of apparent authority. One hundred dollars is valuable consideration, and so statement (c) does not apply.

11.11 Jackson Company was bidding on a government project which included providing construction of laboratory facilities that required a high degree of sophistication because fissionable materials were to be used in the labs. The plumbing was particularly tricky, and this was not easily seen by a reading of the government specifications. Jackson and many plumbing companies knew of the problem, however, and Jackson had difficulty finding a subcontractor. Jackson did find Newtown Plumbing and supplied it with the specifications, telling the company that it was selected because of its great reputation for quality work. Jackson was pleased to interest Newtown and inserted in paragraph 7 of the contract the statement that "Newtown is familiar with the specifications, is aware of the requirements, and is not relying on any statement made by Jackson regarding the project." Paragraph 8 of the document recited that the document "contained all the agreement between the parties." Only after Newtown began performing did it see the difficult problems. Newtown found out this was no surprise to Jackson and now wants to sue Jackson for fraud. Jackson contends that paragraphs 7 and 8 prevent Newtown from beginning suit.

Is Newtown barred from bringing an action for fraud? Decide and state reasons for your conclusions.

The parol evidence rule does operate to exclude evidence that contradicts an explicit term in a written contract which on its face purports to be the entire agreement of the parties. However, the rule does not apply to evidence that would prove fraud or other misconduct. Such evidence does not vary the terms of the contract. It merely shows the presence of fraud, which permits disaffirmance of the contract. The statement that "this contract is not induced by fraud" is meaningless. The law does not permit a covenant of immunity to be drawn that will protect a party against his or her own fraud. Newtown is permitted to attempt to prove by extrinsic evidence that fraud was committed in this case.

11.12 Handel Company owned a $10,000,000 mortgage on the Speer Building and agreed to assign it to Rolo, Inc., in consideration of delivery of 100,000 shares of Rolo common stock. Under the contract both parties were to deposit their respective performances in the Warren Bank by August 15, 19X2. Further, the contract provided that Rolo's properly indorsed stock must be delivered on time, as also must Handel's assignment of the mortgage together with a certificate from a title company reflecting the mortgage to be a valid first lien on the building. Handel deposited the assignment of mortgage on August 1 but was having trouble obtaining the title certificate and had not deposited it by August 15. Rolo, on the other hand, made no attempt to perform the contract. On August 16, 19X2, Handel charged that Rolo had breached the contract and Handel sued for damages.

What success will Handel have? State your answer and reasons for any conclusions reached.

Under the terms of the contract each had to perform at the same time. The contract had concurrent conditions. This called for concurrent performance. Either party could place the other in breach for failure to perform with a valid tender of its own performance. Handel tendered only partial performance. Neither one deposited the necessary title certificate regarding the mortgage. The complete failure of Rolo to attempt a tender does not assist Handel in this case. The contract called for concurrent performances. Handel would lose.

11.13 Tiger Productions was noted for its quality industrial films. The economy was bad, and companies were reluctant to spend money on this fringe area. Tiger did want to deal with Keeton Products and found a sympathetic ear with Albert, Keeton's public relations director. Albert feared that the board of directors would not like the film. Tiger assured Albert that it would guarantee its work to Keeton's "complete personal satisfaction." Moreover, said Tiger, such a promise would be put in writing. Convinced, Albert authorized the film, which was completed in due course. It was an excellent film. It received the top award at the Media Industrial Film Festival, but it shocked the conservative board, which promptly fired Albert. Keeton refused to accept the film and would not pay for it. Tiger wants to be paid and sues Keeton.

What success will Tiger have in its lawsuit? State reasons for your conclusions.

Occasionally, contractors will promise to perform to the personal satisfaction of the other. When they do so, the courts must determine the standard by which the performance is measured. Generally, courts tend to apply the reasonable person test, sometimes called the *mechanical fitness* or *suitability test*. However, if the facts indicate that personal taste, or the subjective standard, was understood by the parties, the only issue is whether the promisee is sincere in his or her dissatisfaction. The above case is a close one. The fact that a film is perceived as having artistic qualities suggests that the personal taste aspect exception to the rule may govern. It is an industrial film, but under these circumstances involving a conservative board of directors holding a particular set of personal values, a court could apply the subjective test. Tiger's only chance then would be in proving that the board's dissatisfaction is a sham. Tiger will probably lose this action.

Chapter 12

Third Parties

12.1 INTRODUCTION

Generally only those who are parties to the contract have rights under the contract. Third parties are "strangers to the contract," as they are not in privity of contract. Two exceptions to this rule are third-party beneficiaries and assignees of contracts.

EXAMPLE 1. Harry Mason agreed to construct a building for Taylor for a price. Taylor decided to breach the contract. Harry felt outrage but did not intend to sue for damages. Harry's brother, John, did not want Taylor to get away with this and so sued Taylor for breach of the construction contract. Brother John is a stranger to the contract and cannot sue under it. John is not within the privacy (privity) of contract with Taylor; only Harry is.

12.2 THIRD-PARTY BENEFICIARIES

An agreement entered into primarily and directly for the benefit of a third person is a *third-party beneficiary contract*. The designated third person can sue the promisor just as if such third party was a party to the contract. The test is whether the contracting parties intended to benefit a third party. One who is only accidentally or incidentally benefited is called an *incidental beneficiary* and cannot sue.

EXAMPLE 2. Winthrop agrees to construct an office building for New Era. Towell has a vacant lot across the street from the construction site. Future office workers would need a close place to eat lunch. Towell, relying on the contract between Winthrop and New Era, constructs a restaurant, intending to cater to office workers. New Era breaches the contract with Winthrop. No office building is built. Towell will suffer a loss but cannot sue New Era for its breach of the contract, as Towell is only an incidental beneficiary who cannot sue on the contract between Winthrop and New Era.

Third-party beneficiaries fall into two classes: donee beneficiaries and creditor beneficiaries. When one of the contracting parties intended to bestow a gift on a third person, a *donee beneficiary contract* is created. On the other hand, if the contracting party obtains the promise of the other to perform the duty of the first party, a *creditor beneficiary contract* is formed.

EXAMPLE 3. Newport owned a successful hardware store which was managed by Mark for many years. Newport contracted with a buyer to sell the going business for $80,000 cash, the buyer's promise to pay the current creditors $10,000, and the buyer's promise to retain Mark as manager for a period of 2 years at a salary of $25,000 a year. Newport's creditors who are to be paid by the buyer are creditor beneficiaries who can sue the buyer. Mark was given the gift of the job by Newport. Mark is a donee beneficiary and can sue the buyer if the buyer should improperly discharge Mark as manager.

In a creditor beneficiary contract, the promisee obtains a promise by the promisor to carry out the promisee's preexisting obligations. However, this contract does *not* excuse the promisee, the original debtor, from his or her debt or obligation. Instead, it provides the creditors with a new debtor in addition to the old one. However, if the creditor agreed to substitute the new debtor for the old one, a *novation* (a new contract) would discharge the old debt. This releases the original debtor. Sales of going businesses or the withdrawal of partners frequently involves a creditor beneficiary.

EXAMPLE 4. X, Y, and Z are partners. The firm has assets and liabilities. X decides to retire and wants her share of the partnership property. P offers to take X's place with the approval of Y and Z. Y, Z, and P agree to pay all the old debts of the partnership and release X. This is a creditor beneficiary contract as regards the new partner P. P will now be liable to the old creditors of the firm, who are now creditor beneficiaries of the contract. X, however, is not released, and if she must pay the old creditors, she then could sue P, Y, and Z on their promise. If the old creditors had expressly agreed to release X in consideration of P's promise to pay, a novation would have occurred and released X.

12.3 ASSIGNMENT

The transfer of a *chose* (right) *in action* is an *assignment*. The transferee is the *assignee*, and the transferor is the *assignor*. The party expected to pay is called the *debtor* or *obligor*. An assignment can be done orally unless there is a statutory requirement that it be in writing.

One of the distinctions between a third-party beneficiary and an assignee is that the former's rights are created at the time of the contract. The assignee's right comes into existence in a later, separate transaction when the assignor, either by contract or by gift, transfers the right to the assignee. Assignments are the foundation of much commercial financing.

EXAMPLE 5. A seller delivers a machine to a buyer on credit. The buyer promises to pay $2,000 in 90 days. The buyer's promise to pay is a chose in action owned by the seller. The seller needs cash and sells (transfers) this right to a finance company for $1,800. When the seller transfers this right, an assignment of the claim occurs, allowing the finance company to sue the buyer directly.

The language of an assignment is frequently expressed as follows: the owner "assigns and transfers" the claim as a right in action. Most contract claims can be assigned. Tort claims, unless reduced to judgment, cannot be assigned. In the absence of a contrary public policy or statute, future wages to be earned by an employee under an existing contract can be assigned even where the employment contract is at will.

Duties cannot be assigned, but many can be delegated. Where the duties of the promisee or obligor would be changed in any material respect or enlarged thereby, the assignment and delegation would be ineffective. Further, where a contract calls for personal skill or judgment of one of the parties, an attempt to assign the contract, and thus require such personal duties to be performed by another, is against public policy.

EXAMPLE 6. Erica is an engineer who has superior writing skills. She is in demand by several technical publications. She is "overbooked," having signed contracts for more than she can handle. Her associate, Bill, is also an excellent writer. Erica assigns and delegates the duty in two of these contracts to Bill. This is an invalid agreement. Authors' contracts generally involve personal skill. One cannot effectively assign them where the right is only earned after performing personal duties.

Assignment of contracts usually occurs when one part is executed and the other performance is in the executory state. But a purely executory contract can also be assigned when the duties of one party are delegated to the assignee. When a duty is delegated, it is assumed by the assignee, and a third-party beneficiary contract is created.

EXAMPLE 7. Sonora Groves contracts to sell and deliver 1,400 crates of Grade B navel oranges to a wholesale shipper in 90 days at $3.50 per crate. Sonora is expert in contracting. Other area growers would like to purchase these contracts for a fee. Sonora assigns this executory contract (both rights and duties) to Mid-Sun Growers, the assignee, for $500. Mid-Sun must now deliver the 1,400 crates to the wholesale shipper who must accept and pay. If Mid-Sun fails in its duty, Sonora must perform. Notice that this contract does not appear to involve personal skill, nor does it enlarge the duties of the party expecting performance.

12.4 RIGHTS OF ASSIGNEES

An assignee "stands in the shoes of the assignor," gaining no greater rights than those possessed by the original contractor, the assignor. If the debtor had a valid defense available against the assignor, it can be used to defeat the claim of the assignee. Notice to the debtor that the claim has been assigned is technically not a condition to the validity of the assignment, but failure to notify could cause the assignee a loss. A payment by the debtor to the original contractor, the assignor, before notice of assignment, for example, is an effective payment barring the assignee from exercising such rights against the debtor.

EXAMPLE 8. A debtor owed a creditor $500 for goods sold and delivered. Later some of the goods were found to be defective, thus creating a right in the debtor to sue for breach of warranty. The creditor assigns his $500 account receivable to a finance company for $300. If the finance company sues the debtor, the defense of breach warranty is available to the debtor. Further, if before the finance company notifies the debtor of the assignment, the creditor and debtor reached a settlement for $200, the finance company's only action would be against the creditor for its behavior.

Defenses include all the rights the original assignor would have been subject to and those the debtor may have against the assignee. A promise by the debtor to waive certain defenses is enforceable as to certain defenses under Section 9-206 of the UCC.

Sometimes an assignor assigns the same claim to several assignees. The issue then arises of which assignee has the better or best claim against the debtor where successive assignments occur. There is a division of authority in the United States when the later assignee was the first to notify the debtor of the assignment. Unless there are special circumstances, the majority rule provides that the assignment first in time is the effective assignment, but a strong minority rule exists in many jurisdictions. Where Article 9 of the UCC is applicable, a perfection of the security agreement determines rights of priority. Generally, the first to perfect by filing a financing statement in the public record would have the greater right in the collateral, here the claim assigned.

EXAMPLE 9. Ace Hardware borrowed money from the bank and signed numerous papers including "an assignment of all accounts receivable" as security for the loan. The bank did not notify any of Ace's creditors. Ace later needed additional inventory from Systems Inc. on credit. Ace signed a credit instrument with Systems which provided an assignment "of all receivables." Systems immediately notified Ace's debtors. Under majority rule the bank would have the greater right against the debtor despite its failure to notify.

An assignment is a *transfer*, not a contract. One may, and usually does, contract to assign a claim. However, in instances where the assignment is motivated by a gift, such transfers may be revoked by the assignor or by the death of the assignor. On the other hand, where an assignee has paid a valuable consideration for the assignment, the law assumes the assignment to be final, and in addition, the assignor makes certain implied warranties in regard to the quality of the assignment. In the absence of an agreement to the contrary, one who assigns a claim for a consideration warrants that (1) the claim or right is legally genuine, (2) there is no defense or limitation on the claim, and (3) the assignor will do nothing to impair the value of the assignment. However, it is important to remember that the assignor does not impliedly warrant that the claim will be paid or that the debtor is solvent.

EXAMPLE 10. Farrow installed a septic tank system for Amuso, an amusement park, on credit, for a price of $10,000. Farrow assigned the claim to Bowe for $8,800. If Farrow had made a mistake and contracted with an unauthorized agent of Amuso, the claim may not be genuine. If Farrow did a poor job, there could be a defense based on breach of contract. If Farrow continued to collect partial payments from Amuso, Farrow, the assignor, is impairing the value of the assignment. Bowe could sue Farrow on the alleged breach of implied warranties but could not sue Farrow if the only failure was Amuso's financial ability. Bowe takes the risk that the debt is uncollectible unless Farrow specifically transfers the claim "with recourse."

Sometimes a contract expressly prohibits assignments. These prohibitions were enforceable under the common law; but certain provisions of the UCC reflect a contrary policy in respect to business accounts. Section 9-318(4), for example, states that a term in any contract between an account debtor and an assignor "is ineffective if it prohibits assignment." In effect, the UCC allows assignment of monetary rights even in the presence of express restriction. In a similar spirit toward free transferability, the UCC directs that any assignment "of the contract" or "all my rights under the contract" will be interpreted as implying a delegation of the performance of the duties of the assignor and the assignee's promise to perform [UCC, Section 2-210(4)].

Generally, an assignment must be of the entire right. At common law, partial assignments were not honored unless all the assignees joined in one action to enforce the assignment against the debtor.

Black Letter Law
A Summary

1. The two exceptions to the rule that only parties to a contract have rights in the contract are third-party beneficiaries and assignees.

2. A third-party beneficiary is a party who at the time of the contract was intentionally contemplated by the parties as having rights in the contract either by a name, class, or other identification.

3. There are two kinds of third-party beneficiaries: donee and creditor.

4. In donee beneficiary contracts, one of the contracting parties intended to bestow a gift on the beneficiary; in a creditor beneficiary contract, one of the parties succeeded in obtaining the promise of the other to pay the other's debt or obligation.

5. An incidental beneficiary is a party named, or not named, who could benefit from the contract but was not intended as a party to the contract and accordingly has no rights in the contract.

6. An assignment is the transfer of a right in action to another; this transfer may be the performance of a contract or can be by gift.

7. Most contract rights can be assigned if they are not tied to a personal performance or do not enlarge the obligations of the obligor; tort and other claims not liquidated generally cannot be assigned.

8. The party who owns and transfers the right of action is called the assignor, the recipient is the assignee, and the party expected to perform is the obligor.

9. Rights can be assigned and duties can be delegated, but the assignor remains bound to assure the performance of the duty by the assignee.

10. When a contract is in the purely executory state, an assignment of the entire contract carries with it, in the absence of an agreement to the contrary, a delegation of the duty of the assignor to the assignee.

11. An assignor is relieved of the duty which he or she delegated only upon the valid release by the obligor through a novation.

12. Where the same right is assigned to different parties, the first assignee in time has the greater right against the obligor.

13. An assignor who contracts to transfer the assignment claim impliedly warrants that the claim is genuine, that he or she will do nothing to impair its collection, and that there are no defenses or claims to it, but the assignor does not guarantee the collection of the money.

Solved Problems

12.1 In order for a court to find a third-party beneficiary contract,

    (*a*) there must be a written agreement.

    (*b*) the assignor and obligee must agree to such.

    (*c*) the contracting parties must have intended that a stranger to the contract have rights in it.

    (*d*) the beneficiary must have been related to one of the parties.

    If the parties meant to benefit another at the time of the contract by having rights in the contract, a third-party beneficiary has been created; statement (*c*) is the answer. There is no specific requirement that a writing is necessary or that there be any special relationship between the beneficiary and one of the contractors.

12.2 Which of the following transactions is likely to result in a creditor beneficiary situation?

    (*a*) A life insurance contract naming a spouse as beneficiary

    (*b*) A sale of a business with the buyer taking over current debts

    (*c*) A bank loan

    (*d*) A construction contract

    Upon the limited facts stated, statement (*b*) identifies a creditor beneficiary relationship. The buyer is promising the seller to pay off the seller's creditors, who then become third-party creditor beneficiaries of that contract. A spouse under a life insurance contract is usually a donee beneficiary.

12.3 Marglow Supplies, Inc., mailed a letter to Wilson Distributors on September 15, 19X1, offering a 3-year franchise dealership. The offer stated the terms in detail and at the bottom stated that the offer would not be withdrawn before October 1, 19X1. Which of the following is correct?

    (*a*) The statute of frauds would *not* apply to the proposed contract.

    (*b*) The offer is an irrevocable option which *cannot* be withdrawn before October 1, 19X1.

    (*c*) The offer *cannot* be assigned to another party by Wilson if Wilson chooses *not* to accept.

    (*d*) A letter of acceptance from Wilson to Marglow sent on October 1, 19X1, but *not* received until October 2, 19X1, would *not* create a valid contract.

(*Adapted from AICPA Examination, November 1981*)

Answer (c) is correct. Generally, most contract rights can be assigned, but an offer to contract is not a contract. The offeree has no right that a person can assign. This is not an option because no consideration was paid for the offer. Since this offer involves a period in excess of a year, the Statute of Frauds, requiring a writing, would apply.

12.4   Fennell and McLeod entered into a binding contract whereby McLeod was to perform routine construction services according to Fennell's blueprints. McLeod assigned the contract to Conerly. After the assignment,

(a)   Fennell can bring suit under the doctrine of anticipatory breach.

(b)   McLeod extinguishes all his rights and duties under the contract.

(c)   McLeod extinguishes all his rights but is *not* relieved of his duties under the contract.

(d)   McLeod still has all his rights but is relieved of his duties under the contract.

(*AICPA Examination, November 1981*)

When a contract is assigned in its executory stage, the assignor still has duties to perform. These duties can generally be delegated but never completely extinguished, statement (c). If the assignee, here Conerly, does not perform, McLeod, the assignor, must. All McLeod's rights are ended, however. There is no evidence here of any breach, much less an anticipatory breach.

12.5   Jane Luft, doing business as Luft Enterprises, owned a tract of land upon which she had intended to build an additional retail outlet. There is an existing first mortgage of $70,000 on the property which is held by the First County National Bank. Luft decided *not* to expand, and a buyer, Johnson, offered $150,000 for the property. Luft accepted and received a certified check for $80,000 plus a signed statement by Johnson promising to pay the existing mortgage. What are the legal rights of the indicated parties?

(a)   Luft remains liable to First County despite Johnson's promise to pay.

(b)   First County must first proceed against Johnson on the mortgage before it has any rights against Luft.

(c)   The delegation of the debt is invalid if Johnson does *not* have a credit rating roughly comparable to Luft's.

(d)   The bank is the incidental beneficiary of Johnson's promise to pay the mortgage.

(*AICPA Examination, May 1977*)

The facts indicate a typical assumption agreement of an existing mortgage on property. The fact that the buyer promises the seller that the buyer will pay the seller's debt does not alter or diminish the original debtor's duty to pay; statement (a) is correct. Here the bank gains a new debtor under this assumption, becoming a creditor beneficiary of the contract between Luft and her buyer, Johnson. The creditor is not restricted as to which party it sues first. In the absence of a clause in the mortgage prohibiting assumption, the debtor can delegate, as this does not impair the creditor's rights.

12.6   On June 1, 19X2, Townsend sold $5,000 worth of goods to Basehart on 30 days credit. Needing immediate cash, Townsend assigned the claim to Capitale Factors on June 5, 19X2. On June 20, one Taylor Industries assigned its $3,250 judgment against Townsend to Basehart. Basehart wanted to use the judgment as a setoff of its debt to Townsend. On July 1 it was discovered by Capitale that a clerk had failed to notify Basehart of the assignment from Townsend. Capitale immediately telephoned Basehart, demanding payment of $5,000. Under these circumstances,

(a)   Basehart has the right of a $3,250 setoff against the debt it owed to Townsend.

(b)   Townsend impliedly warranted the solvency of Basehart.

(c) since Capitale's assignment occurred first, its rights to the full $5,000 are superior to any setoff that Basehart might acquire later.

(d) assignments of accounts receivable must be properly recorded in the public records in order to be effective.

   The answer is (a). Generally, the assignee has no duty to notify the obligor of the assignment, but the failure to do so in a timely manner may cause a loss or create setoff rights to accrue against the assignee. Notice of an assignment prevents the obligor from asserting against the assignee any defense or setoff arising after such notice with respect to a matter not related to the assigned claim. Capitale's delay in notifying Basehart of the assignment allowed Basehart in good faith to acquire a claim which can be used as a setoff of the assigned claim.

12.7 Jones sold his house to Baxter at a good profit. As part of the transaction, Baxter paid cash over the existing real property mortgage on the house held by Second Federal Savings. Baxter promised Jones that she would continue to make the monthly mortgage payments. Under these circumstances,

(a) if Baxter failed to make the payments, Jones may be required to pay Second Federal.

(b) Second Federal is a donee beneficiary of the contract between Jones and Baxter.

(c) Second Federal is an incidental beneficiary of the Jones–Baxter contract of sale.

(d) Second Federal must first exhaust all its remedies against Baxter before proceeding against Jones on the debt.

   The above facts reflect the typical creditor beneficiary situation. However, this does not relieve the original mortgagor, Jones, from his liability; statement (a) is correct. It is true that Baxter has assumed the obligation, but the effect on Second Federal is merely the addition of another debtor to look to for satisfaction of the mortgage loan. Upon default, Second Federal could proceed immediately against its original contractor, Jones.

12.8 Walsh owns and operates a gas station and restaurant on a highway near a beautiful undeveloped lake region. Clark, interested in developing the area, purchased several acres of lakefront property and contracted with Mahoney, a building contractor, to construct an elaborate hotel and 10 beautiful cottages. After learning these facts from Clark, Walsh expanded his restaurant and gas station in contemplation of a substantial increase in business. Subsequently, Clark changed her plans and breached her contract with Mahoney. Clark promptly notified Mahoney not to commence construction, and Mahoney complied with Clark's instructions.

   Walsh is now suing Clark for breach of contract. Walsh claims that he is a third-party beneficiary under the contract between Clark and Mahoney and entitled to damages for the cost of expanding his business and the profits he would have earned had the contract been performed. In his suit against Clark, Walsh will

(a) win in that he is a third-party creditor beneficiary.

(b) lose in that he is a third-party incidental beneficiary.

(c) win in that he is a donee beneficiary.

(d) win in that Clark and Mahoney have acted fraudulently.

(Adapted from AICPA Examination, November 1973)

   Clearly, Walsh would benefit from the faithful performance of this contract, but he is a stranger to it and not within the exceptions called third-party beneficiaries; the answer is (b). Walsh is considered an incidental beneficiary and as such cannot sue on another's contract. Here his interest was not contemplated by the contracting parties, and therefore he has no rights. There must be an intent on the part of the contracting parties that the promisor shall assume a direct obligation to the third party before such party has any rights under the contract. The benefits which would flow to Walsh from the performance of this contract are merely incidental, indirect, or consequential.

12.9 Sage Corporation owed Tovar $30,000 for goods and services received. Tovar needed cash and assigned the right of action to Barnet for $26,000. Tovar needed more money and in obtaining a loan from his bank signed many papers. One of the papers contained an assignment of all Tovar's accounts receivable. Tovar did not realize this. Which is the correct statement of the situation?

(*a*) Under the majority American rule regarding successive assignments, the first assignee in time has the better right against Sage, the obligor.

(*b*) Under the English rule, the last party to notify Sage (the obligor) has the better claim to the $30,000.

(*c*) If neither of these assignments were in writing, they would be unenforceable.

(*d*) Tovar can unilaterally rescind these assignments anytime before payment.

The majority rule in the United States is that the first assignee in point of time prevails over later assignees, statement (*a*). The minority rule, called the English rule, allows the greater right to the party who notifies the obligor first. Even under the majority rule, if the obligor has happened to pay a later assignee, that party will be allowed to retain the payment. Generally, there is no requirement that assignments be in writing.

12.10 Bayless sold goods to Havlin on credit, Havlin agreeing to pay $5,000. If Bayless assigns this claim to Palmore Factors for $3,500, and with no additional contract language, which of the following commitments did Bayless *not* undertake?

(*a*) Bayless, the assignor, warrants that Havlin will pay the $5,000.

(*b*) Bayless warrants she will do nothing to defeat or impair the assignment.

(*c*) Bayless warrants that the claim is genuine and has no defenses other than those stated or apparent at the time of the assignment.

(*d*) Bayless warrants that she has no knowledge of any fact that would impair the value of the assignment.

Statement (*a*) is the answer. One of the disadvantages of an assignment is that there is no implied warranty or guaranty that the claim will be paid, only that it is a legal claim. In order for the assignee to sue the assignor for the default of the obligor on grounds of insolvency, for example, the assignee must have obtained an express guarantee of such, i.e., a "with recourse" assignment. All other statements reflect the warranties of an assignor who transferred the right to another for value.

12.11 Porter was a professional hockey player under a 5-year contract with Viking Enterprises, which was also the corporate owner of the professional hockey franchise in the city. During the second year of the contract, Paul Viking, the president and controlling shareholder of Viking, assigned the franchise and Porter's contract to Polar Sports, another corporation. Porter did not wish to play for Polar, having received a lucrative offer from another franchise which he accepted. Polar officials were incensed over the breach of contract and filed a lawsuit seeking to have Porter enjoined from playing for the other franchise. Porter contends that once this contract for his personal services was assigned to another without his consent, his duty under the original contract ended.

How absolute is the rule that personal service contracts cannot be assigned without consent of the other? Answer the question and state the outcome of this lawsuit.

Porter's argument that personal service contracts can't be assigned is generally true provided they are indeed based upon a personal relationship between the parties. However, the rendition of services by a professional player to a professional club is normally not affected by the personalities of the successive corporate owners. In this case, Porter would have to show some special relationship between the original corporate owner and himself that permits the general rule to apply. After all, the shareholders of Viking could accomplish the same thing as an assignment of Porter's contract by selling their stock to Polar and Porter could not legally complain. Porter would lose this case and would be enjoined from playing for another franchise during the remaining term of the original contract.

12.12 Under the terms of a contract between the State Road Department and Taylor City, it was agreed that Taylor City would maintain the Taylor Bridge, which was within the city limits. Failure to maintain the bridge properly would subject the city to a reduction in the amount of general road funds provided by the state. The city, in a winter budget move, laid off several workers, and the bridge maintenance crew was the first to go. Heavy snow, which normally would have been removed, was the principal cause of a car accident in which Axeltoon, a city resident, lost his life. His estate, seeking compensation for Axeltoon's widow and children, sues the city for breach of its contract with the State Road Department.

What must the court find in order for the estate to succeed in a breach of contract action? State reasons for your conclusion.

In order for a party to sue successfully for breach of contract, it must prove that it had rights in the contract. Each contracting party does have rights, and occasionally, a third party has rights. Such third parties are called third-party beneficiaries. To qualify as such, the court must be satisfied that the contractors intended to benefit such third party. Axeltoon was not a party to the contract, and his only presence was that of a traveler who would benefit from proper maintenance. This benefit is incidental. While the breach by the city in its promise to the state could result in loss of funds, the parties were only interested in providing the most economical and convenient method of doing the necessary work on the highway. Axeltoon was only an incidental beneficiary of the contract, and he has no rights to be determined under the contract, although his estate is not necessarily barred from suing under other theories.

12.13 Lester, a siding contractor, delivered construction material for the school board under a contract which expressly provided that "any money due under this contract *cannot* be assigned without the consent of the School Board." Lester had difficulty meeting his payroll and had earned $13,500 under the contract. Unfortunately, he was not to be paid until the school budget was approved. Lester's bank agreed to purchase this money claim for $11,750 and gave written notice of Lester's assignment of the claim to the school board. The board, upon the advice of legal counsel, refused to honor this assignment, pointing out the express language of the contract. In fact, once the budget was approved, the board made $3,000 in payments to Lester until the bank sued the school board, demanding the full $13,500.

What is the status of the contract provision prohibiting the assignment of monies already earned by the assignor? Decide this action and state reasons for your conclusions.

Generally, courts will honor contractual provisions prohibiting assignments of claims. They do so based on the common law. However, the UCC has several provisions in which an opposite rule governs. This contract was for goods and therefore bound by the UCC. Section 2-210 regarding sales and Section 9-318(4) dealing with secured transactions allow the assignment of money due despite a contractual prohibition. Accordingly, the legal advice given the school board was incorrect under the UCC. Once the bank notified the school board, the latter must pay the assignee, not Lester, the original contractor. Payments made to Lester cannot be deducted from the amount due the assignee, here the bank. The school board, after paying the bank the full $13,500, must seek from Lester the return of the $3,000 improperly paid to him.

Chapter 13

Termination—Discharge

13.1 GENERAL

Contracts are terminated or discharged in a number of ways. A contract may be discharged by performance, breach of contract, agreement, and legal excuse.

13.2 PERFORMANCE

Generally, nothing but exact and complete performances discharge a contract. Partial performance does not satisfy a contractual obligation, but some recovery of such performance may be allowed under the doctrine of unjust enrichment, or *quantum meruit*.

EXAMPLE 1. A painter was hired by a general contractor on a government contract. The painter was overscheduled and undersupervised. The work was poor, and the painter abandoned the job but sued for the value of the work performed. The unexcused breach by the painter does not allow recovery for partial performance unless the benefit conferred exceeds the damages suffered by the injured party. Part performance does not satisfy a contract. The painter would recover nothing.

Where partial performance of a breaching party is actually accepted by the other party, liability is limited to the amount of the benefit received by the one accepting the performance. The nonbreaching party, however, is under no duty to accept the benefit, and if it is rejected, no recovery is possible for the breaching party.

In addition to partial performance, questions of recovery arise under the doctrines of substantial performance and tender of performance.

13.3 SUBSTANTIAL PERFORMANCE

Substantial performance, unlike partial performance, is performance enabling the party performing to sue successfully for the contract price. When a party has performed under the contract, except for some minor deficiency or deviation from the terms not caused by bad faith, full recovery of the contract price is allowed less the amount necessary for the repair of the minor deficiency or deviation. This doctrine of substantial performance is generally observed in construction contracts.

EXAMPLE 2. Zero Construction Builders agreed to construct a two-story residence according to blueprints and specifications for the owner at a cost of $80,000 by July 2, 19X3. Zero ran into some trouble and finished by August 10, 19X3, having received in progress payments of all but $20,000 of the contract price, which it now demands. The owner cites the delay, floor molding strips that are "classic" rather than the specified "modern," and the fact that the back entrance is 3 feet from the west wall rather than 6 feet as per blueprint. Zero admits it made honest mistakes. The owner contends this is only partial performance. Zero shows that these deviations and the delay entitle the owner to a $500 credit for damage. The substantial performance doctrine would apply here, allowing Zero a recovery of $19,500.

If, however, the minor deviations were willful or made in bad faith, the court can refuse to permit a recovery based on the contract price. This restricts the breaching party to suing under partial performance, that is, the amount of the "benefit" received (i.e., *quantum meruit*) and accepted by the nonbreaching party.

13.4 TENDER OF PERFORMANCE

Tender of performance is the offering to perform with the apparent ability to carry out the promise made in the contract, i.e., ready, willing, and able to perform. If refused by the other party, this tender discharges the contract and excuses further attempts to perform by the tendering party.

Further, the party whose tender of performance is excused has the right to sue for damages for breach of contract. This rule applies to executory contracts, but does not entirely apply to a tender of money in a partly executed contract. An offer to pay money for consideration already received by the promisor which is refused by the other party does excuse the party tendering the money from further interest penalties and provides for a release of any security. However, it does not discharge the debt.

EXAMPLE 3.   Add Groceries is owed $500 from Barney's Bar and 10 bushels of cantaloupes from the grower, who, in a tight-money situation, was prepaid by Add. If Add refused to accept Barney's tender of the $500 and the grower's attempt to deliver the cantaloupes because Add wanted no more taxable income in 19X2, the $500 debt is not discharged but the duty to deliver the cantaloupes is discharged.

13.5 DISCHARGE BY BREACH

Where the contract is in the purely executory state and one party clearly refuses to perform the material terms, the contract is breached to the extent that it excuses any further duty owed by the nonbreaching party. However, a technical or minor breach does not have this severe effect; it allows an action for damages but does not entirely discharge the contract. A major or material breach is one that goes to the substance of the agreement and impairs the bargain.

EXAMPLE 4.   A property owner hired a company to build a fallout shelter, the owner paying $500 down. The company promised quality performance and guaranteed no water seepage in the vestibule of the shelter. The walls bulged and seepage was observed. The company abandoned the job. The owner wants money returned and damages. This contract is discharged by a material breach of contract by the company.

Section 2-106 of the UCC, governing the sale of goods, gives specific definitions of discharge behavior. A *termination* occurs when either party puts an end to the contract other than by breach. Here, all executory promises or portions are discharged, but any rights based on prior breach or performance survive. *Cancellation* occurs when either party puts an end to the contract for the breach of the other.

13.6 ANTICIPATORY BREACH

When before the time for performance it appears that a contracting party will not or cannot perform, such party is guilty of *anticipatory breach*. When a party repudiates or renounces his or her obligation before the time of performance, the promisee may elect to rescind the contract and sue for damages, or may wait until the time for performance. Under the UCC, Section 2-610(a), the promisee can wait for a commercially reasonable period of time.

EXAMPLE 5.   City Electric Company sued Cairo Auto Company for failure to fulfill a contract to purchase electricity for a period of 5 years. During the third year the auto company closed its factory. The electric company can charge anticipatory breach, consider the contract discharged, and sue for the minimum bills called for in the contract even though the 5 years have not passed.

Generally, a premature breach of a promise to pay money in a contract in which the other party had performed is not subject to an anticipatory breach. For example, a statement by a promisor that he will not pay the note due at the bank next month *is* a repudiation but does not permit the bank to sue immediately for the debt. In all other cases, however, the promisee has a number of options when faced with repudiation. The promisee may ignore it and sue at maturity, treat it as a breach and sue for damages, or rescind the agreement.

13.7 AGREEMENT TO DISCHARGE

Parties may mutually agree to end their contract. Such agreement requires all the elements of contracts, including the presence of consideration. Except where one or both parties have fully performed under the contract, an agreement to rescind has mutual consideration by definition, i.e., each party agrees to forbear from requiring a duty from the other. This is called a *mutual rescission*. Further, the parties may enter into arrangements in which a new agreement discharges the other by merger or novation.

13.8 MERGER

A *merger* occurs when a right has been enveloped by a new or higher right. This is seen when an open account merges into a promissory note or a tenancy into outright ownership of a leased property.

EXAMPLE 6. A wholesaler owes a manufacturer $5,000 for goods received. The bill has not been paid, and the manufacturer demands a more formal payment arrangement. The wholesaler signs a promissory note for $5,000, due 6 months from date, at 16 percent interest, and secured by accounts receivable owned by the wholesaler. The old $5,000 debt is extinguished by the doctrine of merger. The old debt is merged into the new evidence of the debt, the $5,000 promissory note.

EXAMPLE 7. An airline flight attendant rented a townhouse for 3 years. After 1 year the owner sold the townhouse to the flight attendant. The unexpired 2 years of the lease merged into the greater right, full ownership of the townhouse by the flight attendant.

13.9 NOVATION; ACCORD AND SATISFACTION

Novation is the substitution of a new contract for an old one, which is thereby extinguished. Its effect is similar to mergers but occurs in those instances in which the parties expressly extinguished the old agreement. A common example of novation is seen where a debtor obtains the promise of a third party to perform the debtor's promise to another *and* in which the creditor agrees to the substitution of the debtors, one for the other.

EXAMPLE 8. An inventor transferred patents to a promoter for his promise of royalties and employment. The promoter assigned this contract and patents to a corporation. The corporation and inventor later modified the original agreement and substituted a new agreement. The inventor was not paid on her original employment contract by the corporation. The inventor then sued the promoter. The second agreement was a novation of the first by the express terms of the contract. The promoter was discharged as the original contract was discharged.

A contract is also discharged by accord and satisfaction. This occurs when a party gives a substituted performance in satisfaction of an existing legal duty (see Chapter 7, Consideration, Section 7.11).

13.10　DISCHARGE BY LEGAL EXCUSE

Contracts must have and must continue to have a legal purpose or they are void. Some contracts were originally valid but became invalid by reason of a change in the law or the effects the law places on some future event. The contract is then said to be discharged by legal excuse or operation of law. Common circumstances include (1) subsequent illegality, (2) destruction of the subject matter, (3) death, insanity, or illness, and (4) those claims barred by bankruptcy and statutes of limitation.

13.11　SUBSEQUENT ILLEGALITY

Public policy changes, and what was once lawful may now be unlawful. The legislature is a frequent source of changed public policy altering the effect of a previously valid contract. A contract to supply beer to a tavern for 5 years in a county which votes to go dry before the 5 years have passed is a classic example of subsequent illegality. But the rule is broader than alcohol cases.

EXAMPLE 9. Fidelity Lie Detector agreed to supply Plaza Department Store with polygraph service for 5 years at a specified fee for each examination. The state later enacted legislation requiring all polygraph operators to be legally certified. Each operator must now have a college degree and prove special competence. Fidelity's operators cannot qualify. The unexpired contract period is discharged by illegality. Neither Fidelity nor Plaza could sue the other for breach of contract.

13.12　DESTRUCTION OF THE SUBJECT MATTER

A contract is discharged if through no fault of either party the subject matter of the contract is destroyed. Further, the destruction of that which is necessary for the performance also excuses further performance by either party.

EXAMPLE 10. A sprinkler company agreed to install a sprinkler system for a warehouse. Midway through the installation the warehouse was destroyed by fire without fault of either party. The company wants to recover for part performance on *quantum meruit*. The subject matter of the contract was the "creation" of a sprinkler system. The continued existence of the building was necessary for creation in this instance. The destruction of the realty excuses both parties. Neither party could sue under the contract.

The identity of the subject matter is the critical test in applying this rule. If a builder, for example, agrees to construct a building which is destroyed by a hurricane when half completed, the builder is not excused. The builder's subject matter was the creation of a structure. The builder is required to start again at his or her own expense. Because of this rule, the issues of impossibility of performance and acts of God play a role in contract formation. Generally, impossibility of performance or a loss caused by an act of God does not necessarily excuse one from a contract. Accordingly, written contracts frequently provide that such events causing failure of performance do excuse.

EXAMPLE 11. A builder agrees to construct a warehouse according to specifications but provides that he "will not be liable for delays or loss caused by acts of God, strikes, or any other reason beyond the reasonable control of the builder." An earthquake damages the building before completion. The builder, according to the contract, can recover for his partial performance at the contract rate. The risk of nonperformance for that cause, the act of God, has shifted to the owner by the express terms of the contract. Some courts will imply that acts of God excuse performance.

A promise to deliver a particular racehorse, or 500 crates of oranges from a specified grove, identifies the subject matter as that horse or those oranges. The destruction of either discharges the contract. However, a promise to sell and deliver 500 crates of oranges the seller privately "intended," but did not express or imply to the other, to supply from this source identifies the subject matter as only any 500 crates of oranges. Therefore, a freezing of the seller's grove will not discharge the contract by the operation of the rule regarding destruction of the subject matter.

EXAMPLE 12. A seller of plywood drawer bottoms agreed to build to Oak Ridge Furniture Factory specifications. The factory intended to place these bottoms in its product, but the factory burned down. The factory no longer has need for the drawer bottoms. It claims the contract is discharged by the destruction of the subject matter. The court will rule that there was no discharge. The subject matter of the contract was the manufacture of plywood drawer bottoms. This was not discharged. The fact that these drawers are now of no practical use to the factory is immaterial.

13.13   DEATH, ILLNESS, OR INSANITY

Death, personal inability, or insanity of the contracting party does not, as a general rule, discharge a contract. Most contractual duties can be carried out by the representative of the party. But where the contract calls for distinctly personal effort yet to be performed, such events do discharge contracts and excuse the party. Promises by surgeons to operate, a lawyer to defend a client, or an author to write a book are promises of a decidedly personal nature and qualify as exceptions to the rule that death, illness, and insanity do not discharge a contract.

EXAMPLE 13. Mosco had odd tastes and plenty of money. He contracted with Italian Auto for a special car to be built for him, delivery December 1, 19X3, at Port of Miami. The features of the car were to most people eccentric. They included garish colors and chrome treatment in the "1950s" style. The price was $82,000. In late November 19X3, Mosco was killed in a boating accident. His wife was named personal representative of the estate. Her taste, except for her selection of Mosco, was excellent. She refused to accept this "personally designed car" and refused to pay, contending that death terminates a contract. However, all the representative has to do is pay the purchase price, and, accordingly, this contract is valid and enforceable.

13.14   BANKRUPTCY AND THE STATUTE OF LIMITATIONS

Technically, a debt listed in a bankruptcy schedule and discharged by the Federal Bankruptcy Court is not completely discharged. This discharge does, however, offer a legal excuse not to pay if the debtor elects to invoke it by a special procedure. In a similar way, a creditor who delays an unreasonable time in suing for breach of contract may also find his or her remedy barred at the election of the debtor. This reasonable time is the period beyond the time allotted by each state during which a legal action must be instituted. These time periods are found in laws called the *statute of limitations*. In each state the statute operates against stale claims and prescribes a period from as short as 1 year to as long as 20 years for certain rights. It applies only to relief at law, not equity courts. There is no fixed period for seeking equitable relief, although unreasonable delay, called *laches*, can bar a claim in equity. Under the UCC, Section 2-725, the period within which a lawsuit must be instituted for the sale of goods is 4 years.

EXAMPLE 14. A creditor supplied various pieces of boat equipment to a debtor over a 3-year period. Six years after the first sale the creditor filed suit for payment for items delivered as long as six years earlier. The debtor invokes the 4-year statute of limitations in the sale of goods. The creditor claims all the items were part of one big contract which ended 3 years ago. However, the invoices and bills showed separate purchases. Only those deliveries within the last 4 years can be sued upon.

Revival of debts whose remedies are barred by bankruptcy or the passage of time under the statute of limitations can sometimes be achieved without new consideration. A new promise or other conduct indicating acknowledgment of the old debt and an intention to pay is enforceable provided it meets a particular formality. In some states this formality includes a signed writing promising to pay the old claim.

13.15 IMPOSSIBILITY AND IMPRACTICALITY

While the law recognizes death or disability in personal contracts, and destruction of the subject matter in others, as legal impossibilities excusing further performance of discharging contracts, other events causing impossibility do not normally excuse or discharge. Ordinarily one desiring to protect himself or herself would therefore be required to identify such legal excuse as an express term in the contract itself.

EXAMPLE 15.   A builder contracted with an owner to finish construction of an addition by December 1, 19X3. Despite the builder's good relations with his own workers, they joined in a sympathy strike with the rest of the industry. It is now impossible for the builder to complete the addition by the contract date. The builder can be sued successfully for breach of contract by the owner. The builder should have placed a clause in his contract which would have excused him by reason of "strikes, delays in delivery, or any other reason beyond the control of the Builder."

The UCC, in Section 2-615(a), introduces the concept of impracticality by which nondelivery or delay in delivery of goods can be excused where "performance as agreed has been made impracticable by the occurrence of a contingency the non-occurrence of which was a basic assumption on which the contract was made . . . ." This matter will be treated further in the chapter on sales.

Black Letter Law
A Summary

1. As a general principle nothing except complete and exact performance discharges a contract.

2. An exception to the general principle is the contractor who can place his or her performance within the doctrine of substantial performance.

3. Substantial performance occurs where the performance is complete in all respects except for some minor deviations which were not made in bad faith.

4. The only recovery allowed a party who only partially performs is to sue in *quantum meruit* for the benefit received and retained by the other party.

5. A material breach of contract excuses performance of the other party who is said to be discharged from the contract but may sue for damages.

6. An anticipatory breach or repudiation occurs before the date of contracted-for performance by one party clearly expressing by words or conduct that he or she will not perform when due.

7. Where one party has fully performed and the other, before his or her promised performance to pay money, announces that he or she will not perform, the general rule provides that no anticipatory breach occurs which would permit an immediate action for breach.

8. An agreement to discharge occurs expressly, by release and novation, or by implication, in merger.

9. Some contracts are discharged by reason of death.

10. Death of the party expected to perform personal services, or whose existence is necessary, discharges the contract, as does physical inability by reason of illness or incompetency.

11. A subsequent illegality discharges an agreement which was otherwise valid at the time of the contract.

12. The destruction of the subject matter of the contract discharges the contract.

13. The legal obligation to perform may be excused by discharge in bankruptcy or the passage of time specified by the statute of limitations.

Solved Problems

13.1 A builder promised to construct a garage with a second-story apartment according to specifications for a total price of $55,000. Under which of the following circumstances can the builder properly sue for the contract price of $55,000?

(a) If the builder spent $70,000 in constructing 90 percent of the garage
(b) If the builder was ordered off the premises by the owner before he started work
(c) If the builder substantially performed, less damages for minor deviations
(d) If due to subsoil conditions the builder was unable to perform at all

Generally, only complete performance of the contract allows the contractor to sue for the contract price. Substantial performance, however, is an exception which allows an action for the contract price with the right of the other party to seek a reduction for the damages caused by the minor (but not bad faith), deviation, statement (c). To construct 90 percent of the job is usually a partial performance case, in which circumstances one cannot sue for the contract price. Where the contract is in its executory state, as indicated in statement (b), the measure of damages is different and is usually an action for the profit of the job.

13.2 Anticipatory breach or repudiation permits certain behavior by the nonbreaching party. Which of the following does it *not* permit?

(a) To sue immediately
(b) To wait for the date of the promised performance
(c) To refuse to accept performance later if the nonbreaching party has not changed his or her position
(d) To elect to do nothing

The contracting party suffering an anticipatory breach by the other has a number of options including each statement except (c). If the party who breaches by anticipation changes his or her mind and now desires to perform at the time set for performance, the other must accept such tender of performance, provided the nonbreaching party has not, in reliance on the other, changed his or her position to his or her detriment.

13.3 Which of the following does *not* indicate a breach of contract?

(a) One party prevents the other from performing.
(b) One party notifies the other that he or she will not perform on the contract date.

(c) One party refuses to tender performance at the contract date of performance.

(d) One party notifies the other that he or she may not be able to deliver the goods on the promised date.

With the exception of statement (d), all actions constitute evidence of a breach of contract. A statement that one *may* not be able to perform suggests anticipatory breach. However, in order that it qualify as such, the repudiation must be explicit and final. Statement (d) does not indicate a clear repudiation of the contract.

13.4 Monroe purchased a 10-acre land site from Acme Land Developers, Inc. He paid 10 percent at the closing and gave his note for the balance secured by a 20-year mortgage. Three years later, Monroe found it increasingly difficult to make payments on the note and finally defaulted. Acme Land threatened to accelerate the loan and foreclose if he continued in default. It told him either to get the money or to obtain an acceptable third party to assume the obligation. Monroe offered the land to Thompson for $1,000 less than the equity he had in the parcel. This was acceptable to Acme, and at the closing Thompson paid the arrearage, executed a new mortgage and note, and had title transferred to her name. Acme surrendered Monroe's note and mortgage to her. The transaction in question is a(n)

(a) assignment and delegation.

(b) third-party beneficiary contract.

(c) novation.

(d) purchase of land subject to a mortgage.

(*Adapted from AICPA Examination, November 1981*)

Statement (c) is the answer. Where it is the intention of both parties to an existing contract to substitute a third party for one of the parties, a novation occurs. It is not a third-party beneficiary contract since the creditor, Acme, did not obtain an additional debtor but a new one, discharging the old contractor. For the same reason there is no delegation. A new contract was entered into between Acme and Thompson as the old note and mortgage were canceled.

13.5 Denton delivered 4,000 crates of grapefruit to the buyer, Laddle, on credit. Laddle agreed to pay $6,700 on November 1, 19X3. Laddle was in financial trouble and, having had good relations with Denton, wanted to be up front with him. Accordingly, on June 1, 19X3, Laddle notified Denton not to expect payment on November 1 since Laddle wouldn't and couldn't pay. Which is the correct statement?

(a) Denton can sue Laddle immediately for punitive damages.

(b) Denton can sue Laddle immediately for anticipatory repudiation.

(c) Denton must wait until November 1, 19X3, before he can sue Laddle.

(d) Denton may either sue immediately or wait for the date of promised performance.

Clearly Laddle is repudiating the contract before the date she is required to perform. However, the rule of anticipatory breach is not generally applicable to contracts calling for the payment of money where the other party has fully performed his or her duty; the answer is (c). Accordingly, Denton must wait until November 1, 19X3, before bringing an action for breach.

13.6 Eppie undertook to stage a production of a popular play. He wired Ariel, a famous actress, offering her the lead role at $3,000 a week for a 10-week run. All the other terms were standard theater contract provisions. Ariel wired her acceptance and began rehearsals and completed the first week with fair success. At this time,

(a) if Ariel was able to continue to perform, a court would probably order specific performance.

(b) if Ariel became unable to perform because of illness, she could hold Eppie to his contract if she arranged for the appearance of a substitute star of at least equal fame and ability.

(c) if Ariel became ill and it appeared that she would miss a substantial number of performances, Eppie might terminate the contract but would be liable for payment for performances given.

(d) if Eppie is declared bankrupt and Ariel refuses to perform further, her refusal would not constitute a breach of contract.

Illness of a contractor is generally not an excuse for failure to perform, but an exception lies for those contracts calling for distinctly personal effort by the party who is ill, statement (c). Courts rarely order specific performance of a personal service contract due to the difficulty of enforcing such an order and the personal rights of a party. Eppie's bankruptcy would have no effect on Ariel's duty to perform for the bankrupt estate, that is, the creditor of Eppie.

13.7 The statute of limitations normally

(a) does *not* apply to written contracts.

(b) has *no* application to unilateral contracts.

(c) requires that the lawsuit be concluded within a specified period of time.

(d) commences (begins to run) from the date of the breach of a contract.

(*AICPA Examination, November 1976*)

The law requires that those with a legal complaint seek relief within a reasonable time. The time is set by state statute and varies in some jurisdictions according to the type of contract. Oral contracts, for example, usually have a shorter limitation period. Statutes of limitation, however, generally have one feature in common: the time begins from the date of the breach of contract, answer (d).

13.8 When a lengthy delay has occurred between the breach of a contract and the commencement of the lawsuit, the statute of limitations defense may be raised. The statute

(a) is 3 years, irrespective of the type of legal action the plaintiff is bringing.

(b) does *not* apply to an action brought in a court of equity.

(c) is a defense to recovery if the requisite period of time has elapsed.

(d) fixes a period of time in which the plaintiff must commence the action or be barred from recovery, regardless of the defendant's conduct during the period.

(*AICPA Examination, November 1981*)

The statute of limitations applies to actions at law, but does not apply to equity actions where the doctrine of laches (i.e., unreasonable delay) operates, statement (b). Where the defendant has during the period acknowledged the claim, it is possible that the period will be extended, using the date of acknowledgment as the date for calculating the new period of limitation. Statement (c) is also correct.

13.9 Golden Clocks manufactures grandfather clocks at its only factory, which is in Alabama. At the plant the workers had special machinery which allowed quality work under assembly line conditions. National Express was doing a promotion on these clocks and ordered 2,000 of them for May delivery. National Express sent out beautiful brochures promoting this sale. In April the plant suffered a severe fire which closed the plant. Golden Clocks is a solvent company, and National Express wants damages. What is Golden Clocks' best defense?

(*a*) The fire was an act of God, and acts of God excuse performance.

(*b*) Both parties contemplated the continued existence of the plant at the time of the contract.

(*c*) It would be inequitable to sue for damages under these circumstances.

(*d*) Golden Clocks had not purchased business interruption insurance.

The best defense would be legal excuse by reason of the destruction of the subject matter, statement (*b*). If the parties understood that the factory was to continue in existence in order for this contract to be performed, the destruction of the plant, without fault of the owner, would provide an excuse. Acts of God generally do not excuse performance unless such an excuse clause is expressly placed into the contract, but there is some authority to the contrary.

13.10 Info, Inc., was an information service which would provide up-to-date information of any kind for a fee. Taylor, a bookie, wanted to know the latest race results and hired Info to provide them during the winter horseracing season for a flat fee. Info rented a room in a hotel whose east-facing rooms overlooked the racetrack. A powerful zoom lens provided accurate race results to Info, which it immediately telephoned to Taylor. During the season the state legislature made illegal the communication of any race results by anyone within 15 minutes of any race. What is the status of the unexpired term of this contract?

(*a*) A contract legal when made remains legal until full performance.

(*b*) It is voidable by either party, if the parties wish.

(*c*) It remains in effect if an express provision of the contract stated that a subsequent illegality shall have no effect on this contract.

(*d*) It is discharged by subsequent illegality.

The executory portion of this contract is discharged by operation of law; the answer is (*d*). The parties have no option but to discontinue the contract, and each party is fully excused from its remaining performance under the contract.

13.11 Grant was awarded a contract to repair and renovate the city swimming pool for a price of $65,000. Grant was nearly finished with the task when a riot erupted in the city. The rioters did not overlook the swimming pool, and they damaged it extensively. Grant appeared before the city council and asked that the original contract be amended to compensate for the substantial additional cost necessary to fulfill the contract. The city council refused and ordered Grant to proceed and do his duty. Grant now argues that there was a destruction of the subject matter which excuses him from further performance. Further, the application of such rule, he contends, allows recovery for the work completed before the riot, which he calculates is 90 percent of the contract price.

What success will Grant have with this argument? State your decision and reasons for your conclusions.

It is true that a contract is discharged if through no fault of either party the subject matter of the contract was destroyed. Further, where repairs or additions are to be made on an existing structure, the accidental destruction of the structure discharges the duties of the parties. Grant's contention is that the continued existence of the pool was assumed by the parties and it was destroyed by the rioters. This, however, is not correct. The old pool is still there, though in damaged condition. Where the building or structure to be repaired is not destroyed but the contractor's work is damaged and it must be redone, performance is still possible. It is the contractor's duty to redo the work to complete his undertaking.

13.12 Carlotta was lonely, and Ripper Dance Studios was interested in teaching her to dance. After completing her first series of lessons under a $1,000 contract, she was informed that she had great potential for the dance. Her second contract was for $3,500, and like the first, the signed writing contained a clause stating that the contract was "noncancellable and nonrefundable." Just after Carlotta had signed a third contract, this time for $4,800, she suffered an illness which forced her into a wheelchair. She now needs money for medical bills and wants the return of the $4,800. The studio maintains that the contract expressly denies her a refund.

What legal theory is Carlotta's best chance for the return of the money? State your answer and reasons for your conclusion.

Death, personal inability, or insanity generally do not excuse a promisor from his or her obligation unless the performance can only be performed by the party so affected. The subject matter of the contract was lessons for Carlotta *personally*. Without her presence and participation, there could be no performance. Accordingly, her illness excuses further performance, and the contract is discharged by impossibility. The argument contending that the parties expressly provided for this possibility is met with the argument that the words chosen by the dance studio in its written contract do not show that the parties anticipated her death or illness as no excuse. Because the contract required her personal participation, Carlotta can probably argue discharge by impossibility of performance due to illness.

13.13 Carl Stronhart, a local contractor, entered into a contract with Bennet Township for the construction of a storm sewer system in the canal district. The contract documents specified in detail the type and quality of material to be used in the work, what the work was to amount to, and where it was to be done. The only procedures not mentioned were the mechanical details of excavation and construction. Stronhart had never incorporated and was the sole owner of his contracting business. When the sewer contract was about 75 percent completed, Stronhart suffered a fatal heart attack. His estate, through the personal representative, attempted to carry on the sewer work but fell far behind. The township could wait no longer and declared the contract in default. The township then sued the estate of Stronhart for damages.

What defense will the estate attempt to offer in this lawsuit? State the defense, your conclusion regarding the case, and reasons for such.

Generally, death does not discharge contracts, and the personal representative of the decedent is responsible on all contracts entered into by the decedent in his lifetime. However, in this case the estate may wish to bring these facts within an exception to the rule. This exception provides that where the agreement is for services which involve the peculiar skill of an expert, who alone in the contemplation of the parties can perform, death will discharge the contract. The same also holds true in circumstances where distinctly personal considerations are at the foundation of the contract. The estate should try to show that the township relied on the special skill or professional competency of the decedent. Only then could the estate succeed. Unfortunately for the estate, however, the contract documents apparently reflect sufficient detail and specifications for another contractor to perform the duties. In these circumstances, it is difficult to see how the estate can successfully defend on this exception.

Chapter 14

Remedies

14.1 PURPOSE OF REMEDIES

The law cannot order the exact reproduction of the performance expected by the parties to a contract. However, the law does provide sanctions or remedies to encourage performance or to compensate for the loss or injury suffered. Remedies fall into two main categories: money damages awarded by a law court and other (i.e., extraordinary) relief issued by a court of equity.

14.2 DAMAGES: GENERALLY

Damages are monies ordered by the court to be paid by the party breaching the contract. By classification damages may be compensatory, liquidated, nominal, or exemplary (punitive).

14.3 COMPENSATORY DAMAGES

Money awarded to compensate the nonbreaching party for the loss of the expected performance is called *compensatory damages*. Such damages must legally and actually flow from the breach of contract as to cause and effect. Compensatory damages must be proved with reasonable certainty by the injured party, who must also attempt to mitigate the loss. Measures of damages are, however, limited by precedent and do not accommodate all the losses suffered as a matter of fact.

EXAMPLE 1. A department store sells a camera on credit to a buyer for $190. Repeated efforts to collect the price fail. Two years later the store institutes suit. The store must initially pay the filing fee ($10 to $30) and a sheriff's fee to serve the process and engage an attorney to prepare and prosecute the suit. If legally successful, the buyer will be ordered to pay (by judgment) the court costs, the filing fee, the service fee, the contract price, and interest on the debt for the 2 years. The price and interest are compensatory damages; the others are court costs. Notice that unless the contract called for attorney's fees, the store must pay its own attorney.

Damages for different types of contract breaches have traditionally different measures. A delay in performance, for example, is measured by the use value of the performance during the delay. Failure to deliver goods ordered is measured by the dollar difference between the contract price and the market price at the time and place of the breach. These are measures of actual damages. They are many in number according to the type of contract and breach. These actual damages are called *general* damages, as they apply generally to all similar types of contract breaches. Sometimes types of damages are claimed which go beyond the ordinary measures of general damages. When such extraordinary damage is alleged, the injured party is seeking special, or consequential, damages. *Special* damages are those resulting from particular circumstances reasonably known to the breaching party at the time of the agreement. If special damages are not within the contemplation of the parties at the time of the contract, such damages will not be recovered.

EXAMPLE 2. A widow rented out her garage apartment for years. She decided to replace the garage with a new building. The builder agreed to construct and complete by May 1. Several months after the contract and during construction, the widow rented out the apartment beginning May 1 to some newlyweds at the premium

117

price of $425 a month. The builder did not finish until September 1. The widow claims damages for 4 months at $425 a month. The builder proves that the reasonable rental for like facilities in the community is $300 a month. The widow can only recover general damages of $300 a month. The builder did not know at time of contract of the special damages she would suffer, that is, of a premium renter. Special, or consequential, damages unknown at time of contract cannot be recovered.

14.4 LIQUIDATED DAMAGES

When a party expressly sets forth an amount or formula for calculating potential damages for breach, the contract contains what is variously called a liquidated, stipulated, agreed-upon, penalty, or forfeiture clause. What the parties call the clause does not determine its enforceability. When a court upholds such a clause it will characterize it as a liquidated damage clause. Conversely, when a court refuses to enforce such a clause it is because it has found it to be a penalty or forfeiture clause which the law will not honor. A liquidated damage clause will be enforced only if it meets certain requirements. Generally, if (1) the injury caused by the potential breach is incapable of accurate estimation or even difficult to accurately estimate and (2) the sum or formula fixed is a reasonable forecast of just compensation, the terms will be enforced. If both conditions are not met, the clause will be labeled a penalty or forfeiture and be struck down.

EXAMPLE 3. The government withheld $8,300 as liquidated damage for delay in the performance of four construction contracts. The damage clause was $100 a day on one contract and $50 a day on the three others. The contractor contends that these are penalties. The court ruled that today courts do not look with disfavor on liquidated damage clauses and it is up to the breaching party to prove this was unreasonable at the time of the contract.

14.5 NOMINAL DAMAGES

An unexcused failure to perform a contract is a legal wrong. The nonbreaching party may sue even though no actual damages are legally proved. In such cases the party is awarded *nominal* damages, damages in name only. This is usually a token amount such as $1 or a few cents. Court costs can usually be tacked on to the recovery. Sometimes the party suing only wants to label the other as a contract breaker. However, most parties who are awarded nominal damages obtain them because they failed to meet the burden of legally proving that actual damages were suffered.

EXAMPLE 4. A warehouse agreed to store Baker's piano on the fifth floor of the warehouse. Without Baker's knowledge or consent, the warehouse stored the piano in the basement, a breach of the contract. A fire totally destroyed the warehouse and all its contents. Baker cannot recover the value of the piano unless he can show that the piano would not have been destroyed had it been on the fifth floor. Baker is entitled to nominal damages only, a dollar or a few cents.

14.6 EXEMPLARY DAMAGES

Exemplary or punitive damages are awarded on an increased scale over and above the other types of damages. Exemplary damages are levied for the wrong done as aggravated by circumstances of violence or fraud, or wanton or willful conduct, of the breaching party.

EXAMPLE 5. Fern Caterers faced tough competition in town. Fern is vulnerable to breakdown in delivery. Fern contracts with Laslo Rents for backup on delivery in a 2-year contract. Laslo later buys into a competing catering business, and his first act is an intentional breach of the contract with Fern. Fern sues for punitive as well as compensatory damages. Some states allow exemplary damages arising from willful behavior in breaching a contract. In such states punitive damages would lie, but generally punitive damages are rarely granted in contract cases.

14.7   CERTAINTY AND MITIGATION

Damages must be proved with reasonable certainty, and the injured party must attempt to mitigate damages in appropriate circumstances. The precise amount of damages need not be offered, but reasonable proof is necessary. Speculative damages will not be awarded. Lost profit, for example, is generally held to be speculative and not recoverable if it is based on no past experience. If, however, the business has had experience, such sums are provable upon sufficient grounds for such expectation.

EXAMPLE 6.   A builder sued a subcontractor for damages due to defective tile work in 800 bathrooms in a housing project. The builder had actually inspected 75 bathrooms and testified about their condition. The court awarded the builder $7,593 for these defects in the 75 bathrooms. The builder claims that she should be awarded damages for the defects in the other 725 units. The court awarded no recovery for these units. Direct testimony regarding the condition of the other units must be offered. No inescapable inference regarding the 725 bathrooms not inspected can be drawn from the condition of the 75 inspected bathrooms.

The injured party need only take those actions reasonable under the circumstances to mitigate or diminish the damage. The attempt to mitigate, where appropriate, must be made, and the fact that it did not result in diminishing the damage does not affect the rule.

EXAMPLE 7.   A publisher of entertainment passbooks sued a theater chain for its failure to honor 5,000 passbooks. The publisher claimed loss of anticipated profits of $13,000 from the unsold 3,674 passbooks. The publisher was under a duty to try to promote and sell the 3,674 books at a reduced price, tearing out the chain's coupons. The publisher did not try to mitigate damages.

The type of action necessary to mitigate is dependent on the type of contract breached. An employer who wrongly discharges an employee, for example, must prove that the employee could have obtained a position of similar character in the community before using the mitigation doctrine against the injured party.

14.8   OTHER RELIEF: EQUITY

Where the award of money damages is insufficient or inadequate, the court may award equitable relief. The equity court is a court of conscience. It need not, as a matter of law, always grant the relief sought, even if the party has breached a contract. In contrast, a law court which awards damages as explained above must grant the relief requested where it is proved that the contract was breached. The equity court, in determining whether or not to grant extraordinary relief, is guided by certain principles called *maxims of equity*. They include the following: equity aids the diligent; equity abhors delay; equity requires the party seeking relief to come into court with clean hands; and equity is equality.

The extraordinary relief sought in equity includes orders that a party perform an act or cease to so act. It is other than an order for the payment of money alone. Equitable remedies relating to contract enforcement include petitions seeking rescission of the contract, cancellation, reformation, specific performance, injunctions, and accounting.

14.9   RESCISSION

When one requests the court to set aside a contract, the equity court is asked to decree a rescission of the contract. Voidable contracts are subject to this type of relief. They include a defrauded party's request for avoidance as well as the minor's seeking to be relieved of his or her prior promise to perform. Equitable maxims apply in rescission petitions, and frequently the court restricts such a remedy to cases where the parties can be placed back in the *status quo ante*.

14.10 CANCELLATION

Equity courts have broad powers, and in those instances in which a contract was decreed rescinded, the aftereffects can also be addressed. The decree of cancellation is available where, for example, a deed was placed on record in performance of a contract which was later avoided by a rescission. The equity court possesses the power to cancel the instrument of record.

14.11 REFORMATION

Equity courts possess powers to correct or reform an instrument to prevent manifest injustice or to express the real intention of the parties. When the court does so, it orders a reformation of the accused instrument.

EXAMPLE 8. A church contracted with a subdivider for sale of certain property under special terms regarding assessments. The deed placed on record by the subdivider did not contain the promised assessment clause. The church sues for the reformation of the recorded deed to reflect the true agreement of the parties. The court ruled for the church. If an instrument as written fails to express the true agreement, equity may exercise the remedy of reformation.

14.12 SPECIFIC PERFORMANCE

A decree of specific performance is an order of an equity court requiring the contracting party to do what was promised in the contract. A failure to perform as ordered is contempt of court, punishable by fine and/or imprisonment. It is an extraordinary remedy which courts are reluctant to exercise. Further, courts will not decree specific performance when it cannot, as a practical matter, be enforced.

EXAMPLE 9. Trevor contracted to purchase 5,000 crates of Florida avocados from a grower and a vacant lot from a developer, and he hired Laslow as produce manager for a period of 2 years. If the grower refused to ship, the equity court will not usually decree specific performance for goods that are not unique. Land is, by law, unique, and the court would specifically enforce that contract. It would not grant equitable relief and force Laslow to remain in her job, for this would effectively force Laslow into a form of slavery.

When an equity court rules that the remedy at law (money damages) would be adequate, the party may seek law relief. The equity court does have jurisdiction to award money damages but will not do so unless it is also granting equitable relief in the case.

Under Section 2-716 of the UCC, a promise to sell goods is specifically enforceable in instances when the goods are unique or in the case of "other proper circumstances."

EXAMPLE 10. An airline had a fuel supply contract with a dealer. During a national oil shortage the dealer breached the contract. The airline sued for specific performance. The dealer contended that aviation fuel is not unique goods. The court ruled that, under the UCC, the combination of the national oil shortage and the airline's need for fuel constituted such "other proper circumstances," allowing the court to order specific performance.

14.13 INJUNCTIONS

An injunction is a court order requiring a party to do or refrain from doing something. A mandatory injunction is like a decree of specific performance, as it orders an act to be performed. Mandatory injunctions, unlike petitions for specific performance, are usually applicable to noncontractual situations. The prohibitory injunction is an order to refrain from doing an act and is frequently petitioned in contract litigation. The employee's promise not to compete with the employer upon termination of employment, for example, is a common promise that the court may enforce by issuing a prohibitory injunction. This is a powerful remedy, and courts are reluctant to order a permanent injunction, but under proper circumstances will award a temporary injunction.

EXAMPLE 11. An automaker and a franchise dealer have a dispute. The automaker attempted to fire the dealer after 30 years of service under the franchise contract term allowing dismissal for cause if the dealer does not sell up to market situation. The dealer wants a chance to dispute this fact while not shutting down his ongoing business. This is an appropriate circumstance for awarding a temporary injunction pending review of the contract dispute.

14.14 ACCOUNTING

Law courts have the power to enforce contract demands involving an accounting, but equity courts are more likely to apply the relief appropriate to the problem. A withdrawing partner, for example, who was not privy to the partnership books and who felt aggrieved with the offered share would not know how much to sue for. A petition in equity for an accounting would address this problem. The equity court can appoint a special master or referee to examine the books and report findings to the judge. When the court entertains such relief, it is exercising the right to grant an accounting. Accounting is also the appropriate request of dissatisfied beneficiaries under a trust or estate. It provides them access to the status of their interest in the funds by an independent and competent fact finder.

14.15 ELECTION OF REMEDIES AND WAIVER

It is not unusual for a party to have more than one remedy for a breach of the contract by the other party. Sometimes the remedies are mutually exclusive. That is, the injured party must choose which remedy to pursue. Whichever remedy the injured elects, he or she loses the right to pursue the other.

EXAMPLE 12. Robin was a top saleswoman for Tug Company, and the company knew it. Under Robin's contract of employment, she agreed not to compete upon termination for a period of 1 year in the sales territory. Robin left the firm and began her own business in the restricted area. Tug sued Robin in law, seeking the money damages it claimed to have lost by this competition. Tug's decision to seek law relief in the way of money damages is an election of remedies. Tug may no longer consider suing for equitable relief, such as an injunction.

A right can also be lost under the *doctrine of waiver*, which is defined as the voluntary or intentional relinquishment of a known right. For example, the failure of a party to rescind promptly under circumstances where one possesses the right can result in a waiver.

EXAMPLE 13. Don contracted with a builder to purchase a model home for $125,000, closing by May 1, 19X4, with the contract providing that "time was of the essence." Don, having difficulty in obtaining financing, asked the builder for an additional 30 days to find money to close the transaction. The builder agreed. Don then found that his uncle would loan the money but he must first cash some bonds, prematurely. This was done. Don was nearly ready to close when the builder telephoned, saying that "I am sorry but I have changed my mind about the 30-day extension." The builder could be bound on his promise under the doctrine of waiver, as Don, relying on the promise, did change his position.

Where the sale of goods is involved, Section 2-209(5) of the UCC provides that a party who has made a waiver affecting the "executory portion of the contract may retract the waiver by reasonable notification received by the other party that strict performance would be required of any term waived unless the retraction would be unjust in view of a material change of position in reliance on the waiver."

Black Letter Law
A Summary

1. Remedies fall into two main classes: money damages at law and other relief granted in equity.

2. Money damages are awarded by the court to compensate for the loss of expected performance by the breaching party.

3. Compensatory damages must legally and actually flow from the breach of contract.

4. Compensatory damages are either general or special.

5. General damages are those which courts normally consider as the natural result of the particular type of breach of contract.

6. Special, or consequential, damages are those that do not directly flow from the breach but were, or should have been, within the reasonable contemplation of the parties at the time of the contract.

7. A stipulated damage clause in a contract will be enforced if a court finds it to be a liquidated damage clause rather than a penalty or forfeiture clause.

8. A stipulated damage clause is a liquidated clause (a) when the parties had some difficulty in making an accurate estimate of the possible damage at the time of the contract and (b) when the amount set was reasonable in the light of actual or expected damage.

9. Nominal damages, in name only, are trivial money amounts awarded the successful party when such party either suffered no loss or failed to prove loss within the legal rules.

10. Exemplary or punitive damages are awarded to punish a party and are granted in addition to compensatory damages where wrongful conduct of a tortious nature occurred.

11. Damages must be proved with reasonable certainty, and the injured party must attempt to mitigate the damages by reasonable efforts.

12. Equitable relief is extraordinary relief, granted at the discretion of the court in appropriate circumstances, and is other than money damages.

13. In order to be granted equitable relief, the petitioner must show that his or her remedy at law (i.e., money damages) would be inadequate.

14. Since relief in equity is discretionary with the court, many equity maxims guide the courts in deciding such petitions.

15. The most common forms of equitable relief are those granting specific performance of contracts and those granting injunctions.

16. Other forms of equitable relief affecting contracts include rescission, cancellation, reformation, and the granting of an accounting.

17. Specific performance is generally granted to enforce the sale of real property or unique personal property and is also granted, under the UCC, "in other proper circumstances."

Solved Problems

14.1 The Johnson Corporation sent its only pump to the manufacturer to be repaired. It engaged Travis, a local trucking company, both to deliver the equipment to the manufacturer and to redeliver it to Johnson promptly upon completion of the repair. Johnson's entire plant was inoperative without this pump, but the trucking company did not know this. The trucking company was delayed several days in its delivery of the repaired pump to Johnson. During the time it expected to be without the pump, Johnson incurred $5,000 in lost profits. At the end of that time Johnson rented a replacement pump at a cost of $200 per day. As a result of these facts, what is Johnson entitled to recover from Travis?

    (*a*)   The $200-a-day cost incurred in renting the pump.

    (*b*)   The $200-a-day cost incurred in renting the pump plus the lost profits.

    (*c*)   Actual damages plus punitive damages.

    (*d*)   Nothing, because Travis is *not* liable for damages.

(*AICPA Examination, May 1978*)

    Only compensatory damages are available for this breach, and they are those damages that naturally flow from the breach, statement (*a*) is the answer. Since the additional damage in the form of lost profits could have been prevented by renting a pump at $200 a day, such should have been done. Only if Travis knew, or should have known, at the time of the contract that this was the only pump available and such loss of profits (called special damages) could be the result of Travis's delay, could these funds be recovered. The award here will be general damages only.

14.2 Anton agreed to purchase Toby's house for $82,000. Due to financial difficulties he was unable to complete the sale. The market value of the house is $75,000. If Toby sues Anton for breach of contract, what is the proper amount of damages to be recovered?

    (*a*)   The court will award nominal damages, as Anton has financial difficulties.

    (*b*)   Toby should be awarded compensatory damages in the amount of $7,000, the difference between the contract price and the market price.

    (*c*)   This is a typical case for punitive or exemplary damage.

    (*d*)   Since there is no liquidated damage clause, there can be no recovery.

    Toby is entitled to the difference between the contract price and the market price of the house, statement (*b*). The fact that Anton has financial difficulties is immaterial. Anton's conduct was not such as to warrant punitive or exemplary damages; he just couldn't come up with the money. Absence of a liquidated damage clause is not a bar to recovery of compensatory damages.

14.3 Ortez entered into an employment contract with Ronsin & Company by which Ortez was to be a consultant on the company's oil rigs for 2 years at a salary of $65,000 a year. If Ortez was fired without cause after 1 year, which of the following describes Ortez's rights and duties?

    (*a*)   Ortez must find a job immediately and use the wages earned to diminish the amount of damages he suffered.

    (*b*)   Ortez may take a vacation to get over the shock and then attempt to find some job.

    (*c*)   Ortez has a duty to try to mitigate damages, and if he does not succeed in doing so, he can recover nothing.

    (*d*)   Ortez must attempt to mitigate damages by looking for a position of similar rank and dignity in the community.

    Ortez is entitled to recover the full compensation due him under the contract, less any sums earned in a job of similar rank and dignity in the community; statement (*d*) is correct. If he cannot find such a job in his community, he may nevertheless still recover the full amount to which he would have been entitled.

14.4   Ribbon Paving was having a hard time financially. The company finally found Easy Development needing considerable paving in a subdivision. Easy was willing to award Ribbon the job and prepared the contract. Ribbon, in reading the document, found one clause it didn't particularly care for. The clause provided for a completion date of May 1, 19X3, and for each day of delay by Ribbon a damage payment of $5,000 per day. The entire contract price was $55,000. The damage clause

(*a*)   is enforceable as it states a valid liquidated damage clause.

(*b*)   is enforceable provided Ribbon did not sign under duress.

(*c*)   is probably unenforceable if it is not a reasonable forecast of probable losses caused by each day's delay.

(*d*)   is effective provided the parties were in equal bargaining positions.

Liquidated damage clauses must be judged by circumstances at the time of the contract. If the damage which would be caused by delay is difficult to forecast and the sum fixed is a reasonable estimate of just compensation, the clause is enforceable. Here, the amount set per day appears to be grossly disproportionate to the possible loss or injury, and the clause would probably fail, statement (*c*). If the court declares the clause a penalty, it is unenforceable. At first glance it appears to be an *in terrorem* clause, that is, a warning not to breach and hence not enforceable.

14.5   Tonson found a hot business site next to a new park attraction. She contracted to have her take-out food restaurant constructed by Barren Builders for $110,000. Due to financial difficulties, Barren did not start promptly and, after beginning, had to walk away from the contract. In addition to general damages, Tonson wishes to offer the court proof that if the new restaurant had been built within the contract time, it would have earned $42,000 in the first year after completion. What defense should Barren offer to counter this type of proof?

(*a*)   Barren should contend that it had no idea that Tonson expected to make a profit the first year.

(*b*)   Barren should offer that expected profits of a new business are generally speculative and are not certain enough to be included in the measure of damages.

(*c*)   Barren should argue that Tonson should have mitigated damages by purchasing a business interruption insurance policy.

(*d*)   Barren should show that it has insufficient assets to pay such a claim.

General damages in compensation of the injury suffered must legally and actually flow from the breach as cause and effect. They must be proved with reasonable certainty. Lost profits of a new business generally are considered speculative and rarely allowed; (*b*) is the correct answer.

14.6   Great Northeastern Company employed Taylor Security Electronics to wire its Red River Plant for a contract price of $85,000. Taylor delayed and lied to Great Northeastern's president, telling him that the company would perform when it actually had no intention of doing so, being tied up with a more lucrative contract. The president was furious and hired a competitor who needed the work. The competitor finished the job within the original contract time and did a fine job for $80,000. However, the president was not satisfied with Taylor's behavior, and his board of directors agreed. To teach Taylor a lesson, Great Northeastern filed a breach of contract action against Taylor. What kind of damages will Great Northeastern recover?

    (*a*) Nominal

    (*b*) Special

    (*c*) General

    (*d*) Punitive or exemplary

      An unexcused failure to perform a contract is a legal wrong, and the nonbreaching party may sue even though no actual damages are proved. In such cases, the suing party is awarded nominal damages, damages that are in name only; statement (*a*) is the answer. The deliberate act of Taylor in breaching the contract is just that, a breach. The circumstances do not qualify as malicious, fraudulent, or other wrongful conduct. Therefore, punitive damages would normally not lie.

14.7 The remedy of specific performance is available where the subject matter of the contract involves

    (*a*) services.

    (*b*) goods with a price of $500 or more.

    (*c*) fraud.

    (*d*) land.

    (*AICPA Examination, May 1976*)

      Specific performance of contracts is an extraordinary remedy. It is granted in cases of unique property. Land by itself is unique, as there is no other identical location; the answer is (*d*). A contract for the sale of goods can be the proper subject of an action for specific performance provided the goods are unique, or in other appropriate circumstances.

14.8 Special or consequential damages are awarded by the court providing

    (*a*) the damages actually flowed from the breach.

    (*b*) the plaintiff shows that these special damages were likely to occur if the contract was breached.

    (*c*) the defendant had reason to know the particular damages that might flow from the breach at the time of the contract.

    (*d*) they are not unreasonable in amount.

      Sometimes damages are claimed which are not ordinarily expected by the court to occur from that type of breach. When extraordinary damage is pursued, the injured party is seeking special, or consequential, damages. If such damages were, in the judgment of the court, within the contemplation of the parties at the time of the contract, they can be recovered against the defendant; statement (*c*) is the answer.

14.9 Burt was a minor when he signed a contract for the purchase of a car. He finds that he can't continue to make payments and wants to return the car to the dealer. What type of legal remedy would Burt attempt to obtain?

    (*a*) An action for specific performance

    (*b*) A plea for an injunction

    (*c*) An action for a rescission

    (*d*) A bill for an accounting

      When Burt requests the court for an order to set aside the contract, the equity court is asked to decree a rescission of the contract, statement (*c*). Burt will have the burden of proving that he was a minor at the time of the contract and that a reasonable time has not passed since he attained majority.

14.10 The parties entered into a formal written contract. Due to an oversight on the part of both, paragraph 8 calls for an 11 percent commission rather than 10 percent. Several weeks later the party who must pay the commission notices this error and wants it corrected. The other party resists. What type of action must be brought to correct the mistake?

(*a*) Rescission

(*b*) Cancellation

(*c*) Reformation

(*d*) Injunction

Equity courts possess powers to correct or reform an instrument to prevent a manifest injustice or to express the real intention of the parties, statement (*c*). However, the burden will be on the party bringing the suit to prove that the intention was other than that expressed in the contract. This is sometimes a heavy burden in the face of conflicting testimony and the parol evidence rule.

14.11 Tara was a recognized movie character actress who had sung in many successful musical comedy films. She was signed by Pegasus Films for the film *Musical Lights* for the sum of $350,000 plus 2 percent of the net proceeds. It was a fine role in which she was to sing two numbers. The film was to be shot in the Hollywood studio of Pegasus, starting 2 months hence for a 6-week production period. Studio management changed, and the film project was shelved. Pegasus assured Tara that it would provide her with a substitute film. After 2 weeks it offered her a supporting role in *The Last Martian*, to be filmed in the Arizona desert for 5 weeks. It was a straight character role with a serious theme. Pegasus offered her $200,000 plus 10 percent of the net proceeds. This offer was unacceptable to Tara, who sued the studio seeking recovery of the agreed guaranteed compensation of $350,000. The studio defended on the grounds that Tara refused to mitigate damages by accepting substitute employment.

What success will Tara have in suing the studio? State your decision and reasons for your conclusions.

The measure of recovery by a wrongfully discharged employee is the amount of the salary agreed upon for the period of service less the amount the employer affirmatively proves the employee has earned or with reasonable effort might have earned from other employment. Before projected earnings from other opportunities not sought or accepted can be applied in mitigation, the employer must show that the other employment was comparable or substantially similar to that of which the employee was deprived. In this case the other film offered employment that was both different and inferior. Further, it was at a different locale, the roles were substantially different, and the financial terms were different. Tara can collect the entire salary guaranteed under the original contract.

14.12 A buyer entered into a contract with a seller for the purchase of land at a price of $30,000, $3,000 down and settlement and conveyance in 90 days. The contract contained a clause providing that the failure of the buyer to close as promised would result in the forfeiture of the money deposited by the buyer under the contract. The buyer was having difficulty finding the money to close the transaction, as he was expecting money which was tied up in probate. The seller agreed to extend the settlement date for an additional 90 days for a $1,000 payment. The buyer paid the $1,000 but still couldn't come up with the money for closing. Finally, the seller declared the buyer in default and kept the money paid over. Six months later, the seller sold the same parcel of land to a third person for $30,000. The buyer, assuming that the seller lost no money on the deal, sued to recover the $4,000 he had paid to the seller. The seller claims that the terms of the contract, including the stipulated damage clause, settle the issue, as the $4,000 in deposit money is liquidated damages for the buyer's breach of contract.

Can the buyer recover his deposit and the additional $1,000? State your decision and your reasons for any conclusions.

In determining whether a contractual provision provides for a penalty which is unenforceable, or a liquidated damage clause which is valid, several tests are made. First, the ease or difficulty of measuring the damages and, second, the reasonableness of the sum or formula adopted in relation to the extent of the injury. In land contracts, the seller may have many continuing obligations in regard to ownership. These include interest on loans, insurance, taxes, etc., which must be paid until the land is sold. The value of the land is likewise a problem. In many areas or neighborhoods, sales are not frequent enough to allow for an accurate estimate of worth. Under such circumstances, the 10 percent deposit acting as liquidated damages was not disproportionate to the probable damages the seller suffered. As to the other $1,000 paid, such was consideration for a valuable extension of time. The fact that the seller was able to sell the land for an identical price 6 months later does not undermine the reasonableness of the stipulated damage clause. This is a fully enforceable liquidated damage clause. The buyer will take nothing from his lawsuit.

14.13 Oldtyme Development entered into an installment sales contract with Hugh Ritter, a local landowner, by which Ritter sold 30 acres of unimproved land to Oldtyme. This agreement was reached after extensive negotiation which included Ritter's approval of the design and layout of the new subdivision. After the sale and conveyance, Oldtyme discovered that the property was 5.76 acres less than promised. This deficiency required a survey and a redesign of the project. These actions cost Oldtyme $10,270 in expenses. Oldtyme demanded that Ritter reimburse it for these expenses. When Ritter refused, Oldtyme withheld monthly installments under the contract so as to retrieve this money. Ritter then sued Oldtyme for its breach of contract for failure to make monthly payments. Oldtyme counterclaimed for the $10,270.

What theory of damages is Oldtyme invoking in attempting to recover the $10,270? State the theory, a decision in the case, and your reasons for your conclusions.

Oldtyme is seeking compensatory damages that are special in nature. To be recoverable, damages must be the direct and natural result of the breach and within the contemplation of the parties at the time of the contract. Oldtyme claims Ritter knew of its plans and saw that such required the full 30 acres. It would contend that Ritter knew, or should have known, that a deficiency in acreage would require a new survey and redesign of the project. The court could properly find that the deficiency necessitated the survey and redesign. The second requirement—contemplation—is more difficult to prove. It, however, does not require evidence that the parties actually discussed or otherwise actively contemplated each potential damage claim. It is sufficient that damage be such as the parties may fairly be supposed to have considered. Viewing the specific interest the seller, Ritter, took in the design of the subdivision, a jury could reasonably find such contemplation of the parties. The buyer could collect the special damages as compensation for the seller's breach.

Topic Test, Part II

Contracts

It is not enough that the student know basic legal principles which govern business transactions. It is also necessary that one be able to recognize the legal elements in factual situations unaccompanied by a label identifying the issue as one involving consideration, capacity, offer and acceptance, etc. The following questions provide an opportunity to characterize each problem and identify the legal question involved. Whether or not one can predict the outcome, it is important that one be able to identify the legal issue in each situation described.

1. Adam was running for town mayor; the election was to be held on May 5. Larson Badge Company, a local outfit, was pleased on January 15 to sign Adam to a contract for 5,000 campaign badges at $750, delivery March 15. The contract was in writing on Larson's order form which, except for the names, price, and date of delivery, contained no other language. Larson was proceeding nicely with the manufacture of the badges in late February when it suffered an illegal strike by its employees. No product left the plant, and completion of the order had to wait for the labor settlement on May 1. The 5,000 badges were manufactured and finally delivered on May 10. Adam lost the election and refused to pay anything for the badges. What legal principles are involved in Larson's lawsuit for the $750?

2. Johnsone was a clever real estate broker and at times too clever for some clients. He had some difficulty getting a real estate listing from the Taylors, who believed they could sell their property themselves. Johnsone persisted, however, and got the Taylors to sign a multiple-listing contract with exclusive right to sell, orally telling the Taylors that this writing would not prevent them from selling the property themselves and thereby avoiding payment of a commission. The listing agreement clearly precluded this. The Taylors then signed. The Taylors published a newspaper ad and sold their own property. Johnsone was happy for them, and for himself, as he demanded his 7 percent commission. What legal difficulty will the Taylors have to overcome to resist Johnsone's claim for a commission?

3. Gourd's Department Store was ruled by old man Gourd, a hard but fair taskmaster. He paid well but stood for no nonsense from his employees. He expected that they would be all business and keep their personal affairs at home. Santer, the manager of the store's paint department, was going through a difficult divorce action and, in an attempt to save his property, needed the services of Torrence, an expensive attorney. Santer had a cash flow problem, and in January 19X3, he signed over to Torrence his (Santer's) pay for the coming month of March 19X3. At the end of March 19X3, Torrence approached Gourd and demanded Santer's March pay. Gourd ordered Torrence out of the store, stating that he wouldn't honor any such agreement between Torrence and Santer, claiming that he "could fire Santer any day he wanted to." That statement was true. What legal principles should Gourd be aware of?

4. A buyer agreed to purchase vacant land for $7,500. The buyer put $2,500 in escrow with a bank. The written contract provided, among other things, that "in the event of a default in performance by the buyer" the money in escrow would be turned over to the seller. The buyer ran into some financial difficulties and decided not to go through with the deal. The seller

128

demanded the $2,500 from the bank. The buyer ordered the bank to return the money to the buyer. It appeared that as a result of this contract, the seller now owed her broker a $525 commission and her attorney $150, and though she now had another buyer ready to purchase the land, she did not have the cash to pay her broker and attorney the $675 she owed them. What legal principle is involved in this dispute, and what factors will determine the outcome?

5. Brattle sold goods on credit to Mansy Corporation and was unpaid in the sum of $7,200. Warner, vice president of Mansy, was quite ambitious. Warner knew that Brattle could put some pressure on the Mansy stockholders, and so at a cocktail party Warner told Brattle that "if you use your efforts to make me the next president of Mansy, I will personally guarantee the payment of the obligation you are so worried about." Brattle quickly told Warner, "It's a deal." Brattle used his influence, and Warner was elected president of Mansy Corporation. Unfortunately, Mansy did no better under Warner's management. Brattle would like to look to Warner personally for the $7,200. What legal difficulty will Brattle have in this desire?

6. Quick Fix Construction agreed to deliver a certain model prefabricated house to Marion for $47,250. Completion was due on September 27, 19X3. At 3:30 p.m. on that day, Marion arrived at the building site. She found a crash program being executed. Workers were all over the place, slapping on siding, laying the floors, bulldozing the yard, and hooking up utilities. The foreman told Marion to wait until 5:30 p.m. Marion refused and left. At 5:30 p.m. nearly all the work was done with only a service walk, some grading, and blacktopping left undone. Marion claims that the contract expressly stated that "time is of the essence" and that she is not obligated to accept the property. Quick Fix wants to sue for the contract price. What legal principle will Quick Fix attempt to invoke?

7. Florence had never invested in anything sophisticated and wished to try her hand at it. She was intrigued by Aversee, a Hollywood producer who told her that there was an opportunity with a new film. Florence wanted something more specific, and Aversee assured her that "the distribution arrangements are all set, and the distributor will pay $250,000 when the film is delivered." It turned out that Aversee had merely hopes and his plans did not come true. The distributor had indeed been interested in the deal but had not committed himself to it and eventually got cold feet. Florence wanted her $25,000 investment back from Aversee plus damages for deceit. Aversee claims he is guilty only of having a prediction fall through as he used the $25,000 to try to put the deal together and failed. Is Aversee on sound legal ground on these facts?

8. A service station undertook to clean and adjust sparkplugs for Hofmann, the owner of a car. When Hofmann returned for his car, it would not start even though a new battery had recently been installed. An employee of the service station then "rocked" the car and "unjammed" the starter. A rattling noise was heard in the engine. It was soon discovered that a piston rod was broken in the engine. The service station promised to pay for its repair. Hofmann took his car to a garage to be repaired and then submitted the bill to the service station. The station refused to pay the bill. What defense do you believe the station will rely upon under these facts?

9. Leslie, 15 years of age, was severely injured in an accident. She died 71 days later as a result of her injuries. She had no living parent nor a legal guardian. Claims for hospital services and doctors' fees were filed against her estate. The estate ultimately had assets as a result of an insurance settlement for the fatal accident. Leslie had two brothers who would share in her estate. The estate refuses to pay the claims filed by the hospital and the doctors. What defense would the estate attempt to use to bar the collection of such claims? Comment on the probable success of such a defense.

10. Casey's house needed repair and painting. He asked Alma Services for an estimate. Alma surveyed the property and announced that the estimate was $643. Alma placed this amount on its order form together with a description of the work to be performed. Both Casey and Alma's estimator signed the form. At the bottom of the form the following words appeared: "This contract is not binding until signed by the General Manager of Alma Services." While awaiting credit approval by Alma Services, Casey obtained a less expensive price and telephoned Alma Services canceling his order. Hearing this, the general manager signed the form, stating that Casey had already signed the contract. Alma then insisted on sending its repair crew to Casey's house. What kind of legal question is involved under these circumstances?

Answers

1. The question in this case is whether the contract was materially breached so as to fully excuse Adam from his promise to pay $750. The issue is, of course, the time for performance. Normally, time is not of the essence in a contract, and therefore it is not a material term excusing the other for the breach. There was a definite time set for performance, but that by itself does not make time of the essence. Time is of the essence when the parties expressly say it is *or* where the circumstances indicate such. The latter is applicable here. The written contract was silent on this fact, but the badges were for an election which the Larson Badge Company was certainly aware of. This indicates that time was of the essence by reasonable implication. After all, Larson was a local outfit. The facts about the strike are not generally relevant unless the written agreement stated that strikes would excuse performance. The written contract was silent on that point.

2. One who signs a written agreement is generally bound by its clear terms. To suggest that additional terms also applied is to activate the parol evidence rule, which prohibits other evidence to contradict or vary a written contract. There are, however, numerous exceptions to the parol evidence rule, one of which involves evidence of misconduct, such as fraud. It is possible that the conduct of Johnsone, the broker, might be fraudulent. If so, oral evidence may be introduced to prove such and recover relief from the contract for the Taylors.

3. The issue in this case is the assignment of future wages under employment at will. In some states, there are statutory restrictions on this practice, but generally such a claim may be assigned. This is so despite the fact that the employee, when he assigned the claim, could have been discharged by his contractor (Gourd) and never have earned the money assigned. Assignees may sue the debtor, here the employer, and recover.

4. The court would be examining the stipulated damage clause in the written contract and attempting to decide whether or not to enforce it as a proper liquidated damages clause or strike it down as a penalty clause. If the contract is of such a nature that the damage caused by the breach would be uncertain and difficult of proof and the amount does not exceed the measure of just compensation, liquidated damages clauses are upheld. Here the damages seem substantially less than the contract amount, and there appears to be little difficulty in determining the amount of damages. While forfeitures of many real estate deposits are enforced, the relationship between the amount of the deposit and the actual loss here is too great. The court would probably strike the clause down as a penalty, permitting the seller to sue for her general damages ($675) only.

5. The facts indicate that it is a question of whether a promise to answer for the debt of another is binding against Warner. These types of contracts are subject to the Statute of Frauds; that is, some writing signed by the promisor must be available if the promisor objects to introduction of evidence of his oral promise at the cocktail party. Warner would not be liable on his oral promise. This does not appear to be a novation whereby the corporation was released of its obligation. Had the facts indicated such, the oral promise would have been enforceable against Warner.

6. Quick Fix Construction will attempt to show "substantial performance." It will succeed. Substantial, not complete and exact, performance in a construction contract is all that is required. By 5:30 p.m. there had

been substantial performance. There was no bad faith shown here by Quick Fix, only bad timing. Generally, a house is ready to be lived in, to become a home, when it has been substantially completed.

7.　The question here is whether Aversee committed fraud in inducing Florence to invest in the new film. To show fraud, she must prove that a false material statement of fact was made. A statement of prediction is normally not such a statement of fact. However, the statement that "distribution arrangements are all set," if interpreted to mean a firm deal, is factual. If Florence reasonably relied on that statement, an action for fraud is clearly supportable.

8.　Consideration is required in every simple contract. The service station will claim that although it made the promise, it received no valuable consideration for such promise. In this case, the court must decide a close question. If it finds that Hofmann threatened a lawsuit for damage to his car, and in good faith he believed he had a just claim, the promise of the station to pay if he would drop his claim would be supported by valuable consideration. In this case, however, it appears that no threat was made, and a court could find this to be a gratuitous promise. Hofmann is not barred, however, from bringing a tort action against the service station and would indeed be successful if the act of the employee at the service station caused the damage to the car.

9.　The estate might defend on the grounds that contracts of infants are voidable at the option of the infant or her representative. The representative in this case is her estate. This is a good defense for most contracts but will not entirely bar claims for necessaries actually needed by and supplied to the infant. Emergency medical treatment is a necessary, and as the infant had no guardian, some recovery would be allowed. The recovery will not necessarily be the contract price, however, unless that price was reasonable, because an infant is liable for necessaries actually supplied only to the reasonable value thereof. The hospital and the doctors are entitled to recovery for the reasonable value of their services.

10.　This is a question of offer and acceptance. It is important to determine who made the offer, as both Casey and the estimator initially signed the paper. The problem is that the paper, by its own terms, dictates that no contract exists until Alma Services' general manager signs. Such a clause makes the order only an offer by Casey, which he may revoke any time before acceptance by Alma Services' general manager. Since Alma only accepts by signing, a signature after having been notified of the revocation by Casey is not an acceptance. Casey would win.

Chapter 15

Terms and Formation

15.1 SALES

Sales of goods and transactions in goods are governed by Article 2 of the UCC. These provisions supersede the general law of contracts and were enacted with the specific intention of allowing parties great latitude in fixing contract terms while acting in good faith. Both good faith and reasonableness play major roles in applying UCC principles.

A *sale* is defined as the "passing of title from the seller to the buyer for a price," UCC, Section 2-106. It may be a contract for sale, or a present sale, but a gift or a lease is not a sale. *Goods* mean "all things which are movable at the time of identification to the contract for sale." Goods include the unborn young of animals, growing crops, and other identified things attached to realty which are to be severed under certain conditions. Money, investment securities, and things in action are not goods, but rare coins could be goods.

EXAMPLE 1. In 19X2 Stockman makes three contracts with Shepard. He promises to purchase the lambs of Shepard's flock during the year 19X3, the winter wheat, and Shepard's accounts receivable. In a legal dispute, Article 2 of the UCC would govern issues regarding the sale of the lambs (unborn young) and winter wheat (crops) but not the accounts receivable (things in action).

15.2 REALTY—GOODS

Things attached to realty are tested under Section 2-107 of the UCC. Growing crops and timber, if sold apart from the land, are goods. Minerals and the like and a structure or its materials can be goods or realty. The test for these depends on which party is to sever them from the land: if by contract the seller is to sever, these items are goods; if the buyer is to sever, they are realty. For "other things" attached to realty, the test is whether the thing is capable of severance "without material harm to the realty."

EXAMPLE 2. Nora has a greenhouse, a strawberry crop growing, a room air conditioner in her bedroom, and a fence along the south end of her farm property. If, under a contract to sell, the greenhouse and fence are to be severed by Nora (the seller), these items are goods. Strawberries are crops and therefore goods. The room air conditioner is a fixture, classified as "other things" under the UCC and will be classed as goods provided it can be removed from the premises without material harm to the realty, i.e., the room in the house.

In applying the rules of Article 2 of the UCC, a number of basic concepts must be examined. They include such topics as mixed contracts, merchants, formation of sales contracts, requirements and output contracts, the Statute of Frauds, and identification.

15.3 MIXED CONTRACTS

A contract dealing with goods is necessary before Article 2 of the UCC is applicable. Accordingly, it is not uncommon for parties to argue that the UCC provisions are not applicable to the solution of the dispute, as the contract called for the performance of services, not delivery of goods.

However, when a contract contemplates the performance of both goods and services, it is a *mixed contract*.

EXAMPLE 3. King's Fancy Restaurant serves delicious meals. The restaurant provides no take-out service. King's might contend that it is really selling services, not food, which is goods. However, the UCC specifically states that for the purpose of warranty law such services are goods, Section 2-314(1).

EXAMPLE 4. A hair-tinting at the local beauty salon and a blood transfusion at the hospital can be subjects of this issue. Some courts treat them as goods and others as services. In a few states a statute settles the question.

Generally, a mixed contract is a sale of goods if the goods part is the predominant part of the contract. If the thrust of the contract appears to be for goods and a substantial part of the performance involves goods, the rules of Article 2 of the UCC apply. The dollar amounts attributed to each aspect of the contract provide some guidelines.

EXAMPLE 5. A motor manufacturer agreed to sell a dealer franchise, parts and accessories, inventory, work in progress, equipment, leasehold improvements, service vehicles, demonstrator cars, and accounts receivable to a buyer. The agreement was reduced to writing but signed only by the buyer. The manufacturer changed its mind about the transaction, refusing to perform. It contends that there is no memorandum signed by it. The buyer argues that this was a service contract. The court found that the major part, in both quantity and value, consisted of goods, not services or intangibles. Accordingly, Article 2 of the UCC operates and a signed writing is required. The manufacturer wins.

15.4 MERCHANTS

In 16 areas of Article 2 of the UCC, a professional buyer and seller of goods is bound by a different general rule. Such a professional is called a *merchant* and is defined in Section 2-104(1) of the UCC as one "who deals in goods of the kind or otherwise by his occupation holds himself out as having the knowledge or skill peculiar to the practices or goods involved." This merchant is considered to have specialized knowledge regarding the goods and business customs. The term "merchant" is broad enough to include those who employ an agent or broker.

EXAMPLE 6. Mark, a 17-year-old student, was recently hired to work as a clerk in a hardware store after school. Mark knows little of the hardware business. Mark is an agent for a merchant, and his actions bind the store as a merchant under the UCC rules.

EXAMPLE 7. Tony is a farmer who regularly sells wheat to the local grain dealer. Tony fits the definition of a merchant in some states by court decision. Other states have held that he is not a merchant.

Prominent areas in which the merchant rules differ from the general UCC rules are found in firm offers, implied warranty of merchantability, silence in the face of a confirmatory memorandum, and offers and acceptances where additional or different terms are being introduced. These will be treated in the sections that follow.

15.5 FORMATION OF SALES CONTRACTS

The contract rules of offer and acceptance are not rescinded by Article 2 of the UCC. There are, however, some modifications in respect to the manner of acceptance, implied terms, and additional terms.

15.6 MANNER OF ACCEPTANCE

A contract for the sale of goods may be made in any manner sufficient to show agreement, including the conduct of both parties which recognizes the existence of such a contract (UCC, Section 2-204). Even if the contractual moment is undetermined, or many of the terms are left open, the contract stands if the court finds that "there is a reasonably certain basis for giving an appropriate remedy."

EXAMPLE 8. The court finds the buyer in possession of the seller's goods and as having had some dealings with the seller. Although the evidence does not indicate when the offer and acceptance took place and what price was agreed upon, relief could be granted if the court found that "the conduct of the parties" recognized the existence of an agreement.

A similar open approach by the UCC is found in language allowing acceptance "in any manner and by any medium reasonable in the circumstances" (UCC, Section 2-206). Accordingly, an order for prompt or current shipment can be accepted by a prompt promise to ship or by prompt shipment. Further, the beginning of a requested performance may be an acceptance, but the offeree who is not notified of acceptance within a reasonable time may treat the offer as having lapsed.

EXAMPLE 9. The buyer, by mail, offered to purchase 10 Model H Compressors at $750 per unit. The crating and preparation for shipment may be the act of acceptance if done within a reasonable time. Failing this, a notification of acceptance should be made promptly. The seller could have accepted by sending a telegram if such medium was reasonable under the circumstances.

15.7 IMPLIED TERMS

The UCC provides "gap fillers" as well as supplies specific rules for resolving disputes. It fills gaps when it declares terms in a contract when the parties were silent. If, for example, no price was mentioned, the provisions of Section 2-305 reflect the manner for determining price. If the parties left the price for later agreement, the price is a reasonable price at time for delivery. A similar rule governs when no price was mentioned by the parties, unless the reason for the failure to set a price was the fault of one of the parties. In such a case the other party has the right to cancel the contract or fix a reasonable price. Frequently, the price is set by some standard formula or index, and sometimes the reference fails. In such case, the result is the same: reasonable price at time of delivery. Even where the contract provides that one of the contracting parties will set the price, the court will enforce such clause provided the party setting the price acts in good faith.

EXAMPLE 10. Orson made two contracts. In the first contract, Barrow was to deliver three cords of wood for Orson's fireplace and charge a price which would be set when Barrow found out what it cost to pay his help for cutting the logs. Barrow never looked into his wage costs for cutting the firewood, despite Orson's urging to do so. Orson could cancel the contract or set a reasonable price because it was the fault of Barrow that a price was not set. In a second contract with Young for the sale of storm shutters, Young stated that she would give Orson a price charged by comparable outfits at the county seat. It developed that this reference was unreliable as only two companies sold shutters in that town, and at widely different prices. The court would set a reasonable price.

In a similar way; the UCC supplies delivery and time provisions in a contract silent about such. In the absence of a specific term for performance, the time for performance is a "reasonable time." Where no place of delivery is set forth, the UCC supplies the term: the place of delivery is the seller's place of business; if there is none, then it is the seller's residence. If at the time of the contract the goods are known to the parties to be at a third place, that third place is the place of delivery.

EXAMPLE 11. Both the seller and buyer are lazy and busy. The buyer orders 1,000 Shafer valves. No other terms are mentioned. A "reasonable price," probably the market price, will be enforced, with delivery within a "reasonable time" at the seller's place of business.

It is important to note that a *quantity* term will *not* be supplied by the court. Quantity is the one term which the UCC requires to be contained in a writing which is otherwise sufficient.

15.8 ADDITIONAL TERMS

A definite and seasonable expression of acceptance or a written confirmation sent within a reasonable time is an acceptance. Even if the acceptance contains additional terms to or different terms from those contained in the offer, a contract is formed. This result is a departure from the common-law rule that an acceptance must be identical to the offer. The "mirror-image," as it is sometimes called, is abandoned by the UCC for sales of goods.

Under the UCC, Section 2-207(1), a definite and seasonable expression of acceptance or a written confirmation operates as an acceptance even if it states terms additional to, or different from, those offered or agreed upon, unless the acceptor has clearly made his or her acceptance conditional on these other terms. If it does not appear that the offeree means to counteroffer or reject the offer, a contract exists. The question is then whether the offeree's different or additional terms are a part of the contract. Generally, the different terms won't be, but the additional terms that do not materially alter the offer can become part of the contract if both of the parties are merchants and the offeree did not previously object, or does not object within a reasonable time after receipt of the acceptance. If the offeror specifically prohibited additional terms, then the offeree's additional terms are only proposals. This conflict and search for the complete terms of the contract has been called the "battle of the forms." This is in recognition of the habit of commercial firms of swapping printed forms while contracting. The buyer's form is sometimes known as the *purchase order* and the seller's form as an *acknowledgment order*.

EXAMPLE 12. A manufacturer sent a purchase order to its supplier for 1,000 switching modules, at $35 per unit, 2-year complete warranty. The supplier, using its acknowledgment form, accepted the order, placing a price of $36 per unit, and a 1-year limited warranty. There is a contract since the supplier did not condition the acceptance. Price is generally material, and accordingly, the silence of the manufacturer does not affect the original price. Also, the warranty change is material and would not amend the contract. The terms in the offer, the purchase order, would govern.

EXAMPLE 13. A manufacturer sent a purchase order to its supplier for 10,000 Ace fasteners at 30 cents per unit. The supplier, using its acknowledgment form, accepted the offer, noting that there was a "30-day return policy on rejected items." This additional term could become part of the contract if the manufacturer does not object in writing within a reasonable time. If merchants were not involved, this additional term would not become part of the contract unless the offeror expressly agreed to it.

15.9 REQUIREMENTS AND OUTPUT CONTRACTS

An illusory promise is not a binding promise, and no contract is formed. Accordingly, a clause in a contract which allows one party not to be bound if it so desires is an agreement which binds neither party.

EXAMPLE 14. Ace Manufacturing enters into a written agreement under which it promises to pay $40 per unit of flanges up to a total of $25,000 in any one year, for three years, for as many flanges as "Ace may order." Ace is not, thereby, promising absolutely to purchase any. This is an illusory promise by Ace, and it cannot provide the basis for consideration for the seller to be bound to sell under such terms.

Requirement and output contracts, while appearing similar to illusory contracts, are nevertheless enforceable under the common law and the UCC. Section 2-306 broadly validates agreements to purchase all one might "require" or "need" in one's business. Likewise, the seller's promise to sell and deliver all of his or her "output" or a percentage thereof, or his or her "production," is a promise constituting valuable consideration for the other's promise. The UCC offers some safeguards to prevent an unfair advantage for one of the parties. Section 2-306(1) states that "no quantity unreasonably disproportionate to any stated estimate or in the absence of a stated estimate to any normal or otherwise comparable prior output or requirements may be tendered or demanded."

EXAMPLE 15. Fancy Freeze was a small ice cream manufacturer with a monthly output of 8,000 gallons. Tongue In Cheek Restaurant had a big demand for this ice cream, and it signed a contract for 50 percent of Fancy's monthly output at a specified price for 2 years. Six months later, Fancy Freeze was purchased by a large ice cream company which proceeded to triple the production of its Fancy Freeze plant. Tongue In Cheek could invoke the provision of the UCC regarding a quantity that was unreasonable.

15.10   CONSIDERATION, FIRM OFFERS, AND THE UCC

Generally, every promise needs valuable consideration, but not all promises require such under the UCC. Two exceptions to the rule are present in firm offers and in modification of sales contracts. First, a *firm offer* is an offer by a merchant to buy or sell goods, made in a signed writing, promising to keep the offer open for a period. A firm offer is effective for no longer than 3 months. If no specific time is mentioned, a reasonable time is presumed, but in no event can it exceed 3 months. No consideration is needed for this seeming "option," provided it meets the above UCC requirements. An option, for consideration, is of course enforceable under the UCC. Second, once a sales contract is formed, it may be modified without additional consideration from both sides.

EXAMPLE 16. Computerland had two Model 8885 home computers left in stock. Racer wanted one but didn't have the $2,800 sales price. He prevailed on Computerland to sign a paper offering to sell Model 8885 at $2,800 to Racer at any time within the next 30 days. This is a firm offer enforceable against Computerland.

EXAMPLE 17. Computerland and Racer agree to the sale and purchase of a Model 8885 home computer for $2,800, delivery in 30 days. Racer learns that he could purchase the same computer for $2,500 at another store. Racer complains to Computerland. Computerland agrees to $2,600, a modification of the old contract. Computerland would be bound on this modification, despite the fact that it received no new consideration for the promise.

15.11   STATUTE OF FRAUDS

Contracts for the sale of goods for a price of $500 or more must comply with the UCC's Statute of Frauds (Section 2-201). Basically it asks for a writing signed by the party against whom enforcement is sought. But there are important exceptions which allow oral testimony to support proof of the contract. Proof can come in a variety of ways, arising out of (1) a signed contract, (2) a signed memorandum reflecting a previous oral agreement, (3) a confirmation, (4) a special manufacture, (5) an admission in court or pleadings, (6) a proof of payment made and accepted by the seller, or (7) a showing that goods have been received and accepted by the buyer.

If the party offers proof by a signed writing, it need not be a formal one but it must indicate a contract was made. Even the signature need not be full; initials will do, as will the letterhead on stationery, or even the company name on an invoice. The writing need not contain all the terms of the contract, but quantity must be indicated and the contract is enforceable only to the extent of the quantity of the goods mentioned.

EXAMPLE 18.   A tilemaker used her memo pad to work out the price and quantity of a potential order, ending with "2,123 tiles for $885.50 plus tax." She tore the paper off the pad and handed it to the buyer, who said, "We have a deal." The tilemaker now wants out of the bargain and contends that there is no signed writing. The buyer argues that paper from the memo pad has the tilemaker's name printed at the top. This could be a signing within the meaning of the UCC.

EXAMPLE 19.   A signed memo indicates a contract was entered into for the sale of "all the pipe for your house." The pipe supplier contends that "the quantity of goods is not stated on the memo." *Held*: The memo as it stands identifies quantity sufficiently and is a sufficient writing.

A confirmatory memorandum signed by one party can be used as evidence of the contract against the other who received it and did not sign. This rule applies only to merchants. If the merchant receives a letter or other writing indicating a contract had been formed, this merchant has 10 days to object to this in writing. The merchant's failure to object to it within 10 days permits the court to admit the memo against him or her in evidence.

EXAMPLE 20.   The granary operator telephoned the purchasing agent of Federal Mills. Federal orally agreed to the purchase of 4,000 bushels of rye at $3 per bushel. The granary later in the day dispatched a letter to Federal, stating, "Happy that we could accommodate you for 4,000 rye, shipment will follow." There was no signature, merely the granary's stationery letterhead. If, upon receipt, the purchasing agent remains silent for 10 days, not objecting in writing, the memorandum can be used by the granary to prove the contract. Note that the price was not mentioned, but the important item, quantity, was stated.

Specially manufactured or tailored goods have long been an exception to the Statute of Frauds. The UCC continues the rule in Section 2-201(3)(a) by allowing oral proof of a contract for an item of goods to be manufactured to the buyer's specifications. It is necessary, however, that the contract be entered into under circumstances reasonably indicating that the goods are for the buyer, that the goods are not suitable for sale in the ordinary business of the seller, and that such seller has made either a substantial beginning on their manufacture or a commitment for the procurement before receiving notice of buyer's breach.

The most common provision allowing enforceability of an oral contract for the sale of goods is found under the performance exception, UCC Section 2-201(3)(c). If the goods have been received and accepted by the buyer, oral testimony can prove the contract. Further, if payment was accepted by the seller, this manner of proof is allowed to satisfy the statute. The contract is enforceable only with respect to the goods for which payment has been made and accepted.

EXAMPLE 21.   A buyer made two oral contracts, one to purchase wheat and the other to purchase rye. The seller insisted on payment before delivery of the rye, but delivered the wheat on credit. Both contracts can be proved by oral testimony, fitting the performance exceptions of the UCC.

Admission in court, in pleadings and the like which indicate that a contract was made, satisfies the statute and allows enforcement of an oral contract to the extent of the quantity of goods admitted, UCC, Section 2-201(3)(b).

15.12   IDENTIFICATION

The UCC introduces the concept of *identification* in sales transactions. As to that property in goods, it means to describe a status between no title and full title to goods. Frequently, buyers who contract for goods do not provide for title passing at the time of contract. Nevertheless, under the *principle of identification*, buyers can gain valuable rights and can suffer certain losses heretofore only activated by passage of title. Section 2-501 refers to this special property interest, which also includes an insurable interest in the goods. This means that when the goods are identified to the contract, the buyer has an immediate insurable interest in the goods.

EXAMPLE 22. Ace Supply ordered 10 cartons of assorted staples from a wholesaler, delivery in 30 days. There is no mention of title. If the wholesaler orders its employee to pick out the cartons and mark them for future shipment, an identification of the goods to the contract has occurred. At this point, Ace could enter into a valid insurance contract covering these goods. Likewise, if there was a breach by the wholesaler, Ace has special rights that may be used in regard to these cartons of staples.

Identification can occur by reason of the explicit agreement of the parties where the goods are in existence and the parties specify such goods. Further, when there is a sale of future goods, the identification occurs when goods are shipped, marked, or otherwise designated by the seller as goods to which the contract refers. In the case of crops, identification is achieved when crops are planted or otherwise become growing. For the unborn, identification occurs when conceived. The crops must be those which are to be harvested within 12 months or the next normal harvest season after contracting, whichever is longer. There is likewise a limitation on contracts for the unborn; they must be born within 12 months from contracting.

15.13 UNCONSCIONABILITY

Bad bargains are usually enforceable, but some agreements, while not fraudulent, are so oppressive that courts have identified them as unconscionable. The rise of consumer credit for the purchase of goods and the concomitant burdens placed on those unprepared for the rigors of the marketplace have fueled the recognition of legal relief from such oppression where no established remedy exists.

In the sale of goods, UCC, Section 2-302, while providing no specific guidelines, vests the court as a matter of law with the right to refuse fully or partially to enforce unconscionable contracts. However, the other side is permitted to offer evidence that the contract is not unconscionable by showing its commercial setting, purpose, and effect.

This subject is more fully dealt with under Reality of Consent (Chapter 6), where it can be compared with its pathological cousins, fraud and duress.

Black Letter Law
A Summary

1. Article 2 of the UCC governs transactions involving the sale of goods, i.e., tangible personal property.

2. Goods means all things movable at the time of the identification to the contract for sale.

3. A contract for service is not governed by Article 2, but by general contract law.

4. A contract calling for a performance which involves goods and things other than goods is a mixed contract and is ruled by Article 2 if the goods portion dominates the contract.

5. Certain performances are considered goods by the UCC, such as food served in restaurants, or are defined as goods by state statute or case law, as, for example, blood supplied to a patient in a hospital.

6. Under the UCC, in 16 instances a merchant is bound by special UCC rules.

7. A merchant is one holding himself or herself out as having special knowledge about the goods involved in the sale.

8. Merchants, for example, cannot rely upon the doctrine of consideration to excuse them from liability under firm offers.

9. The method (and manner) of acceptance under a sales contract is any method that is sufficient to show agreement.

10. An order for goods can, in the absence of an instruction to the contrary, be accepted by prompt shipment or notice of a promise to ship promptly.

11. The UCC provides numerous gap fillers to supply meaning to the parties to a sales contract, including fixing time for performance, open price term determination, and the place and manner of delivery of goods.

12. In the absence of an agreement to the contrary, the place of delivery is the seller's place of business; if none, then it is the seller's residence.

13. An acceptance which contains additional or different terms can be an acceptance of the original offer unless the offeree expressly conditions his or her acceptance.

14. Where additional or different terms are placed in the acceptance, those terms which do not materially alter the offer become part of the contract if merchants are involved and the offeror-merchant did not object.

15. Requirement and output contracts are valid and enforceable, but the parties are protected from excessive demands by a UCC provision that monitors reasonableness.

16. A sales contract needs no new consideration when modified.

17. In contracts for the sale of goods for a price of $500 or more, a signed writing is required or some special proof must be offered by the party attempting to enforce the contract.

18. Evidence that the goods have been delivered and accepted or that they have been paid for is special proof permitting oral testimony of the contract.

19. Specially manufactured, or custom-made, goods are not bound by the UCC provisions regarding a writing.

20. Admission in court, or in pleadings, dispenses with the need for a signed writing showing the sale of goods.

21. A merchant who remains silent for 10 days after receipt of a writing confirming an oral sales contract cannot object to oral evidence which attempts to prove that the contract was entered into.

22. Identification occurs when the seller in some manner designates or sets aside the goods as destined for the buyer in accordance with the terms of the contract.

23. Identification under the UCC allows the buyer a special property in the goods, even without the passage of title, and also enlarges the seller's remedies in the event of a breach of contract.

Solved Problems

15.1 Martin, a wholesale distributor, made a contract for the purchase of 10,000 gallons of gasoline from the Wilber Oil Co. The price was to be determined in accordance with the refinery price at the close of business on the delivery date. Credit terms were net/30 days after delivery. Under these circumstances, which of the following statements is true?

(*a*) If Martin pays upon delivery, he is entitled to a 2 percent discount.

(*b*) The contract being silent on the place of delivery, Martin has the right to expect delivery at his place of business.

(*c*) Although the price has some degree of uncertainty, the contract is enforceable.

(*d*) Because the goods involved are tangible, specific performance is a remedy available to Martin.

(*AICPA Examination, November 1976*)

The price for goods may be expressly set by the contract, or it may indicate how the price is to be set at a later date; (*c*) is the answer. Section 2-305 of the UCC provides that if the parties so intend, they can conclude a contract of sale even though the price is not settled. In such a case, a reasonable price at the time of delivery is the contract price. Delivery, in the absence of a contrary agreement, will be at the seller's place of business.

15.2 Roberson Supply offered to sell Executive Office 40 barrels of Magic Cleanser, FOB Roberson's warehouse. Executive accepted the offer by writing: "We will buy 40 barrels at your price; send 1 barrel within 10 days." Under these circumstances,

(*a*) a contract was formed on Roberson's terms.

(*b*) Executive's reply is a counteroffer.

(*c*) a contract was formed on Executive's terms, provided Roberson did not object to the additional term.

(*d*) since both were merchants, no contract could be formed.

Section 2-207 of the UCC provides that a definite and seasonable acceptance operates as an acceptance, even though it states terms additional to or different from those offered. Whether the additional term, here "send 1 barrel within 10 days," becomes part of the contract is dependent on several factors. One, are both parties merchants and, two, did this term materially alter the offeror's terms? If both are merchants, which they appear to be, and this is not a material alteration, the additional term would become part of the contract effective upon the offeror's failure to object within a reasonable time, statement (*c*).

15.3 Marko's Specialty Copper was in high demand, and it was an excellent time to strike a deal with Electrical Components. Electrical agreed to purchase 30 percent of Marko's production for the next 18 months at $1.52 per pound. Six months later, Marko's competitor was making great strides in the market. The going price was now $1.37 per pound. Electrical told Marko that it could not pay the old price in the face of the competition Electrical faced on its level. Marko relented and stated that the new price for the remaining term of the contract would be $1.47 per pound and placed this agreement in writing. On these facts,

(*a*) Marko could sue Electrical if it refused to pay the $1.52 contract price.

(*b*) since merchants were involved, the writing was not necessary.

(*c*) Marko can only collect $1.47 per pound for the production delivered subsequent to the new agreement.

(*d*) Marko received no new consideration for the reduced price, and therefore the original contract still stands.

The correct answer is (c). Modification of a sales contract under Section 2-209(1) of the UCC requires no additional consideration, and Marko is bound by its promise to reduce the price for the unexpired term of the contract. Marko was under no legal obligation to modify the contract because of the change in economic conditions, but once having agreed to the change, the promisor is bound by his promise. This is an output contract which is valid and binding on both parties.

15.4 Base Electric Company has entered an agreement to buy its actual requirements of copper wiring for 6 months from the Seymour Metal Wire Company, and Seymour Metal has agreed to sell all the copper wiring Base will require for 6 months. The agreement between the two companies is

(a) unenforceable because it is too indefinite.

(b) unenforceable because it lacks mutuality of obligation.

(c) unenforceable because of lack of consideration.

(d) valid and enforceable.

(*AICPA Examination, November 1980*)

Section 2-306 of the UCC validates the practice of parties who enter into requirement or output contracts; and so the answer is (d). This agreement, if made in good faith, is valid and enforceable. It is definite in that Base must order what it needs from Seymour and Seymour must sell Base what it needs. Both parties are bound to perform; mutuality of obligation is present as they both have absolute duties to perform, each to the other.

15.5 Andersen wrote Matz, setting forth specifications for a printing press of a unique nature to be constructed to order, and asked for a firm price offer. Matz telegraphed Andersen 1 week later, saying:

> Offer to construct as per your letter for twenty thousand
> seven hundred cash on November delivery. Offer terminates
> 2 days.
>
>   Matz

The telegram omitted the words "seven hundred" when delivered to Andersen. Andersen immediately phoned Matz and stated, "I accept as stated in your telegram." Matz said, "Done." On the basis of the above facts and assuming *no* further writing,

(a) *no* contract resulted since Matz did *not* intend to sell the press for $20,000.

(b) neither party is bound because of mutual mistake.

(c) if Matz completed the contract and delivered the press to Andersen, Matz would be deemed to have made an implied warranty against infringement of any patent held by others.

(d) Andersen probably *cannot* assert the Statute of Frauds as a defense to a suit by Matz if Andersen notifies Matz that he will *not* take the goods after Matz has completed about 40 percent of the work.

(*Adapted from AICPA Examination, May 1974*)

Sales contracts for the price of $500 or more require a writing signed by the party to be charged or some other special oral proof. Section 2-201(3)(a) of the UCC, dealing with the Statute of Frauds, provides for several exceptions, one of which includes specially manufactured goods. If, before notice of repudiation, the seller has made a substantial beginning of manufacture of the goods and they are not suitable for sale to others in the ordinary course of business, oral testimony of the contract is admissible, statement (d). Andersen will therefore be prevented from using the Statute of Frauds against Matz. This was a unilateral rather than a mutual mistake, and, generally, such mistakes are not grounds for relief.

Only the offeror made an error, and the error was not of such magnitude as to be clearly recognizable to the offeree. The warranty of infringement in this case is made by the buyer, not the seller, when the buyer is the party supplying the specifications.

15.6 Which of the following would be enforceable under Article 2 of the UCC?

(*a*) An oral promise to keep open for 10 days an offer to sell a $499 chain saw.

(*b*) An oral promise to keep open for 3 months an offer to sell a $650 camping tent.

(*c*) A promise to sell a company all the machine oil "it may want" at $6 a barrel for a period of 11 months.

(*d*) A hardware store's oral promise to refund $50 on the $300 chain saw that a buyer purchased for what she claimed was an excessive price.

An oral agreement to amend an existing sales contract is enforceable despite the absence of new consideration and, unless the Statute of Frauds is applicable, without a signed writing; statement (*d*) is the answer. The attempt to create a "firm offer" in statements (*a*) and (*b*) fails because the promise must be made by a merchant and in a signed writing; the $500 threshold is not applicable. Statement (*c*) attempts to create a binding promise in the nature of a requirements contract but fails since the statement is "wants" rather than "needs" or "requires"; such is an illusory promise which is no legal promise.

15.7 Cutler sent Foster the following offer by mail:

> I offer you 150 Rex portable electric typewriters, Model J-1, at $65 per typewriter, FOB your truck at my warehouse, terms 2/10, net 30. I am closing out this model, hence the substantial discount. Accept all or none. (signed) Cutler.

Foster immediately wired back:

> I accept your offer re the Rex electric typewriters, but will use Blue Express Company for the pickup, at my expense of course. In addition, if possible, could you have the shipment ready by Tuesday at 10:00 a.m. because of the holidays? (signed) Foster.

On the basis of the above correspondence, what is the status of Foster's acceptance?

(*a*) It is *not* valid because it states both additional terms to and different terms from those contained in the offer.

(*b*) It represents a counteroffer which will become a valid acceptance if not negated by Cutler within 10 days.

(*c*) It is valid but will *not* be effective until received by Cutler.

(*d*) It is valid upon dispatch, despite the fact that it states both additional and different terms.

(*AICPA Examination, May 1978*)

The answer is (*d*). This was a definite and seasonable acceptance which became effective by the use of the wire, which was a medium acceptable in the circumstances, UCC, Section 2-206(1)(a). The additional term assumes delivery consistent with the offeror's "your truck." The reference regarding time of delivery was a question, not a term. Between merchants, the offeree's terms become part of the contract unless they represent a material alteration of the contract or the offeror objects to them within a reasonable time.

15.8 Devold Manufacturing, Inc., entered into a contract for the sale to Hillary Company of 2,000 solid-state CB radios at $27.50 each, terms 2/10, N/30, FOB Hillary's loading platform. After delivery of the first 500 radios, a minor defect was discovered. Although the defect was minor, Hillary incurred costs to correct the defect. Hillary sent Devold a signed memorandum indicating that it would relinquish its rights to recover the costs to correct the defect, provided that the balance of the radios were in conformity with the terms of the contract and the delivery dates were strictly adhered to. Devold met these conditions. Shortly before the last shipment of radios arrived, a dispute between the parties arose over an unrelated matter. Hillary notified Devold that it was *not* bound by the prior generous agreement and would sue Devold for damages unless Devold promptly reimbursed Hillary. In the event of litigation, what would be the basis upon which the litigation would be decided and what would be the result?

(*a*) Devold will lose in that Hillary's relinquishment of its rights was not supported by a consideration.

(*b*) Devold will win in that the defect was minor and the substantial performance doctrine applies.

(*c*) Hillary will lose in that the communication constituted a waiver of Hillary's rights.

(*d*) Hillary will win in that there was a failure to perform the contract, and Hillary suffered damages as a result.

(*Adapted from AICPA Examination, May 1978*)

It is true that under Section 2-209 of the UCC a party who has made a waiver may retract by reasonable notification, but not if such retraction would be unjust in view of a material change of position in reliance on the waiver; statement (*c*) is the answer. It would be unjust to retract this waiver when the other party fulfilled the conditions that Hillary set up. Additionally, no consideration is necessary to make a waiver binding.

15.9 Almovar Electronics was closing out several lines of electronics parts which were becoming outdated. It sent a letter on March 8 to Conduit Sales & Service Company, one of its biggest retail customers, offering the entire lot at a substantial reduction in price. The offer indicated that it was for "immediate acceptance." The terms were "cash, pick up by your carrier at our loading dock and *not* later than March 15." It also indicated that the terms of the offer were *not* subject to variance. The letter did not arrive until March 10, and Conduit's letter accepting the offer was *not* mailed until March 12. The letter of acceptance indicated that Conduit would take the entire lot, would pay in accordance with the usual terms (2/10, net/30), and would pick up the goods on March 16. Which of the following *best* describes the legal relationship of the parties?

(*a*) The acceptance was *not* timely, and hence there was no contract.

(*b*) The different terms of the acceptance are to be construed as proposals for changes in the contract.

(*c*) The different terms of acceptance constituted a rejection of the offer.

(*d*) Since both parties were merchants and the changes in the acceptance were *not* material, there is a valid contract.

(*Adapted from AICPA Examination, May 1979*)

Where the offer explicitly demands that an acceptance be made only as in the offer, the UCC provisions allowing acceptors to state different and additional terms are not applicable; the answer is (*c*). It does seem that there was some delay (2 days) in mailing the letter of acceptance after receipt of the offer, but as a matter of law, it cannot be said that delay was unreasonable. This reply was, under the circumstances, a rejection and counteroffer.

15.10 Lalo Freight ordered spare parts of a specific nature from the Mitsu Machine Foundry, setting price and delivery instructions. Which of the following would *not* be an effective attempt at acceptance of the offer?

(*a*)   The foundry's prompt shipment of the order

(*b*)   A prompt notification of acceptance of the order

(*c*)   A prompt notice that "the order has been received"

(*d*)   A prompt dispatch of a notice of acceptance of the order

   All statements except (*c*) describe a valid manner of acceptance of this order (i.e., offer) under Section 2-206(1)(b) of the UCC. A notice that the order has been received merely communicates the fact that the offer has been communicated to the offeree. No contract would be formed by that action.

15.11 By telephone, a buyer ordered 300 Ansi valves for a total price of $3,000 from the seller. The seller accepted the offer over the telephone and promised to ship the valves promptly. Under which of the following circumstances could the Statute of Frauds be used to *defeat* the oral contract?

(*a*)   The valves were manufactured to the buyer's specifications.

(*b*)   The valves were received and accepted by the buyer.

(*c*)   The valves were prepaid by the buyer before delivery.

(*d*)   The telephone conversation was recorded.

   The recorded telephone conversation, statement (*d*), does not qualify as satisfying the requirements of the UCC's Statute of Frauds or providing an exception to it. The other methods form exceptions under Section 2-201 of the UCC. Thus, oral testimony regarding delivery and acceptance, prepayment, or special manufacture of goods not suitable for sale in the ordinary course of business would be admissible in evidence to prove the contract made over the telephone.

15.12 Taylor, professionally an accountant, spent a lifetime collecting walking canes as a hobby, and his collection was the envy of many. At retirement, he decided to reduce his collection substantially and began selling many of the canes. Farrell, a fellow collector, had long wanted to acquire Taylor's pair of "walnut, Bavaria, circa 1535." Taylor finally sent a letter to Farrell which ended with the following: " . . . and I know how long you have waited for my Bavarian walnuts, so if you still want them at $2,000, let me know as I will hold them for you for 10 days." Under these circumstances,

(*a*)   Taylor has granted Farrell an option.

(*b*)   Taylor has made a binding contract with Farrell since he knew what Farrell's response would be.

(*c*)   Taylor must hold the offer open for 10 days.

(*d*)   Taylor's letter must be dated in order to have any effect.

   The question is whether Taylor has made a firm offer under the UCC, Section 2-205. A firm offer cannot be revoked, despite the absence of consideration, provided it meets the requirements that it be in writing, signed by a merchant who promises to keep the offer open. Further, it cannot exceed 3 months. The only issue here is whether Taylor is a merchant. A merchant includes one who deals in goods of the kind or otherwise by occupation holds himself out as having the knowledge or skill peculiar to the practice or goods involved. It appears that Taylor, despite being an accountant, may also be a merchant in these circumstances, and must hold the offer open for the 10 days, statement (*c*).

15.13 Goods are identified to a sales contract under which of the following circumstances?

(*a*) When title is passed to the buyer

(*b*) When the buyer writes telling the seller that he or she wants the 10 typewriters ordered to be the first 10 that come off the assembly line next week

(*c*) When the farmer informs the buyer that he or she will plant the contracted-for wheat next week in the south field

(*d*) When the seller in his or her warehouse marks the buyer's name on a dozen boxes of assorted gloves ordered by the buyer

Section 2-501(1)(b)(c) of the UCC characterizes the goods as identified to the contract in numerous instances. When the ordered goods are marked by the seller, an identification occurs; statement (*d*) is the answer. Title is a greater interest than identification. Instructing the seller to identify in the future is not sufficient, nor is an intention to plant a crop. If and when the crop is planted, an identification occurs.

15.14 The identification of goods under a sales contract fixes the buyer with certain rights in the goods. Which of the following is *not* among such rights?

(*a*) The buyer has an insurable interest in the goods.

(*b*) If, upon the seller's breach, the buyer is unable to effect cover from the goods, the buyer can replevy them (i.e., get them back) from the seller.

(*c*) The buyer has a right to have goods replevied from the seller if the goods are shipped under reservation and the buyer satisfies the security interest.

(*d*) The right to claim title in the goods.

All statements except (*d*) are correct in that they allow the buyer under those circumstances to have extraordinary legal rights in the goods which are not yet the buyer's under full title.

15.15 Goode, a potato farmer, and Sharpe Chips, a manufacturer, engaged in lengthy face-to-face negotiation concerning potatoes and the spring planting. The parties were at an impasse until one evening the president of Sharpe telephoned Goode at his farm, found him in a good mood, and immediately struck a deal. Goode agreed to plant and sell 100,000 sacks of Kenneback potatoes, delivery May 19X3. Goode continued to be pleased with the deal the next morning and so wrote a letter to the president of Sharpe telling him, "How glad I am to have made a deal with you for 100,000 sacks of my potatoes at $58,000 and rest assured that I will meet the May 19X3 delivery." Sharpe received the letter the next day, but the president's mind was not on the deal as he had just learned that he was being replaced. Goode's letter lay in the file for a month until the new administration took over. They then telegraphed Goode telling him that, "We have no contract with you. Repeat, we have no contract." Under these circumstances,

(*a*) since Sharpe signed no writing, there is no valid contract.

(*b*) Goode could not be held on his promise to sell.

(*c*) Article 2 of the UCC does not apply to growing crops.

(*d*) Goode could defeat Sharpe's reliance on the Statute of Frauds.

A confirmatory memorandum signed by one party as evidence of an oral agreement can be used against the recipient provided he was a merchant and did not object to the memo within 10 days after receipt; statement (*d*) is correct. Sharpe Chips was a merchant, and Goode's letter confirmed the oral contract since it was not objected to within 10 days.

15.16 Adderly Construction was building miniwarehouses and orally contracted with Secure Products to install overhead doors for 200 of the units at a price of $90 each. Secure purchased the prefabricated disassembled doors from a foreign manufacturer, with Secure bound under the contract with Adderly to furnish all labor, materials, tools, and equipment to satisfactorily complete the installation of the overhead doors. The overall project was besieged with problems from the beginning, including numerous work disruptions and strikes. As a result, the doors were not installed for some time. Even then the parties engaged in a difference of opinion regarding Secure's performance. This dragged on until finally, after 4 years, Secure Products sued Adderly on the oral contract. The statute of limitations for bringing an action under a sales contract for goods is 4 years, but is 6 years under a contract for services. Adderly is claiming that this is a contract for the sale of goods, not services. Secure is contending that this was a service contract.

Was this a contract for the sale of goods or a contract for services? Decide and state reasons for your conclusion.

A contract which calls for the sale of goods and also for services is a mixed contract. To determine whether it was goods or services requires an examination of which performance was predominant. This can be done by examining the thrust or purpose of the contract. Is it the rendition of services with goods incidentally involved, or the contrary? Here the predominant reason for the agreement appears to have been the procurement of overhead doors, with the installation being incidental. As such, it is a sale of goods and the statute of limitations under the UCC, Section 2-725, providing for a 4-year limitation period governs. Secure Products may not continue this action, as its legal rights are barred by the passage of the statutory period.

15.17 Volk Contractors was bidding on a military runway project and asked Cember Steel for a bid on a certain quantity of steel. After some delay by Cember, Volk received a letter from Cember on April 23, 19X2, which in substance stated the following:

> "We regret that this bid was delayed. However, we are pleased to offer you all the structural steel you specified, including steel girts and pulins, for $172,000. This price is predicated on a price of $0.1175 per pound of steel, and we would expect to adjust the price on this basis to actual tonnage used in the project."

Volk was delighted with this letter and, relying on Cember's letter, submitted a bid to the U.S. Air Force. Volk was awarded the prime contract. Two days later Cember wired Volk that its offer was revoked. Volk promptly notified Cember Steel that it was holding it to its written offer.

What theory will Volk press to hold Cember to its written offer? What success will Volk have? Decide and state reasons for your conclusions.

Volk Contractors will maintain that Cember Steel could not revoke the written offer as it was a firm offer under the UCC. Section 2-205 of the UCC sets forth the requirements of such a firm offer. The offer must be in writing, must be signed by a merchant, and is effective for the time stated but no longer than 3 months. Unfortunately for Volk, the UCC section has one other requirement: the offeror must give assurance that the offer will be held open. Such language is missing from Cember's letter received on April 23. It is merely an offer, not a firm offer. It may be revoked any time before the offeree's acceptance. Volk Contractors will not be able to sustain an action against Cember Steel on the theory of a firm offer.

15.18 In September, a plastics manufacturer submitted a price quotation to Novelty House for plastic toys. The price quotation was specific, as were the other terms under which the manufacturer would do business. Among the terms was one in which ownership of the eight plastic molds remained with the manufacturer but could be purchased by Novelty for a fee.

The quotation ended with the language that "this offer is good for 15 days only, and all terms contained herein are part of the contract." Novelty was interested in the offer but delayed until November 14 when it prepared and sent out a purchase order at the prices quoted, but with Novelty's own terms and conditions. The face of Novelty's purchase order expressly provided that it would not be bound by any changes in the order unless agreed to in writing. Further, term 6 of the purchase order clearly stated that "all molds used in the manufacture become the property of Novelty upon request." The manufacturer was pleased with the order and sent its acceptance-acknowledgment, which also stated that "this contract is subject to the terms and conditions of our quotation pertinent to this sale." Some time later the toys ordered under the contract were manufactured, delivered, and paid for. Later, Novelty wanted more of these toys under a new contract, but the manufacturer quoted a higher price. At this point, Novelty demanded the molds as its purchase order allowed. The manufacturer refused, citing the terms in its quotation and acknowledgment control.

Does Novelty have the right to the eight molds? Decide and state your conclusions and reasons therefor.

This is a case of the so-called battle of the forms. It is important to determine who made the offer and whether the acceptance was unconditional. At first it appears that the offer was made through the quotation by the manufacturer. However, the 15-day time limit indicates that this offer lapsed by passage of time. The purchase order then became the offer, and the offeror's terms dominate where the acceptance has different or additional terms. If these latter terms in the acceptance are material, or are objected to by the offeror, they do not become part of the contract despite the fact that this transaction is between merchants. The terms that materially alter the offeror's terms refer to ownership of the molds. Such a change will fail unless the offeree expressly limited acceptance to its terms, UCC, Section 2-207(2)(a). Further, the offeror's purchase order stated that it would not be bound by changes unless agreed to in writing by the offeror. Novelty is entitled to the molds without payment of any additional money.

Chapter 16

Risk of Loss and Title

16.1 INTRODUCTION

There are advantages and disadvantages to the possession or ownership of goods. The owner has the enjoyment and use of the item and the freedom of sale or disposal. But goods become lost, damaged, stolen, or sometimes seized by creditors. In sales transactions these rights and risks are in a state of transition. The deliberate or merely fortuitous timing of the transfer of rights dictates who loses when there is loss, seizure, or damage. While it is true that insurance may be provided to cover many of these risks, one must know who suffers the risk of losses which are uninsured in part or in whole and, more importantly, who must proceed against the carrier or insurer.

The study of risk of loss and title requires a consideration of the risk of loss when there is no breach of contract, risk when there is a breach of contract, title to goods, issues regarding sale-or-return and sale-on-approval contracts, and bulk transfers.

16.2 RISK OF LOSS: NO BREACH

Where goods are being shipped to a buyer and a loss or damage occurs, the risk is determined by the terms of the shipment contract, UCC, Section 2-509. Parties can expressly agree that the seller or buyer is to suffer the risk, but they rarely do so expressly. Instead they employ commercial "shorthand" through the practice of including the term *FOB*, meaning "free on board" of risk and expense.

16.3 FOB

FOB is a delivery term used by contracting parties in the sale of goods. When stated, it means that the seller must ship the goods to a named place by placing the goods in the possession of the party who is to accept them. If this party is a carrier, for example, the seller must make a reasonable contract for carriage of the goods, provide documents if necessary, and promptly notify the buyer of shipment, UCC, Section 2-504. If the place cited after the FOB designation is the place of shipment, the seller's expense and risk end when the goods are placed in the possession of the carrier for shipment.

EXAMPLE 1. A seller in Dayton, Ohio, agreed to ship to a buyer in Portland, Oregon, 500 Shaefer valves, FOB Dayton, Midland Trucking. The valves are damaged while being loaded on the truck at the seller's place of business in Dayton. The seller suffers the loss. If, however, the valves were damaged after the Midland truck left the premises, the risk of uninsured loss would be on the buyer. The buyer would have to pay the seller's invoice and sue the carrier, if appropriate.

If the FOB place is the destination, the seller's risk and expense continue until delivery at the destination to the buyer, UCC, Section 2-319. At the destination the seller, or its agent, must put the goods at the buyer's disposition and give the buyer reasonable notification. This is a tender of delivery at the point of destination. Any necessary documents must also be offered. The buyer is allowed a reasonable time to take possession of the goods. Once these conditions are met, the risk of loss and any further expense rest with the buyer.

EXAMPLE 2.   A Detroit buyer ordered a carload of lumber from a Seattle seller, FOB Detroit via Shortline Railroad. Upon arrival in Detroit, the carrier placed the boxcar on a siding 1 mile from the buyer's place of business. Shortline notified the buyer of the arrival and availability for unloading. This was a tender of delivery. The buyer delayed in getting the lumber due to personnel shortage. During the night thieves stole the lumber. The theft occurred after notification. The risk of uninsured loss falls on the buyer. The buyer must pay the seller the full invoice price.

The language used by the parties after the FOB term is an important contract term. If it is FOB a particular vessel, car, or other vehicle, the seller must, at his or her own expense and risk, load the goods on board. If a vessel is called for, the buyer must name the vessel and the seller must contract for a proper bill of lading, UCC, Section 2-323.

16.4   FAS TERMS

The delivery term *FAS* refers to "free alongside ship" at a named port. The seller need only deliver the goods alongside the vessel in a manner usual in that port, UCC, Section 2-319. The seller must obtain a receipt for the goods from the carrier, who issues a bill of lading. Risk of loss passes to the buyer at this time. In all cases, required documentation is a condition to effective tender of delivery and passage of risk.

16.5   CIF TERMS

The *CIF* contract refers to a price the buyer must pay which includes *c*ost (of the goods), *i*nsurance, and *f*reight charges. The risk of loss passes at the point of shipment, as in FOB shipment contracts. The duties of the sellers, however, are somewhat broader. The seller must deliver the goods to the carrier, obtain a proper bill of lading, pay the freight charges, obtain and pay for an appropriate contract of insurance, and forward the necessary documentation to the buyer. The term *CF* refers to the same contract except that insurance is not provided for, UCC, Section 2-320.

16.6   BAILMENT DELIVERY

Not all buyers take delivery from a carrier in a shipment contract. Buyers may agree to collect the goods at some third place where the goods are in possession of a *bailee*, someone other than the seller. The issue is then raised at what point in the attempted transfer to the buyer does the risk of loss pass? If a negotiable document of title has been issued by the bailee, the receipt of such document by the buyer passes risk. If no such document was issued, the risk can pass in either of two cases. One, when the bailee (the third party) acknowledges that the goods are held for the buyer or, two, when the buyer receives a written direction or document allowing him or her to collect the goods. In the latter case the buyer has a reasonable amount of time to present the document to the bailee before the risk shifts to the buyer.

EXAMPLE 3.   Acco Liquors keeps its scotch and rye inventory at a public warehouse. The warehouse issued a negotiable receipt for the scotch, but not for the rye. Acco agrees to sell 100 cases of scotch and 50 cases of rye to Gables. Risk of loss passes regarding the scotch when Acco indorses and delivers the warehouse receipt to Gables. If the warehouse telephones Gables and informs it that the rye is ready to be picked up and Gables confirms, the risk of loss for the rye passes at that time.

16.7 COD

Some shipments are made *COD*, "collect on delivery". Despite the implication of the word "delivery" in the term, a COD shipment is, for risk of loss purposes, treated as an FOB shipping point contract, and therefore the risk of loss passes at delivery to the carrier.

16.8 RISK: GENERALLY

The UCC provides a catchall provision for situations in the transfer of goods not covered by the other specific rules. Where the goods are neither being shipped nor being picked up from a bailee, the risk of loss is simply settled. If the seller is a merchant, the buyer must receive the goods before the risk passes. If the seller is not a merchant, the risk passes when the seller tenders delivery of the goods.

EXAMPLE 4. Laura telephoned a salesman and informed him that she had decided to purchase the rocker she saw at the store showroom. The salesman wrote up the sale, telling Laura that he would put a "sold" ticket on the item. She could pick it up today or tomorrow. Before Laura got to the store, the sprinkler system malfunctioned, damaging store merchandise including Laura's tagged rocker. The store suffers the loss as the risk does not pass until the buyer receives the rocker. The store is a merchant.

16.9 RISK OF LOSS: BREACH OF CONTRACT

In general, the risk of loss usually falls totally or partially on the party who breaches the contract, UCC, Section 2-510. This can occur when the seller, for example, tenders nonconforming goods to the buyer. In addition, even after delivery where the buyer originally accepted the goods, a later but proper inspection allows grounds for a revocation of acceptance. In this event the buyer may treat the risk as having remained with the seller but only to the extent of any deficiency in the buyer's insurance coverage.

EXAMPLE 5. A+M Truck Rental accepted 100 replacement shock absorbers from Super Shock. They appeared to be in order. One month later the shocks were discovered to be unfit for use and did not meet contract specifications. Only attempted use could reveal this defect. A+M notified Super of the revocation of acceptance. Before the goods were returned, the shop was burglarized and all goods were taken, scattered, or missing. No negligence in safekeeping was shown. The truck rental had no insurance covering this theft. Super Shock suffers the uninsured loss of the 100 shock absorbers. Super Shock breached the contract by sending nonconforming goods.

A buyer can likewise breach a contract and suffer risk of loss. When conforming goods have been identified to the contract and the buyer breaches, the seller may, to the extent of any deficiency in his or her effective insurance coverage, treat that loss as on the buyer for a commercially reasonable time. Of course, if the risk has already passed to the buyer, the rule is superfluous.

EXAMPLE 6. A Nashville seller demanded that a letter of credit be issued before an October 3 delivery of goods to a Tulsa buyer. The contract called for FOB Tulsa, Safe Pacific Railway, October 1. The buyer failed to obtain the necessary letter of credit by October 3. The goods were substantially damaged in transit on October 4. By contract, risk of loss did not pass to the buyer, but by reason of the buyer's breach of contract as to identified goods, the buyer suffers the uninsured loss.

16.10 TITLE TO GOODS

The UCC rules governing risk of loss resolve many of the common legal problems flowing from shipment and transfer of goods. The UCC does this without regard to the question of title to the goods. The drafters of the UCC did not abolish title questions but did remove title as an issue in certain areas. There are, however, instances in which title is important, and the UCC provides rules for settling this point. The parties can expressly agree to the moment when title passes to identified goods. In the absence of an agreement, title passes to goods identified to the contract when the seller completes his or her performance with reference to the physical delivery of the goods. Where there is a shipment contract, title passes at the time and place of shipment; in destination contracts, title passes upon tender of the goods at destination. Further, the fact that the seller retained a security interest in the goods does not alter this rule. If documents of title are to be delivered, the time of their delivery determines the passage of title.

EXAMPLE 7. The state levied an inventory tax on "title owners to goods as of January 1." The seller sold goods to the buyer, reserving title in himself for a credit sale. The contract called for an FOB shipping contract. The seller delivered the goods to the carrier on December 29. The goods reached the buyer on January 3. Title is in the buyer, it having passed on December 29. The seller completed his performance by delivery to the carrier. The buyer must report the goods as part of her inventory on her tax return.

16.11   VOID AND VOIDABLE TITLE

The fact that a buyer of goods purchased in good faith for value without notice of any defect in title does *not* always vest such purchaser with valid title. In the first place, a thief cannot pass title to stolen goods. Thievery means larceny or the taking of goods from another without the owner's permission. A robber, hijacker, or burglar who forcibly or secretly seizes goods is clearly a thief within this rule. Also, a party who sells goods given to him or her for only temporary possession is likewise a thief (larceny by a bailee) and can pass no title to goods in most, but not all, situations. On the other hand, a party who obtains goods by fraud or false pretenses or under a breach of contract has the power, though not the right, to pass title to others. This title is said to be voidable. A thief, however, holds a void title.

EXAMPLE 8. Handl hijacked a truckload of wire casings and sold them for a fair price to a wholesaler, who purchased them innocently. No title passes to the wholesaler. If the owner can trace the goods to the processor, no matter how remote, the goods can be retrieved. Thieves can pass no title, as their title is void.

EXAMPLE 9. Tonsar purchased 200 cases of condensed milk from the seller, giving a check on an overdrawn bank account. If Tonsar sold the milk to a good-faith purchaser before the seller disaffirmed the contract on the grounds of fraud, the purchaser gains valid title. Tonsar's title was voidable, not void.

A buyer with a voidable title can pass title to goods to a good-faith purchaser for value. A party with a void title cannot pass title unless the entrustment principle allows an exception.

16.12   ENTRUSTMENT

Section 2-403 of the UCC allows title to pass in instances where the transferee had possession but not title. An owner of goods who entrusts them to a merchant who deals in goods of that kind gives such merchant the power, though not the right, to transfer title to a good-faith purchaser in the ordinary course of business.

EXAMPLE 10. Circle Supply *sells* and *stores* portable silos in the farming community. A farmer delivers two of her silos to Circle for storage only. Circle inadvertently sells these silos to a third party, who buys them in the ordinary course of business. The farmer had entrusted the silos to a merchant who also sells silos. The farmer cannot retrieve the silos and must seek a remedy against Circle only. If Circle only stored silos, title could not pass to innocent third parties.

A buyer of goods who permits the seller to retain possession of goods purchased would also be subject to the entrustment doctrine and risk of loss of title. However, such buyer does not lose its interest in identified goods left with a seller for a commercially reasonable period of time against the *creditors* of the seller, UCC, Section 2-402.

EXAMPLE 11. A retailer selected and paid for goods but left them with the wholesaler for delivery in 30 days. Two weeks later the creditors of the wholesaler obtained an order seizing all the wholesaler's goods, including those belonging to the retailer. Unless this possession was for a commercially unreasonable time, the retailer does not lose his interest in the goods. On the other hand, had a purchaser in good faith bought the goods from the wholesaler, title would pass.

16.13 SALE OR RETURN AND SALE ON APPROVAL

The buyer's creditors may seize goods in the possesion of the buyer on the assumption that the goods belong to the buyer. However, the buyer may have some goods on trial or on approval, or at least have the right to return them to the seller. The UCC provides that when the buyer has made a contract whereby the buyer can return goods, even though they conform to the contract, the contract is either a *sale or return* or a *sale on approval* (trial). In sale or return, title passes to the buyer; in sale on approval, it passes only after the buyer approves.

EXAMPLE 12. A seller delivered cotton goods to a jobber under a sale-or-return contract and a knitting machine under a sale on approval. Before the jobber had decided whether or not to keep the machine and before she had attempted resale of the cotton, the jobber's creditors had obtained an order seizing the property of the jobber. The cotton goods can be seized; title has passed. The seller still owns the knitting machine, as the jobber had not yet approved the sale.

Approval can be express or by implication during the trial period. Selling the item, using it beyond the trial period, or pledging it as collateral for a loan are examples of conduct indicating approval.

Where the parties to the contract do not clearly indicate whether the sale is on approval or is a sale or return, the UCC provides a test in Section 2-326. A sale is one of approval (or trial) if the goods were delivered primarily for use. It is sale or return if the goods were delivered primarily for resale.

EXAMPLE 13. Carlo Limited delivered machinery to Florida Dredging with the assurance that the machinery could be returned if Florida was not pleased with its performance. Florida Dredging has been plagued with vandalism, and before it had an opportunity to test the machines, vandals seriously damaged all of them. Florida was not at fault. Title had not passed to Florida, and the loss remains in Carlo, the seller. The machines were delivered primarily for use, not for resale.

EXAMPLE 14. Flavor Nuts shipped two cases of cashews on credit to the Blue Nuttery with the understanding that "if they don't sell, send them back." Blue Nuttery's assets were seized by a trustee in Federal Bankruptcy Court. Title had passed to the buyer because these goods were delivered primarily for resale; therefore it was a sale or return.

The UCC does not prohibit the parties from expressly agreeing that title passes or does not pass, or that risk of loss or damage is placed on one or the other. In the absence of such an explicit agreement, however, the above rules govern the risk question except in consignments.

16.14 CONSIGNMENTS

Sale on approval is subject to an important exception regarding title to goods delivered to a buyer who maintains a business conducted under any name other than the seller of the goods. In order to protect creditors of buyers who might be misled by the presence of unowned inventory or other property of a merchant, a sale on approval is not available to such seller in regard to the buyer's creditors. These sales are sometimes called *consignments* or *on memorandum*, a practice by which the seller attempts to name the buyer as agent to sell the seller's goods. Protection for the seller is available in the UCC by the use of Article 9, Secured Transactions, under which a security interest can be placed on public record by the use of a financing statement. Section 2-326(3) of the UCC also permits sellers to utilize any existing state law regarding appropriate signs in the establishment. However, this protection for the seller would be unnecessary where the person (buyer) conducting the business is generally known by his or her creditors to be substantially engaged in selling the goods of others.

EXAMPLE 15.   A wholesaler wanted to sell its posters to several college seniors who rented a storefront near the university under the name "Post Patterns." Post was short on cash, and the wholesaler named it as agent, delivering all posters on consignment, or memorandum, with the understanding that title to unsold posters remained in the wholesaler. This is a sale or return despite the express agreement. If the state had a sign law, compliance with the law by posting a sign saying that "All Posters Displayed Here Are the Property of the Wholesaler" would protect the wholesaler should Post Patterns have financial trouble and its creditors seek to seize its assets.

16.15   BULK TRANSFERS

Not all owners of goods may sell them free of claims of their general or unsecured creditors. When merchants attempt to transfer a major part of their goods, supplies, or other inventory, not in the ordinary course of business, Article 6 of the UCC, the Bulk Transfer Law, must be honored. The requirements for the buyer are simple. The buyer must demand from such a seller a sworn list of creditors and their addresses. The buyer and seller prepare a list of the property, and the buyer notifies the seller's creditors about the sale at least 10 days before taking possession of the goods or making payment, whichever happens first, UCC, Section 6-107. This notice must be given personally or by registered or certified mail.

EXAMPLE 16.   York Auto Parts was in business trouble and decided to sell its inventory and equipment to its competitor, Flag Parts. Flag wanted a clean deal and quickly paid cash and took all the property. York's supplier then learned of the sale and demanded that its bill for $3,000 be paid by Flag. Because Flag did not comply with the Bulk Transfer Law, the supplier can either reclaim the goods transferred or, if they are already disposed of, obtain a judgment against Flag for the value of the goods transferred by York.

This potential lien or charge on the goods of a merchant does not encumber the goods forever, however. The time limit on creditor action is 6 months from the date that the transferee took possession, provided the sale was not concealed. Also, an innocent third party who buys from a transferee who failed to comply with the Bulk Transfer Law takes free of any claim. Where there is a compliance, an omitted creditor has no rights under Article 6 of the UCC, being left to his or her original action against the contracting party.

EXAMPLE 17.   Asper Clothing wanted a new location and so sold out its old store to Mod Times, which demanded a bulk transfer affidavit of creditors. Asper omitted Wooling Corporation, its largest creditor, to which it owed $6,200. Mod Times saw to it that those creditors listed on the affidavit had personal notice and received their share of the purchase price. Only then did Wooling learn of the transfer. Wooling's only rights are against its contractor, Asper, provided Mod Times had no knowledge that Wooling had been left off the list in the affidavit.

The manner in which the creditors get paid in the case of a bulk transfer is not uniform, as the UCC offers the enacting states different techniques, including the duty of the bulk transfer buyer to see to the application of the proceeds of the sale. In all states, however, the seller and buyer must prepare a schedule of the property to be transferred [UCC, Section 6-104(1)(b)], and the transferee must preserve the list for 6 months.

The objective of the Bulk Transfer Law is to make subject to it those enterprises whose principal business is the sale of merchandise from stock, including retailers, wholesalers, and manufacturers. However, a number of transactions involving bulk transfers are exempt from this law. For example, a transfer to a secured creditor of such goods is not a bulk transfer within the act. Also, transfers made under judicial process, such as bankruptcy or a sheriff's seizure, are not bound by Article 6. Finally, the purpose of the law is to protect unsecured creditors of the seller; a bulk sale contract with a solvent buyer who assumes the debts of the seller, and gives notice of such, is a contract which need not comply with the provisions of the Bulk Transfer Law.

Black Letter Law
A Summary

1. The search for title is de-emphasized in the UCC, which relies on certain incidents between the parties to determine risk of loss and transfer.

2. Where goods are being shipped and an uninsured loss or damage occurs, the risk is determined by the terms of the shipment contract.

3. Generally, an FOB (free on board) designation in the contract fixes the place where risk passes from the seller to the buyer.

4. In an FOB shipment contract, the risk passes to the buyer when the seller has placed the goods in the hands of the carrier for immediate shipment under an appropriate contract and notifies the buyer.

5. In an FOB destination contract, the risk does not pass to the buyer until the goods are ready for the buyer at the destination.

6. CIF and COD designations are treated for purposes of risk as FOB shipment contracts.

7. Where delivery is not by shipment, the goods being at some third place in the hands of a bailee, passage of risk is determined by whether or not the bailee has issued a negotiable document.

8. Where a negotiable document of title has been issued, the receipt of the document by the buyer shifts the risk to the buyer.

9. Where a nonnegotiable document, or no document, has been issued by the bailee, risk passes when the bailee acknowledges that the goods are being held for the buyer or when the buyer receives a written direction or document allowing him or her to collect the goods.

10. The catchall provision of risk and title passage applies to all other situations by fixing passage of title at the time the buyer takes receipt of the goods if the seller is a merchant, or when the seller tenders delivery of the goods if the seller is not a merchant.

11. Contract designation of risk passage is subject to the exception which places the risk of loss in cases of breach of contract on the party who breached the contract.

12. Title to goods generally passes when the parties expressly or impliedly agree that it shall pass.

13. Thieves cannot pass title to another except if the entrustment principle is applicable.

14. Those who possess a voidable title by reason of fraud, breach of contract, or infancy, for example, can nevertheless pass good title to goods if sold to a good-faith buyer in the ordinary course of business.

15. An owner of goods who delivers possession of goods to a party who sells such goods can lose title to the goods if sold to a good-faith buyer in the ordinary course of business.

16. In sale or return and in sale on trial, the buyer has entered into a contract by which the buyer may return the goods even if they conform to the contract.

17. In the absence of an agreement to the contrary, title and risk of loss pass to the buyer in sale or return, but not in sale on approval until such approval.

18. If the contract leaves doubt about whether the sale is for approval or return, the issue is determined by whether the buyer took the goods for use (approval) or resale (return).

19. A consignment is transfer of possession to buyers who normally sell the goods, but in the meantime title is retained by the seller.

20. A consignment occurs when a seller transfers possession but not title to the buyer for the purpose of resale, and is effective against the buyer's creditors providing state sign laws are complied with, or the security interest is perfected under the secured transactions law.

21. When a merchant enters into a contract to sell all or a major part of his or her inventory to a single buyer, both buyer and seller must comply with Article 6 of the UCC, the Bulk Transfer Law, unless the buyer is solvent and, at the time of the sale (transfer), gives notice that he or she is assuming the debts of the seller.

22. The Bulk Transfer Law does not apply to goods transferred to a secured creditor of those goods, nor does it apply to transfers made under a judicial process such as bankruptcy or a sheriff's sale.

Solved Problems

16.1 Citation Industries of Newark sent a purchase order for 20 drums of XL Cleanser to Faswell Chemical of Dover, Delaware, shipment FOB Dover, via Calen Trucking. Faswell sent a prompt acknowledgment and then delivered 20 drums to Calen Trucking. Only after shipment did Faswell discover that six of the drums were Grade SL rather than XL. Faswell telegraphed Citation notifying the company of the fact and reducing the purchase price by 15 percent. Before delivery, Calen Trucking had a strike, and the shipment was lost along the way. Under these circumstances where is the risk of loss?

(a) With Faswell, since it shipped nonconforming goods

(b) With Citation, since this was an FOB shipment contract

(c) With Faswell, since this was an FOB destination contract

(d) With Citation, since it only shipped "for accommodation"

Where goods are to be shipped under the terms of a sales contract, these terms normally settle the issue. This was an FOB shipment contract, which means that risk passes to the buyer at the shipping point. However, this rule does not apply where one of the parties has breached the contract. Faswell sent nonconforming goods, which is a breach of contract, and the loss follows such breach; statement (a) is the answer. Since Faswell had already accepted the offer, it cannot be the beneficiary of the rule that a shipment of nonconforming goods does not constitute an acceptance if sent for "accommodation only"; that is, the seller notifies the buyer that the shipment should not be considered as an acceptance of the offer, but rather is to be viewed as a counteroffer which the buyer may accept, UCC, Section 2-206(1)(b).

16.2 In connection with risk and expense associated with the delivery of goods to a destination under a sales contract, the term "FOB place of destination" means that

(a) the seller bears the risk and expense.

(b) the buyer bears the risk and expense.

(c) the seller bears the risk but *not* the expense.

(d) the buyer bears the risk but *not* the expense.

(*AICPA Examination, May 1977*)

An FOB destination contract indicates that the parties have agreed that the expense of shipment and the risk of loss continue in the seller until proper delivery at the destination; statement (a) is correct.

16.3 Duval Liquor Wholesales, Inc., stored its inventory of goods in the Reliable Warehouse Company. Duval's shipments would arrive by truck and be deposited with Reliable, who would in turn issue a negotiable warehouse receipt to Duval. Duval would resell the liquor by transferring the negotiable warehouse receipt to the buyer, who was responsible for transporting the liquor to his or her place of business. In one of the sales of liquor to a retailer, the liquor was badly damaged, and a question has arisen about who has the risk of loss, Duval or the retailer. If the contract is silent on this point, when does the risk of loss pass to the retailer?

(a) When the goods have been placed on the warehouse's delivery dock awaiting pickup by the retailer

(b) When the goods have been identified to the contract

(c) When the retailer receives the negotiable warehouse receipt covering the goods

(d) When the goods have been properly loaded upon the retailer's carrier

(*AICPA Examination, May 1979*)

The parties agreed that delivery was at the place of a third party, a bailee of the goods. Further, a document had been issued by the bailee in the form of a negotiable warehouse receipt. In such circumstances, transfer of risk and property occurs when the buyer receives the negotiable document, statement (c).

16.4   In connection with a contract for the sale of goods, the term "CIF" means that the price includes

   (*a*)   the cost of the goods exclusive of insurance and freight.

   (*b*)   the cost of the goods plus freight but exclusive of insurance.

   (*c*)   the cost of the goods plus insurance but exclusive of freight.

   (*d*)   the cost of the goods, freight, and insurance.

   (*AICPA Examination, May 1977*)

   When the parties employ the term "CIF", they intend that the seller will include in the invoice the cost of the goods, insurance appropriate to the contract, and the freight charges; statement (*d*) is the answer.

16.5   Under a contract for sale on approval, unless otherwise agreed, what happens to "risk of loss" and "title" upon delivery to the buyer?

   (*a*)   Risk of loss but *not* title passes to the buyer.

   (*b*)   Title but *not* risk of loss passes to the buyer.

   (*c*)   Risk of loss and title pass to the buyer.

   (*d*)   *Neither* risk of loss *nor* title passes to the buyer.

   (*AICPA Examination, May 1977*)

   A sale on approval is a conditional contract for the sale of goods. Until the buyer approves or otherwise exercises a property interest in the goods delivered to him or her, the risk of loss and title remain with the seller, statement (*d*).

16.6   A Los Angeles wholesaler sold to a Boston men's store certain clothing for the price of $2,161, FOB Los Angeles, via Denver-Chicago Trucking. The goods were delivered to the trucking company, and the men's store was notified of the shipment. The store refused delivery when the truck arrived unless the trucker agreed to unload the goods inside the store. The trucker refused to unload, and the goods were kept by the trucker. They were subsequently lost. The wholesaler demands the invoice purchase price from the men's store. Which statement is correct?

   (*a*)   The wholesaler wins since it made a proper delivery to the trucker in Los Angeles, where risk of loss passed to the buyer.

   (*b*)   The wholesaler wins because the men's store should have accepted the goods and sued the trucker for breach of contract.

   (*c*)   The men's store wins since the wholesaler made an inadequate shipping contract.

   (*d*)   The men's store wins since the trucker was the agent of the wholesaler.

   Statement (*a*) is correct. In an FOB shipment contract, here Los Angeles, the risk and expense shift to the buyer at Los Angeles. At that point the seller no longer has any interest. The buyer's only action would be against the trucking company.

16.7   Smedley stole 200 hindquarters of fresh beef from the shipping dock of a packer. If Smedley should attempt to sell this beef to others, what is the state of the title to the beef?

   (*a*)   Any purchaser would gain a void title, i.e., no title at all.

   (*b*)   A good-faith purchaser for value gains a voidable title.

(c) The title is valid if the goods are sold by Smedley to another in the ordinary course of business.

(d) A valid title passes if the packer should fail to report the theft within 24 hours after discovering the loss.

Thieves cannot pass good title to goods stolen from others; statement (a) is the answer. Only in entrustment situations can a larceny result in a transfer of title. Smedley was not entrusted with the beef; he stole it.

16.8 Entrustment is a principle by which a party having no real title can nevertheless pass a valid title to others. Under which of the following circumstances does title pass?

(a) When a stolen ring is sold by a jeweler who had knowingly purchased it from a thief

(b) When a stolen ring is sold by a jeweler who had unknowingly purchased it from a thief

(c) When a stolen ring, unknowingly purchased from a thief, is sold to a good-faith buyer in the ordinary course of business by a jeweler who only repairs rings

(d) When a ring, left by its owner for repair only, is sold to a good-faith buyer, in the ordinary course of business, by a jeweler who sells and repairs rings

Entrustment is an exception to the rule that thieves cannot pass title to stolen goods. If a party voluntarily turns over possession of an item to another party who regularly sells such items, the risk of an improper sale is present, statement (d). If a seller sells goods deliberately (larceny) or accidentally to a good-faith buyer in the ordinary course of business, title to the goods passes to the buyer. The one who entrusted the goods would have an action only against the seller.

16.9 In a sale or return, which of the following does *not* occur?

(a) The buyer can return the goods if he or she doesn't sell them.

(b) The buyer suffers the risk of loss until he or she returns the goods.

(c) Title to the goods passes to the buyer.

(d) The buyer does not have to pay until he or she approves of the purchase.

Only statement (d) does not occur. A sale or return is a real sale. The buyer owes a duty to pay for the goods on the agreed terms. There is a condition, however, that the goods may be returned for reasons stated in the contract. Until that decision to return is made and communicated to the seller, however, the sale is complete.

16.10 A farmer contracted to purchase a new haystacker using his old unit as a trade-in. Under the directions of the seller, the farmer indorsed and mailed in the title certificate to the old unit to the seller. The farmer, however, was allowed to retain possession of the old unit and use it until the new haystacker was available from the seller. During this period, the old unit caught fire and was destroyed in the farmer's field through no fault of his. Whose haystacker was destroyed in terms of suffering the risk of loss?

(a) The dealer, as possessor of the title certificate, suffers the loss.

(b) The farmer suffers the loss since he should have had the haystacker insured.

(c) The farmer suffers the loss since he was not a merchant and had not yet tendered delivery of the old unit to the dealer.

(d) The farmer suffers the loss because the dealer would only be liable if he had taken receipt of the old unit.

Section 509(1) of the UCC governs this situation by providing that where the seller is not a merchant, the risk passes to the buyer on tender of delivery. Since the farmer was not yet in a position to offer to perform, that is, tender the old unit for the new unit, risk of loss remains with the farmer as the seller of the old unit; statement (*c*) is the answer.

16.11 Trader, Inc., shipped 24 bales of card waste to Woolmar, a manufacturer of woolen cloth. The goods had not been ordered by Woolmar. Trader asked Woolmar to store the goods for it and, if Woolmar wanted to purchase any, to send Trader the invoice price. Later Woolmar found it had use for seven bales and sent the purchase price to Trader. Woolmar then ran into financial trouble and went into bankruptcy. The creditors of Woolmar contend that the 17 bales of card waste belong to Woolmar. Trader wants the 17 bales returned. Which of the following is correct?

(*a*)   Title passed to Woolmar when it did not return the bales.

(*b*)   Title to the 17 bales did not pass to Woolmar.

(*c*)   Title passed to Woolmar when Trader shipped the goods and made a proper contract for transportation.

(*d*)   In a destination contract, once the goods reach the buyer, the risk of loss passes to Woolmar.

This was not a shipment contract, as Trader sent the goods without any agreement with Woolmar. The only agreement here was storage of goods. Accordingly, until the parties agreed that the title to the 17 bales was to pass, there would be no change in ownership; statement (*b*) is the answer. In such circumstances there was no sale or intention to enter into a sales contract, and without such the agreement was for storage only. Trader is entitled to the return of its property temporarily stored with Woolmar.

16.12 Auto Leasing gave possession of an automobile to a used-car dealer to show to a customer but did not deliver the certificate of title. The dealer, representing herself as the owner, sold the car to the customer and failed to remit the proceeds to Auto Leasing. In these circumstances,

(*a*)   automobiles cannot be sold without a title certificate.

(*b*)   the dealer was a buyer in a sale-or-return contract.

(*c*)   this was *not* an instrument situation.

(*d*)   the case will be decided on the entrustment question of whether or not the customer was a buyer in the ordinary course of business.

This was an entrustment situation. Certificates of title are important for questions of public policy regarding theft and enforcement of traffic regulations, but they are not a muniment (evidence) of title which conclusively establishes ownership. The issue here is whether or not the customer was a buyer in the ordinary course of business, statement (*d*). An ordinary customer who will use the car is probably such a buyer. However, if the customer was another dealer, who should know the need for a title certificate, the result might be different.

16.13 A wholesaler jeweler delivered to a retailer two diamonds. They were never returned because within 10 days of receipt they were stolen. The parties had had previous dealings, and where no sale was made, goods were customarily returned to the wholesaler. The memorandum between the parties provided that "the title remains in the wholesaler, but the risk of loss is on the buyer." Under these circumstances,

(*a*)   The wholesaler loses, as parties by contract cannot determine risk.

(*b*)   The retailer loses both under contract terms and under principles of sale or return.

(*c*)   all sales on approval, regardless of contrary agreement, place loss on the seller; accordingly, the wholesaler loses.

(*d*)   a buyer on sale or return is not liable for loss not caused by his or her negligence.

This is a sale-or-return contract which specifically provides for the risk on the buyer. Under either principle the buyer, here the retailer, suffers the loss, answer (*b*). Parties by contract may agree to any risk of loss.

16.14 The bulk transfer provisions of Article 6 of the UCC

(*a*) make void any sale between parties in which there was noncompliance.

(*b*) apply to the sale of a barbershop.

(*c*) put the burden of compliance with the seller.

(*d*) put the burden of compliance with the buyer.

If parties agree to a transaction without compliance with the Bulk Transfer Law, the sale is valid as between the parties. However, the buyer suffers the risk of loss of the goods it purchased, or even personal liability for their value. For example, the sale of a service business with little or no equipment is not a bulk transfer, even though there may be some inventory of supplies involved. The purpose of the law is to protect creditors of businesses that deal in goods and that were sold inventory and other supplies on credit. Statement (*d*) is the answer, for in a bulk transfer, the burden of compliance is on the buyer, who must begin the process by demanding a sworn affidavit from the seller identifying the seller's creditors and their addresses. The buyer and seller prepare a list of the property, and the buyer personally notifies the named creditors.

16.15 Bosell's Fine Shoes is not doing very well. Bosell is being pressured by her creditors. In which of the following situations would a transfer of inventory be subject to the Bulk Transfer Law?

(*a*) Transfer of 30 percent of Bosell's inventory to Arnold, her most aggressive unsecured creditor

(*b*) Surrender of the goods to the sheriff who is levying on the goods

(*c*) Transfer of Bosell's whole inventory to Top Shoes, the strongest retailer in town, who gives public notice that it is assuming all debts of Bosell

(*d*) A general assignment for the benefit of all creditors

Section 6-103 of the UCC lists a number of exceptions to the Bulk Transfer Law, which include three of the above, but not statement (*a*). The other types of transfers are specifically listed as exceptions. In statement (*c*), for example, it is required not only that the assumption be made but also that the transferee be solvent after becoming so bound. Accordingly, if "strongest" suggests solvency, the exception is met on these facts.

16.16 Adamson Boutique was having financial troubles and wished to sell all its inventory and equipment and its lease. Tarson Chain liked the location and offered $30,000 for the entire assets. Unknown to Tarson, Adamson's creditors were owed over $42,000. Adamson kept this secret because he feared that if Tarson learned of this, it might blow the deal. Accordingly, when Tarson demanded a bulk transfer sales affidavit, Adamson listed only those creditors whose claims together totaled $16,000. Tarson took the list and gave appropriate registered mail notice to those listed on the affidavit. Tarson accepted the affidavit as fact although it did wonder why Lane Fabrics, one of Adamson's suppliers, was not listed on the affidavit. The appropriate 10-day delay was honored, and those creditors notified appeared to collect their debts. Seven months later Lane Fabrics and several other creditors learned of the transfer. Meanwhile, Adamson had fled the jurisdiction. What rights do Lane and the other unlisted creditors have against Tarson Chain? Decide and give reasons for any conclusions.

Article 6 of the UCC places a duty on the transferee (buyer) of goods in bulk to obtain a sworn affidavit from the seller from which it can proceed. The buyer-transferee may rely on this affidavit, provided it has no knowledge of any other creditors of the seller. If the information that Lane Fabrics had dealt with Adamson was the buyer's only knowledge, such buyer takes free of claim by the omitted creditor. The buyer in a bulk transfer situation need not seek out additional creditors of the seller, but is merely required to practice commercial good faith. The other creditors, likewise, would have no right against Tarson or the goods. Their only rights are against Adamson, if they can find him.

16.17 Diane, of Phoenix, Arizona, traveled to Santa Fe, New Mexico, to visit a precious stone dealer, McCase Stones, to purchase a quantity of jade and turquoise. At the store she learned that if she took personal possession of the turquoise in New Mexico she must pay a considerable tax. If she ordered it shipped to her home, it would pass tax-free. She took the jade with her and left money and her address to ship the turquoise. McCase packaged the turquoise in two parcels, properly addressed them, and, using registered mail, delivered them into the hands of the post office. McCase did not insure the parcels as the firm had its own insurance policy which had a 6-month occurrence clause. Diane received only one parcel of turquoise, not knowing that two had been sent. She was a jewelry artisan and had placed the parcel aside until she had need of the material. When she opened the parcel 10 months later, she discovered that only one-half of her order was in it. McCase's insurance did not cover the loss because more than 6 months had elapsed from the time of the shipment. Diane sued McCase for failure to deliver the contracted-for stones.

What principle of law is involved in this dispute? Decide the lawsuit, giving reasons for any conclusions reached.

The issue is risk of loss where shipment is being made to the buyer. Contract language usually determines risk of loss. Section 2-504 of the UCC states the general principle that where the seller is authorized or directed to send the goods to the buyer, unless otherwise agreed, the seller must put the goods in the possession of a carrier, make a proper contract for carriage, provide any necessary documents, and promptly notify the buyer of the shipment. It appears that the seller, McCase, performed these acts. Notification of shipment was made when McCase was delivering the jade stones to Diane in Santa Fe. The Uniform Commercial Code assumes that a "shipment" rather than a "destination" contract is the usual manner of contracting. In shipment contracts buyers suffer the risk of loss once the goods reach the carrier for immediate shipment. This was done here. Diane's only relief is against the post office.

16.18 Margate Tire Sales received a shipment of 150 steel-belted tires from Fleming Rubber Company on consignment with an invoice which stated that "goods must be purchased within 20 days of receipt or they will be automatically invoiced to your account." One month later Margate's former wife obtained a judgment against Margate for past-due alimony, and the tires, among other assets, were seized by the sheriff. Fleming has evidence that the tires were shipped on consignment and that title was not to pass until the goods were sold by Margate. Fleming Rubber demands its tires back and attempts to recover possession from the sheriff's levy.

What is the status of title to the 150 tires under these circumstances? Decide and give reasons for your conclusions.

Parties may set forth their agreement about when title passes, but in regard to consignments, the UCC does not permit such an effect in detriment to the buyer's creditors. Section 2-326 of the UCC permits an effective consignment, keeping title with the seller as long as certain provisions are met. If, for example, Margate carried on business in the name of Fleming Rubber, the consignment would be honored. Further, if the state had a sign law and the parties observed it, or in the absence of such the seller complied with Article 9 of the UCC and filed a financing statement "perfecting its security interest," the consignment would be honored. Since none of this appears to have occurred, the seller loses his rights in the tires, having only a contract claim for the price against Margate.

Chapter 17

Warranties

17.1 WARRANTIES

A *warranty* is an assurance that goods will conform to certain standards or qualities. A breach of warranty allows an action for damages and, in some instances, a rescission of the contract. The study of warranties encompasses consideration of warranty of title; warranty of infringement; warranties of quality, including express warranty, implied warranty of merchantability, and implied warranty of fitness; federal statutory warranty; disclaimers and exclusion of implied warranty, privity requirements, chain of distribution, and product liabilty.

17.2 WARRANTY OF TITLE

Unless otherwise agreed, every seller of goods warrants that the title is good and the transfer is rightful. Further, the seller warrants that the goods delivered are free from any security interest or other encumbrance which has not been made known to the buyer, UCC, Section 2-312.

EXAMPLE 1. A buyer purchased a dairy and its equipment from a farmer, including a bottle hooder. The bottle hooder was only leased by the farmer. Later the buyer sold the dairy to Tesdale and, not knowing the bottle hooder was leased, included it in the sale. The lessor of the bottle hooder, hearing of this sale, reclaimed his property. The buyer had to settle Tesdale's claim for $1,100. The buyer can sue the farmer for breach of warranty of title to the bottle hooder. The farmer had no title to sell.

EXAMPLE 2. As a condition to a capital loan, Mason granted a lien on all his equipment to the bank. Later, he purchased a new pipe threader, turning in his old one as part of the purchase price. The sale of the old threader is a breach of warranty of title and the assurance that there is no encumbrance on the goods.

17.3 DISCLAIMER OF TITLE

The seller can agree with another that no warranties of title exist, or sell in such circumstances that the law assumes the buyer has such notice.

EXAMPLE 3. In preparing the bill of sale the seller included the language, "I hereby sell, quitclaim, transfer, and convey all my right and title, if any I have . . . ." This is the language of the *quitclaim deed*. If the seller had title, it passes. If not, the seller cannot be sued for breach of warranty of title.

EXAMPLE 4. A statement by the seller that she will sell the "watch which I found at the company picnic" is notice which indicates to the buyer that no warranty of title is being made.

Circumstances may indicate to another that the seller does not claim title in himself or herself. A sale can be made by one other than the owner. Such sales carry no warranty of title. Auctioneers, sheriffs, executors of estates, and mortgagees selling at foreclosure are parties selling without such representation of title.

EXAMPLE 5. A judgment was against the owner of a townhouse. The sheriff entered the premises under a writ of execution and seized all the furniture, including a piano. On a certain day the furniture was offered for sale to the highest bidder. The high bidder was awarded the piano. Later the neighbor of the owner returned to town and traced her piano to the high bidder's residence. The neighbor proved that her piano was merely being stored while she had been abroad. The neighbor could retrieve the piano. The high bidder cannot sue the sheriff for breach of warranty of title. When the sheriff sold the piano, he did not claim title in himself. He makes no warranty under such circumstances.

17.4 WARRANTY OF INFRINGEMENT

In the absence of an agreement to the contrary, a merchant seller warrants that the goods are delivered free of the rightful claim of any third person by way of infringement. Nonmerchants only make this warranty by express agreement.

EXAMPLE 6. A distributor sells automatic dish-dispensing machines to a dealer. The dealer sells a number of these machines to various buyers. The dealer is sued in federal court for patent infringement, the plaintiff charging that a device on the equipment infringes the plaintiff's patent. The dealer may look to the distributor for protection on the basis of the warranty against infringement.

Sellers who comply with the special orders of a buyer are protected from a claim of infringement; the role of guarantor is reversed by Section 2-312(3) of the UCC, which provides that buyers who furnish specifications to sellers must hold the seller harmless against any claim of infringement arising out of compliance with such specifications.

17.5 WARRANTIES OF QUALITY

The buyer needs more from the goods than title or freedom from claims against them. The buyer needs the goods to perform, taste, operate, appear as such, and so on. The buyer's dissatisfied expectations may result in a finding of breach of warranty of quality. Three types of such warranties are important: express warranty, implied warranty of merchantability, and implied warranty of fitness for a particular purpose.

17.6 EXPRESS WARRANTY

Any affirmation of fact or promise made by the seller to the buyer relating to the goods may become an express warranty. The goods must conform to these representations. The scope of any affirmation of fact or promise is broad and includes language or conduct upon which the buyer relies. Accordingly, statements made on labels, in newspaper advertisements, on tags, or in catalog descriptions could form the basis of an express warranty. Further, the supplying of a sample or model is treated as an express warranty commitment. Even a seemingly vague word about quality may have a definite legal meaning under the circumstances.

EXAMPLE 7. A racehorse owner's statement that the horse she was selling was "sound" constitutes an express warranty of fitness as a racehorse. The term "sound," though generally vague, has a specific meaning by racing custom. This was breached by a showing that the horse was "high-nerved" and therefore disqualified from racing.

Providing a sample or a model as the basis of a bargain is a particularly effective way of creating a warranty that the whole will conform to the sample or meet the model's specifications.

EXAMPLE 8.   A retailer, at a time when soap was scarce, purchased 25 cases of soap from a wholesale broker who represented that the soap purchased was the quality he offered. The retailer sold the 25 cases to satisfied customers. The retailer thereupon ordered 100 more cases of the soap. This soap was different. It was unfit and did not correspond to the original soap. Since the 100-case purchase was made on the basis of the previous 25-case purchase, there was a breach of warranty of quality. This was a sale by sample.

Not all language or conduct proves an express warranty. Some sales conduct is characterized as *puffing*, general words of commendation of the product. An affirmation of value of the product, or a statement reflecting only the seller's opinion or commendation of the goods, does not constitute an express warranty.

EXAMPLE 9.   Examples of puffing and statements of value:

> This rug is excellent.
> It's a $10 value.
> It's the finest on the market.
> Fantastic, it's fantastic!

EXAMPLE 10.   Examples of express warranty statements:

> This car delivers 30 miles per gallon of gas.
> This fabric has been treated for shrinkage control and won't shrink or stretch out of fit.
> This sweater is 100 percent virgin wool.

Advertising frequently uses ambiguous language to describe the quality or expectations of a product. Those matters which are factual can be the basis of an express warranty.

EXAMPLE 11.   The city was interested in buying a used machine. The sales offer referred to a "1980 model, excellent condition, can be shown in operation." The machine, a diesel engine, was actually manufactured in 1974. There was an express warranty that the engine was manufactured in 1980. Such reference is an affirmation of fact having the natural tendency to induce the city to buy the unit.

An express warranty can be created after a sale. Further, since modification of a sales contract does not require additional consideration, it is not uncommon that express warranties are created without new consideration. The warranty card frequently found in boxed merchandise is a common situation where an additional warranty takes effect after the purchase. The execution and return of the warranty card by the purchaser can result in an express warranty according to the terms contained in the card's offer. This does not disturb the existence of any other warranties previously created.

An express warranty cannot easily be disclaimed or excluded. That is, the seller cannot take away in one part of the contract something granted in another part. However, an oral express warranty can be disclaimed by a written contract containing an entireties clause. Silence and inaction of a seller constitute the only way to prevent creation of an express warranty of quality.

17.7   IMPLIED WARRANTY OF MERCHANTABILITY

A warranty that the goods sold shall be merchantable is implied by operation of law in every sale by a merchant with respect to goods of that kind, under the provisions of Section 2-314 of the UCC. This warranty arises even when the merchant's goods are sold in a package or sealed container, and also when there is no practical method for the seller to determine merchantability. If sued by the buyer, the merchant must look to his or her supplier for relief.

EXAMPLE 12. A man alleged that he was severely burned when the contents of a household detergent container spilled on him. The man sued the grocer. The grocer regularly deals in detergents; she is a merchant; she makes an implied warranty of merchantability. The grocer can only sue the supplier once the grocer is sued by the customer.

A product is merchantable if it possesses those attributes that arise from the course of dealing with or usage of trade regarding such goods. Specifically, Section 2-314 of the UCC demands that the goods must be such as

(1) pass without objection in the trade under the contract description.

(2) in the case of fungible (interchangeable) goods, are of fair average quality within the description.

(3) are fit for ordinary purposes for which such goods are used.

(4) run, within the variations permitted by the agreement, of even kind, quality, and quantity within each unit and among all units involved.

(5) are adequately contained, packaged, and labeled as the agreement may require.

(6) conform to the promises or affirmations of fact made on the container or label if any.

This list is not conclusive, but does inform the seller of the buyer's minimum expectations of the goods. The UCC's warranty expectations concentrate on assuring the utility of the goods for the purpose for which they are usually sold by the merchant. There is no implied warranty that a harvesting machine be attractive, for example, or that a cow won't trample down a fence or perform some act contrary to known experience or the known forces of nature. A harvesting machine should harvest; a cow should give milk, etc. However, additional expectations, resulting in an implied warranty, can occur by reason of the course of dealing or usage of trade.

EXAMPLE 13. A farmer purchased a secondhand combine from a dealer. It broke down during its first use. It needs some parts and repairs. The dealer claims there is no implied warranty of merchantability. The farmer offers to show that it is the custom in that farming community for used farm equipment to be "under a 50/50 warranty." The farmer shows that the seller pays 50 percent of repairs and the buyer the other 50 percent. If proved, this implied warranty is created by "usage of trade."

The fact that the seller did not know that the implied warranty of merchantability was breached, or was unable to prevent a breach, does not excuse the seller. It exists without fault of the merchant seller.

EXAMPLE 14. A buyer bought 2,000 day-old chicks, all of which died of avian leukosis (bird cancer), from the Spring Mail Order House. At trial Spring proved that there is no way to determine whether or not newly hatched chicks have leukosis and that there is no medicine available to prevent the disease. Nonetheless, the buyer wins. The purpose of the UCC is to hold the seller responsible when inferior goods are sold to an unsuspecting buyer. The only proof required is that the goods at delivery were not of merchantable quality.

The UCC does not specifically refer to secondhand or used goods. A number of states have, by case law, found an implied warranty extending only to that appropriate to the contract description. Some states have denied an implied warranty for used goods.

17.8 IMPLIED WARRANTY OF FITNESS

A seller, by his or her conduct or language, can be bound by the implied warranty of fitness for a particular purpose. This warranty can be imposed on nonmerchants as well as merchants. Where the seller at the time of contracting has reason to know of any particular purpose for which the goods are to be used, an implied warranty that the goods shall be fit for such purpose may attach to the sale. It is only necessary that the buyer then relies on the seller's skill or judgment to select or furnish suitable goods.

EXAMPLE 15.   A painter purchased rope from a retailer. The painter used it for scaffolding support. It broke while in use, and the painter was injured. The rope performed as ordinary rope judged by its thickness and material. There is no breach of an implied warranty. Unless the retailer knew, or should have known, the expected use of the rope for scaffolding support and recommended (or selected) the rope, no particular implied warranty of fitness for a particular purpose (here scaffolding support) was created.

It is necessary therefore for the seller to have reason to know the intended use *and* recommend or select the goods in order for the fitness warranty to arise. The concern is whether or not the court finds that the buyer was relying on the seller's judgment in the selection of the goods for the particular purpose.

EXAMPLE 16.   Able needs an electric pump for his three-stage lawn sprinkler system. Able does not know what size pump is necessary to do the job. He describes his sprinkler system and his need for a pump to the saleswoman. The saleswoman recommends a 2-horsepower electric pump. Able purchases this pump. The pump does not accomplish the task. A 3-horsepower pump should have been used. The saleswoman breached the implied warranty of fitness for a particular purpose.

EXAMPLE 17.   The facts are the same here as those in Example 16, except that the reason the 2-horsepower electric pump did not perform the task was that this particular pump was defective. It did not meet the standard of 2-horsepower electric pumps. Since the saleswoman is a merchant, the implied warranty of merchantability operates and is breached by this sale of a defective pump.

17.9   FEDERAL STATUTORY WARRANTY

The UCC is not the exclusive source of statutory warranty law. Each state is free to create statutes treating certain aspects of warranty law, and all have done so. In the federal system a number of statutes deal with the safety and quality of goods. This consumer protection legislation generally authorizes a government agency to oversee certain aspects of product creation and distribution. In 1975 Congress enacted the Magnuson–Moss Warranty Act, legislation which added to the rights of a consumer in regard to certain sales.

This act does not affect the UCC provisions, which may and do coexist with the act's provisions. Like the UCC, the act attempts to make more effective the rights of the buyer of goods. Unlike the UCC, the act is applicable only to sales to ultimate consumers for personal, family, or household purposes. Further, the sale of goods must be for a price of $10 or more, and only written express warranties are covered. If the seller makes a written express warranty about a product, he or she cannot disclaim implied warranties in the same contract. Further, the seller must elect to label the warranty prominently as a "full" or "limited" warranty, although such warranties may be limited in time. Failing to so label makes the express warranty a full warranty, requiring, among other things, the seller to repair or replace defective goods within a reasonable time without charge. The warranties must be on display before sale. Limitations are permitted only under the label of "limited warranty." Under the act, the term "merchantable" means that the product will perform as represented in a "safe" manner.

The Federal Trade Commission monitors the act under which it can bring an action. Consumers likewise can sue or bring an action to seek relief under informal procedures as set up by the sellers.

17.10   DISCLAIMERS AND EXCLUSION OF IMPLIED WARRANTY

The UCC places a heavy burden on sellers in regard to implied warranties. Nevertheless, it allows their exclusion or modification by providing specific methods in Section 2-316. Where conflicting conduct occurs, the law does not favor the seller negating warranties and allows, in some instances, parol or extrinsic evidence to explain or supplement by course of dealing or usage of trade. Some words and conduct are clearly disclaimers of implied warranties of quality:

(1) Clear statement or understanding that the goods are:
   (*a*) "As is"
   (*b*) "With all faults"
   (*c*) "In its present condition"
(2) Conduct
   (*a*) As to defects which could be observed, those present after the buyer has fully examined the goods, model, or sample.
   (*b*) The buyer refuses the seller's request to examine the goods and such would have revealed a defect.
(3) Course of dealing, course of performance, usage of trade:
   (*a*) On previous occasions, in different contracts, a slight blemish on fruit has not been objected to by the buyer (course of dealing).
   (*b*) During the contract performance, each shipment of Christmas trees had up to 5 percent deficiency in length specifications with no objection by the buyer (course of performance).
   (*c*) It is the custom in Harvest Valley that 2 percent of the potatoes supplied to wholesale produce buyers can be "shrimps" (usage of trade).

The subtler and more common business way to exclude implied warranties is to follow the formula provided by the UCC. Warranty of merchantability can be excluded by the seller's express language that he or she excludes such. However, the seller must use the word "merchantability" in the exclusion. This can be done orally; if done in writing, such writing must be conspicuous. On the other hand, there can be no oral disclaimer of a warranty of fitness for a particular purpose; it must be in writing and be conspicuous, but no particular words are necessary. The UCC approves the common statement that "there are no warranties which extend beyond the description of the face hereof." Such qualifies as a valid disclaimer of the implied warranty of fitness. Note that it does not satisfy the merchantability disclaimer.

EXAMPLE 18. A buyer sued a new-car dealer for breach of implied warranty of merchantability. The car burned up due to a defective brake assembly. It was argued that the statement in the express warranty card disclaimed this warranty. The card stated, "This warranty made being expressly in lieu of all other warranties, express or implied, and all other obligations on its part." The buyer wins. The language used does not contain the word "merchantability" or statutorily approved expressions such as "with all faults" or "as is."

EXAMPLE 19. A company purchased a used diesel engine from a dealer, signing on the front of a one-page contract which had printing on the reverse. Above the company's signature was the statement "SEE REVERSE SIDE FOR DISCLAIMER OF WARRANTIES." The engine failed, and the company sued for implied breach of warranty of merchantability. The dealer contends that a valid disclaimer was on the reverse side of the contract page. The company proves that the one-page contract was attached to a pad with a carbon under the first page. Only *after* signing and completing the contract did the company get to read the reverse side of its copy of the contract where the exclusion of the warranties was effectively printed. The court held that this disclaimer of exclusion was not conspicuous. The buyer wins.

17.11 LIMITATIONS AND MODIFICATIONS

A cousin to exclusions and disclaimers of warranty is the set of limitation provisions of the UCC found in Section 2-719. Consequential damages may be limited or excluded unless such would be unconscionable. Limitation of such damage to persons who are injured by consumer goods is considered *prima facie* unconscionable. Consequential damages are those special damages flowing from the breach of warranty but which were within, or should have been within, the contemplation of the parties at the time of the contract.

EXAMPLE 20.   Kunkel Corp. sold 3,000 valve fasteners to Reole Machines Co. with an express warranty but with a specific limitation that it would "not be liable for consequential damages." Fifty of the fasteners failed, and Reole's assembly line was shut down for 3 days, causing workers to be idle and also resulting in the loss of some raw materials. At the time of the contract Kunkel knew its goods would be used on Reole's assembly line and what harm defective goods could cause. Accordingly, Kunkel would have been liable for these special, consequential damages but for the limitation of liability contained in the contract.

17.12   PRIVITY REQUIREMENTS

An action for breach of warranty is a contract action. Generally, only parties to a contract can sue unless they qualify as third-party beneficiaries. In warranty actions, however, the privity rule is no longer absolute. More recent rules regarding parties in the chain of distribution and product liability must be noted.

17.13   CHAIN OF DISTRIBUTION

Despite the adage that strangers to a contract cannot sue, many states today allow parties in the chain of distribution of the goods to sue for breach of warranty. These cases began to appear in regard to dangerous items and food and now extend to other products.

EXAMPLE 21.   Burns purchased an Ace toaster from Bumbles' Store under an Ace toaster express warranty to purchasers. Technically, Burns is in privity of contract only with Bumbles, the store that sold him the toaster. Bumbles and Ace are in privity with each other; Burns is not in privity with Ace. Today, in many states Burns can sue Ace for breach of the express warranty, either because he is a third-party beneficiary of the express warranty or just because he is in the chain of distribution.

17.14   PRODUCT LIABILITY

Not all losses are purely property losses. A breach of the warranty or a defect in the product may cause personal injury to parties who purchased the goods or those who come in contact with the goods. When an action is brought for personal injury rather than property losses, the courts may label it a "products liability" case. Two classes of plaintiffs appear in these actions: those who purchased the product in the chain of distribution and those who do not appear in the chain of distribution. The purchaser has a choice of remedies, including warranty, negligence, or, in some states, strict liability.

EXAMPLE 22.   Taylor purchased a tank of propane gas from Flak Products which Flak had obtained from the West Gas Company. The tank exploded without fault of Taylor, and she was injured as a result. Taylor has a choice of legal theories to sue both parties: implied warranty of merchantability, negligence, or, in some states, strict liability. In warranty Taylor need only prove she purchased the tank and it exploded without any contributing action on her part. In respect to negligence Flak owed a duty to Taylor to use reasonable care and failed in this duty thus causing the injury. In strict liability Taylor need only show that the tank was dangerously defective when it left the hands of Flak and that the defect caused the injury. Strict liability is placed only on merchants.

These choices of legal theories are not made lightly by the plaintiff's attorney, as each has its own requirements. An action on warranty is generally the easier to prosecute. The plaintiff wins if he or she proves the warranty and shows the injury from the breach of it. On the other hand, negligence requires not only the task of showing that a duty was owed to the plaintiff by the defendant and that there was proximate causation, but also the sometimes difficult burden of proving that the defendant fell below the duty of a reasonable person. Strict liability would usually be the favorite of the injured party, but its application is restricted to only those items or products which are inherently dangerous if defectively made. Further, whichever legal theory is pressed, the plaintiff must be aware of the statute of limitations. Not all grounds have an identical period within which the lawsuit must be filed.

The extent of product liability on the seller-manufacturer in respect to personal injury of those other than the contracting buyer or others in the chain of distribution is not so clear. In some states remote parties can recover, and in others not. The drafters of the UCC offered the states several alternative sections in regard to these third parties as to warrant of liability. The most enacted version of Section 2-318 of the UCC allows recovery to members of the buyer's family, or household, and to guests in the buyer's home. Further, these parties must be individuals who might reasonably be expected to use, consume, or be affected by the product. States have not uniformly applied this section.

EXAMPLE 23.   A woman purchased a vaporizer from the drugstore and stored it away. Several weeks later her sister needed it for her infant son who had the croup. The sister lived down the block but on the same street. The sister set up the vaporizer in the infant's room and then left the room. The vaporizer was defective and spewed boiling water on the infant, who died. The infant's estate sued the drugstore on a warranty theory. The drugstore contends that the infant was not a member of the aunt's family or household within the meaning of Section 2-318 of the UCC. The court ruled for the infant's estate, deciding that the infant was a member of the family.

EXAMPLE 24.   A college student was employed in the kitchen of a sorority house. She was not a sorority sister. Her hands were burned by a defective detergent. The student sued the grocer for breach of warranty. The grocer successfully defended on the grounds that the student was not a family member, a member of the household, or a guest in the buyer's home.

Product liability litigation is much broader than actions for breach of warranty. The UCC does not address the other actions which a party personally injured may sue upon. The distinctions between a buyer in the chain of distribution, sometimes called a *vertical third party*, and one having no contractual thread with the sale of the product, a *true remote party* or *horizontal third party*, play a role in the success of the action in many states. In those cases, warranty theories are less important than the particular stage of development of doctrines of negligence and strict liability in the state.

Black Letter Law
A Summary

1.   A warranty is an assurance that goods will conform to certain standards or qualities.

2.   Warranties can apply to title, infringement, or quality.

3.   Warranties can be created by express will of the seller or by operation of law based on conduct and circumstances.

4.   An implied or statutory warranty of title to goods exists in most sellers for value of goods.

5.   The warranty of title can be expressly disclaimed or be otherwise not applicable to certain types of sales.

6.   The warranty of title assures the buyer more than that of title; it includes the representation that the goods are free from any claim or encumbrance.

7. Buyers who instruct a manufacturer-seller with the specifications for goods do not get a warranty of infringement from the seller but rather make one themselves.

8. The principal warranties of quality are express warranties, implied warranties of merchantability, and implied warranties of fitness for a particular purpose.

9. Any affirmation of fact or promise made by the seller to the buyer relating to the goods may become an express warranty.

10. A seller cannot disclaim an express warranty.

11. Statements about value or the worth of goods are considered puffing and are not express warranties.

12. A warranty is created where a sample or a model is made part of the bargain.

13. Only merchants are held to the implied warranty that the goods sold are fit for their ordinary use.

14. The implied warranty of merchantability may be disclaimed or excluded by the conspicuous use of the word "merchantability" in the disclaimer or by the use of language such as "with all faults" or "as is."

15. The law imposes on all sellers the implied warranty of fitness for a particular use when the buyer makes known his or her needs or the seller has reason to know the particular needs of the buyer who relies on the seller's judgment or selection of the appropriate goods.

16. The implied warranty of fitness can be disclaimed or excluded only by a writing which is conspicuous or by the use of words such as "with all faults" or "as is."

17. In addition to other principles, warranties can be created by course of dealing or usage of trade, and they likewise can be disclaimed through these methods.

18. Some warranty protection exists on the federal and state levels by statutory protection, the most notable of which is the Magnuson–Moss Warranty Act.

19. The amount of damages that may flow from a breach of warranty and the time within which one must sue can be contracted for by the parties under the limitations and modifications sections of the UCC.

20. Consequential damages can, by contract, be excluded, but not effectively in regard to damages for personal injuries.

21. The privity-of-contract rule has generally been relaxed as a condition to a remote buyer suing a seller or manufacturer of goods.

22. Most states allow buyers in the chain of distribution to sue sellers up the line in the chain for breach of warranty.

23. Product liability generally refers to the dispute between sellers, manufacturers, and wholesalers of goods who are sued by buyers and others who have suffered personal injury from the product.

24. A party personally injured from a product or good may have the choice of remedies of negligence, strict liability, or warranty in some situations.

25. For those parties who are not in the chain of distribution, but are nevertheless personally injured from the goods, the UCC provides a formula which includes the members of the buyer's family, household members, or guests as third-party beneficiaries.

Solved Problems

17.1 Ace Auto Sales, Inc., sold Williams a secondhand car for $9,000. One day Williams parked the car in a shopping center parking lot. When Williams returned to the car, Montrose and several police officers were waiting. It turned out that the car had been stolen from Montrose, who was rightfully claiming ownership. Subsequently, the car was returned by Williams to Montrose. Williams seeks recourse against Ace Auto Sales, who had sold her the car with the usual disclaimer of warranty. Which of the following is correct?

(a) Since Ace Auto Sales' contract of sale disclaimed "any and all warranties" arising in its sale to Williams, Williams must bear the loss.

(b) Since Ace Auto and Williams were both innocent of any wrongdoing in connection with the theft of the auto, the loss will rest upon the party ultimately in possession.

(c) Had Williams litigated the question of Montrose's ownership to the auto, she would have won since possession is nine-tenths of the law.

(d) Ace Auto will bear the loss since a warranty of title in Williams's favor arose upon the sale of the auto.

(*Adapted from AICPA Examination, May 1981*)

Statement (d) is the correct statement. Unless otherwise agreed, every seller of goods warrants that the title is good, the transfer is rightful, and the goods are free from any encumbrance not known to the buyer. A disclaimer of a quality warranty has no effect on the warranty of title.

17.2 The Uniform Commercial Code provides for a warranty against infringement. Its primary purpose is to protect the buyer of goods from infringement of the rights of third parties. This warranty

(a) applies only if the sale is between merchants.

(b) must be expressly stated in the contract, or the Statute of Frauds will prevent its enforceability.

(c) protects the seller if the buyer furnishes specifications which result in an infringement.

(d) *cannot* be disclaimed.

(*Adapted from AICPA Examination, May 1981*)

In the absence of an agreement to the contrary, a merchant seller warrants that the goods are delivered free of the claim of infringement, but not when the seller complies with specifications supplied by the buyer, statement (c). Under such circumstances, the warranty is reversed to the benefit of the seller under Section 2-312(3) of the UCC. Both parties to such a sale need not be merchants, but the seller must be a merchant.

17.3 Marco Auto, Inc., made many untrue statements in the course of inducing Rockford to purchase a used auto for $3,500. The car in question turned out to have some serious faults. Which of the following untrue statements made by Marco should Rockford use in seeking recovery from Marco for breach of warranty?

    (*a*) "I refused a $3,800 offer for this very same auto from another buyer last week."

    (*b*) "This auto is one of the best autos we have for sale."

    (*c*) "At this price the auto is a real steal."

    (*d*) "I can guarantee you that you will never regret this purchase."

(*AICPA Examination, May 1979*)

     Any affirmation of fact or promise made by the seller to the buyer relating to the goods may be an express warranty. The fact in this case was that seller refused an offer for a certain sum last week, statement (*a*). Statements (*b*) and (*c*) express no more than puffing, or words of general commendation. Statement (*d*) is too vague in its guarantee.

17.4 A homeowner injured his foot when it was cut by a lawnmower blade. The accident occurred when the homeowner cut the grass on his hill by mowing up and down rather than working the slope lengthwise. The homeowner sued the seller. Which of the following contentions would be the most advantageous for the homeowner?

    (*a*) He should contend that the lawnmower was dangerous but the instructions only warned the user by a sign on the back reading, "Keep hands and feet from under mower."

    (*b*) He should contend that his negligence is no defense to a strict liability action.

    (*c*) He should contend that the mower was defective since the blade was too sharp.

    (*d*) He should argue negligence, contending that there were no instructions on the machine regarding its use on slopes or hills.

     Since it appears that the injury occurred as a result of the *method* of using the machine, one can't argue that the machine was designed improperly. It would be best to direct the court's attention to the particular danger of mowers on slopes. If it could be shown that the company had reports of numerous similar injuries, a case could be made for the company's negligence in failing to warn of the particular hazard; statement (*d*) is the answer.

17.5 A farmer purchased a used combine from the dealer. The written contract provided that "there are no warranties on used machines." The combine broke down during the first 90 days after purchase, and the dealer fixed the machine, demanding payment from the farmer for 50 percent of the repair bill. The farmer paid that amount, as this was the practice in the community. This used combine was sold with

    (*a*) an express warranty covering 50 percent of the repair bills.

    (*b*) a warranty of 50 percent repair created by trade usage.

    (*c*) an implied warranty of fitness for a particular purpose.

    (*d*) no warranties whatsoever.

     This attempted disclaimer does not meet the requirements of the UCC since it does not use the word "merchantability." There could be an implied warranty even though these are secondhand goods. However, the more obvious warranty will be the one established by trade usage, statement (*b*). There were no express warranties given, nor did the conduct of the parties suggest a fitness warranty.

17.6 While attempting to sit down on a newly purchased chair in the home of another, Finley suffered a serious back injury when the chair collapsed. Under what circumstances could the seller of the chair escape liability to Finley?

   (*a*) Finley was a guest in the home.

   (*b*) Finley was a member of the family in the home.

   (*c*) Finley was a burglar who attempted to rest during his break-in.

   (*d*) Finley was a member of the household of the family.

     Section 2-318 of the UCC allows recovery to third parties to the contract who might be expected to use, consume, or be affected by the goods. These anticipated parties are members of the buyer's family, members of the buyer's household, or guests in the buyer's home. Statement (*c*) is the answer since a burglar, obviously, does not qualify. The rights of these third parties are for personal injury only.

17.7 Thompson Sales sold Kramer an expensive movie camera. Thompson wishes to disclaim the implied warranty of fitness for a particular purpose. Which of the following will effectively disclaim this warranty?

   (*a*) The fact that the camera was widely advertised as used by Hollywood professionals.

   (*b*) A written statement which states that "any and all warranty protection is hereby disclaimed."

   (*c*) A conspicuous written statement indicating that "there are *no* warranties which extend beyond the description contained in the contract of sale."

   (*d*) An inconspicuous written statement which specifically disclaims all implied warranties.

     The UCC expressly provides that the language in statement (*c*), if in writing, will effectively exclude the implied warranty of fitness for a particular use. Statement (*d*) reminds the reader that a written disclaimer must be conspicuous.

17.8 In connection with a contract for the sale of goods, in which of the following ways can the implied warranty of merchantability be disclaimed by the seller?

   (*a*) By an oral statement which mentions merchantability

   (*b*) By a written statement without mentioning merchantability

   (*c*) By an oral statement which does *not* mention merchantability

   (*d*) By an inconspicuous written statement which mentions merchantability

(*AICPA Examination*, *May 1977*)

     The implied warranty of merchantability can be excluded by an oral as well as a written disclaimer, but it must mention the word "merchantability," statement (*a*). If in writing, it must be conspicuous and the word "merchantability" must, of course, be used.

17.9 A buyer asked a retail paint dealer to recommend a paint to cover the exterior walls of the buyer's house. The buyer reported that the stucco was in a chalky or powdery condition. Hearing this, the dealer recommended Paintall, supplying the buyer with directions for its use. The buyer was delighted and bought Paintall. Under these circumstances,

   (*a*) the dealer made an express warranty with the sale.

   (*b*) Paintall's manufacturer made a limited warranty with the sale.

   (*c*) the dealer is not bound on a warranty of merchantability.

   (*d*) the dealer is bound under an implied warranty of fitness for a particular use.

Where a buyer relies on the judgment of a seller who had reason to know the buyer's particular purpose, an implied warranty of fitness for that purpose is imposed; the answer is (*d*). The dealer made no express statements regarding the paint but is bound as a merchant on an implied warranty of merchantability.

17.10 Faste Food Market sold hot sandwiches in sealed plastic bags labeled "Sealcal." The bagged sandwiches were produced by a manufacturer and packager for self-service markets. One sealed bag, containing both a roast beef sandwich and a well-disguised sharp bone, was purchased by a buyer, who suffered a severe laceration of the tongue when taking his second bite. Under these circumstances,

(*a*) Faste Food is liable for breach of an express warranty.

(*b*) Faste Food is not liable under the "sealed container exception" from the warranty of merchantability.

(*c*) Faste Food is liable for breach of implied warranty of merchantability.

(*d*) The Sealcal label, listing ingredients, is not making an express warranty, but is merely puffing the product.

Faste Food, regardless of its care, makes an implied warranty of merchantability that its food is fit for human consumption. A sharp bone in a roast beef sandwich is a foreign object, and thus there is a breach of implied warranty; the answer is (*c*). The statement of ingredients on the label describes the product and, as such, qualifies as an express warranty made by the manufacturer of Sealcal.

17.11 Keeton, an avid sailor, purchased a 29-foot wooden sailing sloop from Edwards after some intensive negotiations. Keeton's interest in the boat was first gained through Edwards's advertisement in *Sailing Monthly*. The ad gave the sloop's specifications and nature of furnishings. The bill of sale finally signed by Edwards contained the details in the advertisement and other technical data, but did not mention Edwards's numerous oral assurances to Keeton that "the sloop will become watertight once placed in the water and allowed sufficient time to make up." Keeton placed the sloop in the water, allowed sufficient time for the planking to swell, or "make up," to form a watertight hull. Despite this, the sloop continued to leak and could not be sailed. Dry rot was then discovered, requiring substantial repair expense. Keeton wants to sue for breach of warranty.

What warranty action can Keeton advance? What defense can Edwards offer? State the result of such a lawsuit and reasons for your conclusions.

Keeton should claim a breach of an express oral warranty. Edwards assured Keeton that the boat would become watertight when placed in the water. It did not. Edwards on the other hand would invoke the parol evidence rule under Section 2-202 of the UCC. There are writings in this contract in the form of the advertisement and the bill of sale. The referenced UCC section excludes any additional oral agreement or terms when a written agreement is intended by the parties to be a final expression of their agreement. However, unless the writing was so intended as a complete and exclusive statement of the terms, evidence of consistent or additional terms is admissible. If the trier of facts believes that such statements regarding the seaworthiness of the sloop were made by the seller, then Keeton, the buyer, would win her warranty action, as those oral statements were not inconsistent with the writings, nor were the writings shown to have been the complete and exclusive statement of the agreement.

17.12 Tropic Construction contracted to install certain pipelines between several Caribbean Islands for local governments. Tropic decided that it needed a certain type of pipe and thought it had found what it was looking for from Coated Pipe Company of Long Island, New York. Tropic executed and sent its purchase order to Coated. In the order the quantity, price, and shipping terms were listed; also stated was the specification that the pipe was to be "coal tar enamel-lined." Coated duly accepted the order and shipped the goods according to specifications. Upon installation, Tropic discovered that the lining was not compatible with the coral reef environment and that the pipeline had to be replaced. With such a heavy expense facing the company, Tropic looked for a "deep-pocket defendant." It sued Coated for breach of contract.

What type of warranty must Tropic prove to win the lawsuit? How is this warranty created? Answer these questions and state the winner of the lawsuit, giving reasons for your conclusions.

Tropic must prove that an implied warranty of fitness for a particular purpose was given by Coated Pipe Company. Then Tropic must show that the warranty was breached in that the pipe as lined was not fit for the particular purpose used, here a Caribbean pipeline. In order to prove this warranty, it is necessary for Tropic to have relied on the judgment of Coated, which had reason to know Tropic's particular purpose in purchasing the pipe. In this case it does not appear that Tropic informed Coated of the particular need or requested a recommendation. Tropic directed the specifications, which got it in trouble. Had Coated sent Tropic pipe with a different lining, even if it was more appropriate, that would have been a breach of contract. On these facts it appears the loss was caused by an inappropriate product freely ordered by the buyer. Tropic would lose.

17.13 Buck was the coach of a minibaseball team for teenagers. The regular playing field was unprotected from the afternoon sun. Buck was reluctant to advise the players to use sunglasses until he was attracted to a TV commercial about Playfree Shades. It offered "instant sun protection by the press of a trigger" and concluded that these were specially designed for the young professional ballplayer. Buck liked what he saw of them at the drugstore and purchased a dozen for the team. The shades could be pressed open or closed at the touch of a spring button. The team liked them although the pitcher broke his the first day when they dropped on the pitcher's mound and shattered. The players were a little uneasy about that. The next day the shortstop, in attempting to catch a high infield fly ball, was hit in the eye by the ball, which shattered the shades into small slivers, one of which pierced his eye. The eye was lost.

What types of action can be brought against Playfree Shades? State the answer and decide the lawsuit, giving reasons for your conclusions.

Three types of action can be considered: warranty, strict liability, and negligence. In warranty it is possible that both the implied warranty of merchantability and fitness for a particular purpose would be applicable. The manufacturer and drugstore are both merchants and so make the merchantable warranty. The manufacturer certainly knew of the intended use and, in fact, solicited that use, and so a fitness-for-a-particular-purpose warranty could be present. In both cases, however, the injured party was not the buyer. He was a remote party, and the state law regarding such action by parties not in privity would have to be considered.

Strict liability is broader, however, especially in regard to barrier of privity of contract. This liability falls on sellers of products sold in a defective condition unreasonably dangerous to the users. These glasses certainly qualify here. The fragility of the lenses and their splintering behavior suggest a strong case for strict liability. Privity of contract is unnecessary for an action in negligence against the manufacturer. The glasses fell below the standard of care in respect to design and the material used therein. Of course, there may be some assumption of risk as the boys and coach all saw how dangerous the glasses were after the pitcher's experience. Nevertheless, at the very least the manufacturer had a duty to notify prospective users of the dangerous tendency of the glasses to splinter.

Chapter 18

Sales Performance and Remedies

18.1 INTRODUCTION

Contracting parties rarely set forth the particulars concerning a failure to perform or other like breaches of contract. The UCC provides these particulars and their effects in detail, supplying the legal system with both consequences and standards to apply to the rights and liabilities of the contracting parties.

18.2 PERFORMANCE: GENERALLY

The parties are generally required to perform as promised. In sales law the seller is to deliver conforming goods in a timely manner and the buyer is to accept and pay for them. When the parties each attempt to perform according to contract, they are *tendering* performance. If the tender occurs, but is refused, a common breach of contract results.

18.3 SELLER'S PERFORMANCE

Technically the seller is obligated to make a *perfect tender* of goods to the buyer. If the tender fails in any respect to conform to the contract, the buyer may reject the goods under Section 2-601 of the UCC. Nonconformance includes failure to deliver and also breach of warranty.

EXAMPLE 1. Wind Products shipped 30 electric razors to Key Sales in response to an order for 25. Wind's invoice reflected a lower unit price for 30 as Wind believed that at the lower price Key would be glad to receive more. Key Sales can reject the 30 under the perfect tender rule. Wind breached the contract. Key has the option of accepting 25 as ordered, and paying the appropriate contract price.

Not all shipments by the seller show such a final or material breach. If the seller has reason to believe that a change in the tender would be acceptable, or if enough time remains for delivery of conforming goods to correct the seller's nonconforming performance, i.e., cure, the contract may not be breached.

EXAMPLE 2. Swarte was a reputable businessman but, with honorable motives, often sent nonconforming goods to his customers. He shipped a new model of a paint sprayer 2 weeks before the scheduled delivery date of the now obsolete model the retailer had ordered. If the retailer objected, Swarte would have 2 weeks to correct his performance, i.e., effect a cure.

The seller is interested in the buyer's acceptance, which the buyer indicates by express language or other conduct. Approval usually occurs after the buyer has inspected the goods, indicating that upon inspection the goods conform, or that despite nonconformity the buyer approves of them. Delay by the buyer in rejecting the goods, as well as the buyer's inconsistent conduct as to the goods, can also be an acceptance.

EXAMPLE 3. Goods were delivered to a buyer when her personnel were too busy to process incoming shipments. It was customary in the trade that a reasonable time was 2 weeks. The written contract provided that return of defective or nonconforming goods must be made within 15 days of delivery. The courts would enforce an acceptance of nonconforming goods by a buyer's delay under these circumstances.

18.4 BUYER'S PERFORMANCE

The buyer must pay for the goods. In the absence of a contrary agreement, the buyer is entitled to inspect the goods before acceptance. In COD (collect on delivery) sales, the buyer has no right of inspection before payment, thus delaying the right to inspect until payment is made. The duty to pay is activated by the buyer's acceptance of the goods. Even nonconforming goods can be accepted if the buyer fails to make an effective rejection. An acceptance is not necessarily final, as further inspection or use may permit the buyer to revoke the acceptance provided the defect (1) was one that was hidden or latent, (2) was not discoverable at the time of the original inspection, (3) was discovered within a reasonable period of time, and (4) substantially impairs the value of the entire bargain, UCC, Section 2-608.

EXAMPLE 4. Fourteen Model TC compressors were delivered to Randy Manufacturing. They were inspected by the buyer and found to be conforming, and the invoice price was paid. Upon use, two of the compressors were found to have shorted. Randy wants to exercise a right of revocation of acceptance of all 14 units. If the failure of the two units "substantially impairs" the value of the entire bargain to Randy, the bargain may be revoked if done within a reasonable time.

Goods must be rejected in a clear manner. The buyer must specify the defects complained of to the seller. A failure to *particularize* the defect in the seller's performance is an acceptance of the goods.

EXAMPLE 5. Bruce Ceilings sold ceiling tile to Ye Woode Restaurant. After Bruce installed the tile, Ye Woode vaguely complained about the tile as being second rate. Ye Woode ignored demands for payment of the invoice. Bruce finally sued. Ye Woode now offered to show the court that it rejected the goods. This is an ineffective rejection. Ye Woode must specify the defect in relation to the contract description and offer to return or not use, if practical. It may also be noted that a failure to object in a timely and specific manner has the effect of preventing the seller from effecting a possible cure in its performance.

A buyer must pay a seller in cash unless otherwise agreed, or where custom or other dealings indicate a contrary method. An acceptance of a check by the seller is a conditional tender and will be effective should it clear payment. A seller may object to the tender of a check, but if so, the buyer is then allowed a reasonable opportunity to tender cash.

18.5 BREACH AND REMEDIES: GENERALLY

The anticipated performance is that the seller delivers conforming goods which are accepted by the buyer who pays the purchase price in a timely manner. Breach of contract occurs in a variety of ways and at different times. These variations will be treated under the topics of partial acceptances; anticipatory repudiation; material breach; substituted performance; impracticability, impossibility, and frustration; buyers' remedies; and sellers' remedies.

18.6 PARTIAL ACCEPTANCES

Some buyers will accept some but not all of the goods. If they have grounds for doing such, the seller has breached the contract. The buyer need pay only for that part accepted, and then at the contract rate. The buyer may also, in addition, sue for breach of contract. This partial acceptance must include no less than a commercial unit. A three-piece suit, for example, cannot be partially accepted ("I'll keep the coat and trousers, but not the vest.") as the suit is one unit.

The term "commercial unit" also has a quantity connotation which relates to the level of commerce at which the sale takes place. For example, a jobber or wholesaler who resells *only* in quantities of full pallet loads would be justified in refusing to accept from a manufacturer-seller only part of a pallet load, even if this were a number of complete and conforming "units of the product." Under some trade circumstances anything less than a full truckload or carload could be less than a commercial unit.

18.7 ANTICIPATORY REPUDIATION

Anticipatory repudiation, or *anticipatory breach*, occurs before the date of contract performance. Here one of the parties anticipates breaching the contract. When one party expresses this intention by words or conduct, anticipatory repudiation is said to have occurred, and this creates rights in the other party. The nonbreaching party has several options: to suspend his or her own performance, to treat the contract as canceled (and sue if he or she wishes), or to wait a reasonable time to see whether or not the breaching party may change its mind, UCC, Section 2-610.

EXAMPLE 6. Horst agreed to sell and deliver to Romney 100 bales of hops at the rate of 20 bales per month during March, April, May, June, and July. In May Romney wrote Horst that he would not take any more hops. Horst sued immediately for breach of contract. Horst has the option to cancel the contract and sue for damages immediately where the contract is repudiated before performance.

The party who repudiates the contract may retract his or her breach, provided certain events have not foreclosed this option. If the other party, for example, has treated the repudiation as final, or has materially changed his or her position, the repudiating party cannot retract. Otherwise, the repudiator may retract, making allowance for a loss occasioned by the retracted repudiation, UCC, Section 2-611.

The doctrine of anticipatory repudiation does not operate to suspend the duty of mitigating damages. The nonbreaching party can wait a reasonable length of time to see if performance is forthcoming if such hope is consistent with the circumstances. It has been held that where there is an absolute repudiation in the delivery of goods which are subject to rapid price changes, a delay in attempting to mitigate damages by *covering* (purchasing substitute goods) may be unreasonable.

EXAMPLE 7. A farmer under a contract to deliver bushels of wheat informed the grain dealer that he could not plant the wheat because of the rainy weather. The farmer told the dealer to look elsewhere. At the time of this repudiation the market price for wheat was 4 cents a bushel above the contract price. The dealer did not cover. Instead, the dealer waited to see if the farmer would perform. By delivery date the spread in the price was 14 cents a bushel. The dealer sues for the difference (10 cents) between the contract price and the market price at the time of the delivery date. The dealer can only recover 4 cents a bushel as damages. The dealer waited a commercially unreasonable length of time to effect cover under the circumstances of rapidly changing prices.

18.8 MATERIAL BREACH

A *material breach* is a serious or substantial breach of contract allowing the maximum remedy in appropriate circumstances, including the rescission of the entire contract. The UCC refers to such instances when it uses language about whether or not the breach "substantially impairs the value of the bargain." Some breaches of warranty can impair the bargain and permit a rescission. In installment contracts, however, Section 2-612 of the UCC somewhat limits the buyer's power to reject or rescind the entire contract. If, for example, a tender of an installment is nonconforming, the rejection is allowed only if the nonconformity substantially impairs the value of that installment and cannot be cured. Further, if the seller gives adequate assurance to cure the defect, the buyer must accept that installment. The entire (installment) contract can be treated as breached only if the default with respect to one or more of the installments substantially impairs the value of the whole contract. The acceptance of the nonconforming installment(s), without notification of cancellation or the bringing of a lawsuit charging breach of contract in regard to installments, reinstates the contract.

EXAMPLE 8. Purpose Mining contracted to sell 500 carloads of coal from its mine. The contract set forth the quality standards of the coal, which was to be delivered at the rate of 20 carloads a week. Four carloads which were delivered during the second week fell well below contract description and could not be used by the buyer for its regular purposes. Such nonconformity substantially impairs the value of the installment and can be rejected by the buyer. Whether this breach substantially impairs the value of the whole contract would be a question of fact. If, for example, the 500 carloads were a minimum for the buyer's production run and no substitute goods could be purchased (i.e., no cover), the buyer might successfully argue substantial impairment, thus permitting rejection, and therefore rescission of the entire contract.

18.9 SUBSTITUTED PERFORMANCE

Where, through no fault of either party, either the method of delivery of the goods or the carrier becomes unavailable, a commercially reasonable substitute may be used, UCC, Section 2-614. Likewise the buyer's method of payment may fail by reason of government regulation. In such a case, a seller may withhold or stop delivery pending a suitable substitute in the manner of payment. If the seller has already delivered the goods, a substitute method of payment, in accordance with the regulation, is proper unless the regulation is discriminatory, oppressive, or predatory.

EXAMPLE 9. An exporter has delivered goods to an importer on credit, with payment due in 60 days. Because of an internal economic upheaval in the importer's country, cash credits are frozen. However, under the new regulations it is still possible to settle payments by barter. The importer has computer machinery in a third country and offers this to the exporter in payment. The machinery can be sold in the third country generating enough proceeds to pay the exporter. The exporter may, under the substitute performance section of the UCC, be required to accept this tender of payment. The exporter cannot claim breach of contract.

18.10 IMPRACTICABILITY, IMPOSSIBILITY, AND FRUSTRATION

In general, mere difficulty, or possibility of loss, sometimes called *subjective impossibility*, neither discharges a contract nor relieves the party from his or her duty. Accordingly, a seller's loss of an expected source from which the seller would fulfill his or her duty, or a drastic rise in the price of material which makes the bargain not only expensive but perhaps financially disastrous to the seller, will not normally excuse the seller. The so-called legal impossibility, or objective impossibility, however, does offer relief. This is observed in cases where personal services (or personal relationships) dominate the performance of the party who dies, becomes ill, or even goes insane. Further, a promisor is excused under the doctrine of legal impossibility where the law has now made such performance illegal, or where the subject matter has been destroyed. The UCC does not, however, repeal these principles of contract law, nor does it attempt to retard their development, but it does provide additional relief on the grounds of impracticability. Section 2-615 of the UCC therefore offers sales contractors some excuse for failure of presupposed conditions. Delay or even nondelivery can be excused if the seller can show that performance has been made "impracticable by the occurrence of a contingency the nonoccurrence of which was a basic assumption on which the contract was made." This includes a seller's compliance with a governmental regulation or order.

EXAMPLE 10. Leroy Chemical provides raw materials to drug companies. Leroy sells a binding agent which is a controlled substance, the supply of which is from two sources. One of the sources is foreign and has just been banned from supplying its customers. Leroy cannot live up to its commitments with drug companies A, B, and C. Leroy may contend commercial impracticability in that the parties had a basic assumption that these dual sources of supply would continue to be available.

If commercial impracticability does not totally preclude, but only impairs, delivery, the seller must allocate among his or her customers in a fair and equitable manner. The seller must notify the buyers of such delay or impairment. The buyer then has the option of either accepting the allocation or terminating the contract.

Sometimes a party attempts to escape liability on grounds of "frustration of purpose," meaning economic frustration. Simply stated, the performance of the contract is no longer of value to one party. Unlike the impossibility doctrine, performance is literally possible but supervening events have essentially destroyed the purpose for which the contract was made. This defense has been troublesome to courts, which have been quite restrictive in its application.

18.11 BUYERS' REMEDIES: GENERALLY

Generally, a buyer's remedies are against the goods or against the seller for breach of contract damages. When there is nondelivery, the buyer may seek the goods but in most instances must be satisfied with money damages. Recovery of the goods by means of a *replevin action* (a law action in which the court seizes the goods) is always allowed if the buyer has title to the goods. This right is now extended to certain other instances. The UCC has extended the right of recovery of goods by way of replevin in those cases where the goods are identified to the contract and the buyer proves that cover is unavailable. If the goods had been shipped under a reservation of title (a security interest), the buyer can demand the goods upon payment, thereby satisfying the security claim. Further, under Section 2-502 of the UCC, a buyer who learns of a seller's insolvency within 10 days of the buyer's prepayment installment can replevin identified goods by tender of the full purchase price.

EXAMPLE 11.   Lauren Fabricating orders 3,000 linear feet of specialty coil strip steel from Royal Extruders. Before delivery Royal's creditors attempt to levy on all inventory. If the steel has been identified to the contract, and Lauren can prove it cannot buy substitute goods (cover), the action of replevin would succeed in allowing Lauren possession.

EXAMPLE 12.   Lauren Fabricating ordered 3,000 linear feet of specialty coil strip steel from Royal Extruders on credit. Royal shipped the steel, reserving a security interest in itself. During transit Royal learns that Lauren is in financial difficulty, and Royal now attempts to divert the shipment to a better customer who will pay a better price. If Lauren tenders full payment for the goods, it can demand and recover the goods under a replevin action.

An *action for specific performance* seeks an order of an equity court for delivery of goods as promised. It differs from replevin in that such a lawsuit is in equity and addresses the discretionary side of the court. Further, neither title nor identification need be shown. It is not, however, a common remedy, and courts rarely grant specific performance for goods unless the item is unique. Section 2-716(1) of the UCC not only widens the applicability of the action for specific performance to include goods that are unique, but also permits this remedy to be sought "in other proper circumstances."

EXAMPLE 13.   Babber Supply ordered 500 metal art frames from Testor Industries, delivery in 60 days in time for the once-a-year local art show. Testor has had great demand for these frames from other customers and decided to put Babber "on hold." Generally, Babber could not force Testor to supply them, as the goods are not unique. Further, the circumstances are not such as to allow the drastic remedy of specific performance. Babber could only bring an action for damages.

EXAMPLE 14.   An airline contracted with an oil dealer for jet fuel for an extended period. An international oil shortage placed a premium on fuel, and the dealer found other customers who would pay more than the airline's contract price. The airline demands specific performance. The fuel is not unique, but the combination of scarcity and the dire need of the airline may be "proper circumstances," permitting the court to order specific performance of the contract.

The most common remedy against the seller is for money damages. When the breach is failure to deliver or is delivery of nonconforming or defective goods, the buyer may treat the contract as terminated and may sue. The usual measure of damages is the difference between the contract price and the cost of cover, together with any incidental or consequential damages. Incidental damages include reasonable commercial expenses. Inspection fees and transportation charges are common items of incidental damages.

EXAMPLE 15.   A citrus grower orders a Matlock 630 irrigation pump from Renfrew Machine for $30,000. The seller experienced difficulty in making delivery by first sending the wrong model and then failing to replace it. The buyer purchased a comparable pump from Tayco Company (cover) from Tacoma, Washington, for $32,000. The grower had to employ an engineer to discover that the first tender was nonconforming and to advise the grower about a comparable purchase. The engineer's inspection fee qualifies as incidental damages and can be recovered. The $2,000 difference between the contract price and the cost of cover is recoverable also, as is the extra transportation expense. Damages to citrus trees for lack of proper water during the period cover was sought would be consequential damages and may or may not be recovered.

Consequential damages are those losses resulting from the general or particular requirements and needs the seller had reason to know about at the time of the contract. They are recoverable if such losses could not have been prevented by cover or otherwise. Where the buyer does not attempt to cover, the general measure of damages is the difference between the market price and the contract price plus the incidental and consequential damages, if any. The market price is determined as of the time the buyer learns of the breach. The place is that where tender was required or, in the case of rejection or revocation of acceptance, the place of arrival, UCC, Section 2-714.

EXAMPLE 16.   Dash Industries ordered 3,000 pallets, at $20 each, FOB seller's plant, delivery in 60 days. A strike at the plant forced the seller to shut down. At the time Dash learned of this, the price for comparable pallets was $21.50 at the seller's place of business. At the time of the lawsuit, the pallets are $15. Dash can recover the difference ($4,500) between the market price at the time it learned of the breach and the contract price.

Of course, any payments the buyer makes before the breach by the seller are recoverable. Where the goods turn out to be not as the contract specified and the seller no longer has the right to cure, the buyer may recover the loss resulting from the ordinary course of events. The measure of damages for a breach of warranty is basically the difference at the time and place of acceptance between the value of the goods accepted and the value as warranted, UCC, Section 2-714. In proper cases consequential damages as well as incidental damages may also be recovered.

EXAMPLE 17.   Allen Corporation purchased a three-stage stamping machine warranted to press 30,000 discs during an 8-hour shift with no more than 1.5 percent rejects. The machine needed adjustments by the seller's engineers before it could be put on-line. Despite the best efforts of Allen and the seller, the machine never reached a volume in excess of 20,000 units per shift. Allen offers that a machine which produces 30,000 units per shift would increase Allen's profits by $10,000 a month. The expected life of the machine is 30 months. The damages could be $300,000. If, in addition, this inefficiency caused other damage that the seller had reason to know about at the time of the contract, consequential damages would be allowed.

18.12   SELLERS' REMEDIES

Sellers want the purchase price the buyer promised to pay. If the goods have been delivered and accepted, the seller sues for the contract price which is the proper measure of damages. However, at times the seller must play a mixed strategy, one that adopts the policy of trying to limit losses. This is seen in the remedies of refusing to deliver the goods, stopping goods in transit, and reclaiming what was delivered. Goods can be stopped in transit for one of two reasons: a breach by the buyer or buyer insolvency. If stopped for breach of contract, the stop order can only be used to halt carload, truckload, planeload, or larger shipments. However, the buyer could prevent this by offering a cash payment.

EXAMPLE 18. Cedar Rapids, Ltd., shipped a half-truckload of cane chairs to Rusty Interiors via Donnick Truck Lines. While the goods were in transit, Rusty's promise to provide a recent credit reference was breached. Cedar Rapids cannot effectively order a stop in transit for breach of contract for less than a truckload. If Cedar had learned of insolvency of Rusty, such a stop order would be proper.

Even after the goods have been delivered to the buyer, a limited right to reclaim the goods exists. Under Section 2-702 of the UCC, where the goods were sold on credit and the buyer becomes insolvent, the seller may demand their return if notice is made within 10 days of the buyer's receipt of the goods. The seller is not restricted to the 10-day limitation if the buyer in writing had misrepresented his or her solvency to the seller within 3 months before delivery of the goods. Another party who buys from such an insolvent buyer takes free of this right (i.e., has good title) if he or she purchased in good faith in the ordinary course of business.

Where the goods are retained, stopped in transit, or reclaimed, the seller has certain duties to these goods in the matter of resale under Section 2-706 of the UCC. This sale must be made in good faith and in a commercially reasonable manner. If less money is received at the resale than that which was contracted for, the difference is recoverable plus incidental damages, less expenses saved in connection with the buyer's breach. The sale may be public or private. Notice of time and place must be given to the buyer for a public sale, which generally should be where there is a recognized market. In private sale the seller must give reasonable notification to the buyer of the seller's intention to sell.

EXAMPLE 19. A shipment of hardware was effectively stopped in transit by the seller who now wishes to sell the ordered goods. There is no recognized market for these goods in the area. The seller notifies the buyer in writing that after 30 days the seller will solicit hardware retailers for private sale. As the goods were identified to the contract, this practice is permitted.

Where goods have been delivered to a buyer who refuses to pay, the price is recoverable as it is in cases where the goods are identified to the contract and such goods cannot reasonably be sold, UCC, Section 2-709. The seller is therefore holding the goods for the defaulting buyer, and a resale is possible. Where, however, the goods are not accepted, or where the contract is repudiated, the general measure of damages is the difference between the market price and the contract price at the time and place of tender of delivery. Incidental damages can also be recovered. If the application of this general rule fails to place the seller into a position similar to performance, the seller may show what profit he or she may have received from the sale.

EXAMPLE 20. Argo Nuts contracted to sell 1,000 cases of cashews to Taggert Foods at $50 a case. Later, Taggert was overcommitted and notified Argo that it could not accept the nuts. At the time and place of the tender, cashew nuts sold for $49 a case. Argo would have made a profit of $5 a case. Section 2-708(2) of the UCC allows the seller to recover the lost profit of $5,000.

18.13 LIQUIDATED DAMAGES

The buyer and seller may, of course, by contract set forth specifically the consequences of the breach, UCC, Section 2-718. These clauses in contracts are sometimes called *stipulated damage clauses*. The code uses the term "liquidated damages." If the amount set, or formula provided, is reasonable in the light of anticipated or actual harm, such a clause is enforceable. Further, the difficulties of proof of loss and the inconvenience or nonfeasibility of otherwise obtaining an adequate remedy assist in evaluating the enforceability of the clause.

EXAMPLE 21. A car dealer took a $1,000 deposit on a $5,000 automobile. The sales contract specifically provided that the deposit constituted the liquidated damages in the event of a breach by the buyer. The buyer changed her mind about the purchase. The liquidated damage clause was found to be excessive, it being 20 percent of the purchase price. In such a case no showing of UCC requirements of actual harm, difficulty of proof, or inability to obtain an adequate remedy would be possible. The 20 percent penalty is excessive on its face.

18.14 LIMITATIONS OF REMEDIES

Buyers and sellers may expressly place limits on the liability should a breach occur. Such clauses are allowed if not in conflict with other UCC principles. A potentially substantial damage that commercial parties attempt to contract away or limit is the risk of consequential damages. The parties may exclude or limit such damages unless the exclusion or limitation is unconscionable. Limitation of such damages for injury to person is *prima facie* unconscionable under Section 2-719 of the UCC.

EXAMPLE 22. A production company ordered 30 special molds for its machine facility. The price was tightly negotiated. The seller was aware of the intended use of these molds and knew that should they fail to meet specifications, the buyer's assembly line would be shut down at great expense. These damages would be consequential. The contract specifically excluded consequential damages. Should the molds fail and the production line be shut down, these damages have been contracted away. The buyer, the production company, would lose.

EXAMPLE 23. Abbaca Products manufactures and sells a batting practice set for children aged 10 to 15. Abbaca has made the set as safe as the item can be, but one can still get injured because no design could prevent certain risks in connection with the swing of a bat. Abbaca sells these sets with a written form requiring a release from each child regarding injury and excluding consequential damages from the use of the item caused by a defect in the item. Generally, the seller cannot exclude consequential damages for injury to persons.

Black Letter Law
A Summary

1. In sales law the seller contracts to deliver conforming goods in a timely fashion and the buyer to accept and pay for them.

2. Sellers must make a perfect tender of delivery of conforming goods though sellers may correct (i.e., cure) their performance before the contract date of performance.

3. The buyer's acceptance of the goods occurs when, by language or other conduct, approval is shown after opportunity for inspection.

4. Unless otherwise agreed, the buyer must pay for the goods in cash at delivery, as the acceptance of a check is conditional on the funds clearing.

5. Unless otherwise agreed, as in COD shipments, the buyer has a right of inspection of the goods before payment.

6. Goods must be rejected by the buyer in a clear manner; a failure to particularize the defect of the seller's performance may be an acceptance of the goods.

7. Buyers may accept that part of the goods which is conforming and pay only the contract rate for such.

8. A party breaches a contract by anticipatory repudiation when before the date of performance he or she indicates a clear intention not to perform the contract.

9. In cases of anticipatory repudiation the nonbreaching party has several options, and unless one of these options is exercised, the breaching party may still perform at the contract time for performance.

10. When a breach of contract is major or, in fact, substantially impairs the value of the bargain, it is said to be material, and it allows rescission of the contract and complete excuse from further performance.

11. A material breach of an installment in an installment contract allows rescission only where the breach substantially impairs the value of the whole contract and the tendering party cannot cure the breach.

12. Impracticability of performance, allowing the party an excuse from performing, occurs by reason of the failure of presupposed conditions.

13. The destruction of the plant in which the parties contemplated the manufacture of the goods could qualify as an occurrence of a contingency which was a basis upon which the parties had contracted.

14. Buyer's actions against goods include replevin when title has passed and in some instances where identification occurred; an order for specific performance is permitted in situations dealing with unique goods or in other proper circumstances.

15. In cases of nondelivery the buyer's money damages are usually those measured by the difference between the contract price and the cost of cover together with any incidental or consequential damages.

16. Consequential damages are those losses resulting from the general or particular requirements and needs the seller had reason to know about at the time of the contract.

17. Sellers' remedies against goods include stoppage in transit and reclamation after delivery within 10 days after the buyer's receipt of the goods.

18. A seller can recover the contract price in cases where the goods have been accepted, or where they have been rejected and cannot reasonably be sold.

19. Where delivery is wrongfully refused, the seller's usual remedy is for damages, which is the difference between the market price and contract price at the time and place of delivery.

20. Stipulated damage clauses are enforceable as liquidated damage clauses, provided the amount or formula is reasonable in the light of anticipated or actual harm.

21. Parties may expressly limit liability in cases of breach except as to future injury to persons, of which attempted limitation or exclusion is *prima facie* unconscionable.

Solved Problems

18.1 Gibbeon Manufacturing shipped 300 designer navy blue blazers to Custom Clothing Emporium. The blazers arrived on Friday, earlier than Custom had anticipated and on an exceptionally busy day for its receiving department. They were perfunctorily examined and sent to a nearby warehouse for storage until needed. On Monday of the following week, upon closer examination, it was discovered that the quality of the linings of the blazers was inferior to that specified in the sales contract. Which of the following is correct insofar as Custom's rights are concerned?

    (*a*) Custom can reject the blazers upon subsequent discovery of the defects.

    (*b*) Custom must retain the blazers since it accepted them and had an opportunity to inspect them upon delivery.

    (*c*) Custom's only course of action is rescission.

    (*d*) Custom has no rights if the linings are of merchantable quality.

(*AICPA Examination, November 1980*)

    The seller has apparently delivered goods that could be rightfully rejected and returned. The buyer's failure to reject could be an acceptance. Acceptance occurs when the buyer indicates approval of the goods or delays in rejecting them. The delay here seems justified on these facts as there is no requirement that the inspection be immediate. An inspection by the next business day would not be in excess of a reasonable time; statement (*a*) is the answer.

18.2 The Balboa Custom Furniture Company sells fine custom furniture. It has been encountering difficulties lately with some customers who have breached their contracts after the furniture they have selected has been customized to their order or the fabric they have selected has been cut or actually installed on the piece of furniture purchased. The company therefore wishes to resort to a liquidated damages clause in its sales contract to encourage performance or provide an acceptable amount of damages. Regarding Balboa's contemplated resort to a liquidated damages clause, which of the following is correct?

    (*a*) Balboa may not use a liquidated damages clause since it is a merchant and is the preparer of the contract.

    (*b*) Balboa can simply take a very large deposit, which will be forfeited if performance by a customer is not made for any reason.

    (*c*) The amount of liquidated damages stipulated in the contract must be reasonable in light of the anticipated or actual harm caused by the breach.

    (*d*) Even if Balboa uses a liquidated damages clause in its sales contract, it will nevertheless have to establish that the liquidated damages claimed did not exceed actual damages by more than 10 percent.

(*AICPA Examination, November 1980*)

    Stipulated damage clauses are enforced if they qualify as liquidated damages. Here, the manufacturer-seller is viewing uncertain damages for breach due to the selectivity of its customers' orders. If the amount Balboa sets is reasonable in the light of anticipated or actual harm, the clause is enforceable; the answer is (*c*).

18.3 Cox Manufacturing repudiated its contract to sell 300 televisions to Ruddy Stores, Inc. What recourse does Ruddy Stores have?

(a) It can obtain specific performance by the seller.

(b) It can recover punitive damages.

(c) It must await the seller's performance for a commercially reasonable time after repudiation if it wishes to recover anything.

(d) It can cover, that is, procure the goods elsewhere, and recover any damages.

(*AICPA Examination, November 1979*)

The actions for specific performance and punitive damages are extraordinary remedies and generally are not available under these circumstances. Cover, the purchase of substitute goods, permits the buyer to recover damages that resulted from such action, statement (d). Once the seller has breached, the buyer need not wait to sue, as the right of action accrues immediately.

18.4 Badger Corporation sold goods to Watson. Watson has arbitrarily refused to pay the purchase price. Under what circumstances will Badger not be able to recover the price?

(a) If Watson refused to accept delivery and the goods were resold in the ordinary course of business

(b) If Watson accepted the goods but seeks to return them

(c) If the goods sold were destroyed shortly after the risk of loss passed to the buyer

(d) If the goods were identified to the contract and Badger made a reasonable effort to resell them at a reasonable price but was unable to do so

(*Adapted from AICPA Examination, May 1978*)

Statement (a) is the answer. An action for the price cannot be maintained if the goods were retained by the seller and the seller has resold them in the ordinary course of business. The other statements offer examples of situations where the invoice price of the goods can be recovered. In statements (b) and (c) title and risk have passed. In statement (d) the goods have no value in the marketplace and the seller is allowed full recovery, provided the goods have been identified to the contract.

18.5 On February 1, 19X5, Colonial Industries ordered 10,000 feet of 2-inch pipe in 20-foot lengths from the Eire Steel Company. Delivery was to be made on or before March 15, time being of the essence, FOB the buyer's loading platform, cash on delivery. Eire Steel accepted the order. On February 15, Eire informed Colonial that its biggest customer had just purchased and taken delivery of its entire stock of 2-inch pipe and that it would be impossible for Eire to deliver the pipe until May 15, at the earliest. Colonial demanded that Eire perform as agreed; Eire apologized but reiterated its prior position that it was now impossible for it to perform until the middle of May.

(a) Eire's action on February 15 constituted an anticipatory repudiation of the contract.

(b) Colonial must cover (procure the same or similar goods elsewhere) within a reasonable time in order to determine the damages recoverable.

(c) If Colonial waits for performance by Eire and tenders the amount due on March 15, it can recover damages of the difference between the contract price and the market value on March 15.

(d) Because Eire had sold and delivered its entire supply of 2-inch pipe, it can successfully plead impossibility of performance in order to avoid liability.

(*Adapted from AICPA Examination, May 1975*)

When a party informs the other that it will not perform as promised on the contract, an anticipatory repudiation of the contract has occurred, statement (*a*). Cover is rarely an absolute duty. This is not a case of impossibility because the seller by its free act caused the failure.

18.6   Tropic Shoe Manufacture of Hialeah, Florida, received an order for 2,000 assorted pairs of summer casual shoes from Fabulous Shoes in St. Louis. Fabulous asked for 30 days credit as it was putting on a big sale. Unknown to Tropic, Fabulous was in financial trouble. Tropic shipped the shoes FOB Swift Trucking, Hialeah, Florida, only to learn 2 days later of the financial trouble at Fabulous. Tropic wired Swift Trucking to return the shoes. The order constituted only a third of a truckload. Under these circumstances,

(*a*)   since risk of loss passed at Hialeah, Tropic has lost all its interest in the shoes.

(*b*)   knowledge of financial trouble is sufficient to exercise a stop-in-transit order.

(*c*)   even if Fabulous is insolvent, it can prevent the stoppage by paying cash.

(*d*)   Fabulous has not breached the contract; accordingly, the seller can exercise this right of stoppage for full truckloads only.

   Tropic possesses a right of stoppage in transit when the buyer is insolvent. Insolvency means the buyer's inability to meet debts as they mature. However, such a buyer, even if insolvent, has the right to pay cash and demand the goods, under Section 2-702(1) of the UCC, statement (*c*) is the answer. The right to order a stop on less than a full truckload is restricted to insolvency situations; for breach of contract only a full truckload can be stopped.

18.7   A tree farm was approached by a wholesaler for an assortment of Christmas trees. Knowing that the wholesaler supplied such trees to city florists, the tree farm demanded a top price of $12,000, which the wholesaler agreed to pay. The trees arrived in several lots and were baled in such a manner as to make inspection impossible before delivery to the florists by the wholesaler. The trees were nonconforming, a fact communicated to the tree farm. The wholesaler had to rent a lot and hire a clerk to sell the trees at salvage prices before Christmas. Under these circumstances,

(*a*)   the wholesaler need not pay the $12,000, but its recovery is restricted to the funds received at the salvage sale.

(*b*)   the tree farm is entitled to the purchase price of $12,000.

(*c*)   the wholesaler can recover the incidental damages incurred in the salvage sale, plus consequential damages resulting from the inability to supply city florists.

(*d*)   the wholesaler is restricted to recovering the difference between the contract price and the market price at the time it learned of the breach.

   The measure of damages for nondelivery by the seller is the difference between the market price and the contract price at the time when the buyer learned of the breach, together with incidental and consequential damages, less expenses saved in consequence of the seller's breach, statement (*c*). This case reflects incidental damages in trying to sell the nonconforming goods. It shows consequential damages suffered by the buyer, who could not furnish its customers (the city florists) Christmas trees, a possibility the tree farm knew about at the time of the contract.

18.8   Tuttle was putting on a convention for doctors at Miami Beach. Tuttle needed table decorations for the banquet and learned that a local Indian reservation had done some clever things with coconuts. In visiting one site in the Everglades, she discovered a unique situation, craftspeople who could cut a coconut in such a way as to make a miniature operating room. Kinsi, the chief, had three craftspeople who were able to do this. Both Tuttle and Kinsi calculated that if the order was given immediately, the three people working full time could provide the table decorations. Tuttle left a $2,000 deposit on a $4,200 order. Production was begun and was going well when one of the craftspeople drowned in a boating accident. As was the custom of the tribe, no work was done for a week after the death. The contract is breached by Kinsi. In this situation, what is the correct statement?

(a) Unless the contract provided an excuse for acts of God, the contract was legally breached by Kinsi.

(b) Tuttle's only recourse is either to accept the completed decorations or to sue for damages.

(c) The facts of the situation suggest the defense of commercial impracticability.

(d) Tuttle could obtain an order for specific performance against Kinsi.

Statement (c) is correct. Delay or even complete nondelivery can be excused if the seller can show that the performance has been made impracticable by the occurrence or nonoccurrence of a contingency which was a basic assumption on which the contract was made. Tuttle was aware of the circumstances under which these goods were to be created. Tuttle must have understood that the continued existence of the three craftspeople was a contingency upon which performance hung. Whether or not the funeral and mourning customs were also within the contemplation of the parties is another matter, but not altogether unlikely. Acts of God do not usually excuse unless stated in the contract. However, where personal services are contemplated, death does excuse. Tuttle could demand the decorations which had been completed and pay the contract rate for them.

18.9 Which of the following remedies is *never* available to a buyer who ordered goods which were not delivered?

(a) An action for the contract price

(b) An action for specific performance

(c) A replevin action

(d) An action for consequential damages

The buyer does not have a remedy by which he or she can sue for the contract price; the answer is (a). Only the seller has such a remedy, usually when the seller has delivered conforming goods which have been accepted. In all other instances stated above, the buyer could, under proper circumstances, have the appropriate remedy.

18.10 Branson sold goods on credit to Lansing, who took possession of them on November 1, 19X3. Branson was induced to grant credit to Lansing on the basis of a marvelous credit representation contained in a letter to Branson from Lansing dated July 14, 19X3. Lansing began selling these goods to its retail customers on November 3, 19X3. By the time Branson discovered Lansing's deceit in misrepresenting its financial condition, Lansing had sold 30 percent of the goods. Branson learned of the insolvency of Lansing on November 5, 19X3. Under these circumstances,

(a) Branson has only until November 11, 19X3, to demand return of the goods Lansing still has in its possession.

(b) since Lansing made a fraudulent statement in writing, Branson can recover all goods, including those sold to Lansing's customers.

(c) Branson has until December 1, 19X3, to reclaim what goods Lansing still has in its possession.

(d) Branson has until November 15, 19X3, to demand the return of goods not sold to Lansing's customers.

Section 2-702 of the UCC allows the seller certain remedies in respect to goods when the seller discovers the insolvency of the buyer who has received the goods. Generally, the seller may demand return if such demand is made within 10 days of the buyer's receipt of the goods, statement (*a*). There is an exception where the buyer has misrepresented his or her solvency in a writing made within 3 months of the receipt of goods. In such a case, the 10-day limit does not apply. In this case the written statement was more than 3 months old, and thus statement (*b*) is not effective. Goods sold by the buyer to customers in the ordinary course of business cannot be retrieved, despite the circumstances.

18.11 Memory Motel ordered a certain floor covering from Tallin Fabrics, and after considerable delay, installation was made. Memory paid for the installation but, from the beginning, was not satisfied. Memory's specific complaints were looked into by Tallin, but the problem could not be corrected. One month later Memory notified Tallin in writing that the carpeting was bad, that it did not lay properly, and that Memory rejected the carpeting and demanded its money back. However, Memory did not tear out the carpeting and tender its return to Tallin. Memory sues for recovery of the purchase price which it paid Tallin.

What defense will Tallin bring in response to this action. Decide, stating your reasons for any conclusions.

Where a buyer refuses to accept, or having accepted, attempts to revoke its acceptance, the buyer must tender the return of the merchandise. Tallin would naturally attempt to say that the buyer's actions are louder than its words since the buyer continues to use the carpeting. The buyer will argue that the tender or offering to perform has a broader meaning. It need not return the carpeting to the seller, as Section 2-602 of the UCC merely requires that after rejection the buyer must hold the goods with "reasonable care at the seller's disposition for a time sufficient to permit the seller to remove them; but the buyer has no further obligations with regard to goods rightfully rejected." The UCC recognizes that many items, bulky in character and expensive to transport and store, may be the subject of a rejection. The UCC places the burden on the seller for defective goods, and the need for the buyer in situations such as this to take up the carpeting at great expense is not present. Memory Motel should recover its purchase price and damages for this breach.

18.12 After lengthy negotiations, Artemis, a highway contractor, ordered paving material including sealing compounds from Laffler Chemicals. There were no disclaimers of warranties included in the documentation, but Laffler was well known in the industry. From the beginning the material supplied was subject to complaints by the supervisors on the job. Each time Artemis would pay an invoice for delivered goods, it would pass on the complaints. The contract was completed, and Artemis was being challenged by the state highway construction inspector's office for substandard performance on that section of the highway in which Laffler's product was used. If Laffler is sued by Artemis, what issue will likely be raised under these circumstances?

State your decision and reasons for your conclusions.

Laffler's best defense is to argue that an effective rejection of the product was never made. A buyer must particularize the defects so that cure, if possible, can be attempted. Otherwise, the goods are accepted, not rejected. The evidence is strong that Artemis did not properly reject the performance. However, an action for breach of warranty might lie. Laffler is a merchant and makes the implied warranty of merchantability. This means that the goods should be fit for ordinary use. If the defect claimed by the state against Artemis was caused by Laffler's product, damages can be seen as flowing from the breach. An action for breach of warranty would seek in damages the difference in value between the goods accepted and the value they would have if they were merchantable, Section 2-714 of the UCC. This looks like a tough case for Artemis in the question of causation and proof of damages. Artemis knew the material it was using was not up to standard but used it anyhow. Artemis may face a very expensive "make good" on this project.

18.13 Grotten got a bit carried away at an auction for the sale of some Oriental rugs. By the time he left the auction, he had bid in $12,320 for several rugs. He fled and refused to pay for or accept delivery of the rugs, staying away from the auction house. Finally, the auction house sued Grotten. In its complaint it alleged that an auction was held, Grotten was the successful bidder on three Oriental rugs for a total purchase price of $12,320, and the rugs still remained at the auction house, but Grotten refused to pick up the rugs and pay the purchase price. At trial the auction house introduced only that evidence which supported the allegations made in the complaint.

Under these facts, is the auction house entitled to recover the $12,320? Decide and state reasons for your conclusions.

The auction house will have some difficulty in attempting to collect the purchase price of $12,320. It is true that where the buyer accepts the goods, but refuses to pay, the contract price is the proper measure of damages. However, where there is no acceptance of the goods, the usual measure of damages is the difference between the market price at the time and place of tender and the unpaid contract price, together with any incidental damages, but less expenses saved in consequence of the buyer's breach, Section 2-708 of the UCC. The damages can be greater than such a measure would bring provided the seller activates other principles. For example, Section 2-703 of the UCC allows the seller, when the buyer wrongfully rejects acceptance of the goods, to sell the goods and recover the difference. Or in Section 2-709, the seller may bring his or her case for an action for the *price* if the goods were identified to the contract and if the seller is unable, after reasonable effort, to resell them at a reasonable price, or the circumstances indicated that such effort would be unavailing. Under the facts in this case, the seller made no attempt at trial to bring its case within the provisions that allow recovery of the price. The auction house has neither alleged nor proved a case for the price. It must be satisfied with the usual measure of damages.

Topic Test, Part III

Sales

1. Juno Computers manufactured and delivered 30 personal computers to Nick Computer Sales under the express written understanding that title remained in Juno until these units were sold to customers in the ordinary course of business. Nick was having trouble with his former wife, who obtained a $30,000 money judgment for past-due alimony. Finding no personal assets at Nick's bachelor pad sufficient to satisfy the judgment, the former wife directed the sheriff to levy on the inventory in Nick's store. Among the items seized by the sheriff were 16 as-yet-unsold computers from Juno's shipment. Juno asserts that the former wife has no claim to the 16 computers. What legal principle is the former wife relying upon in her claim to the computers?

2. Sanders went to a hardware dealer and told the dealer that she needed a weed cutter for her country place. She explained that the elevations on the property made the task of cutting around certain improvements quite difficult. The dealer understood the problem and thought that the most respected product in weed cutting equipment, manufactured by Flare, Incorporated, should be used. The dealer recommended Flare's Model 17A. This model was an excellent device, but it did not accomplish the task for Sanders although she followed the accompanying written instructions. The dealer can prove that this model is the best on the market and that no model could effectively accomplish the task Sanders has before her. What legal issue is involved in this case? Can Sanders under these circumstances demand the impossible from the dealer?

3. Marson entered into an agreement by which he would sell ten truckloads of muck to Farrel on 30 days credit, delivery at Marson's field. Farrel spent the first week picking up six truckloads, but when he attempted to pick up the remainder, Marson refused to let him load any more, citing information received that Farrel was insolvent. Farrel admitted to Marson that he was indeed in a tight cash-flow situation and that, despite the credit agreement, he was "willing to pay cash on the barrelhead for the last four truckloads." Marson refused and demanded the purchase price for the entire ten truckloads. Farrel was angry because, though insolvent, he was beginning to get back on his financial feet. Farrel threatened to sue Marson for breach of contract, citing the agreement as allowing 30 days for payment. What principle does the seller have to rely on in refusing to deliver the remaining four truckloads? Is it appropriate here?

4. The market for copper tubing was fluctuating widely when Tamper Products agreed to purchase 2,000 feet of Glaskow Short for $32 a foot from Raison Tubing. This was a high price, but Tamper wanted to make sure of its supply to fill an expected lucrative order which would require that amount of such tubing. One month later the market price had dropped by 40 percent and Tamper asked for an adjustment on its price from Raison. Tamper can prove that it can make little or no profit from its contract if it must pay the contract price for the tubing. Tamper refuses to pay the invoice price, vaguely mentioning that the UCC contains a provision which specially gives relief to the particular type of problem facing Tamper. What provision of the UCC is Tamper talking about? Does it apply to this situation?

5. Fly-By-Night Blacktop Company offered to repair and blacktop the parking lot for Fabler Restaurant. Fabler, a shrewd businesswoman, rejected several offers from Fly until she finally got the price she wanted. She did this by getting Fly to itemize the actual cost of materials, the sealer, gravel, etc., and add 15 percent for labor and another 5 percent for profit. The resulting contract price was $6,250. Fly performed; but at such close margins, he used inferior materials and exercised some shoddy workmanship. Fabler's complaint for correction of the condition went unheeded as Fly-By-Night contended that it made no express or implied warranties of performance. Fabler is baffled, but believes in her heart that there must be a solid implied promise to do a good job in this contract. Under these facts, what type of implied promise of quality might Fabler try to press on Fly-By-Night? What will be one of her legal problems in this regard?

6. When Arnold, a college professor, retired, he turned his lifelong hobby of rock collecting into a small business by opening a shop to sell semiprecious stones. For a while he prospered and was encouraged to expand by the easy availability of credit from suppliers. However, his lack of business experience began to show, and he soon began to fail. On the other hand, Arnold's brother-in-law, Willard, considered himself to be a top businessman. Willard offered to take over the shop and inventory, lock, stock, and barrel, for $6,500. Arnold owed his suppliers over $7,000 and thought this was the only alternative under which they could be paid. Not a day was lost in the business, because Willard paid Arnold the $6,500 and took over on the day of the agreement. The store immediately began to prosper. However, before Arnold could begin to pay off his creditors, he suffered a stroke and his finances became shaky. Arnold's suppliers are upset and are looking around for satisfaction of their debts. How wise was Willard in this contract? Is there any reason for Willard to be concerned with the suppliers' problems?

7. Baines and Arthur entered into an oral contract for the purchase and sale of two 4-ton Model 834T air-conditioning units. Arthur, the seller, demanded a $200 deposit for the two units which were being sold to Baines for $1,200 each. Arthur then received some good news from a local motel which had just changed hands. The new owners were renovating the premises and wanted all-new air-conditioning units. They were willing to buy all that Arthur had at a premium price as the motel's reopening was imminent. Arthur decided to delay delivering the two units to Baines. Arthur knows that in good faith he couldn't deny that the oral contract took place, but believes there must be some legal technicality available as he had often heard the old joke that "an oral contract ain't worth the paper it's written on." Is there a technicality that Arthur can advance which would give him some leverage in dealing with Baines, who contends that there is a breach of contract? How strong is Baines's case for breach of contract?

8. Flavore Foods ordered 10 flasks of food coloring from Tech-Colors under a written agreement which called for mechantable goods. Immediately upon delivery Larson, Flavore's laboratory technical analyst, identified the shipment as nonconforming because the coloring was not of average quality. Larson recommended that the shipment be returned but found that the production manager had a problem. It seemed that a large order had to be filled, and some coloring was needed. Accordingly, Flavore used one-third of a flask from the Tech-Colors shipment and wired Tech-Colors to pick up the remaining flasks for return. In its wire, Flavore set forth, with particularity, the chemical defect in the coloring. Tech-Colors ignored the telegram and, instead, demanded the purchase price as shown on the invoice. What principle of law allows Tech-Colors to sue for recovery of the purchase price? How successful will Tech-Colors be in its lawsuit?

9. The union at Atwell Oil Refinery called a strike, leaving only supervisory personnel manning the essential posts in the refinery. Atwell, anticipating a long strike and some difficulty with its supervisors getting through the picket line, purchased a large supply of meat and other

foodstuffs so that the supervisors could be fed on the premises. Surprisingly, the strike was quickly settled, and the manager was ordered to sell all the food remaining in the plant. Atwell sold the food to PubCom, a local advertising firm, for approximately 22 percent of its cost. For PubCom the purchase was timely as it was putting on a big promotion and could utilize the steaks and other meats for an evening affair. The steaks, however, were bad and caused illness to a few of PubCom's officers as well as several prospective commercial clients. The advertising firm and its guests want to sue Atwell. What is Atwell's best defense to this action for breach of an implied warranty?

10. Rodeo Targets supplied Sharp Ranges with shooting targets for several years. The most recent order, for 7,000 targets, was delivered just before a new manager for Sharp had taken over the daily operation of the range. The new manager had been doing business with a different target manufacturer in her previous job. When she saw the 7,000 targets that had arrived from Rodeo before her new assignment, she decided to send them back to Rodeo with the comment that they were "markedly inferior." True to her word, the manager shipped all 7,000 targets back to Rodeo. On November 3, 19X3, Rodeo wrote to Sharp Ranges, informing it that the targets were conforming goods, that the manager's personal dislike was the sole cause for the revocation of the acceptance, and that Sharp was "hereby notified that Rodeo will sell Sharp's 7,000 targets at a private sale on November 10, 19X3." Assume that Rodeo received only 50 percent of the invoice price at the private sale for the returned targets. Will Rodeo be entitled to recover the balance from Sharp Ranges?

Answers

1. As a creditor of the buyer (Nick), the former wife is relying on the rule that consignment contracts are ineffective against creditors unless the consignor complies with a state sign law or perfects a security interest by filing a claim of lien in the appropriate state office. There is no indication of such compliance in this case. Where buyers possess goods on consignment, they mislead others about the ownership of the property. While the former wife is perhaps not the type of creditor the UCC drafters had in mind, she legally qualifies as such. Juno will lose.

2. The legal issue in this case is whether or not the dealer is bound under a warranty to supply a product that performs the task the buyer needed done. Accordingly, it appears that conduct necessary to establish an implied warranty of fitness for a particular use has been established in favor of the buyer. The buyer made known her needs, and the dealer recommended a product which the buyer relied upon. Yes, buyers can ask for the impossible if the sellers so commit themselves.

3. It is true that the buyer has negotiated a contract allowing 30 days credit and indeed he is not in breach of the agreement. However, Section 2-702 of the UCC allows the seller to demand cash in cases where insolvency occurs, and even reclaim goods in cases where no more than 10 days have passed since delivery. The UCC also allows the seller to demand cash for goods already delivered in addition to refusing further delivery without full payment. The buyer's threat in this case is hollow; it is not a real legal threat.

4. Tamper is interested in having Section 2-615 of the UCC made applicable to its problem. This provision allows for an excuse by failure of presupposed conditions. Tamper believes that its performance has been made impracticable by the occurrence of a contingency, the nonoccurrence of which was a basic assumption on which the contract was made. Tamper's problem is that a rapid rise or fall of prices, even of great magnitude, is rarely grounds for invoking this provision of the UCC. Price changes are traditional and normal risks of contracting parties which, in the absence of express language to the contrary, each party assumes for itself. This situation does not qualify as an excuse under Section 2-615.

5. It is always implied that a party will perform its contract, but the degree to which the party performs usually involves a quality commitment. If this is a sales contract, and Fly-By-Night is a merchant, Fly impliedly made a warranty of merchantability. Therefore, under these facts, Fly did breach the contract. However, Fabler might have had a problem having the contract characterized as a sale of goods rather than a contract for services but for the manner in which she negotiated the contract. The itemizing of the bill of materials, which constituted 85 percent of the contract price, is very helpful to Fabler. In a mixed contract, the test is whether goods or services dominate. Here, from a monetary point of view, more goods were purchased than labor. Fabler appears to have a strong case that this was a contract for the sale of goods, and therefore an implied warranty of merchantability would apply.

6. Willard was not a wise businessman. He should have considered the fact that he was purchasing inventory and equipment in bulk and that the Bulk Transfer Law must be honored if the buyer wishes to get a clean title to the goods. Article 6 of the UCC spells out the respective duties of the buyer and seller in these situations. Willard should have demanded an affidavit from Arnold, setting forth the suppliers' names, addresses, and debts. Willard's failure to obtain such a list, followed by notification to each creditor of the pending sale, and his failure to follow the procedures outlined in Article 6 before taking possession of the goods and paying the purchase price are costly mistakes for him. All this places on Willard the risk of taking the goods subject to the claims of Arnold's creditors who were his suppliers. Willard will have to answer to these suppliers.

7. Arthur has a technicality which he can raise in the nature of the Statute of Frauds. Under the UCC, goods sold for a price of $500 or more must have written memorandum or some other special proof, or the contract cannot be enforced. One of the special proofs is "with respect to goods for which payment has been made and accepted," UCC, Section 2-201(3)(c). The problem here is determining whether or not a $200 deposit is sufficient payment to allow oral proof of the contract. Since two units are involved, at $1,200 each, it is clear that Baines is at most entitled to one unit, and that is what she will get. While it is true that the oral agreement was for two units, Baines's problem is that a part payment for less than the price of one unit limits her "proof of the contract" to a single divisible unit. To put it another way, if a part payment of $200 could be used to prove a contract for two units at $1,200 each, it could just as easily be used to prove a contract for 20 or 200, and, clearly, such a "hunting license" would not be acceptable to a court.

8. Flavore may have solved its business problem, but it created a legal problem when it used goods it knew were nonconforming. The law does not permit mixed signals on this matter. Flavore has legally accepted the shipment, allowing the seller to sue for the contract price. Section 2-606 of the UCC specifically states that acceptance of goods occurs when the buyer "does any act inconsistent with the seller's ownership." Use in manufacture under these circumstances is an inconsistent act. Flavore may have an action for damages, but such amount of damages will only reflect a diminution of the invoice price since Flavore must keep the goods.

9. Atwell's best defense is to argue that it made no warranty, either express or implied, regarding the foodstuffs it sold to PubCom. Since Atwell is an oil refiner and is not a seller of foodstuffs in the ordinary way, an implied warranty of fitness for ordinary use (merchantability) does not apply to Atwell's sale of the meat. Atwell is not a merchant of foodstuffs. Further, in regard to PubCom's clients there is also a question of privity to the contract in the first place.

10. Rodeo certainly has a case for breach of contract and had rights which entitled it to the purchase price when Rodeo shipped conforming goods which were initially accepted as they had been in the past. The trouble is that, in exercising its right to resell the goods on the buyer's behalf, Rodeo did not follow the rules. Rodeo could sell at either a private or public sale, but the rules of Section 2-706 of the UCC must be followed. If the seller chooses the course of a private sale, the seller cannot just unilaterally set a date for the sale, but rather must give the buyer reasonable notification of the intention to resell. Here, Rodeo attempted a private sale under public sale rules. Rodeo can sue for damages only.

Chapter 19

Form and Content

19.1 INTRODUCTION

One of the most useful forms of commercial writing is the negotiable instrument, now called *commercial paper* under Article 3 of the UCC. This type of instrument has been used for centuries by merchants, traders, and bankers as a means of facilitating trade. In medieval Europe the use of such financial instruments saw expression as part of what was known as *lex mercantores* (the law merchant). That part of the law merchant called *negotiable instruments law* was later codified by the English as the Bill of Exchange Act, which in turn was followed by enactment of the Negotiable Instrument Law (NIL) by most American states around the turn of the twentieth century. The NIL was restated and modernized in a draft first submitted to the states for adoption in 1953 in the form of Article 3 of the UCC. Every state ultimately enacted that article.

19.2 THE ADVANTAGE OF COMMERCIAL PAPER

Commercial paper (negotiable paper) is understood in business to be nearly as valuable as money and is preferred by creditors over mere contracts calling for the payment of money. Because commercial paper must contain certain language, the commitments made are easily recognized, and its transfer to a creditor creates certain favorable presumptions in his or her favor. For example, such a creditor is presumed to have paid consideration, an event that a mere contract creditor must first offer and prove before successfully suing the debtor. Further, certain defects in the creation or transfer of the commercial paper may be cured by this transfer (called *negotiation*) to another. Contract paper, on the other hand, does not improve with transfer (called *assignment*).

This is not to say that contract paper (nonnegotiable) is valueless. On the contrary, it is as legally valuable as negotiable paper provided no defenses to the contract are raised. It is in regard to defenses that negotiable paper reveals its superiority.

EXAMPLE 1. Carson possesses and owns two documents. One is commercial paper by which the signer promised "to pay $500 to the order of bearer," and the other is a $500 IOU, or a mere promise to pay $500, which is not in negotiable form. Carson can successfully sue on both documents. However, if the signers (debtors) have legal defenses to both documents, Carson will have a legal advantage on the commercial paper document only.

19.3 DEFINITIONS

Article 3 of the UCC lists four types of commercial paper: drafts, checks, certificates of deposit, and notes. A writing which meets the essential requirements of commercial paper is a *draft* (bill of exchange) if it is an order, while a *check* is a draft drawn on a bank and payable on demand. A *certificate of deposit* is an acknowledgment by a bank of receipt of money with an engagement (promise) to repay it; a *note* is a promise to pay money other than a certificate of deposit, UCC, Section 3-104.

While those are the specific statutory types of commercial paper, such instruments may also be classified as either two-party or three-party paper.

195

EXAMPLE 2. A buyer wishes to purchase a $90,000 house, and the bank will loan him $80,000 for 30 years at 13 percent interest per annum. At settlement the bank will usually ask the buyer to sign an instrument promising to repay the money on the above terms. This paper is usually two-party commercial paper, a promissory note, or note. It reflects the buyer's promise to pay to the order of the bank the stipulated sum. The buyer is one party (the maker), and the bank is the other party (the payee).

EXAMPLE 3. At the closing of the above sale the bank will give the seller the $80,000 on behalf of the buyer who borrowed the money. The buyer will usually pay the remainder of the purchase price, $10,000, in the form of a check, which is three-party paper in that the buyer signs an order drawn on a bank to the order of the seller. The buyer is one party (the drawer), his bank is a second party (the drawee), and the seller is a third party (the payee).

19.4 TWO-PARTY PAPER: NOTES

A *note* is tangible evidence of a promise to pay money. It can represent the only agreement between the parties, but frequently the maker who signs the promise to pay agrees to do other things as part of the transaction. Accordingly, notes are frequently more specifically named.

A *mortgage note*, for example, refers to a transaction in which the maker of the note has also placed a lien or mortgage on his or her real property as security for the promise to pay.

EXAMPLE 4. As part of the process of buying a house for a price of $95,000, a buyer signed an $80,000 note and another document called a *mortgage*. In the mortgage the buyer placed a lien on the house she bought with the $80,000 proceeds. The buyer paid the seller the balance of $15,000 due for the purchase of the house. The house is security for the promise made in the mortgage note. It appears, however, that the buyer made a bad bargain in that the house was worth only $78,000. The buyer is also having trouble making the monthly payments on the note. The payee of the note, who is also the holder (called the *mortgagee* or *assigns*), forecloses on the mortgage. Upon public (judicial) sale, the house is sold and brings in only $75,000, which is reduced to $70,000 after deduction of the legal expenses of the action. The life of the mortgage is at an end, but the note survives. The $10,000 unpaid to the payee can still be recovered by enforcing the note.

In a similar way a *security agreement note*, *conditional sale note*, or *chattel mortgage note* is created, but in these cases the lien is placed on tangible personal property. If the personal property is intangible, such as a stock certificate or contract right, the term *collateral note* is frequently used, although that phrase is broad enough to include other property as well.

Sometimes *bonds* qualify as notes. They are commercial paper if they possess the requisites set forth in the UCC. Frequently, however, a bond will contain additional language which disqualifies it from being treated as a negotiable instrument.

EXAMPLE 5. Magic, Inc., issues $3 million worth of corporate bonds, promising to pay back the money with interest to the holders. The terms of the bonds provide that the names of the owners are to be registered on the corporate books. The provision regarding registration violates the commercial paper rules, as such must pass freely from hand to hand without registration. The bonds, while evidencing valid and valuable contract rights, are nonnegotiable, and therefore they are not notes. Legal disputes concerning them would be governed by contract law, not by Article 3 of the UCC.

On the other hand, the certificate of deposit is specially mentioned in the UCC as commercial paper qualifying as a note. A *certificate of deposit* is a promise to pay for money received, signed by a bank as maker, but it is more than a deposit receipt. The term *CD* is sometimes used in bank and loan association advertising to indicate committments other than commercial paper. Many advertised CDs are not negotiable instruments, as the institutions issuing them frequently require that registration is necessary or that the payment will not be made without the surrender of a passbook or other requirements which violate Article 3 of the UCC.

The term *judgment note* merely describes a note which contains language granting the holder special rights in the event of the maker's default. The payee or subsequent holder is authorized to act as agent for the maker upon default and "confess judgment" in an action which the payee or holder instituted. This provision operates to assist such creditors to gain a judgment rather quickly in those few jurisdictions which honor the clause.

19.5 THREE-PARTY PAPER: DRAFTS

Drafts are commercial paper drawn by a drawer on a drawee to the order of the payee. Unlike two-party paper, drafts are normally used to transfer funds rather than create credit instruments. A draft may be used as a credit instrument, but in practice its function is more to facilitate transfer of credits. Drafts include checks, the most numerically popular of negotiable instruments. A *check* is a draft drawn on a bank, as drawee, on demand. A *cashier's check*, while not a legal term, is normally a check drawn by a bank on itself. A *bank draft*, on the other hand, is a check drawn by one bank on another bank. *Certified checks* are regular checks in which the drawee bank has, after issue by the drawer (its customer), accepted by signing on the face of the instrument, thus making the drawee bank an acceptor primarily liable on the check.

A *trade acceptance* intends also to be an accepted draft, but the drawee is not a bank. A trade acceptance is a draft, usually drawn by a seller of goods on the buyer of goods as drawee, and payable to the order of the seller.

EXAMPLE 6. By contract, a seller agrees to sell and deliver 400 crates of celery for $4,000 to a buyer who agrees to accept and pay for them under a 30-day trade acceptance. The seller will send with the goods a draft he or she has drawn on the buyer to the order of the seller in the amount of $4,000. The instrument states that it "is payable 30 days after sight." The celery arrives and is inspected by the buyer, who finds it conforming. The buyer then signs the accompanying draft on the face, dates the instrument, and returns it to the seller. The seller now has a trade acceptance, which he or she can hold for 30 days from its accepted date or which the seller can immediately negotiate to another holder who is willing to accept it for a price.

19.6 FORM OF COMMERCIAL PAPER: GENERAL

The presence of certain necessary language and the absence of other words determine the negotiability of an instrument. Historically, this special paper has been referred to as "a courier without luggage whose countenance is its passport." Simply stated, the paper must contain no restrictions on transfer and payment and must be recognizable as commercial paper by examination of the form only.

EXAMPLE 7. A check, otherwise in negotiable form, contains the legend that "this check is given in payment of merchandise and is subject to all the terms of the sales contract this date." This paper is not negotiable since it appears on its face to have *luggage*, that is, the reader must refer to another document or facts outside the paper to determine the right to payment.

The form, not the underlying integrity of the document, is what is essential. If it is in the proper form, it is negotiable even if, for example, the necessary signature is a complete forgery. The party who actually signed the document, the forger, would be liable on it even under the assumed (forged) name.

19.7 NECESSARY LANGUAGE

Section 3-104(1) of the UCC requires that every negotiable instrument must be "(*a*) signed by the maker or drawer; and (*b*) contain an unconditional promise or order to pay a sum certain in money and no other promise, order, obligation or power given by the maker or drawer except as authorized by this Article; and (*c*) be payable on demand or at a definite time; and (*d*) be payable to order or to bearer." Each element is important and must be met. Notice that (*b*) includes three elements.

EXAMPLE 8.   Astrid has in her possession a paper which reads: "The undersigned promises to pay to the order of Astrid the sum of $500, (signed) Theodore." This paper qualifies as a promise under the above rules as promissory two-party paper.

EXAMPLE 9.   Astrid has just taken out her checkbook and filled in a check. The check now reads, "Last National Bank, Dayton, Ohio, December 13, 19X3, Pay to the order of Baker's Department Store, the sum of twenty-five dollars, $25.00, (signed) Astrid." Astrid has just created a negotiable instrument of the *order* type (draft or check) which is three-party paper, here a check.

As can be seen, the necessary language can be terse and yet qualify as commercial paper. Further, it is not necessary that the exact words be used, only the exact meaning. However, commercial practice suggests that traditional language makes the instrument more acceptable.

EXAMPLE 10.   Terrence wrote a letter to Sam Smith reading, "Dear Sam, I promise to pay you, Sam Smith, or anyone you direct me to pay, $500. Very truly yours, (signed) Terrence." Using the letter form does not adversely affect the legality of this document. It is negotiable, although its business use might be limited because of the form used. It qualifies as a note, two-party paper.

EXAMPLE 11.   If, instead of promising to pay Smith, Terrence wrote a letter reading, "Dear Sam, I hereby order Taylor to pay you, Smith, or anyone you nominate, the sum of $500. (signed) Terrence," this unusual letter would also qualify as commercial paper. It is a three-party instrument, a draft in which Terrence is the drawer, Smith the payee, and Taylor the drawee.

One can see that the note (promissory paper) has two parties on the face of the instrument, the maker and the payee. The maker signs and thereby promises to pay to the order of a named person or bearer. Three-party paper, drafts, does not have a signer promising to pay; rather the drawer who signs "orders" another to pay. The idea of the word "order" is found in the use of the traditional verb "pay." Further, the fact that paper is either two-party or three-party does not mean as a matter of law that each party must be a different legal person. Indeed, one person could play all three roles and such paper would still qualify as a negotiable instrument.

19.8 PROMISE OR ORDER TO PAY

The popular use of printed legal forms prevents a great deal of litigation over whether the questioned instrument contained a promise or order to pay money. Yet the printer or other scrivener could fail to state this requirement by using language that does not indicate that the maker "promises" or the drawer "orders" the payment of money.

EXAMPLE 12.   "I owe C. D. Brown $50,000." "Due Brown and Smith, $50,000, value received." "IOU $50,000." These statements have been held not to qualify as promises to pay.

EXAMPLE 13.   "John Smith, you are authorized to pay Thomas the sum of $50,000, (signed) Smedley." It was held that the drawer did not order the payment but merely authorized it, and thus it fails to qualify.

The traditional "promise to pay" for notes and "pay" for drafts are the safest ways in which this UCC requirement can be met.

19.9 SIGNATURE AND WRITING

The UCC does not require any particular form or writing surface, type of writing instrument, or form of signature. Paper is the traditional commercial writing surface; pen, typewriter, and print are the common writing instruments. Occasionally, the newspapers report the cashing of a check written on wearing apparel or a watermelon, or suchlike, but these oddball incidents only support the view that legally such would not be prohibited.

Of more practical significance is the signature of each party who appears on the paper. A signature is merely an external act showing an actor's intent to assent to the terms of the instrument; the manner in which this is accomplished is not inhibited. Even a forged signature is a signature of the forger.

EXAMPLE 14. (*a*) Henry places an "X" on the paper; this can be his signature even if he never uses that mark again. (*b*) Brown's wife writes her husband's signature on the instrument under his direction since his writing hand is broken; this is Brown's signature. (*c*) Laslow signs the note by typing his name in the appropriate place as a comaker of the note, while his wife signs in cursive; both have "signed" the paper.

It is generally poor business practice to sign an instrument using an alias, but it is not illegal unless done for a fraudulent purpose. The reason why most sign in the same manner each time is for ease of authentication for "legal paper" and, sometimes, because without such discipline other parties may not be obliged to act.

EXAMPLE 15. Abe Ford opened a checking account at a local bank. He signed a customer's agreement—a signature card, which, among other items, states that the bank will honor drafts (i.e., checks) containing a facsimile of his signature on the card. Abe, while attending a charity ball, is socially pressured into making a donation right on the spot. He executes a $500 check to the order of the charity and signs it "A. Ford." The check bounced. The bank did not honor the alias its customer used since their contract spelled out the requirements. Nevertheless, this check is a good negotiable instrument although the drawee owed no duty to the drawer to honor it.

19.10 SUM MUST BE CERTAIN

It is essential that the amount of money be firmly stated on the instrument. The UCC allows certain exceptions to the rule that the sum must be certain; the thrust of these is that calculation or determination of the sum must be possible and the method must be clear. Thus, an instrument is negotiable even though it is payable

(1) with stated interest or stated installments.

(2) with stated different rates of interest before and after default, or a specified date.

(3) with a stated discount or addition if paid before or after the date fixed for payment.

(4) with exchange or less exchange, whether at a fixed rate or the current rate.

(5) with costs of collection or an attorney's fee, or both, upon default.

These exceptions do not include many provisions that creditors may wish to include to protect the financial integrity of the instrument.

EXAMPLE 16. A creditor contended that a security agreement that the debtor signed was negotiable. In examining the document the court ruled that while it might be theoretically possible for a security agreement to qualify as a negotiable instrument, such is not normally the case. The agreement examined contained a promise of the buyer to *pay taxes*, to *procure insurance* from a company approved by the creditor, not to remove the purchased car from the filing district, and to make other commitments in addition to the payment of the money. All this "luggage" destroyed negotiability.

The reader of the document must be able to ascertain the amount of money payable. Sometimes the amount fixed is in conflict on the face. If there is no rule of construction to rescue the instrument, it fails to state a sum certain and the instrument is nonnegotiable.

EXAMPLE 17.   Orson, as maker, signed a paper otherwise in negotiable form which read "the sum of $500, payable in 12 monthly installments of $50 each." There is no sum certain because $500 and $600 are stated. If, however, the $500 was written in words ("five hundred dollars"), the rule of construction would apply and the instrument would be interpreted as a $500 note since words govern numbers where there is a conflict.

An instrument payable "with interest," but in which no interest rate is stated, is payable at the legal or judgment rate set by the statute of the particular state.

19.11   PAYABLE IN MONEY

A negotiable instrument must be payable in money. Under Section 1-204(24) of the UCC, money is a "medium of exchange authorized or adopted by a domestic or foreign government as part of its currency." Further, an instrument payable in currency or current funds is payable in money.

EXAMPLE 18.   An instrument reads, "I promise to pay bearer 500 Swiss francs." This is payable in money. The signer, the maker, must satisfy this note with 500 Swiss francs *or* the number of dollars the stated francs will purchase at the current buying rate at the time of demand. However, had the note included the words "payable in Swiss francs," the note could be satisfied *only* in Swiss currency; nevertheless, it is negotiable.

19.12   DEMAND OR DEFINITE TIME

All negotiable paper must be payable on demand or at a definite time. Failure to supply a definite time often results in a *demand* or *sight* instrument.

EXAMPLE 19.   "I promise to pay bearer $500, (signed) Mark" or "Last Bank, Pay to the order of Tom, (signed) Taylor." Both are payable when the holder demands payment, which he or she may do at any time. The first is a demand note; the second is a check which is, by definition, a draft drawn on a bank on demand.

EXAMPLE 20.   "I promise to pay to bearer the sum of $600, 90 days from date, (signed) Elsa." At this point the document is nonnegotiable as it is undated; a date is necessary here to fix a definite time. The holder has the authority to complete the instrument by filling in the correct date.

Sometimes the date of maturity is determined when the holder first presents the instrument to the drawee for acceptance. The drawee at this time signs (i.e., accepts) and dates the instrument, thus establishing a date for payment.

EXAMPLE 21.   A seller draws a draft on a buyer payable to the order of the seller "30 days after sight." When the payee-seller or other holder presents the draft to the buyer for his or her signature (acceptance) and dating, the maturity will be 30 days after that date.

Many instruments have, in practice, more than one maturity date because they include *acceleration* or *extension clauses*. In installment instruments, for example, the business necessity for such is obvious.

EXAMPLE 22.   In temporary payment for a car which Dyer purchased from her neighbor, Dyer signed a note for $2,400, payable $200 per month until full payment. If Dyer fails to pay an installment, the holder can only sue for each monthly payment as it comes due. The note could have read "in the event there is a default in any installment the entire balance becomes due." Such a clause is an acceleration clause.

EXAMPLE 23. A note contained the following language, "Payment due March 2, 19X4, but full amount shall become payable should the maker sell or otherwise transfer his residence. The maker, however, is given the right to extend the maturity of this note for a period of 6 months, provided written notice is given the payee at least 30 days before March 2, 19X4." The note contains an acceleration clause in favor of the payee, or holder, and an extension clause in favor of the maker.

The UCC broadly validates acceleration clauses, allowing the instrument to mature earlier by reason of an event or even the will of the holder. Extension clauses in favor of the maker are also permitted, but here the paper must ultimately set some future time at which the maker must pay the instrument. A clause calling for payment "30 days after my death," while certain to happen, is not a definite time under the UCC. The maker's objective could easily be achieved by employing a definite time and providing for an acceleration upon death. Accordingly, a maker's promise to "pay 200 years from date, provided this note shall be payable in full 30 days after the death of the maker," meets the UCC requirements.

Sometimes the party expected to pay wishes to satisfy the debt before maturity but not pay the unearned interest. The maker cannot so repay unless the instrument permits it. When this permission is included, it is sometimes called a *prepayment without penalty clause*. The words "on or before" or "within" have been held to allow such prepayment.

19.13 PAYABLE TO ORDER OR BEARER

The words of negotiability appear on the payee line. This line must reflect that the party entitled to payment is either the possessor of the instrument (bearer) or a named party who is authorized to name another to be paid (order paper). Accordingly, each instrument must on its face be payable either to order or to bearer. An instrument is payable to order when by its terms it is payable to the order or assigns of any person therein specified with reasonable certainty, or his or her order, or when it is conspicuously designated on its face as "exchange" or the like and names a payee.

EXAMPLE 24. A paper reads "Adam, pay to Adam, or anyone he names, $500, (signed) Adam." This is negotiable because "anyone he names" is, while not recommended from a business viewpoint, a substitute for "order of" and qualifies as payable to order. Notice that this is a three-party paper, a draft, in which one party played all three roles.

EXAMPLE 25. A note which on the payee line reads that it is "payable to bearer," or "payable to order of bearer," or "payable to holder" is in all three cases payable to bearer.

The language on the payee line is of central importance as it names the intended owner of this valuable document, and UCC language or its equivalent must be used. A statement, for example, on the payee line that it is "payable upon return of the instrument properly indorsed" is expressly ineffective, and the instrument is nonnegotiable.

Bearer paper grants ownership of the paper to the possessor and includes the following language: "to bearer," "to order of bearer," "to a specified person or bearer," "to cash," "to order of cash," or any other indication which does not purport to designate a specific payee.

EXAMPLE 26.

(a) "I promise to pay holder" is acceptable but not recommended.

(b) "I promise to pay to the possessor of this document" is good, and, like (a), acceptable but not recommended.

(c) "I promise to pay to Rasco, *the* bearer," is bad, being neither order nor bearer paper.

(d) "I promise to pay to bearer, Rasco," is bad, for the same reason as stated in (c).

(e) "I promise to pay to Rasco *or* bearer" is good and is bearer paper.

(f) "Pay to the order of one keg of nails" is good; it is bearer paper.

(g) "Pay to the order of _____" is bad; under the UCC this is neither order nor bearer paper, only incomplete paper.

Where an instrument is payable to both order and bearer, the instrument will be interpreted as order paper unless the words "the bearer" are handwritten or typewritten (UCC, Section 3-110(3)).

19.14 NONNEGOTIABLE LANGUAGE: GENERALLY

The potential for negotiability can be unrealized by failure to use the necessary words above, but it can also be thwarted by adding language which destroys the form. One of the most common ways in which it is impaired is by making the promise or order conditional. Three aspects of conditions are contingencies, the particular fund doctrine, and other transactions.

19.15 CONTINGENCIES

A promise or order to pay upon the happening of a contingency destroys the negotiable character of the instrument. A promise to pay such as "when my daughter marries," or "when the proceeds from the sale of my house are received," or "when my son turns 21 years old," even if the event happens, is fatal language. This is so even if the event is certain to happen eventually, e.g., death. It is important to note the difference between a contingency bringing an acceleration or extension clause into effect and an attempt to use the date of a contingency's occurrence as the sole date of maturity of the instrument. The test is whether or not the party promising to pay or ordered to pay is absolutely liable for the amount stated.

EXAMPLE 27. A maker executed an instrument to the order of her dentist, promising to pay $480 in monthly installments of $20. The note also contained the language "that in the event of the death of the payee, all payments not due at the time of death shall be discharged and fully canceled and the note retired." This is nonnegotiable because there is a condition to full payment, i.e., the survival of the payee until the full-maturity term of the note.

19.16 PARTICULAR FUND DOCTRINE

Generally, if the signer fails to expose his or her entire legal personality to liability on the instrument, the promise or order is conditional and therefore nonnegotiable. This has not prevented makers and drawers from stating on the instrument that the payment of the instrument is to come from a particular fund. If the promise or order refers to payment *only* from that fund, the instrument is nonnegotiable. If it is interpreted to be merely a reference, it can be negotiable.

EXAMPLE 28. A retailer signed a trade acceptance upon which he included the following: "This is temporary payment for inventory purchased, the sale of which will provide the proceeds to satisfy this obligation." This reflects a typical business intent of a retailer, but if the language is interpreted to mean that the paper will *only* be paid from the proceeds, the instrument is nonnegotiable.

There are two statutory exceptions to the rule regarding a particular fund. An instrument is considered unconditional even though it is limited to payment out of a particular fund if (1) it is issued by a governmental agency or unit or (2) it is limited to payment out of the entire assets of a partnership, unincorporated association, trust, or estate.

EXAMPLE 29. Middletown Drainage District, a governmental unit established to make raw land usable through the construction of drainage canals, raised funds by issuing instruments which are payable "only out of the sale of land owned by the District." If otherwise negotiable, these notes come within the governmental agency exception.

EXAMPLE 30. Ace Hardware is a partnership composed of father and son. An instrument is signed, "Ace Hardware, by John Ace, partner." It provides that "this note is payable from the entire proceeds of the firm." This instrument is negotiable.

The particular fund rule does not, however, prohibit mention of the particular fund or asset from which satisfaction is expected, only that the holder of the instrument is not limited to that expected source. Mere bookkeeping or other references do not make the instrument conditional and therefore nonnegotiable.

EXAMPLE 31. The following were held to be mere notations or references and did not destroy negotiability: (*a*) "Charge to my no. 1913 account." (*b*) "Charge same to drawer's account according to registered letter sent." This, however, was held to be a condition: "Payable only out of rental receipts received from Sixton Properties."

19.17 OTHER TRANSACTIONS

Mere references to other transactions or the underlying transactions do not destroy the unconditional character of the instrument. The issue turns on whether the language merely provides a memorial to the underlying transaction or whether the payment of the instrument is subject to some other document or circumstance. If an instrument recites that the promise or order is "subject to the terms and conditions of (another understanding)" or "subject" to some transaction or other event, the instrument fails its test. Further, a promissory note which recites that it is "secured by a mortgage of this date and *subject* to all its terms" is clearly nonnegotiable.

EXAMPLE 32. The following destroy negotiability:

(*a*) "Subject to any setoff because of defect of goods."

(*b*) "Provided order no. 6782 is delivered by December 1, 19X3."

(*c*) A draft payable "on presentation of release of claim signed by the payee."

(*d*) "On condition that Smith & Co. have become legally liable."

(*e*) A check stating that "the bankbook of the depositor must accompany this check."

It is not the content of the outside document to which the instrument is made subject that destroys negotiability, only the fact that one must refer to something beyond the face of the instrument itself to determine liability. However, parties may limit the life of a negotiable instrument because the passage of time is a fact, being neither a contingency nor a transaction.

EXAMPLE 33. A draft provided that it was "void if not cashed within 60 days." These words printed on the face of the instrument will be enforced as an agreement to shorten the life of the instrument to less than the statutory period prescribed by law; the draft was held to be negotiable.

19.18 INDIFFERENT LANGUAGE

Unless the rules mentioned above apply, the creator of an instrument is free to place considerable additional language on the instrument without affecting negotiability. The writer may refer to the underlying transaction, place a seal, fail to date it, antedate it, or postdate it. Section 3-105 of the

UCC specifically approves mere references which intend to indicate the transaction which gives rise to the instrument. Further, the courts are instructed not to infer a condition where questionable language is used.

EXAMPLE 34.   A check was signed and delivered in prepayment to a grower. The check included the words "for berries to be delivered to us by June 8." This is marginal or questionable language. If the court infers that "to be delivered" is a condition to payment, the words are more than a recital of the underlying transaction; they would destroy negotiability. However, the court ruled the check to be negotiable as the court would not infer a condition.

The above case poses a close question and illustrates the presumption of finding for negotiability when possible, as authorized by the UCC. This philosophy is reaffirmed by the rule that where future performance is expected of a party, notice of such on the paper does not affect negotiability. Therefore, a recital that the instrument was given for a promise yet to be performed, an executory promise, cannot be interpreted as an implied constructive condition.

The UCC specifically mentions certain language that does not affect negotiability. This "legally indifferent" language as to negotiability may, however, be important for business purposes. Section 3-112 of the UCC includes as not affecting negotiability the following: absence or presence of statements such as "value received," terms concerning default in the instrument and the collateral, promises to protect collateral or give additional collateral, confession of judgment clause, waiver of laws, and even statements regarding the instrument as being given in "full settlement or satisfaction of an obligation."

EXAMPLE 35.   The state of Florida exempts the head of a household from execution of judgment to the extent of $1,000 of personal property. A note providing "The maker waives all rights of homestead or head of household" would nevertheless be negotiable while the clause itself would not be enforceable.

EXAMPLE 36.   A check was sent by the debtor-drawer to her creditor and contained the legend "The cashing of this check by the payee evidences full payment of all claims owed by the drawer to the payee." This "voucher check" is negotiable.

19.19   INCOMPLETE INSTRUMENTS

If the party signing meant to create a negotiable instrument, the fact that a necessary element is missing will not necessarily prevent the document from becoming completed into a negotiable one. When completed as authorized, it is as effective as if it had been so created at the time of signing. As will be noted later, even where the document was not completed as authorized, it is possible for certain third parties to enforce it.

EXAMPLE 37.   Turner signs his personal check in payment of merchandise and delivers the check to the dealer, who asks that the amount be left blank as he does not have the correct price at this time. The dealer, before sending in the check for collection, either accidentally or deliberately writes in an incorrect figure. The check is now a completed instrument and is negotiable. As between the drawer-customer and the dealer-payee, the drawer is liable only for the correct amount. However, if this wrongly completed document gets into the hands of third parties who may have greater rights than the dealer, called *holders in due course* or *holders from a holder in due course* (to be discussed later), the drawer may be liable to these third parties for the incorrect amount.

19.20   AMBIGUOUS TERMS

The UCC attempts to make certain that those who examine a document can determine quickly whether or not the instrument is negotiable. Some common errors or miscues are addressed in Section 3-118 of the UCC, which provides certain presumptions. For example, where there is doubt whether the instrument is a draft or a note, the holder may treat it as either. Where interest is to run, but is not specified, the *judgment rate* at place of payment runs on the instrument; this is sometimes called the state's *legal rate*. Instruments can be handwritten using pencil or pen, can be typewritten, or can be printed. The UCC assists in interpretation by stating that handwritten terms control typewritten and printed ones, and typewriting overrules printing. Words always control figures except that if the words are ambiguous, then figures control.

Black Letter Law
A Summary

1. A negotiable instrument is an unconditional promise or order to pay a sum certain in money on demand or at a definite time.

2. By UCC definition there are four types of negotiable instruments: notes, certificates of deposit, drafts, and checks. Collectively these are known as commercial paper.

3. Negotiable instruments are also classified as two-party paper and three-party paper; notes and certificates of deposit are promissory two-party paper, while drafts and checks are three-party paper.

4. Drawers sign drafts and checks; makers sign notes and certificates of deposit; all direct payment to the order of payees.

5. The third party on three-party paper is the drawee on whom the drawer orders payment to be made to the payee.

6. A promise or order is conditional, and therefore nonnegotiable, if it is payable only out of a particular fund, or is dependent on the happening of an event, or is subject to another agreement or transaction.

7. Where payment is to be made out of a particular fund of a governmental agency or where the entire assets of an unincorporated association, partnership, estate, or trust are committed, the instrument is, by statutory exception, negotiable despite the naming of a specific source of funds for payment.

8. Every negotiable instrument must be payable "to the order of" a specified person or "to bearer."

9. A promise or order to pay a "named person *or* bearer" is negotiable, while one payable to a "named person, *the* bearer" is not.

10. A negotiable instrument is payable at a definite time; it may, however, contain an acceleration clause hastening maturity or a clause extending the date of maturity to a further definite time.

11. Mere reference to other transactions, terms binding on default, provisions for attorneys' fees and costs of collection, and confession of judgment clauses do not affect negotiability; however, a promise or order to pay taxes or insurance, for example, destroys negotiability.

12. Where a party signed a document intending it to be a negotiable instrument, the holder may supply any necessary language to complete the document.

13. The fact that the instrument was issued for an executory consideration does not destroy negotiability since the court will not infer a condition; there is a presumption in favor of the negotiable character of the instrument.

Solved Problems

19.1 Protective Coatings, Inc., sold goods to a farm supplier, made out a document payable to the order of Protective Coatings in the sum of $367.67 (the invoice amount), signed the document, and named the farm supplier the drawee. The farm supplier then signed the document and returned it to Protective Coatings. Protective Coatings, needing cash, indorsed and sold the instrument to a credit company. What is the name of the document created?

(a) Cashier's check

(b) Bond

(c) Trade acceptance

(d) Certificate of deposit

When a seller draws on the buyer to the seller's own order, the seller is attempting to create a trade acceptance, answer (c). It is three-party paper of the draft variety, in which the buyer, the drawee, signs on the face, thus becoming the acceptor. Bonds and certificates of deposit are two-party promissory paper. A cashier's check has a bank both as drawee and drawer.

19.2 A lessor rented certain territory to Rainbow Oil Company. The terms of the lease provided that the rental payments were to be made by "either draft or check." Rainbow Oil offered the lessor an instrument which recited as follows: "To: Treasurer of Rainbow Oil Company, Pay to the Order of Lessor, $5,000, (signed) Rainbow Oil Company, Payable through First National Bank." The lessor contends that Rainbow did not satisfy the contract terms. Under these circumstances,

(a) the oil company breached the contract.

(b) the oil company offered a draft and therefore complied.

(c) since this was a check, the oil company did not breach the contract.

(d) this is a promissory note and therefore qualifies as a draft.

A draft is a three-party instrument in which the drawer orders the drawee to pay to the order or bearer. Rainbow Oil Company was both drawer and drawee, and the lessor was the payee of a draft. The oil company complied with the terms of the contract, statement (b).

19.3 A buyer purchased a trailer on credit. Among the instruments signed by him was a document, otherwise negotiable in form, in favor of the seller, in the sum of $4,815.60, which had the following language, "This note is given as evidence of the balance of the purchase price of certain personal property purchased under a conditional sales contract of even date herewith, executed by the maker hereof as buyer and the payee hereof as seller." This language

(a) transforms a note into a certificate of deposit.

(b) makes the document conditional and therefore nonnegotiable.

(c) is a mere reference and does not affect negotiability.

(d) ties the underlying transaction to this trade acceptance.

A statement reciting that which gave rise to the transaction does not affect negotiability; statement (c) is the answer. This is a note by a private party, not by a bank, and therefore it cannot be a certificate of deposit. Also, it is not a three-party instrument such as a trade acceptance.

19.4 A husband delivered a $10,500 promissory note to his wife at the time of the divorce in settlement of future payments of alimony. Several months after the divorce, the former wife remarried and under applicable state law all duty to pay alimony ceased. Under these circumstances,

(a) since the underlying transaction is discharged, the note is also discharged.

(b) the note stands by itself and is not automatically affected by the status of the underlying transaction.

(c) the note is always subject to the underlying transaction which gave rise to it.

(d) notes may be used for commercial transactions but not for marital transactions.

The mere fact that the note was given for an obligation which may or may not be enforceable does not automatically affect the legal character of the negotiable instrument, which is a "courier without luggage"; the answer is (b). As between the parties some defenses may be raised, but the document itself is not affected and third parties who take the note may gain greater rights than the original payee.

19.5 A $5,000 document, otherwise in negotiable form, was payable to the order of William Film Laboratories. It appeared that there was no such legal entity. It was a fictitious trade name that Williams used under which she lawfully did business. Which is the correct statement?

(a) The instrument is not payable to order or bearer.

(b) The use of an assumed name does not affect the negotiable character of the instrument.

(c) The instrument is bearer paper.

(d) Since the payee named does not legally exist, the document is legally worthless.

This instrument is legally good, statement (b). Since the payee was Williams doing business under a fictitious name, the instrument is payable to her as such. It is order paper and would require an indorsement and delivery to further negotiate it. Under the UCC it would only be bearer paper if the name of the payee was not meant to signify any particular person. In such an instance, the paper would be bearer paper and require no indorsement for further negotiation.

19.6 An instrument otherwise in negotiable form in the sum of $10,000 contained the following language: "With interest payable semiannually and in case of maker's death or marriage this note becomes canceled and the obligation of the maker ceases." Under these circumstances,

(a) this is a valid acceleration clause.

(b) the maker has a valid extension clause.

(c) since death terminates contracts, only the language dealing with marriage destroys negotiability.

(d) this is a conditional promise to pay, and hence it is nonnegotiable.

This promise to pay only if a certain event did not come to pass destroys the instrument's claim to negotiability; the answer is (d). The references to death and marriage both adversely affect negotiability.

19.7 A maker signed a $5,300 instrument otherwise negotiable in form and payable in monthly installments. The instrument provided that in the event that any installment became overdue, the holder could demand the full balance on the note. A default occurred, as the maker was unable to make the payment because he was unjustly fired from his job. Which is the correct statement?

(*a*) The default clause creates a penalty and is unenforceable.

(*b*) This is a valid acceleration clause.

(*c*) If the maker can prove that he had good financial reasons for a default, the clause is ineffective.

(*d*) The instrument does not state a definite time for payment.

This is a valid acceleration clause commonly found in promissory notes, statement (*b*). The purpose of the acceleration clause is not to punish anyone for violation; it only serves to protect the payee from long delays in cases where the maker has evidenced irresponsibility for whatever reason. Such a clause makes a loan more attractive to a lender and thereby enhances the borrower's opportunity to obtain credit. It is not against public policy.

19.8 A CPA's client has an instrument which contains certain ambiguities or deficiencies. In construing the instrument, which of the following is *incorrect*?

(*a*) Where there is doubt whether the instrument is a draft or a note, the holder may treat it as either.

(*b*) Handwritten terms control typewritten and printed terms, and typewritten terms control printed terms.

(*c*) An instrument which is payable only upon the happening of an event that is uncertain as to the time of its occurrence is payable at a definite time if the event has occurred.

(*d*) The fact that the instrument is antedated will not affect the instrument's negotiability.

(*AICPA Examination, November 1980*)

Every negotiable instrument must be payable upon demand or at a definite time; statement (*c*) is the answer. Whether or not the event which determines the maturity has occurred is irrelevant. One must be able to tell from looking at the instrument that it is in negotiable form. This is a nonnegotiable instrument. The other answers are correct and reflect statutory rules of construction and allowances.

19.9 Rapid Delivery, Inc., has in its possession the following instrument which it purchased for value.

March 1, 19X0

Thirty days from date, I, Harold Kales, do hereby promise to pay Ronald Green four hundred dollars and no cents ($400.00). This note is given for value received.

Harold Kales

Harold Kales

Which of the following is correct?

(*a*) The instrument is negotiable.

(*b*) The instrument is nonnegotiable, and therefore Rapid has obtained no rights on the instrument.

(c)   Rapid is an assignee of the instrument and has the same rights as the assignor had on it.

(d)   The instrument is nontransferable on its face.

(*AICPA Examination*, *November 1980*)

Every negotiable instrument must be payable to order or bearer. Such words, or their equivalent, are missing from the payee line. Accordingly, this document reflects a contract right, not a negotiable one. As an assignee, Rapid may enforce this contract; statement (c) is correct. The fact that an instrument is nonnegotiable does not destroy its legal character; it means only that the special benefits of negotiability to the holder do not apply.

19.10 An instrument reads as follows: "$7,500, Palo Alto, California, October 1, 19X3. Sixty days from date I promise to pay to the order of cash at First National Bank, Sunside, California, value received, with interest at the rate of 25 percent per annum. This instrument arises out of a personal service contract yet to be performed. (signed) Con Sultant." Which of the following statements about this instrument is correct?

(a)   The excessive interest rate makes this nonnegotiable.

(b)   Only checks can be payable to cash and be negotiable.

(c)   Since this was given for future services, the holder has notice of a condition to payment.

(d)   The instrument is negotiable on its face.

Sultant has created a promissory note payable to bearer; statement (d) is the answer. The interest rate could be excessive under certain conditions, but that does not prevent the instrument from meeting the form requirements. Payable to bearer by use of cash, or other designation, is available to writers of two-party paper and three-party paper. Notice that the instrument was given for executory consideration; this does not give notice of a condition to payment.

19.11 Anderson purchased a home from a developer who lent him the money to complete the purchase. Anderson signed what appeared to be a promissory note for $100,000 and executed a real estate mortgage to secure this promise. The developer had not lived up to certain representations and warranties regarding the house, and Anderson ceased making monthly payments on the paper. In the meantime the paper and mortgage had been transferred to a third party, who, after unsuccessfully demanding that the monthly payments continue, finally foreclosed on the mortgage. It became legally important to Anderson to establish that he did not sign a negotiable instrument. If he did not, Anderson can raise the developer's breaches against the third party. Anderson's attorney was interested in some language she found on the note. At the bottom of the instrument it read that "a real estate mortgage was given with this note and the terms of the said mortgage are by this reference made a part hereof."

What contention must Anderson advance in order to support his position? What defense should the third party marshal?

The issue is whether the promise made by Anderson was an unconditional promise to pay. This must appear on the instrument itself, and one is not permitted to look to other documents or extrinsic evidence to support this premise. The phrase "are by this reference made a part hereof" tells the reader that the mortgage terms are also the note's terms. Thus, the note is subject to another instrument, a violation of the rule regarding negotiability. The only defense for the holder to argue is that this is a mere reference to the underlying agreement and thus the instrument is negotiable in form. Unfortunately for the holder, making another instrument a part of the note violates the rule. Anderson will win his contention.

19.12 Yost signed the following document and delivered it to the Red River Finance Company:

> Tampa, Florida, 16 March 19X3 $1,252.50
> For value received, I, we, or either of us, the under-
> signed promise to pay to the order of _____ in
> _____ monthly payments of $_____ each and the last
> installment of $_____ on _____ at the rate of
> 12 percent per annum. This transaction arose under
> the authority of the Finance Loan Act in which the
> payee is a licensed member.
>
> (signed) *Samuel R. Yost*

Yost defaulted on the document, and it became important to determine whether it was in negotiable form. Yost has taken the position that it is at most an IOU, while the finance company claims that it is a bearer negotiable instrument.

What problems does the finance company have with its position?

Apart from the obvious fact that the sum certain only appears at the top of the document and not after the engagement to pay, there may be an issue about the time for payment. However, the most difficult issue is the complete absence of a payee. Every negotiable instrument must be payable to the order of a specified payee or to bearer. This is payable to the order of _____ . It is an incomplete document, not a negotiable instrument. By construction the court might find the amount by virtue of the figure listed at the top, and, in the absence of a definite time, construe it to be a demand note unless the other words are interpreted to require a reference to a particular date. However, the instrument is clearly nonnegotiable because of the absence of a payee.

19.13 Sanford executed a document otherwise in negotiable form which contained her promise to pay to the order of Tepper Industries the sum of ten thousand dollars "within two (2) years after date." At the time of its delivery the instrument was undated, but an official at Tepper saw its absence and filled in the actual date of issue, May 10, 19X0. This document was made and delivered up by Sanford under the terms of a complicated business deal, the complete terms of which were contained in several other lengthy documents. A dispute arose between Tepper and Sanford, and in the meantime the document had been transferred to a creditor of Tepper, who was now demanding rights under the document. Sanford is willing to pay the document but wants credit for certain setoffs under her other agreements with Tepper. Accordingly, it is important to Sanford to contend that the document she signed promising to pay the $10,000 was nonnegotiable.

What position should Sanford attempt to present which will challenge the negotiability of the instrument?

Every negotiable instrument must be payable on demand or at a definite time. When Sanford delivered the document to Tepper, it was not a negotiable instrument because it was undated where a date was necessary to determine the maturity date. However, the holder has the authority to complete the instrument, at which time it becomes negotiable. There is an additional question, however, and that is the meaning of the phrase "within two (2) years after date." Courts have had some trouble with such words but have determined that the phrase is the equivalent of "on or before." This means that the maker must absolutely pay at the end of the period but has the option of paying before the maturity date without interest penalty, i.e., unearned interest. The instrument is negotiable. Sanford will not succeed in sustaining her position.

Chapter 20

Transfer and Negotiation

20.1 NEGOTIATION: GENERALLY

Negotiable paper is created so as to be transferable from one person to another. This transfer can be either by assignment or by negotiation. When negotiable paper is transferred subject to the rules of Article 3 of the UCC, it is negotiated. When it is not so transferred, an assignment usually takes place.

EXAMPLE 1. Hanson is the named payee of an $8,200 note he wishes to sell to Orwell. Hanson delivers the note to Orwell for $7,000 but fails to indorse it. Hanson has transferred the note by assignment; it has not been negotiated. The law of assignment will govern certain rights in this situation, not Article 3 of the UCC.

The fact that one "assigns" a negotiable instrument rather than "negotiates" it does not, by itself, impair the obligation. Such means only that the rules of contract govern rather than Article 3 of the UCC.

20.2 PAYEE LINE

The payee line on the face of the instrument is the starting place to determine the method to be employed in negotiation of the instrument. If the paper is payable to the order of a named person, the signature of that person on the back of the instrument (an indorsement) is necessary, as well as the voluntary transfer of possession (delivery) of the document. The designation must be strictly obeyed. If the instrument names multiple payees (or indorsees), all must sign the instrument unless it is payable to one *or* the other. If, on the other hand, the face of the instrument shows it payable to bearer, then no indorsement is necessary; delivery alone can effect a negotiation. It follows that the nature and types of indorsement are frequently important issues.

20.3 INDORSEMENTS

The signing by one party on the back of a negotiable instrument together with any additional language is called an *indorsement*. The party signing is called the *indorser*. The UCC names four types of indorsements: blank, special, restrictive, and qualified. Their use informs the reader of the instrument of three things: (1) the method to be employed in further negotiations, (2) any restrictions or conditions placed on the collection of the proceeds of the instrument, and (3) any guarantee of payment or collection made by the indorsers. The transferee of unindorsed order paper who paid value has, unless expressly agreed otherwise, the right to an unqualified indorsement from the transferor.

20.4 BLANK OR SPECIAL

Every indorsement is either blank or special, thus directing the method of how the instrument is to be further negotiated. A *blank* indorsement permits further negotiation by delivery alone; a *special* indorsement requires that in addition to delivery, the indorsee must sign.

EXAMPLE 2.   The face of a note recites that it is "payable to bearer." The possessor of this note need not sign (indorse) it in order to negotiate it to another owner. However, if the face recites that it is "payable to the order of Falstaff," Falstaff must indorse it in order to negotiate it further. If Falstaff merely signs "Falstaff," he has indorsed it in blank. If he had added the words, "pay to Page," he would have created a special indorsement whereby Page, called the indorsee, must sign and deliver if he, Page, wishes to negotiate it further. Note that special indorsements need not use the word "order"; only the face of the instrument requires such.

Negotiation to a party, whether by blank or special indorsement, permits the receiving party to become a holder. A *holder* is a person who is in possession of an instrument drawn, issued, or indorsed to him or her, or to bearer, or in blank.

EXAMPLE 3.   The face of the note reads "Pay to bearer." The instrument is lost. A finder keeps it; the finder is technically a holder.

EXAMPLE 4.   If the face of an instrument reads "Pay to the order of Buckingham," who also possesses the note, then Buckingham is a holder. If Buckingham sells and delivers the note to Lear without indorsement, neither Buckingham nor Lear is a holder. Lear is transferee for value, with the right to demand an indorsement unless the parties had agreed otherwise. If Lear gets Buckingham to sign on the back "Pay to Lear, (signed) Buckingham," Lear now becomes a holder upon repossession of the note.

The UCC permits blank and special indorsements at the will of the owner. Thus, even if the instrument had a blank indorsement or was originally bearer on its face, the holder may elect to force himself or herself and/or the next party to transfer by indorsement and delivery. Where there are numerous indorsements, the liability of each is governed by the order of time at which they signed, and among themselves, extrinsic evidence is permitted to prove such order.

EXAMPLE 5.   Essex executes a note for $500 in favor of bearer and delivers it to Norfolk in temporary payment of goods. Norfolk sells it to Avon Bank, which demands that it be indorsed. Norfolk indorses in blank. Avon Bank then writes above this signature, "Pay to Avon Bank." Although the instrument was a bearer note when created, the subsequent action by Avon Bank has changed the blank indorsement by Norfolk into a special indorsement.

20.5   RESTRICTIVE INDORSEMENTS

Every indorsement is either blank or special, and it is also either restrictive or nonrestrictive. A restrictive indorsement is shown by language placing some limitations on recovery of funds promised or drawn for, or regarding their use. Section 3-205 of the UCC identifies a restrictive indorsement as one which (1) is conditional; or (2) purports to prohibit further negotiation; or (3) includes the words "for collection," "for deposit," or "pay any bank" or like terms signifying a purpose of deposit or collection; or (4) otherwise states that it is for the benefit or use of the indorser or another person.

EXAMPLE 6.   Adam drew a check on White Bank payable to the order of Baker for $500. Baker was about to sell the check to Smith in payment of feed to be delivered next month. Baker wrote the following indorsement on the back of the check: "Pay to Smith on condition feed is delivered by August 10, 19X3, (signed) Baker." This is a special and restrictive indorsement of the conditional type.

This restrictive language in the indorsement which conditions payment is authorized despite the fact that had it appeared on the face by the drawer, it would have made the check nonnegotiable. A restrictive indorsement is binding on all subsequent parties except a few in the bank collection process such as intermediary and payor banks, UCC, Section 3-206(2).

An indorsement which reads "Pay to Star *only*" is also a restrictive indorsement, but it has no legal effect because restrictive indorsements do not prohibit further negotiation. Subsequent parties may ignore the "only" and further negotiate it. However, the most common restrictive indorsement, frequently worded "For deposit only," has considerable legal significance. In a sense it locks the document into a bank collection mode, which is normally the bank collection system, and while still negotiable, a bank which receives such an instrument would be liable for conversion if it did not deposit the money into the required account. All subsequent parties, including those who assist in collection, are informed of the ultimate right of the indorser to the proceeds. Further, any primary party (a maker, for example) remains liable to the party in whose favor the restrictive indorsement was made.

EXAMPLE 7.   Nym was paid by her employer through a check in which she was named payee. Before sending the check to her bank for collection, Nym placed on the back of it the words "For deposit only, (signed) Nym." The check was stolen from Nym's desk. It later reached a good-faith purchaser who contends that the instrument was bearer paper and he is entitled to the proceeds. This purchaser does have rights, but unfortunately for him, he holds the proceeds for Nym as he takes with notice of the restrictive indorsement.

A restrictive indorsement naming one person as the new indorsee, but designating the real owner of the proceeds as another, is also a restrictive indorsement. It creates a trust. An indorsement reading "Pay to Sam Black for his son, John, as his birthday present" is an illustration of a restrictive indorsement of the trust type. The named indorsee has the power, but not the right, to divert the proceeds. All dealing with such an indorsement may ignore the rights of the named beneficiary, provided they have no actual or constructive notice that such indorsee is acting contrary to his or her trust duties.

20.6   QUALIFIED INDORSEMENTS

If an instrument is not honored, and certain conditions are met, every indorser, whether special or blank, restrictive or nonrestrictive, engages that he or she will pay the instrument unless he or she has signed by a qualified indorsement. The usual words of qualification are "without recourse."

EXAMPLE 8.   Borse was having trouble with some of his retail customers who would give checks in payment which failed to clear by reason of insufficient funds. Borse's major trade creditor, Marks, was pushing him for bigger and more immediate payments on his outstanding account. Borse explained that he was doing his best and to show his good faith he would indorse and deliver to Marks all checks received from his customers. During 1 week Borse received 30 checks from customers to his order. Borse immediately indorsed them "Pay to Marks, without recourse, (signed) Borse." This is a qualified indorsement. Should any of these checks bounce for insufficient funds, Marks could not demand that Borse make them good.

A qualified indorsement tells future parties to the instrument that the indorser does not guarantee that the person ultimately required or expected to pay the instrument has the money or even the willingness to pay it. Such indorser does not say that the paper is legally valueless, but only that he or she won't guarantee the collection of the money. The indorser, if a transferor for value, warrants to subsequent parties that they can, in effect, obtain legal judgment against the parties liable on the instrument. Such warranties include representation that the title is good, that the signatures are genuine, that no alterations were made and that the qualified indorser has no knowledge of any defense good against him or her.

20.7   PARTIAL NEGOTIATION

Section 3-202(3) of the UCC provides that in order for an indorsement to be effective, it must convey the "entire instrument or any unpaid residue." If it purports to transfer less, it operates only as a partial assignment.

EXAMPLE 9. Bertran is the payee of a $10,000 note given to her by her client as a legal fee, payable 2 years from date. The client has been making sporadic payments on the note, and Bertran gave receipts for them. When only $5,000 was left owing on the note, Bertran sold and delivered it to Carter for $4,000, telling him that $5,000 had already been prepaid and indorsing the note, "Pay one-half to Carter, (signed) Bertran." It later became important to determine whether the instrument had been legally indorsed. It was held that this was not an indorsement as to the residue, only a partial assignment, and therefore no negotiation. Had the indorsement itself indicated that one-half was paid and the remaining half was being negotiated, the indorsement would have been effective. One must look to the instrument itself for the facts; special outside agreements or notice cannot be employed.

20.8 ALLONGE

An indorsement must be written by, or on behalf of, the indorser on the commercial paper or on an *allonge*, a paper so firmly fixed thereto as to have become a part of it, UCC, Section 3-202. Firmly fixed means pasted, stapled, or otherwise firmly attached; it does not mean an attachment by paper clip.

EXAMPLE 10. A couple were the payees of a $4,298 note, and they delivered it to a seller as part payment for land. The couple did not sign the note on the back, but executed an assignment of deed of trust (assignment of mortgage), which among other language recited that the couple "have indorsed, assigned, and transferred the note" to the seller. The maker of the note defaulted, and the seller attempted to hold the couple as unqualified indorsers, claiming that they had signed an allonge. Since an allonge is a paper so firmly attached to an instrument that, in effect, it becomes part of it, this was not an allonge. The paper (deed of trust) was not attached to the note, much less firmly attached.

20.9 ADDITIONAL INDORSEMENT LANGUAGE

The indorser may include other language and not affect the negotiation, and in it may reduce or enlarge his or her responsibilities. Section 3-202(4) of the UCC expressly states that words "of assignment, condition, waiver, guaranty, limitation or disclaimer of liability and the like" do not disturb the character of an indorsement.

EXAMPLE 11. A used-car dealer was the payee of a $978 promissory note executed by an auto purchaser. The dealer sold the paper to a finance company and indorsed the instrument as follows: "Full repurchase. Pay to Breton Finance Company, without recourse, except that Amstel Used-Car Dealership agrees to purchase from Breton Finance Company in accordance with its Dealer Protection Agreement." The auto purchaser defaulted, and the finance company sued the used-car dealer on the note. The court ruled that this was a qualified indorsement since "without recourse" was used. It may be that the finance company can sue the used-car dealer by reason of the repurchase agreement, but that does not diminish the qualified instrument.

Black Letter Law
A Summary

1. A negotiable instrument can be transferred to another by assignment or by negotiation.

2. In order for negotiation to occur, the instrument must contain the proper indorsement when such is required.

3. Bearer paper can be negotiated by delivery alone, while an instrument payable to order, or indorsed to another who is named, must be indorsed and delivered.

4. Every indorsement is either blank or special, restrictive or nonrestrictive, and qualified or unqualified.

5. The party signing the instrument on the back is called the indorser. In a blank indorsement, the endorser names no one; in a special indorsement, he or she names another party, called the indorsee.

6. A restrictive indorsement is conditional, purports to prohibit further negotiation, creates an agency for collection purposes, or states that it is for the benefit of another person.

7. An indorser engages that upon dishonor and the meeting of certain conditions, he or she will pay the instrument, unless the indorser has signed by a qualified indorsement with words such as "without recourse."

8. The fact that one signs as a qualified indorser does not thereby exempt one from warranting that the instrument is legally effective, as the indorser only disclaims guaranty of payment.

9. An allonge is a paper firmly affixed to a negotiable instrument for the purpose of providing room for additional indorsements.

10. The law does not prohibit additional language from appearing in an indorsement and permits statements which, if made on the face of the instrument, would destroy negotiability.

11. One cannot appear to transfer partially the interest in an instrument, since the indorsement must show that the entire interest in the instrument is being transferred.

Solved Problems

20.1 Johnson lost a check that he had received for professional services rendered. The instrument on its face was payable to Johnson's order. He had indorsed it on the back by signing his name and printing "For deposit only" above his name. Assuming the check was found by Alcatraz, a dishonest person who attempts to cash it, which of the following is correct?

(a) Any transferee of the instrument must pay or apply any value given by him or her for the instrument consistent with the indorsement.

(b) The indorsement is a blank indorsement, and a holder in due course who cashed it for Alcatraz would prevail.

(c) The indorsement prevents further transfer or negotiation by anyone.

(d) If Alcatraz simply signs his name beneath Johnson's indorsement, he can convert it into bearer paper and a holder in due course would take free of the restriction.

(*AICPA Examination, May 1979*)

An indorsement "For deposit only" is one form of a restrictive indorsement, and by it each transferee thereafter must do those acts consistent with the indorsement; the answer is statement (a). It is a blank indorsement, but its restrictive nature prevents even a holder in due course from gaining any rights in the proceeds which would be incompatible with the collection direction of the instrument.

20.2 Which of the following is a characteristic of a restrictive indorsement?

(*a*) It *cannot* preclude further transfer or negotiation although it purports to do so.

(*b*) It *cannot* be conditional at the same time.

(*c*) It prevents the party taking the instrument via such an indorsement from becoming a holder in due course.

(*d*) It releases the indorser from liability on the instrument in the event of nonpayment by the party obligated to pay for it.

(*AICPA Examination, May 1977*)

The UCC lists four types of restrictive indorsements, one of which is the indorser's attempt to preclude further negotiation by use of the words "Pay to A only" and the like. However, such language does not preclude further negotiation, statement (*a*). A restrictive indorsement may be of the conditional variety.

20.3 Which of the following is a characteristic of the "without recourse" indorsement?

(*a*) It can only be used where the instrument is a draft.

(*b*) It puts the person acquiring it on notice of some defect or defense which could be asserted against the transferee of the instrument.

(*c*) It modifies but does not completely eliminate the indorser's warranty liability to subsequent holders.

(*d*) It will *not* limit the indorser's liability to an immediate transferee.

(*AICPA Examination, May 1977*)

A qualified indorsement is created by using words such as "without recourse," and it limits the contract liability (in respect to any guarantee of payment or collection) of the indorser but does not completely alter his or her warranty liability as transferor for value. It is modified, however, in that instead of giving an implied warranty of no legal defense to the instrument, the signer only warrants that he or she has no knowledge of such defense, statement (*c*).

20.4 A TV retailer and its finance company entered into an arrangement by which the finance company would purchase 50 percent of all installment notes obtained by the retailer from buyers of TV sets. However, it was agreed that each such note would contain a 50-word statement regarding the repurchase undertaking by the retailer in addition to the indorsement of the retailer. A clerk at the finance company had the statement printed up on a card the size of the installment note. The clerk would then paste the card along the border of the note, after which the retailer would sign. Under these circumstances,

(*a*) the retailer has not validly indorsed the notes.

(*b*) unless the maker of the note gave permission, this act voids the note.

(*c*) an allonge has been created.

(*d*) the retailer would not be bound by the terms contained on this card.

Usually where there is insufficient room on the back of an instrument for further indorsements, the parties use an allonge. This is done by firmly affixing to the instrument a piece of paper for additional valid indorsements. The terms or additional language with the indorsement on an allonge is effective from a contract point of view; statement (*c*) is the answer.

20.5 Gutter was the payee of a $2,320 promissory note due 2 years from date. Since issue, the note has been transferred to A, then to B, and now to C, who holds the instrument which contains the signatures of B, Gutter, and A, in that order, on the back of the instrument. Which is the correct statement?

(*a*) All indorsers are liable in the order they appear on the back of the note.

(*b*) Gutter was both a payee and indorsee.

(*c*) Only those who at one time owned the note could validly indorse the instrument.

(*d*) The law does not require that the indorsers sign in any particular order.

An indorsement is a signature usually on the back of an instrument together with any additional language, but there is no requirement that two or more indorsers sign in any particular order; statement (*d*) is correct. The parties are liable in the order they transferred the instrument, but should the order appear differently, parol evidence is permitted to show the order in which they signed.

20.6 A farmer was the payee of a check sent to her by a creditor in the amount of $320. The farmer had never trusted banks and had always dealt in cash. The local feed store told the farmer that it would take the check in payment for certain goods supplied to the farmer. When asked to sign the back of the check, the farmer, whose suspicion was great, refused to sign and would only deliver the check to the feed store. The store agreed. Under these circumstances,

(*a*) the feed store has no rights in the check since it was never indorsed.

(*b*) the farmer could have protected herself from all liability on the check by using the language "Pay to Bergen's Feed Store only, (signed) Farmer."

(*c*) the farmer has assigned the check to the feed store.

(*d*) the feed store has a legal right to have the farmer indorse the check.

Negotiable instruments can be transferred by negotiation or assignment, and where a necessary indorsement has not been given, the transfer is by assignment only; statement (*c*) is the answer. The restrictive indorsement in statement (*b*) has no legal effect regarding reduction of liability. Generally, all transferees for value are entitled to have an indorsement unless the parties agreed otherwise. Here it appears that they had expressly agreed otherwise.

20.7 Marston First Bank issued a certificate of deposit to the order of bearer. Which is the correct statement?

(*a*) This CD can be transferred by delivery alone despite any future indorsements.

(*b*) A thief could never pass good title to the CD.

(*c*) Once an instrument is bearer on its face, it remains bearer despite subsequent special indorsements.

(*d*) A qualified indorser on this document would not be liable should the bank default on the payment.

A qualified indorsement would limit the liability of the indorser to the extent that he or she does not guarantee payment; the answer is (*d*). At the moment this is bearer paper, and it could get into the hands of a good-faith holder whose title could be clear even though it came from a thief.

20.8 In which of the following instances could one successfully challenge delivery?

(*a*) The payee's son gave the instrument to another on his father's instructions.

(*b*) The payee handed a check to his creditor "under protest."

(*c*) The payee turned over to another a signed and notarized statement which recited that the payee "herewith transfers all title and interest in the said note which is in my safe deposit box, no. 654, Moorehaven Bank."

(*d*) The buyer of a house unintentionally left an indorsed "closing check" on the realtor's desk at the time of closing.

Transfer of physical possession is necessary for delivery; a statement merely giving the location of the document will not be a substitute; statement (*c*) is the answer. In all three other situations, the document left the payee voluntarily and came into the possession of the next holder.

20.9 Which of the following additions to an indorsement signature is *not* an illustration of a restrictive indorsement?

(*a*) "Pay to Able only."

(*b*) "Pay to Able."

(*c*) "Pay Thomas, for benefit of Carling estate."

(*d*) "Pay any banker."

Only the language in statement (*b*) does not meet the test of a restrictive indorsement. The word "only" in statement (*a*), the creation of a trust in statement (*c*), and the term in statement (*d*) signifying a deposit for collection all qualify as restrictive indorsements.

20.10 A qualified indorser who transfers for value is *not* liable

(*a*) if the maker's signature is forged.

(*b*) if the amount of money is altered by a clever forger.

(*c*) if the party promising to pay or expected to pay has a good legal defense to the instrument.

(*d*) if the party promising to pay has no money to pay the instrument at maturity.

A qualified indorser who transfers for value does not guarantee that the instrument will be honored, but the indorser does make certain implied warranties regarding the integrity of the instrument; the answer is (*d*). The indorser could be liable on all the other grounds listed, as well as some others, but does not warrant that there is no defense of any party good against him or her, but only that he or she has no knowledge of such a defense, UCC, Section 3-417(3).

20.11 Granat, as maker, signed a note to the order of Arlene, her niece, in the sum of $2,500 in full settlement of a bitter family dispute over a relative's estate. The note was payable 1 year from the stated date. However, Arlene needed cash immediately and was able to convince her sister, Regina, to purchase the note for cash, but only for $1,000. When Arlene delivered the note to Regina, she commented that "if anyone can get collection, you can do it." Arlene did not indorse the note. Regina was a smart businesswoman, and in no time at all, she persuaded a young banker she was dating that his bank should buy the note. The Ascot Bank did indeed buy the note for a good price, $1,500. The bank demanded and received Regina's indorsement on the note, to which she added "Pay to Ascot Bank, only." At the maturity of the note Granat is resisting payment on several grounds, including a vague charge about "duress." It now becomes important that the negotiable character of the instrument and its negotiation be proved.

Answer the following questions: (*a*) Who is the holder? (*b*) Can Arlene be forced to indorse the note? (*c*) Is Regina guaranteeing payment? State any conclusions reached to support your answers.

(*a*) There is no holder of the note at this time.

(*b*) The bank is the possessor of a note which requires the payee's indorsement for negotiation, and before the bank becomes a holder, Arlene may be obliged to supply an indorsement since there appears to be no express or implied agreement to the contrary. Accordingly, each transferee for value is entitled to the necessary indorsement.

(*c*) Regina cannot rely on the words of her indorsement to escape liability. She did not use words such as "without recourse" to create a qualified instrument. Instead, she employed a restrictive indorsement prohibiting further negotiation which, under the UCC, is ineffective.

20.12 Despite the vicissitudes of inflation, Ralph had one consolation: the house he had purchased years ago for $40,000 had appreciated to a market value of over $130,000. He was also pleased that he owed only a balance of just over $11,000 on his first mortgage. His first unpleasant surprise came when he tried to sell his house for the market price and found that he had to take back a $100,000 note and second mortgage from the buyer if he wanted to sell. The second shock came later when he needed cash and the best he could do was to find a second mortgage company willing to pay only $60,000 for the $100,000 note in which he was the payee from the buyer, secured by the second mortgage. Ralph needed the cash. He signed his name to the back of the note and an assignment of mortgage form to the second mortgage company. The final bit of unpleasantness occurred when his buyer failed to make monthly payments on the first note and mortgage he had assumed and also on the second note and mortgage.

What legal problem will Ralph have if the second mortgage company forecloses on the house and the public (judicial) sale nets less than $100,000? State your answer and any conclusions you reached.

Ralph got rid of his house but not the obligations. He is, of course, still liable on his own note and first mortgage, but in addition, he may have liability to the second mortgage company. It appears that Ralph indorsed the buyer's note with a blank, nonrestrictive, unqualified indorsement. The latter is bad news. By signing without qualification, Ralph may be liable as an indorser of the note he sold to the second mortgage company, provided the company took the appropriate steps, or such steps may have been waived. Had Ralph indorsed the note with the statement "without recourse," he would not be liable to the second mortgage company.

Chapter 21

Holders in Due Course
and Defenses

21.1 DEFINITION

A *holder in due course* is defined by Section 3-302(1) of the UCC as a holder who takes the instrument (1) for value, (2) in good faith, and (3) without notice that it is overdue or has been dishonored or without notice of any defense against or claim to it on the part of any person. It is often essential that a party establish his or her qualification as a holder in due course in order to attain the maximum rights on the paper. When necessary, each element must be met, and the absence of any one bars a person from being a holder in due course. However, the failure of a holder to succeed to the rights of a holder in due course is only important if there is a legal defense to the instrument.

EXAMPLE 1. Cisco sold Talbert a used car by misrepresenting certain facts. In payment Talbert drew a $1,200 check on his own bank to the order of Cisco. Cisco immediately sold and delivered, but did not indorse the check to Fred who, believing that Cisco needed the money that evening and couldn't get to the bank, paid $1,100 for it. Fred had no reason to think that this was other than a legitimate transaction. Talbert, learning of Cisco's deceit, ordered a stop payment, and if sued by Cisco, Talbert has a good defense against Cisco. However, if Fred could establish himself as a holder in due course, Talbert's defense would not be successful against Fred. Unfortunately for Fred, he met all conditions save one: he was not a holder since he neglected to obtain a necessary indorsement.

Accordingly, to be a holder in due course (HDC) it is always necessary to be a holder, that is, one who has possession of the instrument drawn, issued, or indorsed to him or her, or to his or her order, or to bearer, or in blank.

21.2 HOLDER MUST GIVE VALUE

Value is similar, though not identical to, consideration, and only value is required to have been given. It is similar to the doctrine of consideration when money, goods, or services are actually delivered in payment for the negotiable instrument. Further, adequacy of the goods or services is not important. Unlike the doctrine of consideration, however, most *promises* to pay money, to deliver goods, or to perform services are not value. The taking of an instrument in payment of or as security for an antecedent claim is value.

EXAMPLE 2. Franklin was the payee of a $700 note. Oscar offered to paint Franklin's house for the note. Franklin agreed and indorsed the note over to Oscar. Oscar is not an HDC, as he has not yet paid value for the check. Generally, a mere promise to perform, while it qualifies as consideration, is not value under Article 3 of the UCC.

EXAMPLE 3. A payee received a note of $1,225 from a maker and agreed to return the note when the maker's account with the payee was settled. Instead, the payee negotiated the note to her own creditor in satisfaction of a debt the payee owed to the creditor. In a suit on the note, the creditor maintains she took it as an HDC. The maker contends that the creditor gave no value. The maker is incorrect, because the creditor gave value by accepting the note in satisfaction of a debt owed her by the payee.

220

Not all promises to perform in the future fail as value. Two exceptions are found in Section 3-303(c) of the UCC. Value is present when a holder gives a negotiable instrument for another negotiable instrument or makes an irrevocable commitment to a third person. A simple illustration of the former is where a holder buys a note by giving the owner another note or a check. An example of the second exception would be the issue of an irrevocable letter of credit by a bank. If neither of these exceptions applies, the contracted-for value must have been executed. However, one can be a holder for value for the part executed in a partly executed contract.

EXAMPLE 4. A lawyer was retained by a client to try a difficult easement case for a fee of $7,000. The client had two trade acceptances in which he was the named payee, totaling $4,500. As payment toward the fee, the client indorsed and delivered the trade acceptances to the lawyer midway through the case, at which point the lawyer had earned half of her fee. At this time the lawyer had given value for one-half of her fee ($3,500) and is an HDC for that amount of the $4,500 total of the two trade acceptances. If, at that time, the lawyer learns of a defense to the instruments, she cannot improve her position on them by continuing to work on the case.

EXAMPLE 5. A payee deposited certain checks into his bank for collection. The next day the payee drew on his account for a sum in excess of the payee's entire balance before collection of the checks deposited the previous day. The drawer of the deposited checks stopped payment on them. The question arose of whether the payee's bank was an HDC in regard to those checks. The bank contended that it permitted an overdraft on the payee's account in anticipation of the items for collection. The bank is an HDC for value to the extent of its advances to the payee as it acquires a security interest in the paper by having given value (permitting the overdraft).

21.3 GOOD-FAITH HOLDER

A holder in due course must take the instrument in good faith, that is, "honesty in fact in the conduct or transaction concerned," UCC, Section 1-201(19). It is not always obvious what circumstances show bad faith, but knowledge of facts surrounding the creation of the instrument increases the risk of taking in bad faith.

EXAMPLE 6. Pierce began selling advertising campaigns to small retailers in the area. His presentation was impressive, and "to assure good quality" he demanded a $500 promissory note as good-faith security. His campaign was a fraud and was legally less than represented. Pierce sold these promissory notes to X, Y, and Z (three different finance companies). X knew the disreputable manner in which Pierce sells these programs. As to Y, Pierce sold notes at the bargain price of $150 per note. Z knew that Pierce had just started up his business and did not inquire into these programs or how the notes arose. Z also knew that the makers were small but solid businesspeople. X knows too much and cannot take the notes in good faith. Y might be thought to have been obligated to ask questions about why such a big discount was given for such notes. Therefore Y cannot show good faith. Z, knowing little and seeing no suspicious circumstances, could take the notes in good faith and be consistent with the old-law merchant rule that Z is "empty-headed but pure-hearted."

21.4 OVERDUE OR DISHONORED PAPER

The delivery and any necessary indorsement must take place either before the instrument is past due or before there has been a default, i.e., dishonor, of the obligation. The apparent rationale is that if the instrument was not paid when due, or was dishonored, there may be a legal reason for this.

An instrument is overdue if one takes it after the stated maturity or, if it contains an acceleration clause, after one has knowledge of the default or the acceleration having been activated. In installment notes, knowledge of default in an installment of principal is fatal to taking as an HDC.

EXAMPLE 7. Williams was the holder of a $500 note payable $100 per month beginning April 1, 19X3. On May 1, 19X3 Williams offers to sell the note to Margoles for $300. Margoles inquires about the April payment and is told by Williams that the maker will pay, that "he just needs a little prodding." This is true. Unfortunately for Margoles, she has knowledge of a default in the principal and cannot take as an HDC.

Notice of default in an interest-only payment is not legally notice of default prohibiting one from taking as an HDC. Notice that a draft requiring acceptance was dishonored is notice of default.

Not all instruments have a fixed maturity date; some are payable on demand. Here there are no precise guidelines for determining maturity. If the prospective taker knows there has been a demand and dishonor, the result is clear. Otherwise, the question is, When is a demand instrument overdue? The general answer is a reasonable time after issue, that is, the date on which the instrument reached the first holder. When dated, such date is the presumed date of issue. Reasonable time is measured by considering the type of instrument involved, the custom and usage of trade, and the particular facts and circumstances involved.

EXAMPLE 8. · On May 18, 19X3, a retailer needing credit for purchase of Christmas inventory established a $2,000 line of credit with her bank and executed a demand note. The bank negotiated the note to Smith on December 15, 19X3. The retailer has a defense to the note by reason of a dispute with the bank in failing to provide the full line of credit. The retailer now contends that Smith did not take as an HDC since he purchased 7 months after issue. Applying the guidelines of the nature of the instrument, custom and usage, and the particular facts, Smith took before it was overdue. First, a note is expected to be outstanding longer than a draft. Second, the circumstances surrounding the loan (purchase of Christmas inventory) suggest that the bank wouldn't expect payment until after the Christmas season and the retailer's collection of her receivables from her customers.

The UCC is more specific in defining "reasonableness" where a check drawn or payable in the United States is involved. The holder should take it within 30 days after issue.

EXAMPLE 9. David drew a check in Chicago on his New York bank for $500 on May 15, 19X3, in favor of Peters. Because of a dispute David stopped payment on May 18. Peters negotiated the check to Harold on June 2, 19X3. Here, Harold could be a holder in due course if he meets the other requirements.

21.5 NOTICE OF CLAIMS OR DEFENSES

An HDC must take the instrument without notice of claims of others to the instrument or defenses of the parties to the instrument. In addition, there are some special situations in which one cannot qualify as an HDC. A person cannot acquire HDC status by buying an instrument at a judicial sale, by taking it under legal process, by taking over an estate, or by purchasing a bulk transaction not done in the transferee's ordinary course of business, UCC, Section 3-302(3).

EXAMPLE 10. Timon reads the legal notices in the local newspaper and is interested in three items: a notice of judicial sale of notes owned by an insolvent factoring outfit, an offering by the VanBuren estate of a $15,000 trade acceptance, and an advertisement by Farson Mortgage Brokers stating that it is closing down part of its operation by selling all the notes and mortgages it holds on property in a neighboring county. If Timon buys at the judicial sale, or if she purchases the trade acceptance from the estate, or if she buys in bulk from the mortgage broker, she will not qualify as a holder in due course.

Section 3-304 of the UCC also lists other circumstances which affect the right to take as an HDC. These include the knowledge of a voidable transaction, or of a legal discharge (to the extent thereof), and the taker's awareness that a fiduciary is handling an instrument for his or her own interest.

EXAMPLE 11. Brutus knows that Pompey's son was in an automobile accident. Pompey shows Brutus a draft drawn by Happy Insurance Company for $3,000 payable to the "order of Pompey for the benefit of his son, Claudius." Brutus knows that Pompey has a hot tip on a horse and could use the cash right now. He offers Pompey $2,200 for the draft. Brutus cannot be a holder in due course since Pompey is a fiduciary (for his son) and Brutus has knowledge that Pompey is going to use the money for Pompey's own benefit.

If the prospective holder knows that the maker or drawer is insane, that the maker or drawer is an infant, that one has been defrauded, or that the paper was stolen, good-faith taking is barred.

Further, if the paper appears to have been tampered with, or is inconsistent with other documents to which the instrument refers, the holder may not qualify as an HDC.

While knowledge of circumstances tends to raise questions to the prospective holder, the UCC sets forth certain events that are not by themselves suspicious. They include the antedating or postdating of the instrument; knowledge that the instrument was issued in return for an executory promise or accompanied by a separate agreement; knowledge that an indorser didn't own the paper but signed as a guarantor (an accommodation party); or, even if the instrument was incomplete at issue, ignorance that it had been improperly completed. Further, one can't assume that a fiduciary is going to violate his or her duty without some evidence of such. However, an awareness of the circumstances in which the paper arose, or an arrangement by which one habitually buys paper from another, makes it difficult for these buyers to take in good faith.

EXAMPLE 12.   Radio Ad Sales Company sold long-term contracts to small businesses in the community. The businessowners paid by installment notes, which Radio Ad Sales sold to an out-of-town factoring company. Certain misrepresentations regarding audience coverage induced several of the makers to sign. By previous arrangement, the factoring company supplied Radio Ad Sales the contract and note forms and was available to supply credit information on businesspeople in the community. Generally, the mere supplying of forms does not preclude one from being a good-faith taker, but combined with other practices, e.g., credit investigation, it puts the factoring company in a relation with the payee—Radio Ad Sales, which committed the fraudulent misrepresentation—such that good faith is missing.

The fact that the payee and the potential holder have entered into a contract by which the payee is to sell future commercial paper will not of itself, under certain conditions, bar the committed buyer from taking in good faith. If, however, the arrangement is such that the potential holder is in the position of knowing a great deal about the source and circumstances of the payer, any damaging information may be imputed to the buyer.

21.6   INCOMPLETE PAPER

When the contents of a paper at the time of signing reflect that the paper was intended to be a negotiable instrument, incompleteness will not prevent its enforcement. One can later take it as a holder in due course even if he or she has knowledge of this fact.

EXAMPLE 13.   Anderson buys goods from Starr and draws a check to the order of Starr, leaving the exact sum to be filled in by Starr when the final figures on shipping costs are available. Starr, about to negotiate the instrument to Hibble, fills in $500 instead of the proper number of $310. Hibble knows that Anderson signed an imcomplete check, but he has no knowledge of Starr's misdeed. Hibble can be an HDC to the extent of the altered amount, $500.

21.7   NOTICE AND ACTION

Notice or knowledge by a prospective purchaser which comes after acquiring the paper or too late for effective action will not bar one from being an HDC. A person is responsible for information which he or she learns by whatever method, but a notice in a newspaper one did not read does not operate to give the person knowledge under the UCC, nor does the unnoticed filing or recording of a document in the public records, UCC, Section 3-304.

21.8   PAYEE AS HOLDER IN DUE COURSE

Though rare, it is possible for a payee to qualify as a holder in due course. Of course the payee must meet all the requirements, and this is difficult for a party who normally has direct contact with the party who executed the instrument in the first place and at the most likely time for legal defenses to have arisen. Agency situations, however, do allow payees to succeed as holders in due course.

EXAMPLE 14.   A husband and wife had separate credit accounts at a store. The wife owed $537, and the husband owed $390. The store had pressed both to make payments, and the wife drew her personal check in the amount of $300 to the order of the store. She instructed her husband to take the check to the store and apply it to her account. The husband, however, told the store to apply the payment to his own account, which the store did. The husband deserted his wife, and the store demands the full $537 it claims the wife owes. The store, despite being the payee, can, under these facts, qualify as a holder in due course.

21.9   HOLDER THROUGH A HOLDER IN DUE COURSE

A holder, assignee, or a transferee who is able to trace his or her title through a holder in due course has all the rights of a holder in due course unless such transferee has been a party to any fraud or illegality affecting the instrument. Further, a prior holder (a reacquirer) cannot improve his or her position by retaking later from an HDC, UCC, Section 3-201(1).

EXAMPLE 15.   A payee indorses and delivers a note to Smith, who takes as an HDC. Smith indorses the note in blank and *loses* it. Baker *finds* the note and sells it for value to Howard, who takes it in good faith but 2 days after the maturity of the note. Since Howard took it after it was overdue, she cannot qualify as an HDC. Further, she cannot trace her title through an HDC. Baker found and passed it on; he is a thief; he did not get title from Smith. Howard's title came from the thief, Baker, not from Smith.

EXAMPLE 16.   A society woman was defrauded into giving her $100 check to Arthur, who negotiated it to Tower, who took as an HDC. Tower sold it to Ferro, who knew of the fraud. Ferro can't be an HDC since he has knowledge of a defense. However, Ferro can trace his title through Tower, an HDC, and therefore succeeds to all the rights of an HDC under what is called the "shelter provision."

21.10   HOLDER IN DUE COURSE AND THE CONSUMER

Because of reports of widespread abuse of the protection granted to an HDC when dealing with consumers, the Federal Trade Commission in 1976 issued a rule which can have the effect of limiting such rights in a consumer credit transaction. The ruling requires that consumer paper recite that the assignees are subject to all "claims and defenses which the debtor could assert against the seller of goods or services obtained with the proceeds. . . ." Failure to so notify is an unfair or deceptive act or practice under Section 5 of the Federal Trade Commission Act. Further, a number of states have enacted statutes denying the status of holder in due course in specified consumer transactions.

EXAMPLE 17.   Laura purchased a wig and a 4-year wig service contract from a wig salon and executed a note payable in 24 monthly installments of $14 each. The wig salon had a contract with a finance company, which undertook to buy some future notes and contracts the wig salon might obtain. Laura's note was transferred to the finance company at a 25 percent discount. Several months later the wig salon went out of business, and Laura found it impossible to obtain the wig servicing for which she had contracted. She made no further payments to the finance company. Under the FTC regulation, this contract is a consumer credit transaction requiring a prominent notice to appear on the paper specifically informing all holders of the contract that it is subject to defenses and claims by the debtor. Laura can raise the contract defense against the finance company.

21.11   DEFENSES: GENERALLY

A holder in due course takes free of the more common legal defenses to liability on the instrument, and for that reason it is important to take as an HDC. The HDC takes free of personal or limited defenses, but not free of real, universal, or absolute defenses. Defenses can arise in a variety of ways and at different times during the life of the paper.

EXAMPLE 18. The payee-seller lied to the maker-buyer of the note regarding the quality of the goods being sold. The payee indorsed the note in blank and lost it. It was picked up by a finder, who indorsed it and sold it to a third party, who purchased it in good faith. A defense regarding fraud arose at the time of issue; the defense of nondelivery (thievery or conversion) occurred later. The HDC is free of these types of defenses.

21.12 REAL DEFENSES

Real defenses are effective against all parties, including those who have the rights of an HDC. Sections 3-305(2), 3-404, and 3-407 of the UCC include infancy; such other incapacity, duress, or illegality as renders the obligation a nullity; fraud in the execution; discharge in insolvency proceedings or any other discharge of which the holder has notice when he or she takes the instrument; forgery; and material alteration. This list is not as impressive as it may first seem, as it really just reaffirms that only the most grievous situations would result in a denial of liability.

21.13 INFANCY AND INCAPACITY

Infancy is a defense to the extent that it is a defense to a simple contract. If state law allows complete disaffirmance, an infant has a defense good against any holder including a holder in due course. As to other types of incapacity, however, these are real defenses provided the state law declares the particular obligation to be a nullity.

EXAMPLE 19. Marvin, age 17 years, executes an installment note to a jeweler for a diamond ring he is giving to his girlfriend. In this type of contract, state law permits complete disaffirmance to those under 18 years of age. Marvin would have a complete defense to the note.

EXAMPLE 20. State corporation law permits companies to guarantee debts of other corporations only if their charter so permits. The corporation statute does not, however, prescribe a penalty regarding the obligation. Favore, Inc., through its president, indorses a note guaranteeing another corporation's debt. This is in violation of the statute, as Favore's charter is silent on this point. However, unless state law declares this unauthorized act by the corporation to be a nullity or void, Favore does not have the real defense of incapacity.

21.14 DURESS AND ILLEGALITY AS REAL DEFENSES

Generally, duress and illegality are merely personal defenses but can qualify as real defenses good against even those holding the rights of an HDC when the state law describes the obligation gained thereby as a nullity.

EXAMPLE 21. Benson is so enraged when she finds her employee has cheated her that she places a pistol to the employee's head and orders him to sign a promissory note as restitution for the missing funds. Such conduct is outrageous and has been called gross duress. Generally, such conduct provides a real defense in that no note was meant to be created.

EXAMPLE 22. The payee was the holder of a $2,000 check drawn on the First Bank by the Tower Loan Association. The payee, who had paid nothing for the check, indorsed and delivered the check to Second Bank, which paid the payee. The $2,000 check did not clear, and Tower, insolvent, was closed down by government order. The receivers of Tower resist liability as drawee on the bounced check on the ground that the check was drawn and issued in violation of a state statute that prohibits loan associations from issuing any check without receiving immediate consideration. The statute, however, was silent on the effects of this illegal act. The HDC would win against the receivers since only a personal defense existed. It is well established that a negotiable instrument given in an illegal transaction is nevertheless enforceable in the hands of an HDC unless expressly made void by statute.

Relatively few criminal statutes address the transaction per se. They merely provide criminal sanctions for the specified criminal acts. Accordingly, most commercial paper transactions involving illegality or duress are not specifically made a nullity, and therefore these qualify as personal defenses only.

21.15 FRAUD AS A REAL DEFENSE

Fraud in the execution, or *factum*, renders the instrument void and is therefore a defense valid against an HDC. Section 3-305(2)(c) of the UCC describes the circumstances creating this defense as "such misrepresentation as has induced the party to sign the instrument with neither knowledge nor reasonable opportunity to obtain knowledge of its character or its original terms."

EXAMPLE 23. Makers sued to cancel two promissory notes for home improvements. An HDC resisted such cancellation. The makers testified that they signed the papers thinking they were contracts for improvements, not notes. The makers proved that the forms were designed to deceive and trick persons. The court ruled that it was a real defense since the makers also proved that they were not negligent in looking over the papers.

The above is a close case on the facts, as the burden is on the party to prove not only that one did not know the character of the instrument, but also that one was not negligent. The test is a subjective one, with the result often based on the education, literacy, and mentality of the party claiming the defense.

21.16 DISCHARGE AS A REAL DEFENSE

Two types of discharge are effective against an HDC and those with such rights: discharge by insolvency proceedings and those discharges known to the holder at the time of taking the instrument, UCC, Sections 3-305(2)(d) and (e).

EXAMPLE 24. Farnsworth has financial trouble. He had signed a number of promissory notes and then found himself named as a debtor in a federal bankruptcy proceeding. If Farnsworth lists the notes in the appropriate schedules, they are dischargeable under the law, and if he is granted a discharge, he has a real defense to the instruments. However, the notes themselves are not necessarily discharged, as other signers may still have responsibility on them.

EXAMPLE 25. Tonner executed and delivered a bearer note to Salazar. Salazar indorsed and gave the note to his daughter as a wedding present. The daughter, not wishing to hold the note until maturity, decided to sell it to another. Before she did so, however, she crossed out Salazar's indorsement so that he would have no liability on the note. The party who bought from the daughter, even if an HDC, has no rights against Salazar since the holder had notice of the discharge, here by cancellation, when he took the instrument. He is, however, an HDC for all other purposes.

21.17 FORGERY AND MATERIAL ALTERATION AS REAL DEFENSES

Any unauthorized signature is wholly inoperative as that of the person whose name is signed unless the person ratifies it or is precluded from denying it, UCC, Section 3-404. The real or absolute defense of unauthorized signature (formerly called *forgery*) is effective against all parties who attempt to press liability on it. The unauthorized signature can appear in different positions on the instrument and under a variety of circumstances.

EXAMPLE 26.   Oscar is a playboy, and his father has had to get him out of trouble on past occasions. Oscar signs his father's name as drawer on a blank check form Oscar took from his father's desk. He also found on the desk a check payable to his father; he wrote his father's signature on the back of this check. He was able to transfer both checks to good-faith purchasers for value before maturity. The father would not be liable on his "own" check and would not have lost title on the other check on which he was the named payee. These are unauthorized signatures, a defense valid against all including an HDC. If, however, the father indicated that he reluctantly approved these misdeeds, he may have ratified the acts and cannot plead forgery.

Material alteration is similar to forgery in that it provides a complete or real defense to that part of the instrument which is altered. Like forgery, a material alteration attempts to have the reader of the instrument believe incorrectly that the parties have undertaken specific responsibilities on the paper. Holders in due course may, however, recover under the terms of the paper that the parties did sign. These terms are identified as the "original tenor of the instrument." A party is not bound to the new undertaking seemingly created by the alteration unless he or she acted in such a way as to permit this alteration to happen by negligence in drawing or making the instrument, or by later acts of ratification.

EXAMPLE 27.   As an advance on several installment contracts she was to obtain, a drawer signed a customer's draft drawn on Midwestern Bank with the figure "500" typed in with considerable space between it and the dollar sign. This check was issued to the payee, who deposited it into a new account in Falls Bank created by the payee. At the time of the deposit, however, the check contained on the payee line the name of the new account which the payee had created and the sum of $22,500 which was imprinted on it with a checkwriter, and with two 2s and a comma having been typed in front of the "500." Falls Bank permitted withdrawals in excess of $500, and when the check did not clear, it looked to the drawer and payee. The payee had disappeared and was later found dead. The drawer claimed material alteration. Falls Bank pressed its rights as an HDC, charging negligence. It will be a question of fact as to whether the drawer prepared the draft in such a way or acted in such a way that she substantially contributed (negligence) to the material alteration of the instrument, Section 3-406 of the UCC. If the drawer was negligent, she will be liable for the full amount Falls Bank is out.

While raising the money amount on the instrument seems the most obvious form of material alteration, the concept is not so limited. Any alteration is material which changes the contract of any party thereto in any respect including making changes in number and relations of parties, improperly completing an incomplete instrument, or adding to it or removing any part of it, UCC, Section 3-407.

21.18   PERSONAL DEFENSES: GENERALLY

If a defense does not qualify as a so-called real, absolute, or universal defense, it is called a *personal* or *limited defense*. The latter type is the most common circumstance, and those who have the rights of an HDC succeed against such defenses.

Basically, any breach of agreement, the existence of a cause permitting rescission, or the presence of any legal excuse for not performing can be utilized here. One really revisits all the events that can go wrong with contracts or those grounds that make a bargain unenforceable. They include the consideration defenses, breach of contract, capacity, reality of consent, illegality, discharge, and claims.

21.19   CONSIDERATION AND PERSONAL DEFENSES

Commercial paper is generally given as temporary payment for something that the payee possesses or is to deliver, such as services or goods. When consideration is not delivered, or if received, it does not fulfill the agreed terms, the charge of failure of consideration is raised. Want of consideration (that is, a gratuitous promise) or total or partial failure of consideration is ineffective against an HDC.

EXAMPLE 28.   A payee, claiming he owned nine swine, sold them to the drawer, who drew a check payable to the order of the payee. The payee sold and indorsed the check to a department store, which paid cash for the check. The federal government reclaimed the swine from the drawer, charging that the swine had been stolen from the honor farm at the federal penitentiary. The drawer stopped payment on the check when he lost the pigs. The department store, an HDC, can recover against the drawer since total failure of consideration, i.e., loss of the swine, is a personal or limited defense.

Want of consideration occurs when the party delivering up the instrument to another never expected to receive anything for it. An uncle's check to his nephew as a birthday present, for example, is without consideration, and the defense is a mere personal one should the check reach the hands of a party having the rights of an HDC.

21.20   BREACH OF CONTRACT

Failure of consideration can, of course, include a charge of breach of contract. For purposes of commenting on defenses, it is a catchall phrase. One can breach a contract in many ways. Included in them would be a breach of promise regarding delivery of the instrument. Nondelivery is only a personal defense.

EXAMPLE 29.   Makers executed a $15,000 promissory note payable to bearer. The makers gave the note to their son-in-law for safekeeping in his business office, it being stored for future holders of a mortgage the makers executed. The son-in-law later borrowed $12,000 from a finance company and delivered up the $15,000 bearer note as security for the loan. The son-in-law defaulted on the loan, and the finance company as an HDC demanded payment from the makers, who defended on the grounds of nondelivery of the instrument. This defense is not available against an HDC.

Further, even if nondelivery is accompanied with an unauthorized completion of an incomplete instrument, the defense remains a limited one and is not available against the rights of an HDC.

EXAMPLE 30.   An employer, about to go on vacation, signed 10 blank checks which the secretary was instructed to fill in with the correct figures and to deliver to future creditors. If the secretary improperly completes the checks by naming others as payees or by putting in wrong amounts, the defense of nondelivery of an incomplete instrument is purely personal. The same effect would be true if a robber opened the safe and performed in like manner.

21.21   CAPACITY AND REALITY OF CONSENT AS PERSONAL DEFENSES

In some states the defense that one is an infant, is mentally incompetent, or lacks authority may be only partially effective and therefore, under certain circumstances, may not be available against an HDC. Accordingly, to the extent that state law allows, these are not absolute defenses; they are personal.

Lack of reality of consent is examined in cases involving charges of fraud, misrepresentation, mistake, duress, and undue influence. These grounds are generally personal defenses except when the parties can claim that the fraud went to the execution of the instrument or when gross duress is involved. The more common type of fraud, however, is only a personal defense and is called *fraud in the inducement* or *procurement*. Basically, the party signing meant to sign a negotiable instrument but did so on the fraudulent misrepresentation about some aspect of the transaction giving rise to the creation of the instrument.

EXAMPLE 31.   A buyer alleged that he signed a check in payment of a car upon the representation by the dealer that the title was good. In an attempt to assure himself of this fact, the buyer, as drawer, wrote on the check, "Car represented to be free and clear of liens." The dealer negotiated the check to a holder who took as an HDC. Fraud in the inducement or procurement is merely a personal defense and not available against the holder.

21.22 ILLEGALITY AND DISCHARGE AS PERSONAL DEFENSES

The fact that the underlying transaction giving rise to the instrument was illegal does not usually affect its legal integrity when it reaches one with HDC rights. Where, however, public policy has generated specific law (gambling, usury, and the like) which not only makes the act illegal, but also marks documents arising from the transaction as void or a nullity, the defense is real. Otherwise, in most instances, the defense of illegality, for whatever reason (Sunday bargains, immoral agreements, and the like), is strictly personal.

Discharge of a party can be achieved in a number of ways, but unless it is accomplished by insolvency proceedings, or the holder knows of such, it is personal only.

EXAMPLE 32.   Berber has two notes outstanding. In respect to the first note, Berber has just made her last payment. Unfortunately, Berber did not take possession of the note, and the creditor has negotiated it to another. As to the second note, however, the payee had recently purchased goods on credit from Berber and the price was in excess of the outstanding balance on the second note. Berber has discharged her liability on the first note by payment and on the second note by reason of a setoff for the same amount her creditor owes her on a separate and independent transaction. However, if either of these notes reaches an HDC, the defense of discharge will be ineffective. It is personal defense only.

21.23 CLAIMS OF THIRD PARTIES

Sometimes the party expected to pay has no defense, but others involved with the paper do. Section 3-306 of the UCC states that, generally, the "claim of any third person to the instrument is not otherwise available to any party thereon unless the third person himself defends the action for such party." Simply stated, the undertaking of the obligor is to pay the holder of the instrument, and the claims of others against the holder are generally not his or her concern.

EXAMPLE 33.   Fay executes and delivers a check to a payee. The payee uses the check to buy a car from Parks. The payee indorses, delivers, and sells the check to Parks, who falsely represented to the payee that the car has traveled only 12,000 miles. Parks, of course, does not take as an HDC. Fay knows that the payee was defrauded, stops payment, and refuses to pay Parks. Fay cannot set up the payee's claim and must pay Parks unless the payee should intervene in the lawsuit and assert his claim.

However, in the case of a stolen instrument or restrictive indorsement, the obligor can, so to speak, mind another's business. The obligor can argue another's case, if it can be shown that the person through whom he or she holds the instrument acquired it by theft, or that payment or satisfaction to such holder would be inconsistent with the terms of a restrictive indorsement.

EXAMPLE 34.   Ten negotiable bearer turnpike bonds ($1,000 each) were stolen when the owner's home was burglarized. The bonds were later sold to a buyer. When the buyer demanded payment from the Turnpike Authority, the maker, the Turnpike Authority raised the defense of lack of delivery by reason of larceny. The buyer was unable to show he was a holder in due course. The maker, the Turnpike Authority, had no defense of its own, but there was no doubt about the fact of the theft. The defense of nondelivery therefore is available to the maker under Section 3-306(d) of the UCC.

Black Letter Law
A Summary

1. A holder in due course (HDC) is a holder who takes the instrument for value, in good faith, and without notice that it is overdue or has been dishonored, or of any defense against or claim to it on the part of anyone.

2. Value is any money, property, goods, or services actually delivered in payment for the instrument, as are also promises negotiable in form, irrevocable commitments to a third party, and settlement of antecedent debt.

3. Good faith means taking honesty in fact in the conduct or the transaction.

4. Instruments with a stated maturity date are overdue the following day; demand instruments are overdue when more than a reasonable time after issue has elapsed, except that checks drawn or payable in the United States are presumed to be overdue more than 30 days after date.

5. Holders who purchase at a judicial sale, from estates, or in bulk cannot qualify as holders in due course.

6. Holders who have knowledge that the instrument was originally incomplete, that it was postdated or antedated, or that there is an executory promise still to be performed for the paper may nevertheless still qualify as holders in due course.

7. A holder who knows the paper was incomplete in some necessary aspect when issued can become an HDC to the extent of the authorization; if the holder did not have such knowledge, he or she can be an HDC to the full extent of the unauthorized completion.

8. Once a holder becomes an HDC, subsequent knowledge or events cannot alter this status.

9. A holder, assignee, or transferee who can trace his or her title through an HDC has all the rights of an HDC, with the exception of reacquirers and those who were themselves a party to any fraud or illegality affecting the instrument.

10. Under Federal Trade Commission rules and some state statutes, the status of holder in due course cannot be enjoyed by purchasers of instruments given in a consumer credit transaction.

11. Defenses to liability are real or universal or are personal or limited.

12. Real defenses are available against all parties, including those with the rights of an HDC; personal defenses are ineffective against those having the rights of an HDC.

13. Real defenses include forgery; material alteration; fraud in the *factum*, or execution; discharge in insolvency proceedings; and, under certain circumstances or state laws, infancy, capacity, duress, other discharge, and lack of capacity.

14. A legal defense that is not real or universal is personal.

15. Personal defenses include lack of reality of consent, want or failure of consideration, non-delivery, breach of contract or warranty, and any other defense to a simple contract.

16. In order to determine whether illegality, duress, or incapacity is a real defense, one must look to see whether the document arising out of the transaction has been declared a nullity under the state law.

Solved Problems

21.1 Marston purchased a promissory note at a 20 percent discount from the seller, who was the indorsee. Unfortunately, Marston knew nothing of the rules of commercial paper, and all he received from the seller was a signed statement reading, "I hereby transfer my $6,000 note to you and without further liability of any kind whatsoever." Under these circumstances, Marston

(a) cannot ever become a holder in due course.

(b) can never get paid from the maker.

(c) can never succeed to the rights of a holder in due course.

(d) has not paid value.

   Marston can never become an HDC under these facts, statement (a). Since the seller has no duty to indorse by reason of their contract, Marston can never become a holder, a status necessary to be an HDC. This does not mean that Marston may not have the rights of one. If the seller or a previous holder qualified as an HDC, Marston would be the beneficiary of the so-called shelter provision. Purchase at a discount is value. Even if Marston does not succeed to the rights of an HDC, the obligation must be paid unless there is a valid legal defense to it or a claim by others.

21.2 Directo wishes to purchase a $3,000 note she learns she can buy for $2,000. In which of the following circumstances would she have failed to pay value?

(a) She gives the seller her personal check for $2,000.

(b) She cancels the seller's debt of $2,000 in payment for the note.

(c) She executes a contract to deliver $2,000 worth of landscape material to the seller's residence.

(d) Upon the seller's request, she hires the seller's incompetent nephew.

   Directo would have paid value in all these situations except (c). A valuable promise not yet performed does not qualify as value. Satisfying an antecedent debt, (b), and giving another negotiable instrument, (a), are indeed value, as is performing an act requested by the seller, here the hiring of the nephew, (d).

21.3 The Third National Bank accepted for collection a $2,300 check payable to its customer and drawn on another bank. Before this deposit, the customer had an account balance of $1,200. At which point can the Third National Bank become a holder in due course in all or some part of the $2,300 check it now holds for collection?

(a) When it informs the customer that it will honor checks up to $3,500 drawn by the customer.

(b) When it has cashed checks totaling $2,350 for the customer.

(c) It can never have such rights.

(d) Fourteen days after receipt of the $2,300 check for collection.

A bank does not give value for a deposited check when it credits the check or notifies the customer that he or she can draw on such. However, the bank does give value to the extent that its customer, the depositor, withdraws money against that credit, statement (b). Here the bank has paid value as an HDC to the extent of its security interest of $1,150.

21.4 Acme operates a check-cashing establishment and counts as its habitual customers many of the young smart set in the prosperous office building in which it has offices. Acme has been having some trouble with a few checks that certain young executives have been cashing through Acme. On several occasions certain bounced checks were only made good when Acme threatened suit after the drawers mumbled something about illegal poker losses. Under these circumstances,

(a) Acme can continue to take these checks drawn by those parties as long as they only complain and do not ultimately refuse to pay, and still take in good faith.

(b) unless Acme participated in the illegal poker games, it can take in good faith.

(c) Acme has information which, if not sufficient to give notice of a defense, is sufficient to require further inquiry into the origin of these checks.

(d) Acme could never qualify as a good-faith taker with such drawers' checks.

It is not wise to have too much information about the origin of negotiable instruments if one wants to take in good faith. Acme now has information that some of the checks from these parties may have arisen out of an illegal transaction, a poker game, which is a defense to liability. This information is sufficient to require a prospective good-faith taker to inquire further and assure himself or herself of the true character of the underlying transaction; statement (c) is the answer. It is too much to say that Acme could never be a good-faith taker.

21.5 On April 1, 19X3, Allen offered to purchase a trade acceptance dated March 1, 19X3, from Tucker, the payee. The draft provided that it was payable "30 days after acceptance," but it had not yet been accepted. Under these circumstances,

(a) if Allen purchased it now, he would be taking it when it was overdue.

(b) if Tucker told Allen that the drawee had refused to accept it but would pay it 30 days from April 1, 19X3, Allen could not take it as an HDC.

(c) Allen cannot purchase an unaccepted draft and still qualify as an HDC.

(d) this trade acceptance becomes overdue on April 16, 19X3.

Notice that a draft requiring acceptance was dishonored is notice of default; the answer is (b). The maturity is set by the acceptance, and a refusal to accept prevents such establishment.

21.6 Which of the following cannot have the rights of a holder in due course?

(a) A purchaser after maturity from an HDC

(b) A purchaser who failed to get a necessary indorsement from the HDC

(c) Where a party repurchased an instrument from a complaining HDC, who charged that such party knew the paper was bad

(d) A payee

All the parties mentioned in the above statements except (c) could qualify as having the rights of an HDC. However, a reacquirer cannot improve his or her original position by taking through a holder in due course. However, if the reacquirer was originally an HDC, he or she remains such.

21.7 Which one of the following situations is *not* cause for concern to a prospective buyer of installment notes who desires to take as a holder in due course?

(*a*) The buyer has a close business relationship with the payee, who is in the business of originating the notes.

(*b*) The installment notes are based on credit purchases by consumers.

(*c*) The payee offers to sell only those notes whose installment payments of principal have been in arrears for over 30 days.

(*d*) The payee offers to sell only those installment notes issued under contracts where the payee is not yet due to perform his or her duties under the contract.

　　Mere knowledge that the consideration for the note is in its executory state does not prevent one from qualifying as an HDC; statement (*d*) is the answer. It is knowledge that the payee breached his or her duty which is fatal. Taking a note in default by reason of an overdue installment on principal is taking in bad faith. Further, a close business relationship with the payee who originates this paper may sometimes result in the holder who buys from the payee being the alter ego and therefore bound by any defenses against the payee. In consumer credit situations, the note must contain a legend making buyers aware that all defenses to the note are available even against good-faith takers. The latter is a Federal Trade Commission regulation which, in effect, prevents one from qualifying as an HDC.

21.8 Troy fraudulently induced Casper to make a negotiable instrument payable to the order of Troy in exchange for goods she never intended to deliver. Troy negotiated it to Gorden, who took with notice of the fraud. Gorden in turn negotiated it to Wagner, a holder in due course. Wagner presented it for payment to Casper, who refused to honor it. Wagner contacted Gorden, who agreed to reacquire the instrument by negotiation from Wagner. Which of the following statements is correct?

(*a*) Casper would have been liable if Wagner had pursued his rights on the negotiable instrument.

(*b*) Gorden was initially a holder in due course as a result of the negotiation to him from Troy.

(*c*) Casper is liable to all parties except Troy in that it was his fault that the instrument was issued to Troy.

(*d*) Gorden can assert the rights of his prior holder in due course, Wagner, as a result of the repurchase.

(*AICPA Examination, May 1979*)

　　Statement (*a*) is correct. Wagner took the instrument as an HDC, and had he sued at that time, he could have defeated the defense raised by Casper. Gorden's reacquisition does him no good. While it is true that a holder who can trace his title through an HDC succeeds to the HDC's rights, there are several exceptions to this rule, and this instance is one of them, as a holder cannot improve his original position by reacquiring the instrument. The other exception to the rule is where the holder was a party to a fraud or illegality affecting the instrument.

21.9 Martindale Retail Fish Stores, Inc., purchased a large quantity of fish from Seashore Fish Wholesalers. The exact amount was *not* ascertainable at the time, and Martindale, rather than waiting for the exact amount, gave Seashore a check with the amount left blank. Seashore promised *not* to fill in any amount until it had talked to Martindale's purchasing agent and had the amount approved. Seashore disregarded this agreement and filled in an amount that was $300 in excess of the correct price. The instrument was promptly negotiated to Clambake & Company, one of Seashore's persistent creditors, in payment of an account due. Martindale promptly stopped payment. For what amount will Martindale be liable to Clambake? Why?

(*a*)   Nothing, because Martindale can assert real defense of material alteration.

(*b*)   Nothing, because Clambake did *not* give value and the stop order is effective against it.

(*c*)   Only the correct amount, because the wrongful filling in of the check for the $300 excess amount was illegal.

(*d*)   The full amount, because the check is in the hands of a holder in due course.

(*AICPA Examination, May 1979*)

   While it is true that the instrument was originally incomplete in a necessary aspect, it was later completed and reached the hands of an HDC. That is one of the risks taken by a party who creates an instrument by signing it when incomplete. Clambake is an HDC and did pay value by taking the instrument in payment of an account due, an antecedent debt; the answer is (*d*). The stop-payment order initially prevented payment, but ultimately the drawer must respond to the demand of the HDC.

21.10 Marlin ordered merchandise from Plant to be delivered the following day and gave Plant a check payable to his order drawn on Marlin's account in First Bank. It was agreed that the check would *not* be transferred unless delivery was received and accepted. The goods were *not* delivered, and Marlin notified Plant that he exercised his right to rescind. Plant, nevertheless, negotiated the check for full value to Rose, who took it in good faith and without notice of any defense. Rose then negotiated it for full value to Quirk, who knew of Plant's breach of the agreement. Marlin promptly stopped payment on the check and refuses to pay it. Under these circumstances, which of the following statements is correct?

(*a*)   Marlin would have a valid defense in a suit by Rose for the amount of the check.

(*b*)   Marlin would have a valid defense in a suit by Quirk for the amount of the check.

(*c*)   Despite the fact that Quirk cannot personally qualify as a holder in due course, he can assert Rose's standing as such.

(*d*)   A stop-payment order will not prevent a holder in due course from collecting from the bank.

(*AICPA Examination, November 1978*)

   This is an example of the operation of the shelter provision by which a holder from another HDC gains all the rights of an HDC; statement (*c*) is the answer. The bank has not signed the check, and therefore it has no liability to parties who sue on the instrument. Thus the stop-payment order does, in effect, prevent an HDC from taking from the bank. Quirk has knowledge of the defense, but that only prevents him from taking as an HDC; it does not prevent him from taking as an assignee or transferee from an HDC.

21.11 A 17-year-old son brought his father with him to a used-car lot to purchase a car. Agreement was reached, and the dealer told the father that "certain papers had to be signed" for the loan of $2,200. The father and son both signed a number of papers, including a note as comakers in the amount of $3,000. The note was negotiated to a good-faith HDC. Under these circumstances,

(*a*)   the charge by the father that he didn't know he was signing a negotiable instrument, just "some legal papers," makes his defense a real one of fraud in the execution, or *factum*.

(*b*)   if the state allows infants to disaffirm automobile purchase contracts completely, the son has a real defense.

(*c*)   the father and son here can prove fraud in the inducement, good against the HDC.

(*d*)   representing to the makers that the note was for a loan of $2,200 when it really was for $3,000 is a material alteration.

Minors are allowed a real defense to the extent the state law allows such a defense, statement (*b*). Since this state follows the traditional rule of full disaffirmance, the son is not liable to an HDC. Fraud in the *execution* requires that one had no reasonable opportunity to obtain knowledge of the terms or character of the instrument, but the father *knew* he was "signing legal papers." Accordingly, he is held to one of those papers being a negotiable instrument. There was fraud in the *inducement*, but that is only a personal defense and is not available against an HDC.

21.12 The signatures of three makers appeared on a note. Upon default it appeared that one signer, De Paul, had only schooling at a special class in public school and was not able to read except simple words—and then only with reading glasses which he was not wearing at the time. Further, it appeared that De Paul signed only after being told that he was signing as a "character reference." If an HDC appears against De Paul, his best defense would be

(*a*) illegality.

(*b*) duress.

(*c*) fraud in the inducement or procurement.

(*d*) fraud in the execution, or *factum*.

The first three defenses are personal and would do De Paul no good even if true. Fraud in the execution is a real or universal defense and would be his best chance, statement (*d*). The facts suggest that he might be successful in proving such ground.

21.13 Executive Hotel signed a $122,667 note in favor of Electric Furnace Company for work in connection with the installation of a new system. The note reached the hands of an HDC. At maturity the hotel charged that the furnace company had breached the contract and, in an attempt to prevail against an HDC, proved that under the state law the furnace company was required to possess a state regulatory license. The furnace company did not possess such a license. The penalty was a fine of $1,000 upon conviction. Under these circumstances,

(*a*) the hotel has only the personal defense of illegality and would lose.

(*b*) the hotel is able to select an excellent defense, that of illegality, a real or universal defense.

(*c*) poor workmanship is a real defense.

(*d*) the hotel has no defenses at all to offer the court.

Illegality is generally a personal defense unless state law makes the transaction a nullity or void, statement (*a*). Here, the only penalty for violation was a fine; the legislators left undisturbed the integrity of a document arising from the contract. Poor workmanship, qualifying as a breach of contract, is only a personal defense.

21.14 A tractor owner hired a company to repair a tractor. The owner drew a personal check in the amount of $700 in partial payment of the repairs. The company negotiated the check to the supplier the following day. The supplier presented the check to the owner's bank, but it was returned with the words "payment stopped" on it. The owner seeks to avoid liability on the grounds that the tractor was improperly repaired. What type of defense is this?

(*a*) Breach of contract

(*b*) Mistake

(*c*) Undue influence

(*d*) Third-party claim

The defense raised is one of the garden variety defenses in commercial life, that of breach of contract, statement (*a*), a claim of partial or total failure of consideration.

21.15 To pay for six horses supplied to Colder's farm, Colder drew a check on the Sixth National Bank payable to the order of Fabius. Colder's check-printing machine incorrectly printed the amount of $6,230. The handwritten amount was $16,230. Fabius was in financial trouble and wanted to get these funds as quickly as possible and so sent her foreman over to City National Bank for payment after having indorsed the check in blank. Colder did not have an account with City Bank, but the bank officers there knew him. Because of the conflict in amounts, the officer at City Bank telephoned Sixth National Bank and was told that Colder's account had a balance sufficient to pay the $16,230. City Bank then cashed the check for that amount. The foreman took the cash and then immediately ordered four *bank money orders* made out to different creditors of Fabius, commenting to the bank officer that "these money orders are to settle some of Fabius's creditor problems, but we have problems with other creditors and I hope the boss can straighten things out." Later the Colder check was dishonored by reason of a stop payment made on it by Colder because of discrepancies in the delivery of the horses. City National Bank honored its money orders and now claims to be a holder in due course of the $16,230 check.

What type of contention will Colder try to establish against City Bank? Decide and give reasons for any conclusions reached.

Colder, as drawer of the check, might want to charge that value was not given and that City Bank did not take the check in good faith. As to value, it is true that after cashing the check the foreman "returned" the money to the bank in exchange for money orders, but once value is given, it suffices. The money orders were negotiable instruments and qualify as value. As to good faith, the issue is whether a dollar number irregularity on the face of the instruments gives a prospective holder notice of defects or defenses. It did put City Bank on notice to do some investigation, which it did. Further, it was not a serious discrepancy. The UCC itself has a rule of construction which assists in this type of situation: handwriting governs printing. The argument that City Bank learned of some trouble that might have put it on guard is met with the point that it learned this *after* having qualified as an HDC. To be effective, notice of a defense must be received at such time and in such manner as to give a reasonable opportunity to act on it. City Bank is an HDC and can recover from Colder.

21.16 A creditor pressed a debtor to satisfy an unpaid debt. The debtor prevailed upon a bank to loan him some money to satisfy part of the debt. The bank issued its money order (check) in the amount of $1,200 payable to the order of the debtor and another for $3,000 payable to the order of the creditor. The debtor delivered both of these checks to the creditor's agent. This agent refused to credit these checks to the debtor's account as he was suspicious about how this money was obtained. He questioned the debtor and also demanded that the balance of the debt be paid off the following week while he checked out the situation. The agent then contacted the bank's president and learned that the loan was induced by the debtor's mortgaging of property which he had already encumbered with the creditor. The president of the bank immediately stopped payment on the money orders and claimed that they were obtained by the false representation of the debtor. The creditor, now claiming to be a holder in due course, sues the bank on the checks as the drawer.

What defense can the bank advance to escape liability from the creditor who now owns the checks? Decide and state reasons for your conclusions.

The bank should charge that the creditor's agent had too much information regarding the origin of the bank money orders to qualify as a good-faith taker. While it is true that satisfaction of an antecedent debt is value, the creditor unfortunately (for him) took what proved to be an unwise course of action. Had the creditor simply satisfied the antecedent debt, and thus given value, and then straightforwardly presented the checks for payment, he would likely have been an HDC. Instead, he chose to investigate the origin of the proffered payment. This action was fatal to the creditor because the investigation revealed that the debtor had defrauded the bank in order to obtain these instruments. Such knowledge is fatal, and it destroyed the creditor's chance of taking as a holder in due course in this situation.

21.17 A couple purchased some vacant New Mexico land sight unseen under a contract which provided that they were entitled to receive a certified property report and that until they had inspected the property, they could rescind the transaction up to 6 months. The couple also signed a $6,000 installment note for the purchase price. The payee-developer sold the note and all the contract documents to Statton for $4,200 ten days after the issue of the note and contract. The documents revealed that the couple had not received a copy of the certified property report and had not yet inspected the property. Two months later the couple inspected the land, found it not as represented to them, and, pursuant to the contract, elected to rescind the contract by notifying the payee, who in the meantime had gone bankrupt. The couple stopped paying on the installment note. Statton is upset and intends to sue the couple on their installment note.

What argument should the couple present to defeat Statton's claim that he is an HDC? State your answer and any conclusions you have reached.

It appears that unless Statton can prove he is a good-faith taker qualifying as an HDC, he will be unsuccessful in recovering on the installment note. The couple will charge that Statton knew all the details of the transaction, including the fact that the couple were not given a copy of the certified property report as required. Knowledge of such a defect in the transaction does undermine Statton's good-faith status. Further, buying at such a large discount (30 percent), while not in itself bad-faith taking, is a factor in addition to the undelivered certified property report. Added to this is the fact that the sale to Statton occurred just 10 days after the note originated. Statton knew too many negative things about the underlying transaction to qualify as an HDC.

Chapter 22

Liability of Parties

22.1 LIABILITY: GENERALLY

Part 4 of Article 3 of the UCC sets forth a number of technical aspects regarding the liability of the parties to the instrument or those who have handled the instrument. Signatures, their undertaking, warranties of the sellers, representations of holders, and conditions to liability of secondary parties are treated in detail.

22.2 SIGNATURES

The UCC makes little demand as to what actually constitutes a signature, but sign one must, as no person is liable on an instrument unless his or her signature appears thereon, UCC, Section 3-401(1). A signature can be made by use of any name, including any trade or assumed name, or by word or mark used as a substitute for a conventional written signature. However, intent of a signing party is not so easily ascertained although, in the absence of language to the contrary, the signer meant to bind himself or herself personally. The UCC also presumes that, unless the signature clearly indicates otherwise, one means to bind oneself as an indorser.

EXAMPLE 1. "I, Homer Brown, promise to pay . . . , (signed) Homer Brown" (a maker), or "(signed) Homer Brown, Witness" (clearly a witness, not a maker or indorser). A signature at the lower right-hand corner of a draft is assumed to be the *drawer's*, and if on a note, it is assumed to be the *maker's*. A drawee's signature *anywhere* on the paper, front or back, is treated as the *acceptor's*.

Where one intends to sign in a representative capacity, as an agent, for example, the person must be extremely careful in the use of the words employed.

EXAMPLE 2. The following are clear: "Harry Taub, by (signed) Fabus Wicks, Agent." "Magic, Inc., by (signed) Torrey Cannon, President." If the signers were indeed authorized to sign, they incur no personal liability on the document. Further, if an agent merely signs the principal's name and not his or her own, the agent is not liable.

Where the role of the signer is not clear to the reader, a party not intending to be bound may nevertheless suffer liability. This is especially true if the instrument should reach a third (remote) party, that is, a party other than the one who dealt with the signer.

EXAMPLE 3. Harold Nelson signed a promissory note as follows: "Harold Nelson, Agent." It was made payable to a bank for his employer's loan. The bank could not prevent Harold from offering testimony or other proof that he signed it for his employer. If, however, the bank transferred the note to a third party who had no notice that the real maker was Harold's employer, Harold could not introduce the same evidence against the third party and would be liable on the note. In this example only the bank was an *immediate party*.

EXAMPLE 4. On another note, Harold signed "Fred Townson" and under that name, "Harold Nelson." This produces the same result as in Example 3. Harold could be liable to a third party, as he failed to include a showing of a representative capacity.

It is safest to name the principal and use the word "by," or similar language, so as to escape unintended liability. In regard to principals which are organizations, Section 3-403(3) of the UCC rescues the careless. Where the name of the organization is preceded or followed by the name *and* office of an authorized individual, the representative nature will be presumed. Thus, the words "Magic, Inc., (signed) Torrey Cannon, President," for example, would qualify.

22.3 SIGNATURES AND FICTITIOUS PAYEES

Subtler than the act of a forger who signs the drawer's name or the thief who steals a signature-writing machine from an office are the improper (criminal) acts of parties in a firm who have power to sign, or have legitimate access to the signing ritual, or provide names of payees to their employer. In these situations the unauthorized signatures are found on the *back* of the instrument in the form of a forged indorsement of the payee's signature. A drawer or maker generally has no liability when the payee's signature is forged, but by reason of estoppel and UCC rules, the principal (drawer or maker) can be so bound when the forged indorsement was done by a faithless agent under the fictitious payee situation.

Section 3-405 of the UCC provides that an indorsement by any person in the name of the named payee is effective if " . . . (b) a person signing as or on behalf of a maker or drawer intends the payee to have no interest in the instrument; or (c) an agent or employee of the maker or drawer has supplied him with the name of the payee intending the latter to have no such interest." The last circumstance is illustrated by a dishonest purchasing agent who must provide the accounting department with the names of suppliers who are due money from the firm. This purchasing agent supplies a fictitious payee and will later indorse and then negotiate the instrument.

EXAMPLE 5. Attleboro has authority to sign the firm's name to vendor payment checks. In order to draw money for himself, i.e., embezzle, he names a payee who is seemingly authentic, a payee who would normally be named or might be named. Attleboro names Townsand, a former creditor of the firm, as a payee. The accounting department prepares the check and sends it to Attleboro's office for signature and mailing. Attleboro signs and keeps the check. He later "indorses" Townsand's name and negotiates the instrument. If a bank paid out on this check, it technically would not be following the firm's order *to pay Townsand*. However, the UCC treats this type of forgery as an effective indorsement and places the loss caused by Attleboro on the firm who employs him.

22.4 SIGNATURES AND IMPOSTERS

Section 3-405(1) of the UCC provides that an indorsement by any person in the name of a named payee is effective if "(a) an imposter by use of the mails or otherwise has induced the maker or drawer to issue an instrument to him or his confederate in the name of the payee . . . ."

EXAMPLE 6. Mark, a small-town politician, receives a letter purportedly from Governor John Poller, a national figure. The letter states that if Mark is able to induce the townspeople to send $1,000 to cover expenses, the governor will appear in town for a local affair. Mark decides to foot the bill himself. He sends his own $1,000 check to the address listed. He makes the check payable to "John Poller." The imposter receives the check at his address, indorses it, and cashes it. Mark, not the bank, suffers the loss. Mark intended the imposter to have the check since he delivered it to him. As to the bank, assuming it used good commercial practice, the imposter's signature of John Poller is, in the words of the UCC, an "effective indorsement."

A subtle but important distinction should be noted in this regard. If the check had been sent to the governor's office where a clerk stole it and forged the indorsement, the result would be different. The issue is, did the maker or drawer make *delivery* to the imposter? If such delivery was made, the imposter rule applies.

22.5   ACCEPTORS, DRAWEES, AND FORGED DRAWER'S SIGNATURE

Drawees are not liable by reason of the fact that their names appear on the instrument. It is their assent, by signing, which evidences commitment. Drawees who sign become acceptors. Acceptors are similar to makers in that both engage to pay the instrument absolutely. Further, an acceptor admits to all subsequent parties that the payee exists and that the payee has the capacity to indorse.

EXAMPLE 7.   A draft is payable to the "order of Brown," an infant. The drawee accepts the draft. Brown negotiates it to Tucker. The drawee-acceptor cannot use the fact that Brown was an infant as a defense to the suit.

A drawee's failure to accept (sign) or pay the draft is called a *dishonor*, and while it does not create any rights in the holder against the drawee, it does affect other parties to the instrument. An acceptor's failure to pay a draft permits the holder to sue those who may have liability on the instrument.

Since the drawee has no liability on the instrument until he or she accepts it by signing, or incurs no potential loss until he or she pays it, the act of accepting or paying can create a problem when it turns out that the drawer's signature was forged. Accordingly, the drawee who pays or the acceptor who signs (accepts) will not be able to charge the apparent drawer's account. Even worse, the drawee who pays or accepts may not retrieve the payment from a holder in due course who obtained the payment or is the beneficiary of the acceptance.

EXAMPLE 8.   Two drafts were seemingly drawn by Sutton on Price in favor of Rudding. They were finally negotiated to Neale, a holder in due course. Upon demand the first draft was paid by Price to Neale. The second draft was accepted (signed) by Price and later paid, again to Neale. Only then did Price discover that the drawer's signatures had been forged by Lee. (Lee was hanged for these forgeries.) Price sued Neale to recover the payments since Price could not demand them from Sutton, the apparent drawer. Price alleged, among other grounds, "mistake." In this famous 1762 case, the English court ruled that the drawee, by paying or accepting the draft, admitted the genuineness of the drawer's signature and may not recover back against a holder who was a good-faith purchaser. The case is cited as *Price v. Neale*. This principle is restated in Section 3-417 of the UCC.

22.6   MAKERS

A *maker* is a primary party and is one from the beginning of the instrument, unlike a *drawee*, who becomes a party only after signing (i.e., accepting) the instrument. Makers have a primary duty to pay and are liable until the statute of limitations has run out, or they are discharged in bankruptcy, or they are discharged by proper payment. Like the acceptor, the maker engages that he or she will pay the instrument according to its tenor at the time of the engagement or as completed pursuant to rules governing incomplete instruments.

EXAMPLE 9.   Martha signed a $500 promissory note due 1 year from date, leaving the name of the payee blank at the request of the party taking the note. Martha never saw the note again until 3 years after its maturity. Martha now sees that the note appears to reflect a $1,500 principal amount and shows the names of complete strangers on both the payee line and the back where indorsements appear. She refuses to pay interest after maturity since she was ready to pay on the due date but no one came forward to collect the money; she is willing to pay only $500. Since Martha signed when the instrument was incomplete, she must honor it however completed against the rights of a holder in due course. She is bound to pay after-maturity interest since it was not a "domiciled instrument," that is, payable at a particular place, at which time the maker should have the money waiting for the holder, an act which stops the running of interest. As to principal, Martha will be required to pay only according to the original tenor of the instrument, the amount of $500, unless her negligence in some way contributed to the material alteration in favor of a holder in due course.

By signing, the maker admits to all future parties on the instrument that the payee does exist and that such payee had capacity to indorse at the time the maker executed the document. Like the drawee who pays, or the acceptor, a maker who pays a holder in due course cannot recover such payment should he or she subsequently discover that the maker's own signature has been forged or that the terms of the instrument have been materially altered.

22.7 DRAWERS AND FORGED INDORSEMENTS

Drawers of checks or drafts are technically secondary parties and do not engage to pay the instrument. A drawer has a secondary liability, that is, the drawer engages that upon dishonor of the draft and any necessary notice of dishonor or protest, he or she will pay the draft to the holder or any indorser who takes the instrument.

EXAMPLE 10. Tuff Produce drew two drafts: one, a check in favor of its trucker, Wheels Transport, and the other, a draft on its retail customer, Greengoods, who was named as drawee, to the order of Tuff Produce. Greengoods took the produce, signed the draft, and returned it to Tuff, who indorsed it and negotiated it to a creditor. This is a trade acceptance. Tuff's bank dishonored the check to Wheels Transport because of insufficient funds, and Greengoods refuses to pay the accepted draft. Wheels Transport and the holder of the trade acceptance, the creditor, both look to Tuff for recovery. Even though Tuff, as drawer of the check and the draft, had only secondary liability, Tuff may have to honor these demands provided it has been properly notified. On the check Tuff is liable since the reason for the dishonor of the check was insufficient funds. Tuff is liable for the draft because the act of drawing it was an engagement to pay it if it was dishonored after acceptance and Tuff was properly notified.

Of course, like an indorser, a drawer of a check or draft can sign "without recourse." By so drawing, the drawer informs future parties on the document that the drawee is obligated to the drawer and is expected to pay, but that the drawer does not guarantee that the drawee has funds to honor the draft.

There is one exception to the rule that a drawer who fails to sign without recourse could be relieved of further liability by reason of the failure of the drawee to have funds to pay. It occurs in the unlikely event of bank failure in regard to drawers of checks. If the drawer had sufficient funds on deposit for a reasonable time and the holder delays collection to a point beyond which the bank no longer has funds, the drawer is released from paying again.

EXAMPLE 11. A drawer executed and delivered a check for $300 to the order of the payee on March 10, 19X3. The payee negotiated the check to a holder on March 20, 19X3. The holder ultimately sent the check to the drawee's bank on April 20, 19X3. The bank cannot pay because it was closed by order of the state comptroller on April 18, 19X3. It appears that the bank will pay off 30 cents on the dollar. If the drawer had sufficient funds in the bank for 30 days after issue of the check, and thereafter, and assigns its right to the holder, the drawer is excused from payment. Thus the holder gets 30 percent of the $300, or $90, and has no claim against the drawer for the remaining $210, UCC, Section 3-502(1)(b). In most instances today, the deficiency would eventually be made up through payment by the Federal Deposit Insurance Corporation.

This rule is broad enough to include not only drawers but also makers and acceptors in similar positions. On instruments with a stated maturity, delay after that time activates the rule. In the case of demand instruments, it is that time after a reasonable time after issue, but in regard to checks it is 30 days after date or issue, whichever is later, UCC, Section 3-503(2)(a).

Like the maker and acceptor, the drawer of a draft admits against "all subsequent parties including the drawee the existence of the payee and his then capacity to indorse."

22.8 INDORSERS

One not signing as a maker, drawer, or acceptor signs as an indorser unless the paper shows otherwise. By signing and delivering up the instrument, the ordinary indorser has indorsement liability, and if he or she sells (not gives) the paper to another, the indorser incurs warranty liability. *Indorsement liability* refers to the legally implied promise of the indorser that the instrument will be paid. *Warranty liability*, however, refers to certain implied representations made by a seller of the instrument (even nonindorsers who transfer by delivery alone) regarding the legal integrity of the instrument. Indorsement liability occurs by signing. Warranty liability occurs by selling or presenting for payment or acceptance.

EXAMPLE 12. A maker signs and delivers a $500 note to the order of the payee. The payee indorses and delivers the note to X, who indorses "without recourse" and sells to Y, who indorses and transfers to Z as a gift. At maturity the maker refuses to pay and gives two reasons for his refusal (dishonor of the instrument). First, the payee defrauded him, and, second, he hasn't any money. The first reason is a legal reason and speaks to the legal integrity of the instrument; the second reason speaks to the financial integrity of the party expected to pay. The payee is liable on his indorsement contract, that is, guaranty to pay if proper notice is given to him (see Section 22.9 and Section 22.11, Example 18, for presentment, dishonor, and notice of dishonor). By selling the paper the payee has made a warranty contract to X, his buyer, and since he signed (indorsed), to all subsequent parties as well. X, however, by signing without recourse has made no indorsement contract but has made some warranties by selling to Y. By signing (indorsing), Y has made an indorsement contract to Z but no warranty since he received no value for it. Z, by demanding payment—called *presentment* here—is also making warranties about the instrument to the maker.

22.9 WARRANTIES: PRESENTMENT

Technically, a holder can hardly be said to have liabilities by reason of his or her contract with the instrument. After all, a holder seems to possess only rights; yet liability questions arise by virtue of the holder's claim to the instrument itself, i.e., title to the paper. However, just holding the instrument is not a permanent condition; the holder must either negotiate it to another or present it for payment or acceptance. When these acts occur, the subject of warranties arises.

Parties presenting paper for payment or acceptance, even if they do not sign the paper, make certain warranties to the person who in good faith pays or accepts. Section 3-417(1) of the UCC provides that those who obtain payment or acceptance (as well as any prior transferors) warrant that they have good title to the instrument, that they have no knowledge of certain forgeries, and that, under certain conditions, there is no material alteration to it. Material alteration refers to changes in the number or relations of the parties, unauthorized completion, or additions to the writing or removal of any part of it, UCC, Section 3-407.

EXAMPLE 13. Brennan is the indorsee of a $5,000 promissory note signed by Mason in favor of Payne, the payee. At maturity Brennan shows the instrument to Mason and demands payment. This is called *presentment for payment*. By this act Brennan has made certain implied representations which, if they later turn out to be false, permit Mason to demand return of the payment from Brennan.

EXAMPLE 14. A maker executes and delivers a note to the order of Paul. Paul loses it, and the finder forges Paul's signature on it. The note eventually finds itself in the hands of a good-faith purchaser for value. The purchaser demands and obtains payment from the maker, who only later learns of the forgery. The maker must deliver up the note to Paul, who still owns it and is entitled to payment, as no one can take good title through a forged indorsement. The maker can now sue to retrieve the payment from the purchaser, who impliedly warranted upon presentment that he had good title. On the other hand, had this been a bearer instrument which the purchaser took as an HDC, the warranty of good title would not have been breached since the integrity of an *unneeded* signature is immaterial.

One who presents for payment or acceptance also warrants that he or she has no *knowledge* that the signature of the drawee, maker, or drawer has been forged. As seen above in regard to signatures of the payee and necessary indorsee, the warranty is absolute. As in forgery situations, the presenter warrants certain matters regarding material alterations, but they are not as complete as is the warranty of good title.

Owners of paper may sell the paper to others and doing so makes implied warranties of transfer. These warranties do not extend in favor of those who obtain the instrument as a gift.

EXAMPLE 15.   A maker delivered a note to a payee in the sum of $500. The payee indorsed and delivered it to her church to be used in the building fund. The maker has a good defense to the note. The church sues the payee on her transfer warranty that "there is no defense good against her." The church would lose. No warranty is made to a transferee who gave no value or consideration for it. The church received the note as a gift.

Section 3-417 of the UCC lists four warranties of transfer to those who pay consideration: (1) the title is good; (2) all signatures are genuine or authorized; (3) no defense of any party is good against the transferor; and (4) the transferor has no knowledge of any insolvency proceeding in respect to the maker, acceptor, or drawer of an unaccepted instrument. Indorsements play a role in the scope of these warranties. If the transferor sells without indorsing, the warranties are made only to the immediate transferee; otherwise the warranties are made to all subsequent holders who take in good faith. Even an indorser who signs as a qualified indorser, and is thus relieved of indorsement liability, is still bound by nearly all the warranties (or transfer)—but a qualified indorser does not warrant that there is no defense against him or her, but only that he or she has no knowledge of such a defense.

EXAMPLE 16.   A maker signs and delivers a $500 note to the order of the payee. The payee indorses in blank, writing "without recourse," and sells the note to X for $300. X negotiates by delivery alone to Y for $350. Y indorses "without recourse and without warranty" to Z for $375. At maturity Z demands payment from the maker, who has a good defense. Z cannot sue Y since Y signed without warranty, nor can Z sue X since X never indorsed the note, and although an implied warranty was made by X, it does not run beyond Y. Z may be able to recover from the payee, who, while signing without recourse, nevertheless warrants that he "has no knowledge of a defense." If the payee indeed had no knowledge of a defense, Z is probably stuck with an uncollectible note.

22.10 ACCOMMODATION PARTIES

Most negotiable instruments contain commitments from parties having a real interest in the transactions, e.g., buyers, sellers, creditors. However, some parties place their signatures for the purpose of increasing the creditworthiness of the paper and, by doing so, incur liability. These parties are called *accommodation parties*, and the person for whom this commitment is made is called the *accommodated party*. An accommodation party's signature can appear anywhere on the paper, including as maker, drawer, indorser, or acceptor.

EXAMPLE 17.   A son wishes to borrow $500 from the bank. The bank is reluctant to lend the money, but it will if the father signs the note. The bank prepares a note, has the father sign as maker, and names the son as payee. The son now indorses the note and delivers it to the bank, which gives the son $500. The father is the accommodating party, and the son is the accommodated party. The father signed as maker, and all subsequent parties can treat him as such. Only between father and son is the son a "real" party, the "real" maker of the instrument.

An accommodating party who must pay the instrument can sue only the accommodated party. In practice this would seldom happen, because the usual reason for accommodation is that the accommodated party has few assets and/or poor credit, which is why he or she had to be accommodated in the first place. Suit would not likely bear fruit.

The father in the above example could have signed as an indorser and been liable as such, including the right to be notified upon default. Parties who have notice of the fact of accommodation have no less legal rights against such party, but such knowledge becomes more meaningful after maturity. For example, some behavior by the creditor can release an accommodation party. Without such knowledge there would be no possibility of release. Section 3-415(4) of the UCC reminds us that an indorsement not in the chain of title is notice of its accommodation character.

22.11 INDORSEMENT CONTRACT: GENERALLY

The owner of a negotiable instrument ultimately wants it paid. A principal reason for frustration of this wish is that the party expected to pay is financially unable to do so. The owner then looks to others, the indorsers and drawers, called *secondary parties*, for payment.

Every unqualified indorser engages that upon dishonor and any necessary notice of dishonor and protest he or she will pay the instrument and each will be liable in the order in which he or she indorsed, which is presumed to be the order in which the signatures appear on the instrument, UCC, Section 3-414.

The important conditions to liability, called the *conditions precedent*, require that the owner of the instrument proceed both carefully and quickly to fulfill these conditions.

EXAMPLE 18. Harold holds a $5,000 promissory note which matured last week. He is not worried since he has an indorsement from Tanner on the back. Tanner is the wealthiest merchant in town. The maker had financial trouble, and so Harold decided to give him a few more days before demanding payment. Harold should be worried. He should have demanded payment from the maker on the date of maturity (presentment for payment), received a refusal (dishonor), and immediately notified Tanner that he would look to him for payment (notice of dishonor). Harold, by his failure to take necessary actions, has released the indorser from secondary liability. Only the maker remains liable to Harold.

22.12 INDORSEMENT CONTRACT: EXPRESS WAIVER OF CONDITIONS

Unless the paper reflects that the parties have waived the conditions of presentment, dishonor, notice of dishonor, and, where necessary, protest, the failure to fulfill the conditions results in the release of the secondary parties. Many printed promissory note forms contain such a waiver, and many checks sent through banks contain such releases.

EXAMPLE 19. A promissory note has the following sentence written near the bottom of the page: "The undersigned, whether maker or indorser, waives demand, notice of nonpayment, and protest." This waives the conditions precedent.

The language or conduct does not have to be that explicit. The statement "no protest" or "presentment or notice of dishonor waived" is explicit conduct and is sometimes found stamped on the back of checks forwarded for collection. Many times, however, notice of presentment and dishonor is no news to the indorser, and he or she, by implication, waives the notice of dishonor.

22.13 INDORSEMENT CONTRACT: PAYMENT AND COLLECTION GUARANTEED

If the indorser waives the conditions, his or her liability is fixed, as the indorser was entitled to the fulfillment of the conditions. Some indorsers do more than waive conditions; they establish a particular liability by signing "payment guaranteed," or "collection guaranteed." Either has the effect of waiving the conditions precedent of proper presentment, dishonor, and notice of dishonor. However, the ultimate effect is more significant than simple waiver.

One who signs "payment guaranteed" may be sued immediately at maturity, even without the holder first proceeding against the primary party, UCC, Section 3-416(1). On the other hand, an indorser who signs "collection guaranteed" is entitled to demand that the holder exhaust his or her remedies against the acceptor or maker before making claim on the indorser.

EXAMPLE 20. Bradlee was the payee of a $500 note from Sause. Bradlee offered to sell the note to Hart. Hart, not wishing to be burdened with technicalities should Sause default, demanded and received a "payment guaranteed" indorsement from Bradlee. If Hart is not paid at maturity, he may sue Bradlee directly. If Hart had, instead, obtained a "collection guaranteed" indorsement from Bradlee, Hart would have been required to try to collect from Sause to the extent of obtaining a judgment before looking to Bradlee unless Sause was insolvent or it appeared useless to pursue him, UCC, Section 3-416(2).

22.14 INDORSEMENT CONTRACT: CONDITIONS TO LIABILITY

Presentment, dishonor, and notice of dishonor, and, in the case of international drafts, protest, are necessary actions before most unqualified indorsers must pay the instrument.

Presentment is a demand either for payment or for acceptance. It must be done at a particular time and in a certain manner. Notes, two-party paper, need only be presented for payment; drafts, three-party paper, sometimes must be presented for acceptance before presentment for payment.

EXAMPLE 21.   A note due August 1, 19X3, contains the indorsements of X, Y, and Z. The holder must appear before the maker on that date prepared to hand over the note upon payment. The maker is permitted an opportunity to make a reasonable examination to determine whether the note is properly payable, but she must pay the note before the close of business on the day of presentment, UCC, Section 3-506(2).

This is not to say that presentment cannot be made by mail or through a clearinghouse, but the place for presentment must be at the place of business or residence of the party to accept or pay, or, if a specified place is named, at that place, UCC, Section 3-504(2). Drafts which require a presentment for acceptance are permitted to be considered by the drawee to be without dishonor until the close of the next business day, and the holder in a good-faith attempt to obtain an acceptance may allow postponement for an additional day. Drafts which by their terms provide for acceptance, or are payable elsewhere than at the residence or place of business of the drawee, or whose date of payment depends upon such presentment, must be presented for acceptance before presentation for payment, UCC, Section 3-501(1)(a).

EXAMPLE 22.   A holder is in possession of a trade acceptance which has not yet been accepted. It is payable "30 days after sight." Until it is presented for acceptance, the maturity date is undetermined. The holder must first present it for acceptance before presentment for payment. A refusal of the drawee to sign a proper demand for acceptance would be a dishonor, requiring the holder immediately to give a proper notice of dishonor.

The time for presentment depends on the document. Sight and demand instruments require presentment within a reasonable time after date or issue, as do instruments that have been accelerated. Reasonable time is determined by the nature of the instrument, any usage of banking or trade, and the facts of the particular case. Checks drawn and payable in the United States have a more definite period. A drawer is liable 30 days after date or issue, whichever is later, but an indorser is liable 7 days after his or her indorsement. Late presentment discharges an indorser but only releases the drawer in the unlikely event that the bank goes insolvent during the late period.

EXAMPLE 23.   Barret draws a check on a Chicago bank on August 10, 19X3. The payee indorses and delivers the check to Feison on August 15, 19X3. In order for Feison to make a proper presentment so that if the check fails to clear she can hold the indorser liable, Feison must make presentment for payment, or initiate collection, by August 22, 19X3, 7 days after the indorsement by the payee.

If the party that is expected to pay, or accept, refuses without legal excuse, a dishonor has occurred, and the holder must immediately take the next step to bind the indorsers by giving notice of dishonor. An immediate telephone call to the indorsers is effective, but writing is usually safer. This is done by sending sufficient information of the dishonor to the indorser through the mail or by any reasonable manner "before midnight of the third business day after dishonor or notice of dishonor."

EXAMPLE 24.   A holder dispatched a registered letter, return receipt requested, to an indorser, notifying him of the dishonor. The indorser refused to accept the letter, and it was returned to the holder. This was good notice of dishonor, as the law permits that written notice "is given when sent although it is not received," UCC, Section 3-508(4).

Banks must move even more quickly, as notice must be given by a bank by its *midnight deadline*. This is midnight of the next banking day following the banking day in which it witnessed a dishonor, or is given notice of the dishonor.

An international instrument, that is, one drawn as payable outside the United States, requires an additional formality, that of protest. A *protest* is a certificate of dishonor made under the hand and seal of a United States consul or vice consul, or a notary public, or any other person authorized to certify dishonor, UCC, Section 3-509.

EXAMPLE 25. A drawer from Toronto, Canada, visits Buffalo, New York, shopping for a car. She decides to purchase one and gives a check for $8,700 drawn on the Greater Toronto Bank to the order of the Buffalo dealer. The dealer indorses the check and delivers it to his manufacturer, which promptly presents it to the Greater Toronto Bank for payment on August 10, 19X3. On August 11 the check is dishonored for insufficient funds. The manufacturer mails a letter to the Buffalo dealer on August 13 notifying him of the dishonor. This action is timely, i.e., within 3 days, but since this is an international check, it should have been protested by having the Toronto bank's authorized officer swear to the dishonor. The manufacturer has lost the dealer as a guarantor and can look only to the drawer.

Note that although the drawer was not given notice of dishonor, her liability does not diminish. Notice is excused since the drawer's act caused the dishonor and such result will be no news to her.

22.15 INDORSEMENT CONTRACT: EXCUSES AND DELAY

It is beneficial for the holder to have the conditions expressly waived or have facts justifying waiver by implication. If not, the holder must meet the requirements of proper presentment, dishonor, notice of dishonor, and protest when applicable. Although it seems that the holder must act promptly and correctly, the UCC only requires reasonable steps. Moreover, it provides a litany of approved excuses for noncompliance. Some excuses are temporary, and others are permanent. Section 3-511 of the UCC does not seem to expect the impossible, or even the seriously inconvenient. For example, presentment or protest is entirely excused when "by reasonable diligence the presentment or protest cannot be made or the notice given." Death or the institution of insolvency proceedings, for example, entirely excuses, and when a number of parties are involved, as in partnerships, notice to one partner is notice to all. For the deceased or incompetent, notice of dishonor may be sent to his or her last known address or be given to the personal representative. Moreover, where one exercises reasonable diligence and circumstances are beyond one's control, delay is tolerated until the cause of the delay ceases to exist.

EXAMPLE 26. A $1,000 note was due on January 1, 19X3, payable at Lewiston, Idaho. On August 20 of the previous year, the note had been sold to a husband and wife as part of a down payment for some property. The note was not presented for payment on January 1, 19X3, by the wife since she couldn't find the maker, who resided outside the state, in Oregon. The payee and the husband and wife lived in Lewiston. The wife testified that she attempted to contact the maker by telephone, through his parents, and, finally, through his fiancée. The maker finally came to the home of the husband and wife on January 20, 19X3, saw the note, and refused to pay it. The wife then notified the payee of the dishonor. The payee argued that there was a failure to present the note timely for payment. However, the wife's attempts qualify as a proper excuse since the delay in presentment for payment was caused by circumstances beyond control of the holder. The place of payment was Lewiston, Idaho, and no address was given. The holder was not required to go to Oregon to make presentment.

Black Letter Law
A Summary

1. Except for warranty situations, no one is liable on an instrument unless one's signature appears thereon.

2. One who intends to sign in a representative capacity must so indicate on the instrument, or others than an immediate party can impose personal liability on such signer.

3. Representative capacity is clearly shown by use of words such as "by" or "per" and can only be safely omitted when an organization is named and the signer indicates his or her office.

4. When a party in the organization of the drawer or maker designates a fictitious payee, an indorsement by such party is effective; it is not a forged instrument.

5. Where an imposter, by use of mails or other means, induces the maker or drawer to issue an instrument to him or her in the name of the payee, an indorsement by such party is effective; it is not a forged indorsement.

6. Where a maker or acceptor pays, or a drawee accepts or pays upon the forged signature of a drawer or acceptor, such party cannot retrieve payments or be relieved of liability for an acceptance in favor of a good-faith holder who received payment or acceptance under the rule of *Price v. Neale.*

7. A maker or acceptor is a primary party who engages that he or she will pay the instrument according to its tenor at the time of the engagement or as completed pursuant to the rules governing incomplete instruments.

8. Drawers are secondary parties who engage that upon dishonor and any necessary notice of dishonor or protest, they will pay the draft to the holders or indorsers who take up the instrument.

9. Unqualified indorsers are secondary parties and, by their indorsement contract, have liability, provided necessary presentment, notice of dishonor, and protest are met.

10. Warranty liability arises when a party transfers an instrument for value or presents it for payment or acceptance; such warranty extends to all subsequent parties except that it extends only to the immediate transferee when the transfer is without indorsement.

11. Any person who obtains payment or acceptance and any prior transferor who in good faith pays or accepts warrant that they have good title to the instrument; that they have no knowledge of forgery of the maker, drawer, or acceptor; and, under most situations, that there has been no material alteration of the instrument.

12. The warranties of transfer to those who pay value include warranties that the title is good, that all signatures are genuine, that no defense of any party is good against the transferor, that the transferor has no knowledge of any insolvency proceeding in respect to the maker, acceptor, or drawer of an unaccepted instrument.

13. Where the indorser signs either "payment guaranteed" or "collection guaranteed," the indorser thereby waives the performance of the conditions precedent to liability; in the former case, the indorser agrees to pay upon maturity, and in the latter case, the indorser agrees to pay only after collection efforts have failed.

14. The conditions precedent (a proper and timely presentment, dishonor, notice of dishonor, and protest if necessary) must be accomplished within defined time limits.

15. Presentment for payment must be made at maturity of the instrument, and notice of dishonor must be given within 3 days following dishonor or notice of dishonor, except that banks must act within their midnight deadline.

16. International drafts, those drawn or payable outside the United States and its territories, must be protested in order to hold secondary parties liable on such instruments.

17. Parties entitled to the fulfillment of the conditions precedent may waive these requirements; further, there are both temporary and permanent legal excuses which benefit the holder in fixing liability on secondary parties.

Solved Problems

22.1 A corporation was sued on two notes which had been signed in the name of the corporation as follows: "Keystone Insurance Agency, Inc., (signed) Harry Oster, Secretary." The corporate charter contained a provision stating that all contracts and other corporate documents must be signed with a corporate seal. Under these circumstances,

    (a) the failure to use the corporate seal does not invalidate the signatures on these notes.

    (b) the failure to use the word "by" or "per" or like words results in liability in Oster only.

    (c) corporate seals are the only real signatures of corporations.

    (d) both Keystone and Oster are liable on these notes.

      The UCC makes few stipulations about what constitutes a signature, but it is the UCC that determines whether a signature complies with negotiable rules, not individual corporate charters. According to the UCC, a signature can be done in any manner which indicates assent, and so statement (a) is the answer. If authorized to act, the secretary has bound the corporation. The failure to use the word "by" or the like does not disturb the legality of the agency where the name of the organization is preceded by the name *and* office of the authorized individual, UCC, Section 3-403(3).

22.2 Two signatures appeared on a note in which a corporation was also named as maker. In effect, the lower right-hand corner read:

(signed) M. Good

[Corporation Seal] Earle, Inc.

(signed) Dorn

Dorn is an officer of Earle, Inc. She wishes to introduce testimony that she did not sign individually. Which is the correct statement?

    (a) Dorn is personally liable on the instrument.

    (b) Dorn is entitled to show that she signed in a representative capacity if an immediate party sues on the document.

    (c) Dorn is entitled to show that she signed in a representative capacity if a third party sues on the instrument.

    (d) Since Dorn signed beneath the corporate name, she is clearly an agent.

Dorn's signature follows the name of an organization but does not show her office. Dorn could be personally liable on the instrument except that Section 3-403(2) of the UCC permits Dorn to offer proof of her agency if only immediate parties are involved, statement (b). Such an opportunity would not be available to Dorn if a third party were involved.

22.3   A father was the sole owner of a business he operated under the name Raison & Sons. A $2,000 note was executed in the name of the payee which contained the language "we promise to pay" and the following form of signatures:

Joseph Raison & Sons
(signed) Joseph Raison
(signed) Milton Raison, Attorney

Milton claims that he signed as an agent for his father and thus is not personally liable. May Milton offer evidence of his authority if the payee sues on the note?

(a) No, because the words "we promise" conclusively show joint and several liability.

(b) Yes, but only if his father gives permission to offer such a defense.

(c) Yes, since the payee is an immediate party.

(d) No, because Milton did not identify an office that he held.

The answer is (c). As between immediate parties, one may offer testimony or other evidence of an intention to be bound in a capacity other than that of primary party or indorser. Milton's defense is not dependent on the permission of another, but it does raise the possibility that he may not be able to prove his contention. Nevertheless, he has a right to offer evidence of such authorization.

22.4   A husband and wife owned land as tenants by the entirety, but were estranged. The wife wanted to borrow money and approached a lender, falsely stating that her husband would be unable to attend the settlement, but that he could sign earlier. The wife then brought a man to the attorney's office and falsely introduced him as her husband. He signed as such along with the wife as a maker on a promissory note as well as on the mortgage. The lender issued a $15,640 check payable to the order of the husband and wife. The wife signed her name on the back as well as that of her husband. This was discovered only after the drawee had paid the check. Which is the correct statement?

(a) The lender suffers the loss under the fictitious payee rule.

(b) The lender suffers the loss under the imposter rule.

(c) The drawee bank suffers the loss under the forged indorsement rule.

(d) The drawee bank suffers the loss under the rule of *Price v. Neale*.

The lender-drawer suffers the loss under the imposter rule, statement (b). An indorsement by any person in the name of a named payee is effective if an imposter induces the maker or drawer to issue an instrument to him or her or a confederate in the name of the payee. This is not treated as a forged indorsement. *Price v. Neale* deals with the forgery of signatures of drawers and makers, not payees.

22.5   Gull forged the signature of the Mace Company as drawer on two checks, one in the amount of $5,000 and the other for $10,500 drawn on Greene Bank. Gull made the checks payable to the order of himself, signing the Mace Company as drawer. Gull then indorsed the checks and deposited them in a Mexican bank, which indorsed them for collection and sent them to its correspondent bank in New York for collection. Greene Bank, the drawee, paid the correspondent bank, which remitted to the Mexican bank, which paid Gull. It was then discovered that the signature of the drawer, Mace Company, was forged. Gull fled. Greene Bank had to recredit the account of the Mace Company. Which is the correct statement?

(a) Greene Bank can recover the amounts paid from the Mexican bank.

(b) Greene Bank has no action against anyone.

(c) Greene Bank's only action is against Gull, the forger.

(d) Greene Bank is the beneficiary of the rule of *Price v. Neale*.

The drawee is bound to know the drawer's signature. When it pays or accepts a draft containing a forged drawer's signature, payment cannot be retrieved against good-faith parties. Accordingly, Greene Bank's only action is against the forger, Gull, statement (c). The drawee, Greene Bank, is not the beneficiary of the rule of *Price v. Neale*, but rather its victim.

22.6 A corporation, a good-faith purchaser, was in possession of a government check in the sum of $3,041 to the order of Barton. The signature "Barton" appeared on the back. The corporation, without indorsing, deposited the check into its account with the bank. The bank collected the proceeds from the government and gave the corporation credit. Later it was learned that the indorsement of Barton had been forged, and the government demanded return of the proceeds. The bank then charged the item to the corporation, but the corporation argued that it never signed the instrument and cannot be sued on it. What principle of law is involved here?

(a) The rule governing imposters

(b) The rules of a qualified indorser

(c) Presentment-for-payment warranties

(d) Presentment-for-acceptance warranties

When the corporation sent the check on to the bank for collection, it represented, among other things, that it had good title to the instrument. In this case, it did not have good title and therefore breached its presentment-for-payment warranty, answer (c). There is no need to sign an instrument to be liable for breach of this warranty.

22.7 A demand note dated July 17, 19X1, was executed by a corporation and indorsed by Laslo, one of its officers, as an accommodation indorser. Laslo left the corporation in December 19X1. A buyer purchased the note in March 19X2 and found that the corporation was doing no business although there was no indication of any insolvency proceeding having been instituted. In April 19X2 the buyer found Laslo and notified him that the note should be paid. Laslo refused to pay and, when sued, contended that he was not liable. Which would be Laslo's best defense?

(a) Proof that the buyer knew that Laslo was only an accommodation party

(b) Failure of the buyer to make a presentment for payment on the maker

(c) Proof that the buyer was not a holder in due course

(d) The fact that Laslo received nothing from the proceeds of the corporate note

Laslo's liability was one of contract as an accommodation indorser. This liability is activated by fulfillment of the conditions precedent, one of which is a timely presentment for payment. This the buyer never attempted, and so (b) is the answer. There is an excuse under Section 3-511(3)(a) of the UCC if the maker is involved in an insolvency proceeding, but that is not the situation here. Knowledge that one is an accommodation party does not diminish liability in this instance. Since no legal defense is mentioned, the absence of a holder in due course is immaterial.

22.8 A bookkeeper was a financial advisor to a nursing home. In attempting to get the home in better financial shape, the bookkeeper was named as payee of a $6,150 promissory note executed by the home, as maker, payable in five monthly installments of $1,230 each. The bookkeeper indorsed the note to the moneylender, and the funds were given to the home. The note was not paid at maturity, but the moneylender failed to give timely notice of dishonor. At trial it was shown that the bookkeeper had known that the home was in desperate financial shape, that other notes hadn't been paid, and that she had helped arrange extensions on other notes. Which is the moneylender's best argument regarding his failure to give proper notice of dishonor?

(a) Showing that the moneylender is a holder in due course

(b) Showing that the bookkeeper was the real party in interest since she was the payee

(c) Claiming that the bookkeeper waived the conditions by implication, i.e., full knowledge of the default and her actions regarding payment

(d) Showing that the bookkeeper was overpaid by the nursing home and thereby contributed to its collapse

The performance of the conditions precedent can be excused or waived under certain conditions. One may also expressly or by implication waive such conditions. On the basis of the payee-bookkeeper's conduct, the moneylender was reasonably justified in assuming that the payee did not expect or desire presentment or notice of dishonor. It would be no news to her. The answer is (c).

22.9 A negotiable instrument is examined during an audit engagement. If the instrument contains no agreement about a delayed presentment, which of the following is the proper time for presentment?

(a) On the same date that all other negotiable instruments are presented

(b) Ten days after the due date if it is a promissory note

(c) Within 30 days after issue for the usual uncertified check

(d) A reasonable time after the issuance of the instrument regardless of its type

(*AICPA Examination, November 1977*)

Presentment should be made at maturity. Where there is a definite date on the instrument, it should be that date. Demand or sight instruments pose a different question. Most, but not all, require presentment within a reasonable time after issue. In the case of checks drawn on a bank in the United States, there is a presumption that it is overdue after 30 days, answer (c).

22.10 Wilson drew a sight draft on Foxx, a customer who owed Wilson money on an open account, payable to the order of Burton, one of Wilson's creditors. Burton presented it to Foxx. After examining the draft for its authenticity and after checking the amount against outstanding debts to Wilson, Foxx wrote on its face "Accepted—payable in 10 days" and signed it. When Burton returned at the end of 10 days, Foxx told him that he could not pay and was hard-pressed for cash. Burton did not notify Wilson of these facts. Two days later when Burton again presented the instrument for payment, Burton was told that Foxx's creditors had filed a petition in bankruptcy that morning. Which of the following statements is correct?

(a) The instrument in question is a type of demand promissory note.

(b) Wilson had primary liability on the draft at its inception.

(c) Foxx was secondarily liable on the instrument before acceptance.

(d) Foxx assumed primary liability at the time of acceptance.

(*Adapted from AICPA Examination, November 1977*)

Drawers are secondary parties whether the instrument is a check or a draft and have liability provided the necessary conditions precedent are met by the holder. Drawees, on the other hand, have no liability by being named but assume primary liability by signing a draft, statement (d). This is three-party paper, a draft; notes are two-party paper. In this situation one should also note that a sight draft must be honored by payment, not acceptance. Accordingly, there was a dishonor which would release secondary parties.

22.11 Piper bought a 1970 truck from Rover Motors for $850 and received a written warranty that the truck had just been completely overhauled. In payment, Piper gave Rover a check for $250 and executed a promissory note for the $600 balance. The note was secured by a chattel mortgage on the truck. Piper's check bore in the lower left-hand corner the notation "Warranty no. 39; chattel mortgage of same date." Rover, indorsing the check in blank, negotiated it to Joe Brown, a holder in due course. Later, Piper stopped payment on the check after learning that the truck had not been completely overhauled as warranted. When Brown presented the check for payment, the bank refused payment pursuant to Piper's orders. Brown thereupon brought suit against Piper and the bank for nonpayment. Piper's defense was a breach of warranty, and the bank's defense was Piper's instructions to stop payment. Which of the following is a correct legal statement under the circumstances?

(a) The bank has no liability whatsoever to Brown.

(b) Piper's defense is a valid defense against Brown.

(c) A written notice of dishonor must be sent to Piper by Brown.

(d) Now that the check has been dishonored, third parties are also on notice insofar as the promissory note is concerned.

(*AICPA Examination, November 1977*)

On preprinted checks banks *appear* to have some liability by reason of their presence, but the rule that no one is liable on an instrument unless his or her signature appears thereon applies. Thus the bank has no liability to Brown, statement (*a*). Defenses are of value, but if personal, they do not defeat the rights of an HDC, here Brown. Oral notice of dishonor is permissible. By themselves these events give no notice to others regarding the note.

22.12 Wixstad asked Montrose, her father-in-law, to sign a note as an accommodation comaker. Montrose did this for Wixstad as a personal favor to his son. Both indorsed the note for value to Carlton, who had knowledge that Montrose had signed the note for Wixstad's accommodation only. With respect to Montrose's rights and responsibilities, which of the following is correct?

(a) Carlton has the right to treat either or both parties as primarily liable on the note.

(b) Carlton's best basis for recovery is to sue Montrose as an indorser.

(c) Montrose has no liability beyond one-half of the face value of the note plus interest.

(d) In the event Wixstad defaults on the note, notice must be promptly given to Montrose in order to hold him liable.

(*Adapted from AICPA Examination, November 1977*)

The answer is (*a*). A comaker is a maker and has primary liability. Thus the conditions precedent to having liability are unnecessary. The fact that one has notice of the accommodation character of the maker does not diminish one's rights against him. The liability of makers is entire, not partial, regardless of their number.

22.13 Salary checks issued by Feeble Corporation were bought by Desk Check Cashing service. Some of the checks failed to clear because of insufficient funds. Several officers of Feeble told Desk to hold the checks for later. To assure Desk of no loss, such officers, in November 19X2, gave their own personal checks to the order of Desk to be used in case the payroll checks did not ultimately clear. Feeble went into bankruptcy in March 19X3. The service attempted to cash the officers' checks, and payment was resisted by the officers, claiming that they were released because of the long delay in presentment. Which is the correct statement?

(a) One must present checks drawn in the United States within 30 days of issue or the drawer is discharged.

(b) Drawers of checks are never discharged until the item clears.

(c) One must present checks within 7 days of the last negotiation of the check.

(d) Drawers of checks are the beneficiaries of the 30-day rule only when there is a bank-drawee failure involving drawers' funds.

Drawers are only discharged on checks to the extent of the loss suffered by the delay, statement (d). It is true that within 30 days is the proper time for presentment of checks, but the only effect is that the drawer will be released to the extent of his or her loss. The officers suffered no loss as they selected a solvent bank which had its money. The 30-day rule and the 7-day rule do apply in this case to indorsers, the other secondary parties.

22.14 Which of the following instruments must be protested?

(a) A check drawn on a supplier whose business is located in Mexico City

(b) A check drawn in Tulsa by a Canadian visiting in Tulsa on a Nova Scotia bank, and there payable

(c) A trade acceptance by which a French resident draws on an American buyer, payable in New York

(d) A promissory note signed by a Puerto Rican son, the maker, in favor of his mother, the payee, who lives in Miami

Only international drafts need to be protested. Any draft which appears on its face to be drawn or payable outside the United States, or its territories or possessions, is an international draft. Only statement (b) clearly reflects an international draft, as it appears to be drawn payable outside the United States. Unless the draft appears so drawn or payable, it is not an international draft. "No protest" is an express waiver of the requirement.

22.15 Fenston S. Ladue was an indorser on a $5,000 promissory note which was dishonored at maturity upon proper demand. Just before midnight of the second day of the dishonor, the holder mailed a letter to *Foster* S. Ladue, care of general delivery, since, with due diligence, he could not find a present address. Such notice

(a) is effective since it qualifies as a necessary notice given by the midnight deadline.

(b) is ineffective since Ladue's first name is spelled incorrectly.

(c) is effective since it was dispatched within 3 days of dishonor.

(d) is ineffective since one must be sent a copy of the instrument with the notice of dishonor.

Except for banks, one must give a notice of dishonor within 3 days of the said dishonor; statement (c) is the answer. Since the holder apparently did a reasonable act, mailing to the best address he had, the act of so mailing is the notice. A misnomer does not necessarily invalidate a notice of dishonor.

22.16 Higgins purchased a paper from a bank which contained the printed name of the Touchstone Bank as drawee, the figure $130.37, and the words "Pay to the order of," but the payee line and drawer line were blank. Across the top were the words "Personal Money Order" and "Register Check." Printed instructions at the bottom of the check told the buyer to fill in the name of the payee, date the check, and sign on the drawer line. A sentence at the end of the instructions stated that stop-payment orders on this item would not be honored by the bank unless certain conditions were met. Before signing or completing the paper in any way, Higgins lost it on the same day she purchased it. Higgins notified the bank that it was lost and ordered payment stopped. The bank refunded the $130.37. On the same day as the loss, one Walker offered to sell the paper to Fable Check Cashing Service. Walker showed identification, named himself as payee, and signed the check as drawer. Fable Check Cashing Service bought the paper after Walker indorsed it. Touchstone Bank refused to honor the check when Fable presented it.

Does Touchstone Bank have liability on this check? Decide and state the reasons for any conclusions you reach.

At first viewing the instrument looks like a check drawn by a bank on itself since it contains words such as "Money Order" and "Register Check." *Cashier's checks*, checks drawn by banks on themselves, are sometimes called *bank money orders*, a practice that may have misled Fable Check Cashing Service. Whatever it might have seemed, it does not dispense with the rigid requirement of the UCC that no drawee, here the bank, is liable unless it has accepted the draft or certified the check. Further, this is not a traveler's check or the like since it was not signed (the first signature) by the drawer. Fable has recourse only against Walker, the drawer and indorser.

22.17 Perry and Douglas were the major stockholders and principal officers of Perdoug Construction Company. Both were active in the financial affairs of the company, which needed additional capital. Anderson agreed to lend the company $50,000 but demanded that both Perry and Douglas indorse the note. A demand note in the amount of $50,000 was signed on August 2, 19X2, by the Perdoug Company as maker and Perry and Douglas as indorsers. In December 19X2 Anderson sold and indorsed the note to Tucker. By letter dated January 12, 19X3, Tucker notified Perdoug that the note must be paid by January 22, 19X3. This notice was sent by certified mail, return receipt requested. Copies of this demand were mailed to both Perry and Douglas. Perdoug refused to accept the certified letter, and it was returned to Tucker on January 22, 19X3. Two weeks later Perry died and left a considerable estate, but Perdoug ceased to exist. Douglas fled the jurisdiction. On February 20, 19X3, Tucker sued the Perry estate.

What defense might the Perry estate employ in this lawsuit? Comment on its likelihood of success and state reasons for any conclusions.

Every indorser is entitled to notice of dishonor unless such is waived or excused. The Perry estate should attempt to defend on that ground as no formal notice of dishonor was ever attempted. Perry had notice of demand, i.e., presentment, but no notice of dishonor. However, the facts of Perry's involvement with the company and the note suggest a legal excuse. Perry was privy to the financial affairs of the company, and may even have ordered the dishonor of the instrument as an officer by sending back the certified letter. The purpose of notice of dishonor is to provide the indorser with an opportunity to take steps to protect his or her rights against any prior indorsers and the maker. Where one is a party to the dishonor, the notice is accomplished by that fact. It appears that an excuse is available here to Tucker, resulting in liability to Perry's estate.

22.18 Sybil was the manager of AGEE, a food brokerage firm, and was an officer in the company. The firm had enacted a corporate resolution authorizing her and other officers to "indorse and deposit checks payable to the corporation into the corporate accounts at the firm's bank." Sybil had fallen in love late in life and then to a clever con man. His pleas for loans to tide him over resulted in Sybil indorsing 13 checks which AGEE had received from clients to the order of the firm. Sybil deposited them into her personal account, which was also at the firm's bank. Upon discovering this, AGEE demanded that the bank credit the firm's account with the funds it had given to Sybil. The bank set forth the fact that Sybil had the power to indorse, and, besides, the fictitious payee rule applies.

State the issue, give your decision about a lawsuit between AGEE and the bank, and state reasons for any conclusions you have reached.

It is important to the bank's defense that it establish that a forged instrument did *not* occur. If a forgery did occur, the bank either did not pay the item properly or did not handle it properly. It is true that the bank had official notice of the authority of Sybil to indorse corporate checks, so that a forgery did not take place at that time. However, the bank allowed transfer of these funds to an account which it knew or had reason to know was personal. A bank which negotiates checks bearing forged or unauthorized indorsements is liable in conversion to the true owner. Without the corporate resolution, it is clearly an unauthorized instrument. The resolution must make it authorized in order that the bank can win. Here the language and the obvious intent of the resolution give the bank no immunity. An indorsement by Sybil and other officers was authorized only for deposit (delivery) into the corporate accounts. The bank would be liable by reason of a forged or unauthorized indorsement. It must credit AGEE's account and seek relief against the now lovelorn malefactor, Sybil.

Chapter 23

Discharge, Bank Deposits, and Collections

23.1 GENERALLY

Ultimately all commercial paper is expected to be paid and its journey ended. Part 6 of Article 3 of the UCC sets forth the rules governing this termination, while Article 4, Bank Deposits and Collections, mainly relates to the role of banks in the final settlement of money items, a large portion of which are negotiable in nature. This chapter will review these topics.

23.2 DISCHARGE: METHODS

An instrument is not discharged. It is the parties who are discharged, because the instrument itself never had any liability. There are numerous ways in which parties are discharged, some effectively but others less permanently. When viewing discharge, the following concepts must be examined: payment, tender of payment, cancellation or renunciation, impairment of recourse, reacquisition, alteration, certification, unexcused delay, and discharge by agreement, i.e., contract.

23.3 DISCHARGE BY PAYMENT AND TENDER OF PAYMENT

A party having liability by reason of his or her contract under the instrument may discharge this liability by paying the holder having the rights to the document. The consideration for such discharge is not limited to money. Accordingly, payment of a note with a check or another negotiable instrument is full satisfaction, but only if clearly agreed, as there exists a presumption that an additional instrument is given as security only or is conditioned upon clearance. Payment to achieve full discharge must, in any case, involve surrender of the instrument from one having rights to it.

EXAMPLE 1.   A maker, in good faith, is about to pay and take back his $500 note from a holder. The payee, who lost the note after indorsing it, now demands that the maker not pay the holder. Unless the payee supplied the maker with an indemnity, or all parties are joined in a court action under which the court ordered the maker not to pay, the maker may pay the holder despite this claim by the payee, UCC, Section 3-603. Note here that if the indorsement of the payee had been forged and this was a necessary indorsement, the payee had more than a mere claim; he is still the real owner and the maker might have to pay twice.

Payment by a maker who is in reality an accommodation party does not discharge the accommodated party. The accommodating party may sue the accommodated party on the instrument.

A failure to take up the instrument from the rightful owner is not the only concern of the payor (maker, drawer, drawee, acceptor, indorser), as a restrictive indorser may decree how payment must be made. Only banks which are not depositary banks can ignore such restrictive indorsements.

256

EXAMPLE 2.   A payee indorsed a check drawn on Royal Bank, "Pay to Acton, upon delivery of 1982 Ford Escort, (signed) Payee." Acton deposited the check in Terminal National, her bank, for collection. Terminal sent it to Harbour Bank, which presented it to Royal Bank. Royal Bank (payor bank) and Harbour Bank (intermediary bank) need not concern themselves with the restrictive (conditional variety) indorsement and must pay and deliver the proceeds to Terminal National (depositary bank). Terminal National, however, must assure itself that the term of the indorsement (delivery of the car) was accomplished if it has allowed its depositor to draw on uncollected funds.

One can never be quite sure when a final payment has been made. Section 3-418 of the UCC states that payment or acceptance of any instrument is final in favor of a holder in due course or a person who has in good faith changed his or her position in reliance on the payment. Accordingly, one must be sure that the title of the party presenting the instrument for payment is good. One who takes through a forger has no title and, of course, cannot qualify as a holder in due course since the person is no holder. Where there are comakers and one maker pays the instrument, the other comaker is discharged on the note.

Any party making tender of full payment to a holder at or after maturity is discharged to the extent of a subsequent liability for interest and attorney's fees, but not for the debt itself. Further, a holder's refusal to accept such tender wholly discharges those who have a right of recourse against any party making the tender, UCC, Section 3-604(2). Tender is best illustrated by a party physically offering the money to a holder at the proper place, but it also is broad enough to include situations where "the maker or acceptor of the instrument payable otherwise than on demand is able and ready to pay at every place of payment specified in the instrument when it is due," UCC, Section 3-604(3). The party offering to pay must see that the funds actually arrive.

EXAMPLE 3.   A maker was obligated on a $3,910 note payable in certain installments, one payment of $750 due June 1, 19X3. In the early hours of May 30 the maker took an envelope containing three checks drawn to the order of the payee's attorney, as required in the note, to the attorney's office and dropped the envelope through the mail chute on the office door. There were sufficient funds for the checks to clear. The checks were never found. The payee accelerated the payment schedule, but the maker contended that she tendered payment and thus one could not accelerate for default. The note was lawfully accelerated since the checks were never received, delivered, accepted, or cashed by the attorney.

One can always know where to tender payment or performance if the instrument is a domiciled instrument, that is, the paper states a sufficiently specific location where payable. Payable "in Dallas, Texas," is not a domiciled note, but "Farmers Bank, Dallas, Texas," is. Funds deposited at the specified bank (place) by the party expected to pay at maturity satisfy tender.

23.4   DISCHARGE BY CANCELLATION OR RENUNCIATION

One who possesses a right may unilaterally and arbitrarily surrender this right for consideration or even make a gift of it. Willful destruction or mutilation of the paper discharges it by cancellation. It is more likely, however, that the owner may wish to extinguish liability to some but not all the parties. To do this, the owner need only strike out signatures by pen or other device.

EXAMPLE 4.   A holder purchases a note and finds the indorsements of the payee, A, B, and C on the note in that order. B is a friend of the holder, and the holder strikes out B's signature and initials the cancellation. C is discharged as well as B and since C could have looked to B in case of default. The payee and A are not affected by this cancellation.

A holder may also renounce his or her rights against a party on the instrument by so stating in a signed writing delivered up to the party so benefited. Of course this could prove ineffective in respect to subsequent parties not privy to this discharge by renunciation.

23.5 DISCHARGE: IMPAIRMENT OF RECOURSE OR OF COLLATERAL

Any discharge of certain parties on the paper can affect other parties. Sometimes the holder's act of canceling one's liability on the paper is accompanied by a statement that the holder "reserves his rights" against other parties who could have looked to a party discharged by cancellation. Such reservation is effective, but it does not impair the rights of those parties to look to the canceled party.

A discharge can also occur where the holder unjustifiably impairs any collateral for the instrument given by or on behalf of the party or any person against whom he or she has a right of recourse, UCC, Section 3-606(1)(b).

EXAMPLE 5. A $200,000 note was secured by two properties by way of a mortgage. One property was vacant land, and the other was a small duplex. During the term of the note it was negotiated to others before the present holder. The maker had a marvelous opportunity to develop the vacant land, but his bank would not take a second mortgage. The maker asked the holder to subordinate the first mortgage to a new mortgage by the bank. The holder agreed. By changing the first mortgage to a junior mortgage, the holder has impaired the rights of any previous parties, e.g., payee, indorsers, and to that extent they are discharged from liability.

23.6 REACQUISITION

If a payee or indorser should again own the instrument, he or she may find that others have incurred liability since he or she first signed. Those parties who signed after the reacquirer first became bound are, as far as the reacquirer is concerned, discharged from liability. However, if the paper reveals no cancellation of these parties and the instrument is further negotiated, a subsequent party would not be bound by this rule forcing payment, the relief from which comes only when these intervening indorsers seek recovery from the reacquirer.

23.7 ALTERATION

One signing an instrument does not expect the original undertaking to be enlarged or changed. In Chapter 22 material alteration was examined in light of the warranties the respective parties make or do not make. In discharge, one views the possibility that a fraudulent material alteration may completely discharge all parties to the instrument. The alteration must be fraudulent. In this connection it is said that there is no intent to defraud where a blank is filled in the honest belief that the debtor so authorized it or the change is for the benefit of the debtor.

EXAMPLE 6. A lender loaned a farmer $3,500 using a note to evidence the loan. In past similar transactions the lender had been charging 13 percent interest. This time no mention was made of the rate, but the amount was accidentally left off. The lender noticed this later and, feeling that everyone should know about the recent rise in interest rates, instructed his secretary to type in 14 percent and "to use the same typewriter" that was used to type the note. There was a default, and the farmer noticed the 14 percent interest rate. A successful defense of material alteration as a complete discharge would turn on whether the lender's act under these circumstances was fraudulent.

23.8 DISCHARGE BY ACCEPTANCE

Acceptance is signing by the drawee. When the drawee is a bank, such signing is also called *certification*. Section 3-411 of the UCC provides that if the holder of a draft drawn on a bank (i.e., a check) seeks and obtains a certification, the drawer and all prior indorsers are discharged. However, where the drawer seeks and obtains such certification, there is no such discharge.

An improper acceptance can act as a discharge of the indorsers. These acts are called *acceptances varying the draft*, as they change the original contract of the parties. Of course the holder need not take such, but if he or she does, it will act as a discharge only if the other parties do not consent to the variance. However, it must be a real variance, as the UCC specifically exempts those drawers who sign, agreeing to pay at any particular bank in the United States unless the acceptance states that it is to be paid *only* at such bank or place, UCC, Section 3-412.

EXAMPLE 7.   Baker approached a buyer for a signature on a draft in which the buyer was the drawee. The buyer signed, but added the words "Payable at Frontier Bank, Dallas, Texas." When maturity arrived, Baker found no money waiting for her at the bank. Baker gave an immediate notice of dishonor to the payee, who was also the drawer of the trade acceptance. The drawer claims he was discharged by an acceptance varying the draft. The drawer is not discharged since this variance is allowed by the UCC.

However, a bank does not dishonor a check by its refusal to certify (accept) it, as the UCC provides that a check is an item for payment, not acceptance.

23.9 DISCHARGE BY UNEXCUSED DELAY AND CONTRACT

The conditions precedent to liability of secondary parties include proper presentment, dishonor, notice of dishonor, and, when necessary, protest. These conditions, if not met, operate to discharge secondary parties. Accordingly, some holders may seek a reprieve in Section 3-511 of the UCC, which recites that delay is excused when the party is without notice that the instrument is due or when delay "is caused by circumstances beyond his control and he exercises reasonable diligence after the cause for delay ceases to operate."

Indorsers are discharged when they have not been given any required notice or a proper presentment was not made. Drawers or acceptors at a bank, or makers of a note payable at a bank, can also be discharged, provided that during the delay the bank failed and funds had been available for payment. Once the drawer, acceptor, or maker by a writing assigns his or her right to such funds to this holder who failed to collect, having delayed without excuse, such assignors are discharged from liability.

Contract law is fully operative in this area of discharge. Section 3-601(2) of the UCC specifically provides that "any party is also discharged from his liability on an instrument to another party by any other act or agreement with such party which would discharge his simple contract for the payment of money."

23.10 BANK DEPOSITS AND COLLECTIONS GENERALLY

Banks play a prominent role in the creation, negotiation, and collection of commercial paper. Most discharges occur within the banking system, and the legal problems are many. Issues treated in the following sections are those involving the banks as agents, types of deposits and handling of items, depositor's contract, death of depositor, stop-payment orders and stale checks, delay in claiming error, and right of recovery.

23.11 BANKS AS AGENTS

One of the major functions of a bank is its employment in an agency capacity. Taking a check, for example, and collecting the money due thereon are two of a bank's principal functions. The bank is under a duty to exercise reasonable diligence in collection. Most deposited items, i.e., any instrument for the payment of money (but not money itself), whether negotiable or not [UCC, Section 4-104(1)(g)], are presumed to be taken as *general deposits*, the result of which is the establishment of a debtor-creditor relationship once the item has been collected. *Special deposits* occur only where there is delivery to the bank for safekeeping and the property is to be returned to the depositor. This establishes a bailor-bailee relationship. A *specific deposit*, on the other hand, creates a common agency relationship by which banks act as escrow agents. Banks thereby hold money, commercial paper, or other assets to satisfy a demand for a specific purpose. Sometimes the relationship is not clearly established by the parties.

EXAMPLE 8. A loan association was about to foreclose on Brinson's home, as he was in default in the amount of $1,000. Brinson had only $300 in his checking account at his bank when he appeared before the association with a $5,000 check payable to his order and said he was about to deposit it with his bank for collection. An association officer, suspicious about the value of the check, telephoned Brinson's bank and was assured by the bank that it would collect and hold the proceeds to pay Brinson's $1,000 check just drawn in favor of the association. Brinson deposited the $5,000 check in a regular fashion the next day for collection by his bank. The day after that the bank refused to honor a check drawn by Brinson in favor of one Howard in the sum of $4,335, noting "insufficient funds," but took possession of it "for collection" and issued a receipt to Howard. Several days later the $5,000 check cleared, and the bank honored Brinson's check in favor of the association, after which Brinson drew out the remainder of the account. The bank then returned Howard's check, stating "account closed." Howard contends that the bank failed to exercise reasonable diligence in making collection of his $4,335 check. The bank claims that the receipt of the $5,000 check was a special deposit. Howard succeeds against the bank on the grounds that a special deposit will not be presumed. When, for reasons of its own, the bank paid on presentation checks it was not obligated to pay but failed to collect on checks held for collection, it remains liable for such default.

23.12 BANK COLLECTIONS

Banks handle items as depositary banks, collecting banks, payor banks, or drawee banks and, in so acting, must concern themselves with the midnight deadline, posting, warranties, and the order of payment. When a customer hires a bank to collect an item and credit it to the customer's account, the bank is called a *depositary bank*. When it allows one to draw on an item not yet collected, it is not only a depositary bank but also, in effect, a buyer of the item.

EXAMPLE 9. A loan association drew a check on First Bank to the order of Howard and Polse (joint payees) in the sum of $7,500. Howard indorsed and delivered the check to Polse, who deposited it in Sunny California Bank to the account of Faith Corporation of which Polse was president. The check was sent to the First Bank, but was returned because Polse had failed to indorse it. After Polse indorsed the check, it was again presented to the First Bank, by which time the loan association had stopped payment. In the meantime Sunny California Bank had permitted Faith Corporation to draw $2,000 on the uncollected check. Sunny California Bank is now an HDC on the check to the amount of the overdraft, i.e., $2,000.

Generally, a depositary bank which has taken any item for collection may supply any indorsement of the customer which is necessary to title unless the item contains the words "payee's indorsement required," or the like.

The usual procedure by a depositary bank is to credit the amount of the deposit to the account of its depositor. Any collecting bank along the line likewise credits the account of the previous collecting bank or remits to that bank. Ultimately, the item reaches the drawee or payor bank, which debits its own drawer's account. This process has time limits and requires the observance of good commercial practice. Negligence, therefore, can subject any bank involved in the operation to liability.

23.13 PAYOR BANKS

A *payor bank* is one at which an item is payable as drawn or accepted, including, of course, a drawee bank. A bank with authority to pay only upon specific instructions of the drawer would not be a payor bank but rather a *collecting bank*.

EXAMPLE 10. A payroll draft is drawn payable "through" (rather than "on") a bank. Under Section 3-120 of the UCC, such is not a payor bank, but rather a collecting bank, since the word "through" does not constitute an order to pay. If the payroll item is payable "at" a bank, a different relationship is established. In states adopting Alternative (version) A of Section 3-121 of the UCC, the bank is a payor bank, but in those states adopting Alternative B, the bank is only a collecting bank since the word "at" is not an authorization or order to pay the draft.

Payor banks must pay the item or dishonor it before the close of the business day if presented over the counter. If the item arrives through the clearinghouse or the mail, the payor bank has until midnight of the following banking day (i.e., midnight deadline) to decide whether or not to honor it. A banking day is any day or part of a day on which a bank is open to the public for the purpose of carrying on substantially all its banking functions. As a general proposition, a payor bank is under no duty to assign a particular priority to items presented for payment on a particular day. Where an account does not have sufficient funds with which to pay the items presented that day, Section 4-303(2) of the UCC permits—with certain exceptions regarding stop-payment orders, legal process, or certain final commitments of the bank—the bank to pay or accept, certify, or charge the indicated amount to the account of the customer in any order convenient to the bank.

23.14 BANKS AND THE DEPOSITOR'S CONTRACT

A bank and customer are free to make a contract with each other within the bounds of public policy and some UCC rules. It is common to think that the so-called signature card a customer signs at a bank contains the entire terms of their agreement. This is not so. The following topics will treat some typical problems arising from the bank-customer relationship, including death of depositor, stop-payment orders, stale checks, and delay in claiming bank error.

EXAMPLE 11. Ash delivered currency to the bank in denominations of $10, $20, $50, and $100. Without declaring the amount, he handed the currency to a teller who, after dividing the bills into three separate piles, counted them. The teller registered the sums on an adding machine tape and exhibited the tape to Ash, announcing the total as $10,670. The teller prepared a deposit slip, registered that amount on it and on a passbook bearing Ash's name, and handed the deposit slip and passbook back to Ash, who then left the bank. The bank later claimed mistake in that the amount should have been $6,170. The teller testified that after Ash left the bank, he, the teller, discovered that one of the piles of currency contained $510, not $5,010, the latter figure having been erroneously entered on the tape by the teller. Ash claims that the deposit slip and passbook are conclusive evidence of the amount. The court ruled that such deposit slips and passbooks are only *prima facie* evidence of deposit and may be explained or contradicted by the bank in the event of fraud, error, or mistake, but the burden of proof is on the bank.

23.15 BANKS: DEATH OF DEPOSITOR

Section 4-405 of the UCC provides that a bank may pay or certify checks drawn by a deceased party or a party adjudicated an incompetent until the bank has notice of such death or adjudication. Even then, in regard to death, the bank may continue to pay or certify for a period of 10 days after death unless the bank is "ordered to stop payment by a person claiming an interest in the account."

EXAMPLE 12. Morant drew two checks, one dated February 10, 19X3, for $250 payable to her brother as a gift, and the other dated February 13, 19X3, in the amount of $1,050 to a travel service as a deposit on a holiday cruise planned for April. Morant died suddenly on February 14, 19X3. Morant's widower does not like the brother and had also resisted the cruise idea. Had he had the presence of mind to do so, he would have immediately ordered a stop payment on both checks. The checks arrived at the bank on February 23, 19X3, and on the same day the bank learned of Morant's death. Because it was only 9 days after the death of the drawer, the bank could safely pay both checks.

23.16 BANKS: STOP-PAYMENT ORDERS

The UCC allows a customer to have payment stopped on checks the depositor previously ordered the bank to pay. However, such order must be received at such time and in such manner as to afford the bank a reasonable opportunity to act on it. Under Section 4-403 of the UCC, an oral stop-payment order is valid for 14 calendar days. If an oral order is confirmed in writing during the 14-day period, it is good for 6 months, as is a stop-payment order originally given in writing. Of course, one must have authority to stop payment. After all, if a check is certified, the bank is a primary party and a stop order is ineffective. Generally, only the depositor has authority to stop payments except in case of the death of the depositor, but parties having some, but not complete, interest can activate rights against the bank for failure to stop payment.

EXAMPLE 13. A buyer, one of three shareholders of a coal company, bought out the other shareholders on October 29. The deal was consummated that afternoon, but that morning the buyer, who was also an officer of the coal company, visited the company's bank and advised the bank president of the pending sale. The buyer instructed the bank to stop payment on all checks dated after October 27. The bank so noticed this and signed a ledger notice of the order. Through an oversight the bank paid on checks dated later. A loss resulted to the coal company, and the buyer sued the bank for its failure to obey a valid stop-payment order. The bank defended on the grounds that at the time of the order the buyer did not own the coal company and had no right to order a stop payment until he was later elevated to be chief executive of the coal company. The buyer won on the grounds that the bank accepted the order and is now estopped to say that it was not valid when it paid out on a mistake.

It is important to note that the bank's liability for its failure to honor a proper stop order is determined by the actual loss suffered by the drawer.

23.17 BANKS: STALE CHECKS

Stale checks appear in several ways. For example, the failure of a holder to buy a check within 30 days of its issue prevents his or her taking as an HDC since it is "overdue." Another meaning of the term "stale check" is found in Section 4-404 of the UCC, namely, those checks that are outstanding more than 6 months from issue and the duties of banks as to such items. A bank is under no duty to pay a check which is older than 6 months, but it may do so with immunity provided it does so in good faith.

EXAMPLE 14. An insurance company delivered a check dated April 28, 19X2, in the sum of $5,358 to order of a client *and* the client's attorney as joint payees. The client was not satisfied with the settlement and refused to indorse the check. The attorney sued the client for her fee and received a $3,053 judgment. The attorney tried to collect from the insurance company, which defended on the grounds that the $5,358 check was still outstanding and represented full payment of money due the attorney. The court ruled that a check is, of course, not legal tender and that the check was now more than a year old and therefore it was legally stale. Since the drawee is not obligated to pay the check and normally will not do so without consulting the depositor, the attorney can proceed against the insurance company.

23.18 BANKS: DELAY IN CLAIMING ERROR

A bank customer has a duty to examine his or her statements carefully and the signatures on the canceled checks scrupulously. Section 4-406 of the UCC sets forth the customer's duty to discover and report unauthorized signatures or alterations. Unreasonable delay by the customer can result in a loss falling on him or her rather than on the bank. One of the more dangerous possibilities of loss occurs when there is repeated misbehavior of a forger or alterer. In such a case, a customer must bear the loss if an unauthorized signature or alteration found on any other items paid in good faith after the first item *and* statement showing such was available to the customer for a period not exceeding 14 calendar days and before the bank receives notification.

EXAMPLE 15.   A clerk who had no authority to sign her firm's checks began forging the signature of the firm's authorized signer on checks for less than $50 because she knew they were treated as petty cash and were not audited as carefully as checks for $50 or more. Her first forged check appeared with the statement of February 1. The clerk became quite bold and forged a check every week over a period of nearly 9 months before her actions were discovered. The 14-day rule would apply to all those forged checks after the first one because the checks and statements were available to the drawer firm. Any of these checks arriving at the bank more than 14 days after the firm had the opportunity to examine its February 1 statement and the accompanying canceled checks (including the forgery) cannot be charged against the drawee bank. Only the amount of the first check can be retrieved by the firm from the bank which continued to pay out on forgeries of the drawer's signature.

The depositor-drawer has a duty to examine both the signature of the drawer (i.e., one's own signature) and the indorsements when the canceled checks are available. While it is possible that failure to report a discrepancy in regard to either of these matters may be charged against the customer earlier because of negligent behavior, a depositor-drawer cannot under any circumstances attempt to retrieve payments after 1 year for a forged drawer's signature nor after 3 years from the date such statement and check were available in regard to a forged indorsement.

23.19   BANKS: RIGHT OF RECOVERY

In the process of handling items a bank frequently finds itself in the position of initially suffering a loss. In addition to the rights possibly gained as a holder in due course and in the enforcement of warranties, Section 4-407 of the UCC confirms a bank's right to subrogation in situations of improper payment. In substance, subrogation provides the payor bank with the right to stand in the shoes of an HDC, as payee or holder of the item, and even in the position of the drawer or maker against the payee.

EXAMPLE 16.   A drawer drew a check in favor of a payee for $500. The drawer was induced to draw the check through the fraud of the payee. The drawer's bank paid the item although the drawer did not have sufficient funds to cover the check, the bank having been in the habit of permitting overdrafts by the drawer. The bank was never paid by its customer, the drawer. The bank has the right of subrogation (i.e., the right to stand in the place of another) regarding the drawer's rights. The drawer could have sued the payee, and the bank therefore can sue the payee under right of subrogation.

Black Letter Law
A Summary

1.   Parties to an instrument may be discharged by payment, by tender of payment, by cancellation, by renunciation, by impairment of recourse or collateral, through reacquisition, by material alteration, by acceptance, by unexcused delay, and by simple contract.

2.   Only a proper payment by the party expected to pay, made to the rightful owner, who surrenders the instrument, discharges all parties to the instrument.

3.   A refusal of a proper tender of payment by the party entitled to payment does not discharge the tenderer but does extinguish certain rights of the refusing party and releases other parties on the instrument.

4. An intentional cancellation or renunciation of rights against any party on the instrument is effective despite the absence of consideration.

5. A cancellation or renunciation can result in the additional release of those parties who had a right to look to the released parties unless reservation of rights was made, in which case the released parties still must answer to those against whom reservation was made.

6. When a party impairs recourse or collateral, parties entitled to such benefit are released to the extent of the impairment.

7. Where the holder seeks and obtains the acceptance or certification of a check, the holder thereby releases the drawer and all other prior indorsers.

8. In dealing with negotiable instruments, a bank frequently acts as an agent: it acts as a debtor when it collects the proceeds, acts as a possible HDC when it permits a customer an overdraft, and stands in the shoes of the drawer through the doctrine of subrogation when it permits an overdraft by its customer.

9. Under Article 4 of the UCC (Bank Deposits and Collections), an item is an instrument calling for the payment of money whether the item is negotiable or not; money is not an item.

10. The relationship between a bank and its customer (drawer) is a complex one, but generally, it legally requires that the customer exercise promptness and reasonable care and that the bank exercise good faith and act in a reasonable manner.

11. The depositary bank in handling collection for its customers owes the greatest duty in the collection process and must honor the proper instructions of its customer and the terms of any restrictive indorsement.

12. Payor banks, in the absence of any contrary legal instructions, may honor checks received by them during the course of a day in any order convenient to them.

13. The death of a depositor-customer revokes a bank's agency authority only upon notice of such, and even then a bank may pay or certify such a customer's items received within 10 days following the death unless an authorized stop order has been received.

14. Oral stop-payment orders are effective for 14 days; written stop-payment orders are effective for 6 months.

15. Checks become stale after 6 months; after that time a bank may pay, or refuse to pay, a stale check without liability in either event.

16. A customer's delay in claiming error for unauthorized or altered instruments is tested by the customer's responsibility to exercise reasonable care and promptness, and the bank is tested by its duty to pay the item in good faith in spite of the 1-year limitation period for unauthorized signatures of the customer and 3 years by reason of an unauthorized indorsement.

17. Where successive forgeries or alterations were caused by one party, the 14-day rule begins to run from the date the item and the statement become available to the customer; the customer's failure to notify the bank of such a discrepancy prevents the customer from recovering from subsequently paid items of the same ilk.

Solved Problems

23.1 A husband, his firm, and his wife signed as comakers of a $25,000 note. The wife signed for the purpose of lending her name to her husband, who received the proceeds of the loan. The husband died without paying, and the firm was insolvent. The wife was obligated to pay the payee. The wife now attempts to press a claim on the note against her late husband's estate. Under these circumstances,

(a) the note was discharged by payment of the comaker.

(b) death discharges all contracts.

(c) the wife is entitled to a one-third share amount of the note under the principle of joint liability.

(d) an accommodation party can always sue the party accommodated.

  The wife was an accommodation party on the note, despite the fact that she signed as a comaker. As between the party accommodated and the accommodating party, the latter is entitled to reimbursement after having paid the debt; statement (d) is correct. Death discharges few contracts.

23.2 Sommers, along with three others, was a comaker on a demand note payable to the order of the payee. Three years after its execution, the note was indorsed "without recourse" to Sommers. Sommers now attempts to collect against the comakers, contending that he purchased the note. Which is the correct statement?

(a) Sommers purchased three-fourths of the note.

(b) A holder who purchases an instrument from a qualified indorser waives the collectibility of the item.

(c) Payment by a maker who is the real party in interest discharges the instrument.

(d) Sommers should only have paid one-fourth of the note, which was his entire liability.

  The correct statement is (c). Where one comaker makes full payment, the liability of all is discharged and no right of action exists on the note. It is possible that an action might lie on a contract for contribution, but the instrument does not provide the substance of liability. A qualified indorser says that he or she will not back up the payment of the note; this does not, however, undermine the liability of the makers.

23.3 A $5,000 note was payable 1 year from date, interest at 17 percent per annum until maturity and after until paid. The payee had indorsed the note to Fenner before maturity. The maker, at maturity, offered the $5,000 plus the accrued interest to Fenner and demanded the return of the note. Fenner refused the money as he was in the process of a divorce at the time and wished to have little cash in his possession. Besides, the interest rate was attractive. Under these circumstances,

(a) the maker's tender of payment discharged the instrument for all parties.

(b) the payee (indorser) is discharged by the refusal of tender.

(c) this tender by the maker has no effect on his liability.

(d) Fenner can only recover the legal rate of interest, not the contract rate, once a tender of payment has been refused.

  A tender of payment does not discharge the primary party. It does have several effects, however. Any future interest or other penalties are discharged and any parties who are indorsers having liability on the instrument are discharged by this improper refusal to accept payment, statement (b).

23.4   A discharge may *not* be accomplished by

(a)   intentionally mutilating the signature of a party.

(b)   orally renouncing one's right against another.

(c)   striking another's indorsement without consideration.

(d)   delivering a signed renunciation of the rights to the party involved.

     Both the parties and the instrument itself, and therefore all parties, can be discharged by the voluntary act of the holder. The answer is (b) since orally renouncing one's rights against one of the parties is not authorized in Section 3-605 of the UCC. The other methods are specifically set forth in the UCC.

23.5   Barrow was willing to consider Taney as a partner in an upcoming TV pilot show project but wanted some good-faith money put up. Barrow was a great believer in certified checks when he couldn't get cash instead. Taney offered Barrow a personal check drawn by Taney on Labour Bank in the sum of $15,000 payable to the order of Barrow, but instructed him not to cash it since it was "just a good-faith deposit." In order to induce Barrow to take the uncertified check, Taney had to supply Lansing, a prominent citizen, as an accommodation indorser. As soon as Barrow got the check with the indorsement, he took it to Labour Bank and had it "certified." Under these circumstances,

(a)   certification here discharged both Taney and Lansing.

(b)   only Lansing is discharged by this certification.

(c)   only Taney is discharged by this certification.

(d)   these facts suggest discharge by impairment of collateral.

     Where the holder of a check seeks and obtains a certification, the drawer and all prior indorsers are discharged, statement (a). Had Taney, the drawer, obtained the bank's acceptance, i.e., the certification, there would be no discharge. This case does not involve an impairment of recourse or collateral.

23.6   A drawer delivered a $49,600 check to a payee, who sent it to her bank for collection. The bank permitted the payee to draw on the item before collection. The drawer stopped payment, and the bank, which had given value to the payee, its depositor, sued the drawer. The bank claimed it was a holder in due course. The payee had never indorsed the check. Under these circumstances,

(a)   since the bank was never a holder, it cannot be an HDC.

(b)   if the bank never intended to "buy" the check, it remained only an agent for the depositor.

(c)   a depositary bank acting for collection can generally supply any indorsement of the customer which is necessary to title.

(d)   a bank cannot both be a depositary bank and possess the rights of an HDC.

     Section 4-205 of the UCC permits a depositary bank which has taken an item for collection to supply any indorsement of the customer which is necessary to title unless the item contains the words "payee's indorsement required" or the like; statement (c) is the answer. A bank can succeed to the rights of an HDC when it permits an overdraft or otherwise incurs a liability by reason of such deposit.

23.7   An executive requested that a check she drew on her bank payable to an auto dealer be accepted, i.e., certified, by her bank. The bank obliged and deducted the named amount on the check from the executive's account. She then delivered the check to the auto dealer but soon regretted the deal. The executive ordered the bank to stop payment on the item. Since this order was timely given, the bank stopped payment. The auto dealer then sued the bank. Who will win the suit?

(a) The bank will win since a check is not an assignment of funds.

(b) The auto dealer will win since the bank, by acceptance, became a primary party.

(c) The bank will win since it must obey the order of the drawer, its customer, even in regard to certified checks.

(d) The auto dealer will win, as it is a criminal offense to stop payment on a check even when the drawer has a legal reason.

The bank, by certifying the check, becomes a primary party engaging that it will pay the instrument according to its tenor at the time of its signing, the acceptance, statement (b). The certification by the bank ended the authority of the drawer, its customer, to order a stop payment on the item. The bank used poor judgment in obeying this invalid order. It is not a criminal offense per se to order a stop payment, but many states by statute provide criminal penalties for those who stop payment for improper and illegal purposes as in an intent to defraud.

23.8 Which of the following documents is not an "item" within the UCC definition of that term?

(a) $3,000 signed IOU

(b) $1,500 cashier's check

(c) $56,000 mortgage note

(d) $100 bill

An item means any instrument for the payment of money even though it is not negotiable, but the term does not include money itself; the answer is (d). Though not negotiable, the IOU calling for payment qualifies as an item. A real property (mortgage) note is a note, a negotiable instrument calling for payment of money; it is secured by a lien on real property.

23.9 An item looked like an ordinary check. It appeared that the Magpie Company was paying its stockholders their quarterly dividends with a company draft with Magpie as the drawer. A bank was named on the check, "Fifth National of Athens, Georgia," preceded by the words "payable through." Under these circumstances such language

(a) destroys the negotiability of the instrument.

(b) is legally superfluous.

(c) is an order on the bank to pay the item.

(d) gives the bank no authority to pay the item.

An instrument which states that it is payable "through a bank" or the like designates that bank as a collecting bank to make presentment but does not of itself authorize the bank to pay that amount; statement (d) is correct.

23.10 A bank may pay or certify a check drawn by a deceased customer in which of the following situations?

(a) Within 10 days of the customer's death despite the fact that a stop order has been issued by a party having an interest in the account

(b) Within 10 days of the customer's death despite the fact that the bank has learned of the death

(c) Up to 14 days after notice of the customer's death provided no stop payment has been issued

(d) Only up to 10 days from the date of death of the customer

The death of a customer does not automatically terminate the bank's right to pay or certify checks. It may do so within 10 days of a customer's death despite notice of death provided no lawful stop order has been issued, statement (b). If the bank has no knowledge of the death and no stop payment has been issued, the bank has an unlimited time within which to pay or certify.

23.11 A payee of a note sued to collect on the note, which provided for payment of costs and attorneys' fees upon default. At maturity the maker delivered two checks to the payee for the amount due. The maker later stopped payment on the checks. The payee is now trying to collect the principal amount of the note and the costs and attorneys' fees provided for by the note. The maker contends that the provisions of the note cannot be enforced since the note was discharged by the tender of the two checks. The maker argues that the payee should sue him on the two checks which never cleared. Did the maker make a valid tender of payment on the note?

Answer the question and state the principle of law governing this dispute.

The issue in this case is whether one can make a valid tender of payment by means other than money. This is strictly a question of the intention of the parties involved. If the payee wishes, the payee can accept an offer of any medium to pay the instrument, even another negotiable instrument. However, the law will not assume this is the case without clear evidence that such was also acceptable to the payee. The presumption, in the absence of evidence to the contrary, is that another negotiable instrument is merely more security for the note. Further, where a check is taken as payment, the exchange is presumed not to be complete unless and until the check clears.

23.12 A builder obtained a construction loan through a party named Hill. Hill demanded a mortgage on two lots as security for the two notes the builder signed as maker. Each note was for $5,000. After completion of the improvement on one lot, the builder sought release of the lot from the mortgage and note and sent the appropriate amount, $5,000 plus interest, to Hill. Sometime later, Hill sent back a release of the lot from the mortgage and surrendered the note the builder had signed. On the back of the note this language appeared: "Pay without recourse, (signed) Hill, proceeds to be placed to the credit of Chadwick, holder of the note." Later the builder sought the release of the second lot from the mortgage and sent the proper amount again to Hill. Hill cashed the check but never sent back a release or the note. Hill died and Chadwick, the holder of the mortgage and note, refused to deliver up the note or release the mortgage without being paid. Hill's estate has no assets, and Chadwick never received the proceeds of the $5,000 check Hill used. The builder argues that he has discharged the note by payment.

What position can Chadwick take in regard to this claim of discharge? Respond and give reasons for any conclusions.

When the maker of a note pays someone who does not own the note, such payment is no defense to the holder of the note. The maker has a duty to see that the money reaches the proper party, and the risk is on the maker to see that the note is delivered up. Chadwick's contention is valid and is sufficient to require that the builder pay the item again, this time to the party entitled to be paid, the holder of the instrument.

23.13 A church carried a checking account with a bank. Two signatures, those of Mayfair (the financial secretary) and Tynstall (the senior warden), were needed to draw funds. Mayfair forged Tynstall's signature on some 50 checks and used the money to gamble at a dog track. The church finally discovered the loss and demanded that its account be credited. These losses took place over a period of 9 months. The church offered that Mayfair had been a trusted official and beyond reproach for over 20 years and that on those occasions when inquiry was made to see the books, Mayfair managed to be vague. The bank had sent regular monthly statements and canceled checks to Mayfair as financial secretary, and this delayed discovery.

The church also offered that all the suspect checks were drawn to Mayfair personally and many bore the indorsement of the Happy Times Racing Company, a local dog racetrack.

What legal defenses can the bank marshal in refusing to recredit the church's account? Discuss the validity of these defenses under these circumstances.

The UCC provides a number of technical defenses to the bank in this case. The 14-day rule applicable to successive forgeries seems appropriate here. This rule is found in Section 4-406(2)(b), which deals with the customer's duty to use reasonable care and promptness in examining its statements and canceled checks. Most of the checks came within the 14-day rule, and this would effectively bar the church unless the bank's own duty to pay an item in good faith is questioned on these facts. Here, the bank is in a dangerous position. It knew that Mayfair was a fiduciary, and when he named himself as a payee and appeared to use the money personally, the bank was put on notice that the funds may have been misappropriated. Both those events occurred here. Any inquiry by the bank would have disclosed the true situation and prevented further depletion of the church's bank account. In the face of such facts, the bank was held liable.

Topic Test, Part IV

Commercial Paper

1. Faith, a general practitioner of law, disliked trying lawsuits but was a good negotiator. Faith settled an accident case for a client for $15,000, using her best judgment as authorized in her employment contract with Roberts, her client. It had been a good case, and Roberts believed that it could have resulted in a verdict in excess of $40,000. Roberts was angry with Faith and notified her that he would sign no releases despite the contract provisions, which granted Faith the right to so settle. Donald, the potential defendant, appeared at Faith's office and displayed a cashier's check made out to the "order of" Donald. Faith directed Donald to indorse the check as follows: "Pay to Faith, for Roberts, in full settlement of claim, (signed) Donald." Roberts refused to indorse the cashier's check or have anything to do with the settlement. Could Faith negotiate this check to a good-faith holder by signing just her name alone? What legal point is being raised in this case?

2. Harlow was presented with an exciting proposal to irrigate the neighboring valley by the use of an improved irrigation system developed by Wet Systems, Inc. The key to the success of the proposal was approval by the Lincoln County Board of Supervisors, as the irrigation system involved some operations that might be in violation of local laws. Harlow was asked to invest in Wet Systems pending this approval and put up a good-faith deposit in the form of a $5,000 promissory note payable to Wet Systems, Inc. On the front of the note Harlow typed "Deposit, pending Lincoln County Board of Supervisors' approval." Wet Systems indorsed and negotiated the note to its finance company as security for advances to pay for feasibility study costs. The board of supervisors did not amend the laws, and Wet Systems abandoned the project. The note became due, and Harlow denies liability on it. What issue or point of law must Harlow successfully raise in order to avoid liability against one claiming to be an HDC?

3. By written contract Arnold agreed to sell his ranch to Tucker for the sum of $165,000, with $20,000 cash down and the remainder to be paid by certified or cashier's check at the time of closing or settlement. Tucker was a well-known rancher who was used to doing business his way. At the closing he appeared with his personal check made out to the order of Arnold in the proper amount. Arnold threatened to break the deal right then and there unless Tucker provided him with a certified check. Tucker assured him that such caution was not needed and invited Arnold to telephone the drawee bank from whom he would hear that the check was good. Arnold telephoned the drawee bank and talked to the head cashier who, without hesitation, stated that "Tucker's check is always good, just bring it in." Assured, Arnold signed the deed and delivered possession of the ranch to Tucker, depositing the check in his account for collection. The check did not clear, and when Arnold tried to retake the ranch, he found that liens had been placed on it as this ranch deal had been what had held a number of Tucker's creditors at bay. Arnold is outraged and, having little to gain by suing Tucker, sues the drawee bank. What principle of law will give Arnold great difficulty?

4. Pat, a disgruntled office secretary, stole a $3,250 check payable to her employer, an insurance agency; the check had been received for an insurance premium. Over the years Pat had signed her employer's signature to letters, and so she was able to forge a blank indorsement quite

skillfully on the back of the check. She took the check to Selection Motors Acceptance Corporation in order to retrieve her automobile, which had recently been repossessed for back payments. The corporation saw the employer's signature and knew that Pat was a long-time employee there. It took the check in full payment of the outstanding balance and gave Pat the balance of $275. Pat took her car and left immediately for the West. The drawee bank ultimately paid the check, and it was several months before the employer found out about the forgery. The drawer demands that his account be recredited as he now must issue a new check to the insurance agency. What area of negotiable instrument law is involved in this dispute?

5. Terrance is in the business of cashing checks. Sometimes he buys paper whose history is questionable, but he nearly always finds an outlet in parties who are willing to take some risk for a large discount. Terrance had a funny feeling about a $1,200 check which appeared to have the signature of a well-known society figure. The named payee, however, was quite untrustworthy, a fact which allowed Terrance to buy it for $300. Able Finance is interested in the check and is willing to pay $650 for it. Terrance agrees, but states that he will not add his signature to that of the payee's blank indorsement, which appears on the instrument. Able Finance is now having trouble collecting, as a stop payment was issued on the check. Able Finance has heard that the check was given for a poker loss by the drawer. What is the legal position of Terrance in regard to any future liability on this check?

6. A truck farmer sells produce to local wholesalers on credit, drawing trade acceptances on them to the order of the farmer's bank where he gets all his financing. The truck farmer always places after his signature on the drawer line the words "without recourse." When the produce is delivered to the buyer, the named drawee, and the goods are found conforming, the buyer signs (i.e., accepts) the draft and returns it to the farmer, who delivers it to his bank for credit. What is the liability of the farmer should any of these acceptors fail to pay their drafts when due?

7. Professor Fabius was looking forward to a year's sabbatical in Paris at the Sorbonne. She put her affairs in order and asked Mark, her nephew, to forward really important mail. As a token of her appreciation, she issued a check to Mark's order in the sum of $700. Fabius opened a checking account in Paris, but left a balance of $3,000 in her account at the local bank to cover the $700 check. The balance would bear interest in the account. Mark cleverly altered the check so that it read $1,700 and successfully cashed it. When Fabius's checking account statement and canceled checks arrived on August 17, 19X2, Mark did not forward them to Fabius. Fabius arrived home from France on August 6, 19X3, and got around to looking at her bank statements and checks on August 17, 19X3. She then discovered the $1,000 alteration by Mark. She tried to reach Mark, but he had left home for parts unknown. Finally, on August 18, 19X3, Fabius mailed a certified letter to the local bank notifying them of the alteration of the check from $700 to $1,700. The local bank does not want to recredit Fabius's account with the $1,000. What legal point will the bank invoke?

8. Barbara and Nelson had an off-again on-again relationship. Nelson was generous to his friends to the detriment of his finances. If he couldn't loan a friend money, he would loan his name. He did this when his buddy Red bought a car from Barbara's roommate. Red put $2,000 down and executed a $2,500 note due 1 year from date. The roommate did not know Red, and so Nelson agreed to indorse the note on the back. The roommate, as payee, wanted to leave town 3 months before the note matured. Barbara said she would buy the note from her and did so. One month before the maturity of the note, Nelson and Barbara were once again breaking up and Barbara was dating a young entrepreneur, who agreed to buy the note. Nelson learned of this and reminded Barbara that he was an indorser on the note. Barbara told him in front of a witness that "I will do you one last favor; you are free from liability on that note." Nelson was delighted until the note matured and Red didn't pay. The same day that Nelson learned this,

the young entrepreneur telephoned Nelson and told him that he expected Nelson to pay the note. Nelson told him, "No way. Just check with Barbara about that." What legal point is Nelson proposing? Will it succeed?

9. Santan Corporation was the new boy in town. An aggressive and lively firm, it soon captured the hearts of the residents as it employed over 200 people and was growing steadily. The local bank felt the same way and would permit large overdrafts by Santan on a daily basis. One such overdraft was a $50,000 check, which was a down payment for a $350,000 computer system that didn't function properly and, further, the sale of which was riddled with fraud by the seller. This didn't help Santan, which soon went out of business. The $50,000 check to the seller cleared and now rests in the dusty files of the defunct corporation. The local bank is trying to come up with a legal theory it might employ against the seller, but since it is not the owner of the note, it can't qualify as having the rights of a holder in due course. What legal theory would give the local bank rights against the seller?

10. Smally has made a small fortune in the business of buying mortgage notes at discount. He feels that he should not restrict his purchases to that kind of paper only, but finds that there is little market for the less usual types of notes such as family loans and debt adjustments. Smally decided to let people know that he would be interested in any kind of commercial paper. Smally is approached by a local farmer who has for the past 10 years been selling off pieces of his acreage to small buyers making real estate speculations and has been taking back purchase money notes and mortgages. The farmer has about a dozen of these instruments, which he is willing to sell to Smally "if we can get together on the price." What legal point must Smally concern himself with in respect to this proposed transaction?

Answers

1. The issue in this case is whether an instrument containing a restrictive indorsement naming the indorsee as holding for the benefit of another can be further negotiated or can be properly paid by the party expected to pay the instrument. This indorsement does establish a fiduciary situation but by itself gives no notice that the fiduciary is violating her duty under the instrument. A party who pays or who buys this note in ignorance that the indorsee may be violating her duty would suffer no liability. In this case it does not even appear that Faith is violating her duty, although she does have a dispute with her client.

2. Harlow would want to show that the instrument is nonnegotiable. He would contend that the language he placed on the front suggests that the promise to pay was conditional, thus making his engagement subject to approval by the county board of supervisors. Unfortunately for Harlow, the court will not imply a condition since negotiability is favored. Harlow would be liable to an HDC because the note is negotiable on its face.

3. Arnold is faced with the operation of one of the most basic rules of commercial paper: no one is liable on an instrument unless his or her signature appears thereon. The drawee bank made an oral, not a signed, acceptance. Only the latter is valid. Arnold has no relief from the drawee bank on this instrument alone.

4. This is a classic forged indorsement situation. Initially, the drawee bank suffers the loss since it did not obey the instructions of the drawer. The bank paid out to one who, when presenting the check, warranted she had good title. Selection Motors Acceptance Corporation did not have good title because one cannot take title through a forged indorsement. The drawee bank must recredit the account of the drawer and retrieve its money from Selection Motors Acceptance Corporation.

5. Terrance made no indorsement contract since he agreed not to sign. He has, however, made a warranty undertaking to his immediate transferee only. He warranted that there is no defense good against him, UCC, Section 3-417(2)(d). The defense raised is interesting, as it could be real rather than personal. If the

state law provides that notes or checks given in payment of gambling debts are a nullity or void, then Terrance has breached his warranty. On the other hand, if illegality here is merely personal and Terrance can qualify as an HDC, the defense would not be good against him. In that case he would not have breached his warranty.

6. Drawers can sign "without recourse," and trade acceptances are appropriate places so to do. The truck farmer is saying that he does not engage that the buyers who accept these drafts will have the funds to pay them at maturity. As long as only an indorsement contract is involved, the truck farmer has no liability on the instruments should they not be paid.

7. Professor Fabius's timing is unfortunate. More than 1 year has passed since the altered check and statement were made available to her. Since this is a forged drawer's signature, the rule regarding 1 year, rather than 3 years (for forged indorsements), applies. Unfortunately, Fabius allowed the potential forger to have control over the means of checking for errors. Fabius's delay in notifying the bank puts the loss squarely on her shoulders.

8. Nelson does not fully understand the doctrine of "discharge by renunciation." This can only be done in writing, and even then it must be known by subsequent parties. If the new boyfriend did not know of any discharge before his taking the instrument, he may enforce it as it appears, i.e., with Nelson as an indorser.

9. While the local bank cannot qualify as a holder in due course because it does not have right of possession to the canceled check, the local bank may invoke the doctrine of subrogation in attempting to extricate itself from this situation. The bank may, literally, take the drawer's position, that is, of a contractor having an action against one who has breached the contract. The bank may attempt to recover its loss from the seller, the computer company.

10. Smally has a matter he should consider before he purchases these notes from the farmer. Smally could be a holder in respect to value, maturity, good faith, etc., and yet not be a holder in due course. This is so because certain purchasers of negotiable instruments cannot, by statute, qualify as a holder in due course. Bulk sales of commercial paper, not in the ordinary course of business of the transferor, cannot be taken by the transferee as a holder in due course. Smally may wish to make sure there are no defenses of any kind involved before buying these notes in bulk.

Chapter 24

Terminology and Formation

24.1 INTRODUCTION

If creditors always believed that debtors would have both the money and the willingness to pay their obligations, there would be no need for secured transactions. Many creditors, however, require that something of value be "put up for ransom," so to speak, thus permitting the creditor a special interest in some of the debtor's property. When the debtor gives the creditor this special interest, the debtor grants a *security interest* under Article 9 of the UCC.

Not all attempts to create a security interest come within the provisions of Article 9. Among the excluded transactions are those subject to a U.S. statute, a landlord's lien, some mechanic liens, transfers to governmental agencies, certain sales of accounts receivable or chattel paper (i.e., isolated sales), insurance claims (but not proceeds), judgments, and tort claims, UCC, Section 9-104.

The UCC treats these types of agreements—formerly termed (and still commonly called) chattel mortgages, trust receipts, conditional sales contracts, and even consignments—as *security agreements* under Article 9. A bona fide lease of goods is not within Article 9, but a security agreement disguised as a lease would be.

Accordingly, a lease-purchase agreement could be ruled a security agreement where, for example, the total rents combined with the option price equal approximately the market price of the collateral being "leased." In such a situation, the failure of the lessor to perfect his or her interest could be fatal to a claim to superior rights in respect to the leased property.

24.2 BASIC TERMINOLOGY

Secured Party. A secured party is the creditor, lender, or other person in whose favor a security interest is given. The buyer of accounts receivable or chattel paper is also a secured party.

Debtor. The party who owes the debt or obligation that is secured is the debtor, whether he or she owns or has rights in the collateral. The term includes the seller of accounts receivable, contract rights, and chattel paper.

Security Interest. A security interest is an interest in personal property or fixtures requiring payment or performance of an obligation. It can be created only by attachment.

Security Agreement. This is the arrangement, bargain, or agreement made by which the debtor gives to the secured party an interest in personal property as security for the debtor's payment or performance. Generally this is written, but in some instances it can be oral.

Collateral. Collateral is the "put up for ransom" property. It is personal property which is the subject of the security interest, and it includes accounts receivable and chattel paper which have been sold.

Perfection. This is a process by which the creditor, the secured party, gives legal notice to others that he or she has an interest in the collateral. The creditor does this by (1) possessing the collateral, or (2) filing a financing statement, or (3) attaching consumer goods.

Attachment. A combination of three events must occur before a security interest is created: a security agreement must be made, value must be given by the secured party, and the debtor must have some rights in the collateral. These three events constitute attachment.

Financing Statement. This kind of statement is an instrument signed by the debtor which must be filed by the secured party in the appropriate state office in order to give notice to others. It is the most common of the three methods of perfection.

EXAMPLE 1. A farmer needs cash to plant her wheat crop. The bank will loan the farmer $5,000 but demands that the farmer give the bank a lien on the crop. The farmer (debtor) signs a statement giving such a lien on the crop (collateral) to the bank (secured party) which paid the $5,000 (value). The farmer also signed a statement showing her name and address and the crop, together with the bank's name and address (financing statement). The bank took the financing statement and filed it (perfection) in the local county clerk's office.

EXAMPLE 2. When the farmer in Example 1 signed the security agreement, the bank gave the $5,000, and the farmer owned the crop, an attachment occurred which created the security interest in the crop (the collateral).

Floating Lien. The term "floating lien" in secured transactions refers to the options exercised by the secured party in dealing with the future. A security agreement that provides coverage of (1) proceeds, (2) after-acquired property, and (3) future advances utilizes all three techniques by which a floating lien exists.

24.3 CREATION OF SECURITY INTEREST

The secured party's interest in the debtor's collateral becomes initially effective when three events occur. They may happen in any order. When the last event occurs, attachment has taken place and a security interest in the collateral exists. The events are:

(1) The debtor must enter into a signed security agreement giving the secured party the lien unless the lien is created by the debtor giving possession of the collateral to the secured party. The secured party need not sign the document.

(2) The secured party must give *value*. Loaning money is value, as is any consideration. Further, value can be a preexisting debt or a binding commitment to extend credit.

(3) The debtor must have a present or future interest in the collateral.

EXAMPLE 3. A furniture store sold a sofa to Palmer on credit for $900, demanding the sofa and Palmer's other furniture as security for the payment of the purchase price. Palmer signed a financing statement which described all the furniture. This document was filed at the appropriate state office. Inadvertently, the store forgot to obtain a signed security agreement from Palmer. Upon default on the seventh monthly payment, the store attempted to repossess all the furniture listed in the financing statement. Palmer's other creditors objected. There is no security interest here as there is no attachment. No security agreement was entered into.

On the other hand, pledge agreements are valid security agreements, despite the fact that they may not be evidenced by a writing signed by the debtor. This form of security agreement is an exception to the rule that oral security agreements are not valid. A *pledge* is a transfer of possession of collateral to a creditor for the purpose of creating a security agreement.

24.4 LEGAL NOTICE OF SECURITY INTEREST

If someone other than the owner of the property also has rights in it, an innocent third party who might deal with the owner should have notice that the property is somehow encumbered. In a secured transaction this notice is accomplished by *perfection*. The UCC offers three methods of perfection: by possession, by filing a financing statement, and, in regard to sale on credit of consumer goods, by attachment.

24.5 PERFECTION BY POSSESSION

Possession may not really be nine parts of the law, but it does place others on (legal) notice to inquire why another possesses the property. The UCC agrees with this principle by providing that physical possession of the collateral by the secured party is a form of perfection.

EXAMPLE 4. Toledo is negotiating a tight corporate maneuver. She needs ready cash. She has several very valuable paintings in her family. She borrows $300,000 from Star Capital, which takes possession of two of the paintings as collateral for the loan. This security agreement, here a pledge, is oral. The taking of possession is the perfection of the security interest and notice to the world, other creditors, etc., that Star has some interest in the two paintings.

Under the practice called *field warehousing*, the location of the collateral may even be at the debtor's premises.

EXAMPLE 5. Tobuk Chemicals sells chemicals on credit to Ruff Cleansers under a security agreement which requires Ruff to lease to Tobuk 400 square feet in the corner of Ruff's warehouse for chemicals delivered by Tobuk to Ruff for use in manufacture. The area is fenced, and the gate key is in the possession of Tobuk, which from time to time surrenders it to Ruff to take materials out for use. This arrangement is field warehousing. If Tobuk indeed maintains control, then Tobuk is in possession of the chemicals so stored. Therefore, it has perfected its security interest by possession, although the goods are in the debtor's warehouse.

Some collateral can only be effectively perfected by possession. Such collateral particularly includes instruments and documents that are negotiable, but possession may also be considered necessary by a secured party for any item, including jewelry, art objects, etc., which may not be negotiable but may be all too salable, especially by an irresponsible debtor who needs funds.

EXAMPLE 6. Toro Sales accepted a postdated $2,000 check, a negotiable instrument, from a trucker for a trailer air-brake assembly. Toro needed cash to meet that month's payroll. To induce the bank to lend it $5,000, Toro gave the bank a written security agreement on all its current assets, including the $2,000 check. A financing statement describing this collateral was also signed by Toro and appropriately filed. Toro was still short of money and indorsed and delivered the $2,000 check to a holder in due course. Things have gone badly for Toro, and the bank now wants to repossess Toro's current assets, but finds the $2,000 check gone. The bank contends that it perfected its security interest by filing a financing statement. This perfection is not good against a party who took the negotiable instrument in good faith. Possession is the only effective way by which to perfect negotiable instruments.

Not all collateral can be perfected by possession. Accounts receivable and general intangibles, for example, can only be perfected by filing a financing statement. Perfection by possession attaches as of the date of possession and continues as long as such possession is retained.

24.6 PERFECTION BY FILING A FINANCING STATEMENT

The most popular way to give others notice of a security interest in most types of collateral is by filing a financing statement at the appropriate state office. This is called *perfection by filing*. Section 9-402 of the UCC requires only limited information to be included in this document. It need have only the names and addresses of the debtor and the secured party, a description of the type of collateral covered, and the signature of the debtor. More detail may be included, of course, including language sufficient to qualify it as a security agreement. This is not usually done, however, as a short form called *notice filing* is used. Where crops, minerals, growing timber, and fixtures are the described collateral, the legal description of where such items are located must also be included in the financing statement.

EXAMPLE 7. Adams Type needs more capital. Term Capital agrees to lend $100,000 provided Adams executes a security agreement encumbering all its "inventory and equipment." Adams also signs a short piece of paper containing the names and addresses of Adams and Term, listing "all the inventory and equipment of Adams Type Co." This paper is taken by Term and filed in the public record of the state. Such filing is perfection of a security interest by filing.

Many states have two filing locations. One location is a central file for certain types of collateral, and the other is a local place, normally a county clerk's office. Each state has its own rules about place of filing for different types of collateral. Generally, crops, fixtures, consumer goods, farm products, and farm equipment are perfected by filing at the local office. Equipment, inventory, accounts, documents of title, and the like are classes of collateral requiring a central filing, normally the state's office of the secretary of state.

EXAMPLE 8. A hair stylist purchased a stereo system on credit, signing a security agreement and financing statement describing and encumbering the stereo. If the hair stylist purchased the stereo system for her place of business, it qualifies as equipment and must be filed in the state central office. On the other hand, if the stereo system was purchased for home use, it is considered as consumer goods, and the filing would be done at the local office, generally the county clerk's office.

24.7   PERFECTION BY ATTACHMENT

In order for a security interest to exist in the collateral, there must be an attachment. Such attachment is also a means of perfection for most sellers of consumer goods on credit. (Motor vehicles are excepted.) This type of security interest broadly validates the lien of department store sales on credit when the store retains a purchase money security interest in the item sold. This purchase money security interest occurs where the proceeds of the loan are used to purchase the collateral. The store may obtain a signed security agreement and financing statement but fail to file the latter. This perfection by attachment only applies to purchase money security interest in consumer goods, but it is effective only against other creditors and purchasers who had knowledge of the security agreement.

EXAMPLE 9. Mr. and Mrs. Borden contract to purchase an $850 refrigerator, paying $100 down and financing the rest from the store. They sign a security interest and financing statement. The store does not file the financing statement. A purchase money security interest is created, and all three events of attachment occur: security agreement, value given, and ownership of collateral. If Mr. Borden goes into bankruptcy and the trustee tries to seize these goods, the trustee will fail because the store has first priority by reason of its perfection by attachment.

Perfection by attachment takes effect at the happening of all three events. It creates priority in the party owning the purchase money security interest against all creditors, but not against a good-faith purchaser from the debtor who bought without notice of this security interest.

EXAMPLE 10. Mr. and Mrs. Borden made payments of $400 on the refrigerator subject to a purchase money security interest with the store. The Bordens moved out of the state and quickly sold their home and certain furniture, including the refrigerator, to Tanser, who purchased all in good faith for value. The store was not paid the $350 balance due on the refrigerator. The store attempts to repossess the refrigerator from Tanser. The store will not succeed. A perfection by attachment of consumer goods is effective only against creditors, not against purchasers in good faith. Had the store filed a financing statement, its security interest would have been good even against a good-faith purchaser.

Black Letter Law
A Summary

1. A secured transaction occurs when a creditor (secured party) establishes an interest in a debtor's property to secure performance of an obligation.

2. A security agreement is the debtor's grant of an interest in the property (collateral) to the secured party which is in a signed writing by the debtor except where the collateral is delivered to the secured party.

3. A security interest in collateral becomes effective only when attachment occurs.

4. Attachment is the happening of three events: a security agreement was made, the creditor gave value, and the debtor has rights in the collateral.

5. Perfection of the security interest is necessary for the secured party to have any superior rights over other creditors and purchasers.

6. Perfection is the giving of legal notice to the world that the secured party *may* have rights in the debtor's collateral.

7. Perfection is achieved in three ways: by possession of the collateral by the secured party, by attachment, and by the filing of a financing statement.

8. Possession of the collateral by the secured party notifies the world that such party has an interest in it; certain collateral such as negotiable documents or instruments can be effectively perfected only by possession.

9. Perfection by attachment is limited to consumer goods as collateral and is created by purchase money interest in such goods.

10. Perfection by filing a financing statement is done at the local or central state filing office and is the usual way of perfecting security interests.

11. A financing statement is a writing that need only contain the names and addresses of the secured party and debtor, the debtor's signature, and a general description of the collateral.

12. A security agreement can qualify as a financing statement provided it contains the essential statements and signature(s) required in financing statement.

Solved Problems

24.1 Which of the following is included within the scope of the Secured Transactions Article of the UCC?

(*a*) The outright sale of accounts receivable

(*b*) A landlord's lien

(*c*) The assignment of a claim for wages

(*d*) The sale of chattel paper as a part of the sale of a business out of which it arose

(*Adapted from AICPA Examination, November 1980*)

Article 9 of the UCC includes more than just a section governing security interests in personal property, as it does regulate the outright sale of accounts receivable, statement (*a*). Isolated sales of such as part of the sale of a business out of which they arose, or in settlement of preexisting indebtedness, are excluded from the article. Neither the landlord's lien nor wage assignments are covered, UCC, Section 9-104.

24.2 Which of the following requirements is *not* necessary in order to have a security interest attach?

(*a*) The debtor must have rights in the collateral.

(*b*) There must be a proper filing.

(*c*) Value must be given by the creditor.

(*d*) Either the creditor must take possession or the debtor must sign a security agreement which describes the collateral.

(*AICPA Examination, November 1981*)

Attachment must occur before there is a security interest. The three events regarding such are indicated in statements (*a*), (*c*), and (*d*). Accordingly, it is not necessary that there be a filing for attachment, that is, a means of perfection; thus statement (*b*) is the answer.

24.3 Futuristic Appliances, Inc., sells various brand-name appliances at discount prices. Futuristic maintains a large inventory, which it obtains from various manufacturers on credit. These manufacturer-creditors have all filed and taken secured interests in the appliances and proceeds therefrom which they have sold to Futuristic on credit. Futuristic in turn sells to hundreds of ultimate consumers; some pay cash, but most buy on credit. Futuristic takes a security interest but does not file a financing statement for credit sales. Which of the following is correct?

(*a*) The appliance manufacturers can enforce their secured interests against the appliances in the hands of the purchasers who paid cash for them.

(*b*) A subsequent sale by one of Futuristic's customers to a bona fide purchaser will be subject to Futuristic's secured interest.

(*c*) The appliances in Futuristic's hands are consumer goods.

(*d*) Since Futuristic takes a purchase money security interest in the consumer goods sold, its security interest is perfected upon attachment.

(*AICPA Examination, November 1981*)

Although there are three methods of perfecting a security interest, only an interest in consumer goods can be perfected by attachment; statement (*d*) is correct. It appears that Futuristic executed a security agreement, that Futuristic paid value (it transferred the appliance), and that the debtor has rights in the appliance he or she now owns, and thus attachment is accomplished. In regard to a manufacturer, its goods in Futuristic's hands are inventory (not consumer goods at that point), and such a manufacturer loses its security interest when the retailer sells the appliances in the ordinary course of business. Futuristic's lien is not good against purchasers from Futuristic's customers since a perfection by attachment is not effective against them.

24.4 Weatherall seeks to create a valid perfected security interest in goods under the provisions of the Uniform Commercial Code. Which of the following acts or actions will establish this?

(*a*) Weatherall obtains a written agreement under which Weatherall takes possession of the security.

(*b*) Weatherall obtains an unsigned written security agreement.

(*c*) Weatherall obtains a security agreement signed only by the debtor.

(*d*) Weatherall files a financing statement which is *not* in itself a security agreement.

(*AICPA Examination, November 1977*)

Perfection can be accomplished in one of three ways depending on the nature of the collateral. Statement (*a*) cites one of the ways: taking possession of the collateral. By itself a security agreement does not qualify as a financing statement, and so statements (*b*) and (*c*) are wrong. Filing a financing statement when one has no security interest in the collateral does not result in perfection; hence statement (*d*) is also incorrect.

24.5 Maxim Corporation, a wholesaler, was indebted to the Wilson Manufacturing Corporation in the amount of $50,000 arising out of the sale of goods delivered to Maxim on credit. Wilson and Maxim signed a security agreement creating a security interest in certain collateral of Maxim. The collateral was described in the security agreement as "inventory of Maxim Corporation, presently existing and thereafter acquired." In general, this description of the collateral

(*a*) applies only to inventory sold by Wilson to Maxim.

(*b*) is sufficient to cover all inventory.

(*c*) is insufficient because it attempts to cover after-acquired inventory.

(*d*) must be more specific for the security interest to be perfected against subsequent creditors.

(*AICPA Examination, November 1975*)

Any description of personal property or real estate is sufficient whether or not it is specific if it reasonably identifies what is described; statement (*b*) is correct. This language is simple, but clear, and apprises other parties as to what property is subject to the security interest. Accordingly, the lack of more detail is not relevant.

24.6 Andrew asked Judy about the possibility of borrowing $10,000. Judy replied that she would be happy to make the loan if Andrew would provide collateral to secure payment. Andrew gave Judy his promissory note for $10,000, bearing interest at 7 percent, and delivered to Judy convertible bearer bonds with coupons attached. The bonds had a current market value of $12,000. During the period in which the loan was outstanding the bonds increased in market value to $18,000. In addition, one of the interest coupons became due. There is no express agreement between the parties about their respective rights in the interest or profits. Under the circumstances, which of the following is correct?

(*a*) Judy owns the coupon representing matured interest due.

(*b*) Judy may elect to sell the bonds and retain the proceeds in excess of $12,000.

(*c*) If Judy sold the bonds to an innocent third party, the third party would obtain a valid title.

(*d*) Such a financing arrangement must be filed in the appropriate recordation office in order to be valid.

(*AICPA Examination, November 1977*)

Instruments can be the subject of a security interest, but their negotiable character must be taken into consideration. Perfection by filing would impede the rule of negotiation that the instruments be freely transferrable; statement (*c*) is the answer. Accordingly, the only way to perfect negotiable instruments such as those involved here is for the secured party to take possession of them. The fact is that convertible bearer bonds effectively allow either the debtor or the secured creditor to misbehave, depending on who has possession. Had the secured party perfected only by filing a financing statement, the debtor would still have the power to transfer these bonds to a good-faith purchaser. On the other hand, the secured party, Judy, could wrongly do the very same thing.

24.7 Johnson loaned money to Visual, Inc., a struggling growth company, and sought to obtain a security interest in negotiable stock certificates which are traded on a local exchange. To perfect his interest against Visual's other creditors, Johnson

(*a*) need do nothing further in that his security interest was perfected upon attachment.

(*b*) may file or take possession of the stock certificates.

(*c*) must take possession of the stock certificates.

(*d*) must file and give the other creditors notice of his contemplated security interest.

(*AICPA Examination, May 1979*)

The answer is (*c*). Instruments and documents that are negotiable must be perfected by possession in order to gain for the secured party the maximum protection of the security interest. Attachment as a means of perfection applies only to consumer goods in purchase money transactions. Filing would not be completely effective in this case. Notice to other creditors is not required in this instance.

24.8 Field warehousing is a well-established means of securing a loan. As such, it resembles a pledge in many legal respects. Which of the following is correct?

(*a*) The field warehouser must maintain physical control of and dominion over the property.

(*b*) A filing is required in order to perfect such a financing arrangement.

(*c*) Temporary relinquishment of control for any purpose will suspend the validity of the arrangement insofar as other creditors are concerned.

(*d*) The property in question must be physically moved to a new location although it may be a part of the borrower's facilities.

(*AICPA Examination, November 1977*)

The field warehouse technique is one way in which the debtor can gain quick access to goods it owns but has pledged to another by transferring possession to the secured party; statement (*a*) is the answer. The warehouse can be in a building owned by the debtor, but the space must be physically separated and debtor access restricted in compliance with prescribed conditions. Temporary relinquishment is permitted. It need not be in a new location, but it must be in a separate location with sufficient technical barriers to the debtor's access.

24.9 On June 10, Central Corporation sold goods to Bowie Corporation for $5,000. Bowie signed a financing statement containing the names and addresses of the parties and describing the collateral. Central filed the financing statement on June 21, noting the same in its accounting books.

(*a*) Central need *not* sign the financing statement to perfect its security interest.

(*b*) Central must file the financing statement before the sale if a security interest is to be perfected.

(*c*) Central must sign the financing statement in order to perfect its security interest.

(*d*) Central had a perfected security interest in the collateral even before the financing statement was filed.

(*Adapted from AICPA Examination, November 1975*)

The financing statement need be signed *only* by the debtor, and so answer (*a*) is correct. The financing statement need not be filed before the sale. Such filing would be required if it was a purchase money security interest and the secured party wished to preserve his or her interest in the face of prior perfected parties having a security interest in "after-acquired property."

24.10 Marcus purchased a Zomar 21-inch color television set from Hart Appliance, Inc. Marcus made a down payment of $100 and signed a negotiable promissory note and a security agreement. Hart Appliance did not file a financing statement covering the sale to Marcus. Under these circumstances,

(*a*) Hart's failure to file the financing statement will allow subsequent creditors of Marcus to defeat Hart's security interest in the television set.

(*b*) the sale of the television set by Marcus to a neighbor without disclosure of Hart's security interest in the set will result in the security interest being valid against the neighbor.

(*c*) in order to perfect its security interest against any parties who subsequently assert rights against the television set, Hart must file the financing statement.

(*d*) the transaction would be treated as the sale of a consumer good, subject to a purchase money security interest in Hart.

(*Adapted from AICPA Examination, November 1973*)

This is a typical purchase money security agreement involving a consumer good, statement (*d*). Perfection by attachment, therefore, gives the secured party, Hart, a limited perfection against all other creditors, including future trustees in bankruptcy. This perfection would, however, be ineffective against a bona fide purchaser from the debtor having no knowledge of the security interest of Hart.

24.11 Rapide Industries owned a $15,000 account against Trainor Sylan. Rapide was having financial trouble in paying its major lender, Aries Factors. Under strong urging by Aries, Rapide signed a financing statement naming Aries as the secured party, covering the Trainor account receivable. Aries filed the financing statement in the office of the secretary of state. Four months later Rapide was placed in bankruptcy and the Trainor account had by then matured. Trainor is willing to pay but is being pressed to pay by both the trustee in bankruptcy and Aries Factors. Aries claims that its interest is superior to a general creditor since it is a secured party. The trustee demands that Aries provide proof that it has a security interest. The only paper Aries can offer the court is the signed financing statement.

Is Aries a secured party and therefore superior to the interest of the trustee in bankruptcy? State your decision and reasons for any conclusions you reach.

In order to have a security interest one must prove that attachment has taken place. Perfecting an interest one does not have is inadequate. Since there is no evidence of a security agreement, Aries will fail. A financing statement usually does not contain the necessary language creating a security interest. Oral agreements are effective only where possession of the collateral is possible and is in fact accomplished. One cannot possess an account receivable under the meaning of Article 9 of the UCC. Accordingly, Aries will lose and be merely a general creditor which the trustee in bankruptcy represents.

24.12 Superior Restaurant Supply delivered restaurant equipment and supplies to Blue Nose Cafe under the terms of a lengthy security agreement which was signed by the Blue Nose Cafe. A financing statement was also signed and duly filed. The security agreement recited that the interest encumbered was "food service equipment and supplies delivered to Blue Nose Cafe, St Mary's, Pennsylvania." Blue Nose later needed additional financing and entered into a contract with Force Bank whose security agreement recited "all its equipment located at the Blue Nose Cafe." Force Bank perfected by filing, but neither the bank nor Superior knew or bothered to know that there had been a previous filing. Upon default by Blue Nose Cafe both parties are claiming a first lien. Superior contends that the first to perfect by filing has the greater rights. Force Bank replies that in order to have a security interest one must sufficiently describe the collateral.

Who has the higher interest, Superior or Force Bank? State your reasons for any conclusions reached.

The first to file wins where there is a struggle between two who filed. However, the first to file must have a security interest. Force Bank is correct here as it found a fatal flaw in Superior's security agreement. The collateral need not be extensively described, but it must be *adequately* described. "Supplies delivered to" the debtor is not a sufficient description allowing a charge on the collateral. If the secured party is going to select only certain collateral from all the possible collateral, a more definite description must be made. Force wins.

24.13 Fairwell Corporation purchased a new computer system. The price was quite good, but no trade-in was allowed. One of Fairwell's customers, Credite Com, was interested in Fairwell's old computer system but just wanted to rent it. Fairwell calculated that the system was worth about $6,000. Since Credite Com didn't want to buy it, just to lease it, while Fairwell wanted to get its money out of it, Fairwell offered to enter into a lease for 12 months at $500 a month. Further, to make it attractive it would give Credite Com an option to purchase the system at the end of the year for an additional payment of $500. Credite Com liked the idea, and a form lease was obtained, the terms set forth and signed by both parties. Credite Com made three payments on the equipment and then went insolvent. Fairwell wants its property back but finds resistance by the creditors of Credite Com. What legal problem does Fairwell face in attempting to retrieve its leased property?

Answer the question asked and state reasons for any conclusions reached.

The parties may not have intended to create a security interest, but the nature of the terms suggests that the lessor treated it as such. The total rent of the lease was practically the equivalent of the purchase price. This by itself would not make the lease a security agreement. However, the option that was granted the lessee at a price that was only one monthly payment suggests that this was indeed a disguised sale. If Fairwell did not perfect its interest by filing a financing statement, it will stand as a fellow creditor among equals, not as a landlord or secured party, in respect to retrieving the collateral.

Chapter 25

Priorities and Remedies

25.1 SECURITY INTERESTS AND THIRD PARTIES: GENERALLY

The reason for creation of a security interest is to obtain rights in the debtor's property superior to other third parties. The doctrine of perfection assists in establishing this priority. If there is no third party involved, the secured party has rights in the collateral by the contract alone and without regard to the status of perfection. *Third parties* are other creditors, purchasers from the debtor, other security interest holders, receivers, and even trustees in bankruptcy proceedings.

The rules of priority are measured by the time the secured party perfected or attached, but there are exceptions. The trustee in bankruptcy, having the status of a lien creditor, can, for example, set aside certain security interests whose creation conflicts with bankruptcy law. A trustee in bankruptcy has, of course, priority over all unperfected security interests as of the date of bankruptcy and can also set aside a security interest that was obtained within 90 days of the filing of the bankruptcy petition if the secured party was given a voidable preference.

EXAMPLE 1. Dartner was in financial trouble. Her most aggressive supplier was Affel Corp. Affel was pressing Dartner for immediate payment of a 60-day invoice. To push off this pesky creditor, Dartner gave Affel a security agreement and signed a financing statement covering all Dartner's inventory. One month later other creditors forced Dartner into federal bankruptcy court. The trustee in bankruptcy can avoid Affel's security interest as a voidable preference, it having been given for no new value or consideration within 90 days of the date of filing of the bankruptcy petition.

25.2 COLLATERAL AND PRIORITIES

Rights among competing third parties are determined by consideration of several factors. While the manner and time of perfection are important, the type of collateral and even the place of filing a financing statement may also determine certain priority rights. In a number of situations, the characterization of the collateral is of utmost importance. It is always wise to examine the debtor's relationship with the collateral, that is, what it is *to the debtor*, as this may affect a prospective secured party.

EXAMPLE 2. A state has a dual system for filing financing statements. Farm products, for example, are filed locally, while interests in inventory are filed at the office of the secretary of state. Tyler Bank is considering lending money to "Farmer" Brown and taking as collateral a security interest in all the milk he owns, now or hereafter. The fact is that Brown has been out of the active dairy farming business for years and doesn't own even one cow. What he does is deal with many farmers as a broker, buying milk in bulk for his own account. If Tyler Bank should file a financing statement locally, it must show that this wrong filing was made in good faith or else the bank did *not* perfect its security interest since in the hands of "Broker" Brown the milk is not farm products, but rather is inventory requiring filing at the state capital, UCC, Section 9-401(3).

Generally, unless the collateral is the subject of a purchase money interest or crops, conflicting security interests and rights are ranked according to priority in filing, or perfecting, whichever is the earlier, UCC, Section 9-312. Also, the first to file usually has priority if both security interests are perfected by filing. Otherwise, priority is given to the first to perfect.

25.3 COLLATERAL: INVENTORY

The most common method of perfecting a security interest in inventory is by filing a financing statement in the state's central office. Inventory includes raw material as well as the finished products of a manufacturer and goods held for sale by a wholesaler or retailer. The products of farms are not inventory, but rather are treated under the special classification of farm products. Perfection by filing a financing statement on inventory is not a "perfect perfection," however, as inventory is expected to be sold in the ordinary course of business. Such sales release such inventory from any perfected security interest. This is so even if the buyer knew of the security interest in the goods bought.

EXAMPLE 3. On March 1, Lakefront Knitting Mill gave a security interest in "all its inventory" to Marvell Bank & Trust Company, which filed a financing statement on March 31. Lakefront Mill needed money badly and on March 25 borrowed from Brookings, which filed its financing statement on the same inventory on March 25. Needing still more money, Lakefront held a sale of its blankets to its regular customers and, having decided to get out of the sheet business, sold its entire inventory of sheets to a competitor. The blanket purchasers take free of any security interest. The competitor is subject to two security interests, as it did not purchase in the ordinary course of business in the face of two perfected security interests, those of Marvell Bank and Brookings.

25.4 COLLATERAL: CONSUMER GOODS

Goods are considered consumer goods if they are used or bought for use primarily for personal, family, or household purposes, UCC, Section 9-109(1). Perfection can be by possession, by filing of a financing statement, or by attachment if it is a purchase money security interest. As noted earlier, perfection by attachment restricts its protection to that against creditors and other secured parties, but not against good-faith purchasers.

25.5 COLLATERAL: EQUIPMENT

Goods that are used or bought for use primarily to enable a firm to carry on its business activities are considered equipment. This classification obviously embraces an extraordinarily wide variety of items, ranging from machine tools to milking machines. However, it specifically excludes goods which are physically attached to real property, such as air conditioners and lighting fixtures (see Section 25.9).

25.6 COLLATERAL: FARM PRODUCTS

Goods in the possession of a party engaged in farming operations, such as crops, livestock, or supplies, and including the products of farming operations, such as milk, eggs, and cotton, are classified as farm products, not inventory.

25.7 COLLATERAL: CHATTEL PAPER, INSTRUMENTS, AND DOCUMENTS OF TITLE

Chattel paper is a writing or writings reflecting both a monetary obligation and a security interest in or lease of specific goods.

EXAMPLE 4. Leonard's mother-in-law loaned him $100,000 to establish a computer sales store. He is a good salesperson but learns early that he must sell to some of his customers on credit. Leonard decides to provide financing by taking back an installment contract and security agreement on the computers sold to his retail customers. Leonard has run out of money to purchase new inventory and seeks a bank loan. The bank insists on Leonard signing a loan agreement and a security agreement naming all the security agreements and installment contracts he has with his customers. The bank files a financing statement on this collateral, the chattel paper.

A secured party who perfects a security agreement on chattel paper by filing a financing statement rather than taking possession runs the risk that a subsequent secured party who pays new consideration for such chattel paper without knowledge of the previous security interest (here, perfection by filing) has a superior priority.

An *instrument* means a negotiable document or a security, or other writing, evidencing the right to payment of money. Documents of title include bills of lading, dock warrants, and dock receipts or warehouse receipts. These documents may be valuable in themselves and are capable of effective transfer without notice to others. Filing a financing statement on instruments or documents of title is of limited protection. Only possession gives maximum protection.

EXAMPLE 5. A tool company sells expensive equipment. It makes a practice of selling on the basis of 12 monthly installments and requires the buyer to draw 12 postdated checks at the time of purchase. The tool company needs cash, and Risk Bank will lend upon security of those checks as collateral. Risk Bank perfects by filing a signed financing statement covering these checks. This perfection is effective against all who know of this interest and creditors generally. However, if the tool company should negotiate any of these checks to a holder in due course, the holder takes free of the security interest.

If the document or instrument is nonnegotiable, or if no document has been issued, a security interest in the goods can be perfected in a number of ways. The document can be issued in the name of the secured party, the bailee can be notified of the interest of the secured party, or a financing statement on the goods themselves can be filed, UCC, Section 9-304.

EXAMPLE 6. Altamus runs a private warehouse for the storage of pianos. Temple stored her piano there under a vague agreement with no supporting documentation. Temple wishes to give a security agreement in the piano to Marer. Marer could obtain a signed financing statement for filing, or have Altamus notified by Temple of Marer's security interest, or Altamus could create a document naming Marer. Since no document exists, a change in name (from Temple to Marer) would not be possible.

The more common method of perfection of negotiable documents is by possession in the secured party. However, this possession may prevent a debtor from exercising certain powers over the goods. The document can be surrendered by the secured party to the debtor for a period of 21 days without release of the security interest. Such temporary possession of the document may be necessary for the purposes of handling, loading, shipping, transporting, or otherwise dealing with the goods before sale or exchange, UCC, Section 9-304(5). This protection does not preclude the risk that the debtor may make an unauthorized negotiation to a holder in due course or sale to a bona fide purchaser.

EXAMPLE 7. A bank finances Avery's import purchase of straw bags from Jamaica, paying for the negotiable airbill which is made out in the name of the bank (perfection obtained by being named in the document *and* also possessing it). Avery needs possession of the bags for individual packaging and transshipment. The bank indorses and delivers the airbill to Avery for 14 days. The collateral, the negotiable airbill, is still perfected for a 21-day period. However, Avery could defeat this perfection by a negotiation to a bona fide purchaser for value while the airbill is in his possession.

25.8 COLLATERAL: ACCOUNTS AND GENERAL INTANGIBLES

A right of payment for rendition of services or from the sale of goods is an *account* if not evidenced by an instrument or chattel paper. Perfection by possession is not available because of the lack of a tangible presence to the right of claim. Accounts receivable can be used as security, or sold, called *factoring*. In both cases Article 9 of the UCC may be applicable, but an account assignment need not be perfected if it is a casual or isolated sale. Only the transfer of a significant amount or part of the outstanding accounts of the assignor need be perfected under Article 9. General intangibles, such as patents, copyrights, goodwill, and literary rights require perfection by filing a financing statement.

25.9 COLLATERAL: FIXTURES AND ACCESSIONS

Goods attached to real property are *fixtures*, and they may be used as collateral. Goods obtained under a purchase money security agreement and perfected under fixture filing no later than 10 days after attachment result in an interest even superior to a prior real estate interest other than a construction mortgage. The financing statement should be filed at the office where the real property records are kept; a description of the realty must be included.

EXAMPLE 8.   Siers & Co. sold a 4-ton air conditioner to Laddle Construction Company under a purchase money security agreement and filed a financing statement. The unit was installed in the wall of Laddle's administrative office. Siers has priority over the owner and subsequent owners and real property mortgage holders provided the perfection occurred before annexation, or within ten days thereafter.

A homeowner, for example, who attempts to give a security interest in a fixture already installed can do so but cannot provide a lien over prior claimants to real property unless a written release or consent was obtained. In repossession, the secured party may remove the fixture from the realty but must repair any damage caused by the removal. Fixtures include most items attached to realty but not the building materials. Air conditioners, heaters, built-in refrigerators, and the like are common types of collateral qualifying as fixtures. Readily movable equipment such as office machines and business appliances are usually not considered to be fixtures; they are considered detachable trade fixtures and are classified as equipment, UCC, Section 9-313(4)(c).

EXAMPLE 9.   Last Federal Savings put a real property mortgage on Tapper's building and perfected a security interest "on all fixtures now or hereafter acquired." Tapper later purchased a computer, which was installed in its offices. The computer was large, and a wall had to be removed temporarily to install the equipment. Under the UCC, filing a financing statement before installation is a valid security interest superior to the prior Last Federal mortgage.

Goods installed or affixed to other goods are called *accessions* and, like fixtures, may be used as collateral. Generally, if the security interest is perfected before accession, the superiority of the lien is, with some exceptions, assured. An attempt to perfect the security interest after accession is less effective for all other interests unless consent is obtained from the owner and other secured interests.

25.10 MECHANICS' LIENS

Automobiles are goods that are commonly repaired and are subject to the doctrine of accessions and priority. Under common law and statutes, a *possessory lien* is available to those who claim an interest in personal property by reason of repair, improvement, storage, or transportation. These claimants usually urge a superior lien of prior perfected security interest. Section 9-310 of the UCC permits these possessory liens, sometimes called *mechanics' liens*, to have priority over previously perfected security interests *unless* the statute creating the lien expressly subordinates it.

EXAMPLE 10.   Drover Trucking had one of its rigs subject to a security interest in Moto Manufacturing, which filed the appropriate financing statement. The rig broke down in Virginia, and it was taken to a garage for repairs. The expense was high, and Drover decided to abandon the rig, as the repair bill and lien were in excess of its value. Moto wants to sell the rig and pocket the $4,000 it will bring. The lien is for $5,000, and the repair bill is $3,000. The garage sees that it will have nothing if Moto has first access to proceeds. Unless the state mechanics' lien statute says otherwise, the garage has a superior possessory lien on the sale proceeds. The prior perfected security interest is inferior to a possessory mechanic's lien. The garage has the higher priority.

25.11 PURCHASE MONEY SECURITY INTERESTS

Purchase money interests are the beneficiaries of certain favorable rules in the ranking of interests. This type of interest arises in favor of an interest retained by the seller as collateral to secure the price, or taken by one who makes advances that enable the debtor to acquire the collateral, UCC, Section 9-107. Generally, the secured party has 10 days from the date of the debtor's receipt of the collateral to perfect by filing a financing statement. The use of a purchase money transaction is necessary in those instances in which a borrower has already mortgaged his or her future by a previously executed security agreement containing an after-acquired property clause.

EXAMPLE 11. Regional Telephone Company purchased all its major switching equipment from Eastern Electric, signing a security agreement and financing statement covering all "its telephone switching equipment now or hereafter acquired." Several years later Regional needs additional equipment to expand its operation. Hudson Electric will sell new equipment on credit and security against the new equipment but doesn't want to be a second-priority secured party to Eastern on Hudson's own equipment. The purchase money security agreement is the appropriate vehicle for giving Hudson first-priority security on the new equipment it sells to Regional under these circumstances.

The UCC offers the debtor who had encumbered its future with an after-acquired clause an opportunity to offer a first lien on newly purchased equipment to the seller. This is achieved if the secured party on *equipment* perfects at the time of delivery or within 10 days thereafter, UCC, Section 9-312(4). In the case of *inventory* the prospective secured party must meet stiffer requirements. Before delivery of possession of inventory to the debtor, the secured party must perfect its interest *and* notify the holder of the conflicting security interest, UCC, Section 9-312(3).

EXAMPLE 12. Able Hardware was always underfinanced. Able has given Silver Bank a security interest in all its equipment and inventory and "all other equipment and inventory now owned or hereafter acquired." These interests were perfected by filing. In the course of remodeling the store and freshening up its inventory, Able found Gold Bank willing to put up money for new equipment and inventory. However, Gold Bank wanted a purchase money security interest (PMSI). As to the inventory, Gold Bank must perfect before delivery of the inventory to Able and give written notice of its intention to Silver Bank before delivery of possession. As to the equipment, perfection must be achieved no later than 10 days after transfer of possession; no notice to prior secured parties is necessary.

An after-acquired clause which attempts to give collateral to future loans is complemented by the *future advances* clause used in secured transactions. This too belongs to the floating lien theory, as not only is future collateral subject to an old obligation, but a new obligation is secured by old collateral. There are some limitations on these techniques, as consumers and farmers are specially protected. No after-acquired clause can apply to consumer goods received more than 10 days after the secured party gives value. Further, farm products acquired by the debtor in excess of 1 year from the date of the security agreement are likewise beyond the reach of the after-acquired clause, UCC, Section 9-204.

25.12 PRIORITIES

The purpose of a secured transaction is to gain priority over competing interests in the collateral. These parties can be competing creditors, secured parties, purchasers from the debtor, a receiver in an insolvency proceeding, or a trustee in the debtor's bankruptcy. There is no one general rule that answers all these struggles by assigning priorities. Previous discussion reflected some of the nuances regarding these rights.

Generally, however, conflicting security interests rank according to priority in time of filing or perfection. If two conflicting security interests are both perfected by filing, the first to file has priority. If one or both were perfected by a method other than filing, the first to perfect is superior.

If one is perfected and one is not, the perfected one has priority. If both are unperfected, the first to attach has priority. Priority dates from the time of filing or the time the first security interest is perfected, whichever is the earlier.

EXAMPLE 13. Farnsworth requested a loan from First Bank, intending to supply the bank with a security interest in a negotiable warehouse receipt, two valuable watercolor paintings, and her interest as coauthor of a book on corrosive engineering. First Bank filed a financing statement on all three items of collateral: documents, goods, and general intangibles. First Bank did not decide to loan the funds until 4 months later. In the meantime, Farnsworth, in a panic that she would not get the needed money, sold the warehouse receipt and the two watercolors to good-faith purchasers and gave a security interest in the book to Second Bank for a quick, but expensive, loan. Second Bank filed immediately upon loaning the money. The purchaser of the warehouse receipt takes free of both banks' security interests because it was a negotiable document. But the purchaser of the two watercolors and Second Bank's interest in the copyright are both inferior to the interests of First Bank. The security interest of Second Bank attached first, but where conflicting interests are both perfected by filing, the first to file has priority.

EXAMPLE 14. H. C. Pope's Cash Store had Elmo sign a security agreement and financing statement (PMSI) for the new home freezer Elmo purchased on credit. It was not the policy of Mr. Pope to file financing statements on appliances. Thomasville Loan Company loaned Elmo $600 and took back a security interest and financing statement on all Elmo's household goods, including the freezer. Thomasville Loan Company filed the financing statement at the Marengo County clerk's office. Pope's Store has the higher lien under the rule that the first to perfect or first to file, whichever is earlier, has priority. Pope's Store perfected first by attachment, which is allowed for consumer goods.

25.13 PROCEEDS

When the collateral moves free of the security interest to a purchaser, as in sales from inventory in the ordinary course of business, the proceeds of the sales are the new collateral. This could include cash, chattel paper, accounts, and the like. The original perfection of the original collateral suffices in the new collateral, the proceeds, for a period of 10 days after receipt by the seller. Further, if the original financing statement covering the collateral *was the proper place for perfecting the proceeds*, it will continue beyond the 10 days. Of course, a filing identifying the proceeds as collateral perfects a security interest in the proceeds.

EXAMPLE 15. A retailer's inventory of washing machines is subject to a security interest in favor of a distributor, who perfected by filing a financing statement. The retailer sells one of the machines on credit to a customer, who executes a note and security agreement on the machine. This purchase frees the machine from the distributor's security interest, which now transfers to the "proceeds" of the credit purchase, i.e., the note and security agreement. These proceeds are known as *chattel paper*. The distributor has an automatic lien on these proceeds for only 10 days unless (*a*) he separately perfects his interest in the chattel paper, (*b*) his original security interest and financing statement included proceeds, or (*c*) the original security interest was perfected by a filing in the same office as required for the type of proceeds, here the chattel paper.

Section 9-306 of the UCC treats proceeds and even creates a right regarding identifiable cash proceeds where an insolvency proceeding is instituted naming the debtor. Among the rules is the principle that checks not yet deposited in the debtor's bank are within the reach of the secured party's interest in the proceeds.

25.14 RIGHTS OF SECURED PARTIES: GENERALLY

When the obligation is not met by the debtor, the secured party may of course sue for the breach of contract or enforce the security agreement. Where the secured party has possession of the collateral, he or she owes a duty to the debtor in regard to it, as the secured party must protect it and perform those duties necessary to maintain the value of the security. If, for example, the collateral is an interest in which others have responsibilities, such as guarantors of a promissory note, the secured party must protect the interest by giving the proper notice of default to such parties. The secured party may instruct the debtor to do so by contract. While in possession, the secured party has usually contracted for broad powers in regard to the collateral.

The secured party may commingle the collateral if necessary. He or she is, of course, accountable to the debtor for the proceeds should sale become necessary.

EXAMPLE 16. A manufacturer sold merchandise to a retailer under a security agreement which provided that all chattel paper received by the retailer for merchandise sold must be held by the manufacturer. It was not uncommon for cosigners to apear on the chattel paper, but liability was limited to being notified within 30 days of any default. Certain of these obligations became due, but because of a shortage of personnel, the manufacturer notified several guarantors after the 30-day period. The retailer (the debtor) is released from the obligation to the extent that the retailer was damaged by reason of failure to protect the security.

25.15 RIGHT OF REPOSSESSION

The secured party may, unless otherwise agreed, following UCC provisions, repossess the collateral, dispose of it, or accept it as a discharge by retaining it. Repossession ("self-help") must be accomplished without a breach of the peace, UCC, Section 9-503. Where repossession is impracticable, the collateral may be made unusable pending sale or other disposition. The secured party can also bring an action of replevin to gain possession of the collateral.

EXAMPLE 17. Digital-Toll made and sold computer equipment to Data Agency under a security agreement which was silent on the right of repossession. Data defaulted on a monthly payment. Digital-Toll attempted to repossess the equipment, and the employees of Data barred the door. To push aside these persons would likely result in a breach of the peace. Digital-Toll must now bring a law action seeking possession by replevin, which the sheriff must execute.

EXAMPLE 18. To finance production, Regal Stamping assigned its accounts receivable to Payne Financing as security for a loan. Regal defaulted on the loan. Payne may notify the debtors of the accounts receivable and instruct them that payments be made directly to Payne. Obviously, there is no way to repossess accounts receivable in a physical sense; the secured party must resort to administrative means of the type just described to realize the value of its collateral.

25.16 RIGHT OF DISPOSAL AND SALE

The secured party in possession or repossession of the goods may sell or otherwise dispose of the collateral. The goods may be sold at a special sale in their present condition, or the creditor can make reasonable preparations to the goods for resale. The sale can be public or private. Except for consumer goods, the seller must notify the debtor and other secured parties who have notified the secured party of their intent. The secured party's notification must name the date and place of the public sale, and while written notice is preferred, oral notice is not prohibited by statute in most states. There are some situations where a special sale by the secured party is unnecessary. These include perishable collateral, goods that decline rapidly in value, and goods that are customarily sold at a recognized market, UCC, Section 9-504(3). The secured party may buy at the public sale, and the buyers in good faith take free of security rights. Even a failure by the seller to comply with the rules of sale or disposal proceedings does not disturb the new buyer's title.

EXAMPLE 19. Tagget Industries had all its equipment and inventory under security interests with Xanadu, Young, and Zerba. Tagget had several judgment creditors. Tagget finally closed shop when Xanadu repossessed all the equipment and inventory. Young and Zerba notified Xanadu of their security interests. Xanadu sent a notice to Tagget, Young, and Zerba announcing that after 60 days it would sell all the collateral at a private sale. It sold the goods and received $50,000. Xanadu's expenses were $2,100, and its unpaid balance was $39,000. Young and Zerba now have to fight over $8,900. The judgment creditors cannot object to the fact that they were not notified.

It is not necessary to notify other secured parties where consumer goods are being sold. It is enough to notify the consumer, but the secured party has certain restrictions. The goods must be disposed of within 90 days after taking possession. Further, if the secured party intends to retain the goods in satisfaction of the obligation, the debtor is entitled to notice and objection to such procedure. The debtor's silence during this period permits the secured party to retain the goods, but the secured party thereby loses his or her rights to sue for the deficiency (the unpaid balance after credit for the value of the goods). When objection occurs, the secured party must sell the goods under the UCC rules. However, after a default where the debtor has paid 60 percent or more of the purchase price or debt, unless agreed otherwise, the seller must sell the collateral, UCC, Section 9-505. When the secured party properly sells the collateral after repossession, the debtor remains liable for any deficiency and is also entitled to any surplus, provided all other liens on the collateral are paid in full.

25.17 TERMINATION-CONTINUATION STATEMENTS

A filed financing statement is effective for 5 years from the date of the filing. Unless a continuation statement is effectively filed, the security interest terminates should the secured party fail to file the continuation statement within 6 months before the termination date, UCC, Section 9-403(2). A termination statement can discharge all or part of the security interest, and assignments and amendments may also be filed. The debtor's signature is required on the original security agreement, on the original financing statement, and on all amendments to the financing statements. All other documents can be filed containing the signature of the secured party only, including a financing statement which is signed only by the secured party, provided the collateral is already subject to a security interest in another jurisdiction. This exception occurs when the collateral is brought into the new jurisdiction or when the debtor's location is changed to such.

Termination statements should be filed by the secured party upon discharge of the obligation and, in the case of consumer goods, must be filed by the secured party within 30 days after the debt is paid or within 10 days after demand, whichever is sooner. All other termination statements must be filed within 10 days after notice of the debtor requesting such action.

Black Letter Law
A Summary

1. The classification of the collateral is important in determining priorities and requirements for perfections and includes such classes as inventory, equipment, consumer goods, general intangibles, fixtures, instruments, documents of title, and chattel paper.

2. A debtor's sale of inventory to buyers in the ordinary course of business frees such inventory from the lien of a perfected security interest in inventory.

3. Superior rights among competing interests are determined according to priority in time of perfection and, where none, the first party to effect attachment.

4. Purchase money security interests arise in favor of a seller who uses the collateral to secure the purchase price or who advances money that enables the debtor to acquire the collateral.

5. Secured parties who perfect purchase money interest in inventory before its delivery, and likewise notify a prior secured party having an after-acquired clause, have a first lien on the inventory.

6. Secured parties who perfect their purchase money interest in equipment within 10 days of delivery have a lien superior to a prior secured party which has an after-acquired clause in its favor.

7. A secured party which relies on attachment of purchase money consumer goods for perfection is assured of superiority over other creditors and secured parties except for a good-faith purchaser of the consumer good.

8. Article 9 of the UCC, Secured Transactions, broadly validates the after-acquired clause and the future advances clause, which together make up the floating lien theory.

9. Where inventory subject to a perfected security interest is sold, the proceeds of the sale become the new collateral.

10. Even in the absence of a specific grant in the security agreement, the secured party has the right to attempt a peaceful repossession of the collateral upon default.

11. A repossessing secured party has the right to sell the collateral at public or private sale and may bid at the public sale.

12. A failure of the secured party to comply with sale and disposal procedures of the UCC does not deny the good-faith buyer at a public sale of good title to the collateral.

Solved Problems

25.1 The question of priorities is unimportant to which of the following relationships?

(a) The debtor and the secured party
(b) The trustee in bankruptcy and the secured party
(c) A judgment creditor and a secured party
(d) A secured party and a purchase money creditor

The issue of priorities is one that arises between competing creditors over the assets of the debtor. Accordingly, it is relatively unimportant to the debtor's own interest as to which hierarchy is to be observed; statement (a) is the answer.

25.2 The classification of collateral is unimportant in order to determine which of the following issues?

(a) Whether there can be more than one secured security interest over the same collateral
(b) The proper place of filing a financing statement
(c) The procedure to be followed by a holder in a purchase money security interest
(d) Whether a particular method of perfection must be employed

It is important that the collateral (at the time of the creation of the security interest) be correctly classified. Certain goods, for example, can only be perfected by the filing of a financing statement at a particular place. Further, inventory in a purchase money situation requires a different procedure for perfection than does equipment. Only consumer goods can be perfected by attachment alone. However, any collateral can have more than one party owning a security interest in the collateral, and accordingly, statement (*a*) is the answer.

25.3 Baker Loan Company made secured loans to Smith, Jack, and Roe. Smith gave Baker a security interest in her household furniture. Jack delivered Baker his rare-coin collection as a pledge. Roe's loan is evidenced by her promissory note, payable over 3 years in monthly payments and secured by a security interest in the inventory of Roe's Clothing Store, a sole proprietorship owned by Roe. Proper security agreements were made, and financing statements were duly executed and filed with respect to all these transactions. Which of the following statements is correct?

(*a*) A filing of a financing statement is *not* required to perfect the security interest in Smith's household furniture.

(*b*) Baker's security interest in Jack's coin collection was perfected before a financing statement was filed.

(*c*) On filing a financing statement covering Roe's inventory, Baker's security interest therein was perfected for a maximum period of 1 year.

(*d*) The financing statement for Roe's inventory must include an itemization and valuation of the inventory if the financing statement is to be valid.

(*AICPA Examination, November 1973*)

Perfection by possession was accomplished by Baker taking the coin collection, statement (*b*). The furniture as collateral does not qualify as a consumer good in a purchase money situation; accordingly, the doctrine of attachment does not apply. Financing statement filings are effective for 5 years. Financing statements are notice filings, and therefore, only a description that identifies the type of collateral is required and sufficient.

25.4 Bigelow manufactures mopeds and sells them through franchised dealers who are authorized to resell them to the ultimate consumer or return them. Bigelow delivers the mopeds on consignment to these retailers. The consignment agreement clearly states that the agreement is intended to create a security interest for Bigelow in the mopeds delivered on consignment. Bigelow wishes to protect itself against the other creditors of and purchasers from the retailers who might assert rights against the mopeds. Under the circumstances, Bigelow

(*a*) must file a financing statement and give notice to certain creditors in order to perfect its security interest.

(*b*) will have rights against purchasers in the ordinary course of business who were aware of the fact that Bigelow had filed.

(*c*) need take *no* further action to protect itself, since the consignment is a sale or return and title is reserved in Bigelow.

(*d*) will have a perfected security interest in the mopeds upon attachment.

(*Adapted from AICPA Examination, May 1979*)

Inventory financing requires a perfection by possession or by the filing of a financing statement. However, it is important that if the sale is a purchase money sale that the secured creditor perfect and give notice to any prior secured creditors in order to preserve the priority of his or her interests; the answer is (*a*). Purchasers in the ordinary course of business involving inventory take free of the interest, irrespective of knowledge of the interest. Consignments, where there is a retained title, are not effective against other secured parties unless Article 9 of the UCC or an applicable state sign law is observed. Perfection by attachment is not applicable to inventory.

25.5 On May 1, Dixie Corporation borrowed $100,000 from Clark Bank. The bank filed a financing statement on that date. On May 5, Dixie signed a security agreement granting the bank a security interest in its inventory, its accounts receivable, and the proceeds from the sale of its inventory and collection of its accounts receivable. The bank's security interest

(*a*) was perfected on May 1.

(*b*) was not perfected until a copy of the security agreement was filed.

(*c*) was perfected on May 5.

(*d*) attached on May 1.

(*AICPA Examination, May 1975*)

One cannot have a security interest in collateral until there is an attachment. Entering into a security agreement on May 5 fulfills the last of the three elements necessary: value was given, debtors have rights in the collateral, and a security agreement *was made*; statement (*c*) is the correct answer.

25.6 Forward Motor, Inc., is a franchised automobile dealer for National Motors. National provides the financing of the purchase of its automobiles for Forward. It sells Forward 25 to 50 automobiles at a time and takes back promissory notes, a security agreement, and a financing statement on each sale. The financing statement covering this revolving inventory has been duly filed. Which of the following statements is correct?

(*a*) Each automobile sold to Forward must be described and the serial number listed on the financing statement.

(*b*) Sales by Forward to bona fide purchasers for value in the ordinary course of business will be subject to the rights of National.

(*c*) No filing is required against the creditors of Forward since the automobiles are consumer goods in its hands.

(*d*) As against the creditors of Forward, National has a valid floating lien against the automobiles and the proceeds from their sale.

(*Adapted from AICPA Examination, November 1973*)

Statement (*d*) is the correct one. Where inventory filing is involved, a perfection by duly filing a financing statement in the appropriate state office perfects not only the inventory, but also the proceeds of the inventory for a period of 10 days, sometimes called a floating lien. The collateral description is sufficient even if it does not require a listing of the serial numbers of the vehicles.

25.7 Donaldson, Inc., loaned Watson Enterprises $50,000 secured by a real estate mortgage which included the land, buildings, and "all other property which is added to the real property or which is considered as real property as a matter of law." Star Company also loaned Watson $25,000 and obtained a security interest in all of Watson's "inventory, accounts receivable, fixtures, and other tangible personal property." There is insufficient property to satisfy the two creditors. Consequently, Donaldson is attempting to include all property possible under the terms and scope of its real property mortgage. If Donaldson is successful in this regard, then Star will receive a lesser amount in satisfaction of its claim. What is the probable outcome of Donaldson's action?

(a)   Donaldson will *not* prevail if the property in question is detachable trade fixtures.

(b)   Donaldson will prevail if Star failed to file a financing statement.

(c)   Donaldson will prevail if it was the first lender and duly filed its real property mortgage.

(d)   The problem will be decided by taking all Watson's property (real and personal) subject to the two secured creditors' claims and dividing it in proportion to the respective debts.

(AICPA Examination, November 1978)

In this case, Donaldson has a lien on real property only. Any attempt to claim an interest in personal property would be in vain. Fixtures, once personal property, would be real property and would pass to Donaldson. However, if the property was detachable trade fixtures, these are personal property and come within the security interest of Star, and so statement (a) is correct.

25.8   Vega Manufacturing, Inc., manufactures and sells hi-fi systems and components to the trade and at retail. Repossession is frequently made from customers who are in default. Which of the following statements is correct concerning the rights of the defaulting debtors who have had property repossessed by Vega?

(a)   Vega has the right to retain all the goods repossessed as long as it gives notice and cancels the debt.

(b)   It is unimportant whether the goods repossessed are defined as consumer goods, inventory, or something else in respect to the debtor's rights upon repossession.

(c)   If the defaulting debtor voluntarily signs a statement renouncing his or her rights in the collateral, the creditor must nevertheless resell them for the debtor's benefit.

(d)   If a debtor has paid 60 percent or more of the purchase price of consumer goods in satisfaction of a purchase money security interest, the debtor has the right to have the creditor dispose of the goods.

(Adapted from AICPA Examination, May 1978)

The repossession of consumer goods carries with it certain additional responsibilities beyond the usual duties of a secured party. If the debtor has paid 60 percent or more of the purchase price when the secured party repossesses, there is an absolute duty of a public sale, statement (d). This can, of course, be waived by the debtor in writing, but only after default, UCC, Section 9-505.

25.9   Gladstone Warehousing, Inc., is an independent bonded warehouse company. It issued a warehouse receipt for 10,000 bales of cotton belonging to Travis. The word "NEGOTI-ABLE" was conspicuously printed on the warehouse receipt it issued to Travis. The warehouse receipt also contained a statement in large, clear print that the cotton would be surrendered only upon return of the receipt and payment of all storage fees. Travis was a prominent plantation owner engaged in the cotton-growing business. Travis pledged the warehouse receipt with Southern National Bank in exchange for a $50,000 personal loan. A financing statement was *not* filed. Under the circumstances, which of the following is correct?

(a)   Travis's business creditors *cannot* obtain the warehouse receipt from Southern National unless they repay Travis's outstanding loan.

(b)   The bank does *not* have a perfected security interest in the cotton since it did *not* file a financing statement.

(c)   Travis's personal creditors have first claim, superior to all other parties, to the cotton in question because the loan was a personal loan and constituted a fraud upon the personal creditors.

(d)   The fact that the word "NEGOTIABLE" and the statement regarding the return of the receipt were conspicuously printed upon the receipt is not binding on anyone except Travis.

(AICPA Examination, May 1978)

Statement (*a*) is correct. The only effective way to perfect a negotiable instrument is by possession. Accordingly, the warehouse receipt need not be delivered up by the secured party since continued possession preserves the rights of the party holding it. Filing a financing statement is not necessary where one has lawfully perfected by possession.

25.10 Case Corporation manufactures electric drills and sells them to retail hardware stores. Under the Uniform Commercial Code it is likely that

(*a*)   the drills are inventory in Case's hands.

(*b*)   the drills are equipment in Case's hands.

(*c*)   the raw materials on hand to be used in the manufacturing of the drills are *not* inventory in Case's hands.

(*d*)   the drills are considered equipment in the hands of the hardware stores who purchased them.

(*AICPA Examination, May 1975*)

The characterization of collateral depends on the intention of the parties at the time of the contract. Here, the facts that the debtor is a hardware retailer and a large number of drills are involved suggest that they are being purchased for resale. Thus, inventory is the proper classification, statement (*a*). The drills would also be inventory if the stores consumed them in a manufacturing process.

25.11 A homeowner purchased a riding lawnmower, using the bank to finance the item. The homeowner signed a note and security agreement. Upon a default in payment of the note the bank sent its agents to repossess the lawnmower. The homeowner refused to give it up. Later, when the homeowner was absent, the agents returned and took the lawnmower over the strenuous objections of the homeowner's son, who claimed that he was placed in fear by the agents' threats. The homeowner sued the bank for damages.

What defense will the bank raise? How successful will it be? Discuss and state your conclusions.

The bank will claim that under the UCC, and probably under the terms of its own security agreement, it has the right to use self-help by repossession. This is true, but the UCC requires that in doing so the repossessor does not "breach the peace." The facts suggest that the agents may have overstepped their authority under the UCC. When there is resistance to the repossession, one may not perform acts contrary to the public peace. It appears that the bank's defense may be insufficient.

25.12 A jeweler sold a diamond engagement ring on credit to a customer, who planned to give it to his fiancée. The customer signed a security agreement, but the jeweler did not file a financing statement. The customer went bankrupt, and the trustee in bankruptcy was about to sell the ring and apply the proceeds to the payment of the creditors of the customer. The jeweler contends that he has rights superior to those of the trustee in bankruptcy. The trustee challenges that contention on the grounds that the jeweler made a fatal mistake by failing to file a financing statement in the appropriate state office.

How valid is the argument of the trustee in bankruptcy? State your answer and any reasons for your conclusions.

It is true that perfection must be shown in order for a secured party to overcome the rights of a creditor such as the trustee in bankruptcy. Otherwise such a party is just one more creditor as represented by the trustee. Under these facts the jeweler did perfect a security interest sufficient to prevail against the trustee. The jeweler has a purchase money interest in consumer goods and therefore perfects by the doctrine of attachment. This perfection, while inadequate against a good-faith purchaser of the diamond from the customer, is sufficient against all other creditors.

25.13 Taylor Computers was in the business of selling computer systems to small businesses on credit. Taylor would take back a security agreement and financing statement and then duly file the latter in the state office. Rohn Business Services, a debtor of Taylor's, ran into some financial difficulties and defaulted on its debt. This activated Taylor into sending its agents into Rohn's business premises, where they removed several circuit boards from the computer system's central processing unit, thereby making the system useless for Rohn. Rohn objected even more when the whole system was repossessed 10 days later. Rohn heard no more from Taylor until it received a phone call from Taylor notifying Rohn that Taylor was putting up all the repossessed equipment for sale at the used computer monthly trade market sale in 1 week. Rohn had made substantial payments on the equipment and was shocked to learn 2 weeks later that the sale did not bring in sufficient money to satisfy the unpaid balance. In fact, Rohn had been anticipating that it would receive some money from the proceeds of the sale after satisfaction of the balance due.

What are Rohn's rights regarding the actions of Taylor in dismantling the equipment and the way in which the sale took place?

The secured party has the right to repossess and has the right to make the collateral unusable on the premises of the debtor, UCC, Section 9-504. The secured party may also sell the collateral from the debtor's premises. The notice of the sale was oral, and while writing is required in some states, the UCC merely requires a reasonable notification of the time and place. Rohn certainly had such notification. Further, sending the collateral to a recognized market further diminishes the notice requirements where the sale is "of a type customarily sold on a recognized market," UCC, Section 9-504. It is possible, further, that the deficiency can be recovered by Taylor unless otherwise agreed between the parties.

Topic Test, Part V

Secured Transactions

1. Carryback has varied business interests. He runs a small loan company, buys and sells accounts from small service establishments in the area, and has an interest in the sales of complete home vacuum cleaner systems. The latter business is booming, but he must sell most of these systems on credit to homeowners. He employs a mechanic, who installs the vacuum cleaner systems in the homes, as expert talent is required to cut holes properly in walls and place a duct system throughout the house. Lately, he has had some difficulty in being fully paid for some of his operations, as other creditors have beaten him out. For which of the above enterprises must Carryback have some knowledge of Article 9 of the UCC?

2. Bostone has a thriving leasing business specializing in dragline equipment. She has a fleet of 40 draglines, including three different models. Sometimes she agrees that the lessee has an option to purchase the dragline at the termination of the lease, although she prefers not to do this, as she does not want a lot of used equipment out in the marketplace because the availability of such equipment could saturate the market and hurt her business. Nonetheless, Bostone will accommodate an insistent customer and will provide an option purchase price, which she calculates is about one-half of the salvage value at the time of the termination of the lease. She was very disturbed last week when she was unable to take back a dragline leased to Browning Company, which went bankrupt just before the end of the lease. Bostone has learned that a trustee in bankruptcy has taken possession of the dragline. Bostone can provide the written lease agreement, which clearly states that the lessor has a right to immediate possession upon default of the rent payments. Under what circumstances does Bostone have a problem in her struggle with the bankruptcy trustee?

3. Arlow found it quite easy to start up a business on other people's money. Arlow merely had to sign a few legal papers and the inventory and equipment just rolled in. Arlow is a winner and business is great, but he must keep up the momentum. Arlow has learned that it would pay him to use brands of inventory and equipment in addition to those with which he originally started. However, Arlow finds that the new manufacturers are not eager to sell him inventory and equipment on credit. They state that they have no intention of standing in "second place" with present creditors. What type of argument could Arlow advance so as to assure them that they could get a valid first lien on the inventory and equipment they sell to Arlow on credit?

4. Studds operates a fine cabinetmaking shop, in which she uses rather expensive and exotic woods. Due to the nature of the business, it is necessary to have a large supply of these woods handy for use in the fine furniture her craftsmen manufacture. World Wood Importers of Miami is not disposed to sell large quantities of teak, mahogany, lignum vitae, etc., on credit, although it does want to do business with Studds. Studds tells World Wood that she is perfectly willing to sign a security agreement and a financing statement covering the wood. World Wood, mumbling terms like "commingling" and "hard to identify," rejects the offer, stating that it does not like inventory financing because it hates to surrender possession of its property. Studds is persistent, however, and has an idea of how she can interest World Wood in selling her a great deal of such valuable wood on credit. What idea in respect to the commercial financing of inventory does Studds likely have in mind?

5. State law provides for the filing of financing statements at two different locations, depending on the nature of the collateral. Central filing at the state capital is necessary for accounts receivable, inventory, and equipment, while local filing at the county clerk's office is specified for farm products, consumer goods, and fixtures. Franklin is a wholesaler who deals in the sale of eggs and butter. He purchases these items from farmers in the surrounding countryside. Franklin needs money for expansion of his facilities and applies to the bank for a loan. While reading over the loan agreement, he sees that the bank will require that he put up for security all the butter and eggs that he now has or will have in the future. If the bank is to perfect its security interest, where must the bank file its financing statement under these facts?

6. Testor has reluctantly agreed to lend Larry, his brother-in-law, $30,000. Larry has a one-third interest in a patent his deceased father formerly owned covering an innovative sausage processing machine. Larry tells Testor that he will put the patent up for security. Testor proceeds to a stationery store and purchases a financing statement form and fills it in. He is surprised at how little information it requires: his name, Larry's name, their addresses, Larry's signature, the date, and a box stating "Other intangibles," where Testor fills in "sausage machine patent owned by debtor." Testor sends this completed financing statement to the proper state office for filing. Has Testor perfected a security interest in the patent?

7. Folsom Mines ships semiprecious stones to Arts Crafts, a large manufacturer of gift shop merchandise. Arts Crafts sells to gift shops across the country. As orders from Arts Crafts have increased, Folsom has been required to extend credit to Arts Crafts, and in an attempt to protect itself, it has begun requiring Arts Crafts to sign both a security agreement and a financing statement. The latter is filed in the central office for the named collateral which Folsom describes as inventory. Unknown to Folsom, Arts Crafts also sells on credit, and this has caused Arts Crafts considerable trouble due to buyers giving 30-day promissory notes to Arts Crafts for their unpaid balances. What rights does Folsom have in these notes should Arts Crafts run into financial trouble? What issues are raised under these circumstances?

8. Tom purchased a secondhand car. The E-Z Auto Finance Company demanded a security agreement and financing statement be signed by Tom, along with a statement that merely stated "Tom hereby grants a security interest in one 1981 Ford Escort, ID 633447789, to E-Z Auto Finance Company, (signed) Tom." The financing statement was filed in the central office, as required by state law. Tom was in default by over 3 months when the auto finance company sent its agent over to Tom's house to repossess the car. Tom was prepared and had the car hidden at his neighbor's house. This, however, did not fool the agent, who spotted the car, used duplicate keys, and drove the car away. Tom claims that not only was the taking improper but there was no contract right to repossess the car in the first place. Comment on Tom's contentions. What area of secured transactions is applicable here?

9. On January 10, 19X2, Yeager Enterprises entered into an agreement with the Dune Decorator Shop by which inventory would be supplied on credit, with Dune signing both a security agreement and a financing statement covering all inventory both presently supplied by Yeager and after-acquired by Dune. The financing statement was filed on January 15, 19X2. Dune soon became disenchanted with the goods supplied by Yeager and, on February 10, 19X2, began negotiating with Swifty Products. Swifty agreed to supply inventory and required that Dune sign a security agreement and financing statement for the new inventory. Swifty Products delivered its first shipment on February 25, 19X2, and filed its financing statement on March 10, 19X2. It did not check the public record before filing. This influx of inventory did Dune no good, as sales continued to decline, and Dune went into bankruptcy 6 months later. Yeager claims that it has a first claim on both the inventory it supplied and the inventory supplied by Swifty Products. What principle determines the priority of these claims?

10. Jeffers Appliances employed Yost, a new credit manager who had ideas that the company wished to try out. Yost believed the company would have more leverage in collecting delinquent accounts if it included in its credit sales a security agreement provision that called for the security interest to cover all the household appliances now being sold by Jeffers *and* "all other household appliances owned or otherwise hereafter acquired by the debtor." This clause proved to be a valuable tool when there were defaults by purchasers. Jeffers found that the threat to repossess the clothes dryer sold to a customer was greatly reinforced when it was accompanied by the additional legal threat that all the customer's other appliances were also under the risk of repossession. Victoria, a debtor whose dishwashing machine had been purchased from Jeffers, was not intimidated by the threat of losing it because it was not working properly anyhow. However, she challenged Jeffers when it tried to repossess her new Maytag washing machine, which had been given to her by her ex-husband. Has Victoria any legal grounds to resist the reach of the after-acquired clause in this case?

Answers

1. In at least two of his business activities, Carryback must concern himself with Article 9 of the UCC, Secured Transactions. In the purchase and sale of accounts receivable, the UCC provisions must be honored. While an account is not tangible personal property and is not given for security, the provisions of Article 9 are nonetheless applicable. The sale of personal property—the household vacuum systems, which may become a fixture and in which the seller hopes to retain a security interest—is also within Article 9. In order to preserve a lien in this formerly personal property, the seller must comply with the principles of Article 9.

2. A bona fide lease is not a security interest. The problem is that calling something a lease does not settle the matter. A lease may be just a form of a security agreement when the lessee has an option to buy. If the sum of the total lease payments added to the option price is approximately equivalent to the price of the item plus the time value of the outstanding money balances over the period of the lease, a court may interpret the lease arrangement as a disguised security agreement. Any rights such a party might have are governed by Article 9 of the UCC, and accordingly, a failure by the "lessor" to file properly, for example, could release the security interest if it were challenged by another creditor.

3. Arlow should apprise his would-be supplier of the doctrine of purchase money interests. By entering into an agreement by which the supplier is establishing a purchase money interest in the inventory and complying with the rules, i.e., perfecting before delivery of possession and notification of the prior secured parties, the second supplier can have a first lien on his or her own goods even against a previously perfected interest in after-acquired property.

4. Studds should tell World Wood Importers to keep possession, but to do it at Studds's place of business by use of a field warehouse. Studds would rent out a corner of the building to World Wood, who would fence or otherwise enclose the premises (area) and lock it. The key would be in the possession of World Wood's agent. When Studds needs additional inventory, she would have World Wood's agent open the warehouse and remove what she needs. Field warehousing is perfection by possession.

5. The bank will have to look carefully and determine the nature of the collateral in the hands of this debtor. Then the bank must be sure that the financing statement is filed at the place where such collateral must be noted. Butter and eggs look like farm products and, where there is more than one place for filing in the state, are usually filed at the local office. In the hands of Franklin, however, the butter and eggs appear to be *inventory*, as they are goods purchased for resale by Franklin rather than the result of any farming activity on his part. Inventory usually must be filed at the central office. Should the bank err and file at the local office, it could plead good faith, but this might not prevail in the face of a challenge from another creditor.

6. Testor has done acts which constitute perfecting, but he has no security interest to perfect. There is no evidence that a security interest has been entered into by Larry. Most financing statement forms are terse and are not intended to be a substitute for the written security agreement. Testor has no perfected security interest. Therefore, there is an absence of attachment which requires value being given, the debtor having rights in the collateral, and the existence of a security agreement.

7. Folsom Mines has a limited right in the notes as proceeds which flow from the sale of the collateral in which it has a security interest. However, since the security agreement did not include proceeds in its description of the collateral, this lien is only temporary for a period of 10 days. Accordingly, if Folsom does not otherwise provide for protection, contrary interests can intervene.

8. Tom is only half correct regarding the legal right of E-Z Auto Finance to seize the car. It is not covered by the meager security agreement he entered into, valid though the agreement is. However, the right of repossession comes from provisions of the UCC's Article 9 itself and is implied by law to exist unless the parties by contract exclude it. Secondly, E-Z Auto Finance can use stealth to repossess the collateral, provided it does not breach the peace when doing so. The areas of default and remedies are involved here.

9. Generally, where the competing interests have perfected by filing, the first to file has the superior claim. This is bad news for Swifty, who provided inventory later and filed later. Swifty could not have a first lien on Yeager's goods under these circumstances, but Swifty could have a superior right in the inventory it delivered to Dune. Section 9-312 of the UCC requires the secured party who is giving credit for inventory supplied to perfect before delivering the collateral (inventory) in order to succeed over an earlier purchase money security interest, and this party must also notify prior secured parties known to it. Swifty made no effort to check the record. Swifty made both mistakes: not notifying the prior secured party and delivering the collateral before perfecting its purchase money security interest. The after-acquired clause of Yeager's also captures Swifty's collateral. Swifty does have a security interest in its collateral, but this security interest is inferior to the right of Yeager.

10. After-acquired clauses are valuable tools for creditors, but public policy has not completely unleashed them against the consumer. In the sale of consumer goods, the net is only wide enough to reach collateral received by the debtor within 10 days after the secured party has given value. If Victoria's Maytag arrived more than 10 days after Jeffers gave value to Victoria, it is not included as a security interest. There is also the possibility that such a "presently owned and after-acquired" contract might be found unconscionable in itself as being unduly and unreasonably harsh in a given case where the parties were in unequal bargaining positions.

Chapter 26

Formation and Relationships

26.1 INTRODUCTION

Agency has been defined as the fiduciary relationship which results from the manifestation of consent of one person to another that the other shall act on his or her behalf and subject to his or her control, and consent of the other to act (Restatement of Agency, Second, Section 1). Three elements must be shown for this relationship to exist: (1) a manifestation by the principal that the agent will act for the principal, (2) acceptance by the agent, and (3) an understanding between the parties that the principal will be in control.

The subject as taught, however, is quite broad and includes consideration of other relationships that have agency implications. This chapter will deal with terminology, formation, and the relationship between the principal and agent.

26.2 PRINCIPAL-AGENT

The agreement that one acts for another is manifested in many forms and, sometimes, even fictively, as when the court states as a matter of law that agency exists despite the lack of consent of the parties. Generally, however, the agency relationship is consensual.

EXAMPLE 1. Atlas marketed and distributed products for 12 different manufacturers, including the Thout Shovel Company. A third party maintained that Atlas was the agent for Thout. It appeared that Atlas bought products from Thout. There was no evidence of control, but Thout's name was listed in the telephone directory with the telephone number and address of Atlas. Atlas paid for this listing, but Thout did not know about it. Atlas explained that it had been placed for the purpose of facilitating sales of Thout's products. It was held that no agency was shown here, as there must be some manifestation of assent by one person to the other that the other shall act on his or her behalf, be subject to his or her control, and have consented to so act.

26.3 MASTER-SERVANT

In a master-servant relationship, it is assumed that the party hired, the servant, has no right to act in the place and stead of the master since the servant is not authorized to change the contractual position of his or her master. The servant has been engaged to perform a task, generally a physical one. However, nearly every agent could be considered a servant for some purposes. Also, many servants gain agency powers.

EXAMPLE 2. A worker is hired by a homeowner to cut his lawn and do other odd jobs that the homeowner directs. On some occasions, the power mower has run out of gas. The worker, not wishing to be delayed, purchases gas on credit at the local gas station in the name of the homeowner. The homeowner approves of this. The homeowner is both a master and a principal. The worker is for most purposes a servant, but for buying gas he is an agent, despite the fact that he was originally employed to render services only and create no contractual relationships with third persons on behalf of the homeowner.

The distinction between whether one hired is an agent or servant is generally important only in determining whether the party so hiring is bound in contract for the acts of the other. On the other hand, where the issue is solely tort liability, it is relatively unimportant whether the party acted as an agent or a servant.

26.4 EMPLOYER-EMPLOYEE

Generally, such words are the modern description of all parties hired by another and include master-servant and principal-agent. They serve well as substitutes for the servile connotation of the term "master-servant," but also have a precise meaning defined in various statutes such as the Fair Labor Standards Act, Workers' Compensation Act, and Unemployment Compensation Acts.

EXAMPLE 3.   Lee is employed by Ackland Brokerage to bid on wheat in the neighboring farm areas. She does no physical job; she merely signs her name to grain contracts after making a successful bid. She is an agent since she changes the contractual position of Ackland. Lee was laid off. She files for state unemployment compensation, claiming that she is an employee within the meaning of the Act. She would be an employee if she meets the statutory definition of an employee, which is most likely.

Many times it is necessary or profitable for a party to have an agent or servant (employee), but it can also be legally dangerous. Acts performed by others may be the legal acts of the party engaging them. Accordingly, both good and bad legal effects inure to those so hiring. Simply stated, if the party hired makes a contract for another, it is the latter's contract; if one commits a civil wrong, i.e., a tort, while doing a task for another, the liability will also fall on the party so employing the actor.

EXAMPLE 4.   Eric told Francis to purchase 500 bushels of wheat. Francis contracts with a farmer, naming Eric as the real buyer. Eric is contractually bound by this act, although he has never met the farmer. Eric will have to pay the farmer, but he is also entitled to the wheat.

EXAMPLE 5.   While Francis was bargaining with the farmer, the latter indicated that she was not sure she wanted to sell to Eric since another party was interested. Francis, anxious to please Eric with a shrewd purchase, falsely told the farmer that it would be better for her to deal with Eric since the other party's credit was bad. In fact, the other party's credit was perfectly good, and Francis's statement was slander, a tort. Since the tort was committed by Francis while he was acting within the scope of his employment, this tort can also be the responsibility of Eric under the doctrine of *respondeat superior*, i.e., "let the master answer" (for the wrongs of the servant).

26.5 INDEPENDENT CONTRACTORS

There are many business reasons for hiring independent contractors. One reason is the existence of potential liability for both tortious and contractual behavior of employees or agents. An independent contractor is one who agrees to do a job according to his or her own methods and without being subject to the control of the employer except as to the result of the work. Liability for acts of such a contractor does not usually follow the party who hired the contractor.

EXAMPLE 6.   Commings, a logger, testified that he was employed as a contractor by Sulls. He was to be paid $13 a thousand board feet, less $3 if he used a tractor furnished by Sulls. It appeared that Commings employed and paid several people to cut the logs. Commings did not use any of Sull's employees nor any of their hand tools. Sulls did not go out to see whether the logs were cut, and after Commings finished a job, Sulls would tell Commings what property to cut next. Since there was no evidence of "control" in the method of doing the work, one could properly conclude that Commings was an independent contractor.

A number of factors assist a court in determining whether an independent contractor has been employed. The court will need to know what skill is required for the task; whether the worker is engaged in a distinct occupation; what kind of occupation the worker is engaged in—with particular reference to whether, in the locality, the work is usually done by the worker under the direction of a principal or by a specialist without supervision; whether the principal or the worker supplies the tools and place of work; and what method of payment is used, i.e., by time or by the job.

26.6 INDEPENDENT CONTRACTOR: DANGEROUS WORK

Even if the elements of the contract strongly suggest an independent contractor relationship, public policy may not allow its establishment. This is frequently seen in the case of intrinsically dangerous work situations.

EXAMPLE 7. A heavy blast shook a resident's house, causing outside wall rock veneer to fall off, the foundation and chimney to crack, the doors to jam, the floors to buckle, and stones and debris to be thrown on her property. The resident sued the roadbuilder who had hired the subcontractor to blast. It appeared that the roadbuilder had selected the chert (dark rock) pit to be used, leased it from the owner, directed the subcontractor to use that pit, paid for all the chert to be removed, and directed where the chert should be placed on the road. It was held that while the above elements would not by themselves alter the legal relationship, the law states that one who has work done which is intrinsically dangerous cannot avoid responsibility for the acts of an independent contractor employed by him or her when the work is intrinsically dangerous, however skillfully performed.

26.7 INDEPENDENT CONTRACTOR: CARELESS SELECTION AND EXCESSIVE CONTROL

Another exception to the protection apparently gained by hiring an independent contractor is where one has not exercised sufficient care in selecting the independent contractor. Further, even if such care is exercised, the court may find that in fact the employer exercised excessive control over an otherwise independent contractor.

EXAMPLE 8. A newspaper distributor had negligently driven his jeep, causing death and injury in a collision with another car. The publisher was sued for this act. The publisher offered as his defense a written contract with the distributor, which provided that the distributor was not paid a salary; received payment only for papers sold; had no monies for taxes withheld; was not under workers' compensation; and had his own jeep for which he paid all expenses. However, it also appeared that the publisher required the papers to be picked up at a specific time, required the distributor to call into the office at specified times, did not permit the distributor to alter the time or method of handling customers' complaints, allowed the hiring only of juveniles (not adults) as carriers, permitted no control over the price of the paper, and set the size of and control over the delivery districts. The publisher contended that the independent contractor's written contract did not give the publisher all that authority. The court ruled that if one party orders another to perform in such a manner as to constitute a servant or agency relationship, and the employee follows such instructions, the employer cannot complain because he exceeds the contractual authority by which he sought to establish an independent contractor relationship. The publisher is liable as a master or principal.

26.8 AGENTS: OTHER MEANINGS

The term "agent" is not always restricted to the meaning of principal and agent, but is also used to describe other relationships and situations. "Real estate agent," for example, is generally a term meant to describe a party hired to find a buyer or seller of real property. The agent usually is not granted authority to enter into a contract on behalf of another.

EXAMPLE 9. A property owner entered into a listing contract giving a realtor the "exclusive right to sell or contract to sell" certain property. An interested buyer submitted an offer to the realtor, who demanded a down payment, which the buyer then delivered. The buyer and realtor signed a contract for the sale of the property. The owner had already signed away the land to another. The buyer claimed that the realtor was an agent with authority to bind the seller by reason of the listing contract. The court ruled that the listing contract must expressly grant this power to sign on behalf of the seller. Listing contracts generally only authorize a realtor to seek out a prospective buyer or seller; they do not confer agency powers.

On the other hand the terms "special agent" and "general agent" describe one with power to change the contractual status of the principal. A *general agent*, sometimes called a *universal agent*, is assumed to have broad powers over the principal's business, while a *special agent* has authority to bind another in a particular matter or in a limited area. General agency will not be assumed. One must look to the principal's express language to determine that the principal meant to expose his or her legal personality so completely.

Other professional agents include brokers, auctioneers, and factors. Both the terms of their authority and their behavior must be carefully examined by third parties in order to hold the principal liable for their acts.

EXAMPLE 10.   Howard is a food broker. He appears to be a middleman between the manufacturer and retailers. He could be a real agent for the manufacturer, or retailer, or only an independent businessperson. The contract and the behavior of the parties would determine which was the case.

EXAMPLE 11.   Lauren runs a small art gallery which is patronized by new painters. She runs an auction every Thursday evening. When she offers paintings delivered to her for auction sale, she acts as agent for the owner. When the bid is accepted, she frequently signs the memorandum of sale for both buyer and seller. She is a kind of special or limited agent.

A *factor* is one who sells the property of another. When a factor guarantees that the buyers to whom he or she sells will pay for the goods, the factor is known as a *del credere* agent. Such an agent is liable to the principal upon the buyer's default. *Subagents* are parties who have been appointed by the agent without the authority of the principal. Normally, they are considered to be employees of the agent who hired them and not agents or employees of the principal, unless the principal's conduct in some way leads to a contrary conclusion. Agents by necessity are those persons who assume a role which the circumstances demand of a reasonable person. The classic example involves a railroad conductor who attempts to assist passengers after a train wreck. When the conductor employs doctors to treat the injured at the scene, the conductor is acting as an "agent by necessity" for the railroad.

26.9   CAPACITY TO BE AN AGENT

Generally, any person or legal entity has the power to be an agent. Some parties may not be an agent for a particular purpose, or some public policy might inhibit an appointment. For example, a 4-year-old child *could* be an agent for the father when the child purchases milk at a take-out store while the father waits in the car. However, it is certainly not true to state that an infant of any age can be an agent in all cases. Further, an unlicensed person could not be an agent at law, i.e., an attorney at law. It is stated that the incapacity of a party does not necessarily invalidate the act.

EXAMPLE 12.   A 77-year-old retiree was instructed by his brothers and sisters to find a buyer for the family homestead and given authority to sign the contract. He negotiated with a buyer and finally signed for the sale of the property. The guardian of the retiree then claimed that the retiree did not have the capacity to act as an agent for the family. The medical testimony revealed a mental condition due to the damaging effects of arteriosclerosis. The court understood that the retiree could not have grasped the technicalities of the legal and business steps presented to him for appropriate action. The court stated that regardless of the retiree's "overall competence to deal with his personal interest in the family tract, I have no doubt but that he was competent to act as an agent for members of his family." One not clearly mentally ill may act as an agent even though incapable of acting for himself.

26.10   PRINCIPALS

Infants and incompetents may be principals, but they are the beneficiaries of the rule that they may be able to disaffirm the appointment of an agent and the agent's acts under the same conditions as any other act they attempt. One cannot be a principal if the law specifically excludes the practice in a particular area. This rule would prohibit, for example, a banking corporation from appointing agents to deliver newspapers or do other acts not within the authority of the corporate charter or applicable law. In short, the capacity of a principal is that capacity he or she possesses as a legal entity, whether broad or narrow.

26.11 FORMATION OF THE AGENCY RELATIONSHIP

The conduct of the parties proves the agency relationship. Generally, this conduct may be proved by oral testimony, although certain appointments require a written memorandum, such as the authority to convey land. On the whole, in the absence of a specific statute, the common law tolerates a wide range of evidence to establish the relationship. The law, however, does not require a contract of agency, and while agreement is generally necessary, the presence of consideration is not. It is not unusual, therefore, to find agents who acted gratuitously, and yet their acts are binding nonetheless. Further, despite express language seemingly to the contrary, implied agreement to acts of the alleged agent binds the principal.

26.12 AGENTS' AUTHORITY: GENERALLY

Most legal issues arise over the question of the extent of the authority of the agent. In treating this subject the law examines such aspects as actual, or real, authority; express authority; implied authority and incidental authority; ratification; and apparent, or ostensible, authority.

26.13 ACTUAL, OR REAL, AUTHORITY

When a court finds as a matter of fact that one gave power to another to act for one, it states that the agent had *actual*, or *real*, authority. The concepts of express authority, implied authority, incidental authority, and ratification are considered to be within this characterization.

26.14 EXPRESS AUTHORITY

If an agent is appointed by clear language, either oral or written, the agent has been *expressly* authorized.

EXAMPLE 13.   Paula tells Adam, "Buy 500 bushels of wheat, Grade A, for me, and pay no more than $1,500; complete this task by Wednesday." If this testimony is believed by the trier of the facts, Adam is said to possess real, or actual, authority to purchase the wheat, as proved by the express language of Paula. When the authorization of the alleged principal is not so clearly verbalized, the term "implied" or "incidental" is used.

26.15 IMPLIED AUTHORITY AND INCIDENTAL AUTHORITY

Where the language of the principal is not explicit but the court finds the agent's conduct consistent with his or her general authority, it labels the right to be that of *implied* authority. Generally, the issue is not whether there was an agent for some purpose, but rather whether the agent possessed the power to perform the act in question. However, the alleged principal must have authorized the agent to do something. Mere personal relationship, for example, does not by itself evidence agency, no matter how intimate.

EXAMPLE 14. A landowner's outbuilding and personal property were destroyed by a fire started on adjoining property. It appeared that the adjoining owner's fiancée went on the property of her husband-to-be for the purpose of cleaning up the place. She negligently started a fire which spread to the landowner's property. The future husband had neither instructed his fiancée to go on his property nor asked her to clean it up. He did not even know of her presence. The court ruled that such facts were not sufficient to support the contention that the relationship between the husband-to-be and the fiancée was such as to justify charging him with negligence in her burning of the landowner's property. She was neither agent nor servant. She had neither implied nor incidental authority.

Implied authority, as well as incidental authority, is real authority. It includes the authority to perform acts reasonably necessary to achieve an authorized act and also arises from custom and usage.

EXAMPLE 15. Robin told Ben to sell and convey land but did not expressly state that Ben should sign Robin's name on the deed. The act of signing was implied since it was necessary to carry out the task.

EXAMPLE 16. Lane was appointed manufacturer's agent in dealing with fabric wholesalers. Lane was given few instructions. It is the custom in the industry for such agents to commit their companies (principals) for periods of 6 months or longer. Lane so contracts, only to learn from the company that their last buyer could not promise beyond a 3 months' supply. Third parties and Lane, the agent himself, may be protected by the doctrine of implied authority by reason of custom or usage in the industry.

Incidental authority is that which is assumed for ministerial acts that are necessary or convenient to carry out the task, and such authority is closely connected with implied authority.

26.16   RATIFICATION

Ratification is the equivalent of antecedent authority. Accordingly, a totally unauthorized act can be approved by a party (who thus becomes a principal) through his or her subsequent conduct.

EXAMPLE 17. Talbot, a rogue, purchases a stereo from a retailer on credit by falsely representing that his uncle sent him to the store for it. When the uncle learns of this act, he is enraged. He lectures Talbot, but pays the bill. Talbot was an agent for the uncle by the express act of ratification, i.e., payment of the bill.

There are, however, a number of tests which ratification must pass. It must be shown that (1) the principal had capacity or authority at the time of the act of the agent and at the time of ratification, (2) the act was legal and capable of being done, (3) the agent acted in the principal's name, (4) the principal had knowledge of the material facts at the time the principal approved the act, and (5) there was appropriate conduct by the principal indicating approval of the entire act before withdrawal by the third party. If any of these elements is missing, ratification does not take place.

Express, but subsequent, approval can be shown in many ways and in appropriate places, but must be done with the same formality as the original act. Signing one's name to an authorizing statement is, of course, strong evidence.

EXAMPLE 18. A reconditioned used Caterpillar tractor was sold by a salesperson to a buyer. A written contract form provided for disclaimers of liability for any breach of warranty. After the disclaimer provision there appeared the inclusion, "sold with 150-hour warranty." This line ended with the signature of the salesperson. The order form was signed by the buyer, and the entire contract was later signed by the salesperson's principal, the equipment company. The salesperson had no authority to make such a warranty. While the statement regarding the warranty was signed only by the salesperson, the whole agreement, which included this provision, was signed by the principal. It was ruled that the equipment company not only was a party to the contract, but also had ratified the warranty as expressed by the salesperson.

All elements of ratification must be met, and further, the ratification must be complete. The principal cannot approve of some terms and disapprove others. This occasionally occurs where the alleged principal contends that he or she had incomplete knowledge at the time. Further, ratification always refers to the time of the unauthorized act.

EXAMPLE 19.   An investor trusted an agent for her rental properties, but never gave him authority to mortgage or sell. The agent began to mortgage property without authority of the investor, showing false documents. The agent received proceeds from such mortgages in the name of the investor which he deposited in the investor's account in her bank. The bank notified the investor of the receipt of the proceeds. The investor immediately inquired of the agent as to the source of the funds. The agent falsely told the investor that it was from her other rental property. Satisfied, the investor informed the bank that "everything was okay, and had her approval." Sometime later she learned of liens on her property. The investor attempted to disavow authority to mortgage the property, but did not return the proceeds she had received. The court ruled that a principal cannot split an agency transaction and accept the benefits without the burdens. Also, a failure to investigate where the circumstances are such as to put a reasonable person on inquiry may result in ratification despite the lack of full knowledge.

26.17   APPARENT, OR OSTENSIBLE, AUTHORITY

Sometimes an agency is said to exist when no actual authority is present or, more commonly, where authority is clearly exceeded. When this happens, the court applies the doctrine of *apparent*, or *ostensible*, authority, or estoppel, to hold the principal. Apparent authority is based on the principal's manifestations to a third party which reasonably lead the third party to assume an agency. Therefore, it is the conduct of the apparent principal which must first be shown as indicating agency before inquiry is made into the conduct of the party acting as apparent agent.

EXAMPLE 20.   Buford Steel Company has been bothered by Teller, a party who has been falsely representing himself across the country as a Buford selling agent. This party made up printed forms showing the Buford name and trademark, including order forms. In one city Teller rented a small office with the company's name on the door for a period of 3 months. Any party misled by such an imposter may *not* even introduce in court these indicia of the presence of Buford unless it can first show some connection between the buyer and Buford. Buford would not be liable on apparent authority as its conduct in no way induces these buyers to think they are dealing with Buford.

EXAMPLE 21.   A buyer of food vending machines sued a manufacturer for the seller's alleged misrepresentation regarding the product and its use in the buyer's business. The manufacturer claims that the seller is not an agent and provides the court with the signed contract showing the seller to be merely an independent contractor. The buyer, on the other hand, offers evidence that the seller uses the manufacturer's order blanks, that checks for purchases of equipment were sent to the manufacturer, that the door on the seller's office had the manufacturer's legend on it, and that the manufacturer had acknowledged receipt of the buyer's order. There is sufficient evidence here to show apparent authority. The principal, intentionally or by want of ordinary care, caused third persons to believe another (the seller) to be its agent although the seller was not really employed by the principal.

Moreover, as a general principle, an agent has no apparent authority to delegate his or her authority to a subagent. Since most agency relationships are based on the principal's selection of another for personal qualifications, the third party may not assume that the subagent has the same authority as the agent. This is certainly true in matters other than purely ministerial, for example, where discretion or judgment is involved.

26.18   CONTRACT BETWEEN PRINCIPAL AND AGENT

Gratuitous agencies occur, but agencies more commonly arise out of a contract. Such can be express or implied, written, or oral in the absence of a statute requiring such and provided the Statute of Frauds does not apply. For example, an express agency appointment for longer than a year would have to be in writing. Further, the agreement can be articulate or somewhat vague, requiring the law to fill in necessary aspects of the relative rights and duties.

26.19 AGENCY CONTRACT: COMPENSATION

The law assumes that services are rendered for compensation and, without express agreement, a reasonable sum is to be paid. Litigation generally does not concern the amount, but rather whether any compensation at the agreed rate should continue upon termination or whether any was earned at all. For example, real estate agents occasionally must sue for commissions.

EXAMPLE 22.   A real estate agent is hired by an owner of land to find a purchaser for the property. This is sometimes called a *listing contract*, which some states require to be in writing. Generally, the agent has earned the commission if he or she brings the seller a purchaser who is ready, willing, and able to buy. The amount of the compensation is usually set, but the extent of the owner's commitment varies. If the agent has an *exclusive right to sell*, the presence of any purchaser, even if found by the owner, binds the owner to a commission. On the other hand, an *exclusive agency* allows the owner to find his or her own purchaser and thereby escape liability to the agent. The owner cannot, however, hire another agent during the term of the appointment. A *simple listing* permits the owner to engage others, including other agents, to find a purchaser, and entitles the first agent who provides a qualified buyer to receive the full commission.

Some agents are given advances for their performance, although paid only on commissions. Where the amount of the advance exceeds the commissions earned, an issue sometimes arises of whether an overage must be returned. Generally, in the absence of an express agreement or custom to the contrary, advances are treated as minimum salary. Further, it is also assumed that a contract achieved by the agent, but not yet performed, permits the agent to collect his or her commission later, even if the agency ends before the performance of the contract.

EXAMPLE 23.   A broker for Mines Company entered into a contract with a prison, the terms of which were to be carried out several years in the future. Before the performance, the broker died. Mines paid the broker's widow the commissions on the sales delivered under the contract before the death of the agent, but refused to pay the commissions for later deliveries. Mines contends that commissions cease upon the death of an agent. The agency contract is silent on this point. The court found in favor of the widow since there were no further duties to be performed by the broker. It ruled that a sales agent whose efforts are the procuring cause of a sale made during the agency is entitled to commissions even though actual delivery of the article is made after the termination of the agency, providing there is no clear understanding to the contrary.

26.20 CONTRACT: REIMBURSEMENT TO PRINCIPAL

The parties may express the extent of liability of the respective parties, and the mere fact that one is an agent does not immunize the agent from his or her contractual liability to the principal. A breach of contract by the agent, therefore, permits recovery by the principal.

EXAMPLE 24.   A homeowner employed an architect to engage and direct contractors to remodel the house. The architect warranted that the cost would not exceed $17,000. However, the total ran over $39,000, forcing the homeowner to pay those hired by his agent, the architect. The homeowner sued the architect for the difference. The court found that the architect had failed to prepare adequate plans, which resulted in the additional costs. The homeowner is entitled to reimbursement for the overage, less a deduction for the professional fee due the architect.

26.21 AGENCY DUTIES: GENERALLY

An agent has a *fiduciary* and *confidential* role with his or her principal. This is a position of trust and confidence, and it restricts the behavior of the agent. Several of these duties arise quite independent of contract, as they are placed on the agent by operation of law. They include the duty to be loyal, to be obedient, and to account to the principal.

26.22 AGENT'S DUTY: LOYALTY

Loyalty means that the principal's interest comes first. Information and intelligence obtained while under the agency can be used by the agent for the principal's purpose only. Further, without the consent of both, one cannot serve two principals.

EXAMPLE 25. Tremble, trained as an accountant, is hired by Kong Tax Service as its Boston manager and general agent. Tremble now has access to names of part-time tax preparers across the country, including those retired IRS agents willing to do some work. Further, certain methods used by Kong are cost savers and are clever techniques. They are closely held trade secrets. Tremble has a brother-in-law in a small California town who wants to open up a modest tax service there. The duty of loyalty to Kong prohibits Tremble from sharing this information with his brother-in-law.

The duty of loyalty outlasts the agency relationship and includes a duty not to reveal to others trade secrets and other proprietary information obtained while working for the principal. A more common question of loyalty is the *two masters scenario*. Professional agents might advance the point, for example, that they are intermediaries only and therefore not bound to the test of loyalty. To succeed, however, they must indeed show the absence of an agency relationship.

EXAMPLE 26. A builder hired a mortgage banker to find a construction lender and agreed to pay the banker $50,000. The banker found a finance company willing to loan the money and also willing to pay the banker a finder's fee, an arrangement unknown to the builder. The builder backed out of the loan and was sued by the banker for $50,000. Only then did the builder learn of the other fee. The banker claimed he was not an agent, but a "middleman" only, merely serving as a "conduit to bring the parties together," and that the parties themselves make the final deal. The court ruled that a broker who takes or contracts to take any part in the negotiations is not a middleman no matter how slight his role may be. The failure to reveal the vital fact of receiving a fee from the lender is a violation of the fundamental tenet of the agency relation. The banker cannot recover.

Agents must inform their principals when they are a party to the transaction. Since duties still exist after termination, some transactions may still be avoided at the option of the former employer. In the absence of a valid covenant not to compete, the former agent may work, perform, and compete against the old business and adverse to its interest. The former agent is prohibited, however, even in the absence of an agreement restricting revelation, from using secret lists, customer lists, formulas, and procedures which are the property of the former employer.

26.23 AGENT'S DUTY: OBEDIENCE

In the absence of unusual circumstances, an express direction by the principal to the agent must be obeyed even though it would, in the judgment of the agent, be foolish. Failure to obey can result in liability to the agent.

EXAMPLE 27. Acton, a general agent for the Pitson Company, is instructed to deliver "notice of termination" of a contract Pitson has with Weiss Company. Acton believes, rightly so, that such action could constitute a breach of contract and also cause bad feelings, which, in the long run, would be detrimental to Pitson's (and Acton's) best interest. Acton delays carrying out her instructions. By this time Weiss Company has changed its position relative to this contract. Had Acton given prompt notice as instructed, Weiss Company could have sued Pitson for $32,000 damages. Damages in the amount of $49,000 can now be recovered. Under these circumstances, Acton could be liable for the damage caused by her delay in not obeying the instructions of her principal.

Exceptions to the obedience principle exist where the instructions are illegal, where there is a change of facts which make it doubtful the principal would still issue such orders, and where there is an emergency situation in which further inquiry of the principal is not possible.

26.24 AGENT'S DUTY: ACCOUNTING

The agent is under an obligation to keep and render to his or her employer an account of money or other things which the agent has received or paid out on behalf of the principal. The burden of showing compliance is on the agent. One of the more clear cases of violation occurs in the commingling of the agent's property with that of the principal. Such commingling allows the court, in appropriate circumstances, to rule that any failures are the agent's and the successes in such account belong to the principal.

26.25 PRINCIPAL'S DUTIES OF REIMBURSEMENT AND INDEMNIFICATION

The duties of the principal are somewhat less than those of the agent. The principal is not, for example, under a fiduciary duty to the agent. Further, it is possible that the principal pay no compensation in situations where the agent has agreed to work gratuitously. The principal does, however, owe the duty of reimbursement and, when applicable, the burden of indemnification.

An agent who, in the proper course of employment, expends money or incurs expense in the furtherance of the principal's business is entitled to recover such sums. Commands that an agent travel to a certain place or purchase items to be used in the business are common situations of expense where the law assumes reimbursement. Where an agent carries out the principal's instructions and the act is not illegal but results in liability to the agent, the doctrine of indemnification is applicable. For example, it is possible that an agent for a seller may become liable for a breach of warranty in selling the principal's goods. Indemnification for this liability is available to the agent. Sometimes it is not a simple warranty, but a complicated lawsuit.

EXAMPLE 28. An insurance agent issued an automobile policy to a customer. The agent's principal, the insurance company, canceled the policy for nonpayment of premium 5 days before the customer was involved in an automobile accident which injured a third person, who successfully sued the customer and received a judgment for $10,000. The customer has no money, and so the third person sued the insurance agent for the money. The insurance agent asked for protection and monies to defend this lawsuit, but the company refused. The insurance agent hired her own attorney, who won the case and charged the agent $5,236.09. The agent paid the attorney and now seeks recovery from her company. The agent could recover her expenditures necessarily incurred in the transaction of her principal's affairs. An agent compelled to defend a baseless suit, grounded on acts performed in his or her principal's business, may recover from the principal the reasonable and necessary expenses of his or her defense under the doctrine of indemnification.

Black Letter Law
A Summary

1. Agency is a relationship by reason of agreement or operation of law which authorizes one to act for another.

2. When one authorizes another to act, he or she is named as principal and the party authorized is the agent.

3. A master-servant relationship exists where one is appointed to perform physical tasks for a party who has control over the manner of performance of the task.

4. An independent contractor is employed to achieve a task according to his or her own methods and under no control of the employer, except as to the result of the work.

5. An agency relationship can exist without a contract, as where one is appointed to act without consideration.

6. An employer is not liable for the acts of his or her independent contractor except in cases where an intrinsically dangerous task is undertaken or where the employer exercises excessive control.

7. The term "agent," when used with other words, does not necessarily refer to the full meaning of agent, as in "real estate agent."

8. Generally, the incapacity of the agent is immaterial, while that of the principal is governed by the rules of capacity.

9. Agency can be proved by oral testimony, except in situations where a particular statute is involved, such as the Statute of Frauds in regard to the year clause.

10. A principal gives actual authority expressly or by implication, or even subsequently by ratification.

11. A principal is bound by operation of law under the doctrine of apparent agency, or estoppel, where the principal's conduct leads a reasonable third party to assume agency.

12. Even in the absence of express agreement, the agent is a fiduciary; he or she must be loyal and obedient, must account to the principal; and is also subject to the rules of reimbursement and indemnification.

13. A principal is not a fiduciary to the agent, is subject to the rules of reimbursement and indemnification, and, in the absence of a gratuitous arrangement, must compensate the agent.

14. Ratification is the equivalent of antecedent authority, and requires a showing of competence, legality, knowledge of material facts, appropriate evidence of entire approval, no withdrawal of the third party, and evidence that the unauthorized "agent" acted in the other's name.

Solved Problems

26.1 Which of the following is *not* an essential element in an agency relationship?

(*a*) It must be created by contract.

(*b*) The agent must be subject to the principal's control.

(*c*) The agent is a fiduciary in respect to the principal.

(*d*) The agent acts on behalf of another and *not* himself or herself.

(*AICPA Examination, November 1978*)

It is only necessary that one appoint another to act; it is not essential that such arise out of a contract, statement (*a*). The other elements are all part of the relationship.

26.2 To invoke the doctrine of ratification successfully,

(*a*) the agent must have had the legal capacity to have so acted.

(*b*) the agent must in fact be the agent of the principal, although the action taken was totally without authority.

(*c*) the ratification must have been stated expressly.

(*d*) the ratification must be made with knowledge of the material facts of the transaction.

(*AICPA Examination, November 1981*)

Ratification is effective only if the alleged principal has knowledge of the material facts of the transaction, statement (*d*). This approval can be by any conduct, including that of implication. Capacity of the agent is not material, and the fact that the "agent" had no connection with the principal at the time of the act is likewise unimportant.

26.3 The key characteristic of a servant is that

(*a*) his or her physical conduct is controlled or subject to the right of control by the employer.

(*b*) the person is paid at an hourly rate as contrasted with the payment of a salary.

(*c*) the person is precluded from making contracts for and on behalf of his or her employer.

(*d*) the person lacks apparent authority to bind the employer.

(*Adapted from AICPA Examination, November 1981*)

The control or right of control of physical conduct clearly identifies a servant; statement (*a*) is correct. Servants frequently are placed in such a position that apparent authority is present. The method of pay is generally not helpful by itself in determining the true relationship.

26.4 A power of attorney is a useful method of creating an agency relationship. The power of attorney

(*a*) must be signed by both the principal and the agent.

(*b*) exclusively determines the purpose and powers of the agent.

(*c*) is the written authorization of the agent to act on the principal's behalf.

(*d*) is used primarily in the creation of the attorney-client relationship.

(*AICPA Examination, November 1980*)

The execution of a power of attorney is one method by which an agency authority is shown; statement (*c*) is the answer. Power of attorney is not, however, the exclusive method of determining all the rights and duties. Such powers are used in many commercial settings and are not restricted to the employment of an attorney-at-law.

26.5 Marcross is an agent for Fashion Frocks, Ltd. As such, Marcross made a contract for and on behalf of Fashion Frocks with Sowinski Fabrics. The contract was not authorized, and Fashion has disclaimed liability. Sowinski has sued Fashion on the contract, asserting that Marcross had the apparent authority to make it. In considering the factors which will determine the scope of Marcross's apparent authority, which of the following would *not* be important?

(*a*) The custom and usages of the business

(*b*) Previous acquiescence by the principal in similar contracts made by Marcross

(*c*) The express limitations placed upon Marcross's authority which were *not* known by Sowinski

(*d*) The status of Marcross's position in Fashion Frocks

(*Adapted from AICPA Examination, May 1981*)

Except for (*c*) all the above factors have a bearing on whether the conduct of Fashion Frocks led Sowinski to believe that Fashion's agent had authority to make the contract. It is always the conduct of the alleged principal which determines such liability. Custom and usage, the type of office held by the "agent," and previous dealings all assist the court in settling this issue.

26.6 In order to hold the principal liable under the ratification doctrine for the unauthorized act of a party purporting to act as his or her agent,

(*a*) the principal must have been in existence at the time the contract was made.

(*b*) the purported agent must have been acting for an undisclosed principal.

(*c*) the principal must have full knowledge of all the facts regarding the action to be taken on his or her behalf.

(*d*) the ratification must be in writing and made within a reasonable time after the unauthorized action was taken on his or her behalf.

Among the elements necessary for ratification to occur, it must be shown that the principal was in existence at the time of the contract, statement (*a*). Full knowledge is not necessary; just the knowledge of the material facts of the transaction is required. Ratification does not by itself require a writing.

26.7 Winter is a sales agent for Magnum Enterprises. Winter has assumed an obligation to indemnify Magnum if any of Winter's customers fail to pay. Under these circumstances, which of the following is correct?

(*a*) Winter's engagement must be in writing regardless of its duration.

(*b*) Upon default, Magnum must first proceed against the delinquent purchaser-debtor.

(*c*) The above facts describe a *del credere* agency relationship, and Winter will be liable in the event his customers fail to pay Magnum.

(*d*) There is *no* fiduciary relationship on either Winter's or Magnum's part.

(*AICPA Examination, May 1978*)

Statement (*c*) is correct. The agreement suggests a *del credere* agent, as the agent takes the risk of the credit sale of goods owned by the principal. Magnum may look first to its agent rather than the buyer of its goods. Despite the arrangement, Winter is an agent, and all agents owe a fiduciary duty to their principals.

26.8 Gladstone has been engaged as sales agent for the Doremus Corporation. Under which of the following circumstances may Gladstone delegate her duties to another?

(*a*) Where an emergency arises and the delegation is necessary to meet the emergency

(*b*) Where it is convenient for Gladstone to do so

(*c*) Only with the express consent of Doremus

(*d*) If Doremus sells its business to another

(*Adapted from AICPA Examination, May 1978*)

Normally subagents are the agents of the agent unless otherwise authorized by the principal. One exception occurs where an emergency arises, statement (*a*). Under such circumstances, it is possible for consent to the delegation to be implied.

26.9 A sign stating "10 Percent OFF Today Only" was posted at the camera counter at Orson's Department Store. The clerk at the camera counter suffered a heart attack while on duty. After the commotion had subsided, a well-dressed shopper walked behind the counter and cleverly changed the number on the sign from "10" to "30." This imposter sold 10 cameras to customers in a few minutes, pocketed the cash from those who paid cash or made down payments in cash, and fled. The manager, finally realizing that the camera sales counter was unattended and also seeing the changed sign, began to smell a rat. She ran to the store exit nearest the camera counter looking for customers with bags bearing the camera department's distinctive snapshot logo. She stopped four customers at the exit who were happily leaving the store with their "discounted" expensive cameras. Under these circumstances,

(*a*) the customers lose as they dealt with an imposter.

(*b*) Orson's loses under the doctrine of apparent authority.

(*c*) the customers win under the doctrine of implied authority.

(*d*) the customers win under the doctrine of ratification by Orson's failure to stop the other six customers.

Where the conduct of the principal leads reasonable parties to assume an agency, the doctrine of apparent, or ostensible, agency applies; statement (*b*) is the answer. The failure of the store to have the counter staffed may have resulted in the reasonable reaction of the customers. If they purchased the cameras in good faith, they can keep their purchases. It is always the conduct of the principal in relation to the third party's response that is tested. Implied authority suggests some real authority; such is not the case here.

26.10 The Saint Oslo Paper Company purchased new land for planting of trees but needed a number of scrub trees removed. It hired Anker, a layabout who had done some dynamite work when he worked in the oil fields. The company offered him $20 per tree removed, including the stumps. Since Anker had no money, the company bought the dynamite for him and would deduct its cost from the amount Anker would be paid at the end of the task. Which is the correct statement?

(*a*) Saint Oslo may be liable for any damage Anker causes to others while dynamiting, despite the fact that he is an independent contractor.

(*b*) If Saint Oslo just points out the trees to be blasted, it has no liability.

(*c*) If Saint Oslo has a signed agreement with Anker setting forth an independent contractor status, the actual conduct of the parties during the performance is immaterial.

(*d*) If Saint Oslo had not advanced the money for the dynamite, it could have escaped all liability caused by any negligent behavior of Anker.

Where dangerous tasks are to be performed that put others at risk by the actor, the employer may not always use the shield of an independent contractor to protect itself from vicarious liability. Saint Oslo has the possibility of liability under the dangerous task doctrine as well as a possible failure to exercise care in the selection of such a contractor, statement (*a*). It is likely that Saint Oslo has hired an independent contractor, but to no avail.

26.11 John and Mary, husband and wife, owned investment property as tenants in common. One such property was a working farm. Without examining the public record, one Gregory wanted to purchase the land and spoke to John, not realizing Mary's half interest. Gregory offered $75,000 under a lease purchase. John agreed, but when he told Mary she dissented, telling him she would not sell it for less than $85,000. John nevertheless granted the lease with an option to buy. Gregory made rental payments to John, who put the amounts into a joint (with Mary) investment account. At no time did Mary see Gregory or ever authorize John to sell the land. After 6 years, Gregory decided to purchase the property, only to discover that Mary would not sign the deed.

What principle of agency law will Gregory attempt to employ in getting Mary to sign the deed? Will he succeed? Decide, and state the reasons for your conclusions.

Since the evidence shows no actual authority in John to sell Mary's half interest, one cannot look for evidence of implied authority to carry out the mission. Accordingly, the best argument that Gregory can offer is apparent authority. As such, he must show that Mary's conduct in some way misled him as a reasonable person. The issue may well turn on the fact that he had a lease signed by a cotenant and such rental payments were taken by Mary. Whether this acquiescence regarding the lease would lead a reasonable person to consider one has authority to sell is doubtful, especially in the case of land. One normally looks up the record owners of land and does not rely on appearances. Since the only evidence is the rental situation, Gregory will have scant evidence to show apparent authority, or estoppel.

26.12 Roger was an eager young entrepreneur. His uncle owned a vacant lot several blocks from three small but successful restaurants. Roger asked permission of each to park the cars of their customers. Roger would not charge the restaurants a cent, relying instead on tips from the restaurant patrons. Each restaurant owner agreed, but issued a warning that "you are on your own; we pay you nothing and you owe us nothing." They did assent, however, to Roger and his assistants standing at the restaurant entrances and soliciting business. A snappy uniform was devised and worn by all the attendants. Unfortunately, one of the attendants turned out to be a thief, and during one night he stole three expensive cars. Roger did not have insurance for these losses, and his personal assets amounted to very little more than his clothes and a battered old jalopy. The owners of the stolen cars sued the restaurants involved.

What is the legal relationship between Roger and these restaurants? Discuss and give any reasons for your conclusions.

Although Roger, by express agreement of the parties, was not an actual employee of the restaurants, by implication he was their authorized agent for the purpose of parking the cars. Such authorization was manifested by the owners consenting to the presence of Roger and his assistants in front of the restaurant doors to receive customers, to park their cars, and to issue receipts therefor. This is more than apparent authority. Despite the negative agreement, this was really an agency by implied agreement. It was actual authority.

26.13 Nicola was less than delighted with the task of administering the estate of her late uncle. A major portion of the estate was her uncle's antique business, which included a substantial Chinese collection. This had always been a poor mover, although the items were valuable if one found the right buyers. Nicola met Bruce on an international flight to Paris, and their conversation got around to antiques and Nicola's need to dispose of her late uncle's business inventory, particularly the Chinese collection. It appeared that Bruce was truly an expert on many of the items in the collection. Nicola was very impressed and said she would be glad if Bruce would take it on. Bruce whipped a pad out of his briefcase as their 747 was crossing the English Channel and drew up the following document, which Nicola signed:

> I hereby appoint Bruce my exclusive agent to sell that certain Chinese collection now held by my late uncle's estate, for a period of 6 months, for a sum not less than $200,000, and at a commission rate of 26 percent, (signed) Nicola.

When Nicola arrived back at her home 10 days later, she commented happily to her friends on her good fortune in finding a first-class agent to move the Chinese collection. Hearing this, one of her wealthy racetrack buddies stated that he had always admired that collection and would pay $202,000 for it. Nicola eagerly agreed. Bruce was delighted when he heard the news a few days later and told Nicola to send the $52,520 commission (26 percent) check to a numbered Swiss account. Nicola doesn't see it that way.

What defense would Nicola attempt in resisting Bruce's claim? State your answer and any conclusions you have reached.

The creation of an exclusive agency for the sale of property binds the principal to sell to no buyer produced by a *different agent*. Nicola should defend on the grounds that she, the principal in this transaction, sold the collection. This is permitted where the agreement is for an exclusive agent only. Bruce made a crucial mistake. He should have used the phrase "exclusive right to sell" (instead of "exclusive agent"), thereby earning a commission even if the principal sold the item.

Chapter 27

Third Parties and Termination

27.1 INTRODUCTION

This chapter views third parties in their dealings with agents and principals and their rights and duties. Rules governing agents who buy, sell, and possess the principal's property will be treated as well as the effectiveness of notice. The third person's rights in an undisclosed principal situation, tort responsibility of agents and employees, and termination will also be treated.

27.2 AGENT'S CONDUCT

If the third party can offer no evidence of the principal's conduct which suggests agency, the agent's behavior cannot be introduced, no matter how convincing.

EXAMPLE 1. An owner of a car was involved in an accident, and the car was removed to a garage for repairs. The owner owed money to a car finance company. A man representing himself as an insurance adjuster for the finance company instructed the garage manager to repair the car. While the work was in progress, the garage manager received a telephone call, purportedly from the finance company, inquiring about the status of the repairs. A later call was also received by another garage employee. When the garage manager demanded that the finance company pay for the repairs, the company denied all knowledge of having an agent on the garage premises and of any telephone calls. Neither the garage manager nor the employee could identify either the man who had come to the garage or the voices they had heard on the telephone. Under these circumstances, the garage may not introduce into evidence the statements of the "agents" made on the premises or during the telephone calls.

There must be evidence of conduct by the alleged principal, not merely statements of the agent. This does not deprive the third party from offering testimony of the agent. It does, however, preclude the third party from testifying what the alleged agent said until such speaker is somehow independently connected to the principal. The more common dispute, however, does not involve imposter situations, but rather the extent of authority of agents.

27.3 AGENT BUYING AND SELLING

Agents are frequently granted express authority to buy and sell. When they are so authorized, the third party must question what representations to believe. Generally, business usage, the custom of the industry, and certain legal implications determine how much authority an agent possesses where the extent of the agent's authority is not stated. A buyer for a department store, for example, may or may not have authority to enter into a contract purchase from a manufacturer or wholesaler.

EXAMPLE 2. Ace Department Store is highly successful but very conservative. Its buyer for men's suits has no discretionary authority to contract and certainly not on credit. He is a "looker" and "telephoner," through which means he reports back and is only then given specific authority. Most who deal with Ace are aware of this practice. Ace sends this buyer into a new supply area. The buyer becomes excited over some bargain, believes that Ace would agree, and is fearful that delay would be costly. He agrees to purchase a shipment on credit. It is the custom in this supply area for buyers to have the authority to contract and to do it on credit. Ace's conduct in sending the buyer into this area where such a custom exists *is the conduct* which would make Ace liable for the buyer's unauthorized act.

Generally, a buyer can be assumed to have authority to buy, but the law does not enlarge such right to include a credit purchase unless such was necessary and the principal provided the agent with no funds. Even here, the credit arrangement cannot involve commercial paper, as a third party has no basis to assume that an agent has apparent authority to sign a negotiable instrument such as a promissory note or a draft on behalf of his or her principal.

The apparent power of an agent to sell is likewise examined by the surrounding circumstances and custom and usage. Some types of possession of an article reasonably indicate to a third party a power to sell. Clearly, a department store clerk in seeming possession of goods behind the counter has the apparent authority to sell such goods and deliver them up, but then only for cash or, as is the custom today, by approved credit cards.

Mere possession or authority to sell personal property does not by itself imply unlimited authority as to the type of contract that can be made. Thus, unusual contract terms may be unauthorized and not the responsibility of the principal.

EXAMPLE 3. A buyer of roofing material alleged that upon the recommendation of the salesman, he employed and paid for a certain individual to apply the roofing material with the salesman supervising the application. The roof leaked. The salesman guaranteed that the roofing material would keep the roof from leaking for 10 years. The seller contends that the salesman had no authority to go beyond the brochures, invoices, and printed instructions which are furnished with the product. There was no evidence that the seller was aware of the salesman's statement. The jury found for the seller. The court ruled that neither an agency nor scope of authority can be established by the declarations or actions of the purported agent. The express warranty was unusual and inconsistent with the writings. A jury could reasonably find that the third person was not entitled to rely on these statements despite the salesman's claim that he was talking as an agent for the seller.

While an unusual express warranty should be suspect, the salesperson who recommends a product would normally have authority to activate an implied warranty of fitness for a particular purpose and any customary warranty.

EXAMPLE 4. Testa had heard about "clogging," a dance style all the rage. He travels to the local shoe store where he tells the saleswoman of his needs. The saleswoman recommends a particular type of shoe. The saleswoman has bound her principal to an implied warranty that the shoes are fit for a particular purpose, that is, clogging.

27.4 AGENTS: POSSESSION AND NOTICE

Possession may be thought of as nine-tenths of the law, but such by an agent provides the innocent third party with little evidence of apparent authority by itself.

EXAMPLE 5. Chinchilla, a valuable brood mare, was taken to a California ranch by an Arizona owner to be bred. In the past the owner would personally transport the animal to and from California. When Chinchilla was in foal, the California rancher did not notify the owner, but instead made arrangements with a common carrier to ship the mare back to Arizona. The mare died in the van during transport through the hot desert. The owner sued the carrier for the loss. The California rancher signed a declared value limit of $150 with the carrier. The carrier defended the lawsuit on the grounds that the California rancher was an agent for the Arizona owner when it signed the liability limitations. The court awarded the owner damages of $25,000. The rancher was not the agent for the owner when he signed the value limitation. The sole basis for estoppel must rest on the rancher's possession of the mare. Mere possession carries with it no indication of any right to engage in transactions of a serious consequence to the owner of personal property. There is no showing here of express or implied authority by the rancher to ship the mare, and certainly no apparent authority.

A principal can be affected by his or her agent's contact with third persons in more ways than strictly creating contracts. Certain facts and information given to or learned by an agent are imputed to the principal. The agent's awareness is the principal's awareness.

EXAMPLE 6. Able telephones Baker offering to sell certain goods. Baker, unable to make a decision, promises to call back in an hour with her answer. Baker later telephones Able but reaches only his secretary. Baker informs him that she accepts the offer, and to tell Able. Able returns to the office feeling unwell. Distracted by the illness, the secretary does not tell Able of Baker's acceptance. Able dies before learning of the acceptance. The secretary's knowledge under these circumstances is Able's. A contract would be formed.

The secretary above had no express authority to accept notice, but the law would imply such authority by the nature of his position. The effectiveness of notice given to another in the firm is dependent on whether the relationship and circumstances are such that it appears reasonable that an employer should be responsible for the effect of the notice.

EXAMPLE 7. The terms of the contract between a sand dealer and a contractor provide for delivery of sand at certain times and at certain prices, each party being permitted to terminate the contract upon giving the other party 30 days notice of such intention to terminate. The contractor decides that he can get sand cheaper elsewhere. When the driver delivers the next load, he is informed by the contractor that 30-day notice is hereby given and that the driver should inform his boss. The driver forgets about the message. In the absence of a showing of broader authority, notice to the driver is not notice to the sand dealer.

Where agents have express authority, and their position is more than ministerial, any knowledge bearing on the subject matter of the agency is imputed to the principal whether learned before the agency was created or during the employment. This rule can work harshly in cases where large organizations are involved. Such knowledge is not imputed, however, if it appears that the facts or notice was received under circumstances or conduct so as to raise the clear presumption that the recipient would not communicate such to his or her principal. Further, if a party is an agent and has a business of his or her own, it is unlikely that every act or notice is imputed, particularly where the agent acts adversely to the principal's interest.

EXAMPLE 8. A used-car dealer sold several cars to buyers on credit, the buyers signing conditional sales contracts. The dealer sold the contracts to a finance company and promised that new titles would reflect the finance company as lienholder. The dealer had an arrangement with Enterprise Company under which the dealer would be the purchasing agent for Enterprise. The dealer submitted to Enterprise the titles to the cars without notice of liens placed on them. Enterprise, believing the titles to be clear, paid the dealer. The dealer had now received money from this principal, Enterprise, and the finance company for the same cars. The finance company contends that Enterprise had notice of the liens. The court ruled in favor of Enterprise, the principal of the dealer. Here the agent was clearly acting for himself, not his principal, and adversely to the interest of the principal. The dealer's knowledge will not be imputed to the principal. The principal's interest is superior to that of the finance company.

27.5 UNDISCLOSED PRINCIPALS

A principal can issue more than secret intentions to the agent regarding the business, as the principal can direct his or her agent to hide the principal's presence. When a principal does such, there is an undisclosed principal situation. Three parties are nevertheless still involved: the undisclosed principal, the agent, and the third party. The principal may hold the third party to the contract, and the third party has a right not only against the principal, once discovered, but also against the agent. Generally, the third party will not be able to complain that he or she did not wish to deal with the now revealed principal unless it can be clearly shown that he or she had previously announced such, or unless personal service or trust is involved.

Frequently, in litigation, it is the principal who attempts to escape liability either because the principal now regrets the contract or because the principal believes he or she had never appointed an agent in the first place.

EXAMPLE 9. A dancing student sued Lotus Dance, a national dancing school, for the return of amounts prepaid to a local franchisee for lessons not furnished. The Lotus school offered written evidence that the student contracted with the franchisee and that Lotus's name was never used on such contracts. The student proved that Lotus exercised rigid and effective controls over almost every aspect of the franchisee's operation. The court ruled that Lotus was an undisclosed principal and is liable for the contractual obligations incurred by its agent in the course of the agency.

27.6 UNNAMED OR PARTIALLY DISCLOSED PRINCIPALS

Where the third party is aware of the agency but does not know the identity of the principal, a partially disclosed or unnamed principal situation arises. Generally, the third party may hold either party to the contract once the identity is disclosed.

EXAMPLE 10. A detective agency sued an attorney for services performed in its investigation of an insurance claim. The attorney defended on the grounds that he was working for a corporation when he hired the detective agency. The agency admitted that it knew the attorney was representing the client, but did not know the identity. The bill was not paid, and the client corporation became bankrupt. The attorney was held liable although the court admitted that not all states follow that rule. This court stated that if the attorney wanted to exclude himself from liability, he should have expressly provided for that at the time of the contract.

27.7 UNDISCLOSED PRINCIPAL: THIRD PARTY'S ELECTION

Where the identity of the principal is not known, the third party can hold either the principal or agent liable, but may obtain only one satisfaction. The third party must make an election of parties once the identity of the principal is known. The third party usually has a considerable period within which to make this decision. Even after a judgment has been entered against the agent, a principal may be proceeded against if this is the earliest his or her identity is known.

EXAMPLE 11. A promoter, by written agreement with Pankay, agreed to supply the services of musicians at certain times and at specified rates. Claiming a breach, the promoter sued Pankay and obtained a judgment, but no satisfaction. The promoter then learned that a corporation was the real principal. The promoter proceeded to sue the corporation, which defended on the grounds that the claim was now merged in the judgment against the employer (Pankay) and was *res judicata*. The court ruled that, by weight of authority, the promoter had not made a final election which would bar him from proceeding against the principal, now revealed.

27.8 INJURIES TO THIRD PARTIES: TORT LIABILITY

An employee, agent, or servant might commit a tort within the course of his or her duties. When the employee does so, the issue of liability to the principal arises under the *doctrine of vicarious liability* or *respondeat superior*. There are many possible torts, including assault, battery, slander, defamation, invasion of privacy, libel, negligence, fraud, duress, and conversion. (Note that some of these acts are also crimes and may be punishable separately under criminal statutes. See Section 27.12.) When an agent commits a tort within the course of employment or in furtherance of his or her employer's interest, the principal or employer is likewise liable.

Obviously, few principals or employers order their agents or employees to do an act that is tortious. Yet if the court views the act as having occurred within the scope of the employee's duties, then vicarious liability is imputed.

EXAMPLE 12. Harrison owns an office building. His janitor negligently left a broom in a dangerous place at 4:45 p.m. although the janitor was under specific instructions to begin cleaning up no earlier than 5:30 p.m. A lawyer in the building tripped on the broom and injured herself as a result of this "negligent" act that the janitor was not authorized to do. This is a tort. Both the janitor and his employer (master) would be liable to the third party, the lawyer. The incident occurred within the scope of the janitor's employment duties, though the act certainly was not authorized.

EXAMPLE 13. Maddingdale owned a stock car racetrack. He hired Brinson to manage the track. Brinson is therefore both an agent and employee. Maddingdale directed that under no circumstances was Brinson personally to attempt to break up any fight or disturbance during the meets. He was ordered to call the local police instead. A fracas erupted during the third race, and Brinson, thinking that he could handle it, tried to stop it. As he attempted to separate a few of the main actors, he struck a person who turned out to be an innocent party. This is a battery, a tort. While Brinson's act was unauthorized and occurred while disobeying specific instructions, the law would say that the act was committed in furtherance of his principal's business. Both would be liable to the third party.

Not all tortious acts committed by agents or employees seemingly during some phase of their duties are imputed to the employer. Where the court finds that the act is an extreme deviation from the employee's duties or is independently motivated, the actor is sometimes described as being "on a frolic of his own." The employer is not liable for those acts. Automobile negligence cases are the apt illustrations of acts which physically depart from the terms of one's employment or agency.

EXAMPLE 14. Rumpere, a credit adjuster, uses her own car in business but carries no liability insurance. Further, she has no assets. On her way to see a client she telephones her husband and promises to pick up some items at a bakery for him. On her way to the client, she negligently sideswipes another car. She leaves her name and address. She is upset but proceeds to business which she attends to. On her way back to the office, Rumpere finally remembers the bakery. She must now turn back six blocks. During the return she negligently strikes a bicyclist at a dangerous intersection. Rumpere's employer would, like Rumpere, be liable for the sideswipe accident, but would argue that Rumpere was making an "extreme deviation" when she hit the cyclist. Many courts would agree that this deviation excuses the employer from vicarious liability.

The more difficult cases deal with agents charged with the torts of fraud, deceit, or misrepresentation in the seeming performance of their duties of contracting for the principal.

EXAMPLE 15. Two corporate officers, in a successful attempt to induce the transfer of an employee, promised him lifetime employment in their Los Angeles office if he would move. The employee agreed, but the working conditions became intolerable in Los Angeles due to the management practices there. When the employee was told to "like it or quit," the employee resigned. The employee sued the corporation, contending that the transfer cost him $17,500 for moving expenses and other out-of-pocket expenses. The employee proved that the statements made by the two officers were fraudulent. The corporation defended on the grounds that the officers had no authority to offer lifetime employment, much less make fraudulent statements. The corporation was held liable, as it is accountable for the unauthorized acts which are not too far removed from the scope of the officers' authority as hiring agents.

27.9 AGENTS AND THIRD PARTIES

Unless a party contracting makes it clear that he or she is speaking or acting for another, the mere fact of agency does not excuse the agent from contractual liability to the third party.

EXAMPLE 16. Killion granted a broker a 60-day exclusive right to sell a transmission service company. On the agreement, Killion signed his name over the printed word "Owner." The property was sold, but Killion would not pay the commission, contending that the corporation was the owner of the business and owed the commission. Killion was liable because, in order to avoid liability, it is the duty of the signer to disclose his agency. By concealing the fact that the business for sale belonged to a corporation, the individual assumed the status tantamount to that of an agent with an undisclosed principal.

Where the agent can prove he or she had the authority to act and the third person knew of the agency, the agent is not liable for the principal's breach of contract, or even insolvency. A warranty by an agent in the sale of goods, for instance, if authorized, is the responsibility of the principal alone.

27.10 THIRD PARTIES AND NONEXISTENT PRINCIPALS

If the "agent" had no principal or, having a principal for some purposes, did not have authority for the particular act, the agent would be liable on the grounds of breach of warranty that a principal existed or such authority existed, or liable in an action for deceit. The good faith of the agent is generally no legal excuse where it appears that the principal is not bound or does not exist. Some states, by statute, rescue the agent in some situations, as where, unknown to the agent, the principal has died and the agent acts within the scope of his or her previous authority. The knowledge of the third party regarding the situation bears heavily on the question of liability. An indication that one is speaking for a minor, for example, or under circumstances that the agent is no longer sure of his or her authority to act for another, is such knowledge which denies the third party rights against the agent.

EXAMPLE 17. A number of residents reacted quickly to a land developer's attempt to have residential zoning changed to commercial. One Tyson is emerging as the leader of the group by default. An attorney is invited to attend a meeting of the residents. The attorney is present at the meeting when Tyson recommends that the attorney be employed and retained for $750. There appears to be general but vague agreement, but no vote is taken. Other matters are discussed, but the group is unorganized and not completely identified. Tyson's assurance to the attorney that he will be paid would not generally bind Tyson should the group fail to pay. The third party, here the attorney, is aware of the nonexistence of the principal. Had the group voted, those voting might be the principal and Tyson their agent.

An agent who has no principal is observed in promoter cases. There the promoter deals with third parties on behalf of a corporation yet to be formed. Under the rules discussed above, it is easy to see the promoter's individual liability in such circumstances.

27.11 TORTS AND AGENT LIABILITY

Any tort committed by an agent within the scope of his or her authority (or without it) is, of course, the responsibility of the agent. The liability of the agent is both joint and several. The third person can join the agent and principal in the same action (i.e., joint liability) or sue each party in a separate action (i.e., several liability). Only one satisfaction is allowed. Where the principal must pay, the principal is entitled to seek indemnification of the loss from his or her agent, impractical as this may sometimes be.

27.12 CRIMINAL RESPONSIBILITY

If an agent was directed to perform an act in violation of the public policy of the state, both principal and agent are criminally liable. The language of the criminal statute prescribes what acts of the principal are prohibited as well as those of the agent, who, of course, may not successfully argue that he or she is "just carrying out the orders of the employer."

27.13 TERMINATION: PRINCIPAL AND AGENT

An agent has *power* to bind his or her principal. This power, however, can be severed in most cases by the unilateral act of the principal, as the agent's consent is not necessary despite the existence of a nonrevocable contract. The agent can sue for breach of the contract, but this in no way diminishes the power of the principal to terminate the agency.

EXAMPLE 18. A distributor and canner had an agreement under which the distributor was given an exclusive right, provided the latter promised to use best efforts to promote the product and would handle no competing brands. This agreement could be canceled by either party at will. After 20 years of successful dealing, the canner learned that its agent was now handling competing brands and the next day notified the distributor that the agency contract was canceled. The distributor objected to the short notice, which would cause considerable damage to his business. The agency is terminated, but the distributor may prove damages for breach of contract. The court implied an agreement that the cancellation clause be interpreted to mean "reasonable notification of termination" under these circumstances.

Death, adjudication of insanity, and bankruptcy of either party are grounds for termination of the agency by operation of law. Further, the destruction of the subject matter, subsequent illegality, impossibility of performance, or the happening of other circumstances which a court may say as a matter of contract principles discharged the contract ends the agency relationship.

Due to commercial necessity, some events otherwise causing an end to the agency relationship are addressed by state statutes that provide a modification of the general rule.

EXAMPLE 19. Beverton draws a $500 check on her bank. In effect the bank is being ordered to pay the check and is an agent for the drawer, Beverton. Before the check is presented for payment, Beverton dies. Under common law, death terminates the bank's power to pay. However, Section 4-405 of the UCC changes the rule and permits the bank to act as agent to cash the check after the death and, unless a stop payment is ordered, for 10 days after the death even when the bank has knowledge of the death.

EXAMPLE 20. Tomkins granted Henry, his son, power of attorney to sell and convey his farm for a favorable price. Tomkins, now living in Florida, dies suddenly while Henry is negotiating the sale of the farm. After the death of Tomkins, Henry signs a contract for the sale of the farm. In many states, if this power of attorney is recorded, a state statute validates the act of the agent so acting under the statute to transfer the deceased principal's property to an innocent purchaser.

There are, of course, other natural methods of terminating an agency. These include termination by agreement, lapse of time, occurrence of a specified event, and achievement of the specific purpose.

27.14 AGENCY COUPLED WITH AN INTEREST: TERMINATION

There are exceptions to the rule that a principal can always unilaterally terminate the agency, or that death terminates the agency power. This can occur in situations where the principal created an "agency or power coupled with an interest." Where a power is given to the agent who derives present or future interest in the property, such authority can neither be revoked nor be terminated by the occurrence of an outside event.

EXAMPLE 21. Tittle and her business associate, Yeager, tried a flier on a stock purchase, holding the stock in both names. Later, Tittle wanted to sell the stock, and Yeager authorized Tittle to sell his interest in the stock also when appropriate. Tittle has a power, or agency, coupled with an interest. This would not be terminated by the death of Yeager.

EXAMPLE 22. An owner of land signed and dated a mineral deed and delivered it to his brother, complete except for the name of the grantee. The owner authorized his brother to fill in the name of the grantee, including the name of the brother. After the death of the owner, the brother filled in his own name. The court ruled that the completion was valid as the owner had created in the agent, the brother, an irrevocable power coupled with an interest in the person to whom the deed was delivered.

Where the interest of the agent arises only out of the proceeds of the transaction, or from commissions therefrom, or where the agent's only right is to receive by way of commissions or compensation a certain percentage of a sale or collection, the power is revocable, whether by death or otherwise.

EXAMPLE 23.   An auto broker was given the right to transfer the title to an owner's car and sell it for no less than $6,000, with a 22 percent commission to be paid out of the sale. This is *not* an agency coupled with an interest. The broker's only interest arises out of a sale, if and when made.

EXAMPLE 24.   A doctor had a 10-year contract as the medical director for a hospital. The contract with the hospital expressly provided that the appointment could not be revoked or altered during that period. The doctor was fired and resisted dismissal on the grounds that he had an agency coupled with an interest. The court ruled the doctor had no interest in the subject matter independent of the power conferred. The hospital had power to terminate, but whether it could do so with legal immunity from breach of contract is a different issue.

Where there is a pledge or mortgage of an item with a creditor with the understanding that the creditor may, upon default, sell the item at a private sale in satisfaction of the debt, a "power given as a security" is created. This agency cannot be revoked or terminated before payment.

27.15   THIRD PARTIES: NOTICE OF TERMINATION

Third persons do not always know when an agency has been terminated, but they are subject to the rule that irrespective of notice a termination by operation of law (e.g., death, insanity, and bankruptcy) prevents them from holding the principal liable.

However, a termination of the agency on other grounds entitles certain third parties to a form of notice of termination. Persons who have dealt, or are now dealing, with the agency must have actual notice of termination. Other third parties who might know of the agency are entitled to constructive notice. Constructive notice could be some public notice, usually a newspaper announcement in the community where the agency was generally known.

Established customers generally are entitled to a more personal notification. This requirement is not usually difficult to meet, but the rule of personal notification is broader and might include situations involving apparent authority as contrasted with a situation in which a general agent of long-standing has been terminated.

EXAMPLE 25.   An owner of several farms hired a manager to operate them. The manager employed a contractor to bale the hay and instructed him to send the bill to the owner. The bill was paid, and the practice was repeated the following year. This time the owner refused to pay, contending that the manager's authority was revoked after last year's job. The owner proved that while the manager remained on the premises, he was, after the termination, only a tenant. The court ruled in favor of the contractor. The authority of the agent to bind his principal continues even after actual revocation until notice of revocation is given.

Black Letter Law
A Summary

1.   A third party dealing with an unauthorized agent must prove that the principal's conduct justifiably led him or her to rely on the representations of the agent.

2.   When an agent buys, sells, or is in possession of the principal's property, the agent's actions which are consistent with such status, custom and usage, or business practice determine the extent of the agent's apparent authority.

3. Generally, such knowledge or notice the agent possesses regarding the principal's business is imputed to the principal, unless it involves matters where the agent is acting adversely to the principal's interest.

4. Third parties are bound to, and have rights against, the agent and principal in situations involving an undisclosed or partially disclosed principal.

5. A third party does not make a final election to hold the agent or principal liable until the identity of the principal is revealed.

6. The doctrine of *respondeat superior*, or vicarious liability, causes the employer to be liable for the torts of an employee committed within the scope of the employment or in furtherance of the employer's business.

7. The employer's defense to vicarious liability rests on proving that the employee acted independently, in extreme deviation from his or her duties, or during a "frolic of his own."

8. A principal can be liable for his or her agent's misrepresentation or deceit provided it was committed while acting for the principal.

9. An agent impliedly warrants the existence of the principal and, unless otherwise indicated, his or her capacity.

10. Where vicarious liability is involved, the third party may hold the agent and principal either jointly or severally.

11. Unless there is an agency or power coupled with an interest, a principal may revoke the agency at any time despite the fact that the principal may thereby be liable for breach of contract.

12. Third parties who are dealing, or have dealt, with the agent are entitled to actual notice of agency termination.

13. Termination by operation of law does not require notification, and such instances include termination by death, insanity, bankruptcy, and illegality.

14. An agency coupled with an interest is revocable neither by the principal nor by death and is created when the agent has an independent interest in the subject matter of the agency that does not arise solely from the appointment of the agency.

Solved Problems

27.1   Joe Walters was employed by the Metropolitan Department Store as a driver of one of its delivery trucks. Under the terms of his employment he made deliveries daily along a designated route and brought the truck back to the store's garage for overnight storage. One day instead of returning to the garage as required, he drove the truck 20 miles north of the area he covered, expecting to attend a social function unrelated to his employment or to his employer's affairs. Through his negligence in operating the truck while en route, Walters seriously injured Richard Bunt. Walters caused the accident and was solely at fault. Bunt entered suit in tort against the store for damages for personal injuries, alleging that the store, as principal, was responsible for the tortious acts of its agents. Under these circumstances,

(a)   Metropolitan is *not* liable because Walters was an independent contractor.

(b)   Metropolitan is *not* liable because Walters had abandoned his employment and was engaged in an independent activity of his own.

(c)   Metropolitan is liable based upon the doctrine of *respondeat superior*.

(d)   Bunt can recover damages from both Walters and Metropolitan.

(*AICPA Examination, November 1974*)

   The only defense that an employer has when an employee has committed a tort is to prove that the act was an extreme deviation, that the activity was an independent act, or that the employee was on a "frolic of his own." Here, the action during which the tort occurred was an independent activity, statement (*b*). Walters was not an independent contractor. Bunt's only action is against Walters, the tortfeasor.

27.2   An agent's power to bind his or her principal to a contract is generally terminated

(*a*)   automatically upon the commission of a tort by the agent.

(*b*)   instantly upon the death of the principal.

(*c*)   upon the bankruptcy of the agent.

(*d*)   without further action by the principal upon the resignation of the agent.

(*Adapted from AICPA Examination, November 1974*)

   Death of either the principal or the agent generally terminates the agency by the operation of law; statement (*b*) is the answer. Bankruptcy or tort of the agent might permit termination by the principal, but such is not automatic. Notice of termination cuts the power to bind, not resignation itself.

27.3   Brian purchased an electric typewriter from Robert under a written contract. The contract provided that Robert retained title until the purchase price was fully paid and granted him the right to repossess the typewriter if Brian failed to make any of the required 10 payments. Arthur, an employee of Robert, was instructed to repossess the machine on the basis that Brian had defaulted in making the third payment. Arthur took possession of the typewriter and delivered it to Robert. It was then discovered that Brian was not in default. Which of the following conclusions is supported by the above facts?

(*a*)   Arthur is *not* liable to Brian.

(*b*)   Brian can sue either man or both men for damages, but can collect only once.

(*c*)   Neither party is liable since it was apparently an honest mistake.

(*d*)   If Arthur is sued and must make payment of the judgment obtained against him, he has *no* rights against Robert.

(*Adapted from AICPA Examination, May 1977*)

   Statement (*b*) is the answer. Both a principal and agent are liable for torts committed within the scope of the employment. The tort of conversion was involved here. Arthur's error does not diminish this tort, which is the taking of another's property, whether under the impression of correctness or not. Since Arthur followed instructions of the principal, causing him (Arthur) liability, he can seek indemnification from Robert, his principal.

27.4   Gaspard & Devlin, a medium-sized CPA firm, employed Marshall as a staff accountant. Marshall was negligent in auditing several of the firm's clients. Under these circumstances, which of the following statements is true?

(a) Gaspard & Devlin is *not* liable for Marshall's negligence because CPAs are generally considered to be independent contractors.

(b) Gaspard & Devlin would *not* be liable for Marshall's negligence if Marshall disobeyed specific instructions in the performance of the audits.

(c) Gaspard & Devlin can recover against its insurer on its malpractice policy even if one of the partners was also negligent in reviewing Marshall's work.

(d) Marshall would have no personal liability for negligence.

(AICPA Examination, November 1977)

This tort of negligence was committed by an agent while in the scope of his duties. Both the tortfeasor, Marshall, and his employer, Gaspard & Devlin, are jointly liable to the client, the latter under the doctrine of *respondeat superior*. An agent's failure to follow instructions is no defense to the principal. Gaspard & Devlin's can recover on its malpractice policy, as stated in answer (c).

27.5 Star Corporation dismissed Moon, its purchasing agent. Star published notice in appropriate trade journals, which stated: "This is to notify all parties concerned that Moon is no longer employed by Star Corporation, and the corporation assumes no further responsibility for his acts." Moon called on several of Star's suppliers with whom he had previously dealt, and when he found one who was unaware of his dismissal, he placed a substantial order for merchandise to be delivered to a warehouse in which Moon rented space. Star had rented space in the warehouse in the past when its storage facilities were crowded. Moon also called on several suppliers with whom Star had never dealt and made purchases from them on open account in the name of Star. The merchandise purchased by Moon was delivered to the warehouse. Moon then sold all the merchandise and absconded with the money. Which of the following most accurately describes the legal implications of this situation?

(a) Moon had apparent authority to make contracts on Star's behalf with suppliers with whom Moon was currently dealing as Star's agent if the suppliers had *no* actual knowledge of his dismissal.

(b) The suppliers who previously had *no* dealings with Star can enforce the contracts against Star if the suppliers had *no* actual knowledge of Moon's lack of authority.

(c) Star is liable on the Moon contracts to all suppliers who had dealt with Moon in the past as Star's agent and who have not received personal notice, even though they had read the published notice.

(d) Constructive notice by publication in the appropriate trade journals is an effective notice to all third parties regardless of whether they had previously dealt with Moon or read the notice.

(AICPA Examination, November 1977)

The legal implications of the situation are summed up in statement (a). Third parties who have dealt with the agency and those who are currently dealing with the agency are entitled to actual notice of the termination. Knowledge by the third party, wherever learned, is sufficient notice of termination. A constructive notice by publication is adequate notice for those who have not dealt with the agency before.

27.6 Filmore hired Stillwell as her agent to acquire Dobbs's land at a price *not* to exceed $50,000; the land is badly needed to provide additional parking space for Filmore's shoping center. In order to prevent Dobbs from asking for an exorbitant price, Filmore told Stillwell *not* to disclose his principal. Stillwell subsequently purchased the land for $45,000. Under these circumstances, (*a*) Stillwell and Filmore committed fraud when they did *not* disclose the fact that Stillwell was Filmore's agent.

(*b*) absent an agreement regarding the compensation to be paid Stillwell, he is entitled to the difference between the $50,000 limitation and the $45,000 he paid for the land, i.e., $5,000 based upon quasi contract.

(*c*) Dobbs may rescind the contract upon his learning the truth as long as the conveyance has *not* been accomplished.

(*d*) Dobbs may sue either Filmore or Stillwell on the contract in the event of default by Filmore.

(*AICPA Examination, May 1975*)

Where one is an agent for an undisclosed principal, the third party can hold either the agent or the principal liable; the answer is (*d*). It is not fraud to act for an undisclosed principal. Agents are entitled to reasonable compensation in the absence of a specific agreement, but there is no automatic entitlement to a sum calculated in the manner indicated. A third party is generally liable to an undisclosed principal on a contract made by an agent.

27.7 Under which of the following circumstances will an agent acting on behalf of a disclosed principal *not* be liable to a third party for his or her actions?

(*a*) The agent signs a negotiable instrument in his or her own name and does *not* indicate an agency capacity.

(*b*) The agent commits a tort in the course of discharging his or her duties.

(*c*) The agent is acting for a nonexistent principal who subsequently comes into existence after the time of the agent's actions on the principal's behalf.

(*d*) The agent lacks specific express authority but is acting within the scope of his or her implied authority.

(*Adapted from AICPA Examination, November 1976*)

Where an agent acts for a disclosed principal and has actual authority, whether express or implied, the agent will not be liable on the contract he or she makes for the principal, statement (*d*). An agent will be liable on a negotiable instrument if the agent fails to name the principal, but the principal will not be liable. Agents are always liable for their own torts. An agent breaches his or her warranty when the agent acts for a nonexistent principal.

27.8 Wilcox works as a welder for Miracle Muffler, Inc. He was specially trained by Miracle in the procedures and safety precautions applicable to installing replacement mufflers on automobiles. One rule of which he was aware involved a prohibition against installing a muffler on any auto which had heavily congealed oil or grease or which had any leaks. Wilcox disregarded this rule, and as a result an auto caught fire, causing extensive property damage and injury to Wilcox. Which of the following statements is true?

(*a*) Miracle is *not* liable because its rule prohibited Wilcox from installing the muffler in question.

(*b*) Miracle is *not* liable to Wilcox under the workers' compensation laws.

(*c*) Miracle is liable irrespective of its efforts to prevent such an occurrence and the fact that it exercised reasonable care.

(*d*) Wilcox does *not* have any personal liability for the loss because he was acting for and on behalf of his employer.

(*AICPA Examination, May 1978*)

The employer is liable without fault when an employee commits a fault under the doctrine of vicarious liability, or *respondeat superior*; statement (*c*) is the answer. The failure of an employee to follow instructions does not excuse the employer under tort liability if the act giving rise to the tort was committed within the scope of employment. Employees are always liable for their own torts. Most employees are covered by workers' compensation despite their own negligence.

27.9   In which of the following can it be said that the agent possesses *actual* authority?

(*a*)   Apparent authority

(*b*)   Ratification

(*c*)   Agency by estoppel

(*d*)   Ostensible authority

In all but ratification, statement (*b*), the agent is said to have no real or actual authority. Statements (*a*), (*c*), and (*d*) refer to those cases in which the conduct of the principal has led a third person to believe that such authority existed. While at the time the agent acted in a ratification situation the agent had no actual authority, the subsequent conduct by the principal vested real or actual authority. This intentional appointment relates to the time of the act of the agent when he or she improperly assumed authority.

27.10   In which of the following would an agent *not* be liable to the third party?

(*a*)   Where the principal is unnamed

(*b*)   Where the agent committed the tort while "on a frolic of his own"

(*c*)   Where the third party knew that the principal was a minor

(*d*)   Where the principal is undisclosed

An agent would not be liable on his or her implied warranty of existence and capacity of the principal where the third party knows that the principal is a minor, statement (*c*). The agent is liable in undisclosed, and partially disclosed, principal situations, and, of course, the tortfeasor is always responsible for his or her own torts whether on a frolic of his or her own or not.

27.11   A daughter opened a clothing store and permitted her father to act on her behalf on many business dealings. The daughter had an account with a bank and also delivered to the bank a power of attorney in favor of her father. The power of attorney did not expressly state that the father was granted the power to borrow money. The father signed a promissory note, i.e., negotiable instrument, for the loan of money to put into the daughter's business. The promissory note read, in effect, "Daughter, by Father." The promissory note was not paid when due, and the bank is attempting to hold the daughter liable on the promissory note. The daughter invokes the rule that an agent has no apparent authority to sign a negotiable instrument on behalf of the principal.

On these facts would the daughter be liable on the promissory note? Decide and state reasons for any conclusions.

The daughter will probably succeed using this defense. The authority to borrow money on the credit of the principal is among the most important and also dangerous powers which a principal can confer on an agent. Further, the right to sign a commercial instrument, a promissory note, is likewise not easily inferred. Courts are reluctant to find authority to borrow where such authority is not explicitly conferred. Here, the written power of attorney was not clear enough to indicate that such authority had been granted by the daughter.

27.12   An auto insurance company rejected the application of a minor for a policy. The title to the car was then transferred to the minor's brother, who lived several hundred miles away. A new application for insurance showed that the car would be kept in the town where the minor lived and not at the residence of the brother, the new title holder. It appeared that the agent had either approved or suggested the change of title so as to permit the minor to qualify for insurance. An accident occurred, and the company contends that the policy is void. The argument is made that the knowledge of the agent is imputed to the principal.

What type of defense would the insurance company argue against the contention of imputed knowledge? State your answer and give the reasons for your conclusions.

It is true that most notice to and knowledge of the agent is also notice to and knowledge of the principal. There is one exception, however, which the company should attempt to invoke. A principal is not affected by notice to an agent who is acting adversely to the interests of his or her principal and, instead, for the benefit of either himself or herself or a third party. If it can be shown that this technique of changing title was done to assist the agent to make more commissions, or to benefit a friend or customer, at the expense of the company, the exception can be applied. As the facts appear in this case, it is possible, perhaps probable, that a court would find that the agent's conduct was such as to permit the company to invoke the exception and escape liability.

27.13 The president of a construction company telephoned a plumber requesting an estimate on a job, identifying himself as president. The plumber prepared a written contract and addressed it to the construction company. The president signed the contract but did not indicate on the contract that he was signing for the company. Payments to the plumber were made by checks, one of which did not clear. The checks were drawn on a company account, the president being one of the two signers on the checks. The plumber sued the company and the president individually, charging that the president is liable since he did not sign as an agent.

What principle of agency law is the plumber attempting to invoke? State your answer and give reasons for any conclusions.

The plumber is attempting to charge that the president did not name his principal. Thus the doctrine of undisclosed principal operates to the detriment of the agent. However, the circumstances are such that the plumber had notice of the agency relationship. While the safer procedure would have been for the president to sign in his agency capacity, the principal seems disclosed, thus relieving the agency (the president individually) of contract liability.

Topic Test, Part VI

Agency

1. A city water works official was inspecting certain work by a building contractor on a hookup to the city water system. In checking the work at the site, the official jumped down into the excavation to show a worker that the refilling had been done improperly. An argument developed, and the official struck the worker. A second worker who had been shoveling dirt into the hole, then struck the official on the head with his shovel, causing injury. The official sued the building contractor for the tort of his servant. What principle of law will the contractor attempt to use to escape liability?

2. A property owner suffered a fire loss and hired an adjuster to adjust the matter with the owner's fire insurance company. The company contended that the adjuster attempted to defraud the company by fraudulently increasing certain claims of loss. The insurance policy provided that the contract of insurance was void if the insured "shall make an attempt to defraud the company either before or after the loss." The company claimed that the attempted fraud of the adjuster is the act of the owner even though there was no evidence of personal fraud by the owner. Is the owner subject to the fraudulent act of the adjuster, her agent?

3. A purchaser's property was being foreclosed by the seller, who held a mortgage. Among the defenses raised by the purchaser was the claim that, unknown to the purchaser, the real estate broker who brought the parties together worked for both the purchaser and seller and received compensation from both. The purchaser is attempting to reclaim part of the purchase price as that amount which the purchaser paid the real estate broker. What principle of agency law is being presented?

4. Homecleaning Company employed workers and machinery in its business. One employee had worked for the company for 3 years and was requested to sign an agreement that she would not compete with the company after termination of employment. The employee refused to sign the agreement. During the final months of the employee's service in the company, she indicated that she was going to go into business on her own. After leaving the company, she did start up and succeeded in obtaining a number of customers from the company. Is the former employee now free to take away customers from her former employer?

5. An owner hired a broker to find a purchaser for her property for a price of $80,000 "net" to the owner. In August a prospective purchaser inquired about the availability of the owner's property. Such inquiry came to the attention of the broker, who finally supplied such information on September 10. The owner had died on September 7. The purchaser learned of the owner's death on September 12 when he first attempted to contact the owner. The purchaser bought the property from the heirs of the owner in October, the heirs knowing nothing of the employment agreement the owner had made with the broker. The broker demands compensation for his services from the owner's estate, claiming that he found the purchaser. What defense can the owner's estate raise in this claim?

6. An insurance agent was directed by her company not to issue insurance on boats more than 3 years old or worth more than $5,000 without a condition survey. The agency issued a binder in contravention of such instructions, and the insured boat was lost in a storm. The insured sued the company and recovered. The company attempts to retrieve its loss from the agent. What principle of agency law is involved?

7. A seller was given the exclusive right to sell equipment of the manufacturer in certain specified Western states, but no set period of employment was agreed upon. The seller proceeded with necessary preliminary work involving both services and expenditures needed to implement the seller's planned marketing efforts. The manufacturer terminated the agency without notice. The seller contends that the manufacturer is without power to terminate the agency. Does the seller have any rights in this matter?

8. Nine owners of a parcel of commercial property appointed Eric, one of the nine, as agent for the group to sell the property. During the attempt, the offering came to the notice of a business consultant, who called Eric's office and reached one Charles, another one of the owners and who worked for Eric. They discussed the sale of the parcel, and Charles believed it was such a good proposition that he told the business consultant that they had a deal. The other owners objected, charging that Charles had no authority to act for them. Charles claimed that he was an agent for Eric and therefore had authority. The business consultant sued the nine owners on the deal made by Charles, the subagent. What principle of law determines this lawsuit?

9. A husband and wife were considering the purchase of a house and talked to a bank officer regarding the financing. Among the matters discussed was the need for a termite inspection. The banker told the couple that this was necessary and that the bank usually handled this and charged a fee of $15. The bank ordered the inspection, and the report reflected termite infestation requiring a $450 treatment. The bank neglected to bring this to the attention of the couple, who settled the transaction, only learning of the termite problem sometime later. The couple sued the bank on the grounds that it failed to inform the couple of the findings of the termite inspection report. They sought damages for the termite treatment. The bank claims that it is in the business of providing financing, is at arm's length with its borrowers, and is not the agent for buyers. What is the bank's relationship?

10. Falkin owned a summer retreat that he wished placed up for sale. Happy, who ran an auction house, convinced Falkin that an auction would bring the highest price. Falkin expected at least $90,000 for the property, and Happy felt confident that such could be obtained. Falkin signed a contract authorizing the auction "for the highest price available." Happy was to receive 15 percent of the proceeds of the sale. Happy was going to spend a lot of money advertising, and so he made Falkin sign a promise that the appointment of Happy was irrevocable. Happy ran ads and spent considerable money on promotion, but it looked like few bidders would show up. Preliminary talk before the auction was that if someone offered a sum as high as $62,000, it would be unusual. Falkin panicked and ordered Happy not to call the property up for auction. Happy pointed out the agreement terms, rejected the order, and held the auction. The property was sold for $76,000. What principle will determine whether the buyer at the auction is entitled to good title to the property? Did Happy have the right to continue the auction?

Answers

1. The issue is whether the second worker was acting within the scope of his authority so as to make the employer liable for the tort of battery. Here, the employee worked on the outside crew as a laborer. He had no real interest except digging that furthered his master's business. The court held that the act of battery was a substantial deviation from the duties assigned by the employer. The employer, the building contractor, is not liable.

2. The fraudulent acts of an agent which are committed during the course of employment are generally the responsibility of the principal. Here, the acts were clearly meant to fulfill the principal's instructions, that is, to adjust the loss. The property owner loses.

3. This situation involves the doctrine that an agent for one party cannot act for the other party without the consent of both principals. Where the agent acts in a dual capacity without such assent, the transaction is voidable. If the purchaser can prove that he was without knowledge of such dual agency, a defense to the action is possible.

4. Yes, one is free to compete with a former employer unless one has contracted otherwise by a restrictive covenant. One is not, however, entitled to solicit customers from such competing business *before the end of the employment* in direct competition with the current employer's business.

5. An agency generally terminates upon the death of the principal or the agent. Since the purchaser only learned of the property listing after the death of the owner and the heirs had no knowledge, the estate is not liable. Agency ceased.

6. The rule is that an agent who proceeds beyond his or her authority is liable to indemnify the principal for the latter's losses arising from the act. The agent would be liable and cannot escape the losses and throw them on the principal-insurer.

7. Except where there is an agency coupled with an interest, the principal has the power to terminate the agency relationship. Where there is no set period of employment, the contract is at will. However, the principal may not be completely justified in taking such action and must respond to damages when it is shown that the agent, induced by the appointment, has in good faith incurred expenses and devoted time and labor in the matter of the agency without having had sufficient opportunity to recoup such from the undertaking. Where the facts justify it, damages can be awarded against the principal, even in the case of indefinite agency. Under the circumstances of this situation, damages would appear likely, although the agency itself could be terminated because it was at will.

8. The issue is whether a subagent can bind the original principal, in this case the nine owners. Charles's authority comes from Eric, the true agent. The agency relationship is based on the trust and confidence the principal places in his or her agent. The relationship generally is personal, and ordinarily such authority cannot be delegated without the express approval of the principal where the duties involve personal discretion, skill, or judgment. Here, the agent's job was one involving personal discretion, and accordingly, there is no apparent authority to appoint a subagent to make such a contract that only the agent could make.

9. The bank entered into two relationships. One was that of the lender, an arm's length contractor; the other was an undertaking to do the buyer's job (conducting a termite inspection), and this was an agency relationship. Accordingly, an agent has a duty to do his or her job. When an agent fails to do so, as in this case, the agent is liable to the principal. The bank was required to pay for the termite treatment.

10. Where an agent is appointed and those dealing with the agent are aware of the agency, they are entitled to actual notice of termination. The publicity, approved by the principal, placed the innocent buyer as one entitled to actual notice of termination. Accordingly, the third party (the buyer) may enforce the contract of purchase. This was not an agency coupled with an interest since the only interest that the agent possessed was that of a commission as a result of his appointment. Falkin had the legal authority to terminate the agency despite his promise not to so end it, but the agent would have rights for breach of contract, just as Falkin has a right against his former agent for failing to obey his order.

Chapter 28

Formation and Relationships

28.1 PARTNERSHIPS: DEFINITION

The Uniform Partnership Act (UPA), which nearly all states have enacted, defines a partnership as an association of two or more persons to carry on as co-owners of a business for profit. It is not necessary to prove that the parties intended a partnership, only that they intended to do those things that the law considers as constituting a partnership. Each element of the definition will be examined.

28.2 AN ASSOCIATION

An association implies consent of the parties. If two or more agree to operate a business together as owners to make money, but specifically agree that they are not partners, they are nevertheless legal partners. One cannot be forced into the relationship, however. For example, the son of a deceased partner cannot unilaterally be placed into his father's firm just because the father's will provided for the interest to pass to the son.

EXAMPLE 1. A father, son, and daughter formed a partnership to form a printing business. Later the father and a second son entered into a written agreement by which the father assigned his interest to his second son in "name only," the real owner being the father until his death. The second son worked in the firm but had no authority or control in the administration of the partnership and did not share in the profits or losses. When the father died, the second son contended he was a partner. The court held against the second son, ruling that whatever the agreement was between the father and second son, it was not that of a partnership since no consent was given and the father never intended any interest to pass to the second son.

28.3 TWO OR MORE PERSONS

A partnership is composed of legal persons, either natural or artificial. Even the incapacity of a party does not necessarily deprive him or her of the right to become a partner. Infants, therefore, could be partners, though they still possess the right to disaffirm contracts, but could lose their capital investment, which is not returnable where creditors are involved. Further, incompetents, if not adjudicated such, could become partners. Corporations, unless prohibited by statute or their own charter, may qualify as partners. Corporations frequently participate in joint ventures or partnerships and are found in construction (engineering contractors) and exploration (oil companies).

EXAMPLE 2. A building corporation and Bronsen entered into an agreement for the purpose of setting up and operating a grocery and meat market. The corporation would loan cash and use its credit to equip the market. A note in the sum of $20,700 in favor of the building corporation was signed by the building corporation and by Bronsen for the partnership. The market failed, and the building corporation maintains that it was a creditor and that it was landlord of the building. The evidence showed that the parties had entered into a written agreement entitled "Agreement for Joint Venture" and that both had joined in filing the market's name under a fictitious name. The court ruled against the corporation, stating that there is no rule that states that the firm cannot owe one of its partners or that one partner cannot be a corporation.

28.4 CARRYING ON A BUSINESS

The term "business" in this context includes every trade, occupation, and profession which is intended to make a profit. The courts interpret the requirement broadly to include almost all acts, and one attempting to escape the effects of a partnership can only rarely prove that his or her endeavor is not a business under the act.

28.5 AS CO-OWNERS

In co-ownership, there must be an intention of the parties to make each party an owner of the business. Sometimes the assets of the business are not tangible, but the concept of co-ownership is not restricted to tangible property; the concept merely requires that it is to be the intention of the parties that each is an owner of the efforts that the parties place into the firm for the purpose of achieving profit.

EXAMPLE 3. Altman runs a successful public relations firm but needs an inside person. Barbara, although penurious, is bookish, conservative, and dependable. Altman owns a small building where he does business and which is fully equipped with furniture and office machines. Altman has many clients. Altman and Barbara agree to become equal partners, but Altman is to continue to own separately the building and all the equipment. Altman and Barbara are partners. The common ownership is in the success or failure of the firm. Barbara has the possibility of making a profit and, of course, runs the risk of incurring a loss. She has a voice in the management. She has no right to the specific property which, under their agreement, remained the property of Altman.

Parties who do own property together and earn money from its use or sale are not, solely by reason of that ownership, partners. The UPA provides that a joint tenancy, tenancy in common, common property, or part ownership of property does *not of itself* establish a partnership, whether such co-owners do or do not share any profits made from the use of the property.

28.6 INTENTION TO SHARE PROFITS

This last element is many times crucial in determining whether a partnership exists. The UPA provides that the receipt by a person of a share in the profits of a business is *prima facie* evidence that he or she is a partner. This means that such showing places the burden of the party objecting to the claim of partnership to disprove the relationship.

There are, however, certain situations in which this valuable presumption does not arise. The UPA provides that payment received from a business in any of the following circumstances does not, by itself, create a presumption of partnership: (1) as creditor, (2) as wages to an employee, (3) as rent to a landlord, (4) as an annuity to a widow or representative of a deceased partner, (5) as interest on a loan, even though the amount varies with the profits of the business, or (6) as the consideration for the sale of goodwill of a business or property.

These exceptions govern only when unaccompanied by other evidence suggesting partnership. Coupling any of these with some control leads to a strong showing for the existence of a partnership.

EXAMPLE 4. As part of a divorce settlement, a wife obtained a profitable business that harvested and hauled custom grain. When the wife took over the business, she orally agreed to sell the business to an employee for $30,000, payable $6,000 per year, plus interest. The employee put no money down. All the firm's earnings were to be placed in a firm bank account requiring both parties to sign withdrawals until the $30,000 was finally paid. The wife was to receive one-fourth of the profits until fully paid, the employee being entitled to a draw, but the wife would keep the records. The wife's children worked for the firm. One of the firm's trucks was involved in an accident and injured a third party, which sued both the wife and the employee. The wife maintained that she was the seller of the business, not a partner. The driver of the truck testified that he took orders from both the wife and the employee. The court ruled that the wife was more than a seller of the business. The right of control of a business is an incident of proprietorship. Where her control was substantially as great as that of the employee, a jury could find that a partnership existed.

28.7 ARTICLES OF PARTNERSHIP

While some parties unintentionally enter into a partnership, most deliberately and expressly agree to be partners. The terms of this agreement are known as the *articles of a partnership* when the parties sign a written agreement.

EXAMPLE 5. Paxton and Potter visit an attorney and instruct her to prepare a partnership agreement. Paxton is the promoter type, the activist in the proposal. Potter is the "angel," the man with the money. The attorney starts to ask questions about how much each is putting up, i.e., the capital contribution of each, how much time each will spend, what property will belong to the firm, etc. Through this set of queries, the attorney will prepare the articles of partnership which will include such matters as the name of the firm, the term of the partnership, the names of the partners, their duties, the business, the scope of partnership authority, the relative responsibilities of the partners, the capital contribution of each, a listing of the property to be dedicated to the firm, the manner of settling disputes, the sharing of the profits and losses, and the other promises and restrictions on the partners.

28.8 PARTNERSHIP NAME

The firm may not adopt any name prohibited by law. Nor may it adopt the name of another firm if by doing so it would mislead the public or deprive the other firm of its recognized rights. Since the name selected may be other than the exact name of the partners, most states require that the partnership be registered under a *fictitious name statute*.

28.9 ORAL PARTNERSHIP AGREEMENTS

Some partnership agreements are not reduced to writing but are proved solely by the conduct of the parties, including their oral statements. Unless prohibited by statute, an oral agreement is enforceable provided it does not expressly bind the partners for more than a year. The Statute of Frauds also requires a written agreement where the articles contemplate transfer of land. Many oral partnerships are so formed that they escape both the year clause and the transfer of land provisions of the Statute of Frauds.

EXAMPLE 6. A promoter of a proposed shopping center contended he had certain rights against a corporation which held title to the land. The promoter claimed he was a partner with the corporation. He alleged the oral agreement was for the promoter and the corporation to be joint adventurers in purchasing and developing real property, one contributing money and the other services. The corporation contended the Statute of Frauds demands a writing, as this "involved land and would take more than a year." The court ruled this was not a contract for an interest in land, only for land development. Further, in order to bring an oral agreement within the year clause, there must be a *negation* of the right to perform within the year. Here the parties never stated that the agreement could not be performed fully within a year and there was a possibility for complete performance within 1 year. The corporation lost, and the oral partnership agreement was enforced.

28.10 PARTNERSHIP BY ESTOPPEL

Where a person's conduct leads one to think that another is a partner, a third party relying thereon to his or her detriment can hold as a partner the acting party whose conduct caused such reliance. This creates a partnership by estoppel, similar to the apparent, or ostensible, agency doctrine.

EXAMPLE 7.   Tucker rents space with Alonso, who runs a public relations firm. Tucker is in the same business but is just starting out. In showing prospective accounts around, both Tucker and Alonso give the impression that this is a big firm and that they are partners. One of Tucker's suppliers, who does not extend credit to small one-person firms, credibly believes that Tucker is with Alonso and so grants credit to Tucker. Tucker is unable to pay, and the creditor looks to Alonso. While they are not partners, a third party (here, the creditor) may hold Alonso as a partner by estoppel provided Alonso's conduct misled the creditor to rely on the apparent relationship.

28.11   KINDS OF PARTNERS AND PARTNERSHIPS

A number of different adjectives precede these terms and include trading, nontrading, general, limited, universal, silent, dormant, retiring, incoming, surviving, ostensible, special, nominal, and liquidating. These terms are not necessarily mutually exclusive and, in most instances, serve to give particularity and identification to a special effort or status.

28.12   GENERAL AND LIMITED PARTNERSHIPS

A *general partnership* is one in which a number of parties join in a common effort and are equally liable to third persons to the full extent of each member's personal liability. The partners may have agreed to share profits and losses in different ratios, but their liability to third persons is full and complete despite such agreement. They have unlimited liability.

A *limited partnership* is one in which some members have unlimited liability and others limited liability. The former are called *general partners* and the latter *limited partners*. Unlike general partnerships, however, a limited partnership can only be created by a writing, and this writing must be filed in the appropriate state office, similar to a filing of incorporation papers by a corporation. Every limited partnership must have at least one general partner. (Chapter 31 treats limited partnerships.)

28.13   UNIVERSAL PARTNERSHIP

When parties form an association to combine all their property, present and future, they have agreed to a general partnership, which is called a *universal partnership*. Louisiana specifically provides for such a complete undertaking, it being found mainly in family associations.

28.14   SILENT, OR DORMANT, PARTNERSHIP

When a party hides the fact of his or her membership in a partnership, the person is said to be a *silent*, or *dormant*, *partner*. Such situations are not uncommon and frequently occur where parties agree to finance another in some business but, for reasons of their own, do not want others to know of their investment. Legally, however, there is no distinction nor diminishment in liability for the party, who, once discovered, is held as a general partner.

28.15   RETIRING PARTNERS AND INCOMING PARTNERS

When one general partner leaves a partnership, he or she is called a *retiring partner*, while a new member of the partnership is called an *incoming partner*. The partners who continue with the partnership are identified as *continuing partners*.

28.16 SURVIVING PARTNER

Death terminates a partnership and creates in the remaining partners the right to wind up the business. At this point such partners are called *surviving partners* and are entitled to the right of winding up partnership affairs and terminating the business. This is a liquidation of the firm, and such partners remaining are called *liquidating partners*.

28.17 NOMINAL PARTNERS

While one can be a real partner only by agreement, the law treats a relationship as a partnership when it decrees a partnership by estoppel, as when a party permits his or her name to be used as a partner. Such a party may be a *nominal partner*, in name only, with no real interest in the firm. Third parties are not bound by such agreement, however, and may rely on the appearances of this nominal partner.

EXAMPLE 8.   Dr. Braddock planned to retire and sell his practice to three young doctors, who would pay for the practice over the next 5 years. Braddock is interested in seeing the practice prosper so that he can get paid. Accordingly, as part of the contract, Braddock agrees to let his name remain on the clinic doors and promises to walk through the waiting rooms at least seven times a month. He is, however, to have no rights in the partnership of the three young doctors. Braddock is not a real partner. He is one in name only. As to third parties who rely on his appearance, however, he would have partnership liability, as there appears to be an ostensible partnership.

28.18 PARTNERSHIP GOODWILL

The trade name of the partnership is frequently the center around which goodwill gathers and becomes an intangible but nevertheless valuable asset. *Goodwill* has been defined by courts as "that something in business which gives reasonable expectancy of preference in the race of competition to advantage," or "the expectation of continued public patronage," or, simply, "value beyond the tangible capital, stock, funds, inventory or property employed in the enterprise."

EXAMPLE 9.   Lee purchases a lot and shack at the riverside for $15,000. She decides to start a bait and tackle shop and invests $8,000 in inventory and fixtures. It is a sole proprietorship. She adopts the name of "Lee's Worms" and runs the operation well, and after a year, Bascom and Jack, a partnership, wish to purchase the entire business for $35,000. At this time the lot, the inventory, and the other property are worth $25,000. The $10,000 difference is, in effect, the value of goodwill, an intangible asset.

Goodwill is considered an asset in partnerships and must be accounted for among the partners upon dissolution by death of a partner.

28.19 PARTNERSHIP CAPITAL

Partnership capital consists of the contribution required of each partner by their agreement which is the aggregate of the sums contributed for the purpose of carrying on the business and is intended to be risked by them in such partnership.

EXAMPLE 10.   Mye, Gator, and Red decide to form a partnership. Mye contributes $10,000 to capital, Gator $5,000, and Red the use of his pickup truck for 1 year, which they all agree is valued at $2,000 per year of use. Simply stated, the partners agreed that the capital of the firm at the beginning is a total of $17,000.

Sometimes the parties do not make it clear what has been contributed to the capital account.

EXAMPLE 11. A doctor and a pharmacist agree to operate a drugstore. The doctor contributed $10,000 to start. All the pharmacist has is his license, his skills, and his willingness to work. The business prospers, and the pharmacist is permitted to take $100 a week out to live on. The cost of developing a sophisticated drug inventory increases, and the doctor puts more money into the store, $3,000 one time and $6,000 another. The pharmacist needs more money to live on, and they agree that he can draw $200 per week. The business does well, but much of the profit is tied up in inventory. The doctor now retires and needs income. The doctor contends that he has contributed $19,000 to capital while the pharmacist has given nothing. The pharmacist is shocked, arguing that his earnings as an employee would have averaged over $300 per week for the many years of the drugstore's operation had he hired out for his "market value." He therefore concludes that his capital contribution is the difference between compensation actually received and the amount he could have earned elsewhere. He calculates this sum as $12,000. Since the parties had not made an agreement about what constituted capital, the lawsuit would find the pharmacist in a poor position to make the case he is proposing.

Accordingly, it is the common intention of the parties which determines the amount of permanent investment, the capital of a partnership. This may be varied during the life of the firm or even set as a final value in the articles or other agreement of the parties.

EXAMPLE 12. Two partners operated an automobile agency. Their written articles of partnership provided that upon the death of one of the partners the surviving partner was required to pay the estate of the deceased partner the sum of $40,000 for his interest. Ten years later one of the partners died, and the surviving partner tendered a $40,000 check to the representative of the deceased partner. The representative refused the check, contending that the books clearly showed that the capital alone of each partner was over $100,000, and that the capital is a debt of the firm. A lawsuit was brought to enforce the agreement. The court agreed that the capital was a debt of the firm but that the agreement in the articles governed the issue. The deceased partner's interest can and must be surrendered for the agreed-upon $40,000. (It may be noted that the reverse might have been true. Had the capital of the partnership amounted only to a total of, say, $50,000 at the time of the deceased partner's death, the surviving partner would have been bound to pay the deceased partner's estate $40,000, or sell or liquidate the business and split the proceeds.)

28.20 PARTNERSHIP PROPERTY: DEDICATION

It is not necessary that the partnership own any property, although it is likely that it has either some property or the use of such. Partnership property is for the common partnership use only, and no one partner can be deprived of it without his or her consent. In the absence of a contrary agreement it is for equal use. Further, partnership creditors have prior claim against such property as against creditors of individual partners.

Money, personal property, land, intangibles, right to services, (and the use of them) could become partnership property if there is an intent to dedicate them to firm use. Partners hold ownership in such firm property as tenants in partnership. Litigation, however, reveals the common difficulty partners have sometimes in determining what property was ever dedicated to firm use.

EXAMPLE 13. Lon and Mason are partners in the landscape business. They use a special soil spreader Lon has developed, a truck (title to which is held in Mason's name), an old building which is owned by Lon's father, and a gravel pit from which they take material and on which there is a 10-year lease. The soil spreader is unique and may be capable of being patented; the truck is being maintained and repaired from funds of the firm, the taxes and repair on the building are paid by the firm, and the lease on the gravel pit is in the name of Mason for convenience but the rent is paid by the firm. The parties never discussed what property is owned by the firm, and never agreed on the exact amount of capital each has committed to the firm. For each item, a court would have to determine whether any of this property, as opposed to its mere use, was dedicated to the firm.

The fact that some title certificates show ownership in a name other than that of the firm does not foreclose the possibility that real ownership is otherwise. Courts look to the intention of the parties as indicated by agreement or conduct. Generally, however, unless a contrary intention appears, "property acquired with partnership funds is partnership property," UPA, Section 8(2).

EXAMPLE 14. A deed was taken in the name of five persons. Three were children of a deceased partner. It was their contention that since the deed did not recite the proportionate interest of the parties, each takes a one-fifth share as tenants in common. The two others in this case were partners with the father of the children. The property was purchased entirely from partnership assets. The partners contend that the children are entitled to one-third, their father's share. The court ruled that where property was purchased from firm assets, ownership vests in the partnership in proportion to the partnership account. In the absence of other showing, the partners share equally. The children's share is the interest of their deceased father, that is, one-third. The court quoted the old saying that, "The land is his whose the money was."

The presumption of ownership by reason of use of partnership funds is not irrebuttable, however. Where contrary evidence of use and intention is present, the court can rule otherwise.

EXAMPLE 15. A plumbing business was run by two members as partners. The firm was issued a comprehensive liability insurance policy. Sometime later the partners purchased an apartment house and took title in their individual names. The apartment house was not located on the same street as the business. An accident occurred on the premises of the apartment house, and the partners contended that the partnership insurance policy covered the incident. The liability of the insurance company turned on the question of whether the apartment house was partnership property. The apartment house was purchased from firm funds, which, the firm contends, dictates that it is partnership property. The insurance company offered that the building was not used for any firm purpose and that the partners had difficulty purchasing appropriate insurance. The court ruled that the insurance company was entitled to rebut the presumption that property purchased with firm funds was firm property.

28.21 RIGHTS IN PARTNERSHIP PROPERTY

A partner's rights in firm property are common to the other partners. One cannot transfer one's rights in specific partnership property, nor can the creditors of an individual partner levy on such property by reason of a partner's personal obligation. Such a creditor can only have execution issue against the individual partner's interest in the partnership.

EXAMPLE 16. Able and Baker are partners in a bakery. The firm owns two trucks, several ovens, and a building with trade fixtures. Able is having marital and financial troubles. Able's wife and several of his personal creditors demand satisfaction. Able's car and house have been taken away from him, forcing him to use the firm's truck for transportation. Baker objects. Able's wife and his creditors attempt to levy on the trucks, ovens, building, and fixtures. Able, under pressure, transfers all his rights to the truck to one of his creditors. Specific firm property cannot be transferred by one partner without the consent of all. Further, attachment and levy are ineffective on firm property for an individual partner's debt. Able can be prevented from using the truck for personal use. Able's wife and creditors can, however, levy on the *interest* of Able in the partnership by a special proceeding before an equity court.

When personal creditors attempt to levy on a partner's interest in the partnership, they seek a *charging order*. A receiver is appointed who will receive those profits to which the debtor is entitled and channel them to the attaching creditors. The receiver, although a stranger to the firm, is entitled to receive partnership information and, at dissolution, is entitled to the accounting that a partner would receive.

This involuntary assignment of the interest by court order is, however, good cause for the other partners to seek dissolution of the firm. On the other hand, a voluntary, rather than an involuntary, assignment is not by itself sufficient grounds for dissolution.

Title to firm property stays in the firm upon death of the partner unless the death is that of the last surviving partner. Widowers, widows, heirs, legatees, or next of kin have no specific interest in the firm property. Where the last surviving partner dies, his or her personal representative holds title and proceeds toward dissolution and distribution.

EXAMPLE 17.   Lane, Mark, and Norton are partners. The firm owns both real and personal property. All three are flying to a trade convention when the plane crashes. Lane and Mark are killed instantly. Norton survives for 5 days. The heirs of Lane and Mark have no rights to the specific property save what interest will come to their respective estates after the firm's affairs have been wound up and the interests distributed. The representative of Norton's estate, however, in the absence of unusual circumstances, takes title to all the partnership property and would proceed to wind up the partnership affairs.

Under the UPA all property, whether real or personal, is treated for these purposes as personal property.

28.22   PARTNER RELATIONS

Partners stand in fiduciary relationship to each other and to the firm. Secret profits are not permitted, and each must properly account for all firm fund assets. Each partner is entitled to have a formal accounting of partnership affairs, reimbursement for firm expenditures, and indemnity where applicable. A partner is an owner, not an employee, of the business and therefore, in the absence of a contrary agreement, is not "entitled to renumeration for acting in the partnership business, except that a surviving partner is entitled to reasonable compensation for his services in winding up the partnership affairs," UPA, Section 18(f).

EXAMPLE 18.   Douglas and Edwards join together in a partnership. Douglas is to provide the money and Edwards the labor. In the absence of a clear understanding to the contrary, any money paid Edwards is payment out of profits. Accordingly, any draw that Edwards takes from the firm will be charged against his share of the future profits.

Capital placed in the partnership as a permanent investment does not, unless otherwise specifically agreed, draw interest. However, if the partner should make any payment or advance beyond the amount of his or her specific commitment, that partner would be entitled to interest from the date of the payment or advance.

Since the relationship between partners is one of a fiduciary nature and involves changes in rights among partners, it is difficult to ascertain respective rights during this relationship. Accordingly, one partner may not sue the firm or another partner at law for breach of agreement or other duties arising out of the partnership relations.

EXAMPLE 19.   An owner of a service station sold a one-half interest to the buyer and on the same date entered into a written partnership agreement with him. The parties had operated the station for 6 months when a dispute arose regarding the transfer of certain of the firm's property by the buyer. The owner sued the buyer at law, charging conversion of the property. The buyer contended that one partner cannot sue another over firm business. The court agreed but took the case into equity court as one for dissolution and accounting. The court proceeded in this equitable action and adjusted the interest of the parties.

The rule does not, however, prevent one partner or the partnership from suing another for the breach of his or her promise to contribute capital, leaving all other actions involving the business to be adjusted only in equity through a dissolution.

EXAMPLE 20.   Two brothers operated a farm as a partnership under a firm name. An automobile insurance liability policy was issued in the name of the firm. The brothers, on company business, were involved in a car accident, one brother driving and the other a passenger. The passenger was killed, and his heirs sued for damages for wrongful death, alleging negligence (a tort) of the driver, the other partner. The insurance company invoked the rule that one partner cannot sue another partner at law. The court ruled in favor of the insurance company, stating that the firm does not become legally liable and obligated to pay damage for the death of a partner resulting from negligent acts of the other partner committed while engaged in partnership business.

28.23 PARTNERSHIP NOT AN ENTITY

Unlike a corporation, a partnership is generally not considered an entity for most purposes. It has, therefore, only a temporary life, its interests are not completely transferable, it is not a taxpayer (income tax), and its members suffer unlimited liability to those who deal with the firm. In a few ways the firm is treated separately, including the right to hold property in the partnership name and to go or be placed into bankruptcy separately from its members.

Black Letter Law
A Summary

1. A partnership is an association of two or more persons to carry on as co-owners of a business for profit.

2. To find a partnership it is necessary that the parties intended to make each party an owner of the business.

3. An agreement to share profits creates a presumption of a partnership except under specified circumstances which include payments made for debts, wages, rent, annuities, interest, and sale of a business.

4. The Statute of Frauds applies to partnership agreements where the agreed term is beyond 1 year or where the agreement contemplates the transfer of land.

5. A partnership by estoppel is created where a party by his or her actions leads a third party to rely on the appearance of the relationship to the third party's detriment.

6. In a general partnership, each partner has full liability under an agreement that can be oral; a limited partnership agreement must be in writing, meet state statutory requirements of form, and be filed at a public office.

7. Partnership capital is the aggregate amount contributed by the partners as permanent investment in the firm.

8. Partnership property includes those assets the partners dedicate to the firm; property purchased from partnership assets is presumed to be partnership property.

9. Partnership property is for the equal use of partners in the partnership business, and each has no individual interest in specific property.

10. Because partners stand in fiduciary relationship to each other and to the firm, actions that involve secret profits or competition with the firm are prohibited.

Solved Problems

28.1 Jack Gordon, a general partner of Visions Unlimited, is retiring. He sold his partnership interest to Donna Morrison for $80,000. Gordon assigned to Morrison all his rights, title, and interests in the partnership and named Morrison as his successor partner in Visions. In this situation,

    (*a*)   the assignment to Morrison dissolves the partnership.

    (*b*)   absent any limitation regarding the assignment of a partner's interest, Gordon is free to assign his interest at his will.

    (*c*)   Morrison is entitled to an equal voice and vote in the management of the partnership, and she is entitled to exercise all the rights and privileges that Gordon had.

    (*d*)   Morrison does *not* have the status of a partner, but she can, upon demand, inspect the books of the partnership accounting records.

(*Adapted from AICPA Examination, May 1975*)

    Statement (*b*) is the answer—a partner may assign his or her interest in the partnership. However, the partner does not thereby make the assignee a partner. Further, such voluntary assignment does not cause a dissolution of the partnership. The assignee has certain rights to receive profits and share at dissolution, but the assignee has no voice in management and has no right to seek an accounting and/or to inspect the books.

28.2 For which of the following purposes is a general partnership recognized as an entity by the Uniform Partnership Act?

    (*a*)   Insulation of the partners from personal liability

    (*b*)   Taking of title and ownership of property

    (*c*)   Continuity of existence

    (*d*)   Recognition of the partnership as the employer of its members

(*AICPA Examination, November 1978*)

    While a partnership is not a legal entity, the UPA allows that all property, real or personal, can be held in the partnership name, and so (*b*) is the answer. Since the partnership is not an entity for most purposes, there is no continuity of existence. The partners are not employees of the firm, but are the employers, or owners. General partners have unlimited liability.

28.3 Charles Wilson and Donald Black decided to merge their competing business proprietorships. The resulting partnership was established by a mere handshake. The oral partnership agreement did *not* cover profit sharing or salaries. For this partnership,

    (*a*)   the federal antitrust laws do *not* apply.

    (*b*)   the Statute of Frauds does *not* require Wilson and Black's agreement to be in writing.

    (*c*)   the partnership is voidable by the creditors of either proprietorship.

    (*d*)   Wilson is entitled to a reasonable salary for his services as managing partner.

(*AICPA Examination, May 1975*)

    Oral partnerships are not uncommon and, unless the Statute of Frauds is involved, are enforceable. This agreement does not appear to involve the transfer of land, nor, by its terms, must it take more than a year to be fully performed; statement (*b*) is correct. The agreement appears to be enforceable. The federal antitrust laws apply to partnerships, whether created orally or in writing. Creditors have no standing to set aside a partnership. Wilson is a partner, an owner, not an employee. There is no presumption that he is entitled to compensation for his services, as the partners must specifically contract for that among themselves.

28.4   Charles Norman and Walter Rockwell did business as the Norman and Rockwell Company. This relationship was very informal, and neither party considered himself to be a partner of the other. Their stationery was printed with the name of Norman and Rockwell Company. Donald Quirk loaned Rockwell $10,000 for and on behalf of the business. Norman was informed of this but stated to Rockwell, "That's your responsibility; I had nothing to do with it." Rockwell defaulted, and Quirk seeks to hold both Norman and Rockwell liable on the debt. Under these circumstances,

(*a*)   Quirk *cannot* recover against Norman because of Norman's statement to Rockwell, "That's your responsibility; I had nothing to do with it."

(*b*)   Norman and Rockwell are partners by estoppel.

(*c*)   absent a signed partnership agreement, Quirk *cannot* recover against Norman.

(*d*)   the fact that neither party considered their relationship to be a partnership precludes recovery against Norman.

(*AICPA Examination, November 1974*)

Liability by reason of partnership principles does not necessarily require a showing that a partnership existed, only that a third party relied to his or her detriment on conduct which suggested such. The facts of the conduct of Norman and Rockwell show a partnership by estoppel, statement (*b*). Between themselves the two are not partners, but they are barred (i.e., estopped) from stating that they were not partners in their own minds, because their public conduct toward third parties was that of a partnership.

28.5   Webster, Davis, and Polk were general partners in the antique business. Webster contributed his illustrious name, Davis managed the partnership, and Polk contributed the capital. Absent an agreement to the contrary, which of the following provisions would automatically prevail?

(*a*)   Polk has the majority vote in respect to new business.

(*b*)   Polk has assumed the responsibility of paying Webster's personal debts upon insolvency of the partnership.

(*c*)   Webster, Davis, and Polk share profits and losses equally.

(*d*)   Davis is entitled to a reasonable salary for her services.

(*AICPA Examination, November 1974*)

The law supplies many of the terms of a partnership which the partners neglected to articulate. One of them is that, in the absence of a contrary agreement, profits and losses are shared equally irrespective of the disproportionate capital contribution; the answer is (*c*). All voting is assumed to be per capita, that is, by the head. Accordingly, each party is entitled to one vote.

28.6   In 1970, Allen, Burton, and Carter became equal partners for the purpose of buying and selling real estate for profit. For convenience, title to all property purchased was taken in the name of Allen. Allen died, and the partnership real estate and partnership personal property standing in his name are valued at $25,000 and $5,000, respectively. The partnership had no debts. Allen's wife claims a dower right in the real property. Allen had bequeathed all his personal property to his children, who claim an absolute one-third interest in the $5,000 of personal property. In this situation,

(a) Allen's wife has a valid dower right to all real property held in her deceased husband's name.

(b) partnership property is subject to a right of survivorship in the surviving partners; hence, Allen's wife is entitled only to his share of undistributed partnership profits.

(c) Allen's children are entitled to one-third of all partnership personal property.

(d) Allen's estate is entitled to settlement for the value of his partnership interest.

(*AICPA Examination, November 1974*)

Specific partnership property does not pass upon the death of one of the partners; it remains in the name of the surviving partners. Allen's estate will receive the value of his partnership interest, statement (*d*). Which heir(s) get what will depend on Allen's will or, lacking such, state law regarding the estate of a person who dies intestate.

28.7 Wyatt, Cooper, and Hubble informally agreed to share profits and losses. They agreed that each party would do business under her own name and *not* disclose the names of the other parties, and each would assume liability for her own accounts. All parties lived up to the understanding. Unfortunately, Cooper overextended herself and, consequently, filed a voluntary petition in bankruptcy. Cooper's business creditors seek to assert rights against Wyatt and Hubble. Under these circumstances,

(a) Wyatt and Hubble are partners by estoppel.

(b) Wyatt and Hubble can rely on the Statute of Frauds to defeat the claims of Cooper's creditors.

(c) Cooper's activities were *ultra vires*, hence, *not* binding on Wyatt and Hubble.

(d) Wyatt, Cooper, and Hubble are partners *inter se* (i.e., among themselves) and, hence, are all liable for Cooper's debts.

(*Adapted from AICPA Examination, November 1974*)

The agreement to share profits and losses is one of the most significant indicia of partnership. Such sharing raises a presumption of partnership; statement (*d*) is the answer. There is no estoppel situation here since none of the parties led third parties to believe in such a relationship; in fact, just the opposite impression was given. The accused act does not appear to be in excess of the implied authority of the partnership; therefore *ultra vires*, i.e., beyond power, is not applicable.

28.8 Eric, Steve, and John are partners. John was recently admitted to the partnership and is relatively inexperienced. If the partners have made *no* agreement to the contrary,

(a) John plays a subordinate role in the management of the partnership because of his inexperience.

(b) each partner must contribute to losses according to his share of profits.

(c) John is *not* entitled to interest on money he loans to the partnership.

(d) profits will be divided in proportion to the amount of each partner's capital investment in the partnership.

(*Adapted from AICPA Examination, November 1973*)

The failure to agree about shares invokes the rule of the UPA that the partners share profits and losses equally; statement (*b*) is the answer. There are no junior partners, except by agreement, irrespective of experience.

28.9 The partnership agreement of one of your clients provides that upon death or withdrawal, a partner shall be entitled to the book value of his or her partnership interest as of the close of the year preceding such death or withdrawal and nothing more. It also provides that the partnership shall continue. Regarding this partnership provision, which of the following is a correct statement?

(a) It is unconscionable on its face.

(b) It has the legal effect of preventing a dissolution upon the death or withdrawal of a partner.

(c) It effectively eliminates the legal necessity of winding up the partnership upon the death or withdrawal of a partner.

(d) It is *not* binding upon the spouse of a deceased partner if the book value figure is less than the fair market value at the date of death.

(*AICPA Examination, November 1980*)

It is true that a withdrawing or deceased partner is entitled to his or her full share, which, in the latter case, should be paid to the representative of the deceased partner's estate or heir. However, partners may agree that a fixed sum or formula be used to determine this share. That contractual method, here employed, does effectively eliminate the legal necessity of winding up the partnership, statement (c). The death of a partner does dissolve the partnership; one cannot contract away that effect. The law will not revisit the quality of the bargain made by the parties unless there is an act or conduct suggesting fraud or other imposition. A formula that uses the book value can hardly qualify as an unconscionable method for settling the amount of the share even if the book-value share is less than a fair-market-value share. One might also note that the shoe would be on the other foot if the book-value share were to be greater than the fair market value in this type of situation.

28.10 In the course of your audit of James Fine, doing business as Fine's Apparels, a sole proprietorship, you discovered that in the past year Fine had regularly joined with Charles Walters in the marketing of bathing suits and beach accessories. You are concerned whether Fine and Walters have created a partnership relationship. Which of the following factors is the *most* important in ascertaining this status?

(a) The fact that a partnership agreement is *not* in existence

(b) The fact that each has a separate business of his own which he operates independently

(c) The fact that Fine and Walters divide the net profits equally on a quarterly basis

(d) The fact that Fine and Walters did *not* intend to be partners

(*AICPA Examination, November 1980*)

Parties frequently do not articulate the terms of a partnership agreement. In fact, sometimes they do not even intend to create such a relationship but nevertheless do acts that constitute a partnership. One of the most common methods of identifying a partnership is evidence of sharing of profits and losses, statement (c). One can be a partner in one business and still have another, but not a competing, business.

28.11 Millie and Jack were engaged in hauling grain. Millie had two trucks, and Jack offered to perform the labor. Jack was to keep the books, pay all expenses of the operation, and give Millie one-half of the profits as rent on the trucks. A third party had dealings with Jack pertaining to the operation and demanded payment from Millie. Millie contends that no partnership was entered into and that the elements necessary to prove a partnership did not exist here. Millie further offers that she and Jack did not enter into an agreement to share losses.

What elements of partnership appear in this case? State your answer and give reasons for any conclusions reached.

Here there appears to be an association of two persons as co-owners of a business with intent to share profits. The showing of the intention to share profits is *prima facie* evidence of the existence of a partnership and implies a sharing of any loss. This presumption can be overcome by evidence tending to prove the contrary. Here there is sufficient evidence to prove a partnership whatever the parties may choose to call their relationship.

28.12 Howard entered into an agreement with an accounting firm by which he was to receive a set monthly salary in addition to a fixed percentage of the net profits of the firm. Howard was given the title "junior partner" but was to have no other financial interest in the firm and no right or authority to participate in the management of the firm's affairs except as the "capital partners" might authorize from time to time. At the termination of his duties Howard demands the rights of a partner, including an accounting. The firm contends that Howard is no partner.

Under these facts is Howard a partner? Decide and state reasons for any conclusions you reach.

The firm wins this lawsuit. A junior partner is not necessarily a partner since the use of the term does not by itself create such a relationship. There is no partnership where the contract between the parties clearly provides that there was to be no community of interest in the business as such and no right to participate in the management of the business. The elements of a partnership must be met, and co-ownership (indicating the right to share in control) is missing under these facts, which indicate nothing more than the promise of a bonus based on a percentage of the profits of the firm.

28.13 A father and son were in the dairy business until the son withdrew and went into business for himself as a dealer in calves. The son had his headquarters on his father's farm, which had a sign that read, "Father and Son, Dairy Cattle." A telephone was located in the building. The telephone listing was begun with only the son's name. The telephone company sent bills to the son, who paid for them with his checks. Four months later the son requested that the telephone listing with the same number show the name "Father and Son." The telephone company complied, and the bills were sent to the son's address and were paid by him until 7 months later, when a bill in the amount of $1,261 was not paid. The telephone company, unable to get payment from the son, then demanded the amount from the father, charging that he was a partner. There was no evidence that the father knew that the son changed the listing, ever consented to it, or was ever sent a bill from the telephone company.

What principle of partnership law is the telephone company attempting to invoke here? Comment on the probable success of this attempt.

The telephone company wishes to establish a partnership by estoppel. In order for a suit based on this ground to succeed, it is essential to show that the party asserting liability was induced by the misleading appearance to change its position to its detriment. There was no evidence that the telephone company did anything it would not have done, or refrained from doing anything that it otherwise would have done, had it known the facts of the relationship of the father and the son. The telephone company lost this action against the father as there was no conduct by him which induced the telephone company to act to its detriment.

Chapter 29

Partnership and Third Persons

29.1 PARTNERSHIP AND AGENCY

Every partner is an agent of the partnership for the purpose of its business, UPA, Section 9. Accordingly, the conduct of the partners must be observed in the light of the business for which the partnership was formed and the manner in which it conducts its affairs.

29.2 PARTNERSHIP BUSINESS

Third parties rarely have inside information about the exact nature of the partnership business and so must act toward it on the basis of how it appears to them. As a general principle, older legal cases placed emphasis on the distinction of a trading as opposed to a nontrading partnership. A firm whose business it is to buy and/or sell is a *trading partnership*, the traditional commercial organization. A firm formed to perform certain services only was called a *nontrading partnership*. Most combinations of professionals fell in this category. Accordingly, a partnership of doctors, lawyers, or accountants was generally considered to be a nontrading partnership. Although contemporary cases are not decided by this characterization, the courts continue to find it helpful in solving issues of apparent authority.

The significance of this characterization lies in the range of authority imputed to a trading as contrasted with a nontrading partnership. For example, the apparent authority to execute a negotiable instrument would not be found in a nontrading company, but could be considered within the apparent authority of the partner in a trading company.

EXAMPLE 1. An advertising agency was a partnership composed of two partners engaged in the business of selling broadcast time over a radio station on a commission basis. The firm succeeded in selling time for $100,000 to a buyer, who prepaid. The station had financial difficulties and was later unable to deliver the service. In making a settlement with the buyer, who was threatening to sue for breach of contract, one of the partners signed a promissory note (a negotiable instrument) for $40,000 in favor of the buyer, who thereupon agreed not to sue the firm. The nonsigning partner claimed that the other had no authority to sign a negotiable instrument. The court ruled in favor of the nonsigner while commenting that Section 9(1) of the UPA puts the burden of establishing this as the usual way of doing business on the third party. Here, the nature of the business was restricted to sale of broadcast time on a commission basis. The court ruled that there was no showing of a business which required "periodical or continuous or frequent purchasing" or made resort to borrowing a necessity, nor as existing by reason of embarrassments or on account of some fortuitous event.

Some courts note that the attempted distinction between the types of partnership is nothing more than a shorthand rendition of the notion that B is liable for the act of C if B has held out to other persons that C is empowered to perform acts of that particular nature. Accordingly, the fact that a firm is definitionally a nontrading partnership does not prevent an innocent third party from assuming power greater than that granted.

EXAMPLE 2. Alonzo, Baker, and Carlton are attorneys who formed a law partnership. They discovered early on that greater profit is made in getting pieces of the action in other businesses. Carlton is the more aggressive in this area, accepting money from clients to invest in deals that the firm learns of. Ordinarily, a law firm's apparent authority is very limited and would include such things as purchasing office equipment and supplies, hiring a secretary, renting office space, and paying for accounting services. The practice of Carlton, with the consent of the others, of involving the firm in investment opportunities would overcome the slight presumption that this is a nontrading partnership whose scope of business activity is narrow.

29.3 AUTHORITY: ACTUAL AND APPARENT

The type of business being conducted aids the court in determining whether authority exercised was actual or only apparent. Both bind the firm, the latter under the doctrine of estoppel. The same type of reasoning so often found in agency cases abounds in partnership situations. Actual authority is the express, implied, or incidental authority arising from the way the parties intend to do business or later approval by them under ratification.

There are some guidelines for distinguishing those types of activities not likely to be assumed to be authorized without strong evidence to support the propriety of the action:

(1) Selling capital assets of the firm

(2) Assigning partnership property for the benefit of creditors

(3) Selling the goodwill of the firm

(4) Selling such property that it would make it impossible to carry on the ordinary business of the firm

(5) Confessing a judgment or submitting a partnership claim or liability to arbitration or reference

(6) Standing as surety or guarantor for nonfirm business

This is just another way of stating that actions considered to be out of the ordinary course of business should be viewed with suspicion by a third party and that the third party is in that area in which he or she must prove actual or apparent authority.

Unless in the business of buying and selling real estate, partners generally have no apparent authority to sell firm real estate. As a partnership is not an entity, this has historically caused difficulties in title situations. The UPA specifically allows real estate to be held in the partnership name; when it is so acquired, land can be conveyed only in the partnership name, UPA, Section 8(3).

It is not unusual, however, for real property to have been titled in the name of one or more of the partners, and the solution to this legal problem is provided by state real property law. Provided innocent third parties are not involved, the courts treat it under partnership principles.

EXAMPLE 3.   Land was purchased and title placed in the names of individual family members. Several months later a partnership was created among the family members to engage in farming operations. The partnership agreement was oral. Six years later the firm entered into a contract to sell 750 acres of the land to a buyer for $200,000. The firm was the named seller, and one of the partners signed for the firm. A dispute arose regarding the validity of the contract, the buyer arguing that the contract needed the signatures of all the title holders. The court ruled that the fact that the title was held in the names of individuals did not preclude a showing that this was partnership property. As such, one partner, having authority to sell, binds all despite the state of the record title.

29.4 PARTNERS' SIGNING

When one contracts as an agent, the signature should reflect such status, a rule which applies to partnership transactions as well. A partner should recite the firm name and include the word "by" in front of his or her signature. Sealed documents and negotiable instruments particularly should indicate this character.

EXAMPLE 4.   Victor was well known at a bank. Victor brought Mersey to the bank and identified her as his partner in the construction business. Mersey obtained a loan from the bank by signing a promissory note in the name of the construction firm. Victor did not sign the note and contends that he has no liability since neither his name nor signature appears on the note. The bank proved that the loan proceeds were used in the business. Victor's name, in effect, is on the note as the construction firm, a partnership. He, along with Mersey and other partners, if any, are jointly and severally liable on the instrument.

29.5   ACTS OF THE MAJORITY OF PARTNERS

The UPA provides that differences arising out of the ordinary matters connected with the partnership business may be decided by a majority of the partners, UPA, Section 18(h). This assumes, of course, that the matter is not covered by the articles of partnership. A third party is not concerned with the rule unless he or she has timely notice of the actual intent of the majority since the rules of apparent authority connected with firm business protect innocent parties.

EXAMPLE 5.   For the purpose of blocking low-cost South Dakota land into ranches for sale, two local residents joined with an out-of-state financier to form a partnership. The financier contracted with the buyers to sell some of the firm's land which the financier held in his own name. The local residents were displeased with the purchase prices. The financier went back to the buyers, amending the contracts for lower prices but higher down payments. He did not report this to his partners. When they learned of it, the local residents wrote to the buyers that the land belonged to the partnership and warned the buyers to make no further payments without the approval of the other partners. This was the first notice the buyers had of the partnership. The financier put pressure on the buyers to make payments. They did, and the financier gave them deeds. The local residents claim that majority rule governs and that the buyers had notice of the partnership disapproval. The court ruled that the buyers made proper payments, noting that the majority rule does not invest the majority members of a partnership with power to alter contractual rights. The rights of the buyers were not changed by the fact that notice had been served on them; they had already made valid contracts.

29.6   TORT LIABILITY OF PARTNERS

Tort liability of the firm and partners individually is frequently indistinguishable from ordinary litigation involving *respondeat superior* discussed in agency law. If the tortious act was within the scope of partnership business or in furtherance of its interest, both the firm and its members are jointly and severally liable. Usually two types of issues are reported in partnership tort litigation: one, whether the act occurred within the scope of partnership business and, two, where the party sued claims not to be a partner.

EXAMPLE 6.   An aerial acrobat fell 18 feet from a circus rig where she was performing, breaking both heels and suffering injuries to her spine. She alleged that the fall was caused by the absence of a safety loop on the rig due to the negligence of the riggers. One Brady and the circus corporation were sued by the acrobat. Brady claims that he has nothing to do with the circus. The evidence revealed that Brady had engaged in joint activity with the circus for a long time, sharing profits, and that a partnership certificate had been filed years ago. Further, Brady's name was used in the promotion of the circus. The court ruled that even if this evidence reflected only a joint venture with the circus, the effect is indistinguishable from that of a partnership under the law. Brady is also liable for damages.

29.7   CRIMINAL LIABILITY OF PARTNERSHIP

The actor is liable for his or her own torts and crimes. A crime is nonetheless a crime even if it is performed by a partner while in the course of firm business. The issue, however, is whether it is more than a criminal act performed solely by an individual. Simply asked, can a firm which is not a legal entity commit a crime, or can only its partners as individuals do so? The answer lies in the language of the criminal statute.

EXAMPLE 7. A linoleum company, a partnership, was charged with violation of the Sherman Antitrust Act (15 U.S.C. Section 1). It was argued that the indictment should be dismissed as a matter of law because under the law a partnership is not a separate entity and not a "person" within the meaning of criminal law. The court ruled that the indictment stands. Generally, where criminal acts are committed through a partnership, the culpable members of the firm are held criminally liable rather than the partnership itself. The Sherman Antitrust Act, however, changes this rule in regard to antitrust violations. A partnership can violate the act quite apart from the participation and knowledge of the partners as individuals. Conviction of the firm cannot be used to punish innocent partners personally, but a conviction can result in a fine levied on the firm's entire assets, thus affecting the shares of innocent partners.

Black Letter Law
A Summary

1. The type of business conducted by a partnership determines in large measure the scope of apparent authority on which a third person can reasonably rely.

2. A trading partnership, usually buying and selling, or manufacturing, is deemed to have more apparent authority to perform business acts than a nontrading partnership.

3. Certain activities are so unusual that third parties must assure themselves that the partner has actual authority; these include assigning partnership property for the benefit of creditors, submitting disputes to binding arbitration, and selling such assets as would make it difficult or impossible for the business to continue.

4. Generally, a partnership is not a legal entity, but it can hold title and sell both real and personal property in the name of the firm.

5. A majority of partners settles differences regarding ordinary business matters even against those notified of the dissent of other partners.

6. Tort liability for acts of partners or their agents within the scope of partnership business follows the traditional rule of *respondeat superior*.

7. A partnership can be liable for criminal acts where a statute so provides.

Solved Problems

29.1 Jones, Brown, and Smith were partners in the business of selling and servicing cars. Smith borrowed money from a lender, representing that he was soliciting for the firm, and signed a promissory note in the name of the firm. The note was not paid. Under these circumstances,

   (*a*) since this is a trading partnership, a partner could have the apparent authority to borrow money and sign a note.

   (*b*) a partner as agent for the firm can only sign a negotiable instrument if expressly authorized.

(c)　Smith is not liable on this promissory note.

(d)　since this is a nontrading partnership, Smith's act was *ultra vires*.

The scope of apparent authority is broader where the partnership buys and sells; this is commonly called a trading partnership. When money is needed, there is apparent authority not only to borrow, but also to execute a negotiable instrument as well; statement (a) is correct. Smith of course is liable either as a partner or personally as an agent who warrants his authority to execute the document. This is a trading partnership.

29.2　A husband and wife operated a café as partners. They later became estranged, and the wife sued for divorce, leaving the husband in complete control of the café. Two customers entered the café, and without provocation, the husband shot and killed one and seriously wounded the other. The husband was sent to prison for murder, and the wounded customer sued the wife for the tort of her husband, her partner. Under these circumstances,

(a)　this malicious tort was not committed within the scope of the café business.

(b)　the wife is liable both jointly and severally for this tort committed by her partner husband.

(c)　a partnership is never liable for intentional torts of a partner.

(d)　since the wounded customer was a customer of the café, the wife is liable as a partner for the torts of her partner.

The test of liability in both agency and partnership law is to determine whether the tort occurred within the scope of the authority and business of the firm or in furtherance of its interest. On these facts, the killing and wounding seem independent of the firm's business and are connected only by having physically occurred on the premises of the café. The firm is not liable, and, therefore, the other partner, the wife, would likewise not be liable; statement (a) is the answer. The fact that a tort is intentional, a battery here, does not necessarily mean that it is not the responsibility of the firm. If the firm were liable, the wife would be both jointly and severally liable for the tort.

29.3　Hal, Ray, and Sam are in the retail business of selling stereos. Hal thinks it would be a good sales idea if a special sale were to be advertised in which the first 10 customers could purchase any stereo at 90 percent off. Sam thinks it is a horrible idea; he thinks it will make more enemies than friends, as so many people will show up and be disappointed. Hal and Ray decide to proceed with the sale. Sam, unhappy, has prepared and placed a large sign in the window stating that he is an equal partner and any sales of stereos at 90 percent off will ultimately be repossessed. Passersby read the sign and think it amusing. The sales day was a fiasco. Just as Sam predicted, the most aggressive customers got to the store first and bought the 10 discounted stereos. Now Hal and Ray like Sam's idea of repossessing the stereos. Which is the correct statement?

(a)　If third parties know that an equal partner objects to an act, such parties cannot be innocent purchasers for value.

(b)　For ordinary business matters, majority rule governs.

(c)　Not only was the sale a bad idea, but it had the possible effect of giving away firm assets, an act which requires unanimous aproval of all partners.

(d)　A sale at a 90 percent discount is illegal.

It is true that no partner has the apparent authority to give away the property of the firm. But a promotional sale, here of only 10 units, is not inconsistent with business practice, whatever the worthiness of the idea from a marketing point of view. Therefore, in ordinary business transactions, a majority decision governs, statement (b). The fact that the third parties knew of the objection of a minority partner would not, under these circumstances, disturb their purchases.

29.4 Which of the following is likely to be characterized as a trading partnership?

   (*a*) A barbershop

   (*b*) A firm of lawyers

   (*c*) A mom and pop grocery store

   (*d*) A public relations firm

   The term "trading partnership" frequently assists a court in determining the apparent scope of activity which innocent third parties may rely on. Buying and selling items in a routine manner, requiring replenishment of inventory and such, generally characterizes a trading partnership; the answer is (*c*).

29.5 When an innocent third party who deals with a partnership is contending that the acting partner had actual authority to enter into a contract with him or her, which of the following concepts is the third party *not* suggesting?

   (*a*) Ratification

   (*b*) Apparent authority

   (*c*) Implied authority

   (*d*) Express authority

   Only apparent authority suggests a "fictive" authorization, placed there by operation of law by reason of the equity of the situation, statement (*b*). In all other matters the court is asked to determine actual authority, although in the case of ratification the authority is ratified "after the fact" by the conduct of the partnership.

29.6 Which of the following may a partner *not* do unless he or she has the express unanimous assent of the remaining partners?

   (*a*) Assign his or her entire partnership interest to an outsider

   (*b*) Dismiss the accounting firm engaged to audit the partnership's accounts

   (*c*) Submit a long-standing dispute, regarding a partnership claim against a recalcitrant customer, to arbitration

   (*d*) Obtain a short-term loan from the partnership's banker to increase the partnership's working capital

(*Adapted from AICPA Examination, November 1981*)

   Statements (*b*) and (*d*) reflect customary business transactions and certainly would not require unanimous assent. One may assign one's interest to another, which does not, of course, make the assignee a partner. However, the UPA specifically deprives a partner of apparent authority to submit a partnership dispute to binding arbitration. The correct answer is (*c*).

29.7 One of your audit clients, Major Supply, Inc., is seeking a judgment against Danforth on the basis of a representation made by one Coleman, in Danforth's presence, that they were in partnership together, doing business as the D&C Trading Partnership. Major Supply received an order from Coleman on behalf of D&C and shipped $800 worth of goods to Coleman. Coleman has defaulted on payment of the bill and is insolvent. Danforth denies he is Coleman's partner and that he has any liability for the goods. Insofar as Danforth's liability is concerned, which of the following is correct?

   (*a*) Danforth is *not* liable if he is *not* in fact Coleman's partner.

   (*b*) Since Danforth did *not* make the statement about being Coleman's partner, he is *not* liable.

(c) If Major Supply gave credit in reliance upon the misrepresentation made by Coleman, Danforth is a partner by estoppel.

(d) Since the "partnership" is operating under a fictitious name (the D&C Trading Partnership), a filing is required, and Major Supply's failure to ascertain whether there was in fact such a partnership precludes it from recovering.

(AICPA Examination, November 1980)

One can be liable as a partner fictively, that is, by operation of law. It is possible that Major Supply was misled by Coleman into contracting with what it thought was a partnership. If so, Danforth could be a partner by estoppel, statement (c). For this purpose it is not important whether they are partners or not. Under these circumstances Danforth's silence may have been as telling as words, making him a partner by estoppel. Danforth had a clear duty to speak if, in fact, he and Coleman were not partners.

29.8 In determining the liability of a partnership for the acts of a partner purporting to act for the partnership without the authorization of the fellow partners, which of the following actions will bind the partnership?

(a) A written admission of liability in a lawsuit brought against the partnership

(b) Signing the partnership name as a surety on a note for the purchase of that partner's summer home

(c) An assignment of the partnership assets in trust for the benefit of creditors

(d) The renewal of an existing supply contract which the other partners had decided to terminate and which they had specifically voted against

(Adapted from AICPA Examination, November 1978)

In each of the first three statements the UPA specifically requires the consent of the partners in order to bind the firm. In statement (d), however, the third party who relies on the appearances of customary firm business is protected, provided he or she has no knowledge or notice that the act is specifically unauthorized.

29.9 A general partner will *not* be personally liable for which of the following acts or transactions committed or engaged in by one of the other partners or by one of the partnership's employees?

(a) The gross negligence of one of the partnership's employees while carrying out the partnership business

(b) A contract entered into by the majority of the other partners but to which the general partner objects

(c) A personal mortgage loan obtained by one of the other partners on his or her residence to which that partner, without authority, signed the partnership name on the note

(d) A contract entered into by the partnership in which the other partners agree among themselves to hold the general partner harmless

(AICPA Examination, November 1977)

Third parties who deal with a partner in a transaction which is obviously personal in nature cannot rely on the doctrine of apparent authority; (c) is the answer. The firm and all general partners are liable for those acts of a partner which carry on the firm's business, whether wisely or not. The partnership is liable for torts committed by employees in the course of their employment. The fact that the tort is intentional or is a severe violation of company rules offers no legal excuse.

29.10 Grand, a general partner, retired, and the partnership held a testimonial dinner for him and invited 10 of the partnership's largest customers to attend. A week later a notice was placed in various trade journals indicating that Grand had retired and was no longer associated with the partnership in any capacity. After the appropriate public notice of Grand's retirement, which of the following best describes his legal status?

(a) The release of Grand by the remaining partners and the assumption of all past and future debts of the partnership by them via a hold-harmless clause constitutes a novation.

(b) Grand has the apparent authority to bind the partnership in contracts he makes with persons who have previously dealt with the partnership and are unaware of his retirement.

(c) Grand has no liability to past creditors upon his retirement from the partnership if they have all been informed of his withdrawal and his release from liability, and if they do not object within 60 days.

(d) Grand has the legal status of a limited partner for the 3 years it takes to pay him the balance of the purchase price of his partnership interest.

(*AICPA Examination, November 1976*)

The correct answer is (*b*). The doctrine of apparent authority continues even after a partner has retired unless the third party had the legal notice of such retirement required for his or her position. It is important to the firm, therefore, that the proper notification be issued in order to prevent the unwanted liability.

29.11 Two partners operated a dance studio. One of the partners abandoned the business, and the other stepped in to take care of the dance students still entitled to instruction. It appeared that the breaching partner had traveled about the city to promote the studio, but there was no evidence that he had purchased gasoline at any particular service station for such travel. A service station owner sued the dance studio for gasoline purchases charged to the breaching partner personally. The service station owner proved that in the past some of the bills for gasoline purchased by the breaching partner at the station had been paid by partnership checks.

What principles will cause the service station owner the most difficulty in attempting to collect from the dance studio? Comment and state the reasons for any conclusions you reach.

In the first place this is what would be called a nontrading partnership, and the scope of partnership authority is therefore rather narrow. One purchases gasoline for both business and pleasure, and the fact that the station owner cannot show its use for the partnership makes his case weak. Second, there is no evidence that the station owner relied on the partnership, as such, to his detriment. There is very little evidence of apparent authority or estoppel here. The dance studio was not liable in this case.

29.12 Three partners operated a business which manufactured packing crates and other wood products. The firm purchased a tract of timber and was cutting it into lumber for their manufacturing operation. The managing partner, without authority, contracted to sell lumber to a third party. He received payment for the lumber but never informed the firm nor accounted for the money received. The third party demands the lumber from the firm, which refuses to deliver.

How strong a case does the third party have? State the result and the reasons for any conclusions you reach.

Each partner is a general agent of the firm, but only for the purpose of carrying on the business of the partnership. There is nothing in the firm's operation to suggest that it was in the business of selling lumber. The third party chose to deal with one of the partners without knowing anything of the nature of the firm's business and its operation. This ignorance may be fatal since there is little evidence of apparent authority. The firm was not liable on the lumber contract.

29.13 Two parties were partners in a used-car business. Neither owned a car. They worked irregular hours and would do business all around town, both during the day and in the evenings. One of the cars, part of the firm's inventory, while driven by one of the partners on his way home in the evening, struck a third party. The third party sued the firm, which defended on the grounds that the driver-partner was negligent while driving for his own benefit and not within the scope of the firm's business. The third party contends that the use of a car by one of the partners in this instance was of some benefit to the partnership or incidental to the partnership arrangement.

What particular fact will give the partnership the most difficulty in attempting to avoid legal liability to the third party? Decide and give reasons for your conclusions.

The fact that every vehicle owned was for sale at all times, day or night, at any location, will give the firm the most trouble. It is reasonable to assume that under such facts and circumstances that the partnership interest was being served: the partner driving the automobile to and from work. The activity need not be exclusively business, as any reasonable connection with the firm's business will do. The firm was liable for this action.

Chapter 30

Termination of Partnerships

30.1 TERMINATION: GENERALLY

Just as the death of an individual does not end legal issues surrounding the decedent's previous activities, the "death" of a partnership raises a number of problems to be solved by the legal system. The UPA identifies *dissolution* as the change of the relations of the partners caused by any partner ceasing to be associated in the carrying on of the business. On the other hand, *winding up* is the process of settling the affairs of the firm after dissolution. When this process has ended, the partnership has *terminated*.

30.2 DISSOLUTION

A partnership is rather fragile, as dissolution can occur in many ways. Some of these ways create no liabilities, but others do. Just as an agency can be terminated despite a binding agreement, so can a partnership, as it requires the continuing consent of the parties. Section 31 of the UPA provides that dissolution can be caused by (1) certain events without violation of the partners' agreement, (2) the express will of the partner (even if it violates their agreement), (3) any event which makes the continuation of the business unlawful, (4) death of any partner, (5) bankruptcy of any partner, and (6) decree of a court.

30.3 DISSOLUTION: WITHOUT VIOLATION OF AGREEMENT

The partnership articles may provide for dissolution without breach of the agreement. Further, all the parties may agree to the dissolution, or where the partnership is a partnership at will, any one of the partners could act to dissolve it, provided no express or implied rights are violated.

EXAMPLE 1. Gordon Deliveries is a partnership whose members agreed to join for a period of 5 years. After a tough 4-year struggle, the firm is on the brink of financial success. One of the partners notifies the others that she won't join in a renewal of the agreement. This partner may enforce the term of the agreement and dissolve the partnership at the end of 5 years despite the damage such dissolution may do to the future of the enterprise.

EXAMPLE 2. Three parties join in the marketing and distributing of bibles and other religious articles. Their solid reputations are assets in the business, and the articles of partnership provide that the partnership can be dissolved if there is a violation of the "morals clause." This clause lists incidents activating expulsion from the partnership. Partner Walker was picked up in the buff during a police raid on a motel notorious for sexual activity, and the story made all the local newspapers, complete with candid, though censored, photographs. If the incident is fairly within the morals clause of the partnership agreement, Walker can be expelled and the firm dissolved without violation of his rights and over his objections, if he has the nerve to make any.

EXAMPLE 3. Two farmers agree to join efforts in harvesting crops, with the understanding that this will be done at will and the agreement can be dissolved at any time. The partners rent harvesting equipment and put on extra laborers for the season. Midway during the season one of the partners is dissatisfied with the operation because he thought he would be more the boss of the outfit. Unhappy, he notifies the other of dissolution, citing his right to dissolve at will, as agreed. The other partner contends that to quit in the middle of the harvest season with all the commitments they have already made would be costly. Nonetheless, the withdrawing partner is adamant. The courts would rule that, although this is an "at-will" partnership, it cannot be dissolved so as to harm the firm or other partner where, by implication, one can see that the period of operation of the partnership reasonably contemplated was an entire harvest season.

30.4 DISSOLUTION BY PARTNER: EXPRESS WILL

Despite any agreement, a partner can unilaterally dissolve the partnership, but not necessarily without legal liability for breach of contract. Accordingly, partners who wish to dissolve, free of liability, might seek court relief, alleging that they had a legal reason or excuse for dissolution. The UPA in Section 32 provides some guidelines by listing events which courts consider in these actions. Where, for example, a partner has been declared a lunatic, or is incapable of handling or discharging his or her duties, or commits acts prejudicial to firm interests, or acts in such a way as to make it impracticable to carry on with him or her, the court can decree a dissolution. Further, if it can be shown that the firm can only operate at a loss, or other similar detriment, dissolution may be ordered without disability to the petitioning partner(s). The decision to permit dissolution is usually based on how such events affect the firm, except in the case of adjudicated incompetency of a partner.

Even a nonpartner can petition for dissolution, but on very limited grounds such as expiration of the term of the partnership or in at-will situations. This nonpartner could be an assignee of the interest or a creditor who is the beneficiary of a charging order.

Courts do not lightly grant petitions for dissolution, but they are frequently called upon to hear *trifling charges* by squabbling partners.

EXAMPLE 4. Two partners were engaged in a farming and livestock business. Disputes arose over a number of matters, and one party sought dissolution. The evidence included such incidents as arguments about walking across the lawn, the amount of cream furnished one of them for his coffee, the pounding on the house being remodeled while the children of the other partner were asleep, and other incidents of similar magnitude. However, the business was prospering. The partnership had only 1 year to run, and the court was unable to determine that one partner was more responsible for the situation than the other. It ruled that the harsh remedy of dissolution would not be granted, stating that a prosperous, going business would not be dissolved because of friction between the partners. In such a situation the court will not interfere to determine which contending faction is more at fault.

30.5 DISSOLUTION BY ILLEGALITY, DEATH, AND BANKRUPTCY

A partnership can be dissolved by a showing that the law makes the continuation of the firm's business illegal. Death of any partner likewise causes dissolution even in the presence of a specific provision in the articles of partnership that death does not dissolve. An agreement calling for continuation after death, and substituting the personal representative as a new partner, while possible contractually, may be contrary to law applicable to the decedent's estate. The law, when it allows such, views this relationship as that of a new firm.

The bankruptcy of the firm, or of a partner, is a cause for dissolution. Bankruptcy is a federal proceeding by which the debtor either voluntarily or involuntarily is brought before the court for possible liquidation of assets. Mere insolvency, by itself, does not dissolve the firm.

30.6 DISSOLUTION EFFECTS: GENERALLY

A dissolution does not completely end partnership existence, but immediate legal changes do take place. Winding up begins, and as a general rule, the power of each partner to act for the firm ends except as may be necessary to wind up the partnership affairs or to complete executory transactions. Further, a partner in ignorance of the fact that dissolution has taken place is protected where death, bankruptcy, or an act of a partner causes the dissolution.

EXAMPLE 5. X, Y, and Z are partners in an office supply firm which is an exclusive agent for a particular territory. Z is the salesperson, and while she is on the road, X suddenly dies. Z had made a contract with a buyer, a usual type of activity, the day after the death of X. If Z had no knowledge or notice of X's death before the contract was made, both X's estate and Y are responsible for the contract made by Z.

A partner has no right of contribution from fellow partners for his or her acts in partnership business where the partner knows, or should have known, of the dissolution or of the events causing it.

30.7 DISSOLUTION AND THIRD PARTIES

Third parties who deal with partners after dissolution possess rights dependent on the principles of agency with its emphasis on the apparent authority of the member under the facts and circumstances of the case. Dissolutions of partnerships generally are private affairs, and third-party notice or knowledge determines the liability of the firm.

EXAMPLE 6. Arthur and Benny decide to terminate their partnership in which they have been the exclusive distributor of certain hand tools. Arthur has hopes that after dissolution he will retain the distributorship and attempts to keep his business contacts during the winding-up. A buyer visits the firm, knows of the dissolution, but enters into contracts with Arthur on behalf of the firm, the contracts stating that certain tool orders will be accepted for the next 3 months as is usual. The buyer also buys a calculator which had been used in the firm's business. The buyer could not hold the partnership liable for Arthur's act regarding future orders which was the ordinary business of the firm. However, Arthur's act of selling the firm's calculator may be an appropriate act in winding up, and therefore Arthur may have apparent authority to sell it.

Generally if a third party has neither knowledge nor legal notice of dissolution, it may hold the firm liable for usual business transactions. Two exceptions to this rule are where a partner has become bankrupt and where the firm has been dissolved because it has become unlawful to carry on the business.

Parties who have extended credit to the partnership before dissolution must be given actual notice of the dissolution. Those who have not extended credit, but knew of the partnership, are only entitled to notice by publication. An attempt, therefore, to give notice of dissolution is sufficient if the fact of dissolution has been advertised in a newspaper of general circulation in the places at which the partnership business was regularly carried on, UPA, Section 35.

30.8 DISSOLUTION AND CONTINUING PARTNERSHIPS

Partners do not always contemplate dissolution as the end of the business. Sometimes new partners are substituted for old ones, or, alternatively, the remaining partners intend to carry on the business. If this is the case, it is important to secure continuity in the firm, but this raises legal difficulties for withdrawing partners. Firms do not always completely wind up their affairs by selling the assets, paying all debts, and distributing the remainder. Many times this would be impractical and inconsistent with the desire to preserve goodwill. Accordingly, a withdrawing partner continues to be liable to the old creditors who are unpaid even if they have notice of dissolution and withdrawal. Further, the old partner could be liable to new creditors upon failure to give proper notice of withdrawal.

EXAMPLE 7. Deane, Cottan, and Farino were equal partners. At the time of Deane's withdrawal all agree that the assets of the firm are worth $179,000 and that both long-term and current debts total $35,000, resulting in a partnership "equity" of $144,000, or $48,000 each. Cottan and Farino agree to buy out Deane, promising her that they will pay all the debts and give Deane her $48,000. Deane gives notice of her withdrawal to those who extended credit to the firm in the past or had dealings with the firm, and takes out an advertisement in the local paper informing the public of her withdrawal. Under these circumstances, Deane would not be liable for future debts incurred by the firm, but she is still liable to the old creditors, if not to Cottan and Farino, for the past debts of $35,000. Only a novation, that is, an agreement for consideration by which the old creditors released Deane, would excuse Deane from this liability.

The withdrawing partner is released from liability only where the old creditors give a binding release, or where the creditors materially alter the terms of the old obligations without reserving their rights against the withdrawing partner. It is usually stated that the withdrawing partner is a surety on the obligations.

EXAMPLE 8. A retiring partner in an engineering firm notified the firm's creditors of his withdrawal. Nearly seven months later the continuing partners gave promissory notes to the old creditors to replace the old open accounts. The continuing partners went broke and did not pay the notes. The creditors sued the withdrawn partner on the old obligations. He defended on the grounds that the old creditors made a new agreement with the continuing partners, and since as surety he did not consent to this change, he is discharged. The majority court ruled that the withdrawn partner could be discharged if he proved either that the extension of time prejudiced him or that the old creditors assented to his release upon receipt of the notes.

The burden of withdrawing partners in these circumstances is great. In the example above, the dissenting judge noted that the mere act of withdrawing in no way alters one's responsibility and that the indemnity agreement from his partners, or giving notice to the creditors, in no way diminished his liability.

The incoming (new) partner in continuing partnerships may or may not assume the old obligations. When the new partner does so, he or she is personally liable. In any case the new partner's capital contribution, if any, is available for both new creditors and old creditors.

30.9 WINDING UP THE PARTNERSHIP

The right to wind up the affairs of a partnership is a valuable one and is granted to all except those whose misconduct has caused the dissolution, a bankrupt partner, and the representative of a deceased partner. Winding-up duties include gathering assets, paying debts, keeping appropriate accounts, and performing those acts necessary to conclude a proper stewardship. One doing these things must be prudent, enter into only those contracts necessary for the winding-up, and follow the rules of distribution whether by law or contract set by the articles or, in the absence of such, by the rules of the UPA. The partner in charge of winding up is entitled to be reimbursed for his or her expenses.

30.10 DISTRIBUTION OF A SOLVENT PARTNERSHIP

The UPA provides that the liabilities of the partnership shall rank in the order of payment as follows:

(1) Those owing to creditors other than partners, so-called outside creditors

(2) Those owing to partners other than for capital and profits, that is, inside creditors

(3) Those owing to partners in respect to capital

(4) Those owing to partners in respect to profits

EXAMPLE 9.   Hilda, Janice, and Liz form a partnership to operate Creative Crafts Shoppe and agree to share the profits and losses equally. Hilda contributes $20,000 to capital, Janice contributes $10,000, and Liz contributes her outstanding artistic reputation and labor, but no value is given to Liz as a capital contribution. The shop is successful, but after 4 years the partners decide to dissolve and wind up the business. Outside creditors are owed $15,000; Liz is owed $2,000 on a loan to the firm once given to meet a payroll. There is $71,000 in cash assets once the assets of the firm are liquidated. No profits or capital has been withdrawn. Hilda and Janice were silent partners, while Liz was paid an excellent salary to manage the business. The distribution of the money is as follows: first, $15,000 to the outside creditors, second, $2,000 to Liz for her loan to the partnership, third, $20,000 to Hilda and $10,000 to Janice as return of their capital. This is, therefore, a solvent partnership. There is $24,000 remaining which, by the partnership agreement, all three share equally, $8,000 apiece.

One should note the importance of partners having been given credit for their capital contributions. In the above example Liz may have spent much effort in the partnership, but she receives only what the law allows, not what she might deserve, whether more or less. Of course, the articles of partnership could have provided a different dissolution formula.

EXAMPLE 10.   Eleven doctors practiced medicine as partners. Three of them gave notice of termination of the partnership, alleging that it was a partnership at will. The written agreement set forth provisions for termination of the firm by a vote of two-thirds of the members or by unanimous consent. In addition, any partner could withdraw from the firm by giving 60 days notice and the firm paying for the member's interest according to a set formula. The three doctors seek their share of the firm's interest, not on the basis of the agreement, but rather under the provisions of the UPA which allow recovery to the "value of his interest as of the date of dissolution." The court ruled that the statute governs the distribution *unless* the parties have agreed otherwise. Here, the doctors had agreed to abide by a set formula in the articles of partnership. Partners may provide by agreement the amounts to be paid a retiring partner by the surviving partnership.

30.11   DISTRIBUTION BY INSOLVENT PARTNERSHIP

Where the liabilities of the firm exceed the assets, the firm is insolvent and the rules of distribution of assets result in a loss to each partner. The same UPA formula is used as for a solvent partnership, and so the order of preference is outside creditors, inside creditors, return of capital, and assignment of losses. In the case of an insolvent partnership, therefore, the question of distribution is answered in terms of who will lose, and how much.

EXAMPLE 11.   Frank, George, and Harold are partners but made different capital contributions. Frank contributed $40,000 to capital, George contributed $30,000, and Harold contributed only his services. Upon dissolution there is $51,000 in firm property. The firm owes $20,000 to outside creditors. There are no inside creditors at this time. Total liabilities are thus $90,000 ($20,000 owed to creditors plus $70,000 of partner capital). Since to meet the $90,000 in liabilities there is only $51,000 in assets, the firm is insolvent and at this time has losses totaling $39,000. The partners did not agree otherwise, and so the loss is shared equally, $13,000 each. Since Frank contributed $40,000 in capital, his $13,000 loss is deducted from that amount, leaving him with $27,000 of the $51,000 in assets. George contributed $30,000, and his capital is diminished to $17,000 by his $13,000 loss. Harold, having contributed no capital, must now contribute the amount of his loss, $13,000. Harold's $13,000 contribution plus the assets of $51,000 equals $64,000, which is the amount needed to pay the creditors $20,000 plus the $44,000 in capital to be returned to Frank and George. (Harold must pay his loss in this situation. If he refuses to pay, he can be sued. See Section 30.12.)

The above example of distribution governs unless the parties have among themselves agreed to a different method. Conduct showing such different intention allows the court to enforce the agreement of the parties.

EXAMPLE 12. A father was engaged in the chicken hatchery business. His son returned from military service and joined his father in the business. By this time the father had contributed property of a total value of $41,000 to the business. The son was to contribute only his services. Eighteen years later the son died, and a dispute arose over whether the son's estate was entitled to one-half of the business after payment of creditors. The father claims he is entitled to the return of his $41,000 capital contribution first. The evidence revealed that there was always equal division of profits on the tax returns. The father had made a will giving all firm property to the son. Once, before leaving on a foreign trip, the father showed his son that he owned one-half of the property, and initially, upon the death of the son, he showed an intent to split the partnership property equally. The court ruled that there was evidence of agreement that in the event of dissolution the assets were to be divided equally, without (prior) repayment of the father's capital contribution. The son's estate takes one-half of the partnership property undiminished by a deduction for the father's capital contribution, which was ruled, in effect, to have been a gift to the partnership.

30.12 DISTRIBUTION AND MARSHALING OF ASSETS

In an insolvent partnership the members are personally liable for the firm's losses and payment to its creditors. It is possible, therefore, for one wealthy partner to end up paying all an insolvent firm's debts, leaving him or her with only a legal claim against the fellow partners. Where both the firm and the partners are insolvent, the solution is more complicated. The rule is that *firm creditors have first claim on partnership property* and *individual creditors have first claim on the partners' individual property*.

EXAMPLE 13. Broke and Beat are partners. Upon dissolution the firm has assets of $20,000 and debts of $40,000. Broke has no money. Beat has $10,000 personally but owes his bank and other creditors a total of $30,000. The creditors of the firm would receive only $20,000, and Beat's personal creditors would get his $10,000.

The principle by which the court attempts to reconcile the competing interests of firm and personal creditors is called the *rule of marshaling assets*, an equity doctrine utilized in arranging assets in such an order of distribution as to enable all parties having equities to share in a fair way according to their respective interests.

The rule of firm assets to firm creditors and individual assets to individual creditors could work unfairly in some cases and is, therefore, sometimes inapplicable. For example, a partner who has embezzled or converted firm assets and placed them in his or her individual account cannot deprive the firm creditors access to what are actually firm funds. In such cases firm and individual creditors share equally. A more subtle form of conversion occurs where the creditors thought the firm was a sole proprietorship, but in fact it was a partnership with a secret partner. To prevent gross unfairness in such a case, the different creditors share equally. Finally, when it is discovered during winding up that there are no firm assets and no living solvent partners, neither class of creditors has priority in assets found; again, both types of creditors share equally.

Black Letter Law
A Summary

1. Dissolution of partnerships occurs through the acts of the parties, by court decree, and by operation of law.

2. The winding-up process begins at dissolution as the firm discontinues its regular business by liquidating assets, paying creditors, and making proper distribution to the partners.

3. A partner can cause a dissolution at any time by his or her own will, but not always with legal immunity.

4. Dissolution automatically occurs when a partner dies, when a partner becomes bankrupt, or when the business has become illegal.

5. Third parties dealing with a dissolved partnership may rely upon the principles of estoppel and apparent authority in the absence of appropriate legal notice of dissolution.

6. A withdrawing partner continues to be liable for old firm debts despite full assumption of such debts by the continuing partners unless a novation is achieved with the old creditors.

7. The right to wind up partnership affairs is denied to the representatives of the decedent partner's estate, to a bankrupt partner, or to a partner whose misconduct has caused the dissolution.

8. The order of distribution upon dissolution is payment to outside creditors, payment to inside creditors, return of capital contribution, and sharing of the profits and losses.

9. Where sufficient assets are not available to pay fully both the firm's creditors and individual (partners') creditors, the doctrine of marshaling of assets directs that firm creditors have first claim to firm assets and individual creditors have first claim to individual assets.

10. Where circumstances make the marshaling-of-assets doctrine inequitable, both classes of creditors, firm and individual, share equally.

Solved Problems

30.1 Two sisters were partners in a retail merchandising business and entered into a 1-year contract with an agent in New York who was to render services in buying merchandise and supplying marketing information. After 6 months the partnership dissolved. The agent sued the firm for the remainder of his salary under the contract terms. Which of the following statements is correct?

(a) The agent loses, as his authority terminates upon the dissolution of his principal.

(b) The agent loses, since the partnership after dissolution has no legal status.

(c) The agent wins, as a dissolved partnership must pay its debts, which should be done during the winding-up process.

(d) The agent wins, since he sued the proper party, as the two sisters could not be sued personally.

Dissolution of a partnership does not end it; firm affairs continue until termination. Creditors must be paid. The agent is a creditor who has an unexpired contract which has been breached. The partnership liability on this contract continues until it is satisfied; statement (c) is correct. An agent does lose his authority when dismissed, but this does not deprive him of his rights of contract, only his power. The agent could have sued the two sisters jointly rather than the partnership.

30.2 Alexander, Yancy, and Pinzer entered into an oral agreement of partnership formed to operate an insurance agency. Two years later the firm hired an attorney to prepare a written draft of articles of partnership for a 25-year term. The draft was completed and was to be discussed by the partners before approval and signing by them. Pinzer, without the knowledge of Alexander and Yancy, consulted his own attorney and made plans to take over the business himself. Alexander and Yancy learned of this and sued Pinzer for wrongful breach of the partnership agreement.

(*a*) Pinzer's conduct, while unseemly, is legally a dissolution at the will of one of the partners.

(*b*) Pinzer will not be liable if he can prove that he acted in good faith.

(*c*) Pinzer is not liable since this oral agreement was never enforceable.

(*d*) Pinzer will be liable since he stands in a fiduciary position with his partners.

   The oral partnership agreement did not specify the life of the firm. Thus, the partnership was at the will of the partners. Pinzer's conduct was unseemly, perhaps in both manner and method, but under these facts his conduct supports no legal grounds permitting the other partners to sue for wrongful termination; statement (*a*) is the answer. Oral partnership agreements are enforceable. The fiduciary duty does not inhibit one from exercising his or her legal rights, here to dissolve the partnership.

30.3 A mother and son were partners in a demolition firm. The firm entered into a contract with a corporation to perform a particular task. The contract provided that the firm was subject to certain money penalties for delay in completing the task. The mother died just 10 days before the final period set for completion. The firm failed to complete on time. The corporation gave notice of termination of the contract by reason of failure to perform within the time limits set and then sued the firm for the damages it suffered. Which statement is correct?

(*a*) The mother's estate should have been given the opportunity to complete the task.

(*b*) Death discharges most contracts.

(*c*) Death of the mother dissolved the partnership, and her estate had no legal right to demand that it be allowed to complete the task.

(*d*) The mother's estate will not be liable for the breach of the contract by the firm.

   The correct statement is (*c*). Upon the death of a partner, the partnership is dissolved. It continues, however, for the purpose of winding up firm affairs and ultimate termination of the partnership. The process and activities of winding up are the exclusive obligation and right of the surviving partners. The estate of the deceased partner has no right to participate in such winding up or to interfere with the actions of the surviving partner. Death discharges few contracts. The mother's estate is liable for firm obligations.

30.4 Six persons joined in a partnership in the wholesale food business. Three contributed capital in the sums of $20,000, $5,000, and $740. The other three contributed no money. The percentages of interest were set in the articles of partnership. The partners were to share profits and losses according to those percentages. After 8 months of operation, the firm failed, and it was dissolved, having lost $37,000 including capital. Under these circumstances,

(*a*) the capital contribution of each of the three must be recognized or returned unless the agreement was otherwise.

(*b*) the fact that the parties agreed to share profits and losses in a specific way implies that the capital contributions are subsumed in that proportion.

(*c*) the capital contributions here were really loans or advances to the firm.

(*d*)   an agreement setting forth certain percentages of sharing profits and losses refers to losses in operation, and does not include capital contributions.

In order for the partners to be limited to losses incurred only from operations, they must specifically agree to such limitation. There is no evidence stated here of such agreement, and so the answer is (*a*). The contributions of capital are debts of the firm, and all partners must share equally in seeing to the return of such. Capital contributions are not advances, but rather are sums placed for permanent investment.

30.5   A partner's home was being foreclosed by a firm creditor because a mortgage had been given to secure a firm debt. The homeowner contended that the firm had sufficient assets to pay the firm debt and sought the court's aid in having the firm dissolved and applying firm property toward the firm debt before the homeowner's property was seized. What principle of partnership law is being advanced?

(*a*)   The rule regarding a charging order

(*b*)   The UPA principles of distribution of a solvent partnership

(*c*)   The doctrine of marshaling of assets

(*d*)   The principle of indemnification

The homeowner is seeking to have the court apply the right of a partner to have the individual assets and firm assets marshaled, statement (*c*). Each partner has the right to demand that firm property be applied to the payment or security of the partnership debts in order to be relieved of personal liability. The homeowner should succeed in this case. She would be liable only if indeed the firm assets were not sufficient to satisfy the firm liabilities. The term "charging order" refers to a creditor's levy on a partner's interest in a firm.

30.6   Perone was a member of Cass, Hack, & Perone, a general trading partnership. He died on August 2, 19X0. The partnership is insolvent, but Perone's estate is substantial. The creditors of the partnership are seeking to collect on their claims from Perone's estate. Which of the following statements is correct insofar as their claims are concerned?

(*a*)   The death of Perone caused a dissolution of the firm, thereby freeing his estate from personal liability.

(*b*)   If the existing obligations to Perone's personal creditors are all satisfied, then the remaining estate assets are available to satisfy partnership debts.

(*c*)   The creditors must first proceed against the remaining partners before Perone's estate can be held liable for the partnership's debts.

(*d*)   The liability of Perone's estate *cannot* exceed his capital contribution plus that percentage of the deficit attributable to his capital contribution.

(*AICPA Examination, November 1980*)

Statement (*b*) is correct. While a firm is not an entity for most purposes, classes of creditors of a partnership are honored to a certain extent under the doctrine of marshaling of assets. Initially firm creditors get firm assets and personal creditors get personal assets. Since a partner has unlimited liability to the creditors, individual or firm, they need not stop their prosecution of claims until satisfaction is achieved. Statement (*d*) is incorrect since it attempts to apply an equity concept which is not legally true in respect to general partnerships.

30.7   Jon and Frank Clarke are equal partners in the partnership of Clarke & Clarke. Both Jon Clarke and the partnership are bankrupt. Jon Clarke personally has $150,000 of liabilities and $100,000 of assets. The partnership's liabilities are $450,000, and its assets total $250,000. Frank Clarke, the other partner, is solvent with $800,000 of assets and $150,000 of liabilities. What are the rights of the various creditors of Jon Clarke, Frank Clarke, and the partnership?

(*a*)　Jon Clarke must divide his assets equally among his personal creditors and firm creditors.

(*b*)　Frank Clarke will be liable in full for the $200,000 partnership deficit.

(*c*)　Jon Clarke's personal creditors can recover the $50,000 deficit owed to them from Frank Clarke.

(*d*)　Frank Clarke is liable only for $100,000, his equal share of the partnership deficit.

(*AICPA Examination, November 1979*)

Partnership works rather harshly on the solvent partner where the fellow partners fail to pay. Frank Clarke, being a general partner, is liable for the full deficit, statement (*b*). However, he is not liable for the individual debts of his fellow partner unless one of the several exceptions applies, such as where the funds of the firm and individual funds are commingled.

30.8　King, Kline, and Fox were partners in a wholesale business. Kline died and left to his wife his share of the business. Kline's wife is entitled to

(*a*)　the value of Kline's interest in the partnership.

(*b*)　Kline's share of specific property of the partnership.

(*c*)　continue the partnership as a partner with King and Fox.

(*d*)　Kline's share of the partnership profits until her death.

(*AICPA Examination, November 1979*)

A partnership is dissolved by the death of one of the partners. However, a deceased partner's share is personal property in the nature of the partnership interest; statement (*a*) is correct. There is no right in the estate to substitute for the decedent or share in any property apart from the share in the total assets. There is no dower right in the wife to income from her late husband's firm.

30.9　Which of the following will *not* result in a dissolution of a partnership?

(*a*)　The bankruptcy of a partner as long as the partnership itself remains solvent

(*b*)　The death of a partner as long as his or her will provides that the executor shall become a partner in his or her place

(*c*)　The wrongful withdrawal of a partner in contravention of the agreement between the partners

(*d*)　The assignment by a partner of his or her entire partnership interest

(*AICPA Examination, November 1979*)

A partnership is a rather fragile organization, as death, bankruptcy, or the wrongful withdrawal of a partner will cause a dissolution. An assignment of a partner's entire interest does not, however, automatically cause a dissolution, and so the answer is (*d*).

30.10　Kimball, Thompson, and Darby formed a partnership. Kimball contributed $25,000 in capital and loaned the partnership $20,000; he performed no services. Thompson contributed $15,000 in capital and part-time services, and Darby contributed only his full-time services. The partnership agreement provided that all profits and losses would be shared equally. Three years after the formation of the partnership, the three partners agreed to dissolve and liquidate the partnership. Firm creditors, other than Kimball, have bona fide claims of $65,000. After all profits and losses have been recorded, assets of $176,000 are to be distributed to creditors and partners. When the assets are distributed,

(*a*)　Darby receives nothing since he did *not* contribute any property.

(*b*)　Thompson receives $45,333 in total.

(c) Kimball receives $62,000 in total.

(d) each partner receives one-third of the remaining assets after all the firm creditors, including Kimball, have been paid.

(*Adapted from AICPA Examination, May 1975*)

This is a solvent partnership. Kimball will obtain the return of his capital ($25,000), his loan ($20,000), and a one-third share after all the creditors, the capital, and loans have been repaid. This is one-third of the balance of $51,000, or $17,000. Kimball is thus entitled to a total of $62,000, statement (c). Darby gets one-third of the profits ($17,000) since it was an equal partnership.

30.11 Two certified public accountants operated a partnership for 6 years. Under their articles of partnership, either party could withdraw at any time and the buy-out was fixed at 10 percent of the cash receipts for the 5 years following withdrawal. Further, the withdrawing partner was prohibited from competing for a period of 5 years within 25 miles of the business location. One of the partners, Orson, was not satisfied with the performance of the other partner, Lanevelli. Orson believed that Lanevelli did not devote his full time to the business. Orson notified Lanevelli that he was dissolving for breach. Lanevelli claimed that the charge was ridiculous and cited a number of minor grievances he had against Orson. Lanevelli notified Orson that Orson's decision to dissolve would come under the terms of the partnership agreement and that, therefore, Orson would be prohibited from competing under those terms. Orson proceeded to set up a business in contravention of the covenant not to compete.

How would a court react to these positions of the parties? Comment on the principles involved.

In the first place, a court is careful not to order a dissolution of a partnership except for statutory or good cause. If the grievances are as minor as indicated, no order of dissolution will be granted. The court would likely treat Orson's action as compatible with the articles of partnership, making him a withdrawing partner. Accordingly, the partnership ends by reason of its terms of agreement, which will be enforced. Therefore, Orson may not compete. In a similar case, a court commented that one who voluntarily liquidates the partnership by withdrawing therefrom is bound by a noncompetition clause in a partnership agreement.

30.12 Murphy and Lewis formed a partnership to operate a cafeteria for a period of 25 years. Murphy agreed to furnish the money, and Lewis agreed to supervise and manage. A dispute arose between the partners, and Murphy sought a court decree ordering dissolution of the partnership. The evidence revealed that Lewis was a competent manager and, but for the conduct of Murphy, there would be a reasonable expectation of profit under the continuing management of Lewis. In deciding the case, the court stated that "there is no such thing as an indissoluble partnership as there always exists the power as opposed to the right of dissolution." The court refused to order dissolution.

What principles of contract and partnership law is the court bringing to Murphy's attention in this case? Comment on these principles.

Partnership is a personal relationship containing agency principles, and it can be severed by the mere will of one of the partners. Murphy can do this if he wishes. The court is reminding Murphy, however, that he gets no legal dispensation under these facts. Any partner can terminate the relationship, but the pursuit of that course presents the problem of possible liability for such damages as may flow from the breach of contract. Murphy made an unsuccessful attempt to avoid a breach of contract; that is, he couldn't get the court to take him off the hook, so to speak. Murphy can dissolve the partnership, but he must do it without the court's blessing, and he must accept the consequences, whatever they may turn out to be.

30.13 A father contributed $47,500 as a down payment on a motel together with $1,000 in cash to be used as working capital. His son and wife agreed to leave other interests and devote full time to the business of running the motel. They all agreed that each partner would participate in the proportion of 40 percent each for the father and son and 20 percent for the wife. This formula was to be honored at dissolution. The business did not prosper, and by the time they decided to dissolve, the father had contributed approximately $150,000 total to the firm. At this time the father speculated about how much each should get of the book value of the motel business, declaring that he would get 40 percent. A dispute then arose, and at trial, the father testified that the advances he had made to the firm were loans that had to be paid, that is, that he was an inside creditor who had to be paid before any remainder was divided on the 40-40-20 basis of the agreement. The son and wife argued that the father's contributions were gifts to the business, not loans.

What principles of partnership law will the court apply in determining distribution rights? Comment on these principles.

The UPA principles governing distribution of partnership assets are the otherwise applicable law. They govern where the parties have made no contrary agreement, but here there was a specific agreement among the parties, and the court examined the agreement as it was bound to do. The basic agreement was for a special distribution which ignored the greater capital contribution of the father. The court will honor the agreement. The father's behavior and conduct ("I'm entitled to 40 percent") at the time of dissolution suggests that his advances to the firm were indeed gifts, which is consistent with the original partnership agreement in which he placed money in the business *and* at the same time agreed to the 40-40-20 formula. The court will carry out the agreement of the parties. The father's later advances of funds, like his original contribution in excess of the other partners, were donations made by the father to the partnership. The father received only 40 percent of the assets of the firm.

Chapter 31

Limited Partnerships and Other Organizations

31.1 INTRODUCTION

Many forms of organization have some of the features of a partnership or corporation but legally belong to neither of those classifications. These other forms of organization are commonly employed in the realm of business, and accordingly, this chapter will treat limited partnerships, sole proprietorships, joint ventures, joint stock companies, business trusts, unincorporated associations, and franchises.

31.2 LIMITED PARTNERSHIPS

This form of organization must be created pursuant to state statute. Nearly all states have adopted the Uniform Limited Partnership Act (ULPA). As a form of organization, the limited partnership responds to the business need for a partnership while having some of the advantages of the entity concept, particularly the strength of a corporation. Limited partners are generally not liable in excess of their investments. The current popularity of limited partnerships is attributable to the many tax shelters which utilize this form of organization.

Limited partnerships are creatures of statute requiring that written articles (certificate) of limited partnership be filed in a public office; there can be no oral limited partnership agreement.

EXAMPLE 1. Harry, Jane, and Thomas wish to form a limited partnership. They refer to the state statute and follow the requirements of setting forth a firm name, the principal place of business, the nature of the firm, the duration of the partnership, and the names and addresses of the partners. They identify limited and general partners, disclose the capital contribution of each limited partner, and describe the method for determining changes in personnel and continuance of the business in the event of death or retirement of one of the general partners. This document must be properly signed by all the parties, a filing fee paid, and the document deposited in the state's office of the secretary of state and/or the local recording office.

31.3 LIMITED PARTNERSHIPS: GENERAL PARTNERS

The certificate must include the name of at least one general partner who is liable as a general partner and by whom the business is generally conducted. A corporation may be a general partner. The general partners run the business, but they possess no greater rights than those granted by the statute and charter.

EXAMPLE 2. A mortgage banker sued to collect a loan broker's commission of $9,500 for finding a lender of $950,000 for a limited partnership which had one general partner and seven limited partners. The banker contends that he has performed and is entitled to the commission. The firm defends on the grounds that the terms of the lending offer the banker found for the firm require the signatures of both the general partner and the limited partners; accordingly, the banker *did not* find a qualified lender. The banker contends that the general partner must have known that such would be the requirement of the loan, as it is custom and usage. The court ruled that such may be the custom, but the law and statute do not vest the general partner with power to contract for the limited partners.

31.4 LIMITED PARTNERSHIPS: RESTRICTIONS

The law places restrictions on the activities of a limited partner in a limited partnership. The limited partner, unlike a general partner, must make a capital contribution, and it cannot be in services, only in cash or property. The name of the limited partner cannot be used in the firm name unless it is the same name as the general partner. Most important of all, the statute provides a potentially harsh penalty for a limited partner who attempts to meddle in the business. A limited partner who takes an active role in the business, or who interferes with management, becomes a general partner in the eyes of third parties. He or she is then subject to unlimited liability.

EXAMPLE 3.   Howard and his army buddy, Teddy, decided to form a partnership for an offset printing press operation. Howard was luckier than most, having married the daughter of a successful businessperson who was willing to put $20,000 into the operation, but only as a limited partner. Written articles of limited partnership were filed in the form of the certificate required by the state. The articles reflected Howard and Teddy as general partners and Morrison, the father-in-law, as a limited partner. The printing business did not do well, and Morrison, who lived in a distant city, was distressed to see his investment going down the drain. Morrison was a prominent figure in his community and started asking around to see if any printing business was needed since he could give a customer a "good deal." Several local politicians were running for election and pushed business to this out-of-state firm. They said that "If Morrison is behind it, it will be a first-class operation." Morrison then began to advise his two general partners to cultivate political office seekers, spruce up their offices, and do some entertaining. The general partners followed his advice. It turned out they were poor at promotion but good at running up bills. Their creditors, seeing that a successful businessperson was calling the shots, gave the firm more credit than it could handle. Morrison's activities, inconsistent with the role of a limited partner, may permit the creditors to treat him as a general partner with unlimited liability.

The question of control, and the effects this may have on the legal liability of a limited partner, is not greatly litigated. Perhaps this is because it is difficult to define "control," which can take many forms, some of them quite subtle and very difficult of proof. However, overt forms of control or participation, such as those evidenced by written documents or by open dealings with third parties, are easier to prove and, perhaps for that reason, may be avoided by limited partners aware of their potential vulnerability. It should be noted that there is a current legislative trend to allow some minor degree of control by limited partners without sacrifice of their limited liability. Several states have adopted the Revised ULPA which contains such provisions.

31.5 LIMITED PARTNERSHIPS: RIGHTS OF LIMITED PARTNERS

A limited partner has the right to receive profits and compensation as provided in the certificate (articles) of partnership. A limited partner is entitled to have the books kept at the principal place of business, to inspect the books, and to copy them. He or she is entitled to demand a formal accounting and may proceed toward dissolution by an appropriate action upon just cause before a court. However, a limited partner does not have control over the affairs of the business.

EXAMPLE 4.   Benson and Torry are limited partners who had considerable business experience before they retired. Benson's son, Tommy, runs the firm, which wholesales electric light fixtures in the county. Tommy has just received his M.B.A. and decides to apply some of what he thinks he learned. Tommy has set up an elaborate bonus plan for retailers who wish to join in certain promotions. Benson and Torry know the business well. In their youth they had tried a variation of Tommy's plan, with disastrous results. Benson and Torry vote to veto Tommy's proposal. Tommy ignores the veto. Benson and Torry are considering asking the court to remove Tommy as the general partner. The court would not entertain such a petition since the limited partners possess no such right of removal.

The interest of a limited partner is valuable in that it is freely assignable, but as in general partnership law, the assignee is not granted the rights of a limited partner.

EXAMPLE 5.   Sutton is a limited partner in a thriving tax shelter in the form of a limited partnership which purchases movie rights and rents them out. Fantina is impressed with Sutton's interest and offers to buy it, provided it allows Fantina all the rights Sutton has. Sutton represents that this is the case. Sutton assigns his interest in the firm to Fantina, who promptly notifies the limited partnership of the fact. Fantina requests that the partnership books be opened to her. The firm refuses. Fantina, as an assignee of a limited partnership, has no legal right to inspect the books.

Among the rights that a limited partner can enforce, however, is that he or she be consulted and consent to the admission of any new members, limited or general, or, if the certificate so provides, the continuation of the firm upon the death of a general partner. Further, the statute does not prohibit the withdrawal of the capital of the limited partner, if the certificate so provides, on the condition that no general creditors would be harmed.

EXAMPLE 6.   Dr. Abelard invested in a limited partnership on the condition that her funds could be retrieved upon 60-day notification of her intention. Such a provision was reflected in the certificate of partnership. The firm was having trouble during a recession, but was weathering the storm. The firm's balance sheet showed that it was just able to pay its bills. At this time Abelard suffered a heart attack and needed money. She gave immediate notice to the firm of her demand for the return of her capital. Compliance with this request would reduce the amount of capital available for the creditors. Under these circumstances Abelard's request need not be honored despite the provision in the certificate of partnership. The agreement is not illegal, but the law makes its operation conditional on the circumstances at the time the request is made.

31.6   LIMITED PARTNERSHIPS: DISTRIBUTION OF ASSETS

The order of distribution of assets upon dissolution and liquidation of a limited partnership is markedly different from that of a general partnership. It includes six categories. The order of distribution is:

(1)   All creditors, including limited partners who may have lent money to the firm

(2)   Limited partners in respect to their shares of undistributed profits or income on their capital contributions

(3)   Limited partners in respect to their capital contributions

(4)   General partners other than for capital and profits

(5)   General partners in respect to profits of the partnership

(6)   General partners in respect to capital contributions

31.7   INDIVIDUAL, OR SOLE, PROPRIETORSHIP

The common use of phrases such as "my business" or "my company" causes some to assume that the business enterprise in question is an entity, without fully appreciating the fact that the speaker is probably describing a *sole proprietorship*. Unless the speaker has joined a partnership, or formed a corporation, the likelihood is that the business is completely owned by him or her as an individual; it has no legal identity of its own apart from the proprietor.

EXAMPLE 7.   Markum was a self-made man who had prospered for 30 years manufacturing tile in a small building. He generally employed from five to seven workers. Markum was the manager, salesman, and owner. He owned the building, equipment, and two vehicles (a Cadillac sedan and a large truck); had an impressive bank account and a nice home; and had been married for 40 years to his faithful wife Marian. Markum died leaving a will by which all his property was given to his wife, except " . . . to my faithful workers, Lenny and Mark, I give one-half of my tile business, share and share alike."
Markum was a sole proprietor. What are the assets of his tile business? The truck was frequently used around his home and at his lakeside cabin. He had often used the Cadillac on company business to call on

customers. What part of the bank account is personal funds? Is some of the equipment in the building family property? What of the building itself? A third of it was used for years to store Markum's boat and lakeside cabin furnishings during the winter months.

These are difficult questions which Markum's executor must try to cope with, and which a probate court ultimately must answer. As a matter of law all the property was in Markum's name. There was no separate business under the law.

In a sole proprietorship, the owner is the only principal, has complete control, is responsible to no one else, and has more actual authority than the chief executive officer of a corporation, although, in respect to drawing the line between business and personal expenses, the sole proprietor must be careful lest he or she run afoul of the IRS. The sole proprietor has unlimited liability and the potential for unlimited gain, he or she is taxed as an individual, and the business legally ends at his or her death.

31.8 JOINT VENTURE: CO-ADVENTURERS

A *joint venture* is a temporary partnership formed to carry out a single or isolated business effort for profit. The term describes a combination of parties committed to a single venture as contrasted with carrying on a business within the meaning of the UPA. Despite the fact that the conduct of co-adventurers may not suggest a full partnership, the effects, within the scope of the undertaking, are somewhat similar.

Simply stated, third parties can sue the joint adventurers in a manner similar to partnership where the activities of the parties touch third parties. Further, among themselves, while the specific rules of distribution may not be honored, equitable adjustments among the parties follow partnership principles.

EXAMPLE 8.   Barret believes a new theme park is being put together, and he is sure he knows the site selected. He interests two others in purchasing land near the site and holding the land for later development. If these three become co-owners of the land, they are not necessarily partners, and certainly are not carrying on a business. Yet, Barret's actions on behalf of the owners, sometimes called *syndicate members*, could, if authorized, have the same binding force as if it were a partnership. Further, among themselves, the co-adventurers have rights and duties similar to those found in organizations meeting the UPA definition of a partnership.

Usually the management of a joint venture is in the hands of one of the members by agreement of all. The death of one of the members generally does not end the relationship.

31.9 JOINT STOCK COMPANY

A *joint stock company*, or *association*, is formed when the parties agree to place the management of the business in the hands of others, trustees or directors. In effect, it is a partnership with some of the features of a corporation. As in corporations, the death of a shareholder does not automatically dissolve the association, but as in a partnership, members are liable for the acts of the business. The changeability of stockholders, or members, is permitted. The members normally are not agents for the association.

EXAMPLE 9.   Three investors, each owning downtown property, observe that their properties have much in common in respect to renting out space. They decide to coordinate their business practice, get out of the active management, and yet continue to own the properties. They don't want a partnership and have no desire for a corporation. So they commit all their rental space to a joint stock company they form and transfer management to a managing trustee, who alone has the authority to commit the properties for renting. The agreement specifies the rights and duties of the trustee and sets forth the proportionate interests of the three members.

Acts of the trustee can bind the members, but only to the extent of the specific business operation, the renting of space. The downside legal risk is small, as the scope of authority of the trustee is narrow. Under a joint stock company agreement, certificates are issued to the owners. Like shareholders in a corporation, the members can influence and change management policies, etc.

31.10 BUSINESS TRUST

Like a joint stock company, a *business trust* contemplates placing management in the hands of another party, and certificates are issued. Here, however, title to the assets of the firm is placed in the legal name of a trustee under terms which grant the trustee exclusive right to manage and control the business without interference from the owners. The owners' only rights are set forth in the trust instrument. Ownership certificates are freely transferable, and provided the trust instrument grants no authority to the members to manage the business, the owners bear no legal risk of liability by reason of the operation of the trust by the trustee. However, the trustee, being the principal, does have liability for his or her actions, both contractual and tortious.

This form of business organization is known by a number of different names, including *Massachusetts trust*, *common-law trust*, and simply *business trust*. Some state statutes address this form of business organization.

EXAMPLE 10. Baron envied his friend Tallman who seemed to earn good dividends from her trust. Baron learned that Tallman held a trust certificate representing a 10 percent interest in an equipment trust, which had been formed for the purpose of purchasing road-building machinery for lease to contractors. Baron investigated and was impressed by the operation. He found that he could buy into it because one member was willing to sell. After the purchase, Baron, who knew a bit about construction, chided the trustee on his conservative practices. Baron so stirred up the members of the trust that a majority of them ordered the trustee to adopt the business practices which Baron advocated. If, under the terms of the trust agreement, the members can force this change, they may be "in control of or management of," and the immunity from personal liability which members ordinarily have under a business trust would be surrendered.

The difference between a joint stock company and a business trust is that in a joint stock company, the managers or directors are the agents for the owners, the stockholders. In a business trust, the trustees are the principals, and the shareholders (members) are beneficiaries only, not principals or parties to the contract or activity.

31.11 UNINCORPORATED ASSOCIATIONS

Where parties gather to carry out a common purpose, their relationship may be classed as an *unincorporated association*. It can have either charitable or profit-making objectives. Because such associations are not carrying on a business, they are not deemed partnerships. Those who manage or direct them are, of course, liable for their acts. Further, those who approve or vote approval of its activities are likewise liable.

EXAMPLE 11. Old Man Hardheart finally relented and permitted the Spruce Street residents to use his vacant lot for a playground. Ten residents reside on the two blocks near the lot. At a called meeting, eight of the parents agreed to develop the playground and provide it with some simple sports equipment. Danny, the local high school coach, is one of the residents; he and a banker, who volunteered to act as manager, are the leaders of the group. Among the items installed was a pair of horseshoe game pits. In this activity both Danny and the banker made mistakes. First, the residents who approved the plan didn't pay their assessment. Danny, the banker, and the others who voted for the plan are liable for the cost of the equipment and its installation. Second, and worse, the location of one of the horseshoe pits was badly chosen and was a contributing cause to the injury of a spectator when a pitched horseshoe ricocheted off the iron stake and struck the spectator in the face. This tort liability falls on all approving members as principals as well as on Danny, their agent, as he is the tortfeasor who negligently selected the location.

31.12 FRANCHISES

Technically a franchise is not a form of organization, but rather a contractual relationship one makes, whether as a sole proprietor, a partnership, or a corporation. The *franchise* is a contract by which one party, the franchisee, is granted the right from the franchisor to engage in a business offering goods or services under a marketing plan which is usually associated with the franchisor's trademark, service mark, or other commercial symbol.

However, because of the nature of the problems which can arise in this type of commercially intimate relationship and the statutory involvement of some states in adjusting the interests of the parties, franchising raises more than just contract questions.

EXAMPLE 12.   Joslyn is a world-class Frisbee player. He has written a popular book on the sport and is sought out as a teacher and coach. He decides to incorporate, adopts techniques (copyrighted), develops and trademarks certain equipment, and now sells franchises for Joslyn's Frisbee Studio across the country. He runs a tight operation, and the franchise contract provides for strict control over the franchises, including the franchisor's right to veto the hiring of any particular instructor. This control, by contract, might make the franchisee an agent of the franchisor rather than an independent contractor.

The fact that extensive control is many times provided in franchise contracts has resulted in the relationship being uncertain in respect to contract and tort liability. The conflict between the franchisor's strong desire to preserve his or her sometimes delicate asset of goodwill and the need of the franchisee to manage the business can expose the franchisor to the charge of being in a principal-to-agent, or alter ego, relationship with the franchisee. In response to perceived abuses by franchisors, some states have enacted statutes restricting the degree of franchisor control. Their attempts to find a compromise between a supposedly arm's length transaction and a fiduciary relationship seriously test traditional legal principles that have historically distinguished agents from independent contractors.

Black Letter Law
A Summary

1. Limited partnerships must be formally created by complying with the state statute in a signed certificate of limited partnership, which must be filed with the state.

2. A limited partnership must have one or more limited partners and at least one general partner, the latter having unlimited liability.

3. The rights of limited partners are set by statute and the certificate but do not include the right to have their names in the firm name or interfere in the management and control of the business, the breach of which can result in personal liability to such limited partners.

4. The order of distribution of assets of limited partnerships permits limited partners who are also creditors to have equal rights with the other firm creditors and superior priority to that of general partners irrespective of their claim.

5. A sole proprietor, a co-adventurer, or a stockholder in a joint stock company has unlimited liability.

6. A beneficiary of a valid business trust, in which no control is exercised over the management of the business by the beneficiary, is free from personal liability except to the extent of his or her investment.

7. A member who joins in or ratifies actions taken by an unincorporated association is liable for such approved acts of the association.

8. A franchise is generally a contract between a franchisor and a franchisee, granting to the latter the right to use a marketing system which possesses certain intangible qualities, such as trademarks and service marks.

Solved Problems

31.1 Dowling is a promoter and has decided to use a limited partnership for conducting a securities investment venture. Which of the following is *unnecessary* in order to validly create such a limited partnership?

(a) All limited partners' capital contributions must be paid in cash.

(b) There must be a state statute which permits the creation of such a limited partnership.

(c) A limited partnership certificate must be signed and sworn to by the participants and filed in the proper office in the state.

(d) There must be one or more general partners and one or more limited partners.

(*AICPA Examination, November 1979*)

   With the exception of statement (a), all relate to absolute requirements for a valid limited partnership. Value must be paid in by each limited partner, and while cash is the more common form of contribution, property can (also) be contributed. Services may not constitute the capital contribution of a limited partner.

31.2 A limited partner

(a) may *not* withdraw his or her capital contribution unless there is sufficient limited partnership property to pay all general creditors.

(b) must *not* own limited partnership interests in other competing limited partnerships.

(c) is automatically an agent for the partnership with apparent authority to bind the limited partnership in contract.

(d) has *no* liability to creditors even if he or she takes part in the control of the business as long as he or she is held out as being a limited partner.

(*AICPA Examination, November 1976*)

   A limited partner has an interest somewhat similar to that of a shareholder in a corporation in that he or she can own other interests and can sell his or her interest. A limited partner can also withdraw his or her capital if the certificate allows, but not if the rights of the general creditors in the firm's assets would thereby be threatened; the answer is (a).

31.3   Which of the following rights would the limited partners *not* have?

(*a*)   The right to have a dissolution and winding-up by court decree where such is appropriate

(*b*)   The right to remove a general partner by a majority vote if the limited partners determine that a general partner is not managing the partnership affairs properly

(*c*)   The right upon dissolution to receive their share of profits and capital contributions before any payment is made to the general partners

(*d*)   The right to have the partnership books kept at the principal place of business and to have access to them

(*AICPA Examination, November 1979*)

All the above rights exist except that area of control where the limited partners may veto business actions of the general partners, and so statement (*b*) is the answer. The other rights are provided in the Uniform Limited Partnership Act.

31.4   Teal and Olvera were partners of the T&O Real Estate Investment Company. They decided to seek more capital in order to expand their participation in the booming real estate business in the area. They obtained five individuals to invest $100,000 each in their venture as limited partners. Assuming the limited partnership agreement is silent on the point, which of the following acts may Teal and Olvera engage in without the written consent of all limited partners?

(*a*)   Admit an additional person as a general partner

(*b*)   Continue the partnership business upon the death or retirement of a general partner

(*c*)   Invest the entire amount ($500,000) of contributions by the limited partners in a single venture

(*d*)   Admit additional limited partners from time to time in order to obtain additional working capital

(*AICPA Examination, November 1979*)

The Uniform Limited Partnership Act specifically prohibits the general partners from engaging in certain acts that would be to the detriment of the limited partners. The general partners may, however, manage the business provided this does not affect the structure of the organization by change or substitution. Accordingly, the judgment to spend or invest firm funds in a particular way within the general authority of the firm cannot be challenged by the limited partners; statement (*c*) is correct.

31.5   Which of the following is a correct statement concerning the similarities of a limited partnership and a corporation?

(*a*)   Both provide insulation from personal liability for all the owners of the business.

(*b*)   Both can only be created pursuant to a statute, and each must file a copy of the respective certificates with the proper state authorities.

(*c*)   Both are recognized for federal income tax purposes as taxable entities.

(*d*)   Shareholders and limited partners may both participate in the management of the business and retain limited liability.

(*AICPA Examination, November 1978*)

The correct statement is (*b*). Neither a corporate charter nor a limited partnership agreement can be in oral form; both forms of organization require that a written instrument be prepared, executed, and filed as required by state statute. The other three statements are all true of corporations and are untrue of limited partnerships.

31.6 General Cosmetics, a limited partnership created pursuant to the Uniform Limited Partnership Act, is in liquidation. Some of the limited partners are also creditors of the partnership. Under the circumstances, how should the liquidation be accomplished?

(a) First satisfy all creditors, including any creditors who are also limited partners, in order of priority as provided by law.

(b) Distribute any excess remaining after the satisfaction of creditors to limited partners, with the exception of undistributed profits to which the general partners may be entitled.

(c) Satisfy all outside creditors, excluding any limited partners who are also creditors, and then satisfy limited partners for all their claims.

(d) Satisfy all partners whether general or limited for their original capital contribution after all creditors have been satisfied.

(*AICPA Examination, November 1974*)

Unlike the order of distribution for general partnerships, the order of distribution for limited partnerships provides that limited partners who have loaned money to the partnership, or otherwise have claims against it (except as to capital), share equally with the general creditors of the firm. Statement (*a*) is the answer.

31.7 Tommy is an airline captain who earns $95,000 a year. It is all ordinary income, however, and he decides to have a separate business on the side. He enters into a contract with a shirt manufacturer to design and make beautiful white shirts with epaulettes that pilots wear. He takes orders from fellow pilots and has the manufacturer ship the shirts to the buyers. Tommy is doing well. He calls his shirt business Flightime Shirts and has registered the name under a fictitious name law. Tommy places all funds received into a separate bank account. Tommy runs his business as a

(a) limited partnership.

(b) sole proprietorship.

(c) joint venture.

(d) franchise.

Tommy is operating as a sole proprietor, an individual businessman, statement (*b*). He has no partners, has joined with no others in a joint venture, and has not contracted with a franchisor.

31.8 Which of the following interests gives the least protection from the debts that might be run up by the organization?

(a) A beneficiary in a business trust

(b) A general partner in a limited partnership

(c) A passive member of an unincorporated association

(d) A limited partner in a limited partnership

In each of the foregoing there is either protection or some limitation of liability except for a general partner in a limited partnership, statement (*b*), who has unlimited liability. The beneficiary in a business trust, provided he or she does not exercise control or engage in management, remains immune from liability except to the extent of his or her contributed interest. One who does not vote, approve, or ratify acts done by an unincorporated association is not liable for the acts of the association. If "passive" describes such an individual, then that person is not liable.

31.9 Quentin and Roscoe have transferred all their mining interests to Farrel, who will perform the few duties involved in collecting the rental, renewing leases when necessary, making deductions for expenses, and paying Quentin and Roscoe at quarterly intervals. The instrument signed by Quentin and Roscoe is binding for 10 years and gives them no authority over the management of these interests. Quentin and Roscoe were issued certificates of interest, however, which they can transfer. Under the circumstances,

(a)   Quentin and Roscoe are co-adventurers.

(b)   Quentin and Roscoe are limited partners.

(c)   Quentin and Roscoe are stockholders in a joint stock company.

(d)   this arrangement appears to be a business trust.

    A trust occurs when transfer of legal title is made for the use and benefit of another. Here, the parties formed a business trust, statement (d). The declaration of trust signed by the parties sets forth the terms, duration, and purpose of the trust. It deprives the former owners of the right to control the operation.

31.10 Faust always wanted to run a dance studio. Mephisto Dance Systems is interested in Faust if he will put up $20,000. If he will, Mephisto will set him up at a location; do all the promotion; provide literature, music, and office equipment; and assign a consultant for a time long enough to get a successful operation off the ground. Faust eagerly signs on the dotted line. Under these circumstances it is likely that Faust

(a)   is a franchisee operating as a sole proprietorship.

(b)   is a franchisor.

(c)   is an agent of Mephisto Dance Systems, Inc.

(d)   is in a joint venture with a corporation.

    There is nothing to indicate that Faust is anything but a sole proprietor operating a franchise which he has contracted for, and so the answer is (a). Accordingly, he has the sole potential for personal gain, and he has unlimited personal liability. If the franchisor were to exercise too much control, it is possible that in some situations Faust might be an agent. But, on the face of it, one assumes that a contractual franchising situation is an arm's length transaction. A franchisee can take any form of business organization. That is, a franchisor may contract with any party having the capacity to contract: a sole proprietor, a partnership, a limited partnership, a corporation, etc.

31.11 A National Guard unit had an Armory Committee which consisted of all the officers in the unit. The members planned social functions and other activities to promote good public relations in the community. All the officers but one attended the meeting at which arrangements were made and approved for the New Year's Eve ball. During the night of the ball the parking lot had not been sanded or salted, resulting in a dangerous ice condition. One visitor to the ball fell and injured himself in the parking lot. He sued all the officers of the Armory Committee for negligence in failing to have safe premises.

    Who would be responsible for this tort, and under what theory? Decide and give reasons for any conclusions.

    The Armory Committee finds itself in a very dangerous legal position. It is an unincorporated association. While not every member of the committee would be liable for the tortious act, those members of the committee who actively participated, aided, and abetted the affair are liable. Under these facts it would appear that all the members but the one officer who did not attend the meeting would be liable.

31.12 Ricardo was a general partner of Favorite Farms, a limited partnership with Fresco and Tollerence as limited partners. The three were in the business of truck farming: raising produce and selling it to local brokers. Under their business arrangements all checks written by Ricardo had to be cosigned by either Fresco or Tollerence. Business became bad, and

Ricardo was considered to be managing poorly. As they wanted to salvage the firm, Fresco and Tollerence then voted to remove Ricardo, which they did. However, they were not successful in saving the firm, and Favorite Farms went into bankruptcy. Fresco and Tollerence lost over $300,000, and neither Ricardo nor Tollerence had any assets. Fresco, however, was still a wealthy man. The creditors demanded that Fresco pay the outstanding debts as the firm could pay only 10 cents on the dollar. Fresco, citing the $200,000 loss of his own capital contribution, contends that he has suffered enough and also that he is a limited partner.

What success will the creditors have in demanding the other 90 cents on the dollar of unpaid debts of Favorite Farms? Decide and give reasons for your conclusions.

A limited partner does not become liable as a general partner unless, beyond the exercise of his or her rights as a limited partner, such partner takes control of the business. The manner of handling the checking account is certainly significant. Further, voting to remove the general partner, *and succeeding*, is clear evidence of control. Fresco could become liable as a general partner and therefore be liable for the debts of the firm. Tollerence's position in respect to liability is the same as Fresco's, but his financial situation would preclude recovery from him by the creditors.

31.13 Panncost and Addleson were well-known oil well drillers. They entered into an agreement to drill a well and share expenses. Their agreement provided that after Addleson had expended $73,000 on the drilling, he could elect to cancel the agreement. Drilling began, and success was not at hand when Addleson, having spent over $73,000, notified Panncost that he was electing to withdraw from the contract. Panncost continued to drill, now ordering equipment from Ferro-Union Suppliers in the amount of $141,000 to his own account. The drilling was unsuccessful, and Panncost could not fully pay the bill he had run up with Ferro-Union. At this point Ferro-Union learned of the contract between Panncost and Addleson and sued Addleson for the unpaid balance of the drilling supplies.

What legal theory is Ferro-Union relying on? Decide and state reasons for any conclusions reached.

Ferro-Union is relying on the doctrine of joint venture to permit it to sue Addleson. If a joint venture exists, one joint venturer has the authority to bind the other joint venturers by contracts made in furtherance of the joint enterprise. However, the agreement containing the right to withdraw will be effective in this case. It is true that it was a private agreement between two joint adventurers, but the creditor never relied on the existence of Addleson in the first place, as it gave credit to Panncost only. That is, Ferro-Union did not decide to send the goods on the basis of the legal liability of the other (former) co-adventurer, which would be a requirement to liability. Addleson is not liable on these facts.

Topic Test, Part VII

Partnerships

1. Vincent was a man who had not enjoyed much business success until he teamed up with Ralph, his brother-in-law, as a partner in the business of providing inspection reports on home appliances and equipment in housing developments. The partners named the firm Home Inspect Company. Vincent was proud of the company and went on about it to his friend Thomas. Vincent whipped out his checkbook showing checks imprinted with the firm's name and a place for Vincent's signature as "manager." Vincent then showed Thomas how the title certificate to the two company trucks read. Sure enough they were in the name of Home Inspect Company. Vincent even bragged of how he had to sign an income tax return. All this was too much for Thomas, who said that Home Inspect was not a real company. What point is Vincent unsuccessfully trying to make about a partnership?

2. Lorne was an ambitious youth, and by the time he was 16 years of age he personally maintained seven lawns. Antoine, always on the lookout for a "comer," thought that with better equipment Lorne could substantially increase his income. Antoine proposed a modest partnership with Lorne, who had just turned 17 years of age. They were to go 50–50. Lorne took to the new equipment quickly and was progressing nicely when Antoine interfered, suggesting procedures with which Lorne disagreed. Lorne became fed up and abandoned the partnership. Antoine, bitter, wanted to teach Lorne a lesson and so stopped making installment payments on the equipment Antoine had purchased for the firm. The suppliers, unpaid, started pressing Lorne. Lorne contends that he is a minor and is not liable for the firm's debts. The suppliers counter his contention by stating that the Uniform Partnership Act does not prohibit a minor from becoming a partner. Which party is correct in its contention?

3. Fred, Angio, and Pilote formed a partnership. It was agreed that Pilote was to devote full time to the firm, but the others would just contribute capital. Fred contributed $130,000 and Angio $77,000. Pilote worked very hard, and the firm slowly prospered. All were happy except Pilote's husband, who complained of the long hours that Pilote kept as opposed to no time being put in by the other partners, who only dropped by from time to time to look at the books and see how the operation was going. Pilote's reply to her husband was, "Just look at the money I make. I put up no money, but I am an equal partner." Indeed, Pilote did receive one-third of all money distributed. One day, after the accountant had left, Pilote's husband looked over the financial statements and asked Pilote about the meaning of the entry showing capital contributions. There, Fred was noted as $130,000, Angio $77,000, and Pilote $0. "What does it mean?" asked the spouse. Pilote replied that it meant that at one time the two others had put up those sums of money. "Will it matter?" asked the spouse. Will it ever matter that Pilote is credited with $0?

4. After Pilote's husband understood the effect of unequal capital contributions (Question 3), he then thought he saw a disadvantage to his wife being the only one of the three partners who actively worked in the firm. Pilote assured him that she was paid quite well for her work and pointed to her monthly paychecks as proof of that. Her spouse was insistent, however, and

asked Pilote how much of the firm's profits she got compared with the other two partners. Pilote replied proudly that she was to get a full third of the firm's profits. Each of the other two partners also received one-third of the profits. What important legal point is Pilote's husband illustrating to a partner (Pilote) who spends her full time and effort working for the partnership while the other partners need not under the terms of the partnership agreement?

5. Hanson spent a productive and happy life with an insurance agency with two splendid partners. The agency's assets are considerable, and the future income from renewals will bring Hanson a solid retirement. But Hanson wants a clean financial break with the agency as he is moving away. Hanson demands "all his equity" in the business, including the goodwill, equipment, and several cars used in the business, together with his share of the agency's office building. There is, however, some unfinished business in the nature of current debts from some rather large credit purchases, such as for the complete computer system that had recently been installed and is only 20 percent paid for. Under what circumstances can Hanson make a clean legal break from the agency?

6. Drake suffered a minor heart attack, causing his retirement from a busy firm. Drake did not take to retirement easily and was a burden to his wife, Laura. Drake's doctor suggested a new but only modestly demanding business activity. Tom, Laura's brother, needed money to start up The Paper Place, a novelty retail store at Pier 86 in San Francisco. Tom offered Drake a limited partner's interest for $25,000. Laura encouraged this investment, and she asked her brother what her husband's business management duties would be. Is this the type of opportunity that might satisfy Drake by keeping him actively involved in business?

7. Trent was an ambitious CPA who joined a small but prominent firm in his hometown. Several years as an employee convinced him that to be taken in as a partner would be a fine goal. He had observed the payouts to the partners at Christmas time when they split up the profits. Trent's usefulness is observed, and he is being offered a partnership in the firm, although, the partners hasten to add, as a junior partner. Trent now has a copy of the articles of partnership to study. He sees that if he agrees, he will, as a junior partner, have no vote on the methods and procedures used in the office. He had been wanting to get an inefficient clerk fired. Upset, he wonders how it is possible for him to be a partner but have no right to fire. Doesn't the right to control accompany partnership? Explain your answer to Trent.

8. Burke was a woman of many talents. Her interests included participation in an oil lease and partnership in both a car wash business and an auto parts store. She was also the local Democratic committeewoman for her district. She now has an opportunity to buy into a partnership being formed for the purpose of custom-upholstering vintage cars. Since startup costs will be great and the rent must be paid, the new partners intend to sell a few auto stereos and several other exotic auto accessories at huge discounts, just to get their name out into the auto public. What legal difficulty must Burke face in considering this opportunity?

9. Delilah and two others cut hair in Delilah's unisex barbershop. Delilah owned the building, the chairs, and the equipment. All three signed a document entitled a partnership agreement. It provided that Delilah would get rental credit for all her property used in the business before profits would be split. Further, Delilah was in complete control of the shop, and all assignments would be made by her. Upon dissolution for any cause, each partner could leave and have no claim against the others for any reason resulting from the partnership. The State Unemployment Commission has filed a charge against the barbershop on the grounds that the partners are not paying the unemployment tax as required for persons employed in the business. What type of legal argument will the firm try to use against the state? What success will it have?

10. Five electrical engineers decided to join together in forming a partnership for a period of 4 years. Their purpose was the development and sale of electronic systems. The articles of partnership covered most matters, but no mention was made of grounds for dissolution. The firm was doing well after 2 years, and three of the members were besieged with attractive offers from other companies. The three voted to dissolve, but the remaining two partners wanted the firm to finish out the term of the agreement. The three antsy partners contend that majority rule governs partnership decisions. They state further that even one partner has the power to dissolve a partnership. What other principles of law should the three partners be informed of in regard to their proposed action?

Answers

1. Vincent appears to be trying to indicate that the company is separate from its members. In some ways this is correct, but the company is not a complete legal entity. A partnership can, by statute, sue in its own name in many states, have separate assets, use a firm name, file an informational federal income tax return, go into bankruptcy, and even be a partner in another partnership. However, it is not a complete legal entity separate from its partners who have unlimited personal liability for all obligations. The firm exists no longer than any partner remains a member.

2. Both are correct in their initial statements. Minors can be partners, but a minor is always a minor and has the right to disaffirm contracts except for the reasonable value of personal necessaries. A minor does not lose that right by joining a partnership.

3. Yes, it does matter that Pilote is credited with no contribution to the capital account. Unless there is a specific agreement to the contrary, at dissolution the parties who contributed capital are entitled to its return before any profits are calculated and distributed. If the firm is worth, for example, $600,000 at dissolution, Pilote does not get one-third of this amount ($200,000). She gets one-third of what is left after the total of $207,000 in capital contributions has been returned to the other two nonworking partners. This is neither fair nor unfair per se. A judgment on that point will be personal and will depend on each partner's perception of who contributed what, overall, during the life of the firm.

4. Pilote's husband is teaching Pilote some hard lessons regarding partnership law. Since a partner is not an employee of the firm, no matter how hard he or she works, the partner is not entitled to compensation apart from his or her share of profits unless this is specifically agreed by all partners. Accordingly, any money the partner is paid in "wages" is part of that partner's share of profits unless there is a specific agreement that, in addition to his or her share of profits, the partner is to receive additional compensation for working as a manager. Payment of wages to a working partner will not be assumed. Again, this is neither fair nor unfair per se. Whether it is fair will depend on a personal judgment about the relative value to the firm of the capital contributions of the other partners as compared with the value of Pilote's work.

5. One who has debts cannot get rid of those debts unless the creditors release him or her. The fact that the continuing partners promise to pay the outstanding firm debts and hold the withdrawing partner harmless is fine in that it gives the former a person to sue if the debts are not paid. It has, however, no effect on the creditors who gave no binding approval, such as in a novation. Hanson had better visit all the outstanding creditors and see whether he can get a binding release from them. That is the only way he can achieve a clean legal break from the agency, even if he properly notifies all parties that he is leaving.

6. An investment in a limited partnership is quite passive in regard to "business involvement." A limited partner has many legal rights, including the right to inspect the books, demand an accounting, and receive profits and compensation as provided in the articles filed. However, a limited partner has no rights in the management of the business. He or she could be employed as a clerk in the store, or could perform some special task in the business, provided the limited partner did not become involved in the management of the business. In these circumstances it appears doubtful that this opportunity to become a limited partner is one that will satisfy the intentions of the doctor and the hopes of the wife.

7. Trent understands the law. One who has no right to management is likely not a partner. However, it is one thing to have a right to management and another to contract away certain aspects of that right under the articles of partnership. A situation in which a junior partner is given less than an equal vote in some aspects of management is not inconsistent with partnership relations. It is generally a matter of degree. If, however, the junior partner has *no* rights as an owner of the business, then it is questionable whether he or she is indeed a full legal partner.

8. The new business in which Burke has taken an interest seems to deal in the sale of auto parts. She is already a partner in an auto parts business. Partnership involves a fiduciary relationship, and included in this is the implied promise not to compete against the firm. If the proposal contemplates competition or action adverse to her extant firm, she would be in breach of her fiduciary duty.

9. The firm is aware of the rule that partners are owners of a firm, not employees. The state unemployment statute requires that an employee be covered for unemployment risk and the appropriate taxes be paid by the employer. If the firm has no employees, then there is no tax to be paid. The firm's problem is this: the articles of partnership seem mighty sketchy regarding ownership by the other partners. A firm can have no property (in this case Delilah owns all of it personally) and still be considered a partnership, but there must be evidence to indicate that the two fellow barbers are co-owners of the business. They have no control over the management of the firm, and more importantly, at dissolution they are precluded from any interest in the firm. These two barbers are probably employees, not partners. If so, the firm must pay the tax. Further, a partnership cannot be created solely on the basis of the parties claiming to be partners.

10. It is true that any one partner has the power to dissolve a partnership, and it is also true that majority rule governs ordinary business matters, but those are not the issues in this case. The articles of partnership clearly provide for a 4-year term. Accordingly, one can dissolve before that time only on legal grounds without liability. If the three partners wish to dissolve, they can do so and no one can stop them. However, if they do so, they are causing a dissolution by breach of the contract for which they are responsible to the firm and the other two partners, and they can be sued for such act.

Chapter 32

Nature and Formation

32.1 DEFINITION AND SCOPE OF TOPICS

A *corporation* is a collection of individuals, or even one individual, created by statute as a legal person, which is granted powers to contract; to own, control, and convey property; and to carry on a business or operations within the limits of the powers granted. It can, in many ways, act as a natural person and is used for many other purposes than business, although the main interest here will be to examine its business use.

A corporation, when properly formed, exists in the eyes of the law as an entity or separate being from its owners, who are usually called *shareholders* or *stockholders*.

32.2 TYPES OF CORPORATIONS

Corporations may be classified by type, including corporations for profit, regulated, not-for-profit, and governmental. When formed with the intent of carrying out some charitable, benevolent, or educational purpose, it is a nonprofit corporation. Such a corporation has no stockholders; instead it has *members*. However, the entity concept is observed in respect to such corporations.

EXAMPLE 1. Ten families had an interest in seeing that their children developed computer proficiency. Since the individual cost of obtaining such proficiency was high, the families decided to found the Little Genius Club. Working rules were set up when they discovered that the investment and legal commitments had to be recognized and dealt with. The families voted to take advantage of the state statute authorizing the corporate form for nonprofit corporations. The prospective members, the incorporators, signed the articles of incorporation, adopting the name Little Genius Computer Club, Inc. They set forth conditions for membership and responsibilities pursuant to statute. Once the articles are filed and the charter issued, those acting for the club in contract are not personally liable for debts incurred. The not-for-profit corporation has an existence apart from its members.

Cities, towns, and counties are sometimes thought of as corporations, but they are really political subdivisions, some of which may be incorporated pursuant to state law, but they are usually not classified as government corporations. The so-called quasi-public, regulated corporation is seen in power companies, telephone companies, banks, and insurance companies. These are, however, profit-making corporations. Such organizations, in addition to meeting the requirements of the general corporation law, must seek statutory permission to operate in the regulated area.

EXAMPLE 2. Rught and Carrington are longtime residents on a small island 2 miles offshore of a large city. The island has recently become quite popular, and both traffic and business activity have increased. There is no bank on the island, and Rught and Carrington decide to form one. They study the general statute on corporations for profit, prepare articles that comply with the statute, and put as their corporate purpose, "banking." The state will reject the proposed charter. State law provides that banking corporations must be specially approved and demands that such proposed organizations be shown to have sufficient capital, that the participants be of good moral character, and that an economic need be shown. If, for example, the economist who is called upon to survey the need for a bank in the community reports negatively, no charter will be issued.

Observe that if the two residents in the above example had wished to establish a cannery, for example, a nonregulated industry, the charter approval would routinely follow irrespective of weak capital formation, bad moral character of the incorporators or first directors, or the existence of two failing canneries on the island.

Professional associations are a recent form of corporation. Until the last decade it was not possible ethically for professional persons to practice a profession under the corporate form. Largely as a result of pension plans receiving favorable treatment under the corporate form, the canons of ethics have been amended to allow doctors, dentists, accountants, and the like to form profit-making corporations with shareholders restricted to the members of the particular professions. Such corporations are known by different names, including *professional associations*, or *PAs*.

Some corporations are also described by other additional names. A *close* corporation describes one in which the shares are held by a few who manage the firm. Some states allow these to have easy management rules, including the right to have but one director. The term "Sub Chapter S" corporation tells the reader that a corporation's shareholders have unanimously agreed to be treated as a partnership for tax purposes only under the Internal Revenue Code; no more than 35 shareholders may own the company, and there are restrictions on the income that can be earned.

32.3 PROCESS OF INCORPORATION

The typical for-profit corporation is easily created, and although the technical requirements of the general incorporation statute must be met, they are plain reading.

EXAMPLE 3. A, B, C, and D decide to form a corporation to operate an offset printing plant. A is the active member in promotion, while B knows the business and C and D will put up the most money. An attorney is hired to prepare the articles for filing. The group decides on the name Settipress, Inc.; identifies the capital formation; and directs any special charter provisions it wants included. All the parties sign as incorporators and also as subscribers. The filing fee is advanced; the attorney sends in the articles; and a short time later, the accepted articles, now the certificate of incorporation, validate the charter.

At this point the organizational aspects are addressed, and the parties call their original meeting where directors are elected, bylaws are adopted, resolutions are voted, and numerous other details of giving legal life to this new artificial being are taken care of. This corporation appears to be perfectly formed and may be called a *de jure* corporation. This name is given to a corporation whose creation and operation are so perfectly formed that even the state cannot challenge its existence.

A corporation is a legal person for many but not all purposes. It certainly is entitled to the constitutional protection of due process and equal protection of the law, but it is not a citizen of a state for purposes of doing business in another state without seeking a permit or otherwise complying with the law.

32.4 PROMOTERS

Some party (or parties) must actively promote the formation of a corporation. This party is called a *promoter*. Certain rights and duties arise in the course of formation, occasionally resulting in litigation involving the promoter.

EXAMPLE 4. A dispute arose between the incorporators of a corporation and a lessor who leased realty he owned to the corporation. The corporation and its shareholders charged that the lessor obtained a secret profit in subleasing the property. It was claimed that the lessor was a promoter of the corporation and that as such he owed all the incidents of fidelity due that role. The court defined a promoter as "one that is a self-constituted organizer who finds an enterprise or venture and helps to attract investors to form a corporation and launch it into business, all with the view to earning promotion profits." It was found that the incorporation of the business formed was never a part of the plan of the lessor when he began a quest for a partner. Here the lessor was not a party who, from the beginning of his preliminary negotiations, looked to the formation of the corporation as a vehicle for the consummation of his enterprise.

The promoter, once identified, owes a fiduciary duty from the time the promoter begins his or her activities on behalf of the corporation until the promoter turns over the enterprise to a board of directors or stockholders. A promoter may not make a profit, secret or otherwise, unless the promoter has dealt with the corporation in an "arm's length transaction" in which the corporation has an independent board of directors.

EXAMPLE 5. An assignee of a mortgage attempted to foreclose on the property in opposition to the receiver of the corporation. An issue arose over the propriety of the promoter's action in purchasing the realty in January for $240,000, forming the corporation in August, and transferring the property to the corporation in September for a price of $350,000. The sale was not secret, but the promoter's profit was cause for dispute. Some argued that the promoter had breached a duty to the corporation in obtaining the profit. The court ruled that a breach of duty had occurred. There was no independent board of directors, and the corporate action was dominated by the promoter. The fact that the land may or may not have been worth more than $240,000 cannot override the promoter's fiduciary obligation to the corporation. For the promoter to make a profit of $110,000 under these circumstances is unconscionable and in violation of his fiduciary obligation.

There are a number of ways by which the promoter can violate his or her fiduciary duty. The promoter can, for example, "water the stock" by selling property to the corporation for issuance of stock at a price higher than its worth. Or the promoter can charge a high price as compensation for his or her organizational expertise. Shareholders or creditors may show later that this action was unfair and resulted in a dilution of assets. A promoter can be paid a reasonable fee provided the corporation when formed so votes, or, in some states, by statute the promoter is entitled to a reasonable fee plus expenses incurred during his or her performance.

32.5 PREINCORPORATION LIABILITIES

A proposed corporation is not a legal person and therefore is not liable solely by reason of those who attempt to speak for it. However, the organizers and promoters frequently must perform acts to get the corporation started. Those so acting may be personally liable despite the fact that the corporation, when formed, adopts the acts and assumes the liabilities. Such parties are not then released unless the third party agreed that they would be, or never intended to look to the acting parties, or subsequently released them through a novation.

EXAMPLE 6. Two parties representing themselves as officers of a proposed corporation signed a contract and a promissory note in favor of a supplier. The documents all reflected the name of the proposed corporation. When formed, the corporation adopted the contract and the note. The business did not prosper, however, and the supplier decided to sue the two parties. The supplier argued that since there was no principal at the time of the contract, the individuals are personally liable. The court disagreed, ruling that the evidence showed that the supplier had intended to deal with the proposed corporation and not with the two parties. Where the contract is made on behalf of a proposed corporation and the other party agrees to look to the corporation and not to the promoters or organizers for payment, the promoters incur no personal liability.

EXAMPLE 7. An employee was hired as a meat cutter by a partnership. Later, one of the partners offered the employee a job at a new location, representing that such a change would be a promotion and would pay more. The new store was opened and operated by the member as an individual under the name of Mundi Beef Company. The agreement was long-term and provided certain benefits to the employee. Six months later the individual formed a corporation under the name of Mundi Beef Co., Inc., but the same business was carried on at the same location. Ten months later the corporation became bankrupt, and the employee demanded his rights against the individual under the contract. The latter contended that the corporation alone has liability. The court ruled in favor of the employee. There was no evidence that the contract was amended, or that the new corporation had assumed the old contract with the employee's consent, or even that the employee knew that a corporation had been formed. Under these circumstances the individual does not escape liability.

A corporation which adopts a contract made before its incorporation is, of course, liable irrespective of the liability of its promoters or organizers. Adoption can be shown by conduct in addition to an express agreement by corporate resolution. Use of the property purchased, for example, can be such conduct, though it is not necessarily conclusive or all-encompassing.

EXAMPLE 8. A seller sold a bulldozer to a buyer for $1,500 plus the assumption by the buyer of a $20,000 debt still owed on the bulldozer by the seller to a creditor. The buyer used the bulldozer and later formed a corporation of which he became president. The buyer transferred the bulldozer to the corporation, which assumed the $20,000 debt in exchange for stock. It was alleged that the buyer never paid the $1,500 to the seller, and the seller sued the corporation, charging that the corporation also assumed the $1,500 debt. The seller contends that the buyer was a promoter of the corporation and that the seller had sent bills to the corporation. This, contended the seller, showed that the corporation knew about the $1,500 debt. Further, the knowledge of the buyer as president of the corporation that such a debt was due on the bulldozer was legally noted by the corporation. The court rejected that position and ruled in favor of the corporation. It was not liable for the $1,500 debt. Contracts by third persons are not enforceable against a corporation unless the contracts are subsequently adopted either expressly or by implication. The buyer's action in this case was his own and not that of the corporation since he was acting on his own behalf and not for the corporation. Knowledge acquired by corporate officials while acting for themselves and not for the corporation cannot be imputed to the corporation.

Once adopted, contract rights as well as duties are those of the corporation.

EXAMPLE 9. A seller contracted to sell land to a corporation yet to be formed. Later a dispute arose, and the corporation was sued by the seller. An issue arose over whether the corporation could sue, as it did not exist at the time of the contract. It appeared that after the corporation was formed, meetings were held by the board of directors, at which time the land contract presented by the promoters was formally adopted and ratified by corporate resolution. The corporation could sue on the contract. When a corporation adopts or ratifies a contract of its promoters or organizers, such a contract becomes a contract of the corporation, and this is especially so when there has already been part performance under the contract.

32.6   DEFECTIVE FORMATION

A *de jure* corporation is formed when articles are duly prepared, duly executed, and properly filed in the appropriate state office and the parties organize and operate as a corporation. Sometimes parties begin business having done less than that, and third parties attempt to challenge the legal status of the corporation with the objective of pressing liability on the stockholders, officers, directors, or other agents. It is at this point that the term *de facto* status is used. If the corporation can prove it qualifies as such, it is free from this collateral attack by third parties. The defense that it is a *de facto* corporation requires a showing of certain elements, generally that (1) there was a valid statute under which the parties could organize, (2) there was a bona fide attempt to comply with the incorporation statute, and (3) there was actual use of corporate rights and powers.

EXAMPLE 10. An issue arose in the construction of a contract in regard to whether a lending institution was a valid corporation in August. Three parties went into business earlier in April, and the group did not discover until October that no incorporation papers had been filed. They filed in November. There was no evidence showing a meeting of the shareholders, and no attempt was made to show the prior (to November) existence of any completed but unfiled articles of incorporation. The court ruled that there had been no showing of evidence supporting the contention that a *de facto* corporation existed. While mere failure to file its articles and accompanying papers may not, under some circumstances, preclude a corporation from existing *de facto*, the evidence failed to support any showing of a bona fide attempt to incorporate before August. Further, the complete absence of proof of exercise of corporate power before the decisive date is even stronger influence against finding corporate existence. It is true that a *de facto* corporation cannot be attacked collaterally, but inquiry may be made about whether a purported corporation has attained a *de facto* status. Of the three necessary elements, only proof of a valid statute was shown. There was no bona fide attempt to organize in the manner prescribed by statute, and there was no actual exercise of corporate powers by the parties.

EXAMPLE 11. A sales agent sued a president of a corporation, charging a personal breach of an employment agreement. The written contract reflected the employer as a corporation and the president as its agent. The sales agent alleged that while the president did file for an appropriate charter 3 years before the contract, no property was ever transferred to the corporation, the president continued to do business personally, no organization of the firm was accomplished, no capital stock was issued, nor were any corporate affairs conducted through a directorate. The court ruled that the president was guilty of using the corporation as a personal trade name. Since the corporation never organized under its charter, it could not do business as a corporation and, therefore, could not as a corporation enter into the contract sued upon. The president is personally liable.

Usually, however, the fact that the proper articles of incorporation have been filed is strong evidence of at least a *de facto* status. In fact, under Article 56 of the American Bar Association's Model Business Corporation Act, the issuance of a certificate of incorporation is conclusive evidence of compliance. Not all states have adopted the Model Act.

Where a *de facto* defense is unsuccessful, the parties acting may be personally liable. There are, however, instances in which the estoppel doctrine operates to achieve a just purpose. A party who represents to another that he or she is an agent of a corporation may not use his or her own failure against an innocent third party who relied on the representation. Or where third parties have assumed they contracted with a corporation, they may not, under some circumstances, contend release by reason of the failure for a corporation to be formed or be in existence. This theory is called a *corporation by estoppel*.

EXAMPLE 12. Anson signed a contract for the sale of her land as president of Anson Land Corporation. The buyers later decided to try to get out of the contract since it did not appear as attractive an opportunity as they first thought. They looked around for a legal excuse and found that Anson had never established a corporation. A court could apply the doctrine of corporation by estoppel to deny the buyers the defense that there was no seller. The buyers could be estopped to establish the truth.

32.7 FOREIGN CORPORATIONS

A corporation is a citizen of the state in which it is incorporated; it is a domestic corporation in that state. In all other states it is considered a foreign corporation. This characterization does present problems for a corporation when it either does business in another state or merely wishes to exercise legal rights there, such as defending or prosecuting a lawsuit. Under the U.S. Constitution, a corporation is not a citizen entitled to the full privileges and immunities of all citizens.

EXAMPLE 13. Ace, Inc., a North Carolina corporation, lends money to 10 different residents in South Carolina. The borrowers refuse to pay the money back. Ace sues in South Carolina to enforce the contract. The borrowers contend that in South Carolina there is no such "person" as Ace, Inc., a North Carolina person. If Ace has no permit or certificate to operate in South Carolina, the defense is good.

A permit to do business in another state is not difficult to obtain, but it is not always wise to attempt to obtain such. Once domesticated, the corporation is subject to all the laws of the state, including its revenue laws. The latter point is often likely to be unattractive. There are two aspects in this area that generate litigation: first, the invocation of the interstate commerce clause and, second, the "doing business" exception.

32.8 FOREIGN CORPORATIONS: INTERSTATE COMMERCE

When challenged in another state, a foreign corporation might attempt to claim exemption from being required to possess a state permit by contending that its operations there are strictly interstate and *not* intrastate commerce. A state statute discriminating against interstate commerce would be invalid. Accordingly, a requirement that all foreign corporations register to do business would be constitutionally invalid as it would place a burden on interstate commerce. The delicate issue is, when is a corporation registered in one state engaged exclusively in interstate commerce in another state?

EXAMPLE 14. A drug company, incorporated in another state, sued a retailer in New Jersey for breach of contract. The retailer charged that the company did business in the state but had not obtained a permit to do so and therefore could not sue in New Jersey. The company invoked the rule that a foreign corporation engaged solely in interstate commerce need not obtain a permit to do business when it desires to file suit in another state. The company alleged that it sold to a wholesaler who sold the drugs in interstate commerce. Company salespersons did enter into New Jersey just to "promote" sales. The retailer countered with the argument that 18 detail men were working out of a local office that had the company's name on the door. This office had a secretary and a company district manager who was in charge. The detail men traveled throughout New Jersey visiting not only wholesalers, but physicians, hospitals, and retailers who buy drug products in interstate commerce from the wholesalers. The court ruled that the company was not entirely engaged in interstate commerce in New Jersey. The fact that the detail men provided these people with up-to-date knowledge of the company's products, with free advertising, and with promotional material designed to encourage the general public to make more intrastate purchases, and even participated directly in such intrastate sales themselves by transmitting orders from hospitals, physicians, and drugstores they serviced, evidences doing intrastate business. Here, the company will not succeed in its claim to be exempt from state business permit requirements by reason of being solely engaged in interstate commerce. It is clearly involved in intrastate activities and therefore has no right of access to the state courts because it has no permit to do business in the state.

It is generally stated that if the foreign corporation makes no contracts in the state, maintains no office there, and has no agents there, the fact that the firm does make money from the residents does not prohibit the firm from showing it does solely interstate business. The ownership of property, the solicitation of orders, or even an isolated sale will not adversely affect that position. However, the solicitation of orders may require orders not only to be taken, but also to be accepted in the state, or as is seen in the above example, may involve the active participation of salespeople in sales to customers. Such can lead to a denial of the defense of doing business exclusively in interstate commerce.

32.9 FOREIGN CORPORATIONS: DOING BUSINESS GENERALLY

A foreign corporation may not always rely on the interstate commerce position, but rather may forcibly press the argument that it is not doing business in the state at all. Since a local court must be shown to have jurisdiction over a foreign corporation, the plaintiff must prove that he or she served process, that is, gained jurisdiction, on the defendant by serving the defendant in the local state or by using an approved substituted service of process. By analogy to auto accident cases the issue may be illustrated.

EXAMPLE 15. A Texan is driving in Utah when he negligently strikes a pedestrian in Salt Lake City. He returns home to Texas. The Utah citizen wishes to sue for damages in Utah and cannot send a Utah sheriff or other officer to Texas to "serve the papers," i.e., serve process, as such an officer would be merely a "tourist" in Texas. Federal constitutional law has long approved an exception for such suits by approving substituted service through following procedures set forth in the states' nonresident motor vehicle laws. The service is done by pretending that the secretary of state of Utah is the defendant for purposes of the service of process and mailing a copy of the complaint and summons to the Texas resident at his last-known address. Now Utah has personal jurisdiction over the Texas resident.

This legal fiction solves the problem of jurisdiction by assuming that a citizen of one state who drives on another state's highways has impliedly consented to suit. In a similar way states have adopted this technique by enacting what are known as *long arm statutes*, which assume consent to jurisdiction by the doing of certain acts in the state. The statutes apply equally to nonresident individuals and foreign corporations.

EXAMPLE 16. A guest in a New York resort hotel was injured while using a toboggan maintained by the hotel. The guest filed suit in New Jersey, where she resided, against the hotel, a foreign corporation which had no permit to do business in New Jersey. The hotel contended that New Jersey had no jurisdiction over it. The guest used substituted service against the hotel. The issue was whether the guest had proved sufficient minimum contracts in this state on the part of the hotel. The evidence revealed that reservations for the out-of-state hotel were taken by certain New Jersey ethnic centers which had been taking groups to the hotel for over 4 years. A tentative contract to the guest had been mailed to the center, and the guest, responding to the hotel's advertisement to use its direct-wire reservations service, obtained additional rooms through this method. The hotel regularly advertised in New York papers which reached New Jersey residents, in New Jersey papers, and in ethnic centers' newsletters. The court ruled that the extensive advertising and active solicitation in New Jersey were minimum contacts under these circumstances, stating that the long arm statute is not limited to consumer product cases. It allowed the prosecution of the case in New Jersey to continue against the foreign corporation, stating that the suit does not offend traditional notions of fair play and substantial justice.

Courts generally appear more sympathetic to a finding of doing business when they permit a resident to sue a foreign corporation than when it is asserted that a foreign corporation is subject to other state rules, such as its revenue laws. However, some state statutes carry a heavy penalty when a foreign corporation is a plaintiff or defendant and it is held that it is doing business without a license. Such a corporation may be effectively prevented from exercising what it may believe to be its rights for fear of exposing itself to such a penalty.

EXAMPLE 17. A furniture store was sued for goods sold and delivered by a supplier which was a foreign corporation. The state statute made such a contract unenforceable if the foreign corporation had no permit to do business in the state. When the store went bankrupt, the supplier added to its suit the name of the president of the store who had guaranteed the account. The president defended on the grounds that the supplier had no permit to do business and therefore could not sue. The supplier contended that it had neither assets, agents, nor officers in the state and no services were performed in the state. The court ruled that the supplier did, however, make contracts in the state. This is doing business. The supplier could not maintain this suit.

Black Letter Law
A Summary

1. A corporation is an artificial legal being formed under appropriate statutes by incorporators complying with those statutory requirements.

2. Corporations include those classified as profit-making, not-for-profit, governmental, quasi-public or regulated, close, and Sub Chapter S corporations.

3. The process of incorporation includes preparation and signing of the articles of incorporation, pursuant to the applicable statute and a proper filing, which results in the issuance of a certificate of incorporation, which thereby approves the charter of the corporation.

4. A corporation so perfectly formed that it can survive an attack on its legal integrity by the state is a *de jure* corporation; a corporation less perfectly formed, but that can withstand collateral attack by third persons, is called a *de facto* corporation.

5. In order to establish *de facto* status the organizers must show that there was a valid statute under which they could form, that they made a good-faith attempt to incorporate, and that they were users of corporate powers.

6. Promoters are those parties who advance corporate interests by their preincorporation activities; such parties owe a fiduciary duty to the proposed corporation and may have continued liability for their acts even after incorporation and adoption of their acts by the corporation.

7. Corporations are not liable for preincorporation activities performed on their behalf unless they adopt or ratify them, either expressly or by implication, such as acceptance of the benefits involved.

8. A corporation is called domestic in the state of incorporation and foreign in all others.

9. A foreign corporation does not have full access to activity in other states unless it obtains a permit or certificate to do business therein or comes within the exception regarding interstate commerce.

10. A foreign corporation need not comply with another state's certification or registration procedures if it does no business in the state or its activities there are characterized as exclusively interstate business.

Solved Problems

32.1 Smith, a promoter, entered into a contract with Ace Equipment, Inc., for the purchase of equipment for $23,500. Smith contracted for the equipment on behalf of a yet-to-be-formed corporation, Eastern Machinery Co. No mention of Smith's intent or the planned incorporation appeared in the contract. The incorporation has been completed. Smith is

   (a) *not* liable for the $23,500 because of his role as agent for the corporation.

   (b) jointly liable with the corporation for the $23,500.

   (c) primarily liable for the $23,500.

   (d) relieved of liability on the contract when it is ratified by Eastern.

   (*AICPA Examination, November 1973*)

   Smith is exposed and is solely liable, statement (c). Smith did not mention that he spoke as an agent, and Eastern had no notice of such a relationship for any possible anticipated novation. Even if the corporation adopts the contract, Smith remains liable.

32.2 The separate corporate entity will be disregarded if

   (a) one person owns all the shares of stock.

   (b) it was used to effect a fraud.

   (c) there was a partner-subsidiary relationship between two corporations.

   (d) it is used for the purpose of obtaining limited liability.

   (*Adapted from AICPA Examination, November 1973*)

The answer is (b). In the absence of fraud or other wrongdoing the separate entity concept is honored by the court. While there are circumstances in which the relationship between the parent and subsidiary may result in the subsidiary being treated as the alter ego of the parent, there must be a strong showing of a disregard for the corporate entity between those corporations. See also Chapter 33, Section 33.21.

32.3   Korn was one of several promoters interested in organizing Alpha Corporation. Korn entered into an employment contract for the services of Wentz. It was mutually understood that Wentz would perform certain duties and that these might be performed on behalf of a corporation yet to be formed. Korn also entered into an agreement with Bates Company for services to be rendered by the corporation at a future date. The corporation was formed and began operations, but a defective filing prevented compliance with the requirements for legal incorporation. Failure to comply strictly with all the filing requirements probably resulted in

(a)   a *de jure* corporation.

(b)   a *de facto* corporation for some purposes, at least.

(c)   the formation of a partnership.

(d)   the unenforceability of all agreements mentioned.

(*AICPA Examination, May 1974*)

For some purposes it is not necessary that strict compliance be observed to have the organization treated as a corporation. This was not a *de jure* corporation, as the state could challenge defects in organization. It is possible that sufficient compliance would protect the organizers under the *de facto* doctrine, statement (b).

32.4   Assume (in the problem above) that Alpha Corporation was properly formed, and Wentz performed services for the corporation in accordance with his agreement with Korn. If Wentz seeks to recover the compensation agreed upon in his agreement with Korn,

(a)   the corporation is probably liable to Wentz for the salary under the agreement if it adopted the agreement.

(b)   the corporation is probably automatically bound by the preincorporation agreement of Korn as its agent.

(c)   absent express adoption of the agreement by Alpha's board of directors, Wentz may recover for his services to the corporation only from Korn.

(d)   any obligation Korn undertook under the agreement is terminated if Wentz assumes a position with the corporation at the salary specified in the agreement.

(*AICPA Examination, May 1974*)

It is not necessary that a corporation formally adopt agreements entered into for its benefit before incorporation. Conduct can indicate approval. Here acceptance of the work by Wentz suggests adoption; statement (a) is the answer. Some affirmative act of the corporation must be present, as adoption of prior contracts does not automatically follow incorporation, no matter what the terms of the agreement.

32.5   Weber Corporation was incorporated in the state of Delaware. It does all its business in several adjoining states. Under the circumstances,

(a)   Weber's Delaware incorporation was invalid because it does not do business there.

(b)   on the basis of full faith and credit, Weber is a domestic corporation in all states.

(c)   Weber will *not* have to pay corporate income taxes except to Delaware and the United States.

(*d*) Weber should either incorporate in the adjoining states where it does business or otherwise qualify to do business therein.

(Adapted from AICPA Examination, November 1974)

A foreign corporation is not a citizen allowed to move from state to state as a natural person may do under the U.S. Constitution's privileges and immunities section. Generally a corporation must comply with each state's laws regarding doing business, and so the answer is (*d*). The principle of full faith and credit is not applicable here. Weber would be liable for applicable taxes in all states where it does business.

32.6 The Zebra Corporation is neither *de jure* nor *de facto*. As such it

(*a*) can nevertheless recover on a loan which it made to one of its suppliers.

(*b*) *cannot* be liable for torts committed by its agents.

(*c*) *cannot* be treated as a corporation for tax purposes.

(*d*) can nevertheless validly continue to do business as a corporation without fear of legal action by the state as long as it is solvent and pays taxes.

(AICPA Examination, November 1974)

While this organization has no entity status, the law must continue to deal with the consequences of this action. Those involved and using the corporate name would be liable for all torts and, under applicable tax rules, might be liable as a corporation in addition to individual liability. Zebra really cannot validly do business as a corporation. However, it can be treated as a corporation by estoppel and hold the supplier who may be estopped to prove the truth; thus statement (*a*) is the answer.

32.7 Walter Thomas as the promoter of Basic Corporation made a contract for and on behalf of Basic with Fair Realty Corporation for the purchase of an office building. Thomas did *not* disclose the fact that the corporation had *not* been created. Thomas will *not* have any liability on the contract

(*a*) because he made it in the name of the corporation.

(*b*) if the corporation subsequently adopts the contract.

(*c*) if the corporation and Fair Realty enter into a novation regarding the contract.

(*d*) if the corporation comes into existence and rejects the contract.

(Adapted from AICPA Examination, November 1974)

The only way that Thomas can escape the liability he created in this situation is through a release by the other contracting party. Accordingly, if a novation occurs which releases Thomas and substitutes Basic, for example, Thomas will no longer be liable; the answer is (*c*).

32.8 The sole stockholder of a corporation brought an action to prevent the state tax collector from requiring that the stockholder list the stock of the corporation on his personal state intangible tax return. The stockholder points out that the corporation assets consist mainly of intangible property which the corporation lists on its own tax return. Accordingly, the stockholder contends that to require both the corporation *and* the stockholder to pay tax is double taxation. Which is the correct statement?

(*a*) The state is wrong, as the assets of both merge in equity.

(*b*) Double taxation is always illegal.

(*c*) The stockholder and the corporation are separate legal entities.

(*d*) The stockholder would win had the exact property owned by the corporation and the stockholder coincided.

In this case the stockholder learns a basic truth about corporations. They are indeed legal entities separate and apart from their shareholders, or their sole shareholder as in this case; the correct statement is (c).

32.9 An inventor entered into a contract with a promoter. The contract stipulated that certain inventions would be manufactured by a corporation to be formed and that the inventor would be employed for a definite period of time. The corporation was organized, and the promoter assigned the contract to the corporation, which adopted it. A dispute later arose, and the inventor sued the promoter. What additional facts must be shown in order to determine that the promoter is free from personal liability to the inventor?

(a)   The corporate adoption was validly made.

(b)   By contract the inventor released the promoter.

(c)   The corporation was at all times solvent.

(d)   The promoter was one of the original subscribers to the corporate stock at the time of incorporation.

The promoter has only one avenue for release under these facts, and it must involve a binding release by the inventor, statement (b). The fact that the corporation could pay does not affect legal reality that all promoters must face in like situations.

32.10 A roofing corporation was chartered outside the District of Columbia. It obtained no permit to do business in the District and was later sued in the District. Among its defenses was the contention that it was not subject to suit in the District since it maintained no office, agent, or employee within the District. The party suing offered that the company had performed about 60 jobs in the District of Columbia within the preceding 5 years, maintained an answering service there, and was prepared to accept work in the District whenever possible. Is the roofing company doing business in the District of Columbia?

(a)   No, since these are just isolated business events.

(b)   Yes, entering into more than an isolated contract is strong evidence of doing business in the state.

(c)   No, if 60 roofing jobs constituted less than 5 percent of its gross business, it is not doing business.

(d)   No, roofing work is traditionally excepted from the rule.

The above is fairly typical of what constitutes "doing business." Habitually seeking and entering into contracts in a state are both strong evidence of minimum contacts of doing business within the state and place the company within the reach of the long arm statutes of the state; the answer is statement (b).

32.11 A promoter entered into an agreement with a third party to manage the business of a corporation to be formed. The written employment agreement provided that the third party was to "be paid for 1 year at an annual salary of $32,000, renewable from year to year at the option of the corporation." The corporation was formed, and one of its first acts was the adoption of a resolution regarding this employment. The resolution provided, in effect, that the manager "shall be paid an annual salary of $32,000 commencing July 16. . . . " The third party left his old job and entered the employ of the newly formed corporation, but in a disagreement with the directors he resigned in October of the same year. He then sued the corporation for the balance of his salary, nearly 9 months of pay. The corporation contends it is not bound to pay him. The third party offers that the agreement clearly entitled him to such salary.

Is the corporation liable to the third party? Decide and state reasons for any conclusions.

A corporation can be liable on a contract made by a promoter on its behalf before incorporation, but it must expressly or by implication adopt the contract. Here the contracts made by the promoter and the corporation are clearly two different agreements. There was no adoption of the promoter's contract, which specified a year's employment with options by the corporation. The corporation chose to make a new agreement, providing only for employment at the rate of $32,000 per year. Nowhere was there an assurance of a full year's employment. The third party lost his suit in this case.

32.12 A creditor sued for $790, the balance due on an open account for photocopy work and supplies. The creditor named a corporation and its president as defendants. The creditor alleged that the president formed the corporation for "his purposes and conveniences and as a means of attempting to defeat his own personal liabilities for indebtedness incurred for his own account." It appeared that the president owned 98 percent of the corporate stock and was in control of the corporation. The president contends that the bills sent by the creditor name the corporation and that he has not been charged with fraud.

What is the president's principal defense? Is it valid? Decide and state reasons for any conclusions reached.

This is the typical attack made by frustrated creditors when they are attempting to recover from a "one-person" corporation. The defense of separate entity is the president's best defense in this case. It is a solid defense which will subsist in the absence of fraud or overreaching by the president. The latter point is usually the issue in this type of situation. To the extent that the president's conduct was squeaky clean, he is in the clear.

32.13 A party alleged that she had hired an attorney to file all papers necessary for incorporation, paid a fee, acquired a seal from a stationery store, and did business as a corporation. She pressed that the "failure to file the Certificate of Incorporation was not my fault . . . and I had a right to assume that the attorney hired for this purpose would file the certificate."

What particular defense is the defendant raising by the above testimony? How effective is it? Decide and state reasons for any conclusions.

The defendant is raising the defense of freedom from collateral attack on corporate status. She believes that she has sufficiently complied to qualify her firm as a *de facto* corporation. The precise issue before the court was whether an instruction to one's attorney to form a corporation is equivalent to a good-faith effort to incorporate. The court ruled it was not. Since her attorney performed no *public* function in this regard, the court ruled that the defendant failed to show a *de facto* corporation. It stated that at least a colorable attempt must be made to comply with the statutes governing incorporation before the event against which the defense is asserted. Since it was not alleged that any certificate of incorporation was ever prepared, it is unnecessary to consider whether failure ultimately to file a certificate of incorporation is fatal to the defense.

Chapter 33

Powers and Stockholders

33.1 GENERALLY

When examining corporate capacity or power, one must not only look at the state license for the particular activity but also see whether the incorporators intended to vest their corporation with legal capacity to perform certain acts. Corporate power, therefore, is limited both by the police power of the state and by the corporate vitality, or lack of it, placed in the articles of incorporation, i.e., the charter, by its founders. Once granted by the state, the charter vests residual power in the stockholders, within the confines of public policy. The rights and duties of the stockholders will now be examined.

33.2 BASIC POWERS

Corporate powers include the right of a corporation to have a name; to buy, hold a lease, mortgage, and transfer property; to execute and perform contracts; and to sue and be sued in its own name. The acts are performed by natural persons, the agents, but they are nevertheless the acts of the corporation. The corporate agents, however, are not thereby immunized from all types of personal liability by reason of acting on behalf of the corporation. Yet a corporation, although a legal person, can act only through its agents.

EXAMPLE 1. A discharged employee of a corporation sued its officers, charging them with a malicious breach of the employee's contract with the corporation. This charge constituted a tort. The officers contended that the corporation discharged the employee and that an officer's act is protected by reason of the corporate entity. The court ruled that the acting officer can be personally liable for the tort even though the corporation could also be liable. The court stated that a corporation is nothing more than a robot, created by law, possessing only that sensibility which its management and agents bring to it. Most corporate liability does not attach personally to its stockholders, officers, or agents; however, in an action based on torts committed by corporate agents, the choice of naming the defendant against a possible ultimate liability rests with the one wronged.

The right to sue and be sued includes the right of the corporation to be notified of the lawsuit despite the fact that the individual controlling the corporation has been legally notified.

EXAMPLE 2. A subcontractor sued a general contractor and owner of property to recover damages for services performed by the subcontractor. The general contractor had an interest in a construction corporation which bore his name. During the litigation the general contractor made a motion that he be stricken from the lawsuit as a defendant. The court so ruled and substituted the construction corporation in the lawsuit in the place of the general contractor. The lawsuit proceeded, and a judgment was entered against the corporation and the owner. The corporation appealed, charging that the court had no jurisdiction over it. The corporation was correct. Process and service are essential to join a party to a lawsuit in the absence of a waiver. A corporation is a separate and legal entity from a natural person even though the two may have similar names. A corporation and even its sole owner and president are two separate and distinct persons.

The extent to which this exercise of power is in excess of its grant by its founders and that which is illegal by state law concerns a subject commonly known as the *doctrine of ultra vires* (beyond power).

33.3 *ULTRA VIRES* UNDER THE CHARTER

When a corporation is found to act within the powers granted it in its charter, whether by express language or implication, the acts are said to be *intra vires*. Acts outside of such grant are *ultra vires*, and the shareholder may object to such attempted action. Third persons cannot object, however, though the act may injure them.

EXAMPLE 3. A warehouse company sued to prevent a railroad from using its right of way to engage in business allegedly in competition with the company in warehousing and grain buying. Among its arguments the company contended that the railroad was chartered and given the right of way for the sole purpose of operating a railroad. The railroad defended on the grounds that it owned the right of way, that it had the corporate power to lease such for the warehouses involved, and that a stranger to the title, such as the company, cannot question the title of the railroad. The company, in effect, alleged that the acts of the railroad were *ultra vires*. The railroad won the case. The law does not permit third persons having no interest in a corporation to dispute the corporate act. The alleged *ultra vires* act may be objected to by the state, by the corporation itself, or by the persons with whom the allegedly *ultra vires* transactions are had, but not by third parties having no interest in the subject matter.

If the charter permits the act, and the state law does not prohibit it, the act is effective and cannot be challenged by insiders, stockholders, or third parties.

EXAMPLE 4. A minority of shareholders, owners of 25 percent of the stock of Realty Corporation, attempted to prevent the majority of the shareholders from voting the corporation to sign as an accommodation indorser guaranteeing obligations of another corporation. The original charter of Realty Corporation did not authorize it to make any purely accommodation guaranty, indorsement, or contract of suretyship. However, at a called corporate meeting with all the shareholders present, or represented by proxy, the charter was amended to so provide. The minority shareholders voted against the amendment, but it passed nevertheless. The minority shareholders now seek court relief and, while alleging no fraud, contend that it is not in the best interest of Realty Corporation to guarantee such obligation and that such authorization is not present as a corporate power. The court ruled that in the absence of charter limitations, a corporation has power to guarantee debts in those cases where the corporation has a direct interest. Here the charter was validly amended to allow guaranty contracts. The court noted that it is well settled that the court will not interfere to prevent unwise or unfounded acts or policies. Internal management of a corporation will not be interfered with at the instance of minority shareholders unless the evidence shows that the majority are acting without charter authority, or a strong case of mismanagement or fraud is shown.

If the act is determined to be *ultra vires* by reason of an exercise of power in excess of corporate charter authority, express or implied, the effects generally are as follows:

(1) Where neither the corporation nor the third party has performed, neither party can enforce the *ultra vires* contract against the other.

(2) Where both parties have performed, the contract will stand and cannot be rescinded.

(3) Where the contract is partly performed by both, or performed by one and not the other, the equities of the situation will determine the extent to which relief will be given to the complaining party, but usually the defense is not available.

EXAMPLE 5. Ace Peanut Butter Company is an old and conservative company. Ace's corporate charter states that the purpose of the company is to "manufacture and sell peanut butter." Ace could do better financially. New management is brought in, and the new staff members decide that there is a fine market for printing and selling psychedelic comic books. The president, with the approval of the board of directors, enters into a contract with Arlington Iron Foundry for the purchase of a $250,000 multicolor printing press, and a $100,000 contract with Northern Paper Company for printing stock and ink. A longtime stockholder of Ace, Miss Abigail Wilkins, notifies Ace, Arlington, and Northern that she objects. Ace has already received the printing press but has not yet paid for it; Northern has not yet shipped the paper. In states that have not by case law or statute abolished the defense of *ultra vires*, it is likely that Miss Wilkins would succeed only in preventing the performance of the Northern contract. In most states the fact that the press has been delivered, i.e., performance by one party, prohibits the defense from being raised.

The defense of *ultra vires* in contract litigation is weakened by both modern case law and statutory prohibition, and also by the fact that charter purpose or object clauses are now so broadly worded as to permit, at times, "all lawful business." Section 7 of the Model Business Corporation Act, which some states follow, abolishes *ultra vires* as a contractual defense irrespective of the equities of the situation or the state of the performance of the contract. However, this does not relieve the corporation or its directors from *ultra vires* claims made by their shareholders through a stockholder derivative suit.

33.4 *ULTRA VIRES*: ILLEGALITY

It is one thing to challenge corporate power on the grounds that it violates the charter and quite another to charge that it is being exercised in violation of state law. The complaint is really illegality as opposed to breach of contract. All corporate acts can be challenged on grounds of violation of public policy.

EXAMPLE 6. A minority shareholder brought an action against a banking corporation seeking to enjoin the bank from establishing any new branches in any city other than Savannah, where the principal office was located. It was claimed that a state law authorizing such type of banking was unconstitutional. Among the issues before the court was the bank's contention that the minority shareholder, as a stockholder, cannot maintain this challenge because such statute operates to his benefit and he does not show that the operation of the statute injures him in any manner. The court ruled for the stockholder. A stockholder has a right to insist that the corporation, in carrying out its corporate powers, does not transgress state laws.

33.5 IMPLIED OR INCIDENTAL POWERS

When the charter is not specific in guiding the courts regarding prohibited areas, the court relies on the construction of implied or incidental powers. The corporation may argue that its performance is consistent with the immediate furtherance of the corporate business. Common challenges of this interpretation occur in the areas of partnership, gift-giving, and guaranty contracts. Where the charter or state statute does not specifically authorize such actions, the courts must examine the facts to determine that the corporate interest was being served.

EXAMPLE 7. Four construction corporations, three of them foreign, entered into a joint venture agreement to construct a certain relief drain for a drainage district. An engineer was struck and killed by a backing truck owned by one of the corporations. In claims for workers' compensation an issue arose about the liability of all the corporations as joint venturers. One contention was that the corporations were without power to become partners or joint venturers. Here there was an absence of prohibition in the charter and state law regarding such power. Accordingly, since this joint venture was in the interest of the corporations and since the particular activity, large construction projects, requires participation by multiple corporations, the court cannot say that such combination was *ultra vires*.

Corporations may not give property away without specific charter authority. However, gifts for educational, scientific, or other charitable purposes form an exception. Both state corporation law and case law have made this exception applicable in most instances.

EXAMPLE 8. A railroad organized a nonprofit corporation dedicated to charitable, scientific, religious, and educational purposes. Some shareholders objected to this action and the proposed intention of the railroad to transfer a substantial fund to the nonprofit corporation. It appeared that the charter in 1897 had not given any express power to do so despite the fact that it had been amended several times since incorporation. The state statute was silent on the question of corporate gifts. The state supreme court approved the corporate act. The court cited a change in public policy as evidenced by the favorable federal tax treatment of gifts, the passage by 36 states of statutes granting corporations power to make gifts for the public welfare, and the emphasis in modern society on corporate responsibility regarding public welfare.

Just as a corporation may not give its property away, it may not bestow a gift of its credit. Accordingly, when a corporation promises to answer for the debt of another, i.e., a guaranty contract, it must have express authority to do so by charter, or such act must be in furtherance of corporate interests in the particular circumstances.

EXAMPLE 9.   A lumber company was completely owned by a husband and wife. In order to assure the lumber company of an adequate supply of lumber at low prices, the husband bought into a foreign corporation and owned all but two shares of its stock. The lumber company would, from time to time, discharge debts of the foreign corporation from funds of the lumber company and would also guarantee certain obligations of the foreign corporation. In a bankruptcy proceeding it became important whether the lumber company had committed an *ultra vires* act. There was evidence that the foreign corporation and the lumber company had engaged in some operations for their mutual benefit. It was held that under these facts the interest of the party paying and guaranteeing the debts was present so as to make such action appropriate and not *ultra vires*.

Sometimes a corporation is challenged that it has no charter power to acquire stock in another corporation or even its own corporation, the latter resulting in acquisition of treasury shares. Most state statutes permit such action, it being questionable only where such purchase would cause the corporation to become insolvent or otherwise harm those with lawful interests in the corporate assets.

33.6   RIGHTS OF SHAREHOLDERS: GENERALLY

Rights of shareholders include the right to vote, authorize others to vote, inspect the books and records, complain over corporate policy by bringing derivative suits, demand dividends or an explanation for their absence, and exercise their preemptive rights to more stock.

33.7   SHAREHOLDERS: VOTING

Every corporation has at least one class of stock which is entitled to vote for directors, can approve extraordinary policy decisions, and has the right to vote for an amendment to the charter unless otherwise prohibited by statute or charter. As to the specifics of voting, however, incorporation statutes grant wide authority to frame the corporation as the incorporators please.

EXAMPLE 10.   The charter of a corporation provided two classes of common stock, Class A and Class B. Only Class A had voting rights. The holders of Class B had no right to notice of corporate meetings, except the right to vote on certain amendments to the charter which might affect the rights of Class B stock. Class B stockholders assert that they are denied their constitutional rights. The court found no denial of rights and no law which directly or indirectly prohibits the forming of a corporation with the charter providing for two classes of stock, one voting and the other nonvoting. It is purely a matter of contract and does not affect the public.

33.8   CUMULATIVE VOTING

Since the management of a corporation is in the hands of directors, it would not be uncommon for a minority interest to have no representative on the board. A charter provision allowing cumulative voting gives assistance to the minority. Each stockholder may multiply the number of shares he or she holds by the number of corporate directors to be elected. The effect of this is that minority shareholders may, by concentrating (cumulating) their votes, elect the percentage of directors which their stock represents of the total stock being voted. [However, note that, for example, a minority shareholder voting 16 percent of the stock will not be able to elect a director if, say, four directorships are up for election and the majority shareholders (84 percent) vote 21 percent of the stock for each of their four candidates. To be certain of electing a director, the minority shareholder(s) must have a fraction of the stock equal to the fraction of one more than the number of directors to be elected, plus one share.] In some states the right to vote cumulatively is presumed in the absence of charter provisions to the contrary. Other states have left it to the courts to determine whether the charter permits such voting.

EXAMPLE 11. Magic, Inc., has 1,000 shares issued and outstanding. State law and charter authorize cumulative voting. Frank owns 220 shares. All five seats on the board of directors are up for election at the annual meeting. Frank, accordingly, has 1,100 votes to cast. If he casts all 1,100 of his votes for one candidate, that candidate will be elected, because the remaining 780 shares of stock have 3,900 votes and the most they can do is cast 975 votes for each of their four candidates.

33.9 PARTIES ENTITLED TO VOTE

The registered owner of the stock is the proper party to cast a vote of stock possessing voting rights, not the real or beneficial owner of the stock if such is not the registered owner.

EXAMPLE 12. A decedent died owning 112,459 shares (about 24 percent) of a corporation. His will appointed executors and created a trust naming trustees. The executors were given "all the powers granted to trustees" during the administration of the estate. While the estate was being administered, the trustees demanded the power to vote the shares, but the executors resisted. The court interpreted the will literally. The executors held legal power to vote the stock until the administration was finished, at which time the trustees became the legal owner with the concomitant right to vote. Note that the beneficiaries of the trust, namely the children and widow, do not have the right to vote in this case.

This rule regarding legal title does not apply to treasury stock, i.e., where the corporation purchases its own stock. This stock cannot be voted. However, it is possible for a corporation to have legal title to its own shares that are not treasury stock.

EXAMPLE 13. A merger was proposed between two banks, the law requiring the affirmative vote of two-thirds of the outstanding stock for the merger to be approved. One bank had 40,000 shares of stock outstanding, two-thirds thereof being 26,667 shares. A total of 31,688 votes were cast for the merger. It appeared, however, that 9,347 shares voted were held by the bank itself in a fiduciary capacity. Some shareholders stated that a bank cannot vote its own stock. The court ruled that stock held in a fiduciary capacity is not bound by that state prohibition. Treasury stock would be, but not this stock. The bank holds legal title for the benefit of another and may vote this stock in the merger.

33.10 PROXIES AND VOTING TRUSTS

One having the right to vote may transfer it to another. Two common methods are by use of proxies and by transfers to voting trusts. A *proxy* is a grant of authority given by a shareholder to vote his or her shares at a stockholders' meeting. This authority may be revoked at any time before the actual voting. When a party has given his or her proxy, the mere attendance of that party at the meeting does not act to revoke the proxy. Proxy solicitations in large corporations which are subject to securities law are governed by rules of the Securities Exchange Act of 1934.

A more permanent proxy is achieved by the use of the voting trust. A voting trust is a shareholders' agreement by which the vote of the contractors is combined and there is a transfer of the actual stock into the hands of a trustee for a period of time. While there is general freedom as to what terms may be placed in the trust agreement, there are some statutory guidelines including length of the term of the agreement. An agreement which is less than a trust will also be enforced provided it does not contain terms against public policy.

EXAMPLE 14. A retired insurance company president was approached by four organizers who were desirous of forming a new insurance company. All five parties entered into a written agreement to form the company. Among the numerous terms included was the agreement that the retired president would be the president of the new company for 5 years. After formation of the corporation, the stockholders elected the retired president to the position of president for only 1 year, but he took the job nevertheless. A personal problem ensued, and the president was having some trouble meeting all his duties, although this appeared to be only temporary. At the end of the first year the stockholders did not elect the president to another term. The president charged breach of the stockholders' agreement. Among the defenses raised by the stockholders was that the secret stockholders' agreement was void and against public policy. The court ruled in favor of the president, noting that the state aligns itself with the majority of jurisdictions which hold that a contract among corporate shareholders by which they agree to vote their stock in a specific manner is not invalid unless inspired by fraud or will unduly prejudice other stockholders.

Like the shareholders' agreement, the purpose of a voting trust is to concentrate power in the group who combine in such a fashion. However, the shares are surrendered in a voting trust and transferred to a trustee or trustees. The corporate records reveal the legal owners as the trustees. The trust is not entirely favored by law, and many states restrict its life to 10 years.

EXAMPLE 15. Under the applicable state law a majority of stock may approve a sale of all or substantially all of the corporation's assets. Certain shareholders, including a college, entered into a voting trust agreement. The board of directors voted to sell all the corporation's real estate. The college shareholder objected and sued to prevent the sale despite the majority vote, which included those shares held by the voting trust. The college contended that the sale effectively ends the corporate business. The court examined the language of the voting trust and found it sweeping in its powers. The court will enforce the voting trust agreement. The college is bound by its agreement under the voting trust.

33.11   RIGHT TO INSPECT BOOKS AND RECORDS

The shareholder has a right to inspect corporate books and records; however, it is not an unqualified right. If the purpose of seeking such inspection is hostile to the corporate interests, the right can be refused. The burden of showing such hostility is on the corporation.

EXAMPLE 16. Three employees of a corporation purchased one share of stock each and had the stock registered in their names, although the money came from the local union, which received all the dividends. The three employees requested permission to copy the list of shareholder names and addresses. They wanted to write to them outlining a labor relations dispute. After they were refused, they filed suit demanding their rights as shareholders. The issue was then whether the request was for a proper purpose, and "not speculative or [for] trading purposes or for any purpose inimical to the interest of the corporation or shareholders." The court ruled for the shareholder union members. What matters, reported the court, was that the employee shareholders wished to communicate with stockholders in respect to matters of interest and legitimate concern to the shareholders and the company, i.e., harmonious labor relations. It is immaterial for the purpose of this case whether the employees' dissatisfaction was justified.

The legal holders of stock come before the court with a presumption of good faith when they request that they be permitted to make inspection of the corporate records as authorized by the state statute. The beneficial owners of stock, however, do not come before the court with such presumption. While they may not strictly be denied such access, they generally are not permitted to prosecute such an action.

33.12   RIGHT TO DIVIDENDS

Shareholders have a right to lawful dividends, but the time and manner of distribution are determined by the board of directors in their exercise of discretion. Traditionally dividends were payable out of earnings, but state law varies as to when it is lawful to declare a dividend. Generally, the directors in declaring a dividend may not impair capital or make the corporation unable to pay its debts. There are exceptions to the former, however, as statutes generally allow corporations with wasting assets, such as mines or leaseholds, to impair capital while declaring a dividend. Such an exception is not without qualification.

EXAMPLE 17.   A minority stockholder in a foreign oil company brought a derivative action against the parent company, charging it with not dealing fairly with its subsidiary, the foreign company. The parent owned 96 percent of the foreign company. During the past 6 years the directors of the foreign company had paid out in dividends the sum of $108,000,000, which was $38,000,000 more than it had earned. The parent company elected all the directors of the foreign company. The market value of the stock in the foreign company had decreased 50 percent during that period. The foreign company and parent defended on the grounds that state statutes permit corporations with wasting assets to so declare and pay dividends. The minority shareholder also alleged that there was no effort to add to the resources of the company or to use capital resources to advance the company interests. The court ruled in favor of the minority shareholder, stating that the parent company had a duty to account to the foreign company for damages as a result of dividends declared during the 6-year period.

A corporation may retain earnings or surplus for future growth, but such plans must be reasonably foreseeable in the face of the twin restraints of shareholder complaint and internal revenue penalties (taxes) for improper accumulations.

33.13   STOCK DIVIDENDS

Dividends may be payable in cash or property and also in the stock of the corporation. When it declares the latter, the corporation is said to issue a *stock dividend*, which is a distribution to existing shareholders of additional shares and a transfer of such payments into the capital account.

EXAMPLE 18.   Tailor Corporation has 1,000 shares of common stock outstanding of a par value of $100 and which sum it received at original issue. It has a capital account (shareholders' equity) of $100,000. Its first year is successful, and its surplus of assets over liabilities is $110,000. The company could in most states pay a cash dividend if its liquidity is good, i.e., if it has sufficient cash to pay current obligations. Its assets exceed its liabilities plus stated capital. However, the board of directors decides on a policy of growth and wishes to put the surplus to work as permanent investment, and at the same time wishes to give tangible evidence of this policy to the shareholders. Accordingly, the board declares a 10 percent stock dividend, one share for each 10 shares owned. On the company's books $10,000 will be transferred to the capital account.

Generally a stock dividend is not income for purpose of income tax to the stockholder, unlike cash dividends payable from earnings. Cash dividends become an enforceable debt against the corporation unless the cash dividend was revoked at the same meeting that it was declared, was illegally declared, or was rescinded before the declaration of the dividend was made public or the stockholders were notified.

33.14   STOCK SPLIT

A stock dividend is not a stock split, although the difference is not easily observed by the stockholder. In both cases the proportionate interest of the shareholder remains the same after the split. Generally, however, a *stock split* is merely a restructuring of the shares with no concomitant transfer to capital. If the corporation contemplating a stock split had a surplus, they would continue to have the surplus available for cash dividends after the stock split.

EXAMPLE 19.   A children's home was the residuary beneficiary under a will executed by the decedent, who directed 500 shares of Amfil stock to her niece and the remainder of her property to the children's home. At the time of the execution of the will the decedent owned 1,000 shares of the stock. At her death it appeared that the stock had earlier split two shares for one. The children's home maintains that the niece should be given what the will directed, i.e., 500 shares, and the children's home the remaining 1,500 shares. The court ruled that the niece was entitled to 1,000 shares. A stock split, the court reminded the home, does not change the proportionate interest of the shareholder since it adds nothing of substance to the shares. However, stock splits are sometimes followed by an increase in the stock's value, which may occur because the issuance may represent a change in (ultra) conservative corporate policy or even because lower-priced shares may attract a larger buying public.

33.15   PAYMENT OF DIVIDENDS

Directors set forth when the dividend is to be paid to stockholders of record as of a certain date and, of course, the medium of payment, e.g., cash, stock, property, or even scrip. The corporation may rely on the stock ownership records in the corporate books to make the proper payment. Parties may, of course, determine ownership among themselves, but this is not binding on the company. On the New York Stock Exchange, for example, the agreement of the parties is assumed through the Exchange rules. Buyers there would only be entitled to the declared dividend if they purchased the stock before it went *ex dividend*, a date which is 5 business (stock exchange) days before the record date of payment as set by the directors.

EXAMPLE 20.   Maybi Corporation is listed on a stock exchange. The directors of Maybi declared a regular quarterly dividend of 15 cents per share to all common stock of record on October 8, payable October 31. Unless a buyer of the stock purchases it at least 5 business days previous to October 8, she takes the stock ex dividend, that is, without the 15-cent dividend. If by some error the dividend should be credited to her account, she is obligated to surrender it to the seller of the stock.

33.16   PREEMPTIVE RIGHTS

The *common-law right of preemption* is the right of a shareholder to the option of purchasing a new allotment of stock in proportion to what the shareholder already owns. Generally this right does not apply to the purchase of treasury shares, shares issued for a noncash consideration, or those issued as a result of a merger or consolidation.

EXAMPLE 21.   A local telephone company was chartered with an authorized capital stock of 1,000 shares, par value of $10. During its 40 years of existence no more than 420 shares were outstanding at any time, with only 356 shares outstanding at the time that certain nonresidents took an interest in the stock. The nonresidents offered $200 a share for the stock and thereby acquired 203 shares. The local residents, still holding a majority on the board of directors, then voted that the 644 shares unsold would be transferred to such parties as the directors may from time to time approve at $40 a share; and 225 shares were sold at that price. Upon learning this the nonresidents served notice on the board that they would exercise their preemptive right in any such offer. The directors refused, and the nonresidents sued. The court ruled in favor of the nonresidents, stating that they had done nothing except to buy a controlling interest to the sorrow of the residents who are now a minority. The nonresidents were aggressive, but they operated openly. The success of the nonresidents may be distasteful to the residents, said the court, but that does not affect the nonresidents' right to the protection of their preemptive rights.

State statutes are not uniform in their treatment of this right. Some courts do not honor the right if the stock is newly authorized as opposed to authorized but unsold. Statutes and charter provisions dominate the scope of the operation of this right.

EXAMPLE 22.   Under the state statute each shareholder has, unless otherwise provided by the certificate of incorporation, upon the sale for cash of any new stock of the same kind, class, or series as that which the shareholder already holds, the right to purchase a pro rata share thereof. Shareholders in the Kirkley

Corporation sought cancellation or rescission of certain stock issued by the corporation to others. These shareholders alleged that the stock was issued in consideration of certain specified services to be performed and things to be done. The court ruled that the statute by its plain meaning grants a preemptive right for sales of stock for cash. Here the shareholders allege in their complaint a different type of transaction from that contemplated by the statute. The statute would not be applicable to this type of transaction. The shareholders lose.

33.17 SHAREHOLDER SUITS

A shareholder has a right to sue utilizing what is called a *derivative action*. It is an action instituted by a shareholder on behalf of, and in the name of, the corporation. It is not a suit on behalf of the shareholder.

EXAMPLE 23. Minority shareholders, holding 25 percent of Wing Corporation stock, brought a derivative action against another corporation which purchased Wing's entire assets. The minority charged that the majority sold all Wing's assets without notice to the minority in violation of the state statute which required an affirmative vote of at least two-thirds of the shareholders for such an action. The court refused to order a rescission of the sale. The general rule is that the shareholder in a derivative suit is only representing the corporation, which itself must have a cause of action. The failure to call a shareholders' meeting does not come within this complaint. The minority has stated no cause for complaint under a derivative action.

Where shareholders hold a similar complaint, they have a *class action*, or *representative action*. For example, minority interests wishing to gain their preemptive rights might join together in a class suit for the purpose of benefiting that class or group. A derivative suit would be appropriate where the management, for example, is wasting assets, or abusing its discretion and such. There, the victor would be the corporation, which would be entitled to be reimbursed by the offenders.

33.18 SHAREHOLDER LIABILITY

If the corporation is legally formed and operates within the law, shareholders, even if the corporation has but one, are generally immune from liability over and above the permanent investment they made in the corporation. If, for example, a shareholder paid full value for the par, or stated, value stock, or the agreed consideration for no-par stock, the shareholder's liability is thereby limited. There are, however, some instances in which a shareholder may have liability.

33.19 LIABILITY: ILLEGAL DIVIDENDS

The shareholder who receives a dividend from an insolvent corporation, or who receives a dividend payment which causes insolvency, is generally considered liable for the improper payment whether he or she was aware of the illegality or not. The directors who declared the dividend are of course likewise liable. Where the dividend is illegal but no insolvency results, the corporation itself may retrieve the dividend provided the shareholder had knowledge of the illegality.

33.20 LIABILITY: CORPORATE DEBTS

Generally a shareholder is not liable for corporate debts. However, some state statutes provide liability under limited circumstances.

EXAMPLE 24. A bankrupt restaurant corporation suspended its operation in April. In May the employees' union notified the trustee in bankruptcy that the collective bargaining contract was still in effect. The trustee stated that the chances for reopening the contract were slight. The union then notified the individual stockholders that it intended to hold them liable for unpaid wages under the state statute. This statute provided liability on the stockholders if they were given written notice after termination of the employees' services that the employees intended to hold the shareholders liable. The court ruled that timely notice was not given. Thirty days had passed. The stockholders were not liable because the statute was not obeyed by the union employees.

Even where there are such statutes, their application is limited, as in the above case. Such statutes generally do not apply to corporations whose shares are publicly traded.

33.21 LIABILITY: PIERCING THE CORPORATE VEIL

A shareholder, or even a person acting under the corporate form, may be personally liable should the court rule that the form is being used to promote fraud, evade the law, or achieve ends inimical to society. This power is sometimes called *disregarding the corporate entity* or *piercing the corporate veil*, or sometimes *treating the party liable as the alter ego of the corporation*.

It is not fraud to use the corporate entity to avoid personal liability, but there are some circumstances which make that motive inimical to society. Corporations which are shareholders of other corporations, i.e., subsidiaries, are not infrequently attacked on these grounds. The term "alter ego," for example, may be used by the complaining party if the two corporations mingle their books, funds, and operations so as to make the entities indistinguishable. Nevertheless, each validly formed corporation comes before the court with a presumption of separateness and legality.

EXAMPLE 25.   A passenger on an excursion boat was injured in New York by the negligence of the crew. The passenger obtained a $15,000 judgment against the New York corporation and then found that it had gone out of business. The boat was now owned by a new corporation with a similar name in Washington, D.C. which operated the boat on the Potomac. Among the issues before the court was whether the new corporation was a separate entity in the face of the fact that it had the same president as the old, had almost the identical corporate name, and was using the same excursion boat. This evidence was insufficient to disregard the corporate entity. The court commented that although there was some evidence that the New York corporation was simply a shell for the new corporation, and there was some indication that the corporation was underfinanced (a factor in determining the piercing of the corporate veil), there was no evidence that the president was the controlling interest behind the corporation, or even that he had a stake in it.

Where, however, there is such unity of interest and ownership that the separate personalities of the corporation and the individual no longer exist, and the circumstances are such that such separate corporate existence would sanction a fraud or promote injustice, the entity will be disregarded.

EXAMPLE 26.   Two brothers organized a professional soccer team under the name Naturi Seals, Inc. A player named Fabius was signed to a long-term contract. He was never paid his salary and attempted to hold the brothers personally liable. He offered that the brothers had formed three other corporations which held title to different facilities in the marketing scheme, that Naturi Seals was undercapitalized, that the brothers manipulated the funds between Naturi and the other corporations, and that they did not observe any of the formalities in the other corporations which the brothers entirely owned. Further, there were no assets from Naturi to pay its debts, including that of the plaintiff. The court ruled that under these facts the plaintiff is entitled to prove that the corporate entity should be disregarded.

Black Letter Law
A Summary

1. The general incorporation statute provides broad powers to every company organized under it, thereby making it unnecessary that the charter repeat such authority except to state the general purpose or object and any limitations thereon.

2. Where there is no express or implied power to perform an act, the question of *ultra vires*, i.e., beyond power, may be raised.

3. Generally a shareholder may act to prevent or rescind an *ultra vires* act, but this doctrine has limited applicability as a contractual defense due to modern statutory limitations on the doctrine, unfavorable treatment by courts, and the presence of broad corporate purpose clauses in corporate charters.

4. In contract situations the defense of *ultra vires* is most likely still effective (providing there is no statutory prohibition) in cases where the contract is in its purely executory stage.

5. Where the *ultra vires* act involves illegality or failure to observe regulatory law, the state may successfully challenge the act.

6. The doctrine of implied or incidental powers rescues many otherwise *ultra vires* acts such as corporate giving or guaranty contracts.

7. Shareholders have the right to vote as provided in the charter, to execute proxies to others, and to enter into stockholders' agreements and voting trusts.

8. The right of a shareholder to inspect books and records is not unqualified and may not be exercised to the detriment of the corporation; however, an intent to use such information to gain control does not constitute a hostile purpose to the corporation.

9. Dividends are declared and issued at the sound discretion of the directors, and courts will only interfere in such process when it involves declaration of an illegal dividend, or would render the corporation insolvent, or would cause it to be unable to pay its debts, or would be a gross abuse of discretion by the directors.

10. Stock dividends and stock splits result in the issuance of additional shares to existing shareholders with no change in proportion of ownership, but stock dividends are accompanied by a simultaneous transfer of surplus to the capital account, which does not, however, trigger an income tax incidence to the shareholders.

11. Dividends may be paid in cash, property, stock, or scrip, and are payable at the times set by the directors to legal holders of the stock as of a certain date.

12. The doctrine of preemptive right allows stockholders the option of maintaining their relative stock interest in the corporation.

13. State laws are not uniform in the extent to which they provide for preemptive rights; some authorize such rights only if provided in the charter; in most cases, however, the right is not available in situations where the directors are making stock available to others for noncash consideration, as in employee stock options or in merger and consolidation situations.

14. Shareholders are not in a fiduciary relation to the corporation and may sue individually for a violation of their individual rights, as a class or representative, or for the benefit of the corporation itself through a derivative suit.

15. Shareholders have few liabilities provided the corporation was lawfully organized and they have fully paid for their shares; however, they may have to surrender illegal dividends received.

16. Shareholders or others acting in the corporation may have liability when another has successfully brought an action to disregard the corporate entity (piercing the corporate veil), or where it is shown that the corporation was really the alter ego of another.

17. The court does not disregard the corporate entity concept lightly; it will do so only where it appears that separate personalities of the corporation and individuals do not exist and adherence to the fiction of separate corporate existence would sanction a fraud or promote injustice.

Solved Problems

33.1 The decline in the use of the defense of *ultra vires* was *not* the result of which of the following?

(*a*)   The courts usually struck down such defenses as unconscionable.

(*b*)   Corporate charters contained broad general-purpose or object clauses.

(*c*)   Courts were not sympathetic to undoing completely executed but *ultra vires* contracts.

(*d*)   Corporation statutes have generally abolished this defense for contractual purposes.

   All the reasons above are noted as contributing to the decline of the defense of *ultra vires* except statement (*a*). Courts did not find the doctrine unconscionable, but they were reluctant to enforce this technical defense against innocent third parties who dealt with corporations in contractual matters.

33.2 Swan Electric Power Company was incorporated for the purpose of supplying heat, light, and power to the public. The company later began to sell electric appliances to its customers. The state claimed that this was improper, but the court disagreed, ruling in favor of the power company. Which of the following theories supports the ruling of the court?

(*a*)   Profit-making companies should be entitled to make money.

(*b*)   The charter expressly grants such authority.

(*c*)   The only parties who could legally object to this are the shareholders.

(*d*)   Such new business can be considered to be incidental or auxiliary to such express purpose or object.

   The charter purpose or object clause is clear; it does not provide for the sale of appliances. However, the primary objective of the power company in merchandising electric appliances is to stimulate the consumption of electricity. This is a legitimate manner of extending the company's business in furtherance of its charter object, statement (*d*).

33.3 A lumber company's charter called for the sale and distribution of lumber and lumber supplies. The company changed its distribution pattern and sold three surplus trucks to various buyers. In all cases the company sold on credit, receiving promissory notes for the balances. The lumber company then sold the notes to a finance company, which demanded that the lumber company sign with recourse on the notes, obligating it to pay if the buyers (makers) did not pay. Two of the buyers defaulted on their notes, failing to pay the finance company. The finance company now sues the lumber company on its guaranty. The lumber company defends on the grounds that the promise to answer for the debts of another, a guaranty, is *ultra vires*. Under these circumstances,

(a) the lumber company has a clear defense of *ultra vires*.

(b) no corporation has the implied authority to guarantee the debts of another.

(c) the lumber company must pay, as this guaranty was made in furtherance of its own interest to sell the promissory notes.

(d) if the lumber company pays the finance company, the buyers are released from liability to anyone.

Generally, a corporation has no implied power to give away its property or to stand behind others on debts, i.e., guarantee contracts. However, in the absence of express authority in the charter, a corporation can do those acts which further its own financial interests. The lumber company wanted to sell the notes, and the only way this could be done profitably, apparently, was to sell them with recourse. This is in furtherance of its corporate interests and is binding; statement (c) is correct. Payment by the guarantor will not release those primarily liable on the instruments.

33.4 The board of directors by resolution granted an employee an option to purchase 40,000 of its shares at $3 per share for his services. At the time the option was granted, the stock was selling for that amount. Later the stock price rose to $8 a share. A stockholder claimed that the option to purchase new stock should also be given to him. What right is the stockholder attempting to assert?

(a) Preemptive right

(b) *Ultra vires*

(c) Disregarding the corporate entity

(d) Derivative action

When parties do not wish to lose their share in a corporation, they can use the doctrine of preemptive right [statement (a)] to assist them. This applies in situations where new allotments of stock are available to others for cash. In this case, however, the option was for services by the employee, a recognized limitation on the doctrine of preemptive right. It is not a derivative action since the shareholder is not attempting to bring an action for the benefit of the corporation.

33.5 An objection was made by a stockholder that the board of directors had not declared a dividend although nearly $3 million was available for such. The shareholder charged that one of the directors, who was the majority shareholder, combined with the others to refuse to distribute the sum since retention at that time would benefit the majority shareholder. Under these circumstances,

(a) directors have absolute discretion to declare or not to declare dividends.

(b) where a board decision is based on personal interest rather than corporate interest, the court can stop it.

(c) objecting shareholders must always show how they were harmed by the retention of dividend money.

(d) courts have no authority to order directors to declare dividends.

Courts have authority to order directors to declare a dividend but rarely do so, contending that such decision rests in the sound discretion of the board of directors. It is a business judgment, and the court will not substitute its own for that of the managers. However, to prevent fraud, injustice, or self-interest as opposed to corporate interest, the court will act. In this case the stockholder can win if he proves that this retention was for personal rather than the corporate interest, as stated in (b).

33.6   State law provided that "no person shall hold more than two off-sale liquor permits at one time." The charge was made that two corporations have separate permits, but that the corporations are owned, operated, and controlled by the same person or same group of persons. The state law defines a person as including a corporation. The purpose of the legislature in restricting permits was to prevent a concentration of interests in the manufacturing, wholesaling, and retailing of alcoholic beverages. What legal ground is being urged by those charging that the permits should be canceled?

(a)   Fraud

(b)   Monopoly

(c)   *Ultra vires* by reason of illegality

(d)   Disregarding the corporate entity

The corporate independence from its stockholders is to be disregarded when justice demands it. Here the issuance of the permits to what amounts to the same group is an attempt to avoid the clear legislative purpose. Piercing the corporate veil is the initial manner to challenge this, statement (d). Statement (b) is not correct because each corporation by itself could lawfully carry out its corporate purpose. Illegality will be the ultimate ground, statement (c).

33.7   A stockholder requested the right to inspect the books of the corporation, including its bylaws, minute books, and financial records. Her attorney was permitted a limited inspection of the financial records, but examination of the other material was not permitted. It appeared that the stockholder owned only one share. Under these circumstances,

(a)   a party owning even just one share has the absolute right to examine the corporate books.

(b)   a stockholder is entitled to view the records if the request is made in good faith for a specific and honest purpose.

(c)   a stockholder may look, but the attorney may not.

(d)   A stockholder must own at least 1 percent of a corporation's stock in order to be eligible to see the books.

The answer is (b). A bona fide stockholder has the legal right to inspect the books and records of the company when the request is made in good faith for a specific and honest purpose. Unless there is a showing that the stockholder interest is not germane, or the request is being made for vexatious purposes, the corporation cannot deny the stockholder this right.

33.8   A grandson was the beneficiary of a trust estate in which he was to obtain the *income* from the trust estate, and at his death the property would pass to his child, or children. The estate possessed 40,000 shares in an oil company. The company adopted a resolution providing that for every four shares of outstanding stock, one additional share would be issued. No transfer was made on the corporate books from earned surplus to the capital stock account. The grandson claims that the 10,000 shares, the newly issued stock, was income to the trust. The trustee contends that these shares are not income. Under these facts,

(a)   the company issued a stock split, and so the grandson loses.

(b)   the company issued a stock dividend, and so the grandson wins.

(c)   the company issued, in effect, a cash dividend, and so the grandson wins.

(d)   the grandson wins this point.

Where additional shares are to be distributed to existing shareholders on the basis of their present interest, it is either a stock dividend or stock split. A stock dividend is accompanied by a contemporaneous capitalization of earnings. This was not done here; hence it was a stock split. No earnings were distributed. Earnings would be income, and that is all the grandson is entitled to receive. As stated in (*a*), he would lose.

33.9 Tuttle always seems to have bad luck, and she honestly believes that the other person has it in for her. Now she believes that the officers of Sum Corporation are trying to cheat her. Tuttle is a shareholder owning 200 shares of Sum Corporation stock. Sum's board of directors recently declared a stock dividend of one share for each 10 shares owned. Tuttle has not received her 20 shares, and her letters to the company officers proved fruitless. In fact, they are now saying that her class of stock is not entitled to the stock dividend. Under these circumstances,

(*a*) Tuttle can bring a class or representative suit against Sum Corporation and its officers.

(*b*) Tuttle must bring a derivative action.

(*c*) Tuttle can sue the officers personally for fraud.

(*d*) Tuttle has no rights to be adjudicated.

When a shareholder brings an action on behalf of the corporation against action or inaction of management, she brings a derivative action, but when she seeks rights in particular for herself or others in like situations, she must bring a class or representative lawsuit, statement (*a*). There seems to be no fraud alleged here, but rather a question of defining rights under the share contract.

33.10 Upon the death of the longtime president of a corporation, the question of succession raised, among other points, the adjustments of certain interests within the corporation. The board of directors, in attempting to resolve the matter, adopted a resolution under which the widow of the president would be given a monthly payment until further action of the board "in recognition of the long and valued services rendered to this corporation for many years by her deceased husband, the president." Such resolution was made in good faith. A shareholder excepted to this resolution. Which is the correct statement?

(*a*) Giving away corporate funds may be *ultra vires*.

(*b*) A charter must expressly grant directors the power to bestow gifts.

(*c*) State statutes must expressly grant power to bestow gifts.

(*d*) A corporation can only give away money to its own employees, not their relatives.

The correct statement is (*a*). A corporation formed for profit making is not generally authorized to dissipate assets. When it attempts to do so, it may be acting *ultra vires*. Here the court could not find that the payments qualified as a pension, nor did they constitute a gift or contribution to charity. In the absence of some grounds upon which to sustain the payment, the good faith of the directors is of no avail where such action results in misapplication of the corporate assets. Given grounds satisfactory to the court, such actions as making gifts or contributions can be upheld by the courts despite the absence of an express grant of power in the charter or the state corporation statute.

33.11 The charter of a corporation provided that the company was to "advise and assist persons seeking employment and to print material, products, and school supplies of every class and description." The company moved forward in its activities and had progressed so far as to offer a 2-year course preparing persons to take civil service examinations. In doing so the company provided course material, tests, and grading thereof, and offered further coaching when necessary. The attorney general of the state charged that the activities engaged in by the company were beyond the powers of an ordinary corporation chartered in the state. He contended that in order to perform such actions, the company should have been chartered under a special statute regulating educational institutions which required a license from the state board of education.

What type of challenge is the state making against this company? Will it succeed? Decide and state reasons for any conclusions.

The state is charging that this for-profit corporation is performing acts that are *ultra vires* by reason of illegality. It is true that its charter was approved and that the activities it is performing are within the purpose and object clause of its certificate of incorporation. This seeming approval of the charter, however, does not excuse the company from obeying the law. Educational institutions are regulated by the state, and in addition to following regular incorporation procedures, the company must comply with the state regulatory law. The state will succeed in this case.

33.12 A manufacturer relied heavily upon a sales company for distribution and other services. The sales company was having financial trouble, and this caused concern to the manufacturer. A creditor of the sales company was willing to loan money to the sales company, but demanded that a third party stand as guarantor of the loan. The board of directors of the manufacturer considered the matter and finally decided to help, resolving that "a guaranty in this case would be in the company's best interest." The sales company was granted the loan, and the manufacturer guaranteed the payment of it. When the sales company defaulted on the loan, however, the manufacturer declined liability, citing that it was without power to guarantee the debts of another.

Assuming the corporate charter was silent on the subject of guaranties, how successful will the defense of the manufacturer be? Comment on the defense stating your reasons.

When it appears that the best interests of a corporation are involved, or the corporate interest could be furthered, the power to guarantee may be lawfully implied. Where the fortunes of the corporation depend on the financial stability of another, and good faith was exercised by the board of directors, the court will not permit the defense of *ultra vires* to vitiate the promise to answer for the debt of another.

33.13 Farnsworth and others owned 11 percent of the stock of an old and conservative cosmetics company. They did not like the management and its practices. The state statute provided that by following certain notice procedures, stockholders, or their agents, would be permitted, during usual business hours, to examine and copy corporate minutes and records of shareholders' names. Farnsworth complied with the notice procedures, but the company refused her request and filed an affidavit stating that Farnsworth's intentions were hostile. It cited Farnsworth's public statements by which she had suggested that she take over management, or that she be hired as a consultant, or that the company be sold or merged, or that the company initiate a public offering of its stock. Farnsworth did not contest this affidavit.

Has Farnsworth stated just cause for examining the books and copying the names of the stockholders? Decide and state the reasons for your conclusions.

The burden is not on the stockholders to prove their right to see the corporate books because it is theirs as a matter of right. The burden is on the company to prove that a request is not for a proper purpose. The purpose of gaining voting control of a corporation through purchase of stock or solicitation of proxies is not improper. An antagonistic attitude toward present management is not evidential of bad faith or ulterior motive detrimental to the company. Farnsworth, having complied with the notice requirements of the statute, is entitled to have access to the corporate records which she requested.

Chapter 34

Management: Directors and Officers

34.1 MANAGEMENT: GENERALLY

The governance of corporate affairs is held in the sometimes competing hands of three groups: the directors, the officers, and the shareholders. To determine the rights of these competing powers in respect to a particular situation or act requires consideration of the state corporation law, the articles of incorporation, the bylaws, the resolutions of the board of directors, and, of course, the actions of the shareholders.

EXAMPLE 1. Industrial Leasing Corporation is disturbed by a recent Internal Revenue Service ruling severely affecting its profitability on certain types of equipment leases. All similar companies would also be affected by this ruling. The corporate president searches and finds a highly qualified, but expensive, attorney who may be able to pursue this matter in tax court successfully. The attorney informs the president that the legal efforts involved will take at least 3 years and quotes the estimated fees and costs. The total figure is quite substantial, and the commitment of corporate funds would be very large in terms of the size of the firm. If the president was the sole owner, and the company not in the corporate form, he could make the decision by himself and proceed forthwith. This is not true with the corporate form. The statutes of the state of incorporation may have some provision regarding the power of the president, or even the directors, to enter into such contracts. Further, the corporate charter or the bylaws may have restrictions regarding such contracts.

34.2 STOCKHOLDERS AS MANAGERS

Ultimate power for corporate action rests in a certain number of stockholders, duly assembled or represented, who approve a course of action. In effect, stockholders may take any action which is not prohibited by statute or the corporate charter. Approval of an amendment to the corporate charter is an important example of the exercise of such power by the stockholders. However, corporations are usually not managed by their stockholders. The function of stockholders is usually to adopt bylaws or authorize directors to do so, elect directors, and decide broad questions of policy put to them by the directors at a stockholders' meeting, including the consideration of proposed unusual actions.

34.3 DIRECTORS AS MANAGERS

Directors are vested with the duty of the management of the corporation and exercise all those duties not reserved to the shareholders. The extent to which actual management is exercised by a board of directors depends on the size of the corporation and the traditions or practices of a particular firm.

A *director* is a fiduciary who owes undivided loyalty and allegiance to the corporation's aims, may not profit at its expense, and may not use it for personal opportunities or profits which in fairness belong to the corporation. He or she is to use independent judgment and act honestly and in good faith.

EXAMPLE 2. Tom is a prominent citizen whose family has lived in a Pennsylvania oil community for many years. Like his father and grandfather before him, he has been called upon to serve on many boards for both profit-making companies and public charities. Tom and his family own considerable stock in a local oil company of which he is a vice president and a member of the board of directors. He is also a member of the board of the local bank, an insurance firm in a nearby city, the local junior college, and another corporation in the state. He, like his ancestors, is accustomed to sitting on boards. He is not exceptionally brilliant, but he was educated at a prestigious college, and is familiar with the activities of his father when his father was involved with other firms as director. In a sense, Tom belongs to an aristocracy of directors. As a member of these various boards, he obtains an overview of the stream of commerce, the changing business environment, and the interrelationships of different businesses and their activities. What the bank's board of directors sets in the way of loan policy and credit requirements will affect many individuals and firms, including perhaps some of the companies with whom Tom also holds a similar position as a director.

34.4 DUTIES OF DIRECTORS

Typical duties of directors include declaring dividends and deciding upon payment dates; setting the price for stock to be issued (unless otherwise set by charter or statute); establishing value to be received for stock where property, not money, is to be taken; increasing the capital account; adopting bylaws (if authorized by charter or statute); electing officers and agents of the corporation; removing officers; approving large expenditures; entering into contracts which substantially affect the corporation; initiating new policy regarding corporate activity; determining employee relations; and even providing for the selection of future directors or key personnel.

Directors may be *inside* or *outside* directors. Traditionally an inside director was one who was also an officer of the firm, while an outside director was not such, and there was no formal legal difference between the two categories. More recently the definition of "inside director" has been expanded, in relation to the regulation of stock transactions, to include directors who are also major stockholders. Such persons have access to information either not available to ordinary stockholders or available to them only at a later time.

EXAMPLE 3. Tom, in Example 2, would be considered an inside director of the oil company for two reasons: he is both an officer of the company *and* a major stockholder. In the other companies where he sits as a director (the bank and insurance company, for examples), he would be considered an outside director. Some companies traditionally follow one or the other practice, with the trend being to have more outside members, including the presence of union officials.

34.5 DIRECTORS' MEETINGS

A director is not a corporate agent merely by virtue of his or her position and therefore cannot act for the company solely by reason of the status of a director. The board, using collective judgment, alters corporate life. Directors must be given notice of a board meeting unless such notice is subsequently waived or the absent director ratifies the actions of the board taken at the meeting. Meetings of the board must have a quorum, and the requisite number of votes for the approval of the intended act must be cast.

EXAMPLE 4. Minority shareholders and directors called a special emergency meeting of the board of directors for the purpose of removing the president (and majority stockholder) as a director and officer of the corporation and to restrain her from any exercise of her corporate functions. The grounds for the removal were alleged threats that the president was about to remove the minority shareholders from the board. Only the minority shareholders attended, as no notice of the meeting was given to the president. The minority shareholders voted the removal of the president and then filed an action in court to confirm their act. The president charged that the meeting was invalid since she was given no notice and there was no quorum present. The court ruled that the meeting was patently invalid. No functions entrusted to a board consisting of a number of persons can be validly exercised without notice to all. The state corporation law provides that a majority of a board at a meeting duly assembled shall constitute a quorum. Each director must receive proper notice unless waived. Here the certificate of incorporation provided for a minimum of four directors. At the time of the meeting there was one vacancy. The bylaws provide a procedure for filling vacancies on the board. A majority means a whole-number majority (4 of 7, 5 of 8, etc.) of directors, and a quorum remains the same number even if there are vacancies on the board.

Courts are very reluctant to approve informal actions or resolutions taken by means of a series of casual personal meetings with each member of the board by the board chairperson, for example. The concern is that since a board acts on the basis of its collective judgment, all the members should be able to discuss propositions as a group, and "rump metings" do not serve this purpose. Sitting as a board, the group possesses great discretion in regard to what matters can be on the agenda and who else can attend or appear before them at their meeting.

EXAMPLE 5. A director of the corporation requested permission to bring her attorney to all meetings of the board. The board refused, and she brought an action to compel the board to do so, claiming that she has the right to legal counsel at the meetings. Looking to the state law, the court concluded that it is up to the board of directors to determine who shall and who shall not attend board meetings other than the directors themselves. A determination of this question is to be made by the board as a whole and not individually. The circumstances which may suggest the presence of persons other than board members is left to the sound discretion of the corporation through its board of directors.

The articles of incorporation (the charter) set forth the number of directors in a corporation, with some state statutes specifying a minimum number. Today, with the presence of close corporations, the minimum can be one director. However, the idea of collective judgment persists, and accordingly, unlike stockholders at their meetings, a director may not vote by proxy at a board meeting.

EXAMPLE 6. An advertising agency had three directors, a father, a son, and a third person. The agency was in financial difficulty and was helped by the father, who loaned the agency $10,000 under an agreement with the agency corporation which provided that the sum loaned "shall continue to be a loan for 1 year, or sooner, unless said loan is sooner paid by the unanimous vote of the board of directors." Two months later the agency repaid the loan, and at a meeting of the directors a week later the authority for repayment of the loan to the father was discussed. All directors except the son were present, but the son had given his father a proxy to act on the son's behalf. No formal vote was taken on the question of approving the withdrawal of the $10,000 from corporate funds to pay the father. Two months later the agency went bankrupt, and the trustee in bankruptcy sought to recover the alleged preferential payment by the agency to the father. The issue arose of the right of the agency to pay the father. The court ruled that it was an improper payment. The loan agreement was explicit. No formal vote was taken, but even if an informal vote was taken as claimed by the father, the vote could not be unanimous because the proxy of the son was ineffective. The affairs of the corporation are in the hands of its board of directors whose duty it is to give deliberate control to the corporate business, and this requires the physical presence of a director at the directors' meetings; no director can act by proxy.

34.6 DIRECTOR CONFLICT OF INTEREST

A director is not barred from presenting any proposition to the corporation on whose board he or she sits, but due to the fiduciary relationship the corporate interest cannot be compromised. Such director must deal openly, i.e., make full disclosure, and act in good faith. The board's action of approval must be independent from the director as a matter of law and fact. Such a director is called an *interested director*, and only *disinterested directors* can constitute a quorum and provide the affirmative vote. Failing this test, the action is voidable at the option of the corporation, the interested director being obligated to account for any benefit received.

EXAMPLE 7. A management company was awarded a general consulting contract, which the employing corporation now seeks to rescind. The directors of the employing corporation voted unanimously to award the contract. It appeared, however, that a quorum under the bylaw was five members, a majority of the eight members provided for in the bylaw. It was charged that at the meeting there was no quorum of disinterested directors as three of the six directors present were also directors of the management company. The court ruled that, while the action was not void because of the relationship alone, it is voidable. Courts give the closest scrutiny to such an action, and it is voidable if found to be unfair even though there is no taint of fraud. In this case, however, only six out of eight board members were present, and three of these were interested parties. By simple arithmetic there could have been no quorum of disinterested board members present. As to the argument that a subsequent meeting of the board approved the minutes of the previous meeting, the court reminded the parties that approval of minutes is nothing more than an acknowledgment that the secretary properly recorded the acts of the board. It is not a legalization of invalid acts recorded therein.

Some directors are paid compensation for their services, but in the absence of statute or corporate charter authority, such right will not be assumed. Where no charter provision or bylaw authorizes compensation of directors for their services, it is necessary to obtain the appropriate stockholder approval.

34.7 REMOVAL OF DIRECTORS

Once a director is elected by the stockholders at the appointed meeting, usually the annual meeting, he or she is free to serve out the term in spite of the stockholders' wishes, unless there are charter or bylaw provisions to the contrary which are authorized by state corporation law. Accordingly, a director no longer supported by the majority of the stockholders, as in the case of a change in ownership, could remain in that position until the end of the term.

EXAMPLE 8. A director was removed from the board without cause in July and discharged as an employee in September. The articles did not authorize such removal from the board. The state law allows removal for cause or, if the certificate of incorporation so provides, without cause. The director sued to regain his position, to examine the corporate books, and to obtain other relief. The corporation reinstated him in October and then called a special meeting of the directors to consider an amendment of the certificate of incorporation which would allow the removal of directors without cause. The board of directors approved, as did the stockholders. The director was again removed from the board. The court ordered the reinstatement of the ousted director. The court noted that the entire management of corporate affairs is committed to a director's charge upon the trust and confidence that these will be cared for and managed within the limits of the power conferred by law upon the corporation and for the common benefit of the stockholders. The burden and responsibility a director assumes, and the many economic interests the director safekeeps, all give rise to a vested interest in the director's position. Under these circumstances, and for these reasons, a director cannot be removed from the board without cause unless the certificate of incorporation so provides at the time of his or her election.

The Model Business Corporation Act authorizes removal of directors by the shareholders at a meeting called expressly for that purpose.

34.8 CLOSE CORPORATION CONTROL

Some corporations, because of their financial size and/or the number of their shareholders, choose to be managed in the formal manner described above. Other companies operate with a somewhat streamlined form of management. Corporation law in most states provides for the use of *executive committees* of the board of directors, and also cites other devices through which much action can be accomplished without the necessity of formal meetings. Where the statute and charter combine to use these methods, much of the technical procedure regarding corporate action, even of an extraordinary kind, can be accomplished more quickly and simply.

34.9 OFFICERS AS MANAGERS

The officers are agents of the corporation and are usually elected by the directors. They have such express authority as is granted them by the directors, bylaws, and, from time to time, by stockholder approval. Officers bind the corporation when they act within the express, implied, or apparent authority of their positions. The rules of agency govern this aspect. The title an officer carries does not, in most instances, permit others to assume in the absence of other evidence that an officer has a particular authority.

Except for certain minor purposes, the title "president," "vice president," "secretary," or "treasurer" attached to an employee is not considered sufficient manifestation that such titled officer has any particular power to bind the company. It is likely, however, that the president has a great deal of authority by reason of specific instructions from the directors or under the bylaws. A bylaw reciting, for instance, that "the president shall be elected by the directors and shall serve at their will, and the president's duties shall be those of general manager and chief executive officer" is an express grant of power authorizing acts to achieve the broad objectives of the company. The president does not, however, have the implied or apparent authority to do acts which would substantially deprive the corporation of its profits.

EXAMPLE 9.   A corporate president employed a former officer through an oral contract, the terms of which were for the life of the former officer at a fixed annual salary, plus 25 percent of the annual profit of the corporation not to exceed $40,000 per year. At the time of the contract the company had three directors: the former officer, the president, and another. Two of the directors, the president and the former officer, supported the contract, and together they held a majority of the corporation's stock. The contract was opposed by the other director. Six years later the corporation notified the former officer that the agreement was terminated and offered him a consultant's job at $500 per month. He refused and sued for breach of contract. The court ruled against the validity of the contract. It stated that, as a general rule, the president of a corporation has no authority by virtue of office alone to employ agents and servants for the corporation. Even though a general manager may have great power by reason of position, he or she can only employ under usual conditions those usual persons who are necessary to the conduct of the business. An unusual and extraordinary contract for services is not warranted unless it is expressly authorized by appropriate authority. Contracts for lifetime employment are usually, in the absence of express authority, not considered to be within the power of even a general manager to grant. On the question of such authority having been granted by a majority of the board of directors, the court noted that since the former officer was at that time a director, and had an interest in making the contract, his vote in favor of the contract was improper. It is not proper for directors to vote on a transaction in which they are personally involved. Had the director not voted, the vote would have been a tie, 1 to 1, and the proposed contract would not have been approved. Thus, the president never had the authority to offer the contract in the first place, and it would be doubtful that even proper board approval would have been sufficient to allow it. Such an extraordinary contract, including as it did the disposition of corporate profits, would likely require formal stockholder approval.

There is little regulation regarding corporate titles and authority. A corporate secretary traditionally has custody and control of the corporate books, while the treasurer is the fiscal officer. The title "vice president" carries no apparent authority. State corporation law usually allows one to hold multiple positions except that the combination of president and secretary is normally prohibited. The corporate seal is usually held by the secretary, and its affixation on documents purports authenticity of the act, although not conclusively.

34.10 LIABILITY OF MANAGEMENT: GENERALLY

The board of directors, the officers, and the employees of the corporation, when acting within the scope of their authority, are not liable for the contractual and nontortious activity of the corporation. They are liable, however, for their own torts or individual commitments.

EXAMPLE 10.   The general manager of a hardware corporation ordered 19 outboard motors from the seller, delivery to the corporation only upon receipt of the bill of lading indorsed by the bank which financed the transaction. The corporation took delivery without the bill of lading. The manager knew that it had possession without ownership of the motors. Six of the motors were sold by the manager and other employees with the manager's knowledge and consent, and for which the corporation received $2,800. The corporation went into receivership, and the creditors lost all their claims against the corporation. The seller of the motors charged the manager with converting the motors and demanded the $2,800. The manager proved that she acted in good faith and personally received none of the sales money. The manager was held liable for conversion, a tort. The court noted that it is well established that officers of a corporation are liable for any tort of the corporation in which they participate or which they authorize, even though they were acting for the corporation in the commission of the tortious activity. The sale by the manager of property the corporation did not own deprived the seller of his property.

34.11   NEGLIGENCE IN DECISION MAKING

Negligence is a tort and, if committed by an officer or agent of the corporation while acting within the scope of his or her duties, binds the corporation also. A director or officer is not, however, liable for mistakes in judgment which breach no duty in tort law. If the director or officer acted honestly and as a reasonably prudent person, he or she suffers no liability from others, including the shareholders. Ignorance, however, is not necessarily excused by the presence of good faith.

EXAMPLE 11.   Three directors—an accountant, an attorney, and a corporation president—were concerned with certain proposed corporate action by the directors involving financing. None of the three had actual knowledge that the data upon which the decision was based were correct. All, in one way or another, relied upon data supplied by others as being correct and as the material upon which they formed their judgment and voted as directors. These directors could be liable if these figures are incorrect and, with some additional effort, such fact could have been discovered.

EXAMPLE 12.   A minority shareholder of a baseball corporation sued the directors for mismanagement, alleging the failure to install lights for night baseball which contributed to the financial loss of the corporation. It was alleged that other clubs had night baseball and that it was improper for the corporation not to follow suit. The court disagreed that the directors' unwillingness to follow the example of other clubs in scheduling night games constituted negligence. The court stated that directors are elected for business capabilities and judgments, and the courts cannot require them to forego their considered judgment because of the policies of the directors of the other clubs. Since there appeared to be other considerations in the decision of the directors, such as the relationship of the corporation with its neighbors, it cannot be said as a matter of law that the long-run interest of the corporation is being undermined by the present policy.

Corporate managers are protected by the business judgment rule, and policies adopted by them come before the court with a presumption of propriety.

34.12   CORPORATE OPPORTUNITY

The fiduciary duty that directors and officers owe to the corporation prohibits them from taking some benefit or advantage of business opportunities available to the corporation. Proposals that are closely tied to the corporation's type of business must be treated with care by the corporate managers. This does not mean that such parties have no private lives and therefore no private opportunities. If the directors or officers properly reject the opportunity, or if the corporation was not capable of seizing the opportunity, such parties may then act in their own behalf.

EXAMPLE 13.   Nell Diaper Service is a successful operation and is run by an aggressive management, including an active board of directors, consisting of three members. Peter Pan Babysitters, Inc., is up for sale, as the owners are retiring. The owners approached the president of Nell for the purpose of selling the company to Nell. The matter is brought up before Nell's directors, with one contending that the combination is a natural as the diaper service gives a good entry into the babysitting business. The other two directors do admire Peter Pan but think that Nell's money can be better used to expand in other areas. The offer is refused. Three months later the two directors who voted against the proposal turn up as major shareholders in Peter Pan. This would raise a question of usurpation of corporate opportunity. The safest way to avoid this question would have been to have presented the matter to the stockholders for approval or denial.

34.13 DEALING WITH SHAREHOLDERS

Directors and officers are in a fiduciary relation with the corporation for many purposes but are generally not to be considered in such a position regarding individual stockholders. When they contract with stockholders, present or prospective, sensitive issues arise. Of course the rules of fraud and misrepresentation apply should the director or officer wish to purchase or sell personal stock to a shareholder.

EXAMPLE 14. Wodarczyk is a director and stockholder in a moderately sized corporation which, while the stock is not traded on any of the national exchanges, does have public ownership. For a long period of time it has been run by a man who is both the president and the chairperson of the board of directors. Wodarczyk is approached by the president's wife, who confides in him regarding certain marital troubles and her need to employ an attorney. The wife indicates that the divorce will be messy and some things about the management of the firm may have to be aired in court. Wodarczyk is alarmed at the information and decides to sell his stock slowly before these matters become public. Those to whom Wodarczyk personally offers the stock may be able to charge concealment, or silence when there is a duty to speak, depending on the circumstances surrounding the sale. If a prospective buyer, for instance, inquired about why Wodarczyk wanted to sell, almost any response except the entire truth could be considered fraudulent.

The duty of an insider or controlling person regarding such dealings is also treated under the Securities Exchange Act of 1934. Provisions are extensive in this regard, including a requirement subjecting such owners (officers and directors) of 10 percent or more of a company's securities traded on the national stock exchanges to monthly reporting. Further, under federal law it can be considered a deceptive trade practice for a person to take advantage of any inside information knowing it is unavailable to those with whom such a person is dealing.

34.14 CRIMINAL LIABILITY

The officers, directors, and employees of a corporation have no special immunity to the criminal law by reason of their relationship to the corporation. The statutory language determines whether an act committed for the corporation, and for its benefit, can nevertheless be criminal. Good faith by itself provides no protection. This is particularly true in respect to antitrust statutes, environmental legislation, and food and drug laws. It is possible for one to be liable for acts, or failure to act, by one's agents. Some statutes read responsibility as the key element in the offense. Accordingly, the failure of one's agent to carry out a duty if such failure carries a criminal penalty does not shield the principal from prosecution.

34.15 INDEMNIFICATION

Corporate officers, directors, and employees do get sued for a variety of reasons and by different groups. If the action giving rise to such a lawsuit involves corporate business, such parties are entitled to indemnification for the personal expense to which they are put. It is generally stated that indemnification against personal liability is proper for the corporation in any lawsuit or proceeding resulting from any act or decision made in good faith and without negligence.

Black Letter Law
A Summary

1. The power to direct corporate policy rests in three groups: directors, officers and agents, and stockholders.

2. Legally, the stockholders hold ultimate power, but directors and officers manage the corporate affairs.

3. Directors are not corporate agents; they act effectively only as a group lawfully assembled, or by virtue of ratification.

4. Directors and officers are in a fiduciary relationship to the corporation, but are not generally so in regard to individual shareholders.

5. Directors and officers violate their fiduciary duty when they act in self-interest in dealings which are not fair to the corporation, but they may contract with the corporation openly, in good faith, provided there is independent approval of the board of directors.

6. Directors, in the absence of statutes, charter provisions, or bylaws to the contrary, serve for the assigned term, and may be removed prematurely only for cause.

7. Officers and other corporate agents manage the daily affairs of the company and possess the authority ceded to them by the charter, the bylaws, and the board of directors; corporate titles alone do not generally indicate apparent authority, although the title "general manager" suggests broad apparent authority.

8. Directors, officers, and employees, when acting in good faith within the scope of their authority, are not liable for corporate activity; however, they must answer for their own torts or individual commitments.

Solved Problems

34.1 After proper incorporation of Alpha, it was decided to purchase a plant site. Gold, a newly elected director, has owned a desirable site for many years. She purchased the property for $60,000, and its present fair value is $100,000. What would be the result if Gold offered the property to Alpha for $100,000 in an arm's length transaction with full disclosure at a meeting of the seven directors of the corporation?

(a) The sale would be proper only on requisite approval by the appropriate number of directors and at *no* more than Gold's cost, thus precluding her profiting from the sale to the corporation.

(b) The sale would be void under the self-dealing rule.

(c) The sale would be proper, and Gold would *not* have to account to the corporation for her profit if the sale was approved by a disinterested majority of the directors.

(d) The sale would *not* be proper, if sold for the present fair value of the property, without the approval of all the directors.

(*Adapted from AICPA Examination, May 1974*)

Dealings between the corporation and the directors are always subject to court scrutiny. The principal safeguard is the presence of an independent board to evaluate the transaction. A majority of disinterested directors would satisfy this requirement, and if approved by them, an open transaction can be confirmed; statement (c) is the answer.

34.2   Seymore was recently invited to become a director of Buckley Industries, Inc. If Seymore accepts and becomes a director, he along with the other directors will *not* be personally liable for

(a) lack of reasonable care.

(b) honest errors of judgment.

(c) declaration of a dividend which the directors know will impair legal capital.

(d) diversion of corporate opportunities to themselves.

(*AICPA Examination, November 1973*)

Directors have personal liability, but while the standards they must meet are high, they are not personally liable for honest errors of judgment, statement (b). The other statements reflect *prima facie* evidence of director liability.

34.3   Derek Corporation decided to acquire certain assets belonging to the Mongol Corporation. As consideration for the assets acquired, Derek issued 20,000 shares of its no-par common stock with a stated value of $10 per share. The value of the assets acquired subsequently turned out to be much less than the $200,000 in stock issued. Under the circumstances, which of the following is correct?

(a) It is improper for the board of directors to acquire assets other than cash with no-par stock.

(b) Only the shareholders can have the right to fix the value of the shares of no-par stock exchanged for assets.

(c) In the absence of fraud in the transaction, the judgment of the board of directors as to the value of the consideration received for the shares shall be conclusive.

(d) Unless the board obtained an independent appraisal of the value of the acquired assets, it is liable to the extent of the overvaluation.

(*Adapted from AICPA Examination, November 1978*)

There are a number of areas in which the judgment of the directors, if made in good faith, is final. The lack of an appraisal, if in regard to an unusual and substantial asset of a type with which the board had no previous acquaintance, could impair the good-faith defense, but there is no evidence of that here. Accordingly, the value of the assets acquired, and the corresponding payment made for them by no-par stock, is set by the board of directors; the answer is statement (c).

34.4   Laser Corporation lent $5,000 to Mr. Jackson, a member of its board of directors. Mr. Jackson was also vice president of operations. The board of directors, but not the stockholders, of Laser authorized the loan on the basis that the loan would benefit the corporation. The loan made to Mr. Jackson is

(a) proper.

(b) improper because Mr. Jackson is an employee.

(c) improper because Mr. Jackson is a director.

(d) improper because Mr. Jackson is both a director and an employee.

(*AICPA Examination, November 1975*)

While dealings with boards of directors are examined more closely than others, the main objective is still to determine whether the transaction would be beneficial to the corporation. The board's approval validates the action; answer (a) is correct.

34.5 Unless otherwise provided by a corporation's articles of incorporation or bylaws, a board of directors may act without a meeting if written consent setting forth the action so taken is signed by

(a) a plurality of them.

(b) a majority of them.

(c) two-thirds of them.

(d) all of them.

(*AICPA Examination, May 1976*)

Board meetings are intended to be used for the purpose of consultation and consensus after proper notice to all. In the absence of such notice and meeting, the consent of all would be necessary in order to confirm board actions, statement (d).

34.6 Shares of stock without par value may be issued for such consideration (in dollars) as may be fixed by a corporation's

(a) creditors.

(b) officers.

(c) board of directors.

(d) minority shareholders.

(*AICPA Examination, May 1976*)

The answer is (c). The fixing of consideration for no-par stock is traditionally in the hands of the directors. This is a discretionary act involving corporate policy.

34.7 Directors and shareholders met at a social gathering and discussed an offer made to the corporation to purchase its office building. It was informally agreed that the attorney for the corporation, also a director, would prepare the deed. A deed was prepared and held by the bank for later delivery. Before the buyer had a chance to deliver the money to the bank, the deed was withdrawn. Which is the correct statement?

(a) The sale of the corporation's own building is a routine matter, and any officer has the apparent authority to sell it.

(b) The corporation's best defense is that the directors never acted in concert to approve this extraordinary transaction.

(c) An attorney for the corporation who is also a director is, in effect, a double agent for the corporation.

(d) The transfer and sale of the corporation's own building, in which it carries out its business, can only be made at liquidation of the corporation.

This case deals with actual and apparent authority. If the contract was an extraordinary contract, the presence of apparent authority is unlikely. Accordingly, the actual authority must be proved. If all the directors duly assembled and a majority voted in the affirmative, the act was authorized. However, the informal setting in which the approval took place suggests the possibility of an absence of corporate action based upon deliberate conference and sober discussion of proposed measures; the correct statement is (b).

34.8 A minority shareholder of the Franklin Newspaper Corporation sued its principal officer for damages to the *Franklin News*. It was alleged that the officer owned 52 percent of Franklin stock and owned another company which also published a newspaper. The minority shareholder charged that the other newspaper was printed at the Franklin plant at the expense of the *Franklin News* and to its detriment. What legal grounds is the minority shareholder attempting to invoke?

(*a*)   A conflict of interest

(*b*)   An *ultra vires* act

(*c*)   Oppression of minority shareholder interests

(*d*)   A disregard of the corporate entity

   Directors and officers are precluded from doing an act or engaging in any transaction in which their private interest will conflict with the duty they owe to the stockholders, and from making use of their power or the property of the corporation for their own advantage. The minority shareholder is trying to show conflict of interest, statement (*a*). The officer has the duty of showing that he is not using the assets of one corporation for the benefit of another.

34.9 Priller Features Corporation was owned by Steniz, who held 40 percent of the stock, and Laffenwell, who owned 60 percent of the stock. The company ran a country store in the farming district. The store was quite successful despite the bickering and the sniping behavior of the two stockholders, who also worked in the store. The building used for the store was up for sale, and Laffenwell, who controlled two of the three seats on the board of directors (Steniz held the other one seat), voted to decline the landlord's offer to sell the building to Priller Features Corporation. The landlord then sold the building to Laffenwell's attorney, who was also the corporation attorney. Which is the most correct statement?

(*a*)   Majority rule generally makes this board action valid and final.

(*b*)   A minority shareholder can sue for the loss of the profit to him or her.

(*c*)   A minority director can challenge the action of the majority provided he or she is also a shareholder.

(*d*)   Where directors divert a corporate opportunity, the shareholders may sue on behalf of the corporation for the recovery of such damage.

   The answer is statement (*d*). While the courts rarely intervene in matters of business judgment, an action does lie when an officer or director diverts a corporate opportunity. The facts will determine whether this opportunity was favorable to the corporation and whether the corporation had the wherewithal to seize such a purchase opportunity. If both are found to be true, the stockholder's suit is likely to succeed.

34.10 Belkman was a tough sales manager for Abby Company, and he had an "ironclad" 2-year employment contract. Belkman could get nasty on occasion, and he irritated a good customer by his tactics in trying to get faster payment on the customer's account. The customer complained to the president, and the complaint reached the board of directors. After a long discussion the board members voted to fire Belkman. Belkman sued Abby and the directors personally for this act. Belkman charged the directors with maliciously interfering with his contract with Abby. Under these circumstances,

(*a*)   directors have no liability for their votes as directors.

(*b*)   if the board's action was taken in furtherance of the corporate interests, and in good faith, the directors are immune from personal liability.

(c)   if Belkman's behavior in dealing with the customer was justified, he cannot be fired by Abby.

(d)   only the president or general manager of Abby could be liable for the tortious act of the directors in maliciously interfering with Belkman's employment contract.

A party is always liable for a tort he or she commits, whether as an individual, a director, an officer, or even a shareholder. If the directors committed a tort, they would be personally liable even if the company was also liable. However, the directors must commit the tort. Tort liability for inducement of breach of contract is imposed when the agent or director induces the breach for private benefit, or when personal feelings and purposes relative to a third party are involved. If that is not shown, the directors are not liable; statement (b) is the correct answer.

34.11 An action was brought by protesting stockholders against the managing officer to have that officer account for profits made in dealing with the corporation. The protesting stockholders and managing officer owned all the stock of the company, which manufactured luggage. It appeared that the officer owned another company which manufactured luggage frames, which it sold at a profit to the corporation. The officer contends that he revealed to the stockholders that he was making a profit; furthermore, his private company offered the lowest price available in the market, and it would not be profitable for the corporation itself to manufacture the frames.

Assuming these contentions can be supported, can the officer make a profit selling to the corporation he manages? State the principle governing this decision.

Transactions between a corporation and its directors or officers are not prohibited, but rather are ruled by a strict standard of fairness. The interested director or officer has the burden of proving such fairness. As long as his contentions are supported by the evidence, the officer should be successful.

34.12 The president owned 75 percent of the outstanding stock of a corporation. The only asset of the corporation was 82 acres of land along a highway. The president solicited the remaining 25 percent of the shares from the minority shareholder for the sum of $30,000. The next day the president sold all the stock to a third party for a price of $144,000. Upon learning of the sale, the former minority shareholder sued the president for the $6,000 difference between the $30,000 she received for her stock and the $36,000 (25 percent of the $144,000) the president received for it.

What principle of law should the president invoke to defend his action? What success will the former minority shareholder have? State the reasons for your conclusions.

The president should press the argument that as an officer he owes no fiduciary duty to the individual shareholder or prospective shareholder. However, he is an insider, and the circumstances here may show that he had a duty to reveal the special situation. In the absence of Securities Acts, the courts are not in agreement on the extent of one's duty to reveal the special circumstances of this sale.

34.13 September Markets and its president were indicted under a federal statute prohibiting the keeping of food in a warehouse that was rodent-infested. The company had been warned previously, and the president had set up a system to correct the abuse. The system failed. September pleaded guilty, but the president contends that she cannot be held criminally liable because she did not personally participate in the situation which caused the infestation or allowed it to continue. The federal government contends that by virtue of her position in the company, the president can be liable under the statute which punishes those "responsible for the commission of the act." The president maintains that she does not personally supervise the warehouse.

Can a corporate officer be guilty of a crime where he or she had no specific intent to violate the statute and had ordered the firm's employees to correct the abuse? Decide and discuss the principle involved.

One has committed a crime when the facts show one's behavior comes within the sanctioned act. The statute clearly places liability on those "responsible for the commission of the act." If the president was ultimately responsible for the policies and knew full well the situation which would give rise to the offense, her personal intent not to violate the statute is no defense. Not all statutes require that the accused be "aware of some wrongdoing" or perform "conscious fraud." The statute punishes those who have a responsible share in the furtherance of the transaction which the statute outlaws. The fact that the system the president selected to clear up the violation failed does not excuse the responsible party under the purposes of the act. The president is guilty of the criminal act, as is the corporation. Her punishment might be mitigated by the evidence of her attempt to install a system to correct the abuse, but she cannot evade personal responsibility.

Chapter 35

Securities and Corporate Termination

35.1 CORPORATE SECURITIES

A corporation is owned by its shareholders and indebted to its creditors. In respect to its financial relationships with both, a corporation issues securities. A *security* is a share, interest in, or obligation of an enterprise. It is commonly recognized as an investment and can be either certificated or uncertificated. Securities may be of either the *equity* or *debt* variety. Equity securities include stock, warrants, and rights, while corporate creditors may be issued bonds which are debt. Sometimes a security has dual features, for example, when a creditor purchases a convertible bond.

EXAMPLE 1. Masone, Inc., needs to attract investors, but its financial statement is not appealing, although its ability to pay its debts is not questioned. The board of directors decides to issue $2 million of convertible bonds, at 14 percent interest, with a *conversion* feature which allows the bondholder to convert the bond into stock at a price of $15 per share. This action is authorized by the charter. The common stock presently sells at $13 per share. Those who purchase this security are creditors of Masone with the right to become equity holders, i.e., shareholders, by exercising the stated conversion option.

35.2 STOCKS

The capital stock of the corporation is held by the owners of the company. A corporation may have more than one class of capital stock. The amount and character of each class are determined by the articles of incorporation and any amendments thereto. The total amount set forth in the charter is the *authorized stock*. Stock issued by the corporation and held by others is *issued and outstanding*. Such issued stock as is repurchased, or otherwise received by the corporation, is *treasury stock*.

A corporation must have at least one class of stock. The particular characteristics of securities are left in large measure to the imagination of the incorporators or stockholders through the articles and any amendments thereto. One class must be issued with voting rights. The value of the stock at original issue is determined either by the charter or through authority granted to the directors. If the stock is *par value*, for instance, that set amount must be paid to the corporation which then reflects its receipt by inclusion of the sum in the capital account. If *no-par* stock is issued, the directors are usually granted authority to set the price from time to time, and the consideration received is reflected as paid-in capital. Such sums are called the *stated value*.

EXAMPLE 2. Masone, Inc., is incorporated with three classes of stock: common, preferred A, and preferred B. The common is $100 par and has voting rights. Each original shareholder must pay that amount or more. Any excess payment is paid-in capital. Once the stock is issued, the price someone pays for it will depend on the market, as the corporation is no longer involved in the transfer except for recording the name of the holder on the corporate books.

The common stockholders are usually the possessors of the main residuary power in the corporation and have the greatest opportunity for both gain and loss. Buyers of preferred stock, on the other hand, are usually attracted by valuable features not owned by the holders of common stock. Preferred stock may have first right to dividends, assets in event of liquidation, participation in additional dividends, and other attractive provisions.

EXAMPLE 3. Masone, Inc., preferred Class A stock has a number of rights. It will be paid an 8 percent dividend before any other dividend, and if omitted, such right carries to the future; i.e., it is *cumulative*. Should high dividends occur in one year, the Class A stock will share in the dividend even if it exceeds 8 percent as it is *participating*. Further, in the event of liquidation such stockholders receive first distribution after the creditors. Class A preferred has, however, a negative provision in that it is *redeemable* in 10 years because the corporation has set up a fund to retire this stock at that time, and it might be that at that time 8 percent is a handsome return which the holders of the stock would be sorry to have to give up.

Once issued, stock may be transferred to others including the corporation itself. When the corporation receives back its own stock, such shares have the special status of treasury shares. The corporation cannot vote treasury shares, but it can resell them without restriction on the amount received (e.g., stated value, par value).

35.3 BONDS

Corporations frequently borrow money. When they formally raise money under a long-term arrangement, they may issue bonds; when they borrow for a short time, they may issue notes or run up a charge on an open account. The bondholder is only a creditor and thus must share equally with other creditors—the holders of notes, current creditors, and others. However, some bonds are issued with collateral to assure their repayment. Uncollateralized bonds are usually referred to as *debentures*.

EXAMPLE 4. Masone, Inc., issued $4 million of 15 percent corporate bonds secured by a mortgage on the corporate plant and all its equipment. The holders of such bonds are creditors with a lien on these assets of the corporation. In the event of liquidation, bondholders have priority in such assets over and above other creditors not so favored.

35.4 WARRANTS AND RIGHTS

Rather than an outright issuance of stock, some corporations provide a right to purchase stock by way of an option. The motivation for offering such a security may be to attract further investment by present owners, to act as an inducement to obtain the services of certain personnel, or to retain the services of valued executives in the company. Such options are called *warrants*. Short-term options are *rights*, and unlike warrants, they are usually not transferable and expire at a relatively early date.

35.5 CONTRACTING FOR CORPORATE STOCK

Generally one purchases stock for money or property, but stock can be issued for services. It cannot be purchased on credit; for example, a purchaser may not give a promissory note for the stock. Except for cash, directors have wide discretion in determining the value of what is offered for stock, and in the absence of bad faith or unfairness, their judgment will be upheld.

EXAMPLE 5. Certain promoters were issued stock for services rendered and property furnished. Class B stock was sold at par, but Class A stock was issued to the promoters in consideration of their experience in the business, their standing among the corporate clientele, and their personal guaranty in the purchase of certain equipment by the corporation. It was not questioned that the services rendered and the goodwill present were of value to the corporation, but there was a challenge as to the value of the guaranty. The challenger cited a state statute prohibiting "issuance of shares for promissory notes or other obligations of the subscribers." The issue was whether the personal guaranty was a prohibited consideration. It was ruled that this guaranty was not a promise under the statute. Since the guaranty by the parties reduced the cost of the purchase for the corporation, value was received. The issuance of the Class B stock for services, goodwill, and a guaranty promise of a corporation debt was legal consideration.

35.6   CORPORATE SUBSCRIPTIONS

When parties promise to purchase corporate stock, their agreements are called *stock subscriptions*. These occur before incorporation and after formation. Generally the principles of offer and acceptance apply, although preincorporation subscriptions present a problem in that one of the parties does not yet exist, i.e., the corporation to be formed. Such subscribers are merely offerors and become legally bound only after incorporation. A revocation of the offer before incorporation is effective except in those states having a rule to the contrary, such as that provided by the Model Business Corporation Act in making such subscriptions irrevocable for a period of 6 months in the absence of a contrary understanding. The requirement of the form of subscriptions is not uniform, although some statutes require that a subscription be in writing and signed.

Where the corporation is already formed, the subscription is effective upon acceptance, which therefore also makes the subscriber a stockholder.

EXAMPLE 6.   Tarragoin was a major stockholder in Tylle Corporation, which manufactured bearings. He had a great idea for a distribution system but wanted a separate company for this. Viola was interested in this development and felt that both corporations would do well under Tarragoin's plan. Viola subscribed to 1,000 shares of Tylle common stock and signed a document along with Tarragoin to purchase 2,000 shares of a new company called Tylle II, which was in the process of being formed. As the plan was unfolding, Viola became less impressed with the distribution arrangements. Viola now refused to honor either stock purchase commitment. Viola would be bound on the Tylle subscription if the corporation accepted the subscription, but she could revoke the offer to Tylle II, provided there was no statute to the contrary or a court did not find that Viola's promise to subscribe was specifically induced by Tarragoin's promise (or the promises of others) to subscribe.

35.7   STOCK CERTIFICATES

A stock certificate is evidence of stock ownership, but its existence is not mandatory. Failure of a corporation to issue stock certificates does not deprive stockholders of their rights.

EXAMPLE 7.   Fred and Albert were school buddies who began an auto body shop right out of high school. Ten years later they changed their business sign to read "Fred and Albert, Inc.," having formed a corporation. They were simple and hardworking and for the next 25 years labored well and profitably, it being understood that Fred owned 45 percent of the business. The corporate stock book, which came with the corporate kit in the beginning, was never filled out, and all stock certificates were intact. The charter shows an authorized stock structure of 100 shares of no-par stock. Fred died, and his estate shows that he is a stockholder despite the fact that he never was issued any stock. Assuming proof, the 45 percent share will be honored by the court.

Stock is a form of security and, when represented (i.e., certificated) by an instrument issued in bearer or registered form, can qualify as a *registered security* under Article 8 of the UCC. An uncertificated security is not represented by an instrument, UCC, Section 8-102. The UCC governs much of the law of transfer of securities as well as setting forth numerous rights and duties of the corporation and shareholders in regard to this relationship.

The common printed stock certificate form provides a place for the name of the registered owner, the number of shares, and a certificate number. On the back there is an assignment form which permits the registered owner, if not bearer, to indorse and transfer to another or to bearer. Since under Article 8 a registered security is a form of negotiable instrument, the rights of the parties closely track some of the commercial paper rules found in Article 3 of the UCC.

EXAMPLE 8.   A certificate of stock is issued in the name of Hanley for 50 shares represented by certificate no. C 10452. This is a registered, certificated security. She wishes to sell the shares, and her brother instructs her to "just sign your name on the back and mail it to me." Hanley signs her name on the back and mails it, but it is lost in the mail. This registered security is now a bearer security. It is possible for a good-faith purchaser to affect Hanley's rights in the share certificate. If she had signed her name after naming her brother as the new owner (or as having power to transfer the certificate), an indorsement by the brother could better protect her rights in the certificate.

35.8   TRANSFER RULES

A transfer of a certificated security (e.g., stock, bond, warrant) under Article 8 of the UCC can be by delivery alone if in bearer form or indorsed in blank. If in registered form, transfer can be by delivery of the certificate with an indorsement by the registered owner. This indorsement can be on the back of the certificate or by a separate power of attorney or assignment signed by the registered owner. Such owner warrants to the transferee for value that the transfer is rightful, the security is genuine, the security is not materially altered, and the owner knows of no fact which would impair the validity of the security, UCC, Section 8-306.

EXAMPLE 9.   Ronson holds a stock certificate in the amount of 100 shares. She decides to sell these shares to Alfred for $500. She can make an effective transfer of this certificated security by signing it on the back and delivering it to Alfred. Alfred now holds a bearer security, as it is indorsed in blank. Alfred would take this certificate as a bona fide purchaser of certificated securities.

A bona fide purchaser is one who has paid value in good faith with no notice of any adverse claims, provided such purchaser takes delivery of a certificated security in bearer form, or indorsed to him or her or in blank, UCC, Section 8-302. One who presents a certificated security for registration of transfer, or for payment or exchange, also makes a warranty—that he or she is entitled to such transfer or payment or exchange. If an individual is a purchaser for value without notice of any adverse claims who receives a new, reissued, or reregistered certificated security, that individual only makes the warranty that he or she has no knowledge of any unauthorized signature in a necessary indorsement, UCC, Section 8-306.

EXAMPLE 10.   Burton lost his 500-share certificate in Ramblers, Inc., when he moved from one office to another. Attilla found it, forged Burton's signature on the certificate, and sold it to a brokerage house, which resold the certificate. It was still in apparent bearer form by reason of the blank but forged indorsement. Roberts took it for value with no knowledge of its unlawful transfer. Burton did not immediately discover his loss, as he was still in the midst of his major move. Roberts presented the certificate to Ramblers for registration in his name. This was done. By receipt of a new certificate Roberts now has good title to 500 shares provided he had no knowledge of the unauthorized signature (i.e., forgery) by Attilla.

Generally one cannot lose title to a registered security where the signature is forged or unauthorized, and a corporation which honors such signature does so at its peril as it is liable for improper registration, UCC, Section 8-311. In the above example the corporation could be required to issue another 500-share certificate in Burton's name, or if such would result in an overissue, pay damages if substitute shares cannot be purchased on the market, UCC, Sections 8-404 and 8-104.

35.9   LOST OR DESTROYED SECURITIES

A certificated security which has been lost, apparently destroyed, or wrongfully taken must be replaced by the issuer, provided certain conditions are met by the owner. Reasonable notice of such request for replacement must be made before the missing document has been acquired by a bona fide purchaser and a sufficient indemnity bond be given to protect the issuer. Further, the issuer may demand other reasonable requirements.

EXAMPLE 11. A 94-year-old widow went to live with a friend, who took over some of her business affairs. Unknown to the widow, the friend took her stock certificates, signed the widow's name, and sold them in the public market. The purchasers obtained registration of the securities. Twenty-two months later the widow moved out and only then discovered the loss of her stocks and notified the companies. The companies refused her request to issue new certificates to her, charging the widow with failure to notify the issuer in a "reasonable time" as required by the UCC. The issuers, the companies, contend that the widow could have checked her bank account and she then would have seen that dividends on her stocks were no longer being received. The court disagreed with the companies' position. The court noted that the widow was a lonely and trusting person of advanced years, of infirm mind and body, who had every reasonable right to place her trust in a friend who had betrayed her. She was entitled to replacement of the stock and back dividends.

35.10   RESTRICTIONS

Reasonable restrictions on transfer are valid and enforceable. Closely held corporations frequently use such a device to prevent the stock from reaching outside parties. Common restrictions include those granting other shareholders or the corporation the right of first refusal or a stipulation regarding redemption in the event of death of a party or his or her termination from the company. However, a party who is ignorant of such restrictions may gain full title to the stock. Accordingly, an effective way to prevent such an occurrence is to place the terms of the restrictions conspicuously on the certificate itself, UCC, Section 8-204. The corporation has the burden of proving the applicability of the restrictions to the particular purchaser.

EXAMPLE 12. A bank foreclosed on 1,500 shares of stock it held as collateral for a loan. The corporation itself resisted the foreclosure on the grounds that the stock had restrictions on its sale and hypothecation, i.e., mortgaging or pledging the stock to others. The face of the certificate contained the words that it was "subject to . . . restrictions" and referred the reader to the back of the stock certificate. On the back, also in small print, the restrictions were set forth. The court ruled that the placement of terms was not conspicuous within the meaning of the state statute requiring such. However, the corporation was permitted to try to prove that the bank had actual knowledge of such restrictions; if it failed to do so, the restrictions would be ineffective against the bank.

35.11   TERMINATION OF CORPORATIONS

Corporate life is ended or changed in a number of ways. Most corporations end by the failure of those interested in them to proceed further. Accordingly, a few years pass by with inaction, the corporate franchise tax is not paid, and the state automatically orders dissolution by a simple notice procedure. The name of the faded corporation is once again available for corporate use in that state, or depending on the time and the appropriate state law, the corporate form can be revived by the payment of back taxes. This portion of the chapter will deal with the more deliberate acts of parties to terminate a corporation and includes a consideration of merger, consolidation, and dissolution by the acts of shareholders, creditors, and the state.

35.12   CONSOLIDATION AND MERGER

A *merger* is the union of two or more corporations in which one or more of them are dissolved and only one survives. A *consolidation* is a procedure by which two or more corporations are joined together to form a new corporation. Mergers and consolidations are specifically governed by state corporation statutes. Such statutes deal with a number of problems, the more important of which involve the rights of objecting shareholders and the status of contract rights with others who had dealt with, or are dealing with, one of the proposed merging or consolidating companies.

The economic or subjective reasons of the objecting shareholders are generally not the concern of the court, as the decision to merge or consolidate is a business judgment. However, the court can examine the complaint of dissenting shareholders to determine that fraud or unfairness is not part of the proposed plan.

EXAMPLE 13. Holders of 5 percent of the outstanding stock sought an injunction against a merger with a company already owning 81.8 percent of the company. The objection related to the exchange ratio of 2¼ shares of the other company's stock for the holder's shares. The holders charged that the exchange was so grossly inadequate that it constituted a constructive fraud. The lower court examined the financial reports of both companies and concluded that the objection was really based on the passing of the old order or way of business as the old company had for a number of years been gradually acquired by the other. The appellate court agreed. It noted that in the absence of proving that fraud was committed or showing that the terms were so unfair that they would shock the conscience of the court, it is the policy of the state to permit contracting corporations to take advantage of the statutory provisions for corporate consolidation or merger. The statute provides an efficient and fair method which permits a judicially protected withdrawal by a dissenting shareholder from a proposed consolidation through appraisal rights. The validity of the business reason(s) for the merger is not a matter for judicial determination.

35.13 RIGHT OF APPRAISAL

The right of appraisal is a right which inures to dissenting shareholders to have their stock appraised at the fair market value and to demand cash payment for that amount. Since the proposed change in the corporation is severe and extraordinary, the usual majority rule does not govern dissenting shareholders in this situation. Dissenting shareholders must follow the procedures, and failure to comply in a substantial way in timely fashion may prevent them from exercising such rights. Substantial compliance is sufficient.

EXAMPLE 14. Five stockholders of a coal company which merged into a second coal company were sent a proxy statement by which they could dissent to the merger under applicable state law. They were also required to give written notice of dissent before the vote of the joint agreement of merger. Compliance permitted appraisal rights. The five stockholders sent in their proxy objection to the merger but did not give written notice of their dissent pursuant to statute. The five stockholders then demanded their appraisal rights over the corporation's objection of failure to send the written notice. The court allowed the appraisal rights, concluding that the statute should be liberally interpreted to afford a simple and expeditious remedy for dissenting shareholders.

35.14 STATUS OF EXISTING RIGHTS

All the property, franchises, rights, and privileges of the merged and/or consolidated corporation succeed to the new or remaining corporation. Rights against the corporation are not ended but become an obligation of the new or remaining corporation. There is no physical transfer of property necessary in most cases since compliance with the statutory merger or consolidation requirements operates as an automatic assignment of such rights as a matter of law.

EXAMPLE 15. A building corporation furnished ready-mix concrete on a construction site and was not paid. The concrete had been supplied just before the merger of the building corporation into a surviving corporation. The surviving corporation brought a lawsuit to enforce a mechanic's lien for the material furnished by the building corporation. The defendant claimed that the lien was not valid since the statute required a new filing when the party suing did not perform the work. This defense was not valid. The court cited the statute of the state which provided that all the property of each of the constituent corporations shall "vest in such surviving or consolidated corporation" without further deed. The surviving corporation could bring this action without any further filing.

The statutory procedure does not, however, suspend the general principles of contracts. What the merging or consolidating corporation could not sell or transfer, the new or surviving corporation cannot receive. If, for example, a nonassignable right was present in one company, it cannot be transferred to the other.

EXAMPLE 16. A corporate insurance firm entered into an employment agreement with an agent. The terms prohibited the agent from engaging in the insurance business in a specified area for 3 years after termination. The agreement was silent on assignees or successors in interest. Ten years later the corporation merged with a national firm in the real estate brokerage business. The agent was offered a position in the new company, but he declined, opening his own firm in the prohibited area. Issue was raised as to the rights of the surviving firm to enforce the restrictive covenant not to compete. This would be a question of fact. In this case, the facts include an absence of language showing assignability, the presence of the personal character of the employment contract, and the nature of the business. The national corporation does not succeed to the rights of the original corporation.

35.15 REORGANIZATION

Some financially troubled corporations cannot simply fade away, merge, or be consolidated. The corporation may have a large amount of assets whose nature is such that the appearance of a buyer would be unlikely at a forced sale. In addition, many interests may be involved, and there may be a complicated capital structure, franchises tied in heavily with assets, and perhaps a strong public interest to be served.

Most formal corporate reorganizations occur under the procedures set out in the federal bankruptcy laws. Chapter XI, Reorganization, permits the court to rearrange the interests of the creditors and security holders for the purpose of adjusting the capital and debt structure at a minimum sacrifice to the shareholders, bondholders, and secured creditors. Forced dissolution and its concomitant, liquidation, are thereby avoided. The affected parties can voluntarily agree to such reorganization, but squabbling over their respective interests often results in the necessity of court intervention.

EXAMPLE 17. Fast Land Corporation grew quite quickly and prospered for a while. To continue growth the corporation issued many different series of stock, issued some bonds securing certain assets, incurred many debts, and now holds a large area of land worth a substantial amount, provided it is not dumped on the market at a foreclosure or execution sale. A conservative evaluator calculates that continuing in business with some adjustment of all interests could result in only a 20 percent loss in interests. If private agreement could be reached among all these competing interests, the corporation, perhaps with a new capital structure, could survive.

35.16 DISSOLUTION

Corporate dissolution can be accomplished through the statutory method by which the shareholders or the state follows procedures outlined by statute or by the extinguishing of the charter in a judicial proceeding. Where the shareholders agree to dissolve, appropriate documents are prepared and statutory procedures followed. The final act is usually preceded by a notice of publication in a newspaper given so as to inform interested parties of the termination of the charter. Failure to pay taxes due the state of incorporation is a common example of termination by statute. The state officials note the absence of returns and informational filings, and thereafter the termination procedure is followed.

Statutory terminations are usually not challenged, but an attempt to terminate through a court action is another matter. The attorney general, for example, in a *quo warranto* action can challenge the corporation's right to continue in the face of violations of the law. A corporation, originally chartered to operate a certain business, may be found to have engaged in activities which are prohibited.

EXAMPLE 18. A racing company had a state license to stage dog races and permit pari-mutuel betting. The state law prohibits such companies from making political contributions. The company made a contribution to the campaign of a state senator. A political opponent learns of this and complains to the attorney general, who could bring an action seeking forfeiture of the racing company's charter.

Stockholders can cause a dissolution by voting for such under the state statute. However, some parties may have insufficient votes to accomplish this and attempt to achieve dissolution by a court proceeding. State statutes frequently provide that shareholders may petition for dissolution on the grounds that it would be in the "best interests" of the corporation that it be dissolved. One might contend, for example, that the corporation is insolvent and there is little hope for future financial success. Or where the management is deadlocked or the voting power is such that the corporation cannot effectively operate, an order of dissolution might be issued. Deadlock by itself is not usually sufficient grounds for dissolution.

EXAMPLE 19. Suit was brought to dissolve a lumber company because of a shareholder deadlock. Holland, the owner of 50 percent of the stock and one of the three-member board of directors, had sought unsuccessfully to amend the bylaws to include a fourth member so that she (Holland) would have an equal vote on the board. It was alleged that the shareholders were hopelessly deadlocked in voting power as there was a failure to elect new directors for two consecutive years. Holland offered no charge of dissension except a deadlock over dividends, liquidation, and the election of directors. State law vested courts with jurisdiction to order dissolution and liquidation when it is established, among other grounds, that "the directors are deadlocked in the management of corporate affairs and the stockholders are unable to breach the deadlock, and that irreparable injury to the corporation is being suffered or is threatened by reason thereof." The petitioning director contended that the showing of a deadlock is sufficient grounds for the court to order liquidation. The court refused to grant the petition. It could not find on the evidence that the affairs of the company were suffering from this deadlock, but rather found that the company was ably administered by management. More must be shown than a deadlock, as the court can consider the equities of the individual case. The petitioning director has the burden of proof in showing grounds for dissolution.

Corporate rights do not end at dissolution. Statutes usually place custody of these rights, such as they may be, in the last board of directors, or other described parties, as trustees for the rights of the defunct corporation.

Black Letter Law
A Summary

1. A security is a share or interest in, or an obligation of, an enterprise and is of a type commonly recognized as a medium of investment; it can be either certificated or uncertificated.

2. Corporations, by their charters, establish authorized stock, which, when issued, is called outstanding stock; it may have a par value or no-par value, the latter being sold at a stated value which is usually set by the directors.

3. Preferred stock frequently has characteristics of preference such as priority in dividends, participation with other stock in dividends, cumulative rights, and seniority in distribution of assets at time of liquidation.

4. Bonds are corporate debt instruments and qualify as securities when intended as a medium of investment; they are usually certificated.

5. In the absence of fraud or other wrongdoing, the judgment of the directors as to the adequacy of consideration given for corporate stock is final, but promises to pay cannot be accepted as consideration.

6. A subscriber to stock of a proposed corporation is liable when such offer is accepted by the corporation; this is usually implied by the act of incorporation; revocation of such a subscription is determined by contract law in the absence of a statutory rule to the contrary.

7. The Model Business Corporation Act provides that subscriptions to stock of a proposed corporation are generally irrevocable for a period of 6 months.

8. A bona fide purchaser of a security who has paid value and has no notice of any adverse claim gains good title, provided the purchaser takes delivery of a certificated security in bearer form, or indorsed to him or her, or indorsed in blank.

9. A corporation, the issuer, which honors a presentment for registration of a certificated security bearing a forged indorsement by issuing a new certificate must, in most instances, account to the party whose name was forged.

10. Reasonable restrictions on transfer or disposition of stock are upheld provided the transferee had actual notice or the certificate itself contained conspicuous language reflecting such restrictions.

11. Corporations terminate through statutory procedures or court actions.

12. A termination can occur through dissolution, merger, consolidation, or reorganization.

13. The state may order forfeiture of the charter of a corporation for good cause, which may range from statutory grounds of failure to pay taxes to misbehavior; shareholders may also assent to such dissolution.

14. A court can decree a dissolution on the grounds of deadlock of management causing irreparable harm, or oppression or fraud by management.

15. A merger occurs when one corporation is transferred into another, the surviving corporation; in consolidations two or more corporations become one new corporation.

16. Shareholders objecting to a proposed merger or consolidation have certain statutory rights, including the right of appraisal which permits them to demand cash payment for their shares.

17. In merger or consolidation the transferable corporate rights and property are assigned by operation of law, and all debts and liabilities are assumed by the new or surviving corporation.

18. Reorganization can be achieved by a private adjustment of the interests affected, or can be accomplished under Chapter XI of the federal bankruptcy law.

Solved Problems

35.1 Under which of the following circumstances would a corporation's existence terminate?

    (a) The death of its sole owner-shareholder

    (b) Its becoming insolvent

    (c) Its legal consolidation with another company

    (d) Its reorganization under the federal bankruptcy laws

(*AICPA Examination, November 1974*)

    A corporation is separate and apart from its shareholders and is not dissolved just because it may be insolvent. However, its consolidation with another company terminates it existence and that of its fellow company, statement (c). Reorganization under federal bankruptcy laws does not necessarily result in termination.

35.2 Delray Corporation has a provision in its corporate charter as follows: "Holders of non-cumulative preferred stock shall be entitled to a fixed annual dividend of 8 percent before any dividend shall be paid on common stock." There are *no* further provisions relating to preferences or statements regarding voting rights. The preferred stock apparently

    (a) is noncumulative, but only to the extent that the 8 percent dividend is not earned in a given year.

    (b) is nonvoting unless dividends are in arrears.

    (c) has a preference on the distribution of the assets of the corporation upon dissolution.

    (d) is *not* entitled to participate with common stock in distribution beyond 8 percent.

(*AICPA Examination, November 1974*)

    The state permits corporations to fix preferences and rights on different classes of stock. The specific characteristics will be honored. The company lists the stock as noncumulative and is silent on participation. Therefore the holders are only entitled to the 8 percent dividend when earned, as stated in (d).

35.3 Authorized shares means the shares of all classes of stock which a corporation

    (a) has legally outstanding.

    (b) is legally permitted to issue.

    (c) has issued including treasury shares.

    (d) has issued excluding treasury shares.

(*AICPA Examination, November 1975*)

    The corporate charter and any amendments determine the authorized shares, the charter being a contract with the state, and its approval sets the amount and kind of stock legally permitted to be issued, statement (b). Such stock includes both issued and unissued shares.

35.4 The consideration received by a corporation when issuing shares of stock shall constitute stated capital to the extent of the par value of the shares, and any excess shall constitute

    (a) treasury shares.

    (b) earned surplus.

(c)   restricted surplus.

(d)   capital surplus.

(*AICPA Examination, May 1977*)

Money received for the issuance of stock is not earnings and under some state statutes does not qualify as legal capital. However, it is capital of the paid-in variety, or just capital surplus, answer (d).

35.5   Which of the following *cannot* properly be received as the consideration for the issuance of shares?

(a)   Promissory notes

(b)   Services actually performed for the corporation

(c)   Shares of stock of another corporation

(d)   Intangible property rights

(*AICPA Examination, November 1978*)

Generally all the above are proper consideration for the issuance of stock by the corporation except promises to pay in the future, here represented by promissory notes; and so the answer is (a).

35.6   Watson entered into an agreement to purchase 1,000 shares of the Marvel Corporation, a corporation to be organized in the near future. Watson has since had second thoughts about investing in Marvel. Under the circumstances, which of the following is correct?

(a)   A written notice of withdrawal of her agreement to purchase the shares will be valid as long as it is received before incorporation.

(b)   A simple transfer of the agreement to another party will entirely eliminate her liability to purchase the shares of stock.

(c)   Watson may *not* revoke the agreement for a period of 6 months in the absence of special circumstances.

(d)   Watson may avoid liability on her agreement if she can obtain the consent of the majority of other individuals committed to purchase shares to release her.

(*Adapted from AICPA Examination, November 1978*)

A subscription contract with a proposed corporation is binding if made as an exchange of promises with other subscribers or where a statute validates such promises. Under the Model Business Corporation Act such subscription is generally irrevocable for a period of 6 months; statement (c) is the answer.

35.7   Which of the following could not qualify as a certificated security?

(a)   A corporate bond

(b)   A corporate resolution

(c)   A share of stock

(d)   A stock warrant

A certificated security is a share, participation, or other interest in property of an enterprise of the issuer or an obligation of the issuer which is represented by an instrument in bearer or registered form and commonly recognized as a medium of investment. All the above could qualify except for (b), a corporate resolution.

35.8 The managements of Vestalen Products and Sieta Corporation engaged in preliminary negotiations regarding common corporate objectives. Initial review revealed that both companies could benefit greatly from cooperation or even combination. The results of the negotiations were so favorable that the managements wanted to present a plan to the stockholders of each company. However, a problem was identified when the president of Vestalen reminded the negotiators that his company was an old and honored firm, and that a great deal of its stock was held by a large bank which was a trustee for a very conservative clientele. The president believed that change might not be welcome in those quarters. In considering the forms of combination, which of the following might best respond to the concern expressed by the president?

    (*a*)   Merging Sieta into Vestalen Products

    (*b*)   A consolidation of the two into a new corporation named Vesta-Sieta

    (*c*)   A reorganization

    (*d*)   Merging Vestalen into Sieta Corporation

     Assuming that it would be important to continue both the impression and the reality that Vestalen is still in business, the Sieta Corporation should merge into Vestalen Products. A consolidation legally manifests to the world a new corporation. A merger extinguishes one corporation, and it would not be recommended to have Vestalen merge into Sieta. The answer is (*a*).

35.9 Lawhorn was a minority shareholder of Towner Mines, a corporation with wasting assets. It was her considered judgment that the time was ripe for an immediate sale of all the firm's coal mines (the major assets of the company) and dissolution. Coal prices were currently high, as other companies were paying a premium for mines and mine field leases since the Department of the Interior was recently barred from issuing more leases on public land. Lawhorn's judgment was in agreement with the opinions of stock analysts who kept a close eye on the industry. The corporation law of the state permitted dissolution upon the action of a simple majority vote of the shareholders. If Lawhorn attempts to use the courts to do what she can't accomplish at the shareholders' meeting, which of the following grounds should she pursue on the above facts?

    (*a*)   She should charge fraud.

    (*b*)   There are meager earnings, and future success appears negative.

    (*c*)   There is a deadlock of management.

    (*d*)   The directors are using poor business judgment.

     Corporation law places restraint on the courts to enter the area of so-called business judgment. On these facts Lawhorn's only chance is to show that the prospects for the future are bad and that this company, by its nature, cannot turn around, statement (*b*). There is no evidence of fraud or a deadlock of management.

35.10 A car buyer defaulted on his time payments, and the Aster Corporation brought an action against him. The car buyer defended on the grounds of fraud. While the action was pending, the state dissolved the corporation for its failure to pay its corporate tax. Under these circumstances,

    (*a*)   the car buyer wins the lawsuit, as there is no legal plaintiff in existence.

    (*b*)   dissolution does not destroy a corporation's rights.

    (*c*)   Aster cannot be reinstated by payment of tax.

    (*d*)   where one defends on fraud initially, one can only rely on that ground in the lawsuit.

Dissolution ends corporate life as a going business. It does not, however, as stated in (b), abolish any of the corporation's rights. Here the state statute will prescribe in whose hands these rights now exist for purposes such as this. Usually the rights are held by the members of the last board of directors as trustees. Most dissolutions for failure to pay taxes can be set aside and the corporation reinstated by following statutory procedure, which usually requires only the payment of past taxes.

35.11 Minority shareholders, owners of 34 percent of the stock in an apartment hotel corporation, felt that management's acts were both fraudulent and oppressive. It appeared that management and their families took $50,000 from the company and did not account for it other than saying that such sum was invested in another company, for which it gave back a second mortgage on property with the loan to run at 6 percent interest for 20 years. There were no corporate minutes or documents, such as a note or mortgage, to evidence and support such loan.

What type of relief can the minority shareholders request if it is shown that management has done these and similar acts? Will such relief be granted?

The minority have several remedies which might be available to them including a petition to seek dissolution of the company. Such an order is discretionary with the court but is entered where the petitioners can prove fraudulent or oppressive acts which work to the detriment of the corporation. Under similar facts a court ruled that the directors failed to establish fairness of the loan to another company which was controlled by the directors and their families. Such an act could be considered as fraudulent and oppressive so as to permit the court to apply the statute and dissolve the corporation.

35.12 A city required operators of public garages to obtain a license and pay a yearly fee. Three corporations, X, Y and Z, operated public garages, and each had the necessary license. Before the expiration of the yearly license, X and Y merged into Z company. The city then demanded that new licenses be obtained and fees paid for the unexpired period for the locations previously owned and operated by X and Y and now operated by Z.

What legal principle must Z present in order to escape liability for additional licenses? State the principle involved, your decision, and your reasons for any conclusions.

The Z corporation should point to the state corporation laws on mergers and consolidations which generally provide that upon consummation of a merger the surviving corporation shall possess all rights, privileges, and franchises possessed by the former corporation(s): The Z corporation will win since it succeeded to all the rights of the merged corporations which had indeed paid their required license fees.

35.13 Tandor Shields manufactures and sells heart pacemakers. Success came early, as the company invested heavily in expensive equipment and hired personnel who were tops in their field. Modifications of models were frequent, and for this Tandor was beginning to pay a heavy price. Since the field is new, the expectations of the customers are great, and when the pacemakers seemed to fail, the result would be product liability suits. Lyone S.A., a French manufacturer, also makes pacemakers and intends to break into the American market. It believes that its best strategy is to have a plant in the United States for marketing purposes. Lyone likes what it sees at Tandor, especially the sophisticated equipment and expert personnel under long-term employment contracts. However, Lyone does not like the appearance of the ever-increasing number of product liability suits against Tandor.

If Lyone's plans include some investment or relationship with Tandor, what legal concerns must Lyone have? State these concerns and their legal consequences.

If Lyone is considering a merger or consolidation, it will probably succeed to most of the assets and rights of Tandor. This could mean that even the personnel might be included if the employment contracts are assignable. This is possible since the business and objectives are the same. Certainly all the patents and developments in process would belong to the new combination. These advantages must be weighed against the liabilities, however. In merger or consolidation all the liabilities likewise pass to the surviving or new unit. These are assumed by operation of law. Such would include all the present lawsuits and those not yet filed but which might be for past breach of warranty or the like. It might be safer for Lyone to attempt to buy as many of the assets of the firm as possible. There are dangers here also. The employment contracts are probably not assignable under such a transaction, and Lyone must be careful so as to not appear to take all the assets, including the management. This could result in a challenge that Lyone was merely the alter ego of the selling corporation, Tandor.

Topic Test, Part VIII

Corporations

1. Three young business school graduates decided to put their learning to good use and formed a corporation to carry on a business in public relations. It was mutually agreed that Frank was the natural as president and general manager, and he was so appointed when the corporation was formed. This agreement was put in writing and signed by all three. The agreement provided for a 3-year term and contained a clause allowing termination by either the corporation or Frank upon giving 6 months' notice. The corporation was formed, and Frank was voted president and general manager by the other two directors. There was no express corporate action in regard to the employment contract. The firm prospered and, after 3 years, is being considered as a merger candidate by a leading public relations firm. The only difficulty is that the interested firm wants Frank out as an officer before it proceeds further. His "buddies" vote Frank out, and he is discharged. As Frank examines his legal options, what difficulties do you see for him and for his ex-friends?

2. Casca Corporation is the biggest employer in town and is accorded great respect by its bank, Third Federal Bank. Two officers of Casca said they were going into a business venture. They were able to get a loan from Third Federal because the bank knew how influential these two officers were with Casca. The bank always took the quickest way to get results and so promptly deducted the amount of the loan from Casca's bank account upon default—at which time it learned that there was no business venture. The two officers had put the loan proceeds into Casca. The bank had not known that Casca had a financial problem at the time of the loan. What legal principle will give the bank the most trouble in its attempt to support its action? What problem might Casca have in its attempt to retrieve the money deducted from its account?

3. The directors' meetings of Mitchell-Hill were always lively. Norma, the president, was holding her seat and office by luck and the fact that not all the directors would show up for the meetings. Her luck turned bad when one of the five directors resigned, stating that she didn't need the hassle. At a lawfully called board meeting, Norma, also a director, was out of town and couldn't attend. A new director was elected to fill one of the vacancies, and Norma was removed as president. Under the bylaws a quorum is three directors. What principle of law will determine the legality of this action by the directors?

4. A roofing materials company was owned by three stockholders. The company came upon hard times, and as business became poorer Ernest, the president, who held no stock, would only take one-half of his salary at the time, pending improved business, at which time he would receive the back pay. This continued for 6 months, with Ernest owed $11,000. The company did not succeed and became insolvent. The state corporation statute provided that "shareholders are not liable to the corporation's creditors except for salaries and wages due and owing to its laborers and employees for services rendered to the corporation." Ernest is suing the three shareholders for his back salary. What type of defense will the shareholders attempt to raise to escape the statutory liability alleged?

5. Barret owns one-fifth of the outstanding stock of the Manchester Company. She is an outsider and, to some in the company, a troublemaker. Barret learns that the president of the company has just sold to the company a parcel of land which the president recently purchased for himself when he was on an assignment to purchase land for the company. The president made a $20,000 profit on the sale of his land to the company. Barret can prove these facts and brings an action against the president for $4,000, one-fifth of the profit. What principle of corporation law is involved in this case? Can Barret succeed under these circumstances?

6. Fowler was wealthy, but he was careless with his property, including stock that he held in several corporations. He would keep the stock certificates in his desk drawer since, as he explained, "I don't know when I might want to sell them, and it's best to keep them handy." Most employees and visitors to his office knew of his practice. The desk was never locked. One day he discovered that the certificates were missing and mentioned to his secretary that he was going to "notify the companies of this loss at the next opportunity." Fowler delayed notifying the companies until 30 days had passed. When the corporations examined his written request and understood the facts, they refused to supply substitute certificates. How much trouble is Fowler in? Is he entitled to substitute stock certificates? State the applicable legal principles.

7. Hendall Corporation has reached agreement with its supplier, Pine Products, by which Pine will merge into Hendall. Kruger is outraged. She believes this is not the time for such expansion. She is a preferred shareholder who has not been paid her dividend for the past 2 years. Kruger wants her rights which she perceives to be set forth in the preferred stock contract. It states that "Upon dissolution, liquidation, or winding up of the corporation, the preferred shares shall receive $150 per share plus all dividends in arrears." The preferred stock is presently selling for $73 a share. What principle of corporation law will determine Kruger's success?

8. Farwell Sights has eight directors, and the bylaws require a majority, at least five, to constitute a quorum. Six directors are present when a contract with Half Moon Tours is approved. Three of the directors are also directors of Half Moon, and of these three, two are also minor officers of Half Moon. What challenge could a shareholder of Farwell Sights raise regarding this contract?

9. When Weatherby, Inc., needed money, it issued corporate bonds at an attractive rate. The bonds were quickly purchased. They turned out to be a bad deal as the company did not flourish, but most of the bondholders felt comfortable since the firm had many tangible assets. The corporation was dissolved and the company liquidated. Looking to share in the $3 million realized from the liquidation are the shareholders, general creditors, and bondholders. If the bonds are $2 million face value and the general creditors are owed $4 million, how much of the $3 million realized in the liquidation will the bondholders receive? State the legal principle involved.

10. Arlene and Thomas worked hard to develop their company, A & T Corporation, and it was done by seeking investment capital. They are now at the point of no return, so to speak. They own 50 percent plus one share of the outstanding stock. Thomas is worried about losing control. He trusts Arlene, but she is getting married late in life and her husband-to-be seems like an aggressive salesman type. Thomas fears the situation. He and Arlene both have similar ideas about the future course of the company, and both are interested in seeing that it continues. What type of legal device should they consider under these circumstances?

Answers

1. It appears that Frank has a binding agreement with his ex-friends personally by which they could be sued for breach of contract. However, the corporation's duty rests on less firm ground. The corporation did not expressly ratify this agreement. Frank must show that the conduct of the corporation evidences a ratification or adoption. Under these facts this does not seem likely. The principle most troublesome to Frank is that a corporation is not liable for contracts made by its promoters before incorporation.

2. The bank will have difficulty finding the corporation's hand in the loan agreement with the two officers. Since there was no mention of corporate fraud, if fraud occurred it was personal. If the money was borrowed for the benefit of the corporation, some tort liability might be present, but it must be shown that the officers' actions were within the scope of their duties. It certainly appears that the loan *might* be in furtherance of the corporate interest. Or the funds may have been placed in the corporation to protect some private motive or interest of the officers. Casca's problem is the reverse. It should maintain the position that the officers had no authority to borrow money on behalf of the corporation.

3. Quorum rules and voting principles will govern this problem. A quorum under these facts is three members. The meeting met with a quorum and with proper notice. Since the meeting was lawful and a majority voted her out, the president will lose.

4. Stockholders are not generally liable for corporate debts just by reason of being stockholders. A few state statutes, however, provide an exception in those instances in which back salary is due to employees. The stockholders will defend on the basis that the president is not an employee. The question here is a good one. Is the president of the corporation an employee? He certainly is an agent, and a hired one at that. Accordingly he is an employee in the general sense of the word, as contrasted with a director who is not an employee. Further, the pay the president received was "salary." It appears that the president is entitled to recovery against the stockholders.

5. Barret misremembers the appropriate remedy for this type of corporate abuse by the president of the company. Barret is correct in that the profit made by the president, while on a mission for the corporation, is rightfully to be returned. But it is to be returned to the corporation, not to the stockholders. Barret has no private action available. She should have used a derivative action suit on behalf of the corporation against the offending officer. Barret's action to "recover her $4,000" will lose.

6. Article 8 of the UCC provides relief for those whose certificates are lost, destroyed, or stolen. Proper notice within a reasonable time is required, especially before the certificate is wrongly presented to the corporation for a new certificate. Fowler has apparently notified the corporations before anyone has shown up with the missing certificates to request that new ones be issued. The corporations can demand an explanation from Fowler, and may even require indemnity bonds from him, but they must reissue substitute certificates to him.

7. Kruger has run into a technical problem here. It is true that corporate life for Hendall will be permanently altered, but not in a legal way to benefit Kruger's position. In a merger the surviving corporation survives, by definition. Accordingly, within the meaning of the preferred stock contract, there is no "dissolution, liquidation, or winding up." Kruger will not succeed in activating this provision of the preferred stock contract. However, she has a right to dissent and, accordingly, a right of appraisal.

8. The contention that interested, rather than disinterested, directors approved a contract will be the position of the challenger. Three qualified votes were necessary to approve this contract. Since three of the six directors were interested directors, they could not make up a valid quorum to approve the matter. This is not a void contract. It is merely voidable at the option of the corporation.

9. These bondholders apparently purchased debentures, which are bonds unsecured by any particular assets of the company. In reality such bondholders are no better off than general creditors. Bonds may be collateralized, but such was not the case here. Had the bonds been so issued, the bondholders would receive their full $2 million. In this case, however, the general creditors and bondholders share equally in

the $3 million realized in liquidation. Since the debts due the creditors (including the bondholders) amount to $6 million, they will be paid 50 cents on the dollar. The shareholders are even more unlucky, of course, as they are the owners of a business which is valueless, and they will receive nothing.

10. This is the perfect time to articulate their objectives and common goals, reducing them to writing and creating a shareholders' agreement or a voting trust. To a large measure, either of these types of agreement limits the voting powers of the stockholders when issues arise that are contrary to the objectives and goals. A shareholders' agreement is simply a contract to vote a certain way; a trust agreement, on the other hand, is a complete transfer of power to a trustee with specific instruction to vote according to arranged concepts. The shares are surrendered in a voting trust, and the shareholders receive trust certificates.

Index

444

452 INDEX